THE PETTIGREW PAPERS

Ebenezer Pettigrew (1783-1848), of Tyrrell County, was a planter, state senator, and United States congressman. Photograph of a portrait from the Southern Historical Collection, University of North Carolina Library, Chapel Hill.

The Pettigrew Papers

VOLUME II
1819-1843

Edited by
SARAH MCCULLOH LEMMON

Raleigh
North Carolina Department of Cultural Resources
Division of Archives and History
1988

ISBN 0-86526-069-9
ISBN 0-86526-067-2

CONTENTS

ILLUSTRATIONS

FOREWORD

Volume I of *The Pettigrew Papers* was published in 1971. Because of budgetary and staff limitations, volume II has taken longer to produce than originally anticipated. Nonetheless, it is a valuable addition to the social, economic, cultural, and political history of antebellum North Carolina. The rich manuscript collections of Pettigrew family papers in the Southern Historical Collection at the University of North Carolina at Chapel Hill and in the North Carolina State Archives in Raleigh yield important information and insights on planter life in eastern North Carolina. Specifically, the papers furnish essential source materials for studying the family, child-rearing practices, slavery, religion, and agriculture, among many other topics. From these vast collections Dr. Sarah M. Lemmon, professor of history emerita at Meredith College, has had to make difficult choices in selecting documents for a letterpress edition. The skill with which she has accomplished that task is evident in the pleasure one can take in just reading the documents as part of a larger narrative. Dr. Lemmon is now at work on the third and final volume of *The Pettigrew Papers*, which will bring the family's story up to the death of James Johnston Pettigrew at Gettysburg in July, 1863. Poignantly, Pettigrew is a young child and adolescent in the years covered by volume II.

As always, the staff of the Historical Publications Section rendered invaluable service in bringing this volume to print. Kathleen B. Wyche served as the in-house editor who verified transcriptions, edited footnotes to conform to the section's style, and saw the volume through press. Sally Copenhaver assisted in checking transcriptions. Lisa D. Bailey proofread galley proofs and page proofs, and Stephena K. Williams and Trudy M. Rayfield prepared the manuscript for typesetting by encoding it on a microcomputer.

JEFFREY J. CROW
Historical Publications Administrator

March 1, 1988

INTRODUCTION

The Pettigrew Family, 1819-1843

Volume II continues the account of the lives of Ebenezer Pettigrew (1783-1848), who was the only surviving child of the Reverend Charles Pettigrew (c. 1744-1807);[1] his wife Ann Blount Shepard Pettigrew (1795?-1830); and their children.

Married on May 17, 1815,[2] the couple took up their residence at Bonarva, on Lake Phelps in Tyrrell County, North Carolina. Because of the isolation of Bonarva and the high incidence of malaria and bilious fever there from late summer through the fall, Ann Blount (Nancy) Pettigrew spent many months separated from her husband by a three days' journey from Bonarva to New Bern, where her family lived. Ebenezer kept his promise to move to New Bern in 1819; but five months later, after his father-in-law's death, he accepted his inability to adjust to town life and, although he rented a house in Edenton for a short time, made Bonarva his permanent home thereafter. Nancy took the younger children with her on her visits to New Bern, leaving the older ones with their father, a tutor, and a housekeeper until they became old enough to attend boarding school in Hillsborough, North Carolina.

The separation of the family members produced a voluminous correspondence: Nancy and Ebenezer to each other; Nancy to her sister Mary Williams Shepard (who married John Herritage Bryan in 1821); Ebenezer to his sons at school and to their schoolmaster, William J. Bingham; the sons to their father; and, later, the Bryans to Ebenezer.

Between 1815 and 1830 the Pettigrews had nine children: Charles Lockhart (born February 16, 1816), William (born and died July, 1817), William Shepard (born October 3, 1818), John (born

---

[1]Since the publication of the first volume in this series in 1971, additional genealogical information has been received from descendants of the families included in that volume. Mary Pettigrew, sister of the Reverend Charles Pettigrew, married John Verner rather than James Verner. See the genealogical chart, Sarah McCulloh Lemmon (ed.), *The Pettigrew Papers* (Raleigh: Division of Archives and History, Department of Cultural Resources, projected 3 volumes, 1971—), I, xiv, hereinafter cited as Lemmon, *Pettigrew Papers*. (Margaret B. Stephenson to Memory F. Mitchell, December 13, 1978.) William Pettigrew, brother of the Reverend Charles Pettigrew, married Louise Guy Gibert rather than Louisa Gabart. (Martha W. Daniels to Carolyn A. Wallace, February 6, 1983.) Mrs. Daniels suggests the sibling order of the last-born children of James and Mary Cochran Pettigrew as Ebenezer, Jane, Nancy, William, and Elizabeth.

[2]Lemmon, *Pettigrew Papers*, I, xiiin.

August 29, 1820, and died July 21, 1821), James (born January 29, 1822, and died October 27, 1833), Henry Ebenezer (born September 23, 1824, and died December 3, 1831), Mary Blount (born March 12, 1826), James Johnston (born July 4, 1828), and Ann Blount Shepard (born June 30, 1830), at whose birth the mother died. The children then were taken by relatives, leaving Ebenezer alone at Bonarva. Charles, William, and James continued at Hillsborough Academy; Henry and James Johnston lived with their Grandmother Shepard and her then unmarried sons James, Frederick, and Richard in New Bern until Henry's death and Johnston's entrance into Bingham's school; Mary and Ann (Nancy, or Nannie) were taken by their mother's sister Mary Williams and her husband, John Herritage Bryan, and were reared with the Bryans' own children. Nomenclature becomes confusing: Mary Pettigrew called her father Pa, her Aunt and Uncle Bryan Mother and Father, and her Grandmother Shepard Ma.

Prior to 1830, Ebenezer considered himself a small farmer. Although he paid taxes on some 700 acres of land in 1815, much of it was swamp, and Ebenezer struggled to ditch and drain it in order to increase the arable acreage for his crops of wheat and corn. He was interested in soil chemistry; machinery for sawing, ditching, and shelling corn; and improving his livestock. He attempted a herring fishery[3] and a mulberry tree nursery, both with other entrepreneurs, and succeeded in neither. Rather, his successes came when he depended on himself and his own hard work. He borrowed money to purchase additional land, shipped his crops to Norfolk, New York, and Charleston, and even built his own schooner because of the difficulty of securing vessels when he needed them to carry his cargo.

Following the death of his beloved wife, Nancy, Ebenezer became almost a recluse. He drove himself to increase his worldly goods both to take his mind off his great loss and to provide a competence for the future of his numerous children. Whereas in 1815 Pettigrew owned 700 acres of land and seventeen slaves, by 1840 he owned 8,500 acres and fifty-four slaves. His mind was keen and his vision farsighted, so much so that during the 1830s he acquired a reputation as an advanced agriculturalist, and from being a man of very modest means he came to be reputed a man of wealth. While cash was sometimes short, he never denied his children their needs and comforts, nor was he niggardly in contributing to the poor.

---

[3]Settlement of Aligator Fisheries Accounts, April 2, 1822, Pettigrew Family Papers, Southern Historical Collection, University of North Carolina Library, Chapel Hill, repository hereinafter cited as Southern Historical Collection.

After the death of his stepmother, Mary Lockhart Pettigrew, in 1833, Ebenezer expanded the old home plantation, Belgrade, and prepared it for one of his sons. Charles was graduated from the University of North Carolina in 1836 and went to Bonarva to become a planter. He was restless, however—Ebenezer said he had too much Shepard in him—and invested his small inheritance from his Grandmother Pettigrew in a steam mill in nearby Columbia. Unable to make the mill prosper, Charles eventually became the master of Bonarva. William's temperament seems to have been more like that of his father. He concluded his education at the University of North Carolina by withdrawing at the end of his junior year and returned to the plantations, where he was gradually given charge of Belgrade. James Johnston was sent to Hillsborough to Bingham's school at a tender age, and there he was frequently in disciplinary trouble. At one time Ebenezer brought him home to teach him obedience. Johnston's brilliant mind was recognized from his early years, and after Ebenezer had supervised his behavior for some months the boy went on to finish at Bingham's academy and graduated from the university in 1847 with first honors.

During this time period Ebenezer and his two older sons traveled extensively on business, for health reasons, and to extend their education. Having lost his fourth son, Henry, to disease in 1831 and his third son, James, a victim of chorea, by accidental drowning while on a voyage for his health in 1833, Ebenezer took great interest in the physical condition of Charles and William. On various excursions they visited Harpers Ferry; Lexington, Kentucky; Cincinnati; Buffalo; Quebec; Boston; New York; and Philadelphia. Business trips frequently were taken to Norfolk and Baltimore. Interestingly, Ebenezer seems to have been regarded more highly by his business and social acquaintances outside North Carolina than he was at home.

Persuaded to run for Congress in 1835 as a Whig, Ebenezer was elected and served one term. While there he exerted great energy to keep his constituents informed of major speeches and legislation, much to their gratification. He also helped them with their claims against French spoliation and their western land warrants from Revolutionary War veterans. He attempted to secure funds for the improvement of navigation in the sounds and recommended suitable postal routes and postmasters. Pettigrew was a fiscal conservative, an opponent of abolition petitions, and a critic of extravagance and corruption, which he saw personified in Locofocoism. His temperament could not tolerate the House of Representatives and the city of Washington, however, so he declined to stand for a second term. Three of Ebenezer's brothers-in-law also served in Congress: William Biddle Shepard, Charles

Biddle Shepard, and John Herritage Bryan. His son William considered a public career but did not serve during the period covered by this volume.

The two daughters, Mary and Nancy, pursued the usual type of female education of the period. They were taught by lady schoolteachers in New Bern and later in Raleigh, to which the Bryans removed in 1838, and they studied piano from assorted instructors. For some years they attended rather irregularly the schools in which they were enrolled. Then in 1841 Mary Pettigrew and her first cousin Mary Bryan were sent to Miss Breschard's, a good school in Washington, D.C., where they completed their education. In 1843 Nancy became a day scholar at the newly opened St. Mary's School in Raleigh.

Ebenezer, as his father had been before him, was continuously involved with the absentee ownership of land in Tennessee. He visited that state twice, once in 1819 to consider moving there and again in 1843 to attempt to sell his holdings. Ebenezer concluded that his North Carolina swamps were preferable, although he seems to have been generous in aiding less affluent persons who needed a stake to move west.

Other than the family members, Ebenezer's chief correspondent was his dear friend James Cathcart Johnston, a bachelor who lived with his sisters at Hayes Plantation near Edenton. Johnston also owned establishments in Pasquotank County and on the Roanoke River at Caledonia. An extensive correspondence developed exchanging opinions, advice, and offers of assistance, while many business affairs and trips were undertaken jointly by the two men.

Neighbors of the Pettigrews included the Collins family, who lived at Somerset Place but of whom Ebenezer disapproved because they were not devoted to the land and were often absentee owners. He seemed to feel that they patronized him because he lived in the swamps and worked hard. Other neighbors included Doctrine Davenport, Ebenezer's chief overseer; several families, such as the Woodleys, who lived on the canal connecting Lake Phelps and the Scuppernong River; an old enemy named Dempsey Spruill; a cousin on his mother's side, John Baptist Beasley; Sheriff Henry Alexander; several Phelps families; and the carpenter Nathan A. Brickhouse. His father's friend Thomas Trotter, who had moved to Beaufort County, was visited regularly en route to New Bern, but Ebenezer's boyhood friends James Iredell, Jr., and Thomas Haughton drifted away as he ceased to visit Edenton.

The Pettigrew family was Episcopalian, but the correspondence does not indicate any activity in support of a particular congregation. Ebenezer was delighted when Charles and William were confirmed; he himself felt unworthy to receive Holy Communion and declined at one time to serve as warden of the congregation at the chapel established by his father. Yet he contributed to the salary of the minister and was always hospitable to the bishop on his rounds.

Volume II of the Pettigrew Papers ends in 1843. At that time Charles was operating Bonarva, William was operating Belgrade, Johnston was a freshman at the University of North Carolina, Ebenezer was building a house called Magnolia for his retirement home, Mary was finishing school and planning to come to Magnolia to keep house for her father, and Nancy was living with the Bryans in Raleigh and had just entered St. Mary's.[4]

The history of the family will be concluded in volume III.

THE SHEPARD FAMILY

When Ebenezer Pettigrew married Ann Blount Shepard of New Bern, he acquired a large family of in-laws who played an important role in his life. Because of the extensive correspondence with and numerous references to various members of the Shepard family, a survey of the family is presented here.

William Shepard (1765-1819) of Beaufort and New Bern married Mary Blount, daughter of Frederick Blount of Edenton and his wife, Mary Williams.[5] Because Frederick Blount was brother to Ebenezer Pettigrew's mother, Mary Blount Pettigrew, Mrs. Shepard was first cousin to Ebenezer.[6] William Shepard had two known sisters, one of whom, Hannah, married Captain Charles Biddle of Philadelphia in 1778; their son was Nicholas Biddle of Bank of the United States fame.[7] Shepard's other sister, Anne, married one Lardner of Philadelphia; two of their daughters, Catherine and Fanny, are mentioned in the Pettigrew documents.[8] The William Shepards had ten children, who are identified below.

Ann Blount Shepard (Nancy) married Ebenezer Pettigrew in 1815 and died July 1, 1830. See the preceding discussion of the Pettigrew family.

---

[4]All other information in the above essay can be found in the documents printed in this volume.

[5]Shepard genealogical material, Private Collections, Elizabeth Moore Collection, PC 1406, Archives, North Carolina Division of Archives and History, Raleigh, hereinafter cited as Moore Collection, PC 1406, repository hereinafter cited as North Carolina Archives.

[6]Blount genealogy chart, Lemmon, *Pettigrew Papers*, I, xvi.

[7]Allen Johnson, Dumas Malone, and others (eds.), *Dictionary of American Biography* (New York: Charles Scribner's Sons, 20 volumes, 1928; index and updating supplements), II, 243, hereinafter cited as *DAB*.

[8]Shepard genealogical material, Moore Collection, PC 1406.

William Biddle Shepard (1799-1852)[9] attended the University of North Carolina but was dismissed for delivering a commencement address that had been forbidden; this incident became known as the Shepard Rebellion.[10] After completing his education at the University of Pennsylvania, he made his home in Elizabeth City, Pasquotank County, where he practiced law and engaged in planting, politics, and banking. He served four terms in Congress (1829-1837) and two in the state Senate (1838-1840 and 1848-1850).[11] Although Shepard had been dismissed from the university, he served on its board of trustees from 1838 until 1852.[12] William was twice married: to Charlotte Cazenove of Alexandria, Virginia, who died in 1836, and to Anne Daves Collins, sister to Josiah Collins III of Somerset Place and Edenton.[13]

Mary Williams Shepard (1801-1881) married John Herritage Bryan on December 20, 1821.[14] See the following discussion of the Bryan family.

Hannah Biddle Shepard died suddenly in 1818 while visiting the Pettigrews at Bonarva. First interred in the Blount family cemetery at Mulberry Hill near Edenton, her remains were moved in 1831 to the Pettigrew family burying ground at Bonarva.[15]

John Swann Shepard married Maria Long at the home of Cadwallader Jones in Halifax on November 27, 1821.[16] He sought his fortune first in Florida and then was reported in Tennessee. His ultimate fate is not known.

Penelope M. R. Shepard (1806-1835) developed a disease in her arm early in life and was in delicate health until she died.[17] She

---

[9]*Biographical Directory of the American Congress, 1774-1971*... (Washington: United States Government Printing Office, 1971), 1591, hereinafter cited as *Biographical Directory of Congress*.

[10]Kemp P. Battle, *History of the University of North Carolina* (Raleigh: Edwards and Broughton, 2 volumes, 1907, 1912), I, 236-239, hereinafter cited as Battle, *History of the University*.

[11]*Biographical Directory of Congress*, 1591.

[12]Battle, *History of the University*, I, 824.

[13]Ashe, *Biographical History*, VII, 424. William Biddle Shepard married Charlotte Cazenove in October, 1834; he married Anne Daves Collins in May, 1843. See William Biddle Shepard to Ebenezer Pettigrew, August 31, 1834, and Ebenezer Pettigrew to James Johnston Pettigrew, May 22, 1843, in this volume.

[14]Bryan/Simpson Family Bible in the possession of Mrs. Jesse S. Claypoole, New Bern, typescript at North Carolina Archives, hereinafter cited as Bryan Family Bible; Parish Register of Christ Church, New Bern, typescript at North Carolina Archives, Marriages, 128; *Carolina Centinel* (New Bern), December 22, 1821.

[15]Lemmon, *Pettigrew Papers*, I, 630-631; Ebenezer Pettigrew to Mary Williams Bryan, August 24, 1830, in this volume.

[16]*Carolina Centinel* (New Bern), December 8, 1821. The middle name of Swann is given in Shepard genealogical material, Moore Collection, PC 1406.

[17]Works Progress Administration Cemetery Index, North Carolina Archives.

became a Roman Catholic, although the rest of the family was Episcopalian.[18]

Charles Biddle Shepard (1807 or 1808-1843) was graduated from the University of North Carolina in 1827 with the second highest honors, was admitted to the bar the following year, and settled in New Bern. He served in the North Carolina House of Commons one term and in Congress two terms.[19] He was twice married: to Lydia Jones in 1830 and, after her death in 1833, to Mary Spaight Donnell, daughter of Judge John R. Donnell, in 1840.[20] He left three children: Frederick, Margaret, and Mary.[21]

Richard Muse Shepard was graduated from the University of North Carolina in 1829 and became a lawyer in New Orleans.[22]

Frederick Biddle Shepard[23] was expelled from West Point. To judge from remarks in the letters in this volume, Frederick had a highly unstable character.[24] In 1843 he was living in Mobile, Alabama.[25]

James Biddle Shepard, a graduate of the University of North Carolina in 1834, settled in Raleigh and became United States district attorney for North Carolina.[26] His mother moved from New Bern to Raleigh to live with him.[27] A Democrat, he was nominated for governor in 1846 but was defeated by Whig William A. Graham.[28] On October 26, 1844, James married Frances Donnell of New Bern, sister to the second wife of Charles Biddle Shepard.[29]

---

[18]Ann Blount Pettigrew to Ebenezer Pettigrew, December 30, 1824, in this volume.

[19]*Biographical Directory of Congress*, 1591; Battle, *History of the University*, I, 316.

[20]Parish Register of Christ Church, New Bern, Marriages, 133 (December 20, 1830), 136 (March 24, 1840); Burials, 85 (November 24, 1833).

[21]John Hill Wheeler, *Historical Sketches of North Carolina from 1584 to 1851* (New York: Frederick H. Hitchcock, reprint edition, 2 volumes, 1925), II, 120, hereinafter cited as Wheeler, *Historical Sketches*. See also Parish Register of Christ Church, New Bern, Baptisms, 26, 33, 36.

[22]Battle, *History of the University*, I, 793.

[23]The middle name of Blount is given in Shepard genealogical material, Moore Collection, PC 1406.

[24]Ebenezer Pettigrew to James Johnston Pettigrew, April 30, 1843, in this volume.

[25]Ebenezer Pettigrew to Alfred Gardner, December 7, 1843, in this volume.

[26]Battle, *History of the University*, I, 795, 833.

[27]John Herritage Bryan to Ebenezer Pettigrew, January 19, 1836, in this volume.

[28]Battle, *History of the University*, I, 356.

[29]Parish Register of Christ Church, New Bern, Marriages, 138; Wheeler, *Historical Sketches*, II, 120.

THE BRYAN FAMILY

Two connections developed between Ebenezer Pettigrew and the John Herritage Bryan family. First, Ebenezer's wife's sister, Mary Williams Shepard, married John Herritage Bryan;[30] and second, following the death of Ann Blount Pettigrew the Bryans took little Mary and Nancy Pettigrew into their family circle and reared them.[31]

John Herritage Bryan (1798-1870), a native of New Bern, was graduated from the University of North Carolina in 1815 and admitted to the bar in 1819. He entered politics and sat in the state Senate for two terms, then served two terms in Congress as a Whig. In 1838 he moved to Raleigh for family health reasons, although he continued a punishing circuit of superior court practice in the eastern part of the state.[32] Stephen F. Miller recalls Bryan as "very logical and earnest," with an ample forehead, intelligent face, and courteous manner.[33]

John Wheeler Moore refers to the family of John Herritage and Mary Williams Bryan as "large and interesting."[34] There were, in fact, fourteen children, most of whom are at least mentioned in the letters in this volume.

Francis Theodore Bryan, the oldest child, was born on April 11, 1823.[35] He was graduated from the University of North Carolina in 1842 with first honors and delivered the Latin salutatory at commencement. Appointed to the United States Military Academy at West Point, he was graduated sixth in his class, served in the war with Mexico, and was wounded at Buena Vista. He resigned his commission after the war and settled in St. Louis, Missouri.[36]

---

[30]William S. Powell (ed.), *Dictionary of North Carolina Biography* (Chapel Hill: University of North Carolina Press, projected multivolume series, 1979—), I, 255-256, hereinafter cited as Powell, *DNCB*; Parish Register of Christ Church, New Bern, Marriages, 121. John Herritage Bryan's younger brother, James West Bryan, married Ann Mary Washington in 1831; the two Mrs. Bryans should not be confused.

[31]Ebenezer Pettigrew to John Herritage and Mary Williams Bryan, July 12, 1830, and William Biddle Shepard to Ebenezer Pettigrew, July 17, 1830, in this volume.

[32]*Biographical Directory of Congress*, 616; Powell, *DNCB*, I, 255.

[33]Stephen F. Miller, "Recollections of New Bern Fifty Years Ago" (1873), unpublished manuscript at North Carolina Archives, 19-20, hereinafter cited as Miller, "Recollections." Other statements may be found in Battle, *History of the University*, I, 247, 325, 526-527, 711.

[34]John Wheeler Moore, *History of North Carolina: From the Earliest Discoveries to the Present Time* (Raleigh: Alfred Williams and Co., 2 volumes, 1880), I, 490, hereinafter cited as Moore, *History of North Carolina*.

[35]Bryan Family Bible.

[36]Battle, *History of the University*, I, 477-478.

Mary Shepard Bryan (born September 25, 1824) was two years older than her cousin Mary Pettigrew. The two girls were educated together. Mary Bryan married Edwin G. Speight on December 3, 1851. She died in Raleigh, February 23, 1895.[37]

John Herritage Bryan, Jr. (born November 20, 1825),[38] graduated with third honors in the class of 1844 at the University of North Carolina. He was nicknamed "Keats Bryan," but, according to Johnston Pettigrew, he was not well liked by other students.[39]

William Shepard Bryan (1827-1906), called Billy by his cousin Johnston Pettigrew, was a popular student at the University of North Carolina in the class of 1846. In 1850 he moved to Baltimore, where he eventually became judge of the Maryland Court of Appeals.[40]

James Pettigrew Bryan (1829-1887), class of 1849 at the University of North Carolina, became a physician and practiced in Kinston.[41]

Elizabeth Herritage Bryan (born January 15, 1831), referred to as Betsy, was about the same age as Ann Blount Shepard Pettigrew, and the two girls were educated together. Elizabeth married Kenelm H. Lewis in 1856.[42]

Charles Shepard Bryan (1832-1876), class of 1852 at the University of North Carolina, was living in Cassville, Missouri, at the time of his death.[43]

Octavia Maria Bryan was born April 18, 1834. In 1855 she married John C. Winder.[44]

Henry Ravenscroft Bryan (1836-1919), class of 1856 at the University of North Carolina, became a lawyer and, after the Civil War, a superior court judge in New Bern. He was not a robust person but had a physical disability of some sort. He married Mary Biddle Norcott; their son John Norcott Bryan became ill while the family fled from the Union attack on New Bern in 1862 and died within a few days. The Bryans had at least eight other children: Sarah Frances, Frederick Charles, Mary Norcott, Henry Ravenscroft, Jr., Shepard, Kate, Margaret Shepard, and Isabel Constance.[45]

---

[37]Bryan Family Bible; Parish Register of Christ Church, Raleigh, 210.

[38]Bryan Family Bible.

[39]James Johnston Pettigrew to Ebenezer Pettigrew, July 27, 1843, in this volume; Battle, *History of the University*, I, 586, 799.

[40]Bryan Family Bible; Powell, *DNCB*, I, 264; James Johnston Pettigrew to Ebenezer Pettigrew, July 27, 1843, in this volume.

[41]Bryan Family Bible; Battle, *History of the University*, I, 802.

[42]Bryan Family Bible; Parish Register of Christ Church, Raleigh, 213.

[43]Bryan Family Bible; Battle, *History of the University*, I, 803.

[44]Bryan Family Bible; Parish Register of Christ Church, New Bern, Baptisms, 27; Parish Register of Christ Church, Raleigh, 212.

[45]Bryan Family Bible; Powell, *DNCB*, I, 254; Battle, *History of the University*, I, 807, 834.

Isabelle Ann Bryan (born 1837) was described as "a most beautiful babe." In 1874 "Miss Annie Isabella Bryan" was living in Raleigh with her mother and sister Mrs. Mary Shepard Speight.[46]

Charlotte Emily Bryan was born January 27, 1840. She married Colonel Bryan Grimes in 1863.[47]

George Pettigrew Bryan (1841-1864), a captain in the Confederate army, "was killed by a minnie ball under the heart" while leading his company in a charge two miles east of Richmond, August 16, 1864. He had graduated from the University of North Carolina in 1860 and tutored there in Latin until he was commissioned.[48]

Ann Shepard Bryan was born May 8, 1845.[49]

Frederick Richard Bryan (born May 28, 1846) died December 13, 1863, "at his father's plantation near Raleigh."[50]

A Survey of the Papers, 1819-1843

During the period covered in this volume, the chief correspondent is Ebenezer Pettigrew. The collection of letters and documents is enormous, so that difficult choices had to be made concerning those items most important for inclusion. It was decided to stress social history: family life, customs, education, farming methods, slavery, medical knowledge, the westward movement, and travel and transportation; at the same time, perspective was retained by using some selections relating to politics, marketing methods, commodity prices, and banking. The religious element present in volume I is almost entirely missing from the papers of this period.

Taken together, the letters present a narrative of family history during the first half of the nineteenth century. Family life is revealed by correspondence between Ebenezer Pettigrew and his wife, Nancy, and between Nancy and her sister Mary, from 1819 to 1830. Attitudes toward marriage, details of childbearing and rearing of children, and discussions of food and clothing, health care, and social events are set forth, spiced on occasion with a little gossip about the New Bern gentry.

Following Nancy's death, there is less information on family life. Instead, the theme of agricultural development predominates. Ebenezer's correspondence with James Cathcart Johnston of

---

[46]Bryan Family Bible; New Parish Register of Christ Church, Raleigh, 14. The Bryan Family Bible typescript errs in recording her death at the age of three months and seventeen days.

[47]Bryan Family Bible; Parish Register of Christ Church, Raleigh, 215.

[48]Bryan Family Bible; Powell, *DNCB*, I, 255-256; Battle, *History of the University*, I, 672, 719, 812.

[49]Bryan Family Bible. This line has been typed over.

[50]Bryan Family Bible.

Edenton provides the best summary of his farming methods and business enterprises. While Ebenezer served in the United States Congress (1835-1837), his overseer, Doctrine Davenport, wrote him weekly with explicit reports of the activities of sowing, reaping, ditching, sawing, the health and care of his "people," and the like.

Marketing corn, wheat, shingles, and staves involved not only correspondence but also frequent trips to Norfolk, Baltimore, and New York. At first dealing with two mercantile houses located in nearby Plymouth, J. S. Bryan and Thomas and W. A. Turner, Ebenezer increased production to the point that he sold directly to Hardy and Brothers in Norfolk; to Van Bokkelen and White in New York, and later Bryan and Company there also; and to John Williams in Charleston. There is correspondence with Jonathan Eastman and Frederick Vanderburgh concerning the building of farm machinery. The bulk of this correspondence deals with prices and quantities, and from it only letters containing general remarks on economic conditions have been included. Because these years encompassed Andrew Jackson's war on the Bank of the United States, the overexpansion of state credit for internal improvements, and the panic of 1837, there are some interesting opinions expressed, as well as descriptions of the effects of inflation and subsequent depression.

As the Pettigrew children grew up, education became increasingly important. After a series of tutors, the boys were sent to Hillsborough to attend the famous academy of William James Bingham. Ebenezer insisted on regular letters from his sons, to which he responded with firm directions. Bingham reported regularly to the parent, sometimes suggesting the need for certain remarks in a future letter to one of the boys, which suggestions seem always to have been followed. There are both serious and light insights into academy life, discipline, and education of the time.

All three surviving sons went from Bingham's to the University of North Carolina at Chapel Hill, although William spent a few months at Round Hill in Northampton, Massachusetts. Their letters from Chapel Hill describe professors, the two literary societies, studies, monetary needs, and social life in some detail. Not only do Ebenezer's letters contain advice to his sons, but the older brothers likewise advised the younger.

The education of the two daughters was also given attention in letters from Ebenezer to his sister-in-law Mary Williams Bryan. He often stated, however, that he knew little about rearing girls and abided by the recommendations of the Bryans. By the time Mary Pettigrew went to Washington, D.C., to school, she had become a good correspondent. Her letters to her brothers William and James

Johnston are colorful and detailed, while revealing much about the personalities of all three.

The lowlands of eastern North Carolina were unhealthy from late summer until frost; the inhabitants suffered from chills and fever and from bilious fever. Added to this were the usual diseases of measles and whooping cough, with occasional outbreaks of smallpox and cholera. Retaining medical personnel in rural areas seems to have been a problem, judging from the rapid turnover of physicians in the Lake Phelps area. Not only does almost every letter contain information or inquiries about health, but a number of physicians were among Ebenezer's correspondents: Old, Sawyer, Warren, Hardison, Lewis, and others. There are mentions of visiting other physicians, and in one case a dentist, in Baltimore, Philadelphia, and New York. Almost every letter to or from a physician has been included, although most bills were omitted.

The westward movement, which gained momentum after the War of 1812, is revealed in numerous letters from William A. Dickinson, Henry Alexander, Moses E. Cator, and David M. Sargent. Living conditions, soil and crops, the state of law and justice, prices, inflation, and mushrooming towns are described. Some settlers came home again, as did John Baptist Beasley; others like Moses Cator stayed and urged their relatives to join them. Memphis, Vicksburg, central Alabama, and even parts of northern Florida are portrayed by migrating North Carolinians in their letters to Ebenezer Pettigrew.

It is rather surprising to read of the extensive travels undertaken by persons of the period. Ebenezer discussed driving a light vehicle from eastern North Carolina across the Appalachians beyond Salem to Abingdon, Virginia, and then to Nashville and returning in 1817, which trip is described in volume I of this series. Later travels to the west involved a route through Norfolk, Baltimore, Winchester, and Abingdon and on to Nashville. Boats were utilized as often as possible until the "cars" began service; thus, descriptions of transportation by sailboat, steamboat, and railroad are included. In the fall of 1838, Charles and William journeyed from Baltimore to Harpers Ferry, across to Kentucky, up the Ohio River to Lake Ontario, past Niagara Falls and down the St. Lawrence River to Quebec, thence to New York, and back home, a journey of some three months. Details of adventures, accidents, and scenery are found in their correspondence.

Many of the letters contain weather information, including dates of hurricanes, rainfall and snowfall amounts, and facts about major floods, significant freezes, and unusually high temperatures. Such data is found chiefly in letters between Ebenezer and his two older sons, his overseer, and his friend James C. Johnston.

Political events discussed include the major state elections during the Jacksonian period; events in Congress from 1830 to 1844; and opinions on Andrew Jackson, Martin Van Buren, Henry Clay, John C. Calhoun, William Henry Harrison, and John Tyler, expressed from the Whig point of view.

The choice of the year 1843 as the end of this volume was determined by Ebenezer's retirement from active plantation direction and his settlement at Magnolia.

A SURVEY OF DOCUMENTS OMITTED, 1819-1843

In the Private Collections, John Herritage Bryan Collection, PC 6, at the North Carolina Archives there are twenty-two letters written between 1823 and 1843 that have been omitted. Eleven are from Ann Blount Pettigrew to her sister Mary Williams Bryan; seven are from Ebenezer Pettigrew to John Herritage Bryan; two are from Ebenezer to Mary Williams Bryan; and one is from each of the two Pettigrew daughters to the Bryans. The content of all these is unexceptional or, if of special interest, is given in other letters that have been included in this volume. They give ordinary details of domestic life in this period.

In the Private Collections, Pettigrew Papers, PC 13, at the North Carolina Archives there is a wide variety of documents that have been omitted. Some were not used because they are outside the general theme of this volume. Others, such as statements from factors, repeat information that may be found in economic histories and newspaper price lists and do not contribute to the history of the Pettigrew family. Letters from unknown persons and single letters constituting the only correspondence from an individual were omitted unless an unusual event is mentioned.

Commercial correspondents include Blount and Jackson, A. H. Van Bokkelen, Thomas and W. A. Turner, Van Bokkelen and White, Charles Edmondston and Company, Hicks and Smith, Bettner and Wright, Gordon and Townes, John Williams, Bryan and Maitland, Hardy and Brothers, John S. Bryan and Company, George S. Rathbone, John Trimble, Trimble and Wilson, and Williams and Welsman. Only a few examples of their letters have been included.

A dozen or so lengthy letters pertaining to lands in Tennessee were exchanged by Ebenezer Pettigrew with Moses E. Cator and Alfred Gardner and are omitted. They relate to payment of taxes and the continuous effort to sell the property.

Other omitted letters relate to the purchase of farm machinery, to carpenters and other craftsmen, and to efforts to locate better varieties of wheat and clover seed. Correspondents include

Jonathan Eastman, William A. Dickinson, William Woodley, and Nathaniel Brickhouse. There are also a few letters from ship captains John Dunbar and Joseph A. Spruill, who transported Pettigrew cargo, in which they describe voyages or notify of arrivals or returns of vessels.

During 1835 and 1836, after his election to Congress, Ebenezer Pettigrew received a number of social invitations in Washington. It was decided that the Washington scene has been depicted adequately in other printed sources, and therefore these letters were omitted. While in Congress Ebenezer also received numerous letters from his constituents, most of which have been omitted. They deal with routine matters such as postal routes, West Point appointments, new equipment at lighthouses, subscriptions to Washington newspapers, pensions, land patents in the West, and claims against France for naval depredations during the Napoleonic period. Frequently these were forwarded to federal officials, and Ebenezer kept copies with notations of action taken.

The rest of the omitted documents pertain to either Tyrrell and Washington county associates or to old friends and relatives. Among the county correspondents are William A. Dickinson, Sheriff Henry Alexander, and the Phelpses, Brickhouses, Spruills, and Woodleys. Letters from old friends include several from Thomas Trotter and a few to and from James C. Johnston. Family members some of whose letters were omitted because they are repetitive and overlapping include John Herritage Bryan and the Shepards. As Pettigrew became wealthy, there is a scattering of solicitations for charitable funds and personal loans.

The Pettigrew collection at the archives contains for this period seven large volumes with approximately 125 documents mounted in each, as well as seven boxes of papers. Documents omitted number around 800.

The Pettigrew Family Papers in the Southern Historical Collection at the University of North Carolina Library at Chapel Hill contain more than 3,000 items. The most common omissions from this collection are hundreds of receipts—of every size, handwritten and printed, some almost illegible, some illiterate, and for amounts varying from a dollar to several thousands of dollars. There are receipts for purchases of clothing in Baltimore, for newspaper subscriptions, for binding books, for postage, for corn, for repayment of loans, and for many other expenses. There are two folders of receipts and other papers pertaining solely to the operation of the schooner *Virginia Hodges*, plus fifty or so additional schooner receipts scattered through other folders.

Another large category of omissions is that of invoices and other statements of accounts due, totaling nearly 200. There are at least ten statements from doctors who cared for the Pettigrew slaves, as well as invoices for cloth, shoes, and other supplies for slaves, quantities of staple food and some luxuries, educational needs and clothing supplies for Charles, William, and James Johnston Pettigrew at Hillsborough Academy, bar iron and machine parts, and various other items.

Also omitted are most of the letters from the South Carolina branch of the family. One of the cousins from this branch, who later married Charles Lockhart Pettigrew, deposited in the collection a group of letters written to her mother by her Petigru brothers Charles and James Louis, as well as numerous letters exchanged between mother and daughter relative to events in family life in South Carolina.

A small group of papers from 1832 relate to the estate of Nathaniel Phelps, of which Ebenezer Pettigrew was executor.

Judging from the presence of court orders and receipts, Ebenezer must have been the equivalent of county treasurer in 1834-1839. During this same time the Tyrrell County Courthouse was built, and there are about twenty-five documents relating to construction transactions.

William Shepard Pettigrew apparently made numerous friends at Hillsborough Academy and the University of North Carolina. Exchanges of schoolboy correspondence and also some in later years include letters from Albert G. Hubbird, Dennis D. Ferebee, John M. Ashurst, Richard S. Sims, Augustus H. Roby, and Richard B. Creecy, most of which have not been included.

Personal letters have been omitted if they add no new information or repeat what was written in other letters. This group, including family letters and some correspondence with James C. Johnston and Thomas Trotter, numbers close to 100 letters. Correspondence with John Baptist Beasley is part business and part family. Much of it has been omitted, some twenty or thirty documents in all.

A total of approximately 2,888 documents located in the Pettigrew Family Papers at Chapel Hill have been omitted.

METHODOLOGY

The Pettigrew Papers are deposited in the Archives, Division of Archives and History, North Carolina Department of Cultural Resources, Raleigh, and in the Southern Historical Collection, University of North Carolina Library, Chapel Hill. In addition to letters in the Pettigrew collection at the North Carolina Archives, some from the John Herritage Bryan Collection at the same repository have been located and used. The location of each document is indicated thus in the heading: A&H for Private

Collections, Pettigrew Papers, PC 13, North Carolina Archives; A&H, BRYAN for Private Collections, John Herritage Bryan Collection, PC 6, North Carolina Archives; and UNC for Pettigrew Family Papers, Southern Historical Collection.

Most of the documents are originals, and their covers indicate that some were hand delivered and some mailed. Many of the letters written by Ebenezer Pettigrew were transcribed from his drafts. Some letters, especially on business matters, were copied by their senders and only the copies have been preserved; such documents are marked with asterisks (*). Only two letters were transcribed from copies made by a person other than the sender, and these are so indicated.

The documents in this volume have been transcribed and printed as exactly as was feasible. Editorial insertions appear in italics in square brackets ([ ]), while inferred readings of illegible material are given in square brackets in roman type. [*Sic*] denotes factual errors. Material underlined in the original is printed in italics. Letters and words canceled by the writer but still legible are printed within angle brackets (<>), and solidi (//) enclose interlinear insertions. A solidus separates words written at the end of one page and repeated by the author at the beginning of the next page.

Spelling, or rather misspelling, varies greatly, and the editor has interpreted those words that are so grossly misspelled that they might be unintelligible to the reader. Superscript characters have been retained, and superfluous punctuation and flourishes have been eliminated.

Indentation and format of the letters have been standardized. To facilitate use of the volume, the editor has added the place of origin of each document in the dateline position if not given and if known, as well as the date if it does not appear there in the original. Outside addresses have been included, but other notations have been deleted.

An effort has been made to identify as many people and places as possible, with the exception of presidents of the United States, contemporary governors of North Carolina, and other well-known persons, such as Napoleon Bonaparte. Where the writer has given only one name, the other name if known has been added in brackets with sufficient frequency to keep the reader informed. At times identification has been impossible, however; the writer of a letter sometimes used only a common given name or surname. In other cases the records that are needed for identification are missing for the month or year concerned. The editor has searched newspapers, marriage bonds, county tax lists, censuses, minutes of the courts of pleas and quarter sessions, civil action papers, wills, documentary volumes, memoirs, and genealogies. Except in cases where the writer of a letter remains unidentified, no notations concerning efforts at identification have been included. Cross-references appear in footnotes where the editor felt they were immediately valuable, as well as in the index. The editor prepared both notes and index.

Special thanks are extended to the late C. O. Cathey of the University of North Carolina at Chapel Hill, who directed the typing of nearly half the Pettigrew Papers used in this volume; to Frances W. Kunstling, whose knowledge of Tennessee history clarified numerous points related to the bounty lands in that state; to friends and colleagues who assisted with the quantities of typing—Barbara H. Willis and Gayle G. Peacock; to the staffs of the search rooms at the North Carolina Archives and the Southern Historical Collection; and to Susan Marie McDonough, who undertook a bibliographical project in the Carlyle Campbell Library at Meredith College. Martha W. (Mrs. John H.) Daniels provided a number of photographs of Pettigrew portraits, as well as valuable genealogical information. Mr. Thomas Pettigrew assisted in identifying portraits. The editor also appreciates the encouragement, advice, and work of Dr. Jeffrey J. Crow, Kathleen B. Wyche, and other staff members of the Historical Publications Section, Division of Archives and History, who saw the book through press.

SARAH MCCULLOH LEMMON

Meredith College
Raleigh, North Carolina

LIST OF DOCUMENTS
1819-1843
INCLUDED IN THIS VOLUME

1. Ebenezer Pettigrew to James Cathcart Johnston, January 5, 1819
2. Ann Blount Pettigrew to Ebenezer Pettigrew, January 7, 1819
3. Ebenezer Pettigrew to Ann Blount Pettigrew, January 13, 1819
4. Ebenezer Pettigrew to Ann Blount Pettigrew, February 13, 1819
5. Ebenezer Pettigrew to Ann Blount Pettigrew, March 26, 1819
6. Ebenezer Pettigrew to James Cathcart Johnston, April 9, 1819
7. Rebecca Tunstall to Mary Lockhart Pettigrew, April 24, 1819
8. John Gray Blount, Jr., to William Shepard, May 31, 1819
9. Ann Blount Pettigrew to Ebenezer Pettigrew, [June, 1819]
10. Ebenezer Pettigrew to James Cathcart Johnston, August 4, 1819 [copy]
11. Ebenezer Pettigrew to Ann Blount Pettigrew, September 10, 1819
12. Ebenezer Pettigrew to Ann Blount Pettigrew, September 18, 1819
13. Ebenezer Pettigrew to Ann Blount Pettigrew, October 1, 1819
14. Ebenezer Pettigrew to James Cathcart Johnston, December 10, 1819
15. Dr. M[atthias] E. Sawyer to [Ebenezer Pettigrew], January 4, 1820
16. [Ebenezer Pettigrew] to James Cathcart Johnston, February 20, 1820
17. James Moffatt to Ebenezer Pettigrew, February 23, 1820
18. John Swann Shepard to Ebenezer Pettigrew, April 23, 1820
19. Moses E. Cator to Ebenezer Pettigrew, August 8, 1820
20. John C. McLemore to Ebenezer Pettigrew, November 11, 1820
21. Ebenezer Pettigrew to Major Ferrange, March 17, 1821
22. Ann Blount Pettigrew to Mary Williams Shepard, November 16, 1821
23. Durand Hatch to Ebenezer Pettigrew, December 22, 1821
24. Ebenezer Pettigrew's Tax List, 1821
25. Ebenezer Pettigrew to James Cathcart Johnston, February 4, 1822
26. Dr. James A. Norcom to Ebenezer Pettigrew, February 19, 1822
27. Ann Blount Pettigrew to Ebenezer Pettigrew, June 13, 1822
28. Ebenezer Pettigrew to Ann Blount Pettigrew, June 21, 1822
29. Ebenezer Pettigrew to Ann Blount Pettigrew, July 2, 1822

30. Ebenezer Pettigrew to Ann Blount Pettigrew, September 10, 1822
31. Ebenezer Pettigrew to Ann Blount Pettigrew, September 17, 1822
32. John C. Calhoun to Ebenezer Pettigrew, March 26, 1823
33. Ann Blount Pettigrew to Mary Williams Bryan, October 7, 1823
34. Ebenezer Pettigrew to James Cathcart Johnston, January 12, 1824
35. Ann Blount Pettigrew to Mary Williams Bryan, April 20, 1824
36. Ann Blount Pettigrew to Mary Williams Bryan, May 27, 1824
37. Dr. Thomas Old to Dr. Samuel Henry, July, 1824
38. Ebenezer Pettigrew to James Cathcart Johnston, August 3, 1824
39. Ann Blount Pettigrew to Mary Williams Bryan, November 15, 1824
40. Ann Blount Pettigrew to Ebenezer Pettigrew, December 30, 1824
41. Ebenezer Pettigrew to James Cathcart Johnston, January 4, 1825
42. Ann Blount Pettigrew to Ebenezer Pettigrew, January 10, 1825
43. Ann Blount Pettigrew to Ebenezer Pettigrew, January 18, 1825
44. Ann Blount Pettigrew to Ebenezer Pettigrew, January 31, 1825
45. Dr. Thomas Old to Ebenezer Pettigrew, March 17, 1825
46. Ebenezer Pettigrew to James Cathcart Johnston, April 26, 1825
47. David Witherspoon to Ebenezer Pettigrew, June 9, 1825
48. Dr. Thomas Old to Ebenezer Pettigrew, August 5, 1825
49. Receipt from Pettigrew Children's Tutor, September 22, 1825
50. Ebenezer Pettigrew to John Herritage Bryan, October 16, 1825
51. Charles Lockhart Pettigrew to Mary Lockhart Pettigrew, November 12, 1825
52. J. B. O'Flaherty to Ebenezer Pettigrew, March 2, 1826
53. Ebenezer Pettigrew to John Herritage Bryan, April 18, 1826
54. Ann Blount Pettigrew to Mary Williams Bryan, July 11, 1826
55. Ann Blount Pettigrew to Mary Williams Bryan, September 11, 1826
56. Ann Blount Pettigrew to Mary Williams Bryan, October 20, 1826
57. Ebenezer Pettigrew to Ann Blount Pettigrew, November 28, 1826
58. Ebenezer Pettigrew to Ann Blount Pettigrew, December 5, 1826
59. Ann Blount Pettigrew to Ebenezer Pettigrew, December 18, 1826

86. James Cathcart Johnston to Ebenezer Pettigrew, February 17, 1829 [copy]
87. Ebenezer Pettigrew to James Cathcart Johnston, March 30, 1829
88. James Cathcart Johnston to Ebenezer Pettigrew, April 1, 1829 [copy]
89. Charles Biddle Shepard to Ebenezer Pettigrew, May 30, 1829
90. Ebenezer Pettigrew to James Cathcart Johnston, June 5, 1829
91. Ebenezer Pettigrew to John Herritage Bryan, September 1, 1829
92. Charles Biddle Shepard to Ebenezer Pettigrew, October 26, 1829
93. Charles Lockhart Pettigrew to Mary Lockhart Pettigrew, December 18, 1829
94. Ebenezer Pettigrew to Ann Blount Pettigrew, December 27, 1829
95. Ann Blount Pettigrew to Ebenezer Pettigrew, December 31, 1829
96. Ebenezer Pettigrew to Ann Blount Pettigrew, January 5, 1830
97. Ann Blount Pettigrew to Charles Lockhart and William Shepard Pettigrew, January 6, 1830
98. Ebenezer Pettigrew to Ann Blount Pettigrew, January 11, 1830
99. Charles Lockhart Pettigrew to Ebenezer Pettigrew, February 16, 1830
100. Ebenezer Pettigrew to James Cathcart Johnston, March 9, 1830
101. Ann Blount Pettigrew to Mary Williams Bryan, March 9, 1830
102. Mary Williams Bryan to Ann Blount Pettigrew, March 16, 1830
103. Frederick Biddle Shepard to Ann Blount Pettigrew, June 20, 1830
104. Ebenezer Pettigrew to William James Bingham, July 6, 1830 [enclosing letter to his sons]
105. Ebenezer Pettigrew to John Herritage and Mary Williams Bryan, July 12, 1830
106. Richard Muse Shepard to Ebenezer Pettigrew, July 17, 1830
107. Ebenezer Pettigrew to Mary Williams Bryan, August 24, 1830
108. Ebenezer Pettigrew to Mary Williams Bryan, September 23, 1830
109. Thomas Pettigru to Ebenezer Pettigrew, October 7, 1830
110. Nathaniel Phelps to Ebenezer Pettigrew, October 10, 1830
111. Ebenezer Pettigrew to James Cathcart Johnston, December 5, 1830

338. John Herritage Bryan to Ebenezer Pettigrew, September 20, 1840
339. Ebenezer Pettigrew to Moses E. Cator, September 22, 1840 [copy]
340. William Biddle Shepard to Ebenezer Pettigrew, September 28, 1840
341. William Shepard Pettigrew to Augustus H. Roby, October 12, 1840 [copy]
342. John Trimble to Ebenezer Pettigrew, October [1]7, 1840
343. Ebenezer Pettigrew to William Shepard Pettigrew, October 28, 1840
344. Bill of Sale to Ebenezer Pettigrew, October 31, 1840
345. Richard S. Sims to William Shepard Pettigrew, November 18, 1840
346. Hardy and Brothers to Ebenezer Pettigrew, November 23, 1840
347. William Shepard Pettigrew to Ebenezer Pettigrew, November 30, 1840
348. Ebenezer Pettigrew to Mary Williams Bryan, December 29, 1840
349. Henry Alexander to Ebenezer Pettigrew, January 6, 1841
350. Mary Williams Bryan to Ebenezer Pettigrew, January 22, 1841
351. Ebenezer Pettigrew to William Shepard Pettigrew, February 18, 1841
352. William Shepard Pettigrew to Ebenezer Pettigrew, February 18, 1841
353. John Baptist Beasley to Ebenezer Pettigrew, March 29, 1841
354. Edward Stanly to Ebenezer Pettigrew, April 12, 1841
355. John Baptist Beasley to Ebenezer Pettigrew, April 28, 1841
356. Ebenezer Pettigrew to James Cathcart Johnston, May 17, 1841
357. Mary Blount Pettigrew to Mary Williams Bryan, May 27, 1841
358. Ebenezer Pettigrew to James Cathcart Johnston, June 7, 1841
359. Hardy and Brothers to Ebenezer Pettigrew, July 13, 1841
360. John Herritage Bryan to Ebenezer Pettigrew, July 18, 1841
361. James Johnston Pettigrew to Ebenezer Pettigrew, July 20, 1841
362. Mary Blount Pettigrew to John Herritage Bryan, July 23, 1841
363. William James Bingham to Ebenezer Pettigrew, August 17, [1841]
364. Ebenezer Pettigrew to William Shepard Pettigrew, August 19, 1841

415. Mary Blount Pettigrew to James Johnston Pettigrew, March 28, 1843
416. John Herritage Bryan to Ebenezer Pettigrew, April 1, 1843
417. Joshua Skinner to Ebenezer Pettigrew, April 24, 1843
418. Ebenezer Pettigrew to James Johnston Pettigrew, April 30, 1843
419. Hardy and Brothers to Ebenezer Pettigrew, May 19, 1843
420. William Shepard Pettigrew to Mary Blount Pettigrew, May 20, 1843
421. Ebenezer Pettigrew to James Johnston Pettigrew, May 22, 1843
422. Thomas Turner to Ebenezer Pettigrew, June 7, 1843
423. Henry Alexander to Ebenezer Pettigrew, June 21, 1843
424. Jesse Alexander to Ebenezer Pettigrew, July 10, 1843
425. Ebenezer Pettigrew to Charles Lockhart and William Shepard Pettigrew, July 23, 1843
426. James Johnston Pettigrew to Ebenezer Pettigrew, July 27, 1843
427. William Shepard Pettigrew to Ebenezer Pettigrew, August 2, 1843
428. James Alfred Pearce to Ebenezer Pettigrew, August 7, 1843
429. Mary Blount Pettigrew to James Johnston Pettigrew, August 10, [1843]
430. Ebenezer Pettigrew to John Herritage Bryan, August 15, 1843
431. Henry Alexander to Ebenezer Pettigrew, August 20, 1843
432. John Herritage Bryan to Ebenezer Pettigrew, August 26, 1843
433. Mary Blount Pettigrew to James Johnston Pettigrew, September 2, [1843]
434. James Louis Petigru to Ebenezer Pettigrew, September 5, 1843
435. Ebenezer Pettigrew to Charles Lockhart and William Shepard Pettigrew, September 11, 1843
436. Ebenezer Pettigrew to Charles Lockhart and William Shepard Pettigrew, September 17, 1843
437. William Shepard Pettigrew to James Johnston Pettigrew, September 26, 1843
438. William Shepard Pettigrew to Ebenezer Pettigrew, October 3, 1843
439. Ann Blount Shepard Pettigrew to [William Shepard Pettigrew], October 29, 1843
440. William A. Dickinson to Ebenezer Pettigrew, October 31, 1843
441. Ebenezer Pettigrew to James Johnston Pettigrew, November 1, 1843

THE PETTIGREW PAPERS

1819-1843

Ebenezer Pettigrew to James Cathcart Johnston[1] UNC

Bonarva,[2] Jan. 5, 1819

My dear Sir

Your very obliging and friendly letter of 16th Nov. came safe to hand a month after its date, I take the first opportunity of answering it. If your visit to my house and view of my feeble and embarrassed efforts, will be a means of extending your views of improvement, my pleasure from the visit, though I had thought as great as my mind was susceptable, will be greatly increased; but on the other hand if your plans should not succeed to your expectation and be no more than vexation, I hope you will pardon me for having led you into a difficulty and permit me to number it as one more of the unfortunate events of which I am the innocent cause. I thank you for your friendly advice respecting the state of my mind, I know the folly of it, but alas! it is out of my power to control. At this time I write with the greatest difficulty and to collect my scattered ideas gives me real pain; I mention it as an excuse for my stiffness of diction, & inaccuracy which I know you will overlook. I fear my dear friend you have formed too good an opinion of me, all I can say, is, I pray God that I may not by some unfortunate act make shipwreck of it, and that you may never have it in your power to think that you were mistaken; I say think because I know your goo[*d*]ness would never permit you (though disappointed) to expose one for whose wellfare you ever felt so great an interest. As for the happiness which I enjoy in my family I thank my God, it is without interruption. But I have no doubt you can find a great number who would prfer windmills, water mills or canals through low ground to a wife, such perhaps as they have got.

While my dear companion was at Newbern on a visit I bore the seperation tolerably well, but since this is no longer a home, it requires all my fortitude to stay at it and I intended to set out on a visit to her this day, but my overseer went away on Christmas day and has not yet returned, consequently I must stay. To stay here and attend to my business is fulfilling the duty which I owe her and my dear little children I hope it will always be but necessary for me to know my duty to do it, though I should feal as if knives were seperating the flesh from the bones. On the first Inst. I recv[d] a letter from M[rs] Pettigrew, all the family were well except M[r] Shepard who had been very ill, but was better, he was unwell when I was there and I fear for him. My business goes on tolerably well here I find the saw more trouble to keep in order than I expected.

My poor old Mother[3] has been very sick but is better, she is yet in an unsettled state of mind and what is to become of her I know not; I feal for her sincerely but am perfectly unable to relieve her distresses. I engaged your chair when in Newbern it will be done the first of Feb. and [*torn*] will be sent to you in the vessil which carries my furniture [r]ound I thought it unnecessary to countermand the order because if you did not like it when you saw it can no doubt be deposed of.

I hope to have the pleasure of seeing you in this month, in the interval Please to give my best respects to the Ladies and assure your self of the Esteem & regard of your friend

E Pettigrew

N.B. It would give me great pleasure to know that I should live to see you happily married.

James C. Johnston Esqr

[*Addressed*] James C. Johnston esqr
Hays

---

[1]James Cathcart Johnston (1782-1865), son of Governor Samuel Johnston, was a wealthy planter who lived at Hayes Plantation near Edenton his entire life. He never married, and at his death he bequeathed his large estates to three friends—Edward Wood, Christopher W. Hallowell, and Henry J. Futrell. Although his disinherited relatives challenged his will in 1867, the North Carolina Supreme Court upheld a decision favoring the defendants. J. G. de Roulhac Hamilton and Max R. Williams (eds.), *The Papers of William Alexander Graham* (Raleigh: Division of Archives and History, Department of Cultural Resources, projected 8 volumes, 1957—), VII, 269n, hereinafter cited as Hamilton and Williams, *Graham Papers*; Thomas C. Parramore, *Cradle of the Colony: The History of Chowan County and Edenton, North Carolina* (Edenton: Chamber of Commerce, 1967), 78-79; Archibald Henderson, *North Carolina: The Old North State and the New* (Chicago: Lewis Publishing Company, 2 volumes, 1941), II, 812, hereinafter cited as Henderson, *North Carolina.*

[2]Bonarva was named by Charles Pettigrew in 1790. Ebenezer built a house there for his bride. Lemmon, *Pettigrew Papers*, I, 88, 497.

[3]Mary Lockhart Pettigrew, second wife of the Reverend Charles Pettigrew and stepmother to Ebenezer, resided at Belgrade, the "home" plantation, until her death in 1833. Lemmon, *Pettigrew Papers*, I, xix, 8n, 93n, 125, 138n, 208, 380.

Ann Blount Pettigrew to Ebenezer Pettigrew UNC

[*New Bern, January 7, 1819*]

My dear Husband,

You cannot complain of my not writing often. I wish I may not tire you with my letters, though I need not /fear/ for I feel assured that they are always agreeable if they are written in a legible hand, I am sorry to inform you of Pa's indisposition again he has had a very severe attack since my last letter he was confined to the bed several days & is now confined to the room the D^r says it is Reumatism but he has been very sick be it what it may, the rest of the family are well. I expect it will not be very long before we shall see You. I am very anxious for the time to roll round, Pa, has employed them to white wash the house but they have not began to paint—which I am anxious /to/ have done before our furniture arrives how much happiness should I feell if it was where our interest was & We could be always together but we must wait for time to do all things & if it can never be we must be resigned to our lot. I hope you will not forget my flowers in the box also two passion vines, & inquire of Sam for the cypress vine seed which I fogot to bring with me will you also bring what feathers there are as we shall have use for them, & if it is convenient have the wooden things made if not we may buy them here. Pa' sickness confines us entirely we have not been visiting but once neither are we overun with visitors, I mentioned his riding once & by that exposure got a relapse.

I hope Aunt Pettigrew [*Mary Lockhart Pettigrew*] has re-cove/re/d health. I gave Master Charles a dressing for bad behaviour & it offended him so much that he wend down stairs & told of it to Mary who he flees to in all cases of necessity, he has behaved much better ever since, he came after breakfast to rock the cradle by way of making friends. I know of no news worth relating, Geo. Badger[1] is married & is expected down with his wife her sisters & Brothers & a cousin (young lady) also his groomsman W—— Stanly[2] who they say is courting one of the sisters, poor fellow he will get a wife at last. do write soon, remember my love to your Mother and believe m[e]

as ever affectionate yours—
Ann B Pettigrew.

Newbern January 7th 1819—new year I entirely forgot to wish you a merry christmas in my other letter—though it was a very dull one to me my mind dwelt upon upon one subject which I shall ever regret & feel hurt at & distressed at as long as I live my feelings are burried from the world but I suffer the more.

[*Addressed*] Mr E Pettigrew,
Skinnersville,
N.C.

---

[1]George Edmund Badger (1795-1866) married Rebecca Turner in 1818. A native of New Bern, Badger served as a superior court judge (1820-1825) before moving to Raleigh in 1825. He was appointed secretary of the navy by William Henry Harrison in 1841 but resigned when Tyler succeeded Harrison as president. From 1846 to 1854 he was United States senator from North Carolina. Powell, *DNCB*, I, 79-80.

[2]Wright C. Stanly of New Bern, a lawyer, had served in the North Carolina Senate in 1814. John L. Cheney, Jr. (ed.), *North Carolina Government, 1585-1979: A Narrative and Statistical History* . . . (Raleigh: North Carolina Department of the Secretary of State, second, updated edition, 1981), 265, hereinafter cited as Cheney, *North Carolina Government*. He moved to Mobile after this period. A bachelor, he had red hair and always wore spectacles when practicing before the bar. Wright Stanly was a cousin to John Stanly, the prominent Federalist legislator and congressman. Miller, "Recollections," 20.

Ebenezer Pettigrew to Ann Blount Pettigrew UNC

Bonarva Jan 13, 1819

My dearest Girl

I recv^d^ your affectionate letter of Dec. on new years day and yours of that day I recv^d^ yesterday, I am much obliged to you for them; I regret to learn that your Pa has not yet recovered but I hope he is by this time much on the mend. On the receit /of/ your first I determined to go and see him and yourself as soon as Whidby[1] returned from Christmasing, but he staid so long that my business constrained me to stay and also Mothers letter informed us that he was better. No one can be more anxious to see another than I am to see you but positively my business so compleatly occupies me that I know not what to do first. As for Whidby he has turned out to be an obstinate, oppiniated fool, who believes he knows every thing and in fact knows nothing, my dictates he treats with perfect contempt not from disrespect of my person but from an idea of his superior knowledge even of my own business. I set out tomorrow morning for Col. Wiggins' vandue and from thence to Edenton. Immediately on my return I intend to discharge him. What my arrangement will be then I am unable to tell you, but I do not by any means dispair of going on tolerably well. I find Mr Cowan[2] quite a clever fellow, and I think will after a little experience mannage pretty well he is yet coopering. Our Bill would do much better than W. Mother has discharged <Asburn> Ashburn[3] and he swairs he will not remove his family they are there yet; he has had a good many drunken frolicks and abused the old lady very much. Mother has got tolerable well she has not made any complaint to me and I act as though I knew nothing about it, they may jog on as they will.

I hope by the 12 Feb you will see us all pack & package but you must not expect me to stay with /you/ more than a month, but my dearest girl if we part in love and meet in love and continue to love each other in absence and when together let us lift up our hearts to God in praises to him that he has united us in the bonds of marriage. My dear I will never leave nor forsake you and if before marriage I languished for you I yet glory in that union and that affection which I then felt I can assure you has not diminished one attom, I am ready at any time to lay down my life for your happiness;

I have purchased a negroe woman & child she is for a cook and I think will do much better than any we have got unless it is melia she was sold for a good washer and ironer she is 23 years of age and pretty likely, [*torn*] has taken a great liking to her and it so turned [*torn*] head that I had to give him a floging on sunday last.

Do not think that W[*hedbee*]. and myself are always quarriling we have had but one slight jar yet, and /when/ I discharge him I expect to do it without any anger.

Pray kiss my dear little boys for me and remember me affectionately to your Pa, Ma & family and believe me your ever affectionate and Loving husband

E Pettigrew

N.B. I am much obliged to you for the receit for the gout but I shall not be apt to follow it exactly

NB. My saw mill answers very well and with me at her head is good for ten dollars pr day

[*Addressed*] Mrs Ann B Pettigrew
Newbern

---

[1]Whedbee was Ebenezer Pettigrew's overseer at this time.

[2]No Cowan is listed as a head of family in Tyrrell or Washington County in either 1820 or 1830, but several persons by that name are listed in Bertie County in the 1830 census, according to Ronald Vern Jackson, David Schaefermeyer, and Gary Ronald Teeples (eds.), *North Carolina 1830 Census Index* (Bountiful, Utah: Accelerated Indexing Systems, 1976), 41, hereinafter cited as *1830 Census Index*.

[3]Ashburn was Mary Lockhart Pettigrew's overseer.

Ebenezer Pettigrew to Ann Blount Pettigrew UNC

Plimouth Feb 13, 1819

My dearest Girl

I came up to this place to day with the intention of selling my corn but I shall fail to get my price. When I returned home /from [New]/ [*Bern*] I found Mother still in joperdy that family yet with her and Mrs Ashburn very sick what is her complaint no one knows. Doctor Ellis[1] attends her. Anthoney had resisted Whedbee's authority and in the affray Will got from A. a terrable cut on the arm which has entirely disabled him for the present. Anthoney then ran away & has not yet been taken. Do not think that all this has put me out of temper for I assure you I was never more cool and deliberate in /my/ movements every thing else goes on tolerable well Scuppernong has been quite sickly but geting less so, the complaint is something of the Epidemic in a mild form Col. Tarkinstons[2] /wife/ has died of it. I hope you have had the bacon hung up do have the pickle pored from the pork and boild and when cold let it put back to the Pork. I hope to be under way for Newburn before long but I have got to go to Edenton & to Alligator first, two fellows in a fray down there the other day cut a Constable throat but it is said /he will/ get over it. I hope before this your Pa is much on the mend do remember me to him your Ma & family also kiss my dear little children for me and believe me to be my dearest Love your affectionate Husband

E Pettigrew

N.B. I am pretty well recov[*torn*] of [*torn*]. I expect more for Newbern by the first of March I think I shall come in the vessil I have heard that Mr McKinly[3] is dead

E P.

In great haste

Mrs A. B. Pettigrew

N.B. There is to be a steem boat Ball in Edenton the 18th & one in this Place the 22nd so that these places are in high life

[*Addressed*] Mrs Ann B Pettigrew
Newbern NC

---

[1]A Dr. Ellis is mentioned in Lemmon, *Pettigrew Papers*, I, 572, as wishing to buy a horse from William Shepard of New Bern in 1817. He may have been the Dr. James H. Ellis who died in Tyrrell County in 1827. *Raleigh Register*, September 4, 1827.

[2]Col. Benjamin Tarkinton (Tarkenton, Tarkington) of Tyrrell County is listed as a head of family in the 1830 census but does not appear in the 1820

census. Eleven Tarkinton families are listed in 1830 in Tyrrell County, and seven in Washington County. *1830 Census Index*, 183. In Tyrrell County, the wife of Col. Zebulon Tarkington died in 1825. *Raleigh Register*, April 26, 1825.

[3]Ebenezer is probably referring to James McKinlay of New Bern, former president of the Bank of New Bern, who died on February 4, 1819. *Raleigh Register*, February 12, 1819.

Ebenezer Pettigrew to Ann Blount Pettigrew UNC

Bonarva March 26, 1819

My derest Love,

I yesterday put on board our furniture and the vessil Droped down the river I am too meet her at the mouth of river tomorrow about 10. when I shall go on board, for a number of reasons which I will give you when I see you I have determined to /go/ round in her and hope to get with you as quick as the bearer of this but if I should not you will keep Ben and set him to work in the yard and garden untill I see you I will defer every other communication as from the mutiplicity of business it is heard work for me to write or think but in general. I am in health I hope dear Girl you and my little ones are also. and that your Pa is on the recovery. Remember me to them all and believe as always your ever affectionate Husband

E Pettigrew

[*Addressed*] Mrs Ann B. Pettigrew
Newbern

Ebenezer Pettigrew to James Cathcart Johnston UNC

Newbern April 9, 1819

My dear Sir,

Agreeable to promise I send you a few lines although from the present confused and agitated state of my mind it is with great difficulty I put my ideas on paper. I arrived at this place the 3rd after a seven days voyage in which I experienced 72 hours of storm, the first 36 was in Croatan sound where we rode safe, the next 36 was to Leeward of the Royal shoal in which I was in great alarm, in fact there was strong probability I had seen my family and my friends for the last time. The evening of our anchoring to Leeward of the Royal shoal the wind had been light & favourable and the Captain in lufing to get to the place to anchor for the night ran on the shoal, we made every exertion with sails and poles to get of but with no effect; we then carried out an anchor by which we got off.

In 15 minutes after it was carried and before we hove to it, the wind rose so that it would have been impossible for our boat to have lived, and the Pilots who came on board the second day after (for none could venture out the next day though we hoisted a signal of distress) told me that if we had not got off that evening we should certainly have gone to pieces that night.

After my first alarm I consoled myself with this sort of reasoning. I am now moving to a place [*New Bern*] and among a people who I know very little about and that little which I do know has not prejudiced me in their favour. I am tolerably advanced in years and have formed my habits and my friends who are very dear to me they are persons who I have the most perfect confidence in. Does my observation teach me there are any such here? I must answer no. I know I am among a set of sharpers and cannot feal easy when I am where they are and as all is for the best perhaps it has pleased God to give me the watery grave that I may avoid the evil to come & his will be done.

I feal happy in this reflection that I have paid the debt which I owed to my dear Nancy than which nothing ever gave me more uneasiness, though I declare she never demanded; I hope you know me sufficiently to believe that I do not require dunning to pay my debts.

This is the 7th day since I landed & I have not been in one private house except Mr S[*h*]epards, Do not be affraid I shall commence a warfare I shall avoid that by treating them with great distance.

It is with the deepest regret I inform you that I believe Mr Shepard is past hope. He is gradually sinking under the Doctors say a complication of diseases he yesterday had a violent pain in his knee to day he has little or none but I think him no better and I fear the time not far distant when he /will/ close this mortal caier. Mrs S. is also unwell. Mrs P. and children are well She joins me in best respects to the ladies & please to acept assurances of the Esteem & regard of your sincere friend

E Pettigrew

Mr Johnston

Pra[y] write me soon

[*Addressed*] James C Johnston Esqr
Hays
Edenton Post Office

Rebecca Tunstall[1] *to Mary Lockhart Pettigrew* A&H

April 24, 1819

My dear Aunt,

I have taken up my pen to write you by Mr Horten who calld on us a few minutes Monday. I am much pleased to hear you ware well—but am truly sorry to hear of your greate loss I hope Aunt it was not all of your Corn—as it is such a price with us, and not much Cheaper with you Mr Horten Says I think Mr Tunstall Says he Sold his for 6 and a halfe Dollars pr Barrell—Mr Horten says My dear Aunt you think very hard of my not going to see you, but am Sure if you knew how I am Situated you could not think I could leave home at least for Several months back—Mr Tunstall was taken in September with a voilent actack of a Billious Complaint and Continued all the fall and winter spring very unwell—and indeed my dear Aunt I am doubtfull he will never injoy his health again he is much Reduced and allways Complaining with a pain in his stomack Doctr Pugh thinks his liver is affected Oh My dear Aunt if it should please God to take him before me what would becom of me he is at Halifax at this time but was not well. you may be Sure my dear Aunt I Shall allways go to see you when I can with Conveinance—but to say when I can it is out of my power at this time Mr Horten told me you talked of Coming Up with him but gave it out, nothing would have been more pleasing to me then to have Your Company here but it is a Satisfaction I little expect—we are quite lonesome at this time Our Children are all at School Joseph and William at Chapple Hill and Beckey and Mary at Louisburg in Franklin [*County*].[2] Lucy and Peyton goes from home—I am much pleased with your preasend my dear Aunt. I think the Cap a very hansom One, and it fits me as well as if my head had been their to have fitted it on—but, the pattron for Mary is not a neought they are allmost as tall as my selfe. I must give her my preasant—I have Sent you Some Tobacker and I think it very good perhaps Aunt it may be too Strong—by puting it in the Sun it may weaking it Some. I Saw Sister Pugh[3] last week She was not well. as for Peggy[4] I never see her I hear from her often She injoys good health. I am Surprised she never Comes to See us I know she has it her power to do so I am not very well my selfe—<with> I am very much given to a pain in my head and eye every week or two I have an actack I perserved a nice Pot of Peaches last fall for you my dear Aunt with the intenshion of carrying them to you—but Mr Tunstall /Sickness/ pervented my doing so—I wish sincerly you had them but cannot think of trubling Mr Horten with them—My paper is giting short and must conclude with my love to you and Sally. Beleive me my dear Aunt to be your Sincear and

Affectionate Child and Neice
Rebecca Tunstall

P.S. Make my best respets to Ebenz^r and Lady Polly[5] Mr Slatter and Family desire to be Remembered to you Thomy[6] and Family are well—give my love to Rily and all the old set

R Tunstall

---

[1]Rebecca Bryan Barnes Tunstall was a niece of Mary Lockhart Pettigrew. She married Peyton R. Tunstall of Scotland Neck, Halifax County, after the 1795 death of her first husband, Thomas Barnes. Lemmon, *Pettigrew Papers*, I, xix, 115n, 291n; *Raleigh Register*, October 26, 1821. Her second husband was listed in the 1820 census as Paeton R. Tunstall. Dorothy Williams Potter (ed.), *1820 Federal Census of North Carolina* (Tullahoma, Tenn.: Dorothy Williams Potter, 56 volumes, 1970-1972), XXIV, 46, hereinafter cited as *1820 Federal Census*.

[2]Female academies were in operation at Louisburg fairly continuously from 1820 on. Charles L. Coon, *North Carolina Schools and Academies, 1790-1840: A Documentary History* (Raleigh: Edwards and Broughton, 1915), 96-106, hereinafter cited as Coon, *North Carolina Schools and Academies*.

[3]Elizabeth, the older sister of Rebecca Bryan Barnes Tunstall, was the wife of a Mr. Pugh. Lemmon, *Pettigrew Papers*, I, xix, 191, 308.

[4]Possibly Peggy was Margaret, another sister of Rebecca Tunstall. Lemmon, *Pettigrew Papers*, I, xix.

[5]Polly was a nickname for Mary. It is unclear whom Rebecca Tunstall meant.

[6]Thomy was probably Rebecca Tunstall's son Samuel Thomas Barnes, who had married Marina Keys in 1814. Lemmon, *Pettigrew Papers*, I, xix; *Raleigh Register*, February 11, 1814; *Raleigh Register*, October 26, 1821.

John Gray Blount, Jr.,[1] *to William Shepard* A&H

Raleigh May 31st 1819

Yours on the subject of your Tennessee lands[2] was rec^d on my arrival at this place—I am unacquainted whith what has passed between you & my Father on the subject, except what your letter communicates, and that, I do not perhaps understand—If it means only that you will refund any sums which may be paid to persons for identifying, & to Surveyors & chain carriers for resurveying, your lands, I should prefer declining the agency, as it would give me some months labour & could in no way lessen the expenses attending the establishment of my Fathers lands—If however, you wish your lands established & resurveyed, I will undertake to do it for 12 p.c^t which I believe is one half less than any person has yet offered to do it for—I have a connected plat of the lands surveyed in that country, which I think will enable me to find all the lands which have been granted—If your corners can be established, your lands shall be resurveyed and you furnished with a plat &

description of its soil value &c—If they cannot be established I will procure warrants for the amount which may be best, on the same terms, you paying one half of the fees of office—The terms I have proposed would not pay me for going to that country, but as I shall be there & have to attend to business of that sort, it may perhaps pay me for the extra trouble & labour it will occation—Whether I am employed or not it is proper that you should be informed, that it will be necessary that you should as soon as possible assertain whether your lands can be identifyed, and whether there are any interferences with other lands, in order that you may in time avail yourself of the priviledge of obtaining warrants for such as may be lost or taken by better title—It will also be necessary that your Grants should be recorded—The deed from J[*ohn*] G[*ray*] & T[*homas*] Blount to R. D. S[*paight*].[3] and from Speight to W[*illie*]. Blount[4] & the deed from W. B to yourself should all be recorded in the event that your lands cannot be established or the warrants cannot be obtained in your name—Certified copies of the Grants may be had in Tennessee & if the originals cannot be had, they may be recorded—

I shall remain in this place until the 8 or 10th of June and should be glad to know your determination before I leave it

Respectfully your Obdt
J G Blount jr

[*Addressed*] William Shepard Esqr
Newbern
No Caro

[1]John Gray Blount, Jr. (1785-1828), was handling the Tennessee land interests of his father, who ran the Blount mercantile business in Washington, North Carolina. John Gray Blount (1752-1833) had extensive landholdings in Tennessee, as had his brothers William, who died in 1800, and Thomas, who died in 1812. Powell, *DNCB*, I, 179, 182, 183.

[2]Charles Pettigrew likewise had acquired lands in Tennessee and engaged Howell Tatum as his land agent. Sarah McCulloh Lemmon, *Parson Pettigrew of the "Old Church": 1744-1807* (Chapel Hill: University of North Carolina Press, 1970), 83-86, hereinafter cited as Lemmon, *Parson Pettigrew*. Ebenezer Pettigrew first engaged Moses Fisk as his land agent and then changed to Moses E. Cator in 1816. Lemmon, *Pettigrew Papers*, I, 451, 527.

[3]Richard Dobbs Spaight (1758-1802) and his son, Richard Dobbs Spaight, Jr. (1796-1850), both were governors of North Carolina. Beth G. Crabtree, *North Carolina Governors, 1585-1974: Brief Sketches* (Raleigh: Division of Archives and History, Department of Cultural Resources, revised edition, 1974), 53, 80, hereinafter cited as Crabtree, *North Carolina Governors*.

[4]Willie Blount (1768-1835) was a half-brother of John Gray Blount, Sr. Alice Barnwell Keith, William H. Masterson, and David T. Morgan (eds.), *The John Gray Blount Papers* (Raleigh: Division of Archives and History, Department of Cultural Resources, 4 volumes, 1952-1982), IV, 14n, hereinafter cited as Keith and others, *Blount Papers*.

Ann Blount Pettigrew to Ebenezer Pettigrew UNC

[*June, 1819*] Sunday morning—

My dear Mr Pettigrew

I have the melancholly task to inform you of My dear Fathers death he expired this morning between the hours of five & six after very severe suffering he was taken tuesday with a dissentary which was violent in the extreme & which he bore with great patience & calmness—I believe he knew he was going. oh we have wished for you & John wrote for you to come—but our friends & myself think that as you will be under the necessity of returning in a short time it will endanger your health therefore stay untill you finish your business and then come Mama is in great grief & I do not know what will be the consequence—

I am yours
aff—
A B P—

[*Addressed*] Mr Pettigrew

*Ebenezer Pettigrew to James Cathcart Johnston** UNC

Bonarva Aug 4, 1819

My dear Sir,

Your favour of 2nd July did not come to hand untill the last of the month. I was aware of the necessity of shiping wheat early but from disappointments in geting a vessil my wheat is yet in the house, the disappointment is much greater to me in consequence of my intention to set out about the middle of this month for the Western country. My objects are various, one to view the country with <view> an intention to settle and another to have secured the land which Mr Shepard held in that country. The unfortunate circumstance of Mr Shepards death has put my continuing at Newbern longer than /the/ year out of the question; and where I shall go next I am entirely undetermined; Christmas will however make a change be the same better or worse. I am glad to find Doctr Beasley[1] treated you with so much respect & attention; I understand he is marked for his politeness to all Gentlemen visiting the City except his relations who he is less desirous to see in proportion as they get nearer to him in fact when they get within the limmits of Philidelphia desire totally ceases. Bye the bye the<y> greater number of them are such a stupid, degenerate set that he is in a great measure excusable. But let me drop this subject for the farm.

My wheat was much injured by the caterpillar and the north east spell of weather we had about the 10th may. My corn is very likely I think some of it will produce more than I ever had before the seasons of late have been very partial while one <farm> neighbourhood will be very much parched with drouth another will be leting off water and have their corn very much injured. <I could> My farm could not however <ask> wish for a better season to the present time than this. The Lake is 2½ ft below high water and lower than I recollect to have ever seen it but once before. I am taking the advantage of the dry weather and am deepening my canal a foot from below Woo[*d*]leys (which is the farm at the lower end) to above Indian town a distance of about 2 miles. I think it will be of great account in as much as the water when the machinery is going will be a foot lower in the canal about the plantation. This is only the tenth year since I have been working in the canal. <Mr> <I believe> I believe I have writen all I can think of at present and must conclude with expressing a great desire to see and beging you to believe me with great regard your sincere friend

E Pettigrew

[*Addressed*] James Johnston Esqr
New York

---

[1]Dr. Frederick Beasley (1777-1845), an eminent Episcopal clergyman and provost of the University of Pennsylvania, was the son of John Baptist Beasley and Elizabeth Blount Beasley, the sister of Ebenezer Pettigrew's mother. The Reverend Charles Pettigrew had greatly encouraged him in his studies. Lemmon, *Pettigrew Papers*, I, 178n; Powell, *DNCB*, I, 124-125.

Ebenezer Pettigrew to Ann Blount Pettigrew UNC

Raleigh Sep 10, 1819

My dear Girl,

I have just time to inform you that I arrived at this place at 9 oclock, /this mo[*rn*]ing/ in good health and spirits and all well I shall continue on this evening. I have been very much gratifyed with the hills and vallys brooks and rocks. I wish you were with me. Kiss the children for me and believe me your affectionate Husband

E Pettigrew

My hurry arrises from the mail being about to close and know you will be more anxious to he[*a*]r from me now than after I have been gone some time

[*Addressed*] Mrs Ann B Pettigrew
Newbern

Ebenezer Pettigrew to Ann Blount Pettigrew UNC

Abingdon Virginia Sep. 18, 1819

My dear Girl,

I have without any accident of the slightest sort arrived at this place, which is 400 miles from Newbern I found the road better than I expected untill I got to the B[*l*]ue Ridge which for about 40 miles is very ruff the ascent at the Bule Ridge is a mile as steep as I was able to walk up which fatigued /me/ exceedinly, I had to set down and rest 4 times, that walk and the walk up the Pilot mountain (of which I will give you a discription when I see you) together with the thumps I got in the 40 miles spoken /of/ made me so sore that I could scarcely get in and out of the chair but I hope in a day or two I shall be quite over it, all this fatigue has not made me any way sick or low spirited in fact I have had unusual good spirits, I am very much amused with the hills and valleys of this uneven country but of all I have yet seen I should prefer the Haws fields which is near Hillsborough. I think my dear Girl you will be pleased to travil through the up country and I think if I should see next fall I must take you up, & how much I have wished for /you/ when I have been delighted at seeing a distant mountain. I parted with my newbern company at Tarborough and did not travil one mile with another person—untill I got 18 m beyond Salem which is a distance of 200. /m/ I was then overtaken by a young /gentle/man who traviled with me 2½ days in which we crossed the Blue Ridge. I then fell in with a Mr Randolph and will travil with him Nashville. he is quite a clever man and does not drink a drop. I mention these little circumstances my dear Nancy because I know it will be gratifying to you. I think my horses mend. I feal my dearest Nancy great anxiety about the health of yourself and my dear little boys but I hope for the best In the mean time kiss them for me and belive me to be your affectionate and loving Husband

E Pettigrew

N.B. I saw Mr Stevens at Salem and I wrote you from Raligh. Pray write Mother in my absence.

Ebenezer Pettigrew to Ann Blount Pettigrew UNC

Nashville Tennessee Octr 1, 1819.

My dearest Nancy

After a long and fatiguing journey I arrived at this Place yesterday. I stayed a day at Murfreesborough where the Assembly is siting. I am exceedingly disappointed in the country. I expect to go into the Chickasaw nation to either see or survey the land. Heartyly tired I wish I was but on your side of the mountains again. I find here a number of North Carolineans who are all friendly and intimate. My dearest life & Love I never in my life was so desirous to see you, but so it is I must before that can happen travil 750 miles and receive 10 million thumps. I have been very well since I set out. I hope my sweet Nancy you and our dear little boys are in tolerable health. If I should go to the nation to survey the land I shall write you again before I start therefore I will conclude by subscribing myself your ever affectionate and loving Husband

E Pettigrew

I wrote you from Raleigh and Abingdon I hope you have recv[d] them. I was much disappointed this morning on going to the Post office and finding no letter for me

E. P.

[*Addressed*] M[rs] Ann B Pettigrew
Newbern NC

Ebenezer Pettigrew to James Cathcart Johnston UNC

Newbern Dec 10, 1819

My dear Sir

I thank my God, I have once more arrived at this place after a long and fatiguing journey and disastious as respects horses unparaleled having left Nashville the 16 Oct[r] for home. I hope never to see any of /the/ west country again, not liking any of it which I saw nor any which I could have an account of I am satisfyed it has no advantages over that in which I live, and any man who will move to it without seeing is crasy and he who move to it after must be still more so. I hope to see you shortly after Christmas and then I will give you an honest account of all I have seen. I hope to leave this in a few day forever as a home. Edenton and its vicinity forever. The mail is closing and I must conclude by hoping to see you shortly and beging to give my best respect to your sisters and accept my warmest wishes for your hapiness from your much Esteemed friend.

E Pettigrew

N.B. M[rs] P. & children are tolerable well.

I have a hint that there is to be a sale of M[r] Collins'[1] property shortly. If the fourth of the Eastern tract should be offered I should be much obliged to you /if you/ will bid /it/ of or have it done for me

E P.

Mrs P. sends her love to your sisters also

Pray excuse this miserable scrall for I am in a devil of a hurry. they swear dreadfully in Tennessee

James C. Johnston Esqr

[*Addressed*] James C. Johnston Esqr
Hays
near Edenton NC.

---

[1]Three generations of Collinses were neighbors and business associates of the Pettigrews. Josiah Collins (1735-1819) came to Edenton in 1777 as a widower. A merchant, he and others formed the Lake Company to drain the swamps around Lake Phelps and turn them into arable land. It was he who persuaded the Reverend Charles Pettigrew to move to the lake. Lemmon, *Parson Pettigrew*, 44.

Josiah Collins II (1763-1839) lived chiefly in Edenton and visited his lake plantation sporadically. He married Anne Rebecca Daves of New Bern in 1803. Their children were Anne Daves (married William Biddle Shepard); Mary Matilda (married Dr. Mathew Page of Virginia); Josiah III (married Mary Riggs of Newark, New Jersey, in 1829); Henrietta Elizabeth (married Dr. Mathew Page); Hugh Williamson; John Daves; Louisa McKinley (married first Dr. Thomas Harrison and second the Reverend William Stickney); and Elizabeth Alethea (married Dr. Thomas Davis Warren of Edenton).

Josiah III (1808-1863) and Mary built the existing house at Somerset Place on the lake and became noted for their elaborate hospitality. They had three sons who survived, Josiah IV, Arthur, and George, and three who died young, Edward, Hugh, and William. All of the above appear in the letters in this volume. Powell, *DNCB*, I, 404-406.

Dr. M[atthias] E. Sawyer[1] *to [Ebenezer Pettigrew]* UNC

Edenton Jany 4. 1820

Dear Sir

I have never been able until the close of the last year to procure for you in this place a house and lotes suitable for the residence of your family and my success finally was rather the result of accident than expectation. It affords me much satisfaction however to have succeeded in getting the house formerly belonging to Doct Beasley[2] which will be ready for your reception whenever it may be convenient or agreable for you to occupy it—I was compelled to give what may be considered here a high rent $220. and if I have erred in securing the house at that price you must impute it to an over anxiety to have you live amongst and from the knowledge of the facility with which you could erect a new building if you should select this as a place of your permanent residence.

I take this opportunity to acknowledge the receipt of your very interesting letter from Nashville of the 3[d] of October, interesting not only on account of the just views you have taken of the soil climate and state of society in Tenessee but as affording me an additional prof of the friendship and regard of a man who has been so long esteemed and admired by

M E Sawyer

---

[1]Matthias E. Sawyer was a physician in Edenton. He married Mrs. Margaret (Peggy) Hosmer on December 21, 1795, and the couple had five children: Matthias E., Jr., Samuel Tredwell, Margaret, Hellen, and Mary. In 1820 the census showed a family of two adults, four children, and nine slaves. Mary died in 1823 at age thirteen, Mrs. Sawyer died in 1826 at age fifty-eight, and Margaret died in 1827 at age nineteen. The 1830 census listed Matthias, Jr., and Samuel in separate households, living alone. Dr. Sawyer had five young men living at his Edenton home in 1830; possibly they were medical apprentices. He also had twenty-seven slaves.

Dr. Sawyer died in 1835, and in his will, probated in May, 1835, he left everything to Samuel with the injunction to look after Matthias, Jr., and Hellen. Dr. James A. Norcom witnessed Dr. Sawyer's will, indicating that he probably attended him in his last illness. The 1840 census listed only one Sawyer in Chowan County—Arnell Sawyer, not a member of this family. *1820 Federal Census*, XIV, 6; Fifth Census of the United States, 1830: Chowan County, North Carolina, 334, microfilm of National Archives manuscript copy, North Carolina Archives; Sixth Census of the United States, 1840: Chowan County, North Carolina, 208, microfilm of National Archives manuscript copy, North Carolina Archives; Will of Matthias E. Sawyer, Chowan County Wills, Book C, 182, North Carolina Archives; Chowan County Marriage Bonds, North Carolina Archives; *North Carolina Star* (Raleigh), January 6, 1826; *Raleigh Register*, December 15, 1823, September 26, 1826, December 18, 1827.

[2]Dr. John Beasley of Edenton, a physician and cousin to Ebenezer, had died in 1814. Lemmon, *Pettigrew Papers*, I, 178n, 472-473. See also the discussion of the Beasley family in the footnote for Ann Blount Pettigrew to Mary Williams Bryan, September 24, 1827, in this volume.

[Ebenezer Pettigrew] to James Cathcart Johnston UNC

Bonarva Feb. 20, 1820

My dear Sir,

I regret exceedingly that I am constrained to abandon the idea of moving to town at the present, and though I carry my family to the Lake again with fear and trembling as to their health and with a great dislike to the seclusion of my dear wife from society, yet upon cool and deliberate reflection I consider it all important, to prevent me from being plunged in debt still deeper, which in the event of my death would place her and my little children in a very dependant and wretched state. My overseer has conducted my business with credit to himself & to my satisfaction and though I shall continue him, there is a great deal for me to do.

My wish has never been to amass great wealth but an easy competence is necessary and truely desirable. It may be asked, Did you not know all these things before? I certainly did; but I had hoped that the production of my farm would not only sell but command a reasonable price. You very well know the fallicy of such a hope.

Mrs Pettigrew regrets as much as myself the necessity of this movement but I am happy to say it is only requisit for me to mention the importance of an act to get her approbation and perfect willingness, She is at this time singing Psalms in great stile it being sunday.

I shall always feel grateful to my friends in Edenton and its vicinity for their attention to me and their pleasure at a knowledge of my moving among them.

My dear Sir, Yourself and Doct^r^ Sawyer to whom I have writen a similar letter and feel it my duty to account for this apparent whimsical kind of conduct, will pleasure to excuse this frailty of human nature; At the same time I beg the like indulgence from the Ladies of your fa[mi]ly.

It would give us great pleasure to receive a visit from them and yourself this spring; in the interim please to give our best respects to them and [*torn*]

[*Addressed*] James C. Johnston Esqr
Hays

James Moffatt[1] *to Ebenezer Pettigrew* UNC

Edenton 23rd—February 1820.—

Dear Sir,

Your favor of the 20th inst. is received,—Mr Whedbee with the vessel for your furniture arrived yesterday afternoon, which with the assistance of 3 Carts, (1 from Mr Collins, 1 from Dr Sawyer and 1 from Mr Horniblow[2]) & Mr Collins's hands, I have had put on board this forenoon in good order—, the Secretary, side board and safe are left on Deck as they could not be got down in the hold, I hope it will all arrive at the Lake safe, and that you may find nothing amiss.—I shall endeavour, with the assistance of Dr Sawyer to rent your House for the balance of the year on some terms.—

Your friends here are much dissapointed on your declining taking up your residence amongst them with your family, although it is certainly more to your Interest to be where your bussiness is carrying on.—

I should be very happy to have the pleasure of visting you this spring, but situated as I am here, I cannot make you any real promise on that score, it has been planned—sometime ago—between Mr C. & myself to go over next month for the purpose of making some surveys near the Lake, which are wanted, but am rather uncertain.—

Wishing you and your family all the health, happiness and *contentment* which this world can afford.—

I am Dear Sir,
your sincere well wisher
James Moffatt

Give my respects to Mr & Mrs Carraway[3]

[*Addressed*] Ebenezer Pettigrew Esq:
Lake Phelps

---

[1]This was probably the James Moffatt associated with Josiah Collins's business. Lemmon, *Pettigrew Papers*, I, 632n. Census records list no James Moffatt in 1820, but a person by that name is listed in Elizabeth City, Pasquotank County, in 1830. *1830 Census Index*, 130.

[2]This might refer to James Horniblow or Joseph Horniblow of Edenton, sons of Elizabeth Pritchard Horniblow. Mrs. Horniblow was the widow of John Horniblow, who died in 1799, and operated Horniblow's Tavern. Estate Records of John Horniblow, 1799, Chowan County Estates Records, North Carolina Archives; Lemmon, *Pettigrew Papers*, I, 162n.

[3]Perhaps Moffatt refers to Snoad B. Carraway or Jesse Carraway, who may have been brothers. Snoad was associated with Ebenezer's business affairs. He married Penny Lee in 1812 and is listed as a head of family in Washington County in the 1820 census. Lemmon, *Pettigrew Papers*, I, 91n, 426n, 448; Dorothy Williams Potter (ed. and comp.), *Index to 1820 North Carolina Census* (Tullahoma, Tenn.: Dorothy Williams Potter, 1974), 75, hereinafter cited as *1820 Census Index*. He moved to Lenoir County and married again in 1828. See Snoad B. Carraway to Ebenezer Pettigrew, January 21, 1828, in this volume.

Jesse Carraway is first mentioned in the documents in 1813. He was a builder and constructed mills for Ebenezer in 1817 and 1818. Lemmon, *Pettigrew Papers*, I, 454, 561, 604.

John Swann Shepard to Ebenezer Pettigrew A&H

New Bern 23rd. April. 1820.

Dear Sir.

Yours per mail enclosing letters of introduction [to] gentlemen in [Tennessee] I have received for which I am much obliged. enclosed you will find a bond to refund your legacy in case the estate should not be able to pay its debts I should not have demanded from you that Instrument but it is customary and it would have been necessary for me to have given you a bill of sale for the negroes, but this bond will answer every purpose as it will be filed away in the Clerks office which will allways show your title to the negroes--for your edification I have enclosed to you a letter from that infamous Hypocrite Beasely [*Dr. Frederick Beasley*] <from> /of/ Philadelphia. I wish you not to show it to any person but on the return of mother send it to me. I think I discover from the tenor of his letter a little exulting security I have not answered and shall not until until after the 6th of december 1820, which time the judgement that hangs over the head of Wilson Blount[1] will have expired. My reasons for acting in this way are these Beasely I veryly beleave expects to draw from me something which I do not possess in way of evidence with which he may show the sale of the land to be a fraudulent one and upset blounts will and receave the property as the Heir of Blount but I Shall act no way offencive to the fellow but let him tickle himself <whi> with the vain hope until it is out of His power to disturb the Sleeping lion. I am very much afraid that the fellow in this town will succeed in establishing his account because he is a scoundrel all the Church people in this town sympathize with him as the event came I found that Stanly was not [postive] but on the [contrary] was fearful of the event—I have been up the Roanoak since you left this I saw Mr Jones a gentleman of your acquantance when in Tennessee I believe It was mutually understood between you to blow each others fame—my business in the season comes on so rapid that I cannot go with mother to your House I shall travel with them as far as Plymouth and there leave them under the care of his reverence Mr Mason[2] who will attend to the lake and you and him will have room and privacy enough to abuse the clods of our town. William [*Biddle Shepard*] is I dont know where we heard last from him at Philadelphia If you should find him shooting through your swamp you will confir a singular favour on me if you would set him to Ploughing for I am told that is an admirable remady for lunacy—but I suppose he thinks if that is the case we ought all go that business—Mothers health does not improve I wish you would exert your Self to throw this melancholly from her mind and induce her to exercise more—I will give you my opinion of Tennessee when I return

Yours with respec
and aff
John S Shepard

---

[1]Wilson Blount was a brother to James Blount of Mulberry Hill and uncle to Ebenezer Pettigrew, Dr. Frederick Blount, Dr. Frederick Beasley, and Mary

Blount Shepard, mother of the letter writer. Childless, he aided Frederick Blount with his medical education, but later the two became involved in a dispute over his generosity. Lemmon, *Pettigrew Papers*, I, xvi, 53n, 422.

[2]Richard Sharpe Mason (1795-1874) was minister of Christ Church, New Bern, from 1818 to 1828. After a sojourn in Geneva, New York, he returned to North Carolina and settled in 1840 in Raleigh, where he served as rector of Christ Church until his death. Gertrude S. Carraway, *Crown of Life* (New Bern: Owen G. Dunn, Publisher, 1940), 124-128, hereinafter cited as Carraway, *Crown of Life*; *Journal of the Proceedings of the Annual Convention of the Protestant Episcopal Church in the State of North-Carolina . . . 1819* (Fayetteville: Carney and Dismukes, 1819), 3, hereinafter cited as *Journal of the Diocesan Convention, 1819*; *Journal of the Proceedings of the Annual Convention of the Protestant Episcopal Church in the State of North-Carolina . . . 1820* (Fayetteville: Carney and Dismukes, 1820), 3; *Journal of the Proceedings of the Annual Convention of the Protestant Episcopal Church in the State of North-Carolina . . . 1821* (Fayetteville: Carney and Ward, 1821), 3, hereinafter cited as *Journal of the Diocesan Convention, 1821*; *Journal of the Proceedings of the Twenty-Fifth Annual Convention of the Protestant Episcopal Church in the State of North Carolina . . . 1841* (Fayetteville: Edward J. Hale, 1841), 3, hereinafter cited as *Journal of the Diocesan Convention, 1841.*

Moses E. Cator[1] *to Ebenezer Pettigrew* A&H

Williamson County [*Tennessee*] 8th Aug 1820

Dear Sir,

I have a fiew days since Returnd from overton County and have Been suckcessfull in obtaining a warrant for you for 565 Acres, having a Coppey of Flewreys[2] Deed to your Father and also a Coppey of the Later Clause of your Fathers will enabled me to Take the warrant in your own name. Viewing the stricktness of the Law and the Restricktions the Commisioners were laid under I had great doubts of obtaining said warrant and also being informed by several law Characters that it was useless to make the attempt that others of a much Clearer nature had faild. However I <almost> was determined to try the Experiment and suckceeded. I shall Deliver said warrant to Mr McLemore[3] agreeable to your Request (if not otherwise Directed by you) to lay upon the Best terms that I Can Contract with him for. I have no doubt of the phidelity of Mr McLemore the only objection that I have against him is that he holds more warrants than any other man in the state (as i am informed) Consequently he will hardley lay your warrant upon the first Quality of land and his own upon an inferior Quality, as self perservation is the first law in nature as to the Ballance of your land in overton [*County*] which is 235 Acrees. I have offered at one dollar Pr acree upon a Credett payable in Horses at a fair price whether I shall have it in my power to sell it or not for that price I Cannot tell as yet. one great objection to it is that there is no water on it and in short I Know of no water. (I mean a Spring) on the 1000 acre Tract except on the 200 acrees Conveyed to Gatlin.[4] However I do asure you that I have done and shall Continue to do every thing in my power (Consistant with phidelity and integrity) in the premisses to your interest. I omited informing you above that no warrant under the present law Can be obtained unless the land Can be identifyed so that so much is saved through a little industrey. I discover a Clause in the present law of this state an injunction laid on the surveyors of each District in this new purchase to publish at least 3 weeks in a publick news paper the day when his office will be opene[d] for the purpose of Recieveing Entrees and at the same time Requireing all persons Claiming lands within their District by Virtue of a Grant or Grants derived from North Carolina to Cause the same to be processioned before the 1st day of oct 1820 there is also a provision that if such Clayment should not attend and no other person for them that in that Case the surveyor shall strive to Identify such granted lands if in his power. probably you had Better attend to your land Business on the Obian River or git some person to attend to it for you. I have the law now before me.

as to my Traveling Expenses notwithstanding you were so generous as to pay me the three fourths part of it. from an observation you made I Recollect that I promise[d] you to Bear my own Expenses therefore I shall Refund the said traveling Expense Money to you again for if I make a Bad Bargain I am willing to stand to it. we have a great prospect for good Crops altho at this time we nead Rain. myself and familey are in Health Hoping these lines may find you and familey in perfect Health. you promised to write as soon as you Returned Home But have not heard from you since you left hear. only by Adkins Wynne who said he met you on your way home and said you had given up your Sulkey to your Boy and taken Horse and Sadle. I am Dear Sir your Readey friend and Verrey obd[t] Serv[t]

Moses E. Cator

NB M[rs] Cator and familey Join me in love and Complyments to M[rs] Pettigrew and familey to your Mother and to all enquiring friends and you will please to accept the same your self—when you write please to direct your letters to Nashville as usual—

[*Addressed*] E. Pettigrew Esquire
North Carolina
Skinnersville. P. Office

---

[1]Moses E. Cator was a resident of Tyrrell County as late as 1809. By 1816 he had settled in Tennessee, where he represented Ebenezer and several other North Carolinians as land agent. Lemmon, *Pettigrew Papers*, I, 527-528.

[2]Charles Pettigrew had purchased the land in question from Henry Fleury. Lemmon, *Pettigrew Papers*, I, 203n.

[3]John C. McLemore was an active Tennessee land speculator. Keith and others, *Blount Papers*, IV, 141n.

[4]John Gatling had received a grant for a tract adjacent to that of Henry Fleury. This may be a reference to Gatling or his heirs. For a discussion of the confusion concerning location of the tracts, see Lemmon, *Pettigrew Papers*, I, 651-654.

John C. McLemore to Ebenezer Pettigrew UNC

Nashville 11th Nov. 1820

Dear Sir,

Your esteemd favour of the 3d ulto is before me—our friend Mr Sheppard succeded in finding his lands without much difficulty or expence and I understand a considerable portion of it is excellent land,—I was much pleased at his Success for he is a young man I am much pleased with,—but I expect he has some charm in Carolina much more interesting than Tennessee lands, for it was with much difficulty I coud prevail on him to go to the Western District,—make my respects to him & tell him the Snakes are all in their houses, and he will have nothing now to dread but Swamps and muddy places and that they are not so numerous as in his Section of Country—that I shall be glad to hear from him if he has time to write—I saw your agent Cap. Cator some few weeks past he spoke to me about the location of your warrant and talked of selling it if he coud get a fair price. I advised him to sell, he said if he failed in selling he woud get me to locate.—Warrants are dull sale, owing to the great Scarcity of money—We like you begin to feel the *hard times*, the Banks have in a great measure been the cause of all our money difficulties, but as you say, "the people woud have Banks," and now when it is too late begin to curse them—You will see from our papers that our land lottery which commenced on the 1st Inst has to be drawn over again, owing to an error which occurred in the course of the drawing—Wednesday next is the day fixed for the commencement of of the new drawing, as soon as it is over I will endeavour ascertain the number your warrant has drawn and will write you,—Our new State Bank is in opperation, it has made a good start, and we hope it will do well. Our worthy Genl [*Andrew*] Jackson who was appointed to hold a treaty with the Chocktaws has lately succeded in obtaining about Six million of acres [*torn*] lands in the Chocktaw Country East of the Missipippi—will see treaty published shortly. When you have time write me, I shall [be] glad to hear from you.—

With great respect
Your mo obt. st.
Jno. C. McLemore

[*Addressed*] E. Pettigrew Esq
Skinnersville
North Carolina

Ebenezer Pettigrew to Major Ferrange[1] A&H

Bonarva Lake Phelps March 17, 1821

Dr Sir,

From the polite attentions which I received from you when at your house last spring I take the liberty to address you, please to accept my sincere thanks for those attentions and I assure you that if you could find the time, I should be very glad to receive a visit from you this spring or when convenient. My friend Mr Carraway had two of his negroes to run away at Christmas, and there is no doubt but their intention is for the north, he has advertised them with a reward of 100 dollars in the Edenton & Norfolk papers which you probably have seen, but least you may not I will give a small description of them. Their names are Steven & Anthoney, Steven is of yellow complexion, smiling countinace middle size, is pretty handy with carpenters tools, he also had as good cloths as any gentleman would wish to wear. Anthoney is below middle stature, of black complexion, served at the carpenters trade, cloths pretty good. There is no doubt but they will pass the canal; & will endeavour to get to Norfolk. Will you be so obliging as to have a look out for them and you are autorised by this letter to offer privately 50 dollars to any one who will give any information concerning them so that they may be caught. On the receit of this I should take it a favour if you would drop me a line My address is Skinnersville N.C. Your attention to the above request will receive the sincere thanks of my friend Mr Carraway and not less from your friend & obdt. Servt

E Pettigrew

[*Addressed*] Major Ferrange
Lebanon canal
Elizabeth City post office

---

[1]Major Ferrange has not been identified.

Ann Blount Pettigrew to Mary Williams Shepard UNC

Lake Phelps November 16 1821,

My dear Sister,

I received yours of the 1st inst with infinite pleasure and regret extremely it is not in my power to be present at the solemnization of your marriage but my particular situation entirely prevents my having that gratification but be assured notwithsanding my heart most sincerely participates in your happiness and I wish you sincerely every happiness I am very happy in in the idea of your connexion with a worthy object and have just reason to hope and believe /your affections/ are not misplaced but let me give you a piece of advice which I hope will not be unaccepable perhaps we may never have an opportunity of conversing, as I have to pass through a perilous scence which may or may not terminate my existence our lives are in the power of providence but again the subject our happiness or misery in a measure depends on ourselves, be prudent unreserved & condescending and you will always retain the affections of your husband without which their is no<t> happiness in married life, none but dupes would submit to a reverse conduct and cone/c/ted with such a being we could not be otherways than miserable, this sage advice little corresponds with the preparation for a gay wedding, but serious hours will come at last, I suppose the death of Julia Hawks has disappointed you of an attendant, I saw <health> her death in the paper also poor Mr Ward whose death I sincerely regret. he is a great loss to his family. I am very sorry Ma's health is not perfectly restored, my not seeing you was a great disappointment I have looking all the fall for a visit we received a letter from William the other day he was quite well. Mr Pettigrew is in bad health we are all tolerably well. except him. he joins me in love to Mama, self and family and believe me ever your affectionate Sister—

Ann B Pettigrew.

Reccommend to Mama, a cure for her disease. Dr. Mead's Anti Dyspeptic, or stomach Pills, for indigestion, or sour stomach—they have made great cures with us and no doubt would perfectly restore her—

[*Addressed*] Miss Mary W. Shepard
Newbern
N. Carolina

Durand Hatch[1] *to Ebenezer Pettigrew* A&H

near Newbern 22nd Decr 1821—

Dear Sir,

I recd your Favor of 26th Novr Last this moment & Hasten to inform you, there has been for 12 months or there about three Negroes, that is runaways Lurking about my Plantation. I am informed two are yours, About 6 weeks past I was Hunting & came of their camp & when I perceived them I ordered them to stop & return to me or I would kill one of them, they immediately all three Stoped & got behind a tree each of them Presented their Guns at me about 40 or 50 yards of me, I ordered them to Drop their Guns or I woud kill one on the Spot. their reply was we cannot Drop our guns but if you will not Kill us we will lower their mussels & come to you if you will give your word you will not kill not try to take us. I ansd I woud not. & ordered them to come & speak to me, accordingly they came or Two of them came & Spoke to me one yellow man said he belonged to you the other refused to ansr Keeping their guns in good order to defend them selves, & woud not get nearer to Each other than about 10 steps, the yellow Boy appeared to be about 20 years of age & said he belonged to you. I try'd to prevail on him to go Home he Bitterly refused & said he wou'd Die first. for Sir, said he if my master was with you & had as good a gun as yours appear to be & I had nothing to Defend myself I wou'd not be Taken alive by you, he then informed me his name & the cause of his leaving of you which to me appeared to be very Trifling, for him to leave you for, his name I have forgot, I then tryed to prevail on him to let me intercede through Mr Shepherd for him but he still refused to go home on any Terms I then pointd out to him he woud be killed he said yes he expected to be so but he rather Die than return to you, this boy appered to have a good Countinance & spoke Freely to me verry Humble he said he was Shot at a few Days past—they had some of my Hogs then killed as I expected, then I informed them they must leave the Neighbourhood they said they wou'd I told them to take up that they had in possession & be of that Day, Hoping by speeking to them as I Did I coud get some of my Friends & take them before they left their Camp. when I got home too men was at my House & was more at their camp in a very short Time but they were gone & I have heard nothing of them since, the Boy said a Mr Smith had bought a Blackboy of you that was with him & is gone Home to Smith a few weeks past. Smith lives at the Cross roads of Whiteoak River in Jones County & Said he had bought the Yellow Boy also but he wou'd not go to him from what I have been informed Smith has got one negro he said he bought of a Widow lady of your name this is negro nuse but I beleave it to be true. I will give the information you requested of me to give & will assist in taking of them if in my Power

Respectfully I am your
Obt Sert
D. Hatch

Mr E Pettigrew

[*Addressed*] Mr
E Pettigrew
at Lake Phelps—

[1]This was probably Durand (Durant) Potter Hatch, who lived near New Bern and was a friend of John Herritage Bryan. Parish Register of Christ Church, New Bern, Baptisms, 4; Ann Blount Pettigrew to Ebenezer Pettigrew, June 13, 1822, note, in this volume. Durant Hatch represented Jones County in the North Carolina Senate in thirteen sessions between 1800 and 1824. Cheney, *North Carolina Government*, 241, 242, 244, 246, 248, 249, 251, 256, 260, 261, 278, 279, 281.

Ebenezer Pettigrew's Tax List UNC

[*1822*]

List of Taxable property of E Pettigrew in Tyrrell Co

Plantation at the Lake	305 Acres @ 20$	6100
Bee Tree tract—	90— @ 1.66½	150
Swamp at the mouth of canal	4 Acres @ 1.00	4
¾ Estern tract	5250 @ .25	1312.50
	5649	$7566.50
	6455 25	1613.75

1 White Pole
30 Black Ditto. 1822. 33. /B.P./ 1823. 35. 1825

1822 List of Taxable property of E. & Mary Pettigrew in Wasington Co

3 Acres Land on mal [*Maul*] creek @ $6 pr A.	2310
187 ditto on which Mrs Pettigrew lives @ 10$	1870
41¼ ditto adjoining, bought of Willoby Phelps[1] @ $3	123.75
613¼	4303.75

10 Black Poles

[1]Willoughby Phelps of Washington County is listed in the *1820 Census Index*, 358.

Ebenezer Pettigrew to James Cathcart Johnston UNC

Lake Phelps—Feb. 4, 1822

My dear Sir,

With great pleasure I received your favour of 20 Nov. and with not less pleasure did I learn from it that you had, had so pleasant a trip up the country, I hope it has removed that devil you complain of (and which torments me so much) to such a distance from you that you may never more receive a visit from him. I regret very much not having the pleasure of a visit from you, but I poor devil seem to be not in prison bounds, as I once thought, but in close confinement where I can neither visit any one nor they approch me. However I will drop this subject. As respects Doctr Blount[1] & Mr & Mrs S.'s attention to them I feel either too indignant or too insignificant to require of my friends to resent (against their will) slanders against my character, which if true would render me unfit for the company of those I wish to associate with, they must do as they please; but I have the power of /of/ seing and judging for my self. Let us jog on we will get to our journeys end after a while. I am very desirous to move from this place and to sell land and the greater part of the negroes and things belonging to /the/ plantation. Could you in your travils /find any one/ who would buy do send him to me and I would take it a great favour if you would take occasion to mention it if you sould see any person who you thought there was a possability of selling to. Of the value you have some knowledge and there is no place better fited for a quarter and the time may not be very far distant when it would be a comfortable residence for an owner, but I do not wish to wait any longer for a change.

We have it extremely wet and the Lake is within 4 inches of a full head which gives me a good head for sawing, but plank is dul at even 14$ pr Thousand. On the 29 ult. Mrs Pettigrew was delivered of her fifth son,[2] it is a stout healthy child, and she is as well as could be expected. We are all tolerable.

My crop of corn gathered better than I expected and gives me a surplus which I have nearly sold at $3½ pr bbl. I have sown a pretty large crop of wheat which I hope will command a better price than last crop. Mrs P. joins me in best respects to your sisters and please to assure yourself of the Esteem & Regard of your friend

E Pettigrew

[*Addressed*] James C Johnston Esqr
Hays

[1]Dr. Frederick Blount (1778-1823) was the elder son of James and Ann Hall Blount. After studying medicine, he settled in New Bern in 1806. In 1807 he married a widow, Rachel Whitfield Bryan; they had two sons, Frederick S. and Alexander C. Hall, and several daughters. He was a first cousin to Ebenezer Pettigrew and Mary Blount Shepard (Mrs. William Shepard). Lemmon, *Pettigrew Papers*, I, xvi, 388n; Powell, *DNCB*, I, 177-178. The *1830 Census Index*, 137, lists Rachel Blount as a head of household in Craven County.

[2]The fifth son was James, who was lost overboard at sea on October 27, 1833. Works Progress Administration Cemetery Index, North Carolina Archives. See also Frederick S. Blount to John Herritage Bryan, November 7, 1833, in this volume.

Dr. James A. Norcom[1] *to Ebenezer Pettigrew* UNC

Plymouth Feby 19. 1822

Sir,

Happening to be at Mr Turners on the arrival of your letter it was put into my hand with a request that I would answer it: To oblige Mr Turner, & without any intention of obtruding my advice or opinion upon you except to serve you, I have consented to do it.

The Salt of Tartar is a medicine that dissolves & disengages tenacious & viscid phlegm in parts with which it comes in contact; it promotes the secretions; & gently determines to the bowels: it is a good palliative in Hooping cough, but is not so serviceable as mild emetics, of Ipecac or antimonial wine frequently repeated. where the constitution is strong, the patient plethoric, the system inflammatory as indicated by a full strong pulse flushed countenance, hurried & painful breathing &c more active depletion becomes necessary (ie) bleeding & cathartics of salts or castor oil—On the contrary when the patient is weakly & delicate the pulse quick & weak & the constitution frail, less active measures will be found to answer best.

very respectfully
Ja Norcom

[*Addressed*] Mr Eben^r^ Pettigrew
Lake Phelps

[1]Dr. James A. Norcom practiced medicine in Edenton. Lemmon, *Pettigrew Papers*, I, 288n; Wheeler, *Historical Sketches*, II, 124. His son, Dr. John Norcom, practiced in Washington, North Carolina. Guion Griffis Johnson, *Ante-Bellum North Carolina* (Chapel Hill: University of North Carolina Press, 1937), 728, hereinafter cited as Johnson, *Ante-Bellum North Carolina*.

Ann Blount Pettigrew to Ebenezer Pettigrew UNC

Newbern June 13th 1822—

My dear Husband,

You see I do not formally wait for a letter first from yourself but write without a knowledge of your safe arrival at home, which I hope you have without any disasters, there were several cool pleasant days after you left us, Charles & William cried excessively the day you left us to go with you, the little creatures were very disstressed. they still /say/ they wish to go to the Lake William has not forgotton the little dog— I have had as many visitors as I could wish, Mrs Hawks the widow I expected she would have resented her sons disappointment, of a ride in the Carriage, I thought her rather cool though scarcely perceiveable Charles & William have been very unwell, C. was taken in the afternoon with a high fever which continued all night. I was quite alarmed Ma. advised me to send for a Phisician but, knowing the good effect of Salts on him the next morning I concluded to give him a dose and with very great difficulty (for you well know his extreme obsinacy) I forced two spoonfulls down he used every resistance and I left him with a determination to send for a Doc^{t} if he did not get better but not <g>to give him any more Salts, fortunaty what he retain/e/d had the desired effect and he is now pretty well, William was seized with a vomiting which continued all day he is now recovered, so you see I jog on pretty much in old style though I have changed places, Mr Mason has paid us one visit he regretted extremely not knowing you were in town and begged I would appologise to you for his not calling to see you, he seemed really to regret it I believe him sincere; Mrs McKinley has gone to North so you must give her a call— likely you'll see Jhonny Daves,[1] he looks like Death & the cobler— I believe they tell many <unthru> untruths on his Wife,[2] I heard the <the> other day— She gave (the negro who has run away) a very severe scurging and scratched his face all over which I believe a falsehood, this world—this world, oh it is a wicked world so given to slander, I hear a plenty here; Mrs. West[3] was married last night in the most secret manner, Mary Bryan is the picture of happiness she is extremely fond of fashion and has to all appearance a very affectionate husband, they have been a few days to trenton— Mrs. Col. Armstead[4] is very ill <very> with /a/ billious fever it will be a strange event if /she/ comes to Newbern to breath her last, it is said she had but just recovered from a billious attack; I hope my dear Husband you will not spend yours hours so lonely as you immagined as you expected, I feel extremely desirous to see you and most sincerely wish we lived where we never should be sepperated, but alas there is always some alloy, perhaps if we lived in society there would be a greater evil to contend with, after being in society a few weeks, I wonder how we can seclude ourselves /so much/ from the world, though the world is not a desireable one still society has it charms. give my love to your dear Mother— I intend writing next week to her— also remember me to all inquireing friends. Ma [*torn*] in love to you— and believe me my

dear husband your ever [af]f—
companion & sincere friend—
Ann B Pettigrew—

Penelope—setts off for E[*mmitsbur*]gh—Monday she says she wishes—she could carry James with her.

When you come do bring Ma some turnip seed— there are some articles of the memorandum I left out— two turenes for soup—

[*Addressed*] Mr. E. Pettigrew
Skinnersville,
N.C.

[1]This was probably John Pugh Daves of New Bern, the son of Maj. John Daves. The family had lived in New Bern since about 1770. John P. Daves was brother to the wife of Josiah Collins II. Ashe, *Biographical History*, II, 67, 70; Powell, *DNCB*, I, 405.

[2]John P. Daves married Jane R. Henry of New York in 1816; she died in 1827. Ashe, *Biographical History*, II, 70; *Raleigh Register*, February 16, 1816, June 22, 1827.

[3]Mrs. Elizabeth West, widow of John S. West, married Durand Hatch on June 12, 1822, at the home of John Herritage Bryan. *Raleigh Register*, June 21, 1822; Parish Register of Christ Church, New Bern, Marriages, 129.

[4]Elizabeth Stanly Armistead (Armstead), daughter of John Stanly of New Bern, was the wife of army officer Walter Keith Armistead (1785-1845). Lemmon, *Pettigrew Papers*, I, 476-477; Powell, *DNCB*, I, 42-43.

Ebenezer Pettigrew to Ann Blount Pettigrew UNC

Lake Phelps June 21, 1822

My dear girl,

I should have writen you the last week but in the first place it had been so short a time since I left you and next when I intended to write I was quite too unwell arising from the dust of the machine, however I am now tolerable well, but exceedingly lonesome, it seems as though you had been gone two months, but I will exercise all my philosophy and bear with my seperation as well as I can. I have one of the strongest motives, which is, that you are where you wish to be, (enjoying the cumpany of those who are as dear as life to you) and with my perfect will and approbation. I can assure you my dear Nancy that your happiness is and has always been my first object and for two of the best reasons 1st I love and always have loved you better than <my> all other things in this world. 2nd your conduct ever since I knew you always entitled you to every indulgence that was in any ones power to give, and if I know my own heart one of /my/ greatest distresses has been, that I was not in a situation to do what my desire prompted. However I drop this subject for it is but writing what I have one hundred times told you, and if my conduct does not prove the tenderness my heart to you my declarations can never produce conviction in you, that I love. However tender & affectionate words are very greatfull with kind acts.

I shall finish harvist today and should have got done yesterday but was prevented by rain I have had fine weather for it; no rain since I came home untill yesterday and then not near <enou> enough for the corn which is very likely and promisses to be an abundant crop. My wheat is rather better than for several years back though only tolerable; I think it probable I shall not be able to get off with it untill about the middle of July.

I had forgot to inform you of my trip home from Newbern I got to Swift creek to dinner and it began to rain and continued so late that I staid all night; the next /morning/ I got to Mr Trotters[1] to breakfast and in the evening to Jacksons, when I was very unwell with my bowels and the head ache. The next day I got to mothers, who was not very well; she has the fever & agues. the next day to the Lake. when you must know I felt wretched. I was not a little motifyed at being obliged to stay all night within 16 miles of my dear wife & children and almost induced to turn back to Newbern as the evening came on.

I wish you would ask your Ma to have an Epitaph writen for poor Hannah, and send it in your next, and I will when I go on to New York have a tomb stone for her grave. Keep a coppy of the Epitaph lest the letter may be lost. Do write often and particularly and pray take care of yourself. Give my affectionate remembrance to your Mama & all the family. Kiss the dear little boys for me and believe me to be your affectionate Husband

E Pettigrew

N.B. I began to Harvist on Monday after my return on saturday., the wheat fully ripe. June 22. We had a fine rain last Evening & night & the corn is in full season

Mrs Ann B. Pettigrew

[*Addressed*] Mrs Ann B Pettigrew.
Newbern
N.C.

[1]Thomas Trotter was an engineer, inventor, and manufacturer of machinery. A Scotsman, he worked near Edenton for Josiah Collins, Charles Pettigrew, and others until he moved to Prospect Hill, near Washington, North Carolina, prior to 1809. Trotter was a prolific correspondent. Lemmon, *Pettigrew Papers*, I, 91n.

Ebenezer Pettigrew to Ann Blount Pettigrew UNC

Lake Phelps July 2, 1822

With very great pleasure my dearest Girl, I received your affectionate letter of the 13th June on the 23. And no less was I gratifyed to find that you waited for no formalities, You my dear, know that I have always been opposed to anything of /that/ sort /<that>/ between man & wife, and I hope that after this there will not remain one latent spark of it in your breast; nor in your acts; let me tell you that you have the least reason of any one I ever knew. Familiarity begets familiarity and you very well know that I never exercised the least distance or secrecy towards you, no my dear wife my whole heart and soul has been open to you, and I never expect so long as we live to have a secret from you. To be reserved to my dear companion the sweet mother of children and the source of all my comfort, would be like making any part of my own body reserved to my hand or eye.

I am glad your old friends had not forgot you and that you received those attentions which I think you so eminently deserving I am sorry to learn of the childrens indisposition, but the pain & pleasure come together, they are recovered & I hope at this time are quite well. I could have wished you had said something of your own health, whether you had, had any simptoms of your complaint & whether your appetite & strength was improving. these are particulars of much importance to my feelings. Do tell Mr Mason I should have been very glad to have seen him and that his appology is accepted. I have no doubt of his sincerity. With your letter came a Newbern Paper in which was the marriage of Mrs West. All is for the best.

I am very happy in the confirmation of my opinion as respects the happiness of a certain Lady mentioned in your letter. No doubt but her husband loves her with ardour and that he is /the/ man of all others whome she prefered; all those things combined cannot fail to make a couple happy. & Heaven bless the woman who can be kind, affectionate & dutiful her husband where there is any other person of her acquaintance, who she would prefer as one.

I pass the time tolerably composed. I rise by day light and sleep little or none untill bedtime which I suppose arrises from the anxiety <from> /of/ being alone. I find it very distressing to be in the sun, so much so that I do not stay with the hands as much as I expected I should after you were gone. I cordially agree with you in a wish that we were so situated as never to be separated and wish also that we lived in more society, but there are great evils in too much, better for many persons that they lived in the dismals. I think we have had more enjoyment of each others cumpany than if we had lived in the fashionable world, which to me would be exchanging a pleasure, I could always look back at with delight for someting which rarely bears reflecting on. Did we ever spend a day in retired converse which I regreted? No. but m/an/y pleasurable hours have I had in thinking of the past. I have now gone through and answered your letter, let me ask of you the favour of doing the same after the receit. Pray do not be [in] a hurry but write as I do under the idea that you are conversing with me. The hand which conveyed your letter to me carryed one for you to the office which I hope you received in due time. I write thus early from the pure pleasure which I take in conversing with /you/ though through the quil, knowing [*torn*] the same time that I impart a pleasure to them that it has always delighted me pleases and one <to> /who/ takes great interest in /my/ gratification. I see advertised a concert of sacred music also the Elephant to be seen. I hope my dear you will not loose any amusements under a notion of economy, believe me there is not the slightest reason and if I knew it, it would distress me very much I walked out to mothers & back on sunday the 22 with little or no fatigue, she was very unwell that night with the 3rd day fever & ague. We are all tolerable well I hope you are all in the same state. also Remember me to all & believe me your ever affect Husband

E Pettigrew

[*Addressed*] Mrs Ann B. Pettigrew
Newbern

Ebenezer Pettigrew to Ann Blount Pettigrew UNC

Lake Phelps Sep 10, 1822

My dearest Love

With heart fealt pleasure I received your affectionate letter on the 5th Sep. informing me of the compleat restoration of your stomach to its proper tone, I pray God it may continue, and to that end my dear girl let me beg of you /to/ persist in your determination not to trespass on it, and neither to stop from the use of means which you think have been so beneficial to you when ever you think you nead them in the smallest degree. I have now a ten fold pleasure in my trip to see /you/ when I bilieve that while there I placed you in the way which has brought you to the present state. O my dear, all my happiness depends on bringing you through this troblesome world with peace, safty, & Love. Yes what I once promised in ardour of Love I will alway do, not because I promised but because I will it, because it imparts to me the only real happiness this world can give, /& because I Loved you then & Love you no less now./ O Nancy what what would this wourld present to me if you were gone from me? nothing but a dreary void an empty space, for I can with most perfect truth say that you and you alone have occupied my whole affection and warmest Love from the first time I ever saw you. I am very sorry to learn that your Mamas health continues so bad. I wish most sincerely she could be prevailed on to take the pills; Mr Carraway thinks that if he had persisted in them in the early stage of his disease they would certainly have made a cure of him. I do not think the eggs will answer for your Ma now but have no doubt but the pills would; do try and persuade her to take them. I am sorry to learn of Mr Masons indisposition and that we shall loose the chance of geting little James christianed; if he is not gone give my respects to him.

I rejoice with you that our dear children are in good health my pleasure in learning their health was lost in the joy which I felt in your restoration. George promises to attend to the selery I also attend to the cherries and when I returned from visiting you found the peaches fit to dry, all which I had cut, and they made a great show when gathered but dont promise yourself too many, we have had a great job to dry them in this rainy season, they are now nearly dry and I believe all safe. I have the greatest abundance of Figs. O, that you had some of them. The wheat which I shipped before I visited you arrived safe and sold tolerable well and I have received all the articles sent for, all which you are concerned in I think you will be pleased with. I think they come lower than I ever got before; among the most prominent articles are the China (all safe except the 2 sauce ladles got their handles broke, whether my dear would it not be better to have silver) Baithing tub, rocking chair, and supurb knives, which I fear will plague you half to death.

I /am/ now shiping the remainder of my wheat & a parcel of plank to Baltimore. Will you write me in your next whether you wish me to bring your Pelliece when I come. I will take your kind advice not to expose myself; I have not been quite [*torn*] for this week past, but am better today, my complaint is something of what they call the burning ague, every day alike. I cannot tell you when to look for me my business is such, it may be the first of Octr or after the middle, you will hear from me again in due time <again> pray keep on writing. The house I am building is the obsticle, I /have/ 5 workmen now, and expect 2 more next week. Fearing that you may want money I have inclosed you 20 dollars which I hope you will get safe. Mother is quite recovered she desired me to give her Love to you when I wrote. Remember me affectionately to your Ma. Kiss the children for me and believe me your ever affect Husband

E Pettigrew

[*Addressed*] Mrs Ann B. Pettigrew
Newbern N.C.

Ebenezer Pettigrew to Ann Blount Pettigrew UNC

Lake Phelps Sep. 17, 1822

My dearest Girl,

I wrote you dated the 10th Inst. which I hope you have received before this. In it was inclosed twenty dollars. We have been a good deal sickly with fever & ague. James died last week, his complaint was that pain in the neck which he had in the winter it continued to the last. the Doctor says it is a new complaint. Edmond, Melas youngest child died on sunday last, I suppose with worms. I came from Mothers yesterday she & Mrs West[1] send their Love to you and your Ma. She is well. In my last I wrote you I was unwell I am now quite recovered. Frederick [*Shepard?*] is with me he is tolerable well but labours under great costiveness. I have this morning given him a dose of salts. This will be handed you by Mr Spruill[2] or Ben who goes for the purpose of bringing away my runaway. Pray give yourself no uneasyness about my conduct to him. I do not expect to lay my hand on him. I have writen to Mr Bryan concerning Pomp but if he should be from town <but if he should be from town> will you be so good as to get Mr Furlow, Mr Duncan or Mr Bell to go with him and with your assurance to either of them Mr Spruill can get him. I wrote to Mr Bryan the date of your letter requesting him to make arrangments in case of his absence when I sent. If /he/ has got the letter he has no doubt done it. I have sent your Pellice by this opportunity if the trunk will hold my coat you will send it in return that I may not incumber the carriage. Remember me affect. to your Mama

and believe me as ever your affect
and loving husband
E Pettigrew

N.B. Inclosed is the Key of the trunk

[*Addressed*] Mrs. Ann B Pettigrew
Newbern

[1]Mrs. West was a relative of Mary Lockhart Pettigrew. Ann Blount Pettigrew to Mary Williams Bryan, July 11, 1826, in this volume.

[2]The Spruill family in Tyrrell and Washington counties was extensive. The *1830 Census Index*, 176, lists seven family heads in Tyrrell and twenty-five in Washington, the latter including Amelia and Dempsey mentioned in this volume.

John C. Calhoun to Ebenezer Pettigrew A&H

Washington 26th March 1823

Dear Sir,

I have delayed answering your letter of the 12th Novr till after the rising of Congress, in order that I might give you the general opinion, which was entertained of your wine;[1] and am much gratified to say, that with little exception, it has been found to be excellent. It was, however, generally thought, that it would still be better, if instead of the apple brandy, the French, or some other less dissimilar in its taste from the wine, had been used; or if it had been manufactured without brandy at all. These were, however, mere conjectures and probably were erroneous.

Your wine was so much esteem, that I was continually asked, if it could be obtained of the same quality; and I promised to request you to send a cask to Mr Lloyd,[2] Senator from Massachusetts, at Bost[*on*], another to David B. Ogden Esqr[3] of New York, and Virgil Maxcy Esqr.[4] near Annapolis to be sent to Baltimore. I would be much gratified, if you could send each of them a cask, as it would contribute to extend the knowledge and reputation of so fine a domestick wine, they being all gentlemen of the first standing in society.

Very Respectfully
J. C. Calhoun

E. Pettigrew Esqr.

[*Addressed*] E. Pettigrew Esqr of
Lake Phelps
Plymouth
No Carolina

[1]The history of the scuppernong grape and wine-making industry is detailed in Clarence Gohdes, *Scuppernong: North Carolina's Grape and Its Wines* (Durham: Duke University Press, 1982).

[2]James Lloyd (1769-1831) of Boston held a seat in the United States Senate from 1808 to 1813 and again from 1822 to 1826. *Biographical Directory of Congress*, 1227.

[3]David Bayard Ogden (1775-1849) of New York City was a lawyer well known for his presentations before the United States Supreme Court. Joseph G. E.

Hopkins and others (eds.), *Concise Dictionary of American Biography* (New York: Charles Scribner's Sons, 1964), 745, hereinafter cited as *CDAB*.

[4]Virgil Maxcy (1785-1844), a lawyer, served as a Maryland legislator, first solicitor of the United States Treasury, and chargé d'affaires in Belgium. *CDAB*, 656.

Ann Blount Pettigrew to Mary Williams Bryan A&H, BRYAN

Lake Phelps, Octr 7—1823.

My dear sister,

Your letter of the 18th Sept. I received with infinite pleasure, Bonaparte was not more delighted at receiving letters from Europe during his exile at St Helena than I am at hearing from my dear friends, I am very sorry to hear that Mr Bryan has such ill health, you should take good care of him good husbands are very rarely to be found, we are peculiarly fortunate indeed, poor D[oct] Blount's death[1] we heard of, poor unfortunate man, he indeed was the sport of his violent passions, I believe he had many estimable qualities, a good charitable heart he possessed, but he has retreated from the storms of life I hope to experience the forgiv<ness>ing and all attoning Redeemer's love, what a hope, & consolation for dying sinners as we are all by nature. I am extremely obliged to Mama for her affectionate invitation, do assure her it is not for the want of affection, or desire to do so, that I shall not visit her this season nothing could give me more pleasure than to meet my dear brothers and sisters at that time but circumstances will not permit me to enjoy that happiness. I am happy to hear of Penelope's arrival, I hope to see her with John and his wife on their way to Newbern they certainly will come, William we hear nothing from I hope nothing has befallen him, I love him very much, he is an amiable man, but too silent as respects himself.

I am happy your town enjoys such health, it is not the cas<t>e at Edenton, we are pretty well, we have a little D[oct] here who is quite skilful also quite genteel. Quite likely Mrs Mason's nervous head ache is attributed to the right cause, they are like two turtle doves no doubt perfectly happy. Surely Madam Natty's folks are not going to take things as they have done, well it is an evil tide that never turns so they say, who knows what our fortune may be, poor Mrs. Armstead needs all the pleasure she can have to enjoy life, I think these people who are constantly gadding about—from Shocco to Saratoga from thence to the city &c.—are in a state of most perfect derangement. Newbern must appear very dull to Madam Mac [*McKinlay?*]—now—.

Mr Blount[2] died of ague and fever it is said but was bled improperly his friends are very distressed, his wife bore his loss with unlooked for fortitude, fortunate for her she can recover from so great a loss.

Charles, William & James with myself all send Theodore a thousand kisses stale presents to send so far.

Mr. Pettigrew <sends> joins me in love to Mr Bryan—& yourself also to Mama—and the children.

Believe me your affectionate sister,
Ann Pettigrew.

PS. I sent for a cloake like Mama's are they worn by the ladies. do write me if you please, Never write a shorter letter than your last, I have nothing to write but you have an abundance of something that is agreeable to me, anything from our native place in highly interesting—the most trifling occurrence, oh how delightful for bretheren to dwell together. Those who have never been sepperated are unconcious of the happiness they enjoy,

Your aff A B P.

Please remember me to all enquireing friends,

[*Addressed*] Mrs Mary W. Bryan,
Newbern,
NC.

---

[1]Dr. Frederick Blount died on September 5, 1823. *Raleigh Register*, September 26, 1823.

[2]Possibly Nancy refers to the death of Joseph Blount, who had lived at Windsor and who died at Oxford, North Carolina, on September 1, 1823. *Raleigh Register*, September 5, 1823.

Ebenezer Pettigrew to James Cathcart Johnston UNC

Lake Phelps Jan 12, 1824

My dear Sir,

Your highly esteemed favour of July came to hand in due time and would have been answered long before this, but for the information in that letter of your being about to set out on your falls excurtion, at which time I could not know where to reach you with a letter, and since your return I have been too sick untill very late. It is certain I have writen a few letters on business but the labour of thinking was very great. I was taken sick the 12th of October and untill the week of Christmas, I had but little hope of living longer than March; since that I have increased in health, and am only afflicted with rheumatism, it is all over my system but does not yet deprive me of walking and I can put on my cloths, but the hand with which I write, I am not able at this time to shut.

The expressions in the first of your letter were truely gratifying, in as much as they come from a friend who never flatters. If my friendship and Esteem for my friends has not been of the most sincere kind, I have decived myself. But Alas! my old friends have nearly all deserted me. However let me tell you my dear friend that I always considered you as an unshaken one & that you would duely appretiate me, and if I have lost them, I have the consolation of not being conscious of its arising from my unworthiness.

The friendship and esteem of an honest & sincere man is a jewel indeed, but there seems to be such a mass of corruption & duplicity pervading all societies that man appears satisfied with the semblance of it. Whatever I might have been in early life, I am very badly calculated for such prisons now. I am too old to begin to learn the fashions of this learned & polite age, viz. be very civil, do you a favour, go to church on sunday, perhaps receive the sacrement, and cheat on monday a poor unsuspecting man out of half his hard earnings for half a dozen years.

As the fall has passed away without the pleasure of seeing you I hope to have it by or before the spring, but I almost despair. An evenings conversation is a favour which rests with you to give; my time is not my own or you might be certain I would not stay in this low country with my family to endanger their lives and at any rate to be deprived of all pleasure from sickness of some of them all the fall. My house has been an hospital during the whole time & all I can say is thank God we are all alive. I know that I am rong to indulge in melancholy at the corruption of man, more particularly when I see little else; and when I have that which no human being can take from me; *an approving mind*. I thought my business was brought to a close in September, but by an error which was made in their own deed and in their own favour the business has been defered untill another hearing. At sighining I inadvertantly overlooked it and if they insist on having the deed proven as it now is, I shall be obliged to enter a protest. I ought never to deal with persons whose sole object is to get the advantage; but to employ an agent adapted to the business.

Although I have been sick all the fall I have endeavoured to keep my people busy, and have consequently sown 120 acres of ground in wheat, it is all prime ground, sown in good season, looks [*torn*] and I promise myself a good crop. I planted last spring 100 acres of ground in corn, it was in fine order and the season was good, but the chince bug (an enemy I never saw before) attacked it and instead of 1200 barrils I gathered but 600; however from the present price there is not much difference between 6 & 1200 barrils corn.

When in Edenton in September I sunk my debt with M^{r} C[*ollins*]. about 1200 dollars it is now about 2100, which I hope my next harvest will extinguish. Mrs Pettigrew joins me in best respects to the Ladies & yourself and assure yourself of my sincere friendship

E Pettigrew

James C. Johnston Esqr

[*Addressed*] James C. Johnston Esqr
Edenton

Ann Blount Pettigrew to Mary Williams Bryan A&H, BRYAN

Lake Phelps April 20th 1824.

My dear Sister,

I am pleased to know you do not formerly wait for an answer to your letter previous to the last, be assured I duly appreciate your goodness, also /I wish you to know when I am neglectful/ that something unavoidable always prevents my enjoying that delicious pleasure of conversing with my dear Sister through the quil; I am sorry to inform you Mr Pettigrew still continues in the same state, his fingers are very stiff and he suffers very much he desires you will tell Mr Bryan that he should have written <written> him long ere this but he is totally unable, his hands are almost useless. We are happy to hear of Mr Bryan's good health, I hope Theodore has quite recovered, give him a kiss for me. Mr Pettigrew exercises the greatest patience and fortitude although he suffers so much he rarely complains, I flatter myself the warm weather will have some good effect, but it appears as though we shall never have comfortable weather again, I suppose my anxiety over passes the season.

We had a visit from Brother W, last week he was quite well, I rather suspect he has a sligh notion of Miss Nancy [*Anne Daves Collins*], she appears to be a very fine girl much prettier than her Sister Several of the family spent last week on the Lake, they said very much to their satisfaction, they are indeed very dressy, they appear to have been delighted with their visit to Newbern, so gay so hospitable What a place for rich people this Newbern is. I shewed William your letter, he was highly diverted with Cousin Jacky's singular or unappropriate taste in being represented with his arm resting on a pile of books a quile indeed would have been much more suitable, I understand he is a widower for a short time, his wife Mary having taken a visit home with Miss J.

I received a letter from Frederick [*Shepard*] the other day, he complains very much of his relations not writing him, he says Penelope writes once in an age just enough to tell him they are not all dead, his letters are very affectionate he has an affectionate heart.

I am very much grieved to think of not seeing Mother at the time appointed, We heard such shocking news of the Small Pox raging in Washington We thought in unnecessary to send the horses, I understand all communication between Washington and Newbern is prevented. Mr Pettigrew desires to be remembered to Mr Bryan and yourself, also our love to Ma—and family

and accept the same from your aff. sister,
Ann B Pettigrew.

Mrs Bryan

Please turn over

PS Mr Pettigrew says. Mrs Bryan <says> did you have the head ache while you were at Raliegh! this question arrises from some information from William relative to a ball in New bern. Mr Pettigrew has not lost his spirits he is yet fond of joking

[*Addressed*] Mrs Mary W Bryan,
New Bern,
NC.

Ann Blount Pettigrew to Mary Williams Bryan A&H, BRYAN

Lake Phelps May 27th 1824.

My dear Sister,

I dislike sending so much blank paper to my friends which must be the case when I have so little to communicate, that to be candid I have almost formed a dislike for letter writing, that delightful medium for communicating our ideas or expressing our feelings to each other, sepperated friends ought to rejoice at the priviledge of such a blessing to civilization.

Mr Pettigrew's health is something better he now can sleep tolerably well without taking opium, but his hands are still very much contracted so much so that he uses them very little, some of his fingers are almost drawn double, the weather continues so very cold or I flatter myself he would get much better, it is a very great affliction but /he/ bears it with great fortitude, when our afflictions eminate from Divine Providence we ought to be assured they are always for a wise purpose or for the health of our Souls, if we would only believe so we should always boast or rejoice after an illness or visitations in any respect.

Mrs Sawyer[1] was very desireous for me to visit Edenton during the visit of /Bishop/ Ravenscroft,[2] I should have been delighted to have done so but unavoidable circumstances prevented me, The Bishop has a very pious and pleasing character much admired I believe for his exalted piety and sociability of disposition.

I received a letter a few weeks sinse from Cousin Fanny Lardner,[3] she says Mr Bedell[4] is exceedingly admired in Philadelphia, more so than I should have believed possible, I heard him once in Newbern and was rather unfavourably impressed, Fanny L——s letters are elegantly written they are very long and I really view them as something worth receiveing, they contain more news of P—— and our relations than I have heard since I left them, she is not a branch but a different stalk from the Biddles, I rather think her situation is a disagreeble one she expresses great affection for me and I think her sincere.

Do inform me of the state of Mother's health and Penelope, I shall write very soon to both Ma & Sister P. tell P—— Prince Hohenloe[5] will be a charming subject for her next letter I wish we may find the story /not/ a fallacious one I am too far in the woods to know any thing about it.

Mr Pettigrew joins me in love to you all, he is unable to write, do write me as early as possible and believe me as ever your

affectionate sister,
Ann B Pettigrew.

Mrs M—— Bryan—

I was heartily grieved that we were so much disappointed by the Small Pox though before very long I hope to see my dear relations, we had our children vaccinated their arms were very sore.

[*Addressed*] Mrs Mary W. Bryan,
Newbern,
NC.

---

[1]Mrs. Sawyer of Edenton, a family friend, is mentioned several times in the first volume of Pettigrew papers. She was probably Mrs. Margaret Sawyer, the wife of Dr. Matthias E. Sawyer. Lemmon, *Pettigrew Papers*, I, 500, 524, 600, 604, 616; *Raleigh Register*, December 15, 1826. See also Ebenezer Pettigrew to Ann Blount Pettigrew, December 5, 1826, in this volume.

[2]John Stark Ravenscroft (1772-1830) was consecrated bishop of the Protestant Episcopal Diocese of North Carolina in 1823. He recorded in his journal a visit to Mary Lockhart Pettigrew on April 27, 1825. Marshall DeLancey Haywood, *Lives of the Bishops of North Carolina* (Raleigh: Alfred Williams and Company, 1910), 37-38, hereinafter cited as Haywood, *Lives of the Bishops*.

[3]William Shepard's sister Anne married one Lardner of Philadelphia, and Fannie was their daughter. Shepard genealogical material, Moore Collection, PC 1406.

[4]This was Gregory T. Bedell, who had been rector of St. John's Episcopal Church in Fayetteville, North Carolina. *Journal of the Diocesan Convention, 1819*, 3; *Journal of the Diocesan Convention, 1821*, 3.

[5]Hohenlohe was the name of a German princely family in the areas of Wurttemberg and Bavaria. *Webster's Biographical Dictionary* (Springfield, Mass.: G. and C. Merriam Company, 1966), 719.

[Dr.] Thomas Old to Dr. Samuel Henry[1] A&H

Skinnersville, N. Carolina July 1824

Sir,

By the request of Mr Ebenezer Pettigrew, who has been informed of some cases of his Disease from the Town of Washington in this State, successfully managed by you, I herewith transmit a statement of his case, so as to enable you to form a correct opinion of the real nature of his disease, and to advise what will for the future be probably the most appropiate method of treatment.

Mr P. is in about his 42nd year, rather robust in make with some degree of apparent laxity in fibre, of the nervous temperament and nearly approaching a Scrofulous Diathesis. His habits until the last two years have been active if not laborious—shunning alike the indulgencies of the table and the escapes of the bottle. Since the period of puberty he has enjoyed almost uninterrupted health, checked only by those occasional attacks of Fall Fever which the inhabitants of the South are never exempt from. In early life his constitution was delicate and he was strangly threatened with an attack of Phthisis, all symptoms of which however in a few years entirely left him. Within the two last years his manner of living has been more indulgent as to exercise but not less temperate in other respects. Last Fall he had two attacks of Int[*ermittent*]. Fever closely following each other. During convalescence less Bark was taken than the case required and his recovery was slow—cold weather set in and he was attacked with chronic Rheumatism. A system a good deal debilitated by previous Disease in which there existed a strong hereditary predisposition to Rheumatism offered ready access to its influences at that time. The joints of the fingers were first affected with nodosities which gradually became painful, at the same time or nearly so accompanied with soreness & pain in the larger joints, particularly the shoulders, knees, hips & Back. In the large joints it was rather a sensation of stiffness & soreness on motion, than much pain. In the hand and wrist it was more painful, considerable external tumefaction and a very considerable retraction of and rigidity of the Flexor tendens of the fingers. As summer came on the pain & soreness abated slowly but the immobility & rigidity of the fingers has remained nearly the same until this time. I will now give the plan of treatment adopted in the earlier stages of his complaint. The Disease was pretty firmly fixed before medicine was recurred to. As he had been subject to slight attacks of it for some years in the shoulder particularly, and no permanent ill consequences had arisen, the same termination was hoped for in the present instance. When I was first called to him I was lead to notice particularly the situation of the superior extremities, dreading a partial if not entire and permanent rigidity of the joints, which induced me to apply a large Blister to the hand conjointly with the exhibition of the usual internal remedies. This produced but little if any benefit and was succeeded by the use of frictions with a number of stimulant and volatile substances, all of which however if useful at all, were but temporarily so. The internal medicines prescribed were Guiac, Lavin, Camphphor, and opium assisted by Dileunts seperately or variously combined according to circumstances. The violence of the disease was no doubt mitigated but not removed by these remedies, which were continued until the warm weather came when seeing their inefficiency, they were all abandoned, trusting to the change of season to accomplish what medicine had failed to do. The pulse was irritable, but feeble. Depletion in any shape was manifestly injurious, greatly increasing the debility and local Disease. The cold Bath was tried without advantage. Opium produced a more positive alleviation of pain and a greater relaxation and flexibility of the joints than any thing else, but in the more advanced period of the Disease the functions of the stomach became slightly impaired, manifested by occasional nausea & temporary pain in that organ, which occurred however but a few times in all. It was feared the use of Opium might have aided the appearance of this symptom and that its continuance wo^d^ be likely further to enervate its powers. Since the spring he has taken nothing in the way of medicine. His appetite had become good which indeed was generally the case throughout his Disease and he had got quite corpulent—as heavy as he ever was Within the last fortnight he has had several fits of Int. Fever which has somewhat reduced his general health. From this however he is rapidly recovering. The hands & fingers yet continue in nearly the same state, excepting that there is but little if any pain, and no swelling or soreness, now and then a stiffness in the large joints and but little pain or soreness in them. The great object is to restore flexibility & motion to the fingers & hands and to remove the general predisposition which still lingers in the system, liable again to be excited into activity upon the return of cold weather. If this can be effected, it is of the first consequence that it be done immediately.

If practicable, it is very desirable for him to remain on his Farm, while the cure is attempted, as his business must be greatly neglected in his absence. But if you concieve the use of any mineral waters wo^d^ conduce greatly in hastening or add to the facility of the cure he may perhaps be prevailed on to give them a trial. Electricity or Galvanism are remedies that were formerly highly recommended in the management of this Disease, tho more rarely I believe recurred to in the present day. They are probably not destitute of utility. Mercury cannot be born to the extent necessary to do good, I am convinced from my experience with his constitution in other Diseases. From the description I have given, you might presume the Disease to be Gout instead of chronic Rheumatism Altho. I confess there is some similarity to that Disease, I am of the opinion it is the latter, 1st Because Rheumatism is hereditary in his family, his father having been afflicted with at about the same age the Son was first attacked with it. 2nd Because it was not confined to one joint but attacked many at the same time & pervaded the muscular system generally. 3rd From the Disease not being preceded or accompanied by any disorder of the stomach until a late period after its origin. 4th Because Gout in the onset never remains so long, nor does rigidity of the joints arise as a consequence but from repeated attacks.

I hope I have said enough to give you a tolerable correct idea of the situation of Mr P.—such a one as will afford you a successful indication of cure. I think there is a general tendency to rigidity in the muscular fibre and that the chief & important indication is to counteract or remove this State. It being at present in the extremities, on the verge of the sanguiferous system, chiefly in tendinous parts where the vital powers are languid, adds much to the difficulty of the case. But tis possible if the general Rheumatic predisposition of the system is vanquished the local Disease will as consequence yield.

You will be so good as to attend to this communication without delay by sending written advice, together with medicine & & Directions to Mr Ebenezer Pettigrew, Skinnersville Washington County N.C. As this will be handed you by Mr Van Bocklen,[2] Mr P.'s agent in N. York it will perhaps be the most eligible to put in his possession your letter & medicines & he will have an opportunity of forwarding them direct to N. Carolina more expeditiously than by mail.

Yr. Ob: Sev:
Thos: Old

Dr. Sam Henry New York

[*Addressed*] Dr. Samuel Henry
New York
To the care of
M[r] A. H. V Bokkelin

---

[1]No additional information about either of these two physicians has been found.

[2]The Van Bokkelen family was from New Bern and had a mercantile office in New York. Adrian H. Van Bokkelen was living in New Bern as late as 1844, where he was an active member of Christ Church. He died in 1846. *Journal of the Twenty-Eighth Annual Convention of the Protestant Episcopal Church in the State of North Carolina . . . 1844* (Fayetteville: Edward J. Hale, 1844), 3, hereinafter cited as *Journal of the Diocesan Convention, 1844*; Parish Register, Christ Church, New Bern, Burials, 91.

Ebenezer Pettigrew to James Cathcart Johnston UNC

Aug. 3rd 1824. Lake Phelps

My dear Sir,

Having again recovered the use of my fingers so as to write I take up the pen. Though I can write my fingers are yet stiff, I can neither shut nor straighten them, in truth my disease is yet in all my system and I have no hope of ever having the full use of my hands again, but I am resigned to my fate. I think I have had as little depression of spirits this year as any preceding. It was with very great pleasure I received your favour of 12 <Jan.> /March/ and should have answered it due time, but about the first of Feb. I was deprived of that pleasure which has continued untill about three weeks. I regret very much the untoward event which deprived me of the pleasure of your company at the time you mention. I almost dispair. O! what an out of the way place do I live in. It is well adapted for a quarter, but not a residence of the owner. Your company will be always truely desirable to me whether in sickness or in health most I am unable to say. Though you have declined appointing a time of visiting me I still entertain a strong hope of seeing you once more before I go hence. I am sensible of the time necessary to bestow on your several farms, by that which mine requires, but my dear Sir, when a man /has/ two or three he must depend on deputies and has rather more time, than when he commands one in person and has to give dayly orders and see them executed.

Do not think by the account I give you of my health that I am a poor emaciated being with scarce any flesh on my bones. I am as corpulent as I ever was, with a pretty good appetite, yet my physical power is gone. If I was set on the floor it would be with the greatest difficulty, I could get up, I cannot carve a chicken nor can I pull of my cloths. As respects the deceit & dissimulation of mankind my mind is made up. I look for little else, but the misfortune in me is that I am sometimes by an impetuosity of temper constrained to talk of it. I have some curiosity to know who it is that has lately shown you his cloven foot. I see a great degree of unjustifyable selfishness which never fails to excite my ill temper. There is nothing like news in this place, and my pidling concerns must be very uninteresting to you, but that you may know that my mind has lost none of its energy I will give you a short detail of my opperations. Last fall I took the roof off my machinehouse house, also the roof off my barn took down the sheds which covered the machinery between the two houses, added 15 ft to the front of the barn so as to make it 40 ft; the width of the machinehouse, and covered the whole with one roof thereby giving a loft 110 ft by 40, in which is my cornsheler driven by a tub wheel to an upright shaft adding to the whole length of the two houses a Piazza in front 10 ft wide supported from the roof and /on/ the back a 14 ft open shed supported by posts; this I find very convenient and worth five times their cost. Before harvest I spent on the creek which my canal empties into four weeks of 12 hands and am now at work on it, with 20. I hope in about 3 weeks more to make it well navigable for flats and half way up to my canal for vessils of 40 tons. I expect to deepen my canal about a mile in the middle one foot, and to widen it at top on the road side two feet for four miles. Then I know nothing I can do to it for the better. In diging in the savana below the Bee Tree, (for you must know I began a six feet ditch from that place to the creek which my canal empties into.) I find a chaffy soil about 3 ft deep and then a good clay. I think in twenty years it [*torn*] good land. I raised thi[s] season 2300 bus wheat, the crop was [*torn*] by the caterpillars. My corn is pretty likely, not like to be as much injured by chince bug as last year. It has suffered much from drouth, and will be shortened. The disasters which are natural to the crops and their low price takes me hard to it, to pay my debts. I fear I shall not be through next year. You will observe in the Edenton paper my lands offered for sale.[1] The reason given in the advertisment is the true reason. My health does not justify my confining myself here, with all I think if I could have gone away my health might have been restored whereas my disease is but paliated by the warmth of the season and I look forward /to/ another long winter of confinement if not death. Mrs P. & children are in good health, she joins me in best respects to your sisters and Please to assure yourself of the sincere Esteem of your friend

E Pettigrew

James C. Johnston Esqr.

[*Addressed*] James C Johnston Esqr
Hays
Edenton Post Office

---

[1]The *Edenton Gazette* for this year is not extant.

Ann Blount Pettigrew to Mary Williams Bryan UNC

Lake Phelps November 15th, 1824.

My dear Sister,

Your last letter I received with much pleasure; but was much supprised to learn from it you had not received but one from me since last winter, I certainly have written much oftener than that, my letters must have miscarried, although I confess I do not write half as often as my inclination would direct, I am not quite so negligent.

I am happy to hear you have a fine daughter Mary Elizabeth, only one day older than my little Henry. I suppose you have learned I have added another link to my chain of troubles I might add, a house full of boys is enough to craze ones brain. I congratulate you on the good fortune of having a daughter so much more manageable than the other sex. Viz. Betsey Stanly[1]

I promised myself the pleasure of seeing you this fall, but Mr Pettigrew and James have the fever and ague, and Henry is so very young, that I have deemed it prudent to postpone my visit untill February when probably the weather will be comfortable. Mamas inquiry respecting William's notions respecting a certain lady cannot be satisfied by us, I believe he has a wish, but I believe the subject has never been mentioned. I believe whoever looks for great fortune there will be catched, I suspect the riches will go to the sons with the exception of the land given by the grandfather, which without great expenses will not be productive of anything, but enough of this subject of surmises, aded to that, I would not give a cent for /a/ wifes land.[2]

I have had a visit from Miss Eleanor Trotter,[3] who I understand is the belle of Beaufort County, I think she is much improved quite intelligent, when she returned home she sent me a cosmetic for the skin, a transparent soap which I think has benefitted the moth on my face, I am in the full tide of successfull experiment at present. Though Mr P. is doubtfull[4]

The Miss Beaslies who it seems cannot be driven from NC. have returned this fall to Edenton reinforced with the youngest sister,[5] I think the marriage of Betsy B ought to deter them from marring incautiously, what a dreadful misfortune to be left unprotected and without friends and advisers in this miserable world; I congratulated you on the birth of a daughter, but I ought to have reflected on the many ills she probably might be exposed to, true as Dr Johnston says they are the most unfortunate part of creation. If they are, it must be because they have the command of all the other part of the creation. We know to rule is not always the happiest life, more particularly if we have not descretion, they generally carry too much sale though it is well known they are the weaker vessil. E P.[6]

Give my love to Mama Penelope Frederick and all the the family. I suppose you are alone by this time.

Mr Pettigrew joins me in love to you and believe me your affectionate sister.

A B Pettigrew.

Mrs Mary Bryan—

[*Addressed*] Mrs Mary W. Bryan
Newbern,
N.C.

---

[1]These three words appear to have been added in Ebenezer's handwriting and may refer to Elizabeth Stanly Armistead.

[2]Ebenezer apparently wrote the last part of this sentence, beginning with *aded.*

[3]Eleanor was probably the daughter of Thomas Trotter. Trotter mentioned his daughter Elena in a letter to Ebenezer in 1817. Lemmon, *Pettigrew Papers*, I, 559. She was married in 1826; see Ann Blount Pettigrew to Mary Williams Bryan, March 9, 1830, note, and Thomas Trotter to Ebenezer Pettigrew, May 17, 1834, in this volume.

[4]Apparently this phrase also was added by Ebenezer.

[5]Sally and Betsy, two daughters of Dr. John Beasley and Ann Slade Beasley of Edenton, deceased, are mentioned in Lemmon, *Pettigrew Papers*, I, 374; another daughter, Maria W., married Lt. Frederick Norcom at Edenton on May 15, 1828. *North Carolina Star* (Raleigh), May 29, 1828. A fourth daughter, Harriet, had married William R. Norcom earlier in 1824. *North Carolina Star* (Raleigh), March 26, 1824.

[6]Ebenezer inserted and initialed the last two sentences of this paragraph.

Ann Blount Pettigrew to Ebenezer Pettigrew UNC

Newbern December—30th 1824.

My dear Husband,

According to promise I commence with writing you very often your advice to the contrary notwithstanding. I am extremely desireous to hear from my dear husband and children, I would rather be buried in solitude forever than be deprived of their society. absence has the effect to increase my regard, when sepperated from my friends only the fair side of their characters presents itself to me. I cannot reflect on their faults. Newbern is the gayest of the gay at present, almost every night their is a party Fred is a great beaux I do not partake of them, the married folks are excluded almost which suits me extremely well. last evening Ma and myself were at Mrs McKinleys, her house is like a palace she has the most splendid drawing room I ever beheld, quite new and the latest fashion, she told us the furniture of that room cost 1500 dolls it almost surpasses description and to grace the room in a peculiar manner her portrait is on one side and Miss M. Jones's is on the other. Penelope's health is so delicate she cannot partake in the amusements of the evening. Ma had a dinner party the other day when I saw Mr Mason he inquired after your health. I think he has lost his spirits or at least his vivacity.

William arrived a few days before Christmas, he seemed disappointed at not seeing you. he said he would willingly have escorted me to Newbern, he seems to be rather at a loss what to do with the Negroes they are all unwilling to be sold from Newbern, poor mortals! what a state of society is ours, every day I have a more horrible idea of it.

John is expected on saturday unaccompanied with his wife I understand he sold his farm for much more than its value and that he is or seems satisfied to remain where he is—

The death of old Mr Smyth made a considerable change in the family. Mrs Armstead is quite a fashionable woman and looks handsomer than ever, it is supposed she is going to be married to R Orme—she is quite a fine looking woman. Newbern is full of extravagance and fine dressing, the poorest people make a show

Mr Bryan has not returned from the assembly yet, a number of persons have gone to Raleigh with the expectation of seeing Lafayett, but will be disappointed—Mrs Iredell I understand has gone up with her brother Mr Bryan wrote for Mary to hire a carriage and go up, but she I suppose preferred staying because of my being here.

La Fayette will be in Carolina in the spring.[1] He is said to have been fatigued with travelling and requested permission to stay in Washington a short time during the session perhaps for the purpose of resting.

After I had sealed your letter by Mr Woodly[2] sent, I understood Stewart the taylor had not your measure, if you wish to send your measure, let me know what you wish to have done

I am desireous to know whether Mr Morris has arrived or not, and how you proceed do write me.

Penelope is a staunch Roman Catholic. she does not go to the episcopal Church. her feelings I perceive are very acute on the subject, she does not make a show of religion but does not like to be jested with on the subject of her faith.

Give my love to your Mother—to Mrs Warrenton[3]—kiss the children for me Ma joins me in love to you. remember me to to all the family and believe me my dear husband your

ever affectionate wife
Ann B. Pettigrew

P.S. I still continue in the enjoyment of good health, Henry has the colic as usual, James has a bad cold but does not mind it much he is wild as ever, Grace's hand is not well yet but I cannot induce her to wear a rag on it without more trouble than her hand is worth.

[*Addressed*] Mr. Ebenezer Pettigrew,
Skinnersville,
NC.

---

[1]The Marquis de Lafayette visited North Carolina in March, 1825. Johnson, *Ante-Bellum North Carolina*, 140-141.

[2]Perhaps this was Daniel Woodley of Tyrrell County, a carpenter and builder. See other letters in this volume. Woodlys (Woodleys) in the *1830 Census Index*, 207, include Baily, Eli, John, and Samuel in Washington County, and Alay and Hardy in Tyrrell County.

[3]Mrs. Warrenton (Warrington) was an elderly woman who apparently lived near the Pettigrews and served as a housekeeper and companion to Nancy. Lemmon, *Pettigrew Papers*, I, 637, 645; Ebenezer Pettigrew to James Cathcart Johnston, January 4, 1825, in this volume.

Ebenezer Pettigrew to James Cathcart Johnston UNC

Lake Phelps Jan. 4, 1825

My Dear Sir,

I hoped before this to have received a line from you, but as letter writing is distant conversation with ones friends I take up the pen without ce[re]mony to let you know how the world wags with me and be assured I should be no less glad to learn how it is with you, and let me tell you that though I stay so short a time with you and see you so seldom it is very contrary to my wishes; how pleasantly could I spend a fortneight with you if my affairs would allow it; You must be certain how much more agreeable it must be to converse with a friend in whome you have the most perfect confidence and open your whole soul, than to be spending days and weeks with those who are waying every word to see if an unfavourable construction can be placed to it; when I am with the latter discription (which is alas too often) how often do I drop a sigh with deep sorrow, that I cannot be some where else. You will naturally suppose that something has occured lately; I think there is a small party behind the curtain, but I am confident I shall put them down without their ever coming out. Virtue & Truth has for ever borne the test of ages.

We have had a very wet fall and by far the most disagreeable one to sown wheat that I recollect, I however sowed eighty acres, which was nearly what I intended, the ground was not in the order I wished but I have confidence in the land, I planted but a small crop of corn for want of cleared land, it produced tolerably and will /be/ sufficient for use; I /have/ pretty good head of water and am sawing I hope the mill will be of profit to me this winter. I sold last year between 6 & 700 dollars worth of plank, I intend to loos no time with it this winter & spring and am in hopes it will be worth 1000 dollars. I am from a request of my mother about to take possetion of her plantation & negroes, and supply her wants; I know it will increase my troubles, but she is totally unable to conduct it; The plantation is mine at her death and she says most of the negroes. They are all spoiling, the plantion is going to wreck; and I think without any pecuniary expence more than those on it can produce I can make it a valuable place for one of my children. I dislike the increase of business but I must get an overseer for it, a thing she would no do.

As to my health, my fingers are about what they were when I was with you, and I have very little affection else where, I am accordingly able and do take a great deal of exercise, but I have had for some time a pain at intevals and constant soreness in my left side which I thought was a pleuritic symtom, but the Doctor says not, that it is probaby a Scyrrus; I take the liberty to doubt, but I do not like the soreness which has come on in a fortnight and is inconvenient, though I treat it with contempt. I do not see death any where near at hand, but we must all die /and should it happen/ before, you, could I my dear friend venture to appoint you sole executor to my will with a hope that you would act. If I could it is unnecessary for me to tell you that one great distress would be removed at parting from the world; Property is nothing compaired to the manner in which children are brought up, and he must be a bad child indeed who will take none of the advise of his Guardian. Train up a child in the way he should go and when he is old he will not depart from it. I wish no better woman than their Mother, but I have been satisfyed and she is no less so that Mothers cannot manage boys.

After a stay of two years and three month in this solitary abode Mrs Pettigrew set out about the 15th ult. for Newbern [*torn*] were such as to prevent me from going with her, and I got [*torn*] my engineer and a very worthy litle man to go with her, she took the two youngest children and left with me the two eldest, and an elderly lady Mrs Warrington to keep house. I learn they got safe to Newbern and are all well. I expect to go for her the first warm spell in February.

My pecuniary affairs need more than I have. I expect to receive in the course of the Spring what I may want, but it will not be in time; I would /consider it/ a great favour if you /would/ oblige me with the loan of between 3 & 500 dollars. I make this request under a belief of its being perfectly convenient, and if so will you be so good as to place it in the hands of Messrs. Th. & W. A Turner Plymouth,[1] and advise me of it; I /would/ have sent expressly to your house but for the uncertainty of finding you at home. I hope you /will/ overlook the interlineations when I give as excuse for not writing over; stiff fingers, and not being in the habit I make as many the second as first. Please to give my respects to the Ladies and believe me your sincere Friend

E Pettigrew

[*Addressed*] James C. Johnston Esqr
Hays
Edenton Post Office

---

[1]Thomas and William A. Turner, brothers, were merchants in Plymouth, Washington County. They are listed in the *1820 Census Index*, 16. Some of the persons listed as members of their households may have been apprentices or employees, as neither brother was ever married.

Ann Blount Pettigrew to Ebenezer Pettigrew UNC

Newbern—January 10—1825—

My dear Husband,

I received your two letters with very great pleasure your last dated the 4th of January I received a few minutes since I cannot express to you my dear husband the gratifycation I receive in reading your affectionette letters, I spent this morning in returning some of my calls, called on the Smyth family found them in distress at the loss of Mrs Bryan whose death they had lately heard of, I find Madam McKinley extremely polite, remarkably so; I am happy to inform you I have had the pleasure of seeing all my brothers, John staid nearly a week he is wild as ever, made fun for us all the time, but he breaks fast, & looks old, much older than myself, he gives a flattering description of his situation for health & beauty none exceeding his well is 45 feet deep oh! how delighted I should be to live in such a country he says you would have no rheumatism in that country, and it would seem so knowing that yours proceeded from debility occasioned by fall fever.

Mr Bryan returned last week, looks very <beadly> badly; he did not enjoy his health in Raleigh. I would advise him to leave the low country. brother John was much pleased to see me he expressed great desire to see you.

I am sorry to hear of William's indisposition, but am happy to learn he had nothing of the croup I feel greatly obliged to Mrs Warrenton for her extreme care and attention, I am very sorry to hear you have not the teacher I feel distressed at the idea of my dear children being so backward in their education and so far behind other children of the same age.

Mama had a splinded tea party last thoursday evening where I saw a great assemblage of bells and fine dressing music on the Pianno by Miss Betsy Graham,[1] & Miss Susan Gaston[2] one of the sweetest looking girls I ever saw though not handsom I was requested to play, but pled an excuse. Ma requested me to tell you she regretted not having the pleasure of your company. Mr Roberts[3] said your presents would have heightened his pleasure vastly, but he stands as a good man but not sincere therefore I did not believe him altogether, the widow I mentioned in my last looked very languishing as one might expect, I received as much enjoyment as I could sepperated from my dear Husband and children, believe me when I tell you such amusements have very little pleasure for me though you may say I am not in the habit, as you have an excuse always for my good feelings, and perhaps that may be the case, I was the only lady in the room without curles except one or two old women, and got a severe reprimand from Mary for not wearing a wreath of flowers on my head which she sent me for the purpose, I wish to live not for the pleasures this world presents, but for my husband first and family &— James is quite well, and very mischievous. Henry looks tolerable but does not grow he is not near as large as Mary's child. Almost every person I see exclaims at my increased size. I have fattened very much since I came. Ma has so many nice nic, nacks, I attribute it to that.

I wish your plan with your Mother may succeed well without increasing your trouble very much—I approve [*torn*] however—I fear your increased business will ca[*u*]se you [*torn*] yourself more than ever; John has 600 acres of land where he lives he intends raising cotton & having a store a mile from his dwelling, with a clerk, where he intends doing extensive business. he seems perfectly devoted to his wife he seems scarcely to think of any thing else. Ma joins me in love to you—remember me to Mrs. Warrenton and your Mother kiss the dear children for me. and believe me ever

your affectionate wife
Ann B Pettigrew

Mr E Pettigrew.

P.S. Excuse this scrawl I have no black lines—.

[*Addressed*] Mr E Pettigrew,
Skinners-ville.
N—C.

---

[1]Possibly Betsy Graham was the daughter of Edward Graham, a prominent New Bern attorney who served in the state House of Commons in 1797. Miller, "Recollections," 16; Cheney, *North Carolina Government*, 237.

[2]Susan Jane Gaston was a daughter of William Gaston (1778-1844) of New Bern, a distinguished state legislator, congressman, and chief justice of the North Carolina Supreme Court. Miller, "Recollections," 15; *Biographical Directory of Congress*, 933-934; *DAB*, VI, 180-181. Susan Gaston married Robert Donaldson of New York in 1828. *North Carolina Star* (Raleigh), February 21, 1828.

[3]This probably refers to John M. Roberts, who was cashier of the Bank of New Bern. *Raleigh Register*, January 29, 1819.

Ann Blount Pettigrew to Ebenezer Pettigrew UNC

Newbern Janury 18th 1825—

My dear Husband,

I received your letter dated January the 11th this morning with very great gratify-cation, but was very sorry to learn you have been unwell. I hope you will speedily recover with a little care and attention. I fear your walks and attention to your business are too fatiegueing and require too much exposure at this season of the year—do My dear Husband be careful of your health for the sake of your family, I think Ma's two daughters can boast of having good husbands, therefore we should beg them to preserve their lives. I think Mr Bryan an excellent man he <seems> has such an uniform temper, but I fear he is in a bad state of health. he looks very badly he was very sick night before last, was taken with a cold sweat which alarmed Mary very much, but next day was tolerable well—I think his aunt and Mother will live to enjoy their fortunes. and to walk over his grave if they choose. Mama complains of the colic to day and looks very badly, myself and children are very well.

Dr Jones has come to Newbern with his daughters to spend some time, he will soon be a smart widower, but has an odious character. from his immorality, I see him in the street he looks very genteel in deep black, which is indeed only a semblance of grief a perfect mockery of wo. he gave Mary a remedy for rheumatism written on a slip of paper he says he has made many cures I send it, you must understand if you can.—

Newbern still continues very gay. I am invited to a splendid Ball to be given at Mr John Stanleys[1] to-morrow and wish not to go, though I am teazed on all sides I think I shall not be prevailed on,. these parties if I go will cause <to> me to make more purchases than I intended. therefore must borrow some money to carry me through—my 40 Dolls. slipt out of my pocket book for things I really needed very soon, I could not immagine at the lake what use I had for money, but soon found my mistake, but I am very saving and frugal more so than any one I meet with who pretend to dress—.

I was very sorry to hear of poor Shamrocks death poor fellow, Charles no doubt grieved much.

I am sorry to hear you have purchased more land, you had better take care of your mon/e/y, you need not murder your days to make farms for your children, for they will not live on them and they will not thank you, I am sometimes almost tempted to perswade you to move to Edenton. but I know /not/ what is right. certain it is we cannot live forever and while we live let us live, [*torn*] enjoy some of the comforts of society, but as [I to]ld Mr [*torn*] last night, I am not willing to sacrifice all interest for society. I have written your Mother—please give her my love, also Mrs W. kiss the children and believe me whether at Newbern Lake or any other place your aff—wife

A B Pettigrew

Mama sends you her love—

[*Addressed*] Mr E Pettigrew—
Skinners-ville
NC.

---

[1]John Stanly (1774-1833) of New Bern was a brilliant attorney and eloquent speaker for the Federalist party. In 1802 he killed former governor Richard Dobbs Spaight in a duel but received a pardon from Governor Benjamin Williams. Stanly served in Congress, 1801-1803 and 1809-1811, and in the state legislature, for fifteen terms between 1798 and 1827. In the latter year he suffered a stroke from which he never fully recovered. Upon Stanly's death, a two-column obituary was printed in the *Newbern Spectator*, August 9, 1833.

Stanly had eight sons and one daughter. One son, Fabius, became an admiral in the United States Navy; another, Edward, a Whig, served in Congress, 1837-1843 and 1849-1853, before moving to California. Miller, "Recollections," 12-13; Crabtree, *North Carolina Governors*, 54; Henderson, *North Carolina*, I, 485, 507, 509, 570, 611; Parish Register, Christ Church, New Bern, Burials, 84; *Biographical Directory of Congress*, 1644; Cheney, *North Carolina Government*, 238, 240, 263, 265, 266, 268, 272, 274, 275, 278, 283, 284, 286, 288, 290.

Ann Blount Pettigrew to Ebenezer Pettigrew UNC

Newbern Janury 31st 1825.

My dear Husband,

Your affectionate letter I received last evening with very great pleasure and was much relieved to learn you were in tolerable health for the night before I had a distressing dream which ought not to have caused me any uneasiness knowing my dreams never have any signification. I was much shocked to learn the risk you run of being killed by the tree I beseech you in future to keep at a sufficient distance you know how many accidents have happened on the Lake of the kind.

We are all tolerable well several days I was quite unwell with a sore throat and mouth which arose from fevers from some little cold I had taken. I had Henry Ebenezer Pettigrew cristned in Church last sunday he behaved extremely well laughed nearly all the time. Marys baby was christned the same time. I have seen very little of Mr Mason since I have been here he seldom comes to see us—he has a fine daughter which they say delights him very much

Frederick has received a commission to attend & escort Lafayette to the city of Raleigh, but he is undetermined what to do he will /be/ obliged to get uniform hat & feather—and horse &c.—which expence is too great to incur to be thrown aside afterwards, I think the State aught to furnish such expenses—but Carolina like they do not. he is very anxious to go.

Mr Bryan says he is affraid he will be from home when you come—he is anxious to see you. I wish my dear husband you would come some time before we set out for home. Your friends here would be very much pleased to see you get some man to attend to your bussiness, & give yourself a little time for recreation—I was amazed to see Dr Old—in Newbern, I should not have been as much supprised to have seen LaFayette—he made a very short stay—offered to take a letter to you but I had just written by mail—. Newbern continues very gay, so much frolicking that Mr Mason gave a severe lecture from the Pulpit, which had not much effect—. I did not go to Mr Stanly ball—the weather was so bad.

The other /day/ a large company of us went to see a show—tigers a lion monkeys /&c—/ a sight I have never seen before—how delighted Charles and William would have been to have seen the monkey dance. Charles has not improved much in writing. I hope you sometimes give him a lesson. Mama is anxious for Charles to come to N. and go to school she says she will take any & every care of him—but I dislike the distance—sometimes I am almost determined to persuade you to accept of Mr Johnstons offer to go to E. to live for the purpose of educating our children I shall expect to see you very soon my dear Husband [*torn*] excedingly anxious you may be sure, I reckon Mrs W. is almost weary keeping house, give my love to her—& Mother, kiss the children.

I thank you much for the 50 Dollars I find it very convenient

believe me your ever affectionate wife
Ann B Pettigrew—

I wish you would get Mrs. W. to put up some seeds--aspargus seeds also if it will not be too much trouble to bring them. please to get her to look for my receits in the close closet in a ban box, for the receit for hooping cough and bring it—they have it N. we intend keeping the children very close—to prevent their taking it Marys oldest child is in bad health if it should take it—it will be bad.

[*Addressed*] Mr E Pettigrew,
Skinnersville
NC.

[Dr.] Thomas Old to Ebenezer Pettigrew A&H

March. 17th 1825.

Dear Sir.

By a letter lately recd from my friend Mr Ivy I am requested by him to Solicit of you the refusal of the purchase of your Pine Timber if you will under any circumstances dispose of it. He appears to be under the impression that the only objection you have had to sell is the purpose to which the Timber was to be applied (the British service) and that since he has a contract for our Government he might without impropriety make you proposals. altho. from my Knowledge of your sentiments I am lead to believe you intend to retain it for your own use, in communicating the request of Mr Ivy I am performing a duty incumbent on me. You will therefore pardon me for touching on this subject.

A few days ago I recd a present of some very fine pickled oysters from a friend in Va Being very solicitous that Mrs Pettigrew shall receive a share of them I shall make an effort to Keep them as long as possible. Be so good as to send immediately on your return for them—a jar that will hold two gallons.

Yrs &
Thos. Old

[*Addressed*] Mr Ebenezer Pettigrew
Lake Phelps

Ebenezer Pettigrew to James Cathcart Johnston UNC

Lake Phelps. April 26, 1825

My dear Sir,

Your esteemed favour of Jan 30th I did not have the pleasure to receive untill my return from Newbern, which was not untill the latter part of March. My long stay at that place was occasioned by the extreme high tides. To be shut up six or eight weeks in a town where I know but few and perhaps associate with none will be better immagined by you, than I can discribe; I however got out alive, though in a very crippled state; from which I have just recovered. My complaint was a violent cold & cough which seemed to threaten a consumption; I began to think that just at the time I had thought myself free from danger I was about to take it.

I regret that my request to you, has given you the mortifycation to decline a favour to a friend, one I am satisfied you would comply with if in your power, but let me assure you my dear friend that I accept your reasons as fully sufficient, they confirm me in my opinion of your frien/d/ly disposition towards my children if in distress and at all times. In respect to the severity & caprieces of your temper, give me leave to disagree with you, and to say that I am astonished that you should have any such idea of yourself. Please to accept my sincere thanks for the money which you were so good as to direct in the hands of Messrs Turners. It has been received and I have found it very convenint, in settling all the calls which seem naturally to come out of business. At foot is a note for the amount which you will be so good as to accept untill I have something of more worth to give you. I am striving to do something in the gaining way and as usual am in hopes of geting out of all pecuniary difficulties in a year or two, but that has been so old a story that I scarcely believe it myself. My wheat is promising and I hope to rais nearly 2000 bushels. The Lake is at this time very full which gives me a full head for the saw, and I am taking the advantage of it by sawing day and night. I /have/ sold & sent away a considerable quantity, but sawing so constantly fills up the space and I have a good deal on hand. Should you see any one who wants I would be glad if you would recommend me to them. I expect to saw by the fall not less than 200 thousand ft. which if I can sell will put me compleatly above board. The Lake at this time looks delightfully. How glad I should be to see you here! Mrs Pettigrew & the children are at present well, she joins me in best respects to your Sisters and please to accept for yourself the sincere regard & Esteem of your sincere friend

E Pettigrew

James C. Johnston Esqr

N.B. I should have writen you sooner, but I have been since my return so overwhelmed with business that I could not compose my mind sufficiently and I now write you after all have gone to bed, no noise but the saw

E P.

[*Addressed*] James C. Johnston Esqr
Hays
Edenton P. office

David Witherspoon[1] *to Ebenezer Pettigrew* A&H

June 9th 1825

Dear Sir

I wrote to you by Mr Joshua witherspoon he neglected or forgot to take the Letter with him to you—from the Recolection I have of you and the Intimate acquaintance I had with your worthey father indusus me to write to you—as it may be Sum Sattisfaction to you to Convers with you on paper—a number of years past I perchist a valuable tract of land on the oconey River in the fruntiars of Georgia I Give five Dollars per acre I held the mans bond for five thousand Dollars he was a man of large property but faild in makeing ti[t]les to the land the man is Dead. I have brought Suit in Federal Court. /against his Executors/ I Expect to Get my money next fall—I have had to encounter Sc[or]es of Difficuteys in my old age. Can Say I have lost Sum thousands of Dollars by trusting bad men—I purpus Sittleing in Georgia—the Last purches that was maid of the Creek Indians is the most valuable of aney purches that has been made in that State of late Dr Sir I wrote to you Sum years past Respecting your Fathers Sermons and pamplets—he had wrote in his Life time he mensiond them to me the last time I had the pleasure of seing him—he told me he would leave them and I might make such use of them as I might think proper in haveing them printed—as it was his Request it is thought thay ought not to lay Dorment—

now Sir as there has been a long delay in haveing them prined. If you will do me the favour of Sending them on to me by the Maile to Morganton Burk County I will Receve them Doct Askew a clergeman of high Standing was Intimately acquanted with your Father when he was young Says he will Give his aide in prepareing his Righting for the press /if thay want aney/ prehaps there is few Gentlemen more Capable he thinks thay /can/ be sirculated to advantage in the fruntir States now Sir it may be Sum what Gratefeing to you to heare of sum of your /old/ Relatesions two of your Fathers Sisters[2] are alive and Injoys tolerable helth for those of there age thay have Rasd Respetable Famileys Sum of the men are leading Carrectors. also my oldest Sister /Ha[r]bin/ Lives on togolo River She has been a widdow about 16 years She has three Sons men of Buisness her oldest son is Clart [*clerk*] of the Court also a Collo of the County—<hir> through hir Good aeconemy Sinse hir husbands Death /She/ has Doubled the Estate—mostly from the Culture of Cotton. Cultivates about 250 acres of land the Greater part of the first quality—workes about 25 hands—Sister McGemsey also a widow /is Rich/ whare I now write from[3] has two sons prehaps as Respectable young men as aney Rais^{d} in this Sexson of the State. one is a Docter now liveing on Duck River in Columba[s?]. Gets a Extensive practice—there father when he Died was Co^{lo} of Burk County—

The oldest Son W^{m} MGemsey has a Desire to sell his farme thay now live on—I will Describe it to you perhaps sum of your—acquaintane may incline to purchis that lives in that onhealthy part of the Country. it lyes 12 miles /west/ from Morganton on Linvill River on the mane publick Road to tennessee Contains one thousand acres /of land/ there is upwards of one hundred acres of Cleard Land the greater part River bottom of the best quality a quantaty of god [*good*] upland <to> to Cleare. it is one of the handsumest <in> Seats in this part of the Country—there is an Exelent Mill Seat on it. it is one of the best publick stands in burk County—it Can be bought for [5]000 Dollars part on a Credit the Greater part might be paid in young negrows—Cant you send sum of your welthy farmers to purchis (there Reason for <Sell> offering this land for sa[le] thay want to go Yon Duck River—

there is no part of the world more helty than it is heare from this farme there is one of the most beautifull views of the Mountans I Ever beheld—if the Cataby River is wonst made Navigable /for it/ botes will Come with in Eight miles of this farme—it will be Compleated in time—My worthy friend M^{r} McGemsey is desirous I should make this Comunication to you /<about his land>/ as he is onacquaintd with you—prehaps from your numerous acquaintance you might Se Sum person would Incline to purchis—as to my self I Enjoy a tolarable Shear of helh in my old age tho at times I am much afflicted with the Rhumatack paines—My sons that are Grown are Men of buisness thay have good lerning—tho two of them have turnd out to be Medithist preachers my oldest son[4] is liveing in Georgia maryed in that Country in a Respetable family—one of my Nephuse in Georgia lives about 20 from the Indian Line he wants to purchis a drove of Indian horses to sell in the Low Country. I think thay will Suit your Climet. thay will /last/ almost as long as Mules sum of them are the niseist harness I Ever Road. thay say thay will keep fat on Ruf food I think I must

Join <in> him in a Drove /next fall/ thay will sell the price will be modrate Dr Sir I am Respectfully yours &c

D. Witherspoon

E Pettigrew Esqr

Please to give my Respects to Mrs Pettigrew your Lady.

Pos your father wrote a pamphlet on the Death of two Infents an exellent peac I Epect the one on Baptism Equelly so also his advice to his advic to his sons my Relations think as great a peace as thay Ever heard Read—thare is no Dout but thay are worthy of being printed as well as for the publick good So that I shall be much gratifide if you Can mak it Convenant to Send his papers on by the Maile

D. W.

[*Addressed*] E. Pettigrew Esqr.
Terrel County
Lake Phelps
N. Carolina

---

[1]David Witherspoon was a son of Martha Pettigrew, sister to the Reverend Charles Pettigrew, and her husband, John Witherspoon. He lived at Wilkesboro, North Carolina, in 1817, according to a letter he wrote to Ebenezer. Lemmon, *Pettigrew Papers*, I, xiv, 579. David Witherspoon represented Wilkes County in the legislatures of 1795 and 1796. Cheney, *North Carolina Government*, 233, 235.

[2]Other sisters of Charles Pettigrew were Rachel, Mary, Jane, and Elizabeth. Lemmon, *Pettigrew Papers*, I, xiv.

[3]Possibly the writer refers to Flora Witherspoon, who married John McGimsey of Burke County. *The Heritage of Burke County* (Morganton: Burke County Historical Society, 1981), 301. This letter is postmarked Morganton.

[4]Presumably this was George Witherspoon. Lemmon, *Pettigrew Papers*, I, 579.

[Dr.] Thomas Old to Ebenezer Pettigrew UNC

Norfok Va Aug. 5th 1825

Dear Sir,

Frequently and anxiously have I thought since leaving /you/ of the destitute situation of yourself and many other of my friends, in a medical point of view have been placed by my removal from Tyrrell and had not causes of an insuperable nature occurred to drive me from the country I shd have sacraficed other considerations & have remained. The young gentleman of whom I spoke to you has come to Norfolk to see me & brought a very marked recommendation from my friend Dr C. of this state, independently of which his oppertunities have been so favorable that he must I think be well qualified to perform the duties of his profession. His name is Dr Wm C. Warren.[1] His object is to settle permanently in Tyrrell if he commences business at all as far as I can learn from him which is an additional recommendation in his favor If he does <no> so I shall think I have conferred a real favor on you by quitting for it was impossible for me to become satisfied & I coud not be brot. to view myself as finally settled. You will consider this an Introductory Letter for Dr Warren. He will visit very soon after he reaches Tyrrell. The Doctor as I am informed by him has been engaged in practice anterior to this time and is a graduate of the Pennsyl. University.

Since leaving you my health has improved altho I am but just recovered from an attack of Intermittent Fever, by which cause and the necessary attention to some business I have been detained longer than I anticipated in Va I shall however start on monday morning for Washington City whence after stopping a couple of days to admire the Public Buildings & view the magnificoes of the nation I shall proceed to Baltimore, Phila & N. York. From one of these places I will write you again & more lengthily. Present the assurances of my highest esteem to Mrs Pettigrew My complmts to Mr Kennedy[2]

Believe very sincerly yr. friend
Thos. Old

Mr Ebenezer Pettigrew

[*Addressed*] Mr Ebenezer Pettigrew
Lake Phelps,
N.C.

---

[1]Undoubtedly this was Dr. William Christian Warren. *North Carolina Star* (Raleigh), December 8, 1826; Ann Blount Pettigrew to Mary Williams Bryan, February 12, 1827, in this volume.

[2]W. W. Kennedy was a tutor of the Pettigrew children. See the following document, dated September 22, 1825.

Receipt from Pettigrew Children's Tutor UNC

[*September 22, 1825*]

Received from Mr Ebenezer Pettigrew Thirty Nine Dollars in full for three months and one week tuition of children—

W W Kennedy

Septr 22nd 1825—

Ebenezer Pettigrew to John Herritage Bryan UNC

Lake Phelps Oct 16, 1825

Dear Sir,

I received your esteemed favour of 7 ult. about a fortnight after its date, and regret to learn that you did not receive that benefit to your health from your northern tour which was anticipated; I hope to learn from your next though in Carolina that your health has improved. We have all been in good health this fall except William who about two months ago had a sevier attack of bilious fever, but has perfectly recovered; I do not know that Nancy, Charles or the little one /has/ had a fever in six months, James was unwell in the summer, but by a fortunate *guess* of his disease he now looks like a mountain boy.

I congratulate you on the manner which you were elected to Congress, I however with you /regret/ the necessity of you serving, but you must make the best of it. I hope that all is for the best; it was a case in my opinion which should have excited the fears of the people. For the first time in my life I took an active part in the election. I even became a stump orator, and to my great satisfaction we succeeded not only in district but in my county where it was <was> thought our anticaucus candidate would get scarcely any votes, being opposed by all the most active and leading characters of the county but /we/ cryed aloud and spaired not, and got a majority of 12 votes I will attend to your request for David B. Ogden Esqr if to be had of the proper quality which is too often not the case.

I was Edenton last week, where I saw Mr W. Shepard he informed me something about your passing on that way to Congress; and we concluded the better way would be for you to come to my house from thence I will see you safe by water either in person or otherwise to Mr Shepard who says he will then send you to Norfolk. Nancy says she will be very happy if you will think proper to take this rout and bring with you as far as [*t*]his hous sister Mary who can certainly get some of her numerous Brothers to /come &/ return with her as a life guard. I hope I am well enough known to render it unecessary to say any thing as to my desires on the subject as I never propose to do any thing with[*out*] being in good e/a/rnest. Please to inform me on the above subject that I may be in place at the time.

When in Newbern Genl. [*Durand*] Hatch gave me some advertisment of a /runaway/ negroe which he suspected might be in Aligator. Will you be so good as to inform him that on my return home I did with the advertisments as requested and that when in that part of the county at the election I made strict enquir[y] about the fellow and from all that I could learn believ[e] he was not, nor do I believe has been in the county since runaway.

Please to excuse this bad writing, give our love sister Mary and assure yourself of the Esteem of your friend

E Pettigrew

N.B. I have be so discouraged in my bad writing & diction by some of my learned friends that I am wont to give out writing to great men.

[*Addressed*] John H Bryan Esqr
New Bern
N.C

Charles Lockhart Pettigrew to Mary Lockhart Pettigrew UNC

Lake Phelps November 12 1825

My Dear Grandma

I am glad I am able once more to write you a few lins I am sorry to inform you we have a very sickly family. Adam has died very sudden a very strange death. Penny also has<t> lost her child which was very puny from the first the white family are pretty well

I am you affetionate grandson
Charles L pettigrew

Ma says please send her some aggs ma sends her love to you

[*Addressed*] Mrs Mary pettigrew.
Washington county

J. B. O'Flaherty[1] *to Ebenezer Pettigrew* A&H

[*March 2, 1826*]

Dear Sir,

I have been this day honored with your letter of the 26th ultimo. From my present circumstances, I have decided on accepting one hundred & fifty Dollars per annum for my services as Tutor to your children. Should not the situation be awarded to one who might be engaged by your friend Doctor Warren. The salary is small, but you may hereafter find it your interest to increase it.

The Season is now so far advanced, that a decision, in my opinion, ought to be made soon as you may feel yourself justified to do so.

I send this by post & expect an answer soon as you can conveniently give it.

I am Sir
yours respectfully
J. B. O'Flaherty

Washington. N.C
2nd March. 1826.

[*Addressed*] E. Pettigrew Esqr
Skinnersville
Lake Phelps
Washington County
N.C

---

[1]Although O'Flaherty has not been further identified, this letter is included because it illustrates methods of education among rural families. Other tutors to the Pettigrew children mentioned in this volume are W. W. Kennedy, William J. Welles, and D. Stone.

Ebenezer Pettigrew to John Herritage Bryan UNC

Lake Phelps, Ap. 18, 1826

Dear Sir,

I regret to learn from Sister Mary that your health is no better than when you left Newbern, and that you believe you have a confirmed affection of the liver. I hope by the applycation to some of your eminent Physicians you may be restored; whether in the present stage of the disease simples will be useful is doubtful, they may be but paliatives. Calomel in some shape seems to be almost the only remedy. Charcoal in slight bilious affections, or in other words, in a bilious obstruction, of not serious nature, is an excellent remedy. But the way in which you took it, it was as bad as eating so much earth, it should have been heated /immediately/ before taken to expel all that it absorbed. It is I immagine as great an absorbant as magnesia. If I were to venture advice among the thousand who I expect are advising, I should say apply to one of the most Eminant Physicians for a cure & remove with/out/ delay to a healthy part of the country where bilious diseases are least frequent. Also pay strict attention to regimen. It is unnecessary to be persecuted with medicines to a cure, and indulge in eating or live in a climate which affects three fourths of the population with the disease which you are trying to eradicate, for it will return be you never so perfectly restored, if there is any hereditary predisposition.

I was quite mortifyed to learn that you had it in contemplation to take another rout home. I have advised Sister Mary to continue with promise to write you. The difficulty of geting here is I think not so great. You will know w/h/ere you are untill you get to Williams, There are from thence two routs, the one by Edenton & McKeys ferry, the other by Aligator. The latter I think would <be> be the best. You will get a boat or barge at Elizabeth and cross the Sound to Fortlanding on Aligator river, from thence you will get a chair & horse to my house which is 35 miles. Capt. Basnight lives at the landing. M^r^ Ma[jr]. Edmond Alexander & Sam. Spruill live within /two miles of fortlanding/ & Henry Alexander the Sheriff of the county lives with five miles. They all have chairs and I have no doubt you can be accommodated. I am on the best terms with them and will next week at court speak to them on the subject. For the other rout I refer you to our brother William who is all contrivance. He is by promise to visit me on business in the next month, perhaps it would be convenient for him to visit us with you it might be well for you to write him on the subject. You have no doubt heard of my dear wife being deliver of a daughter [*torn*] five weeks ago. She is not in as good health as u[sual] after such events, but I hope will be better in a few we[eks]. I am as common, poor in spirit, but of a sound desposing mind. Please to excuse this abominable scratch. I have not patience to write any better. And assure yourself of the

Esteem your friend
E Pettigrew

Hon. J. H. Bryan

N.B. After writing this beautiful nice letter I read it to the Ladies & Mrs P. directs to give you her most unfeigned respect & Mrs B says you have be been gone five months this day & she is most dead to see you

E P.

[*Addressed*] Hon. John H. Bryan H.R.
Washington City

Ann Blount Pettigrew to Mary Williams Bryan A&H, BRYAN

Lake Phelps, July 11th 1826.

My dear Mary,

I received your letter sent by Mr R (from the ferry I believe) before your first written by the Mail, the removal of the office having made some little confu<si>sion, I was very sorry to learn you had such a disagreeable journey home, I hoped from the pleasantness of the weather you would have had quite an agreeable time, I am sorry Mr Bryan was so unwell, it was a pity you left here that morning—I hope the Beaufort air will benefit him, I hope poor little Mary will get better before long, kiss the children for me.

Miss Caroline is determined to be a fine lady. New York exactly suites her desires, it is to be hoped the old lady will not die, she had /better/ sell off and clear out too.

Mr Pettigrew begs I will tell you, I wrote Fanny Lardner word how many beautiful children you had, Mary continues very quiet and I think improves in beauty. Henry is loosing his fat, he is the fattest child almost I ever saw, William has the fever and ague. slightly one dose of medicine probably will restore hime.

The weather still continues very dry and the garden suffers. Mr Pettigrew is threshing his wheat which is a very poor crop. I suppose Ma, has given you my message respecting the trip to the Springs, my immaginary trip like yours was very short lived, a Castle in Air indeed, I should have given you a circumstantial account you may be sure, what did Ma, think of the plan?

I have had a visit from Mrs Walker, who is a very agreeable woman, they have promised to send their Son and Daughter to see us, she gives Mrs Hines the most exalted character. I understand Mr Bane talks of taking /his/ wife on the circuit he says he cannot bear the separation, he had forgotton her countenance in an absence of 6 weeks, Mr Bryan must have had a very feint rememberance of yours in six monthes.

Mr Stone [*the tutor*] gets along as usual—James likes school much better, Mrs Walker sent him some Pidgeons and Mr W, is erecting a house for them near the barn greatly to his pleasure this is a piece of news worth relating to Theodore.

Aunt P——s relation Mrs West has come to visit her, she is well and says she regrets not having seen your little Mary before she left us, she says you have a great turn for nursing children, thinks I to myself, it is well she is. Give my love to Ma Penelope and family—also remember me to Miss Betsy, write soon a long lettler.

Mr Pettigrew joins me in love to yourself and Mrs [*sic*] B, and believe me your affectionate Sister.

Ann B. Pettigrew.

We received a letter from William the other day he is in fine spirits. and about preparing a speech for the 4 of July—Preacher Wiley[1] is very much admired in Edenton. I learn from a gentleman in Williams distrit that he is a ca[ndid]ate for *CONGRESS* by the particular solicitations [of] his most faithfull, kind, loving, & ever to be depended on *FRIENDS*. Awake!

[*Addressed*] Mrs Mary Bryan,
Newbern,
N.C.

[1]The Reverend Philip Bruce Wiley was an Episcopal deacon and rector of Christ's Church, Elizabeth City. *Journal of the Proceedings of the Eleventh Annual Convention of the Protestant Episcopal Church, In the State of North-Carolina... 1827* (New Bern: Watson and Machen, 1827), 3, hereinafter cited as *Journal of the Diocesan Convention, 1827*; *Journal of the Proceedings of the Seventeenth Annual Convention of the Protestant Episcopal Church in the State of North Carolina . . . 1833* (Fayetteville: Edward J. Hale, 1833), 3, hereinafter cited as *Journal of the Diocesan Convention, 1833*.

Ann Blount Pettigrew to Mary Williams Bryan UNC

Lake Phelps September 11th 1826.

My dear Mary,

Both of your affectionate letters I received after they had been miss sent, at which I was suprised as they were so correctly directed, certainly post masters are very negligent or careless, I was much disappointed several mails at not getting letters, I am fully convinced of the manny provoking occurrences that prevent letter writing with the manager of a family, particularly when there are many children, it is almost impossible sometimes to compose our minds sufficiently—Williams illness was of short duration, but last week he had an attack of bilious fever, but through Divine Providence and medical aid he is much better. he is very often sick at this season. Mr Pettigrew is not well, the children are tolerable—I was sorry to hear of Marys fall and fear the scar will continue, nurses are careless, I am pleased to hear of Francis Theodores improvement wonderful indeed! what posessed you to alter his name, you need not be so choice as to names, you will have enough to procure, it really produced a smile some of Mr Bryans taste I suppose, our object seems merely to distinguish one child from another. James has no middle name—you must look quit beautiful since you have rid yourselves of the tan. my poor children still continue quite bespeckeled and will remain so for life no doubt. instead of Mr Bryans electioneering again, I suspected he would be at home trying hard to cure the dispepsia, he has had a taste and no doubt is a member for life, if Mr Speight[1] does not dose the people too much—They say brother William wishes to distinguish himself in the annals of his country—he has been to see us and is fatter than I ever saw him. I assure you he is quite a plantation man. certainly the Shepards must have inherited that predilection for the cultivation of the soil from the maternal side, though I suppose

Mama would clear herself of that, W. says Mr Wiley is courting Miss Gregory[2]—he also fainted in the Pulpit not long since, from excessive heat—he is much thought of in these parts. Miss H Pritchard[3] said the Edenton people were delighted with him, William came over in a boat to Mr Hatheways.[4] on his return we went down to M^{r} H——s, in the carriage with him and about dark he set off home—Dr [*William C.*] Warren is <not> not married, but I suspect will be before long—when she arrives I will give you an account of her, no doubt she is all perfection as no other would suit one of his taste—I perfectly agree with you that there is more pleasure in immagination than reality—but certainly a change of scene is very recreating—true as Zimmerman says a change from solitude to society enables us to enjoy both.

Our teacher still continues with us and has the Dispepsia, also Mr Woodly has it and is under the direction of the D^{r}—write me soon—I am sorry to hear James is sick but I hope he is better, William said, he had no idea Pennys arm was in such a state—he seems to be convinced it is a scrofulus habit and says she must go to the salts—Please give my love to Mama and family—also my respects to Miss Betsy [*Graham*]—Mrs Warrenton is making a long visit to Aligater of two or three months, but will return in time for me to visit Newbern.

Mr Pettigrew joins me in affectionate rememberances to Mr Bryan and yourself—

Your affectionate sister
Ann B Pettigrew

Mrs Mary Bryan.

[*Addressed*] Mrs Mary W. Bryan,
Newbern
N C.

---

[1]Jesse Speight (1795-1847) of Greene County was a member of the state Senate at this time. He served in the United States House of Representatives from North Carolina, 1829-1837. He moved to Mississippi and sat in the state Senate there from 1841 to 1844, then in the United States Senate from 1845 until his death. *Biographical Directory of Congress*, 1636.

[2]The Reverend Philip B. Wiley married Claudia C. M. Hamilton Gregory on October 26, 1826. *North Carolina Star* (Raleigh), November 10, 1826.

[3]Possibly this is the Miss Hannah Prichard referred to in an 1813 letter in Lemmon, *Pettigrew Papers*, I, 456.

[4]Several Hathaways lived in the vicinity of Bonarva. Lemmon, *Pettigrew Papers*, I, 512n. Burton Hathaway of Tyrrell County and William Hathaway of Washington County are listed in the *1830 Census Index*, 81.

Ann Blount Pettigrew to Mary Williams Bryan A&H, BRYAN

Lake Phelps. Oct, 20th 1826.

My dear Sister,

I received your last with much pleasure, I had been disappoined several mails at not getting a letter, I am suprised at my letters not reaching you, I believe the Post is managed badly, I was really greived to hear of Sally Vails[1] death, it must be a sore affliction to her Mother who I believe has been peculiarly unfortunate in her children, what a sorrowful world this would be without the prospect of a future, it would indeed be a dreary pilgrimage—an incessant toiling for nothing, it is necessary for our happiness and salvation.

Mr Pettigrew has been very sick but I am happy to say has recovered Dr Warren was sick here with bilious fever at the same time, we sent to Plymouth for Dr Norcom, Dr Warren stayed with us 4 weeks and then after his recovery, returned to Scuppernong to resume his business—you will think I had my hands full of nursing, myself and the children enjoy very good health, Miss Mary has learned to exercise her voice, she is not so quite as she was, I promise myself the pleasure to see you all the last of this month or the first of next when I shall stay untill sometime about Christmas.

Mr Woodly is just compleating a well of fine water--it is conducted in pipes from the Lake, after being filtered there by a machiene he has constructted, we think the water will be equal to any below the mountains.

Give my love to Ma & family—remember me to Miss Betsy, Mr Pettigrew joins in respects to Mr B. and yourself—

Your aff sister.
Ann Pettigrew.

[*Addressed*] Mrs Mary Bryan,
Newbern,
NC.

[1]Sarah (Sally) Vail died August 4, 1826, according to the Parish Register, Christ Church, New Bern, Burials, 80. The *North Carolina Star* (Raleigh), October 6, 1826, states that she died on September 17, at the age of fourteen.

Ebenezer Pettigrew to Ann Blount Pettigrew UNC

Lake Phelps Nov 28, 1826

My dear wife,

It is with great pleasure I contemplate the approach of the day for the mail, not because I expect yet a letter from you, but that I may write you being very sensible of your anxiety to hear from home. The evening I left you I got to Swift creek, the next day I got to M[rs] Jacksons and the succeeding morning /cold as death/ was under way long before sunrise and arrived at mothers a little after dusk; there I learned the children were all well but M[rs] Warrington had been sick, and was then better; fealing desirous to see the children & get home, I set out from mothers a little after sunrise and got to the Lake to breakfast, Where I found all well, and things had gone on as well as might be expected. The children are perfectly free from disease, & M[rs] Warrington is well, what her disease is I did not learn but suppose it was some disease common to women. I have taken my bed in the room overhead, Charles sleeps in the cot & William I have taken as my bed fellow, Poor fellow you know he has a failing & M[rs] W. said he would be troublesome, but he is cautious in drinking & by being waked up in the night he has not yet incommoded me. I put my hand in Charles' pocket the other day and among other things took out a box on opening it I found it contained snuf, and on enquiry he told me he had it to clean his teath, I without the show of temper threw the establishent in the fire On saturday I had a slight chil but did not goe to bed, on sunday I was not so well but in the afternoon was better, on monday I had some pains in my limbs, but today I feal tolerable, with my little indisposition I have a good appetite, and hope soon to be well I give you this information because I think it rong to keep secrets from my better half. My mouth had got quite bad, but for these three days I have drank Boneset tea, and it is almost well. Henry is outrageously bad, he is so heavy that I can heardly lift him, he will not come near me. I got a letter from Brother William since my return; he says the report about that girl was false, that [Rogerson] sold her to a man in Alabama. How this world is given to lying? he also says he had got the fifty dollars from Lindsey, which make 350 dollars he has received on my note to him of 383 dollars. I have not yet heard from M[r] Johnston nor have received a line since my return from my New York freind. Fearing you may want or be cramped for money I have inclosed you a twenty dollar note. My dear wife I never quit you with /so much/ composure, bec/a/use I had so great a tie at home, our dear children, but now I am at home & see them wel[l] [*torn*] absence makes a great void /in my/ mind; and but from [*torn*] expectation of soon seeing you I know not how I should get through this world; I can assure you with perfect truth I view your minature with great delight, because it represents that which has been always since I saw it, dearest to my soul. I shall write you by every mail, & hope you will do the same, if it is but to say how you are. M[rs] W. desires to be remembered, also Remember me to your Ma. Sister & B. and assure yourself of the sincere Love of /your/ Husband

E P[ettigrew]

N.B. Kiss poor little Mary for me. Brother Carle came to the Lake on saturday last but did not call to see us [*torn*] You would have been delighted last evening to see little Jim carrying wood to the study. I have begun this morning to take a bottle of Dr Swaim

[*Addressed*] Mrs Ann B. Pettigrew
Newbern North
Carolina

Ebenezer Pettigrew to Ann Blount Pettigrew UNC

Lake Phelps Dec 5, 1826

My dearest Love

It is with double pleasure I contemplate the mail day, as /it/ will not /only/ permit me to converse with you but I hope to receive by the return <of> of the boy a similar conversation than which nothing can give me more pleasure while you are this far removed from my voice.

Since my former letter we have not been so well, I had on the last of the week something like a chill and fevers several evenings; I however feal better to day than since I left you I have taken a bottle of Swai[m]s Panacea which I hope has made a cure of my mouth, the Boneset failed. I can find no more of the Panacea and can account for but 3 bottles and there should be 3 more. I took one some time ago, gave one to S. Davinport and have now taken one. Mrs Warrington has been pretty much in my situation as to chills & fevers but is now better. Poor little Henry has had a bad caugh (but nothing like croup) he last evening had a pain in his ear, he seems quite well today and without caugh. But Poor little James took a fever yesterday after dinner and went to bed, his fever is not so high this morning, he complains a little of pain /in/ the ear, he is still in bed and rests very quiet I am afraid his indisposition arises from some cold he took by runing out on sunday for it was a very sharp air. Mrs Warrington is very attentive to them & I know you have every confidence in me on that subject, then I hope you will give yourself no unnecessary uneasiness concerning them, and if anything should occur serious you should be informed express. It is time for Doctor Warren to return according to his own appointment. I have not been off the Lake since I came home, neither have I heard one word from below Mothers. Except Mrs Miles Spruill, & Wo[*o*]dson no one has been here since my return. Mr Collins was with last week and went away fryday evening to mothers; I went to see him the second morning after his arrival. I found him very clever & conversant. He inveighs stoutly against the present fashionable life, he says nothing can stand a party every night and then sleeping untill ten in the morning. He also gave a bad account of some of our friends across the water. You recollect in a conversation coming from M[rs] Blounts[1] to Edenton on our first visit to that place you contrasted your situation with a certain Ladies in cumpany, but if all or the half is true you may <I> thank God that things are as they have been. My Husband is pure & uncontaminated from the fashionable views of /the/ present age, you can say; at certain hours of the day and night /you can tell/ where your Husband is and that he is at all times where you wish him to be. You know that at the proper time he is attending to our mutual interest; if our dear children are sick you are confident his greatest pleasure is to nurse them. But this is a character I should not give myself; it would come more properly from you. Untill yesterday which was a bad day I have been in the habit of geting up one hour before sunrise, I have made great way in ploughing for corn. Today is very windy and then falling a great deal of rain yesterday & last night, I have them jobing about the barn. M[r] Collins also informed me that M[rs] Sawyer[2] /was/ so low when he left that he expected she must by that time be dead, & that M[rs] Blair[3] had not recovered her mind. By account death must be a great relief to M[rs] Sawyer. Give my respects as formerly and believe me my dear Girl to be your ever affectionate Husband

E Pettigrew

N.B. I have nothing stimulating since the third day after my return, I think the outrageous drinking at present will have the opposit Effect. 2 ocl. P.M. James told me to inform you that he is better which corresponds with my opinion also. E P.

[*Addressed*] M[rs] Ann B. Pettigrew
New Bern
N. Carolina

---

[1]This might refer to Ann Hall Blount, widow of James Blount of Mulberry Hill, who was brother to Mary Blount Pettigrew, Ebenezer's mother, and to Frederick Blount, Nancy's grandfather. Ann Hall Blount was living with her unmarried son Clement Hall Blount at the time of their deaths in 1843. See Joshua Skinner to Ebenezer Pettigrew, April 24, 1843, in this volume. However, both Ebenezer and Nancy Pettigrew refer to her as "Aunt Blount" in earlier letters. See Lemmon, *Pettigrew Papers*, I, 328, 474, 494, 600.

[2]Mrs. Margaret Sawyer died on November 29, 1826. *North Carolina Star* (Raleigh), December 15, 1826.

[3]This was Margaret Sawyer Blair, daughter of Dr. Matthias E. Sawyer and his wife, Margaret. She married George Blair in 1825 and died in 1827 at the age of nineteen. *North Carolina Star* (Raleigh), January 6, 1826; *Raleigh Register*, December 18, 1827.

Ann Blount Pettigrew to Ebenezer Pettigrew UNC

Newbern December 18th 1826.

My dear Husband,

I am pleased at the arrival of Mail day so that I may have the pleasure of conversing with you through the quil, but I have nothing [w]orth co[*torn*] except that I am well, last saturday I had a sick head ache the whole day except that day I have enjoyed uninterrupted good health also little Mary is now very well and I hope will escape the hooping cough, if I were at home I should prefer greatly her having it, but the fear of being kept from my family all the winter is my objection—last saturday William and Frederick arrived here, William has been quite sick ever since, I think he is in bad health. Frederick bore the joke of the Mare and co/a/lt admirably—she did not loose it—he is delighted with Pasquotank—one of Old E[*noch*] Sawyers sons[1] was married and they had a great deal of frolicking—William gave a Ball, all which suited Frederick very well—A son of Mr Poppleston[2] is in town a genteel lookging man—he is studing Law with Iredell[3] of Edenton—The Boys have arrived from Chapel Hill—Richard got the first honor in his class—Charles is very much improved—he is handsome—intelligent—and I think you would be pleased with him—Mama has a house full of us—so many great Boys remind me of the Biddle family. Richard will be an enormous man, he is now only 16—and is as large of Frederick—Education is now so universal that a young Man is not received or respected in genteel company without it—and [*torn*] who [kn]ows his duty, I [see] not why children cannot be well educated—it certainly is the part of a Parent to restrain them—I heard the Boys say it would not cost them near as much but they have to procure their clothes there, and give double the sum it would cost at home—economy is an important thing in raising a family—few exercise it I believe—this is a noisy house at present—so much company—

We yesterday had a visit from Mr. Potter Miss Smyths Beaux he is very homely I think—he complimented you highly by saying he had often heard of your fame which he says has extended to Virginia as the most scientific farmer in our country—so you see you stand as high as the member of Congress with some—the famous potatoe has not yet been baked—it has been shown to many who say it is the largest they have seen—it is now beginning to rot; I have visited very little since I have been here—the weather has been very unsettled, but this morning I set out being apprehensive I should delay too long—and returned some of my first calls—I fear I shall take cold for yester[da]y wa[s] [*torn*] and a sudden change from <hea> warm to very cold weather—I am pleased to hear Doctor Warren and Lady are on the way—I hope they will remain contentedly but I fear the contrary—Mama got a letter from Mary, they had a perilous voyage up the Bay the Steam Boat was obliged to turn back once—and after that had a long and Boisterous passage. I suspect [*torn*] wished herself at home—I hope I shall get a lette[r] [*torn*] mail from you dear Husband for nothing gives me [so] much pleasure I assure you—the weeks appear longer than usual in consequence of my desire for the day to approach. Kiss the dear children for me—remember me to all—the family all inquire affectionately after you—when they are are guilty of little inattentions I am sure it arrises from the negligences of youth—and living in the fashionable world—and not from the want of respect or affection—

Believe as ev[er] your affectionate wife,

Ann B Pettigrew

[*Addressed*] Mr E Pettigrew,
Cool Spring
Washington County
North Carolina.

---

[1]Possibly the groom was William G. Sawyer of Camden County, who married Eleanor L. Shannonhouse in November, 1826. *North Carolina Star* (Raleigh), December 8, 1826. Enoch Sawyer lived in Camden County, which he represented in the state legislature. He was a delegate to the constitutional ratification conventions of 1788 and 1789 and served as collector of customs for the port at Camden. He died in 1827. Keith and others, *Blount Papers*, IV, 198n; *Raleigh Register*, March 27, 1827.

[2]This may refer to John Poppleston of Edenton. Lemmon, *Pettigrew Papers*, I, 303n.

[3]James Iredell, Jr. (1788-1835), of Edenton, served in the state House of Commons in eleven sessions between 1813 and 1827. He was governor of North Carolina in 1827 and 1828. Cheney, *North Carolina Government*, 161, 265, 269, 270, 271, 272, 273, 274, 275, 277, 283, 284, 286, 288, 289, 290. He and Ebenezer Pettigrew were school friends. Lemmon, *Pettigrew Papers*, I, xvii.

Ann Blount Pettigrew to Ebenezer Pettigrew UNC

Newbern, December 26th 1826.

My Dear Husband,

I received your letter on Friday and was much distressed to learn you had been sick, also poor little James & Henry—Henry has never had the ear ache before, I hope by the next Mail to have my anxiety relieved by a more favourable account—for I assure you I have passed a week of uneasiness—a letter once a week /which gives me information/ from my dear Husband and children is a great comfort to me in my absence from them—what a dreary world this would be to me without them—a void which nothing could fill—and knowing you must feel a similar anxiety, I have written once a week.

Mama has been quite sick—but is now up—& looks very badly—Penelope complains very much of her arm, it is now so stiff she can scarce raise it to her head—poor girl she bears her affliction astonishingly well—she seems not to enjoy any amusemet the town affords. Marys cold is nearly well. I hope she will escape the cough Mrs Forlaw[1] tells Mama she is the prettiest of her grandchildren, she is a sweet child. she can walk with the assistance of a hand and get up by any thing—Old Forlaw[2]—came here the other day expressly he said to see my daughter—poor old man is not long for this world I suspect—he is a pitiable looking object.

I am in very fine health—have an excellent appetite which is always the case when my health is good.

I have commissioned Mama to sell my land, I believe she wo[uld] make a better Bargain than any one I could get—you know Mr R. and herself are cronies, therefor she will have the advantage. Mr Forlaw says the lots that Guildersleeve bought for ten dolls, he now offers for 30$ per acre—making 20 on the bargain, which is much more than the value—but honest dealing is out of the question nowadays.

Mr. Mason was here on [teau]sday with his wife—he looks badly—he told me /he/ had a wish to visit you—when at Mackeys ferry[3] & if he could have spared time he should have done so—he was supprised when I told him we lived twenty miles from the ferry. I see no difference in her appearance.

The Smyths gave a great ball last night—we were all invited the messenger enquired whether you were in town or not—I suppose was directed. I suspect they are vexed for not one of us attended—I had no inclination to go.

I had a visit day before yesterday from Mrs Freeman—the Ministers wife—she is a very amiable woman—they have a house full of fashionable ladies from up the country—they must live at a great cost—Mrs Mc K—— visits us, & gives a detail of the movements of the gay—

Frederick Blount goes to all the parties and thinks himself a man I suspect he will get along at the Law—his brother will do his best for him you know he is great for *kin*—he is going to E[*denton*]—in two weeks—

I noticed the latter part of your letter—and be assured I duly appreciate all your estimable qualities—I hope I evince it by my disposition to please—and my undeviating affection for you—as for E[*denton*]—I think it the sink of vice—to believe the perpetrators of such enormities are taken by the hand by respectable people is truly amazing—nothing disgraces—conscience is asleep there Mr M says that Avery[4] is quite a chatty man he has too much milk &

water—composition to reform the profligate—they ought to have the eloquence of Demosthenes & the Sword of the Turks to reform them—poor Mrs Sawyer is dead and I was not sorry to hear it—hers must have been the death bed of sorrow and disgust. I wish our children could be raised out of the state of N—C. every day I live the more throughly am I convinced that the eastern part of N—C— is the meanest part of the world—I sincerely wish my lot had been cast in a more agreeable part of the world—alas! what is wealth when—<when> health—honor happiness—& eternal happiness is at stake—I mean all the lower part of the state—Mama got a letter from Mary by the return of the Carriage, she is much delighted—at P[*hiladelphia*]—they visited the Navy yard—went on board the Gu[*e*]rrier[*e*]—in every apartment of that Ship—she is charmed with all she sees, well she may when She has been in a corner all her life—, if convenint will you bring Mama a Pitcher of fresh butter—it is a scarce article here; they rely on the firken butter—prin[*torn*] I shall expect you the week after Christmas I look for[ward] to the time with pleasure—if my Husband and chi[ldren] were in a desert—it would be more desirable than any other place to me—Mama promises to spend some time in Spring with me—tell Charles James bought ten hogs for his Mother to day—he does all the marketing and shopping—you would be supprised with what facility he calculates. tell Charles to take a little more pains with writing. Kiss our dear children for me—remember me—to all—tell your Mother I have bought her a pretty gown. Mama joins me i[n] loves—Believe me your affectionate wife

A B Pettigrew

[*Addressed*] Mr E Pettigrew
Cool Spring
Washington County
N—C—

---

[1]One Mrs. Forlow, a neighbor of the Shepards, died in 1807. Lemmon, *Pettigrew Papers*, I, 405. Perhaps this refers to one of her relatives.

[2]William Shepard mentions his neighbor Mr. Farlow in an 1817 letter to Ebenezer. Lemmon, *Pettigrew Papers*, I, 587. It is possible that this is the same person. He may also be the Mr. Furlow mentioned in Ebenezer Pettigrew to Ann Blount Pettigrew, September 17, 1822, in this volume.

[3]Mackeys Ferry operated on Albemarle Sound and was located in north Washington County. William S. Powell, *The North Carolina Gazetteer* (Chapel Hill: University of North Carolina Press, 1968), 307, hereinafter cited as Powell, *North Carolina Gazetteer*.

[4]Probably this was the Reverend John Avery, who was rector of St. Paul's Church in Edenton in 1827. *Raleigh Register*, December 4, 1827; *Journal of the Diocesan Convention, 1827*, 3.

Ann Blount Pettigrew to Mary Williams Bryan A&H, BRYAN

Lake Phelps February 12th 1827.

My Dear Mary,

After spending nearly three months in NewBern I have returned home, my visit was lengthened in consequence of Mr Pettigrews indisposition, he went for me in that very cold spell shorly after Christmas which gave him a violent cold a confined him some time and from which he has not yet recovered. I left Ma and Penelope is their usual health. your Daughter was very fat and interesting and has improved in beauty which information will be highly agreeable to you no doubt—NewBern is gay to folly but I did not participate—a certain old Lady plunges very deep in the vortex of fashion—I found her a very entertaining visitor, I like her manners vasly— I was honored with an invitation to take a social dish of tea with her which you know is not common with her—

I suppose you have passed the session very pleasantly in Washington— I should have been much pleased to have had some of your interesting letters, you had such a fine theme I do not know how you could avoid writing, I must reproach you a little for such indifference. I should have written you from NewBern but it was not convenient.

Doctor Warren has returned with his Richmond wife[1] she is a beautiful woman—a fine complection—animated black eyes—and very intelligent—you would be charmed with her— I expect her to see me to morrow to spend some time—they have not yet commenced housekeeping—

Mr Pettigrew joins me in respects to Mr Bryan and yourself—
Believe me your affectionate Sister

Ann B Pettigrew

PS. I did not know the sheet was torn untill I began to write—therefore excuse it.

[*Addressed*] Hon John H Bryan,
H R
Washington City.

---

[1]Dr. William C. Warren married Harriet Innis Alexander of Richmond, Virginia, in November, 1826. *North Carolina Star* (Raleigh), December 8, 1826.

Ebenezer Pettigrew to John Herritage Bryan A&H, BRYAN

Lake Phelps June 18, 1827

My dear Sir,

I received your two favours since I had the pleasure of seeing you this time last year, and have from time to time determined to answer them, but being out of the habit of expessing my opinions on paper, also a total want of any thing that could interest you to write, makes it a labour which I dread to commence.

Please to accept my thanks for the different speaches which you have sent me, also the pen knife. I am glad to learn from your last letter also from Mr Hines[1] that your health is improving. It would have given us a great deal of pleasure to have had yours & Mrs Bryans company with us on your return from Washington City, but I apprehend our solitude would have been too great for you to have borne with composure more than two days. Those parties which you complain of as aggravating your disease, equally unfit the mind for such a place as I live in.

I observe you are a candidate for a reelection to Congress and I suppose cannot fail of being elected, having no opposition. Mr Hines is also a candidate, he has been (since his return from Congress) with us twice. I think his election is certain, Dr Hall[2] is certainly one of the poorest electioneerers in the state, and Hines is one of the best. Mr W. Shepard has also been through his district, but I suspect he is too near sighted, I understand his election is very doubtfull. Sawyer[3] does his business in a very smooth way, does a great deal without seeming to be doing anything, which is certainly the best way to get a permanent hold on the good will of we the sovereign people or in other words we the swinish multitude.

My affairs jog on as usual, the season has been very cold and a part of it dry. It is now seasonable We have had it extremely windy. My corn looks well

Mrs Pettigrew and the children have been in tolerable health, she sends her love to Mrs Bryan, please to give mine also and assure yourself of the Esteem of

Very truely your friend
E Pettigrew

Hon. J. H. Bryan

N.B. I inclose you a part of Mr R. M. White's letter of N. York to me of Ap 28, 1827. Mr White has accounts with me for the debt due from Mr Ogden and takes it to him self.

E P.

Since writing the above I have receivd a leter from Messs V Bokkelen & White dated June 6,—Informing that Mr D. B Ogden had not yet paid his wine Bill.

[*Addressed*] Hon. John H. Bryan
Newbern N.C

---

[1]Richard Hines, an attorney, was born in Tarboro. He served in the state House of Commons in 1824 and was a member of Congress, 1825-1827. An active Episcopalian, he was a member of Calvary Church in Tarboro and a delegate to the Diocesan Convention of 1833 in Warrenton. Between the date of this letter and 1841 he moved to Raleigh, where he joined Christ Church and served as a convention delegate in 1841 and as vestryman. Hines was named to the state central committee of the Whig party at its 1843 convention. He died in 1851. *Biographical Directory of Congress*, 1058; *Journal of the Diocesan Convention, 1833*, 4; *Journal of the Diocesan Convention, 1841*, 3; Parish Register of Christ Church, Raleigh, Burials, 269; *North State Whig* (Washington, N.C.), May 4, 1843.

[2]Dr. Thomas H. Hall (1773-1853) of Tarboro, a physician, defeated Hines for Congress in 1827 and served until himself defeated by Ebenezer Pettigrew in 1835. He had once before represented his district in Congress, 1817-1825. Hall was a Jacksonian Democrat. *Biographical Directory of Congress*, 992.

[3]Lemuel Sawyer (1777-1852), a lawyer in Elizabeth City, served in Congress 1807-1813, 1817-1823, and 1825-1829, after which he was defeated by William Biddle Shepard on the latter's second attempt at election. Sawyer moved to Washington, D.C., where he held a federal position until his death. *Biographical Directory of Congress*, 1565.

William J. Welles[1] *to Ebenezer Pettigrew* UNC

[*June 27, 1827*]

E, Pettigrew Esquire

Dear sir

Having gotten through with the quarter for which I was engaged in the neighborhood of Mess'rs Hodges[2] and Bateman,[3] it is now in my power with pleasure (to myself) to comply with your obliging engagement of me, as making one of your family—and it is hoped, that by a steady and punctual attendance on my part, to the tuition and morals & manners of your children, I shall merit the approbation of madam Pettigrew & yourself.— The time has passed, very agreeably, indeed, during my residence here, having the approbation, I believe, of those persons (whose children I taught;) friendly to my promotion to the hospitality of "the family at the Lake"—

The quarter here ended with the last week preceding this, but as Mr. Hodges has gone on to the city of Raleigh, and requested me to remain with his family during his absence, you will please not expect me at the Lake, until his return, which will be on sunday next, /or/ on monday at farthest—.

I have the honour to be, Sir
very respectfully
Your Hble. Servt
William J Welles

Newport Scupng
27th June 1827

[1]Other than the internal evidence that Welles planned to tutor the Pettigrew children, no information about him has been found.

[2]This might refer to Wilson B. Hodges, who later represented Hyde County in the state Senate and in the Constitutional Convention of 1835. Keith and others, *Blount Papers*, IV, 347; Cheney, *North Carolina Government*, 311, 817.

[3]Possibly this was Daniel Bateman of Tyrrell County, who in 1820 had three sons and three daughters and would have had good use for a tutor. *1820 Federal Census*, LII, 4. He may be the Daniel Bateman who represented Tyrrell in the state legislature in seven sessions between 1815 and 1822. Also, a Daniel N. Bateman served in the General Assembly from the same county nine times between 1825 and 1835. Cheney, *North Carolina Government*, 268, 272, 273, 275, 277, 279, 281, 286, 288, 290, 292, 294, 295, 296, 298, 302. According to Coon, *North Carolina Schools and Academies*, no academies existed in Tyrrell County prior to 1840.

Samuel I. Johnston[1] *to Ebenezer Pettigrew* UNC

Edenton July 15 1827

Mr Pettigrew

My Dear Sir

I am truly obliged to you for the favour confered by writing to me; and ought to have acknowledged the same some time since, but really I have felt so little like writing that I have postponed it from time, I have suffered more than I usually have done lately with my head I do not know what cause to ascribe it to if it be not the unaccustomed on Sundays. I have had service three times during the day—until the last two Sundays—when I had communion & baptisms—and have been so compleatly exhausted that I really had not the ability to perform the third service—but I shall soon be relieved from this pressure of duty as Mr A[*very*]. will return early next month—& I have a notion of spending most of my time after then at Nags Head—I am truly gratified to hear that Cousin James' health has improved so much. I thank God for it and may it please him to restore him entirely. Edenton is about as quiet as <usual> it us/u/ally is. Indeed much more so than it has been for years at an election. There seems to be no excitement on the subject of the election in this place it has been remarkably quiet—It has been healthy up to this time, but I hear that Miss Ann Page is quite sick with fever also Mrs Page son is not so well. James & myself have escaped thus far. the rest of my family is at Nags Head where they enjoy health.

Mr Collins is over but I have had no opportunity of conversing with him. He & The Dr (T. D. W) [*Thomas Davis Warren*] seem to be very friendly, but with you I think it no sign of a wedding the Dr has just returned from his Chattanooga trip, but I have not been able to ascertain what else the convention did but adjourn to meet again in November he was highly delighted with his trip and says there is no doubt but what the Southern University will be established.[2] Edenton will soon be deserted a large number went away on last Saturday & Tuesday. And they will continue to go—I hear that we are to have an opposition boat from Washington, town in this state a very superior steamer Pamplico she will during the Nags Head season, [*go*] there from this place & the towns <on the> in this vicinity & will be a day boat during the winter, to Blackwater, I hope that you may continue well & enjoy yourself at the Springs—My own George who leaves tonight for Chapel Hill—desires his regards to you & his love to Cousin James, please give my love to Cousin James—very truly & sincerly

Your friend
S. I. Johnston

Dr Lewis was in Edenton last Friday, and is quite well—he brought his son Henry over to send him up to Mr Binghams[3]—our friend the Rev Mr Haughton[4] has received a call & accepted it, from Christ Ch. New Berne he spent a few hours with me last Friday—[yrs] S I. Johnston

crops are excellent—

---

[1]Samuel I. Johnston was an Episcopal deacon at this time. In 1835 he was at Calvary Church, Wadesboro; he was ordained priest and became rector there in 1836. Sometime before 1841, he returned to St. Paul's, Edenton, as its rector. *Journal of the Proceedings of the Nineteenth Annual Convention of the Protestant Episcopal Church, in the State of North Carolina . . . 1835* (Fayetteville: Edward J. Hale, 1835), 3, hereinafter cited as *Journal of the Diocesan Convention, 1835*; *Journal of the Proceedings of the Twentieth Annual Convention of the Protestant Episcopal Church in the State of North Carolina . . . 1836* (Fayetteville: Edward J. Hale, 1836), 3, hereinafter cited as *Journal of the Diocesan Convention, 1836*; *Journal of the Diocesan Convention, 1841*, 3.

[2]In spite of the optimism expressed here, the University of the South at Sewanee, Tennessee, was not founded until 1857. *Yearbook of Higher Education, 1980-81* (Chicago: Marquis Academic Media, 1981), 515.

[3]William James Bingham (1802-1866) of Hillsborough graduated from the University of North Carolina in 1825 with first honors and studied law with Archibald D. Murphey. The death of his father, a schoolmaster, caused him to return to Hillsborough in 1826 to take over the Bingham academy. Under his leadership the school acquired a national reputation. He married Eliza, daughter of Judge William Norwood of Hillsborough. In politics he was a Clay Whig. Powell, *DNCB*, I, 161; Battle, *History of the University*, I, 791. See also Coon, *North Carolina Schools and Academies*.

[4]No Episcopal clergyman in North Carolina at this time by the name of Haughton has been identified. However, Thomas Goelet Haughton of Edenton, an 1834 graduate of the University of North Carolina, was at one time an Episcopal clergyman. Battle, *History of the University*, I, 795. The Reverend Richard Sharpe Mason was rector at Christ Church until, apparently, early in 1828. Ann Blount Pettigrew to Mary Williams Bryan, February 19, 1828, in this volume.

[James Louis Petigru to Jane Gibert Petigru North][1] UNC

Sullivans Island, 31st Aug. 1827.

My dear Jane,

The last mail brought your letter from Pendleton informing us that you were no longer Jane Petigru—Well—I hope you will have the grace to be a good wife and that your husband may give a good account of you. I have no idea that a woman should marry at all, unless she is willing to devote herself heart and soul to promote the good of her husband— Men have many ways to show themselves clever fellows—in the service of the state in peace & war; politics and religion, all are before them to choose, & if one shines in these, a moderate neglect of home & family is by the consent of mankind conceded to him. But a woman if she has a sense of virtue and honor is to show it like Solomon's /good/ wife in rising betimes & setting her maidens to work. [*incomplete*]

---

[1]James Louis Petigru (1789-1863) was a South Carolina attorney and cousin to Ebenezer Pettigrew, his father, William Pettigrew (1758-1837), having been brother to the Reverend Charles Pettigrew. Lemmon, *Pettigrew Papers*, I, xiv. James Louis's mother, Louise Gibert, was a Huguenot from Charleston. The change in spelling of the surname occurred about the time that James Louis graduated from South Carolina College in 1809. He became an outstanding Unionist and an eloquent opponent of secession. *DAB*, XIV, 514-515.

Petigru's brother Thomas was a captain in the United States Navy. George C. Rogers, Jr., *The History of Georgetown County, South Carolina* (Columbia: University of South Carolina Press, 1970), 254-255, hereinafter cited as Rogers, *Georgetown County*. He entered the navy as a midshipman on January 1, 1812, and was forced to retire in 1855. The 1812 register of naval officers gives the surname as Pettigrew; in 1822 the spelling changed to Pettigru. "Names, Rank, Pay, and Rations, of the Officers of the Navy and Marine Corps. Communicated to the House of Representatives, February 4, 1812," *American State Papers: Naval Affairs* (Washington: Gales and Seaton, 4 volumes, 1834-1861), I,

Document 90, p. 262, hereinafter cited as *American State Papers: Naval Affairs*; "List of Naval Officers. Communicated to the Senate, February 21, 1814," *American State Papers: Naval Affairs*, I, Document 110, p. 303; "Naval Register for the Year 1822. Communicated to the Senate, January 7, 1822," *American State Papers: Naval Affairs*, I, Document 203, p. 754; James Petigru Carson, *Life, Letters, and Speeches of James Louis Petigru* (Washington: W. H. Lowdermilk and Company, 1920), 314, 316, 322, hereinafter cited as Carson, *James Louis Petigru.*

Another brother, Charles, was an officer in the army; see the letter to his sister from Appalachicola, Florida, April 29, 1835, in this volume. He was a second lieutenant in the Fourth Artillery, serving from July 1, 1829, until his death on October 6, 1835. Thomas H. S. Hamersley (comp.), *Complete Regular Army Register of the United States for One Hundred Years, 1779 to 1879* (Washington: Privately printed, 1880), 689.

Two sisters have been identified. Adele Petigru (1810-1896) married Robert Francis Withers Allston, a South Carolina rice planter. Rogers, *Georgetown County*, 276. The other sister, Jane Gibert Petigru, to whom this letter was written, married John Gough North and was left a young widow with three daughters: Jane Caroline, Mary Charlotte, and Louisa Gibert. See Draft Conveyance, April, 1836, Pettigrew Family Papers, Southern Historical Collection, in which Gibert is misspelled Gilbert.

Other siblings were John (1791-?), Mary C. (1803-1872), Louise (1805-1869), and Harriette (1813-1877). Martha W. Daniels to Sarah McCulloh Lemmon, February 16, 1983. William and Robert are listed erroneously as sons of William Pettigrew in the genealogical chart in Lemmon, *Pettigrew Papers*, I, xiv; actually they were sons of Ebenezer Pettigrew of Ninety-Six, South Carolina.

Ann Blount Pettigrew to Mary Williams Bryan A&H, BRYAN

Lake Phelps Sept 24th 1827—

Dear Mary,

Yours of the 22nd of Aug--I received with much pleasure, I was in bed with a slight bilious fever when it arrived and you may be sure it was doubly gratifying to hear from a relation at such a time, I am now quite well except a bad cold—which is very prevalent here.

I understand Dr Norcom says Frederick was the most imprudent person as respects health he had ever seen. he was very ill—I am supprised at his Northern trip, but ventures makes Merchants—Lem. Sawyer was elected by a great majority, it is useless for a man to oppose him, which certainly reflects on the District.

I suppose you have not prevailed on your husband to cease from serving the public, it must be a fascinating business—I believe some of our county representatives would almost as soon forfeit their lives as their exelections—and probably their families are suffering at home.

Col. Hodges whose house we dined at is broken up, he will be entirely sold out and his family destitute, he had a comfortable living and appeared to be care taking.

We have had a Storm which injured the corn, but nothing else, I can sympathise with regard to the musquitoes with you, since the storm they are worse than I ever saw them, the woods is alive with them, we have no pleasure in our pleasant walks, they seem to be confined to the woods.

The country is very sickly and Dr Warren is constantly employed, his wife continues to enjoy good /health/, I think she is in [*no*] danger, being a very healthy looking woman—I have not seen her for some time—her husbands engagements precludes visiting. The weather is remarkably cool.

I am sorry John and Maria Shepard have had the distress to loose their youngest child, John's letters give us reason to believe he promises himself a vast deal from his move to Florida. I hear he has purchased a most valuable sugar farm in that country, some person told Mr. Caraway, who had seen it: I am very sorry he goes so far—but it is a duty incumbent on us all to provide for a living.

I am glad to hear your son has recovered—I give you credit for the throwing off the fine lady, but I doubt whether you deserve it or not for a housefull of children it an insuperable bar. and of course /it is/ not a voluntary act.

I am much obliged to you for the invitation to visit you, but you know my impediments, therefore I need not apologise, my will is good I assure you— I have a very large troublesome family— Mrs Warrenton has not returned from her summer visit, which commenced in <Ju> May, she is a Quaker is one respect, which is, moving when the Spirit moves—her niece<s> is going to be married to our cousin John Beasly[1] who lost his wife last fall, he has been courting Miss Walker—

I hope you will <will> write soon—give my love to Mama & Penelope—Mr Pettigrew desires <to> his respects to Mr Bryan & yourself—also present mine—and Believe me your affectionate Sister—

Ann B Pettigrew

[*Addressed*] Mrs Mary Bryan,
NewBern,
NC.

---

[1]John Baptist Beasley was the grandson of John Baptist Beasley of Edenton, who died in 1790, and his wife Elizabeth Blount Beasley, sister to Ebenezer Pettigrew's mother. The first Beasley had five children: Joseph; Frederick, identified earlier in this volume; John, who practiced medicine in Edenton; Martha, who married David Ryan after 1790; and Rebecca, who married a Swann prior to 1790. Will of John Baptist Beasley, Chowan County Wills, Book B, 87, North Carolina Archives.

The eldest son, Joseph Beasley of Bertie County, died in 1801, leaving one minor child, the John Baptist Beasley mentioned in this letter. Joseph left all his property to his son and directed that his brother Frederick use it at his discretion to educate the boy. Joseph's will (Chowan County Wills, Book B, 174-175, North Carolina Archives) was witnessed by David and Mary Ryan, possibly the same Mary referred to in Frederick Beasley to Dr. John Beasley, April 11, 1805, in Lemmon, *Pettigrew Papers*, I, 364.

Dr. John Beasley married Ann (Nancy) Slade; she died in 1810. *Raleigh Register*, January 25, 1810. His 1814 will (Chowan County Wills, Book C, 26, North Carolina Archives) mentions four children; see Ann Blount Pettigrew to Mary Williams Bryan, November 15, 1824, footnote 5, in this volume. He made a bequest to his two nephews, John Ryan and the John Baptist Beasley of this volume. Ebenezer Pettigrew was one of the executors of the will.

The younger John Baptist Beasley served in the state Senate from Tyrrell County, 1821-1831, and from Washington County, 1835. Cheney, *North Carolina Government*, 278, 280, 281, 283, 285, 287, 289, 291, 293, 294, 304. He appears in Tyrrell County in the *1820 Federal Census*, LII, 2, as a head of household of five males and three females, and in the *1830 Census Index*, 12, also in Tyrrell.

William Shepard Pettigrew to Mary Lockhart Pettigrew UNC

Lake Phelps 6th October 1827

Dear Grandma'

This being my turn to write, I now have the pleasure and honor of addressing my respects to one who is so nearly related to my Pa's family. my brother Charles and myself have come under an agreement to write alternately every saturday, and I mean to try very hard to exceed my brother Charles in the writing, if not to excel him in my composition, at any rate, I know that my dear Grand-Ma' will rejeice to see our improvements in writing, from time to time. we are glad, both to have so good an opportunity, and such discernment as yours, to stimulate our pens, in this pleasing task. We are all in pretty good health at present, my Pa' and Ma' are both very well, and brother James, and little sister [*Mary*], are now convalescent Those apples which you were so good to send my Ma were very fine. I remain with great respect

Your dutiful grandson
William Shepard Pettigrew

[*Addressed*] Mrs. Mary Pettigrew
Scuppernong
Washington County
N.C.

Lawrence J. Haughton to William Shepard Pettigrew UNC

Scuppernong Dec. 20. 1827

Mr Wm S Pettigrew

Dear Sir

I have had the pleasure of receiving a communication from you and have to thank you for opening a correspondence, the affect of which will not only be an improvement to our young minds, but will also engender the most friendly dispositions betwen us, you /wished/ to be informed by the return post whether your letter shall have been received. Your favor has just now come to hand. We got along very well with my Cousins wild horse.

You could not have regreted more than myself the shortness of my visit at the Lake, and feel assured I shall never loose an opportunity of enjoying the agreeable society of your self and your brother Charles. I should be very hapy to see you in Scuppernong during the gay /season/ of christmas and if you can prevail on your papa to let you leave th delightful /solitude/ of the Lake for a few days do come out, my papa's family is well and with my respect to Charles, believe me your friend

And Ob^t^ Servt
Lawrence J Haughton

[*Addressed*] M^r^ W^m^ S Pettigrew
Lake Phelps

Snoad B. Carraway to Ebenezer Pettigrew UNC

Wheat Swamp, Lenoir County Jany. 21st 1828

My dear Friend

The /day/ I left you, and your interesting family, made an impression on my heart that never can be effaced. The conflicting emotions that agitated and affected my feelings, evinced a week-ness, which would be thought by some, unbecoming the dignity of a man, and perhaps Sir, correctly too, but my kind friend, in me they were the ebulitions of an aching heart emenating from the best feelings of my nature, A retrospective of the last 17 years of my life are well calculated to produce all I have *felt*, and yet *feel*, to describe which, I am entirely incompetent

It is with no ordinary degree of pleasure, I inform /you/ that I was *married* on the *tenth*,[1] am now enjoying the company of an Affectionate *Woman*, and have resumed the business of an agricultural life, to *both* of which I shall devote myself with unremitted attention, The result of such a course is obvious, and to you Sir it is /too/ well known, to require a single remark, in truth all I could say on the subject would be superfluous. happiness, is the great desideratum, and no Man in my Opinion enjoys more than yourself.

I have no news of much interest to communicate The people of this /county/ are embarrased, and many very much distressed A weathy man was sold out the other day, at a great sacrifice. 24,00 acres of good land. with a large and well improved farm and fine buildings of every kind. Sold. $3700. Negroes sold very low. young fellows from 15. to 25 years old went at $225. and the highest price given was $275 Girls. 12 years old. at $140. woman & four likely children at $400. likely young fellow. and an excellent carpenter at $400 Six months credit, Corn has been sold in this neighbourhood at 90 cents pr Bbl. on a credit. Pork at Newbern $350. great quantities of that article has been lost during the warm weather, owing to the great losses in every part of the country I think Bacon will be high next summer.

Low land of excellent quality in this county and Jones. can be purchased at $1 pr acre; their is several tracts contain[in]g several thousand acres each, of as fine land as any in Scuppernong: it abounds with every variety of timber common to our best land; and thickly set with reeds. Very few persons are engaged in reclaiming it, a general dislike to the use of the spade seems to pervade every part of our country.

Mrs Carraway joins me in respects to Mrs Pettigrew and yourself We expect to visit Tyrrel in the latter part of February and intend giving ourselves the pleasure of spending a few days with you, please remember me affectionately to the children to Mr Wells [*the tutor*] & Mr Woodly. And accept the best wishes

of your friend and
respectful Srvt
S. B Carraway

E. Pettigrew Esqr

I have sent by the Waggon your Trunk to the care of Mr Hathaway by whom it will be forwarded—for the use of which please accept my grateful thanks—

[*Addressed*] Ebenezer Pettigrew Esqr
Lake Phelps.

---

[1]He married Harriet Wiggins in Lenoir County. *Raleigh Register*, January 25, 1828.

Ann Blount Pettigrew to Mary Williams Bryan A&H, BRYAN

Lake Phelps, February 19th [*1828*]

My Dear Sister,

Having understood from William that you had another child I take this opportunity of congratulating you on the birth of a fine son. I have no doubt but the stock will be increased eve/r/y eighteen months, very fortunate for us, the breed is so good, so smart, &c—. I suppose you have seen your husbands speech on the slave subject, he was polite enough to send us a copy, and we admire it and think it much to the purpose.

Mrs Warren has a fine son, she had a narrow chance for her life in parturition, she was delivered by her husband, Mrs Norton was present and told me, she had the worst labour she ever saw.

The Madam & the Misses Collinses are on the Lake, appear to be much pleased with it, interest, what a powerful stimulus, Their is a Dr Page[1] also visiting them here, from Virginia, probably on a courting expedition, do not speak of it before Mrs McK— The Lake looks as usual at this season of the year, the wheat we are sorry to think remarkably foward, and the spring frosts will probably serve it, as when you were here, this continues to be the warmest winter I scarcely have known. William our brother appears to be in bad health, I beleive he has been so for some time very fortunate for him he is not encumbered with a family he can <can> now go about for his health, without any cares comparatively—he thinks your daughter far outstrips mine in point of beauty, Mary had a very severe spell in the fall and has not recovered her complexion, she looks very delicate but is quite sprightly.

I have lately been to a wedding down the county, J Beasly was married to Mrs Warrenton's niece Mary Alexander, they had a very nice wedding. I was quite supprised at your having a ball in absence of Mr B. William says Mama is quite gay and in fine health, I was highly pleased to hear it.

I was supprised to hear Mr Mason had left New Bern, your town is unfortunate, in not being able to keep an episcopal Minister, whether is it the fault of Parson or the people? I suppose the Church is closed, a Minister calculated to please the people must be immaculate, he must be divested of his human nature, he must not have the sensibilities of other men, What a world we do inhabit—

Give my love to Mama & family, Mr Pettigrew joins me in love to yourself—

Your aff sister—
Ann B Pettigrew.

P.S. I should be very happy to receive a visit from you this spring. William told me that Mama expected me to /go/ to Pasquotank with her but my situation will not permit it. do conclude to come.

[*Addressed*] Mrs Mary W Bryan,
New Bern,
NC.

[1]This probably refers to Dr. Mathew Page.

Ebenezer Pettigrew to James Cathcart Johnston UNC

Lake Phelps March 25, 1828

My dear Sir,

From the wish you expressed when I was with you to hear from my sick family, I take the pleasure of writing you.

When I got to town the morning I left you, I found a traviler in the ferry boat waiting; I accordingly eat a slight breakfast and at eight set out. When I landed at McKeys, I found a note from Mrs Pettigrew, which I sent you by Davie. My horse was ready and in seven hours from leaving Edenton Wharf I was at home. I found my family in about the state Mrs P. had informed me the day before. They have however all pretty well recovered, ecept poor little James who is in about the same state as when you were last informed. His nerves are all affected, but his right side so much, that it is with difficulty he can walk, his tongue is so much paralised that he can scarcely be understood. It is a sore affliction to us; the Doctor gives us great hopes of his recovery by saying that he has no doubt of it.

I have since my return some pretty sharp twinges of the gout one of the places I suspect is in the back, and if it is in that place, by the Doctors account, my measure of suffering has but begun. / begun.

The frost which we have had since I saw you I fear has killed half my wheat; I am weeding in the furrow for corn my first sown. You may ask, why weed it? There would be too much straw for a second ploughing, it is half thigh high. It is not necessary to remark to you that with such misfortunes and the low prices of produce it is difficult for farmers to make both ends meet, and that without prudence & economy, be them never so industrious, they cannot get along.

The Lake is but barely high enough to saw, I hope to have the greater part of your plank the next week. I saw day & night. The Captain who I expected to send your plank by, says his engagements in Baltimore will not permit him to take it. I expect to be able to get a vessil in the river as soon as it is ready. I have declined altering my saw for the present according to the one I saw at Coffields, untill an experiment is made of a very light gate. The improvement I saw proves one thing, that it is not necessary to have the saw tight to cut a streight line, and I intend having a gate so small as to give almost no weight, an evil I have spent some time in thinking how to obviate.

I hope Miss Fannys health is quite restored before this. Mrs Pettigrew sends her best respects to her & Miss Helen,[1] Please to give mine also to them and assure yourself of the Esteem & Regard of your sincere friend

E Pettigrew

James C. Johnston Esqr

[*Addressed*] James C Johnston Esqr
Hayes
Edenton Post Office

---

[1]The two sisters of James C. Johnston were Frances P. (Fanny) Johnston, born February 25, 1785, and died July 6, 1837; and Helen S. Johnston, born November 29, 1787, and died October 19, 1842. Mrs. John S. Welborn (comp.), *North Carolina Tombstone Records* (High Point, N.C.: Daughters of the American Revolution, 3 volumes, 1935-1939), III, 48-49 (although the entry for the Johnston Family Cemetery in Chowan County erroneously gives 1812 as the year of Helen S. Johnston's death); Ebenezer Pettigrew to James Cathcart Johnston, October 21, 1842, in this volume.

*[Ebenezer Pettigrew] to Moses E. Cator** A&H

Lake Phelps March 30, 1828

My dear Sir,

Your favors of Sep 12, & 27 came safe to hand for which please to accept my sincere thanks, also your kind offer to attend to any of my business though inconvenient. How I have permited <to let> them to lay by me so long unanswered is to me strange, but I have been promising from time to time untill now. As respects the division of the land, I am satisfied, I have perfect confidence in the honesty of your principles. And I now autorise you as fully as a letter can, to deed that part amounting to 106¼, to Mr Johnston for locating the tract, and the other part to amounting to 106¼, to whoever you may think proper to sell to, as it is your interest in the tract according to the agreement between us according to a power of atorney given to you by me over some lands owned by me on Roaring river, from which the land now in question was obtained.

If the above will be a sufficient power for you to secure the lands above mentioned, please to inform me and whatever may be farter necessary and I am ready at any time to do it. What is best or right to do with Mr Frost I am unable to say. I am very much averse to law at any rate but at such a distance is still worse, and whether there is sufficint ground for recovery depends on circumstances. I will leave that subject to your discretion & judgment. I fear Mr Frost will do as great an evil to the land as flooding or rendering it sickley, which is taking of all the valuable timber for the mill. I can have no knowledge of the gentleman and if I should do him injustice I beg his pardon, he may be one of the most honest men. I should be glad if his mill could be stoped but be cautious of law unless your ground is undoubted. Perhaps you could sell to Mr Frost or some other <pers> person at a tolerable price, if so pray do it without delay. I shall be glad to hear that your <trips> last trip to Roaring river is over. Pray what did you sell your part of the land for. I do not think you may have the least hope of geting the ten dollars of Mrs Hooker. I will the next time I see her make one other effort and if I succeed I will inform you. I must be in arrears to you I should like to know how much and how I can pay it. I have some expectation that one of Mrs Pettigrews Brothers will be your state this spring to attend to the lands of family on Obian, if so I will get him to call and settle with you. I should be glad if you will continue your attention to the little [pieces] you have been a while longer. I know not the country it is in or the river it is on or the name of the county town. Our crop of corn last year was abundant, though we had a storm in the fall, it is now dull at 150¢ pr barrel. The cotton crop was very bad, in truth with most persons it was almost a clear mess. The price is about 8 or 9 cents. We have an extreme warm winter, but few frosts in it. There has been two or three this spring which has done some injury to the first sown wheat. The winter has been so warm that a great number of families have lost their pork. There is nothing in this county worth relating. Col. Hodges has failed and moved to Washington, he has left much to part of his debts and others to go without their money. Among those who are to pay his debts as security is Burton Hathaway, he has had the whole of his property sold except his land, and it is expected that will go also. Mrs Ester Alexander the former widow of Asa Phelps & Jeremiah Tarkinton her brother died about a fortnight ago. John Beasley was married this winter to Miss Mary Alexander a daughter of Henry Alexander the sheriff.

Ebenezer Pettigrew to John Herritage Bryan UNC

Lake Phelps March 31, 1828

My dear Sir,

Your favour of Jan. 30 came safe to hand, as well as your inclosed speech on the rights of property, for which please to accept my thanks. I think you did ample justice to the subject. The ideas expressed by the opposition on that question were to me very strange, and proves satisfactorily what will be attempted when there is sufficient power. I hope I shall be out of the way when that day arrives.

I have received from Mr Ogden through my friends, V Bokkelen & White the amount for the wine.

The absence from your family must be a great privation, but to one unaccustomed to it insupportable; and I should suppose the neglect of your professional business by your absence would in the end destroy it. We at this time are in great need in Congress of men of firm, independent principles, and I fear our state can boast of as few on that floor as any other in the Union.

Frederick Shepard & [*Frederick?*] Blount, were with us last week, they say that all were well at Newbern. Shepard had understood that there was a small insurrection on his Plantation, which he was anxious to go home and quell. My family have enjoyed very good health since the fall untill this month, since which time most of them have been complaining. Poor little James my third son has an affection of the nerves, a disease called St. Vitus' dance, which has distressed us very much. He walks with great difficulty and his tongue is so much affected that he can scarcely be understood, we have to take him from school. The Doctor says the disease can be cured but that it is a work of time.

We have had an extraordnary winter, from its mildness my wheat is too forward, some of the first sown is much injured by the spring frosts, of which we have had several very hard ones. Corn appears to be a very heavy article and the holders scarcely know what to do with it. It is thought by most persons that the Tariff, the canals & railroads into the western country will destroy the Bread stuff farmers on the Atlantic. I think their extravagant manner of living and the idleness of the labouring class, will do that without the aid of the industry and enterprise of the west. Mrs Pettigrew sends her Respects to you and Please to assure yourself of the Esteem of your

Obdt Svt.
E Pettigrew

Hon. John H. Bryan

[*Addressed*] Hon. John H. Bryan: H.R
Washington City

Ann Blount Pettigrew to Mary Williams Bryan UNC

Lake Phelps April 15th 1828

My Dear Sister,

Your letter by Frederick I received with much pleasure, your letters always give me great gratifycation, but your last was indeed such a rarity that it produced a twofold pleasant sensation. I think you must be mistaken as respects my being in debt a letter to you, but as I think it an immaterial point among friends I shall not contend—I assure you my mind is now so much engaged that I am scarcely ever sufficiently composed for letter writing—I have almost as much trouble as if I had three infants, I suppose you have heard of poor James's situation. Dr Warren says he can cure him but that it will be <a> some time first, he is now taking mercury and when the weather becomes comfortable, he intends using the cold bath, his disease commenced with a twitching in his right arm and leg but his arm is now quite useless, but notwithstanding all this, he retains his spirits and is disposed to run about and play, which is consolatory to me, if he were depressed I should be miserable indeed—Mrs Warren passed a few days here last week—the Doct. purchased a neat little carriage for the purpose of visiting Virginia, but James's sickness precludes the idea—she cannot go alone & the D^{r} cannot go with her, she has a fine son and they are very fond of it.

Mrs Collins is now at the Lake with her youngest daughter Alethia, who is little older than Henry and a sweet child, Henry and Mary visited Miss. the other day and Mary returned with a Doll, a present which delighted her, never having seen any thing of the kind before. We have constant variations of weather from heat to cold—sunny to cloudy &c, such a season I have never before seen—Mr Pettigrew is unable to determine whether his wheat will be destroyed or not—I heard this morning that Aunt Pettigrew was quite sick with a bad cold, except that she enjoys good health and spirits.

I understand the Stanleys have failed—what a reverse—!

I suppose your husband will soon return, I should suppose he would be tyred of Washington—

I thank you for the frock you sent Mary—also the raisons which were very good—

Kiss the children for me—
Mr Pettigrew desires his respects to you,

believe me your aff sister,
Ann B. Pettigrew

[*Addressed*] Mrs Mary W. Bryan,
Newbern,
NC.

D. Stone to Ebenezer Pettigrew UNC

Plymouth [*Maine*] June 28th 1828.

Dear Sir,

I received your letters about two months after date. Yours which informed me your family had been sick also gave me the pleasure of hearing that they had recovered; I suppose you expect it once a year; and I dont think you will be disappointed often.

But Sir, are you still making improvements on your possesions, have you got through to Alligator with your ditch, and does the water run to or from the Lake I should like to know that. If there were a few more men around you as spirited and enterprizing as yourself about improvements, then might the Dismal Swamp be made to blossom as the rose and to bring forth abundantly. Such men are to scarce; But how are more to be raised, what others have tried by precept you have *attempted* by a still more powerful *stimulus* viz. Example.

I hope when you take a tour to the North you will come as far as the State of Maine. My health has been tolerable good since I returned, better than when I left the Lake. My passage down the river, crossing the Sound & putting up at the *Queens* Hotel I shall not forget very soon; should it ever be my fortune to stop there again I hope [she] will something decent to eat. Agreeable to your request I inform you that you can direct (if you wish) to, /the care of/ Ephraim Jones Esq. Boston. 22 Portland street. (PS) I hope to be where I can send you the animal you wish for, next fall. Last season I was some distance from the seaboard which made it inconvenient to attend to it at the right time.

I have not heard (except by you) from Doct. Warren, I should like to know if he received my letter & whether he remains in Scuppernong yet. Please to let me know /how/ Mr. Woodleys well and water works belonging thereto operate;

He engaged to write to me when he was married I shall expect a letter from him soon please to remind him of his promise.

The provisions which Mrs. Pettigrew provided for me /when I left/ were of great service to /me/ down the river ha[d *torn*] not been for them I believe I should have starved as my appetite was so poor I could not eat any thing they had on board the vessel. Please to write soon and often and let the Boys do so to.

Rememeber me to Mrs. P., my scholars and all my friends who shall do me the honour to enquire after me.

Yours respectfully
D Stone.

Please to direct your letters to me in Plymouth, Maine.

[*Addressed*] Ebenezer Pettigrew Esqr
Lake Phelps,
North Carolina.

Ann Blount Pettigrew to Mary Williams Bryan A&H, BRYAN

Lake Phelps August 4th 1828—

My Dear Sister,

Your kind letter was thankfully received a few weeks since, I assure you it was as you beleived, peculiarly grateful, <at that> for at such a time I am always depressed and all the kindness I can receive is not too much, I am nearly recovered from my late confinement and have a very healthy child, which is a blessing I am thankful for, we think of calling him Johnston, as children are not rarities in our family I will not give a dissertation on his quite disposition, beauty, &c—

The rest of our family are well, James is mending—do you know those cases of St Vitus's dance in Newbern, & how they were cured? Mr Pettigrew has been very unwell, but is now mending. Aunt Pettigrew shews age, is very feeble, but has returned home to day from visiting us, she could not be prevaild on to stay one day longer than the one appoined for her return, set out before breakfast for the benefit of a cool morning, shorty after sunrise, she is really a very remarakable woman of her age.

I am pleased to hear of Mr Bryan's return, your patience I think must have been nearly exhausted, if his was not. A trip to West Point would have been a very pleasant one you must have regretted the disapp<o>intment—can it be possible, that Frederick is making a Northern trip, I merely think so from an expression in Charles's letter, we never hear from him through the quil, has William gone to Tennessee? I extremely regret that antipathy to writing, which prevails in our family, you are not totally exempt, your letters are too short—you know my seclusion so well, you should be more charitable, I have many excuses that none of the family have, a want of something to write which is first, I always fear from the sameness and extreme dullness of my epistles, they are tiresome. How is Mr Stanly poor man I sincerely pity his misfortunes, pity a few years ago would have excited his hatred & contempt, but alas! the destiny of man, how fortunate for us we cannot foresee.

Mrs Warren visited me not long since, her visits are less frequent the addition of one child has obliged her to stay at home—I am very happy to understand that Mama will visit me this November, I wish you would persuade her to stay all the winter with us, do let me know the state of Penelope's arm.

I suppose you will spend next winter in Washington—then you will persuade Mr Bryan not to offer again, and I wish you may succeede—

Mr Pettigrew joins me in respects to Mr B. and yourself and believe me your aff sister.

Ann B Pettigrew.

PS. I do not contemplate visiting Newbern this winter—therefore Mama's visit to me will be truly gratifying, do not permit her to give it over, she is so apt to decline such good resolutions after forming them—

[*Addressed*] Mrs Mary W Bryan,
Newbern,
NC.

John Swann Shepard to Ebenezer Pettigrew UNC

Tallahassee [*Florida*] Septr. 15th 1828.

My dear Sir,

It has been so long since I wrote to you that I am allmost ashamed to acknowledge my negligence but I have been so much engaged in settling in the woods clearing land and s[*c*]ufleing for provisions that I really have had only time to think of my friends. I have often expressed as wish in my own breast that we could live near each other, but I fear our ideas are so different about happiness and prosperity that you will forever be an inhabitant of lake Phelps and I that of lake Jackson (the lake on which live) the advantages of this country over that which you reside in are incalculable. I mean not to say from superior fertility of soil. I believe our lands I mean the best we have are greatly inferior to those you possess but the productions of the country which are common to this latitude are so much more profitable to the cultivator than they are which you cultivate noth our lands grow here in the greatest possible perfection Sugar cane black seed and mexican cotton either of these crops when properly attended will yield to the field hand from 200$ to 250. each the cane I know nothing of its productiveness we are all gitting in seed and preparing to make sugar it is said by the cultivation in Louisiana of that article that it will make from 500 to 600$ per hand and molasses will pay all expenses we are too far south to make grain advantageously but I suppose our [*illegible*] lands when judicioulу managed may average 40 bushels to the acre a production sufficient to secure an abundance of provission without much labour we have a decided advantage over you in point of climate and a climate in my opinion will adapted to your constition one of the most even and agreeble temperature in the cold season rarely below 40° and in the summer here rarely higher than 85° our nights are allways cool and comfortable and the repose invigorating and refreshing as it regards the health of the climate thus far no country can surpass it. I have been here since Mar. 1827. and have not heard of a single case of fever I contend the health must be unusual but those who have resided here for six years say disease is a stranger to their familys if it continues to be thus healthy I have no hesitation in asserting it will be five years hence the most desirable part of the Union the country is gently undulating and abounds with good free stone water I have growing the orange the pungranite the fig the tamerand and the prune which I have no doubt will all do well and in a year or too yield us an abundance of those fruits. I want nothing now but the scuppernong grape the seed you were good enough to send me did not prosper they all died but one and that I gave to a neighbor may I ask of the favour to send me a few more, and inform of the truth of what I understood if there is <one> any grape one seed which will produce the genuine white grape and the balance the varieties of the forest grape for agreeable life and p[lea]sure I want nothing but m[y] relations to be near me If I had them near or a portion of them I should never desire to remove from this favoured belt. cannot all I have said induce you to visit me and look at the country if you should determine to come here after looking at it a man of your energy and enterprise would in one year increse his estate in Value 25 per cent and then your prodution to the hand would be so much much grea[ter than] I fear it is now that you would never regret it our society [is] good and improving dialy many emigrants of the most respectable characters are coming in Tennesses takes all the blackgards and this country the gentlemen of moderate fortunes who desire independence and I wish to God I could number you and a fiew more of my friends with them I wrote to Fred some time ago and advised him to come here when will the enterprise of this family of ours be aroused why will those boys persist and trifling away their lives where they without any advantges to themselves or any person else Visit me this winter and Fred with you. My love to Nancy and all the little ones and beleve me to be your affectionate friend

J S Shepard

[*Addressed*] Ebenezer Pettigrew Esqr
Lake Phelps
Tyrrell county
N. Carolina

Thomas and William A. Turner to Ebenezer Pettigrew A&H

Plymo NC Sep 23 1828

Lake Phelps
Mr Ebenezer Pettigrew

Dear Sir—

Yours of this month, is this day at hand with your two carts.—We send you two boxes, four bags, one saw, & five bars steel, being all the goods, except one Ream paper & a paper parcel, which we recd of the Schr John S Bryan Capt Pike, & VanBokelyn & Whites letter of Aug 30, for you—and the paper parcel and ream of paper, the writer understands you have already received. We find a Stove in our office, which was recd of the Jno S Bryan, at the time we received the above articles for you—but as it is not marked at all—where as your goods are marked with your name, and as it is not mentioned in the Bill of Lading with your goods, and has not been mentioned by you to us, we decline to send it, thinking perhaps it may belong to some one else.

One of your negroes gave us a dollar & said you wished Jack Knives bot with it—We have bot & send you 6 jack Knives for it.

The shoes have been returned to Mr Pender. We have bot you another pair which is about ¼ inch longer—but not narrower. The quality is 20 Cents cheaper—and this is the best we could do, having examined every store in Town—Price of this $1.60—We send you a bottle of snuff, price 25 cents.

Your letter contained one hundred and ninety dollars in North Carolina Bank notes, with a request that we purchase a Bill for about that sum, payable at sight or at a short sight & remit it to Messs Van <K> Bokelyn & White for your account. We have recd the money and will try to purchase the Bill & remit it as you direct.

But are apprehensive one cannot be had for less than 5 or 6 P Cent. We shall enquire in several directions & shall do the best we can—and after all expect to send our own Bill on Charleston payable 21/24th October—We have /sales of/ corn due there at that time, the neat proceeds of which belong to Jesse Averett Esqr of Bertie who refused 5 P Cent for the Bill last week at Windser: But we think he had better have taken it. He has left us to dispose of it for him.

We shall not charge you <a> Commission on the procuring of that vessel. We did this thing once and have been sorry for it ever since. Other merchants in Plymo at that time made those charges—& we did it—but have ever regretted it.

Your goods have not been in our way. Our best respects

Th. & W A Turner

[*Addressed*] Ebenezer Pettegrew Esq
Lake Phelps

Ann Blount Pettigrew to Mary Williams Bryan A&H, BRYAN

Lake Phelps, Oct. 20th, 1828—

My Dear Sister,

I have at length found liesure to write you, after having had a disposition to do so a long time, I regret that you always wait for me to answer your letters when you have so much more to communicate than I can possibly have.

We have had a remarkably healthy family this summer and fall but within two weeks two of my children Mary & Johnston, have been very sick with the flux, which prevails in the neigbourhood at this time they are now much better, I am happy to inform you that James is quite well, but we are obliged to exercise the greatest care and as we believe a derangement of the bowels was the cause of the disease, we frequently give him cathartticks. We have not yet procured another Teacher and I am obliged to bestow some attention on the children, but I find the duties of housekeeping nursing and teaching are not compatable therefore one of them must be neglected, which is the school, the others being indispensable, my time is always usefully employed as I am seldom interrupted by company—which would be very agreeable I assure you sometimes—I devote my Sabbaths to reading the Commentary purchased from Mr Carle. when you were here. it is a very entertaining and instructing work. there are many digressions from the subject or it would be rather monotonous—Dr Warren is quite a literary gentleman and occasionally lends me a late novel, he is still a great politician a violent Adamite and as such he stands almost alone in this county as I do not think much on this subject I have little to write.

The Lake looks rather gloomy at this time the faded foliage of the trees and dying vegetation, forms a melancholly contrast with the green corn and waving wheat with which our fields are generally ornamented with, the low prices of grain keep the farmers depressed in spirits and purse, but my husbands /Spirits/ is better than common. /He says his purse is low/

There has been a great rain in this country, Mr Pettigrew was affraid it /would/ destroy his opperations on the Creek he is clearing out, you recollect a trip we made in a small skiff down the Creek, he says it is much improved by the work performed, Mr Pettigrew estimates the labour at 2000 $—

Mr Collins has been on the Lake greater part of this year without his family, they have not yet returned from their Northern visit, he seems to enjoy the loneliness of this place—such is the effect of age, he is very unlike his family—they are gay and fond of the world, I suppose next year his son will take poss<s>esion, they have increased the number of slaves and houses and find their overseers so faithless that they must give their personal attention, the only alternative for Farmers, the education of the son will cause him to pass many a wretched hour, it will be very unlike New York, the Opera and amusements of various kinds which that great city affords.

I suppose you are now preparing for your trip to Washington. you will be unwilling to see Mr Bryan set out without you—this will be an interesting session—the Presidential contest excites great commotion in all quarters I believe, the strength of the candidates was tested at Tyrrel Court house the other day, and General [*Andrew*] Jackson prevaild by a great majority, Mr Pettigrew was not there, he takes very little interest in it, for which I give him credit—

Do persuade Mama to spend the winter with me—

Aunt Pettigrew is quite well, she is a miricle of health and age—

Mr Pettigrew joins me in respects to Mr Bryan & yourself—kiss the children and believe me your aff, Sister,

Ann B Pettigrew.

[*Addressed*] Mrs Mary W. Bryan,
Newbern,
No Carolina.

[Dr.] Thomas Old to Ebenezer Pettigrew UNC

Murfreesboro. N.C. Nov. 17th 1828

Dear Sir,

I have been waiting to reply to your last favour in order to ascertain whether I shd effect the change I contemplated in my profession & pursuits, <before> that I might apprize you of it. Some time during the last month I visited P. Anne [*Princess Anne County, Virginia*] to examine a Farm that was for sale belonging to George Newton. While negotiating for its' purchase, the Dwelling House (the chief desideratum with me) was consumed by fire. Since then I have leased a Farm lying on one of the Branches of the Elizabeth River and within 9 miles of Norfolk & 1 of Kempsville—I shall remove there at the expiration of the present year—Medicine I expect to abandon entirely—To this resolution I am brought by a variety of considerations—Among the chief I may name the state of my health which is such as to incapacitate me <from> for exposure at night and in bad weather—moreover there is too little /profit/ attached to it, to form an adequate compensation—I am fully aware of the difficulties I shall meet in my new avocation and shall not be surprized if I become altogether disgusted with it. But I think the reasons growing out of the nature of circumstances, preponderate on the other side—My advantages as a Farmer will be great—But on one subject I anticipate much trouble—I mean the management of slaves—Here I am conscious of a great deficiency both in moral & physical energy a quality that is I imagine indispensable.

Believing that you know more of this subject than / than any other person I have met with, I shall be under great obligations to you, if you will give me a few aphorisms or directions on this as well as Farming in general—All that I know of Agriculture which is very little, I think I gleaned from you when I formerly had the pleasure of visiting your House—I shall confidently expect you to bring Mrs Pettigrew & your children to see us when we get fixed in our new home—

I shd have told you when asking rules for the controul of negroes, that they are intended for a set that have been hired out for the last 10 /15/ years and contain some very grand scoundrels—so I guess—I think of trying the culture of cotton for the sale crop—The Farmers here say, it is the only article on which they can make any thing—of the truth of this I have my doubts—so I shall but try the experiment—

The only news I can give, is on the Presidential Election, which absorbs the attention of all here—In this County we gave the General more than two to one & there is I fear no doubt but he will get the vote of this state & Va In N. York by the latest advices the vote is equally divided 18—18—Kentucky & Ohio doubtful—and Mr [*John Quincy*] Adams chance equally so—many of my side have given up for lost I can hardly do it yet, but I fear one week more will compel me to do so.

Pray what has become of my friend Dr Warren—It has been a long time since I heard from him, tho I think he is in debt to me, one letter—I have been expecting to see him & Mrs Warren during the present month, on their way to Richmond—How does the Squire, Haughton get along? as busy and as much from home as ever, I expect.

If I /can/ get you to P. Anne once, I have some hopes of inducing you to purchase a place, there as a summer residence for your family. I know a small Farm for sale which can be purchased for very little, that has on it one of the han/d/somest sites for a dwelling House that I ever saw any where—It is unimproved, but tha[t] wod but afford you an opportunity of indulging your constructive faculti[es] The former proprietor (Williamson of Norfolk) a man [of] considerable taste had prepared a large quantity of Bricks to build the House, which are now lying on the spot uninjured. In front you have the Lynhaven River running in a straight line from the Bay for ¾ mile and its Branches on each side—you have just enough of the Bay to see vessels passing—It is decidedly the most beautiful place I ever saw—in the low country I may add—At all events come let me shew it you—You will then decide—

Please present my respects and those of Mrs O to Mrs Pettigrew and assure her of the great pleasure Mrs O will derive from her acquaintance, and visit if we may be permitted to indulge in the anticipation of its being realized—

Very truly yr friend
Th: Old

[*Addressed*] Mr Ebenezer Pettigrew
Cool Spring Post Office
Washington County
N. Car.

[Dr.] William C. Warren to Ebenezer Pettigrew UNC

Norfolk 24th Nov. 1828

My Dear Sir

I arrived in this place last night in one of the James River Stm Bts: to day the first task I impose on myself, is to report to you some account <of> our journey from Tyrrell &c.

We got to the Ferry the day we left home pretty early in the afternoon, but owing to the contrary wind we were compelled to spend the night with Mr Downing, where we were entertained in very plain style; tuesday we got to Edenton about 12 Oclk and put up at Mrs Wills'—where we were detained all day by the indolence of a Blacksmith, who had to shoe one of my horses. I send the horse to the shop as soon as I got to town, and the sun was almost down before the shoes were put on—Wednesday we traveled 30 miles without much inconvenience to Mrs Warren or our little boy—Thursday we went to Suffolk 23 miles, to dinner & set out from there at 3 P.M. to reach a tavern 10 miles distant; we got to the house about sun set & much to my mortification found there was no entertainment to be had there; the man said he only had tavern License that he might sell spirits by small measure—Thus disappointed there was no alternative but to proceed to Smithfield 12 miles farther—it was very cold and we soon overtaken by night after traveling some time we came to a mill and not knowing whether the road passed over the dam which was immediately before us, I sent Phil to a negro cabin to enquire; he returned & said we must go straight forward I took the reins from him & drove over the dam, which I found so narrow that the carriage was in the most imminent danger of upsetting, indeed the danger was so great we had to get down & lead the horses & then with difficulty, got over—when we got to the other side I found we were at the end of the road. I stopped the horses & went back to the negro house, where I learnd we ought to have gone below the mill. Two negroes volunteered to put us right, which they accomplished by leading the horses about a quarter of a mile through the woods along a cart way. We reached Smithfield at 8. cold & frightened though very thankful we escaped so well. On relating our adventure to the Tavern Keeper he really appeared alarmed—he said the dam was just made & that two days before a cart could not pass over—he said the water was deep on one side & the other not less than 15 feet high, as perpendicular as earth could be piled. Friday it raind & we remained where we were Saturday we rode 35 Mls & Sunday got to Chas City about 3 oclk all safe. We had the pleasure of meeting my Mother at Dr Willcoxs & finding all of my friends in good health. The inclemency of the weather has not permited us to visit much, as yet we have only been Dr Willcox's & Dr Christians as soon as I return to Chas City, which will be in a few days, <I> we shall proceed to Bedford & after remaining two weeks with Mrs Alexander, we shall return to Carolina—

I have had the pleasure to day of receiving your favor for which I must tender my thanks as I know you have a great aversion to writing. I shall certain[ly] [*torn*] to your requests. The cloth for Mr

Woodley & the Lins[ey] will be forwarded immediately to Wright & Williams. E City.

As soon as I got to Chas City I began to look around for your teacher and I have the satisfaction to inform you I have contracted with a young man I suppose every way qualified—he teaches English Latin, Greek & French and speaks the French. The young Gentleman's name is Vaiden, he was raised in my neighborhood & is at present employed as a teacher in Mr Tyler's family—he will not be in Carolina before the 20th of Jany. I have written in great haste & fear you will not be able to read what I have said—Harriet desired me to send her warmest respects to yourself & Mrs Pettigrew—You will both accept mine &

Believe me most sincerely & affectionately
your Friend
W. C. Warren

[*Addressed*] Mr E. Pettigrew
Cool Spring
Washington Cty
North Carolina

[Dr.] William C. Warren to Ebenezer Pettigrew A&H

New London [*Virginia*] Decr 12th 1828——

My Dear Sir,

I promised in my last to write you on my arrival at this place. After remaining a few days in Norfolk I returned to Chas City, where I spent a few days more & proceeded to Richmond, there I passed two nights and a day, which made Decr 4th when we commenced our western pilgrimage. The first day we set out at 10 Oclk, and traveled 22 miles by hard driving, the sixth day we reached this place almost exhausted with fatiegue. The road from Richmd is a bed of clay and is hilly the whole distance—in many places it is hardly passable, the heavy laden western waggons have cut it up & the droves of hogs have made good mortar of the clay.

We have all recovered from the exhaustion of the journey and begin to feel the renovating influence of the mountain air — Edward has improved very much indeed he has not required a grain of medicine since we left home. Mrs Alexander & family are in fine health How the Farmers in this Section make out to live, I cant imagine, and still most of them live in fine houses & have a good deal of property, the Land is barren, rocky & hilly, of course difficult to cultivate, and what produce they raise to sell, attended with great expense in sending it to market Tobacco has been the principal staple, here, but the present low price of it does not justify its cultivation—Hemp is not raised in this neighborhood, but I have conversed with several gentlemen, familiar with its cultivation, and they expect your land is particularly adapted to it. I calculate on receiving all the necessary information, from Dr Massie of Nelson; a wealthy gentleman who has a crop of hemp this year—

Since I left Richm^d^ I have seen thousands of western hogs yesterday & to day five thousand passed this road. what is very remarkable, most of the Farmers here, have to purchase pork, though the present low price of it, makes it as cheap as herrings. The Drovers are glad to sell at $3.50—Corn here is $2. cash— I hope you disposed of your wheat when the price was so high; it sold at one time as high as $2 in Richm^d^ & Flour at $10. lately it has declined & at this time only brings 7—

I was much mortified at the result of the Presidential election in N. Carolina. I never though for a moment that Adams would receive the vote of the State but I had no conception Jackson's majority would be so large.[1] Tyrrell gave a most shameful vote[2] and I am highly pleased that I was not present to witness the exultation of the Heroites. I suspect you were gratified with M^r^ [*James*] Iredell's success in the Senatorial Election though I think he must have been chagrined, by the number of scattering votes—

I feel very impatient to return to Carolina, but I cannot say when I shall get there. We shall remain with Mrs Alexander ten days longer and shall then set out on our return via Richmond, we shall only remain a few days in Chas City & N Kent and probably by the 10th of Jany shall land in Tyrrell—our horses have performed admirably. Shepard is a fine draft horse & has improved on traveling—

Harriet writes with me in kind regards to Mrs Pettigrew & yourself, she is perfectly happy only when she thinks of the Swamps—She however has no thought of suffering me to return without her—

I remain My Dear Sir your most Sincere friend
W. C. Warren

PS Excuse my illegible writing there is so much confusion I have lost my senses

N London V^a^
14 Decr 1828

[*Addressed*] Mr E. Pettigrew
Cool Spring
Washington County
North Carolina

[1]In the presidential election of 1828 Andrew Jackson received 37,857 votes in North Carolina, while John Quincy Adams received 13,918 votes. Cheney, *North Carolina Government*, 1329.

[2]Tyrrell County gave 273 votes to Jackson and twenty votes to Adams. Cheney, *North Carolina Government*, 1329.

Thomas and William A. Turner to Ebenezer Pettigrew UNC

Plymo: NC Dec 12 1828

Dear Sir.

Yours of the 2d is before us. The writer has been absent and is but 2 or 3 days returned—

Corn—the price is not settled. It rules @ 1.75 to $2. No sales @ $2. Sales @ 1.75 on the other side of the sound. Mr Jas D Marburn of Norfolk says in his letter Nov 29, that he does not think it safe to give more than 40 cents per bushel for corn in that market.

If the price in Liverpool be 81 cents the duty is 30. At 90 cents the duty is 20. At 100 cents the duty is 2 cents. This is as near as may be to exclude fractions. You can calculate the charges to Liverpool as easily as we—to these add the duty, and you will see the price it must bear in that port to justify our shipping to England. Observe that altho the Crops are short in Europe, they will import no corn except in England. Observe that as soon as the price reaches 100 cents per bushel in Liverpool the duty is off to 2 cents. We may therefore conclude the price there will not go over 100 cents—and thus we may say with some confidence that the price with us will scarcely go higher than 2$ if so high: For there is no demand in the United States equal to raising or keeping up the price of Corn. Observe also that underwriters insure only that the *quantity* shall arrive--that they take no risk as to *quality*. If you ship Rum—they will underwrite on the quantity; but not that it will arrive 3d or 4th proof. And so of Corn, and other goods. Therefore the shipper of Corn must risk something; /He must risk the damage, not the loss./ The charges of your Corn may therefore be thus stated, supposing you to determine upon sending it to England—

Freight to New York—
Storage in New York
measuring, & storing
Commissions for shipping
Freight to Liverpool
Storage in do—if not sold afloat
measuring & landing
Commissions on sale—
Insurance to New York
Do to Liverpool

Risk on quality to New York
Risk on Do. to Liverpool
Duty in Liverpool—

The demand in England for flour is such as to ship all that we shall make in the United States—This scarcity of flour will tend to increase our consumption of Corn—

We are purchasers of Corn & offer you $1.75 per bbl—payable on delivery. Delivery to suit us—as soon as we may be able to ship it. Place of delivery on board of a vessel at your Canal.

We thus give you all the information we have. Perhaps we may be incorrect in some points. If so, we dont know it. Yours truly

Th & W A Turner

[*Addressed*] Ebenezer Pettigrew Esq
Cool Spring
Washington County

Ebenezer Pettigrew to John Herritage Bryan UNC

Bonarva on Lake Phelps Dec 17, 1828

My dear Sir,

I observe you were not present at the opening of Congress howeve I suppose before this you /have/ resumed your seat.

Although we need and I immagine no state in the Union has sent a more miserable representation to Congress, I yet confess I do no regret to learn in your last letter that you have an idea of declining a reelection to that body. A continuance in it will most certainly injure very much your pecuniary affairs as well as deprive you of that greatest of pleasures, the society of ones family. Whether your mind will rest in a state of reti[re]ment is known but to yourself. I think you would be very restless at Lake Phelps before half the winter was gone. We should be much pleased after you retire into private life if you with Mrs B. would try it for a while.

You express great hopes that the Legislature will do something liberal for Newbern in the way of a railroad. If you wish much done in that way, I would advise you to change your seat, for one in that body, and perhaps something may be done in the process by it, according to your wishes. Newbern has certainly at this time an able representative of her interest, but if I am not mistaken he is not popular, and can /do/ very little with all his eloquence & powers of reasoning.[1] I am justified in saying the case would be very different with you. But at best the internal improvements of North Carolina, so far as I have heard & read would be a disgrace to any civilized people. The plans may be good but I am certain the execution betrays great imbicility. We have great numbers of men who are full of plans, such as no one can execute, if we had the energy & industry necessary. I fear your rail road will be like most other of our great projects. The great men of that section interested meet, organise then retire. One who can make the best speach rises & tells the gaping multitude that which they are all agreed on, the utility of such a work, they then pass a number resolutions towards it execution, the meeting is then dissoved & the next to be done is to have an act of Legislature, and after that go to work, a thing no one is willing to, and if by chance they should commence opperations, there is probably appointed some weak, ignorant or visionary being, at its head, and the funds of the undertaking are exhausted & nothing like the expenditures in return. I am perfectly certain that the great cause of all our failures has has arisen from the inefficiency in one way or other of /an/ head man. What has made nations great at different periods but their leading characters? What has made armies perform wonders but their Generals? When imbacility and ignorence governs the physical energies of a people they cannot be exerted to any profitable extent. It is the height of folly to employ men on great undertakings when large sums of money are at stake without practical knowledge.

I should not be in the least surprised if the Legislature in dispair should dissolve the board and do away the internal improvment system entirely, for generally speaking it is little else than a foolish waste of money.

We received a letter the other day from John Shepard, he is very desirous for us to move to Florida, but Mrs P. says there are too many Aligators & rattlesnakes in that country and we will stay in the unenterprising state of N. Carolina th[ough] I very much regret to stay among such a set of imbeciles.

The 22nd of this month three years ago was the date of the first paper I received from the office of the National Journal. I am desirous to discontinue it. Will you be so good as to pay up for the two last years which is due & stop it, and subscribe for me to the National Inteligencer. Inclosed is fifteen dollars for the above purposes. I do not recollect the amount of a years subscription to the latter paper but if it should be more than $5 please to advance the remainder and I will transmit is in the next letter.

To save myself the trouble of making a will yearly I have made such a one a will answer for few or many children. I was the other day within a hairs breadth of puting it to the test by the fall of a tree. Nothing saved me but cool thought at the time & prompt determination as the tree was falling. Mrs P. & children are tolerable well she sends her respects to you—Please to assure yourself of my Esteem & regard

E Pettigrew

P.S. Please excuse this miserable scrawl for I have not time to write Do not believe that I am averse to internal improvement, by what I say It is worthlessness I am opposed to, but a great friend of any sort of improvment.

[*Addressed*] Hon. John H. Bryan
Washington City
H.R.

---

[1]This is probably a reference to William Gaston, who was serving as the town representative for New Bern in the House of Commons. Cheney, *North Carolina Government*, 292.

Ebenezer Pettigrew to James Cathcart Johnston UNC

Bonarva on Lake Phelps Jan 13, 1829

My dear Sir,

With great pleasure I received your favour's of Nov 17, & Dec 28 & in like manner I received your congratulations on the approach of a new year. That it may be a more agreeable one to you than you say the /last/ has been is my sincere wish. I have begun it with unusual vigor how I am to hold out is uncertain. My mind never tires at business and my body has been at no time more vigorous, though I have had within the last ten days some symptoms of gout in my extremities and I strongly suspect in my stomach; at any rate the pain which I have had there is an unusual one. If my suggestion is correct I suppose I shall be some day stoped in my earthly carear in short order, and I will try and loos as little time as possible untill it does happen. I am now very busily engaged geting the timber for a vessil of about 60 tons, which I am about to build, in partnership with a Capt. Dunbar, we expect to get her ready for the next wheat crop. I have full confidence in my partner the Captain, as an honest, active, industrious man. It not being a material matter with Mr D. Clark,[1] whether his mill is improved now or some time hence and Mr Woodley being rather pressed for time, he has declined it for more leasure. Mr Woodley can be employed in your work after about the middle of June. I think him fully competent to any thing you may want done, neither do I think he will clog the work with any visionary speculations. His general ideas /& managment/ are very superior and I consider myself indebted to him for some of my most valuable plans. Nothing would give me more pleasure than to receive a visit from you. We could then talk over the subject of your mill, but if you cannot give me that pleasure and you think I can make any usefull suggestions in the work, I will meet you on any given day at any place in this or the next month, health permiting and we will go to the seat, where we will talk more to the purpose; Provided no one knows what I am about. It is of importance that the timber for it should be got before the spring, that it may season.

I accept with pleasure your congratulations on my good crop & the prospect of a sale; I hope you will be alike benefited by that event. Though I have at this time not an hour to spare from business I have commenced in Doctor Warren absence the practice of medicine I have been called to & have visited a very sick child eight miles in the country twice last week. Some of our children have been sick but through the assistance of providence they have recovered. Mrs Pettigrew as well as myself are very much gratified at the alteration made in our society on / on the Lake. It is a great affair to have in your neighborhood well bred persons who stand on honour & character. That we shall get along in peace there can be no doubt. Our interests cannot clash in any shape, and if I know my own heart, I feel a very strong disposition that the place should thrive, but the young gentlemans habits of society, and his associates being of the first circle in the nation, forbid that I could be company for him *long at a time* or *very often*. In truth their stay in this out of the way place cannot be to enjoy the society of any one. The reason must be obvious. I hope no one has been taught his station & knows it better than I do.

The most of the money you were so obliging as to loan me I have converted to the paying debts, which my bad crops have caused m[*torn*]tract, purchasing mares to raise mules, and the remainder [*torn*] in building this vessil. I have yet a wish to increase my negroes and shall be glad to receive the money you may collect to the amount we have talked. I have on hand about 600 bus. wheat and 3000 bus corn. I have sown about 100 acres in wheat, my various ditching opperations made me rather too late in seeding some of it, yet I have confidence in the land, it will no doubt command a good price next summer. Mrs Pettigrew joins me in best respects to your sisters. Hoping shortly to see you here or else where, I remain your sincere friend

E Pettigrew

James C. Johnston Esqr.

[*Addressed*] James C Johnston Esqr
Hayes, Edenton P.O.

---

[1]Possibly this refers to the merchant David Clark. Keith and others, *Blount Papers*, IV, 22n, 75. See also the following letter.

*James Cathcart Johnston to Ebenezer Pettigrew** UNC

Hayes. 17th Febry. 1829.—

My Dear Sir

I have delayed writing in answer to your's of 13th of last month hoping to be able to appoint a day when we could meet <at> but my arrangements have been so much deranged by bad weather & other cause beyond my controul that I /now/ find <now> that it will not be practicable and I <cannot> could not think of calling you from home at this inclement season & when you have such full imployment for your time on an uncertainty. I have at length succeedd in collect the money due from Cox tho' at the risk of my life which is /now/ threatened for <fifteen> eighteen months indulgence. I care very little for his threats which like his promises will [no*t*] be full filled.—I now enclose you bills on Messrs Robt Lenox & Son the amt of I [sho]uld have paid you the money could I have seen you but have adopted this course as the most safe & convenient and the bills can be converted into cash at par or perhaps at a small premium by sending them to Mr J. S. Bryan at Plymouth or to the Bank at this place /with/ one of which I should have had to deposit the money for you so that you will have no more trouble in getting it.—I thot farther that /if/ you <might> /should/ want to purchase negroes in Virginia that currency /or United States money/ might be more ready got for the Bill than it could be had for N. Carolina notes.—I hope the arrangement will please you.—The note you will please sign and enclose /it/ in a letter and put /it/ into Mr Collins hands to be held until I see him. I am this particular because there is no safety in our Post Office.—

I am more anxious to see you now than ever and wish very much I could have done so before you commenced your vessel building.—It may be <may> very officious in /me/ to obtrude my advice on one who never acts without well considering what he is going to do who always looks before he leaps and who always get successfully thro' his undertakings I am generally willing to take advice but much more apt to give.—I should have advised you most strenously to have nothing to do with vessels or vessel building the latter cannot <be> /end/ profitable to you, the holding & running them <is> /would be/ still more so. There are several objections to /farmers/ owning vessels first they are a kind of property <that> over which you can have little or no controul you must rely on your Capt the wind & weather the capt you now have may be a very good man and to be relied upon—but the human character is extremely changable and these vi<ss>cissitudes are so frequent <that> & have astonished me so much of late years that I begin to think that a man ought never to <put him> rely on others further than is absolutely necessary and atho' your capt may be a very good man and may continue so, yet he may die and how will you supply his place a good & capable is not so easily found now a days.—Your vessel can^{t} stop until you find one—you are oblige to take up with such as you can get a fellow who perhap by one act of bad conduct will rid you of all further trouble with vessels.—Again with the very best management by merchants who devote their time and attention to /them/ they are expensive & unprofitable. a friend of my M^{r} /D/ Clark who made a large fortune in trade has told me that he never made a cent by /owing/ vessels. his Brother /W^{m}/ sunk six or seven thousand dollars by building & sailing them before he would be convinced of the correctness of his brother opinion—If these merchants of the best management can make nothing [how] is a farmer whose time is take up with /his/ farm to make a profit by vessels.—A farmer who spreads his bread on the land may after many days gather it to gather again but when he scatters it on the water I fear he will not again find it all.—again you will be drawing from & crippling a fund which you have appropriated to a great & important object and which it is of the utmost importance that you should effec/t/ as soon as possible the draining of your Savannah Lands.—I know well the motive that prompts you to build it is the inconvenience of getting your produce to market, I have felt the inconvenience myself but never tho^{t} of owing a vessel a river or canal boat was the summit of my ambition. now Sir let me tell you my plan for remedying the inconvenience which we both labour under—I have given orders to my overseer in Pasquotank to get timber & materials to build a canal boat which will not cost me much and with which I can with my own negroes and at no expence except the toll carry my produce thro' to Norfolk where if does not sell at a fair price it can be shipt a very reduced freight to any other market forgein or domestic. I think norfolk will become a great grain & Lumber market and if it does not the facility of shipping from there to any other is so great that I would much prefer sending my produce there /with my own people/ and shipping it than be subject to the uncertainty & delays of our navigation.—with a boat of kind I think you might count with certainty of having a crop of grain in New York in four or five days whereas by Occacocke it might be a month.—for your lumber Norfolk would be a great market.—/& I have a friend there who would do us both ample justice/ but I /may/ have said to much against your project & too much in favor of my own.—I have been trying to dismount you from your hobby to mount you on mine.—I may be wrong. but /mine/ is a dull & gentle sort of a beast & so low that if I get a fall <it wil> it wont hurt much I hold the rain in my own hands & do not trust to coachmen Hayden the Blacksmith whom I engaged to mak a doz & half of axes for you has been obliged return to the north in consequence of bad health he regreted very much not being able to execute your order before he left. but has taken it on with him & says if he gets well enough it shall be done & the axes sent to his agent at Elizabeth.—My dear friend if you can honorably get off from this vessel engagement even at some pecuniary loss I would advise you to do it will be a source of vexation & trouble to you & no profit.—

Edenton. 17th Febry. 1829.

Exchange $2500

Ninety days after date of this my first of exchange second of this tenor & date unpaid pay to Ebenezer Pettigrew Esqr or his order two thousand five hundred dollars value rec^{d} & charge the same to acc^{t} of y^{r} mos^{t} Obd^{t} Sv^{t}—

Ja. C J

Mess^{s} Robert Lenox & Son
New York

<I promise [One] day after date> /with Interest from 17th of Feby/ I promise to pay James C. Johnston Guardian of Joseph Blount[1] or his order two thousand five hundred dollars value rec^{d} Witness my hand & seal this 17th day of Febry. 1829.—

[*seal*]

---

[1]Possibly this refers to a son of Joseph Blount of Windsor.

Ebenezer Pettigrew to James Cathcart Johnston UNC

Bonarva on Lake Phelps March 30, '29

My dear Sir,

I have at length succeeded in geting the Clapboards & also have had the uncommon good luck to get a vessil to take them on board for you the very day after they are ready. They will be deliver to you by my partner in the vessel, Capt. John Dunbar, who goes to Edenton in his former small vessil, under the customhouse arraingments. Expecting that you may probably be from home, I have agreed to settle the freight of the boards with him. I hope you will find /them/ good. So far as I have seen them, I think them uncommonly fine. I expect they are in number about 2500, which will be about the quantity wanted.

I addressed a letter to you about a fortnight ago by Mr Collins in answer to yours of 17th Feb. inclosing my note to you for $2500 which I presume you have received. In that answer I made some reply to your kind & friendly advise on the subject of vessil building, all which I received with the pleasing knowledge of its coming from my best friend. Had I received it in time it should unquestionably have had its due weight, but my partner the Captain had then gone to Beaufort, for carpenters, and the most of the materials were in the yard, consequently there was no backing or turning. The Keel is laid, the stern, sternpost & frames are up, the spars are got & so far we are going on well. I am pleassed with the master workman and the other hands hired from Beaufort seven in number appear to be good. I feel highly flattered by your remark, that I look before I leap, that I allways consider well what I am going to do and farther that I always get through successfully, all my undertakings. Whether I succeed from good luck or from other causes I leave the /world/ judge. I well know that by patience & persevierance almost anything can be done. I can assure you that the most unremiting exertion will be used in this case. I have this consolation, which is a great stimulous in undertakings at the advanced stage of my experience, that I have never regreted or had cause to regret any thing of magnitude which I have undertaken to do. I have found my works to answer my fullest expectations and what is still important in the extreme to my pecuniary circumstances, they have been profitable so far as could be tested. I have never borrowed money without its being useful to my interest, and I have a strong hope that in four years, when I shall be fifty years old which is the time I have laid out to quit work, that I shall be clear /of/ the world and have a snug interest for my family, when I shall be no more in this vale of tears. When I look at the margin of the Lake, my opperations on the Creek, my canal and the buildings & machinery on it, which are four great works for a man of my resourses, and when I think how dependant I was before these things were done I cannot but thank God that he gave me the power & rejoice that I have had the will to engage in them. However I must bear in mind that the Pitcher cannot go to the fountain so often but it may be broken, and that I may be stranded at last. Under this knowledge I hope I shall never presume too much on my former success or my energy. I very much approve of your plan as respects the canal boat & the Norfolk trade, but you have an advantage over me in that respect. Some of your plantations are on & others are convenient to the river which the canal connects with Norfolk and other of your plantations [*torn*] great rout which will command steam boat conveyance, while I live out of the way and cannot yet command any of those conveniences. Have you ever seen the months of Feb. & March more inhospitable or vegitation more backward. My wheat crop looks tolerable considering circumstances; the fear of frost cannot be entertained and having confidence in the land, I flatter myself with a good crop. With the quantity of rain and my ditches runing into the Savanna & thereby conveying the water from it into my canal, I have been but above water. The Lake is now at a good sawing point and I am taking the advantage of it by loosing no time with the mill. We have all suffered with bad colds & several violent attacks of croup but we are now all well except poor James who is again visited as violent as ever with St vitas dance. Please to give our respects to your Sisters and assure yourself of my sincere Esteem & regard

E Pettigrew

James C. Johnston Esqr.

[*Addressed*] James C Johnston Esqr
Hayes
near Edenton

*James Cathcart Johnston to Ebenezer Pettigrew** UNC

Hayes. 1st April. 1829.—

My Dear Sir

Capt Dunbar has just now handed me your letter <of the 30th> and is now delivering the boards for which I am extremely obliged to you, they came unexpected for the slight hint I gave you that I wanted them had past from my <mind recolle> memory tho' it appears to have remained on yours, an eviden/ce/ not only of your disposition to serve me but of your efficience & promptitude in action. <Many person> /Some persons/ are very much disposed to serve their friend, if it they could do so without exertion /or/ inconvenience and a great many are not capable of exertion even to assist themselves but lean upon any thing that will support them for the moment so on from day to day until at last they are left prostrate without property without friends & alas too often without character—this is <generally> /always/ the fate of men without energy. and self dependence. I have a great talent for moralizing that a few cypress boards should excite it.—I am sorry that I said so much about the vessel not because you <have not abandond> /persevere/ but because I now think that I was half wrong & that you are half right and it is much better to be half right than half wrong—I know you will attribute what I said to the true motive & no other,—the warm interest I feel in your welfare & concerns. You might with great justice have retaliated on me for preparing to build a mill.—a cursed sort of property.—but what is a man to do when he cant get a hoe cake much less a biscuit to eat.—In July

August Sep^{t} & Octr last I had to send constantly twenty miles to get bread for near two hundred mouths.—I calculate on Mr Woodley to do my work on Roanoke Relying on your recommendation and have deferred commencing <oper> active operations until the 1st of July /in the mean time/ the timber will be all got ready for immediate use I have already during the winter gotten 200 cypress stocks 175 oak D^{o} ash & elm hickory & dog wood for the running gear & any castings I may want can be readyly got from Petersburg.—you will by that time have finished your vessel shipt your wheat & laid by your corn and I hope I shall have the pleasure of your company & advice /on the spot/ on which last I think you are in my debt and you shall have a far opportunity of paying in full.—And I shall have the mortification of Shewing /you/ a plantation just the reverse of your snug & neat farm.—large & extinsive but ragged & tattered in some places bare to the skin and almost to the bone. looking very muc[h] like those splendid old mansions in virginia with pillo[w]s, red flannel petticoats & old hats for dead lights in the windows—but I /am/ just about striping off all the old rags and putting on a new suit & I hope in a year or two to make it look as spruce & clean as our negroes do at Christmas when they have on their new clothes. I am just or / organizing a corp of internal improvement of about 30 prime hands to be under my own <com> immediate command to have nothing to do with the crop but to be employed entirely in improving I shall make it a kind of legion of honor.—but woe! I am galloping my hobby too hard. for your comfort.—Can'^{t} you make it convenient to slip over here one or two days <during> next week.—I should be very glad to see you & there is to be great sales of property but I doubt no bargains—the same negroes you saw sold this tim[e] last year will again occupy the same place in the court yard.—I knew /it/ then just as well as I know it now I will not /now/ be the cause of your leaving your business with the expectation of buying as [*torn*] but should be much pleased to see you particularly as I <know not when I shall ha> <shall not be> /<can not>/ shall not be able to <see you> /do so/ before July if not now.—It would perhaps be well to come over & see how things go perhaps it may not be time thrown away.—I send you a <bull> calf of an excellent breed he is not as likely as he ought to be for my overseer has not attended to him so much as the severity of the season required but with a little nursing he will be a fine animal,—

most sincerely your friend
Ja. C. Johnston.

Charles Biddle Shepard to Ebenezer Pettigrew A&H

New Bern NC May 30th 1829

My dear Sir,

If those only, who are able to write interesting letters, were allowed to handle their pens, the post-office-revenue would be a meager one & I, among thousands of others, would be doomed to Keep my thoughts to myself. But thanks to the free government under which we live, every one can write as much as he wishes, what he wishes, & to whom he wishes, even if the only object be the gratification derived from inter course with an absent friend—

The town has been exceedingly gloomy for the last three weeks & I had a *real* apprehension that coffin-hand bills would be necessary or rather that the dissolution would be too speedy even to *strike them off* Van Boklin & White have failed in N York. The news arrived at night & had an archangel summoned us all to *heaven* the good people could not have been more astonished We are, however, recovering from the fright, since the merchants, have discovered that, with one or two exceptions, they are *debtors* & not *creditors* to the bankrupts.

We lately had an interesting law-case decided in our court. James Stanly[1] was Wright's Stanly's security on several notes in the New Bern-Bank. At last W. gets him to sign a note of $10.000, with a view, as J. *asserts* but does not *prove*, to take up the old notes, & have /all/ the <whole notes> /debts/ embraced in one large one. W. did not do it but applied the money to other purposes. Therefore J. says that he ought to be released from the debt. Badger from Raleigh came to appear for J. Stanly & the bank was "cast." A more unjust decision never was declared in a court of justice. It only shows <the spici> that the hostility of the people against the banks is so great that it cannot be restrained even when they are acting as jurors under the obligation of an oath.

A few days ago, I was invited to spend a day or two at Burgwyn's plantation.[2] I visited old Po[ll]ock's[3] farm that contains 3.000. acres of cleared ground. There were five acres of sugar. There was nothing very remarkable or beautiful in the appearance of the plant. The cane is put in the soil, three or five inches below the surface, in a horizontal direction & the sprouts shoot from the joints. Last year he planted an acre in sugar. Part of the cane planted this year was the product of that acre & part he got from Savannah. The former is equally as good as the latter That the sugar-crop may prove profitable I sincerely wish.

Fredk, we hear, has gone to Tennessee & John is a judge in Florida. The latter has not written a single line since his elevation to the bench. Whether dignity or want of time be the cause I cannot say.

Mama is going to Hillsboro' in a few weeks. She can't think of parting with James so soon—

With the hope that little James is recovering & the remainder of the family in good health

I remain
Your aff. Brother
C Shepard.

Give my love to Sister Nancy & Aunt Pettigrew

[*Addressed*]
E Pettigrew Esqr
Cool Spring
NC.

[1]This was probably James Green Stanly (1783-1858), a lawyer who served as clerk of court for fifty years. He was brother to John Stanly and cousin to Wright C. Stanly. Gertrude S. Carraway, *The Stanly (Stanley) Family and the Historic John Wright Stanly House* (New Bern: Tryon Palace Commission, 1969), 21-22.

[2]Shepard probably refers to John Fanning Burgwyn (1783-1864), a wealthy merchant who owned plantations in Craven and Jones counties. Powell, *DNCB*, I, 277-278.

[3]George Pollock (1772-1836), the son of Thomas and Eunice Edwards Pollock, was a wealthy plantation owner and half brother to Sarah Pierrepoint Hunt Burgwyn, the wife of John Fanning Burgwyn. Beth G. Crabtree and James W. Patton (eds.), *"Journal of a Secesh Lady": The Diary of Catherine Ann Devereux Edmondston, 1860-1866* (Raleigh: Division of Archives and History, Department of Cultural Resources, 1979), xviii, hereinafter cited as Crabtree and Patton, *"Journal of a Secesh Lady."*

Ebenezer Pettigrew to James Cathcart Johnston UNC

Bonarva on Lake Phelps June 5, 1829

My dear sir,

I received your favour of Ap 1st by Capt Dunbar together with the Bull for which please to accept my sincere thanks, he is a fine looking animal and I have no doubt will be a great acquisition to my stock, of which the severity of the past winter has made a considerable diminution. I am far from thinking your mill speculation a wild one. I know, no mill that the building would cost too much when the owner had as much use for it as you have. Though my mouths are but few to feed, comparitively speaking yet if mine cost five times as much as it did, the convinience is so great I would have it. At the time of the sale you mention it was not in my power to go to Edenton, I had engaged Dr Warren to go, but his business did not permit. I regret not having the pleasure to see you also the loss of bargins, but all is for the best. I approve of your corp of internal improvement, you will find them I think pay as much or more than if in the crop. My corn is very promising I think more so than last year, it never stood better, and I have not yet seen any chince bugs. I have 103 acres planted. My wheat may be called a fair crop. A part of it suffered from the wet in the winter & spring, and the youngest of it is some blasted by a spell of rain while in the blossom yet I think it will avarage 25 bus. I must begin to harvest next week. From the appearance of the weather I fear a wet and of course a troublesome one, but I have never lost any wheat yet from unfavourable harvests.

Our vessil will be compleated at farthest in three weeks. The Captain is now in Baltimore geting the sails riging & iron work, as soon as he returns she will be lauchėd riged and then loaded, which I hope will be between the 1 & 5 of July. I shall then proceed in her to Edenton for the purpose of taking out the necessary papers, when I hope to have the pleasure of seeing you, and I hope my business & family will permit me at that time to take with you the contemplated trip, in the interim I should be very glad to see you here. Mr Woodley has been closely employed on the Creek, and there has been a great deal of mud taken out, a vessil drawing 6 ft is able to load at my upper thoroughfare at common tide.

I have learned that Messrs V Bokkelen & White have failed under very unfavourable circumstances to their character, I sold a draft on thim dated 15th April to the Branch Bank U. States at Norfolk. I hope it was paid as I have heard nothing from it. It was at sight. I shipped about 4 weeks ago mine and my mothers little last years crop of wheat to Baltimore and am informed that it nets nearly a dollar. I have not yet sold my last years crop of corn, having reserved it for the second voyage of our vessil. I observe it is advancing and I hope by that time it will command a tolerable price.

Mrs Pettigrew joins me in best respects to your sisters and please to assure yourself of Esteem & regard of your friend

E Pettigrew

James C Johnston Esqr

[*Addressed*] James C. Johnston Esqr
Hayes

Ebenezer Pettigrew to John Herritage Bryan UNC

Lake Phelps Sep. 1, 1829

My dear Sir,

Your favour of 24th June came safe to hand & I believe I was at that time in your debt a letter received from Washington. I cannot give as an apology and be honest the heat of the weather, for such apparent neglect, as long as I can ride a dub horse under the saddle 42 miles in one of the hottest days of august, without experiencing any inconvenience after it, but I will say that untill a short time my mind has been so much occupied with a multiplicity of business the very reverse of letter writing that it has been too much labour. I know your liberality will receive this as sufficient apology.

I had the good fortune to draw on V Bokkelen & White at sight about six weeks before he failed, in favour of the United States Bank at Norfolk. I have heard nothing from it since. I feel a great deal of compassion for the helpless part of the stock holders in the Banks but when those who could have the business otherwise, would permit Stevens to remain in office as long as he did, What must we say? Could anyone who knew the concerns of the Bank or the movements of Stevens doubt for a moment that he was a perfectly useless being in it and that he would be (in the refined language of the present refined age) a large defalter. What in old times would be called thief. We know that Stevens is not alone by almost all the rest.[1] There has not been honesty enough found for a number of years past to justify a bank, and I very much fear that the Legislature in the plenitude of their folly will make one exclusively belonging to the State, which will be nothing more than a nursery for theives, but in the language of this polished age *Defalters*. I fear you will think me blood thirsty, but in this day of extravagance, who can be trusted with money? Witness John Haywood[2] & German Baker. If they did not waste, they permited their families. They both deserved the same death. If there is not more work & less extravagance, all confidence will be destroyed.

I shall expect the horses from Mrs Shepard, to drag my dear wife to visit her relations. I am much obliged for your attention to the Sugar cane. I shall be prepaired for it, though I have had but one opinion on the subject of agriculture in this climate & particular soil, which is that wheat & corn juditiously divided are the most profitable. I have in partnership with a Capt. Dunbar, built a vessil this spring of about 63 tons burden She is on her second voyage to Boston, with a load of my corn. The first was with a load of my wheat to New York which commanded a tolerable price.

Mrs Pettigrew recived a letter by the last mail from her Sister Mrs Bryan, informing her of the birth of another fine son [*James*

Pettigrew Bryan] also his name. I am gratified at the good opinion expressed in that name, at the same time I fear that at some future day, there may be cause to change it, for we are all [*torn*] imperfect beings. We congratulate you & your better half on the event, but really I fear we shall be too numerous to thrive. However there is yet an immense unoccupied territory in the United States. Mrs P. and children are tolerable at present she sends her Love to her sister, Please to give mine & assure yourself of my Esteem.

E Pettigrew

John Bryan Esqr

[*Addressed*] Hon. John H. Bryan
Newbern
North Carolina

---

[1]Historical accounts, newspapers, and biographies have been searched unsuccessfully for information on the bank fraud or embezzlement.

[2]John Haywood (1744-1827) served as state treasurer for forty years, beginning in 1787. In 1819 he was accused of dishonest practices, and at the time of his death his accounts were short almost $70,000. Ashe, *Biographical History*, VI, 282, 283, 285; Hugh Talmage Lefler and Albert Ray Newsome, *North Carolina: The History of a Southern State* (Chapel Hill: University of North Carolina Press, third edition, 1973), 319, hereinafter cited as Lefler and Newsome, *North Carolina*; Daniel Miles McFarland, "North Carolina Newspapers, Editors, and Journalistic Politics, 1815-1835," *North Carolina Historical Review*, XXX (July, 1953), 390.

Charles Biddle Shepard to Ebenezer Pettigrew A&H

New Bern NC. Oct. 26. 1829

My dear Sir,

Your long-expected letter came to hand at Hillsboro' when I was on the eve of a departure to the Western part of the State. It should have been answered before this time but I had hoped that my trip would have furnished something new & interesting to communicate & therefore I have delayed so agreeable a duty to this period. I have visited the celebrated gold-mines,[1] that are attracting hundreds of capitalists from all parts of the country & not a small number of persons who were governed by the same motive as myself—curiosity. Many are amassing vast fortunes & some, I fear, are losing them. one man obtains daily $100 from the labour of four hands; others $5, <a pei> from each labourer & some $1. Nothing but the mines is talked of in the West & there is scarcely a man, who is not engaged in them, in [some w]ay or other, either, as lessor, lessee, buyer, seller, or search[er.] In most of them the ore is <of a generally ne> a kind [of] gravel or rock; this is pounded & ground with water & quicksilver, the former [of] which carries off the dirt whilst the latter adheres to the gold & sinks with it to the bottom of the vessel in which the stones are used.

I was very much pleased with the country. It is far superior to the one in which I live. It is healthier, the soil is richer, the mass of the people better clothed, fed & more intelligent than those who live in the neighbourhood of Athens. But it is never the less not to be compared to the Lake-Country. I have never seen such noble growth as that which you can boast of nor such a farm as the one of which you are master. My companion, Col Jones[2] of Hillsboro' formerly of Halifax, is a farmer & whenever an opportunity occurred, I would dilate on the beauty & richness of Lake-Phelps.

We returned to New Bern on 19th inst. Mama thought it best that the horses should have a little rest before they were sent to you. If convenient, she wishes you to help Bill on his way homeward as he is a poor walker. Probably you could Send him as far as Washington. We are in hopes that we shall see Sister Nancy & yourself & family in a short tim[e.] We are always glad to see our brothers & sis[ters] but we shall be particularly so at present, [for] a great revival, among the religious folks in New Bern, has thrown a gloom over the town & I really wish to see some one who can enjoy a laugh without thinking he has committed a sin. old *Madam MAE* has been converted. Divers others have given up the pomp & vanity of this life to become—I was about to say hypocrites but I will be more charitable. However we will talk over these matters when we meet. Mama & the family join me in love to yourself & Sister Nancy & beg me to say they are anxiously expecting you. Believe me your aff. Brother

Ch. Shepard.

[*Addressed*] E. Pettigrew Esqr
Cool Spring
Washington Co.

---

[1]The presence of gold in North Carolina was known shortly after 1800, and mining became extensive after 1825. Mining camps sprang up in Burke and McDowell counties and a gold rush was on by 1829. In 1837 the federal government established a branch mint in Charlotte that operated until 1871. Samuel A'Court Ashe, *History of North Carolina* (Greensboro: Charles L. Van Noppen, 2 volumes, 1925), II, 306, hereinafter cited as Ashe, *History of North Carolina.* For more information on gold mining in the state see Richard F. Knapp, *Golden Promise in the Piedmont: The Story of John Reed's Mine* (Raleigh: Division of Archives and History, Department of Cultural Resources, 1975), and Fletcher Melvin Green, "Gold Mining: A Forgotten Industry of Ante-Bellum North Carolina," *North Carolina Historical Review*, XIV (January and April, 1937), 1-19, 135-155.

[2]Cadwallader Jones (1787-1861), a native of Virginia, was an alumnus of Warrenton Academy. After serving in the navy and as an army officer, he lived in Halifax. Jones moved to Hillsborough and sat frequently on the state board of internal improvements. Henderson, *North Carolina*, I, 563, II, 54; Hamilton and Williams, *Graham Papers*, V, 225n.

Charles Lockhart Pettigrew to Mary Lockhart Pettigrew UNC

Hillsborough 18 Dec 1829

Dear /grand/ Mama

I take this opportunity of writing you a few lines we arrived at Newbern on the evening of the third day after we left your house and remained there two days and we got to Raleigh on the third day there my Papa showed me and my brothers the statue of general Washington and there we me with uncle James Shepherd he stayed there two days and started in the stage to Newbern we went to the circus two night and saw a little boy make a summerset over seven horses and two nights to the theatre and saw some very pretty plays acted and /varius/ songs and amongths them was cold black rose sung we stayed five days in Raleigh and set out for Hillsborough on sunday morning and we had not got five miles before my Papa evedently discovered that Richmond was founderd very bad I like Mr Bingham tolerable well my Papa set out from here the day after he came here all of us sends our love to you

your affectionate grandson
Charles L Pettigrew

[*Addressed*] Mrs Mary Pettigrew
Cool Spring pst.
Washington Co.
N.C.

Ebenezer Pettigrew to Ann Blount Pettigrew UNC

Lake Phelps Dec 27, 1829

My dear wife

The greatest pleasure which I can have on this earth when seperated from my sweet Girl is to converse with her through the quill, a pleasure which I had expected to enjoy on Christmas day, but settling with Mr Davis[1] & then intruders as likewise yesterday have prevented untill today.

I wrote you from Plymouth on monday evening; the next day seting out very early I got to Mothers before 12 & to breakfast, and to the Lake before night. I found my mother well and disposed to employ Stubbs, another year, a thing I shall not object to. I go out there tomorrow for the purpose of settling with him. I shall then have mother to employ whom she pleases. I understand but it is as usual kept a secret that the night after we left, mother fainted and was apparently dead an hour, before she came too. My authority is good.

When I arrived at home Mr Davis was about winding up salting pork, we have a fine parcel, and though it has been warm since I hope there will be none spoiled. Mr D. says it was well rubed, & they have used more salt than in former years. Mrs Warrington & our dear little children were and had been quite well, they seem to be very contented, though little Mary says she wants to see her Ma, & brothers, you /know/ Henry is satisfied if he can see Mrs W. who is eaqually kind to Mary. As well as a quantity of pork, you have three barrils of fat.

I think Mr Davis has been has been very busy since I left he had got not only that part of the Bee Tree which was in wheat two years ago, ploughed up but all that where the potatoes had been planted, amounting to 70 acres, and counting the middle field makes one hundred acres. He also had got all the pines as welll as reeds that were in the Bee Tree cut down, at the same time keeping the mill going, though it has been dry the Lake is about the height it was when we left. I think Mr Davis a worthy fellow & disposeed to do something in this world; his business obliged him to leave me for the present, but he has agreed to commence the next year after the first day of Feb. He wanted more wages but would undertake for the old price, however I thought that $2.50 per month was nothing to be well served also knowing that if you want good servants pay them well I agreed with him for $15 p^r m. I can make out very well the next month, but my dear sons being gone, also my heath I thought, demanded (howevr enegetic my mind might be) some person to assist me, and knew no one who would suit me so well. His fine constitution, his sobriety, his strict attention, are great recommendations, and indispensible to me. M^r [*Nathan A.*] Brickhouse had quite recovered, and had both the houses that were raised before you left finished, he /is/ now gone home, but expects to return in a week. I think him right smart.

One of Lidia's son Joe had been very sick with flux & Mrs Warrington sent for the Doctor, but he was too sick to come, he however came the day before Christmas & went away next morning. I learned from Dr W. that he had been very ill, with something of his old complaint & cold from exposure. Previous to his sickness he was at the Lake & Mrs C. /(the old gentleman was one also)/ invited him & Mrs W. particularly to dine, to which they attended. And such stile the D^r says he has before seen in a few instances, but such as I have never heard of, and such luxury of wines as I am sure I shall never be engaged in; They /the C.s/ were very clever, as much so /as/ it was possible Though they dined at 3^oc they had coffee & the Doctor & M^rs went to Mothers that night, having left Edward there. All this needs no comment from me. I am an independant man. The young man & wife are expected tomorrow.

Moffat is dead. Poor creature! I forgive him, I was not with the [suit], because he steals my pelf, but how can I forgive the wretch who would ruin my character & thereby my happiness in my family forever. I would not live a /day/ longer than my companion had the most perfect confidence in my virtue & honesty & truth. Nor do I believe I could take [to my armes] one who did not posses those qualities in an eminent degree, I thank my God though a wicked sinner that he has had me under his fostering care unto the present day. Untill I returned home my old complaint was much better, the Doctor say from the diaria & discharge of blood, I had some pain yesterday & the day before, but yesterday I drank an infusion of Sasafras & Bay bark root, (a prescription of my own) and was better last night & today. I think the disease originates in the kidneys. I was much disappointed in not geting a letter from you last mail. You see I have filled the paper & have but room to ask you to give my respects to your Ma & family & assure you of the warmest feelings of your Husband

E Pettigrew

Dec 28. I am just informed that Capt. D. was in the storm of Nov. 27. and had to scud 3 days, in all which time the Lady of the Lake behaved well he is now in Aligator river, [not] very well himself

[*Addressed*] Mrs Ann B Pettigrew
Newbern N.C

---

[1]As this letter indicates, Ebenezer employed Davis as an overseer. Seven Davis families are listed in Tyrrell and Washington counties in the *1830 Census Index*, 46-48.

Ann Blount Pettigrew to Ebenezer Pettigrew UNC

Newbern December 31st 1829

Dear Husband

I received your letter from Plymouth with great pleasure, I was sorry to understand that you had been so sick, it was very fortunate you procured the laudnum, I am gratified also that you have placed the Boys so comfortably. I had a letter from William last week he said they were well—Johnston has been very sick with the vomiting and purging, I tried various simples which did not succeed and I sent for Doct— Boyed who gave him a dose of calomel, since I have been giving him stimulents & charcoal and he is much better—his sickness prevented my going to church on Christmas day and as that was the day for administering the sacrement I regretted it—I saw the ornaments of the Church after—the dressing was more splendid that you can immagine wreathes of evergreens festooned in the most beautiful manner, gilt letters on crimson appropriate to the occasion—also a dove made of wax was suspended over the Pulpit, which fell down the day before & was broken—

I am as well as one can expect to be who eats heartily & takes no exercise, before one can walk in town it is necessary to dress & that is sufficient to prevent me—Mrs Mc K—— has returned from the wedding after many hairbreadth escapes <of> /from/ head winds, rainy weather etc—. there were four gentlemen from Richmond & every thing that was great and good—she also investigated poor Frederick's rencontre with Holloway by inquiring of Mr Sawyer from Pasquotank who says he acted honorably & justifyably—the story was circulated through the country much to his prejudice—I fear he has quite too much impetuosity of temper for his good—

I was invited to a party at Mrs Smyths but did not go—not having much desire for such amusements, Mrs Armstead begins to break a little, but is as gay as a lark—

Through the vigilence of the Bank the Stanly negroes are coming from Norfolk, the old man [*John Stanly*] has been very ill—speechless four days so they say they say he is a child in intellect & therefore is not reproachble for any thing that is done. but it is believed he knew nothing of this affair untill after & that caused the paralisis—he frequently cries immoderaly—James & Right Stanly's reputation suffers much for their conduct—I shall be ready to return the first of Feby I long to see you dear Husband & the dear children—kiss them for me give my love to your Mother & Mrs W—

Ma & family send their regards to you

believe me as ever your aff. wife
Ann B Pettigrew

[*Addressed*] Mr E Pettigrew
Cool Spring
Washington County

Ebenezer Pettigrew to Ann Blount Pettigrew UNC

Lake Phelps Jan 5, 1830

I rejoice to see another week roal round that I may have the double pleasure of conversing with my sweet Wife again. I congratulate you on the commencment of a new year may it be <to us> a year of rational pleasure, to us both, is the prayer of your affectionate Husband. It gave me pain to learn in your kind letter of the 23d (which I received by the last mail) that you had been sick, but the same conveyance informed me that you were better; I hope your health is restored, and that you will take all necessary precaution against a return of that dangerous disease. I should have been pleased to learn whether my *Lovely wife*, was in the situation which we both suspected.

In regard to the Rians, I believe I have informed you in a former letter, but I will again say, that I gave Mr Hog[1] a $50 fee & requested him to defend me against, Dave [*David Ryan*] whose suit is in the sup[rime] court; John's [*Ryan*] is in Bertie yet[2] & I must employ yet another lawyer Mr H. being employed in his case. I hope from Mr Hogs statement, at any rate, not to be obiged to pay more than I have received of the estate say $1500 but there is a chance for me to get clear. You will say nothing of the amount.

The continued show & dash of those who are insolvants, may be compaired to a candle in the socket. Just before it sinks it brims up with more brilincy, sinks and is no more seen. There will be a dash with the sums perloined from creditors untill it is extinguished, and then they will sink to be no more seen, unless some fortunate het may set them going again.

I very much pity Mr Stanly, but except his infirmity, with his course he must expect the like. It is the natural consequence of extravagance & the manner of raising children.

I believe I wrote you that I had placed our dear children at Mr Bingams, very much to my satisfaction. I got a letter by the last mail from Charles written on the day I left. He writes as though they were all very well satisfied.

On the day I wrote you last I went to Mothers to settle with Stubbs, after which I left her to employ who she pleased. Stubbs, Jordan Phelps, young Clayton, and Jack Hathaway, were candidates and who do you think she chose? who do you think? Why Jack Hathaway. I have nothing to say on that subject now. Old Mrs Peterson, just went from Mothers the day I passed to her house from [Gi]bbs. I have reason to believe that the object of her visit, was to get in there with her Husband but the poor old Lady, had resolution enough to resist that move.

With regard to my self, I have some times been a little better and then again the same. After settling with Stubbs as above I went to Doctr Warrens, and he showed me a book, giving my case precisely, which rather depressed my spirits, but we must bear up with the ills of this life with firmness. He says mine is a mild case and he has taken me in hand in good earnest. I am now restricted the use of meat, and all grease, also from walking. He applys camphor & vinigar, and I drink the infusion of Bay & Sasafras bark root, which I have great confidence in. He says if these remedies will not cure, I must be laid on my back for a month & <undergo> /be/ Salivated. And I say from the book, that /if that/ will not cure, You know the next. It is not necessary for me to say how much I feel and who most for, and if any act of mine had caused it, I know not what I should do with my self. My dear wife I have not words to express the pleasure which I have always had at your reasonable gratification. And I now declare to you that I am willing to be sacrificed for your happiness, for a sweeter & more deserving woman does not exist. My indisposition while coming home & my low living has lessened my flesh, you frequently speak of the hardness of my hands but, I think they look much more boney than then. My general health is now pretty good & my thinness arises from abstinance. If my situation will permit I shall come for you but I may even be geting /well/ and still be prevented, pray do not be alarmed in that case untill you learn from the servant the facts of the case. Mrs Warrington sends her complements to you Mrs B. & Ma. She & our dear little children are well, Henry had two days last week a cold with considerable fever, but got well with simples. Doctr Warren was informed by his brother t[*torn*] Vaiden had sailed for New Orleans, and that Frederick [*torn*] going but his eyes were so bad, that he had to stop.

I understand from J. Haughton[3] that Mr C[*lement*]. Blounts[4] creditors have made a sale on him to the amount of about $2000. In which they sold his crop of corn, his household furniture, & 4 or 5 of his negroes. These executions [were] levied before the deed in trust. Haughton says he owes more and that the creditors are determined to rush through the deed in Trust. Capt Dunbar has been to see me. he has been doing something to a profit. I expect him on the 20th to take a load of corn from me. Lidia had a daughter on the 3rd Inst. All well The Collins' have not yet made their appearance since Christmas. There is to be tonight at Mr J. Haughtons a ball. The company are invited from Edenton, Plymouth & a select few in the country, among them myself, /among/ my importuners to go is Dr W. but I shall decline it. I am sincerely your aff. H.

E Pettigrew

[*Addressed*] Mrs Ann B. Pettigrew
Newbern N. Carolina

---

[1]Gavin Hogg, an 1807 graduate of the University of North Carolina, practiced law in Bertie County. He moved to Raleigh, where he lived at the time of this letter, and worked with James Iredell and William H. Battle to prepare the *Revised Statutes of the State of North Carolina*. Hogg "had a large practice and a wide reputation" as an attorney. Battle, *History of the University*, I, 182.

[2]The suits probably concerned the will of Dr. John Beasley; Ebenezer was an executor of the will. See Ann Blount Pettigrew to Mary Williams Bryan, September 24, 1827, note, in this volume.

[3]John Haughton was a friend of Ebenezer Pettigrew. He married Mary Hooker of Tyrrell County in 1809. Lemmon, *Pettigrew Papers*, I, 406n.

[4]Clement Hall Blount, brother of Dr. Frederick Blount and Sarah Porter Blount Fuller, was the son of James Blount and Ann Hall Blount of Mulberry Hill near Edenton. He was first cousin to Ebenezer Pettigrew. Lemmon, *Pettigrew Papers*, I, xvi. See also Ebenezer Pettigrew to Ann Blount Pettigrew, December 5, 1826, in this volume.

Ann Blount Pettigrew to Charles Lockhart and William Shepard Pettigrew UNC

Newbern January 6th 1830—

My Dear Children,

It is uncertain whether your uncle James will go up to Hillsborough or not as the Academy is now in such a flourishing state here, if he does not this letter will be carried by Mr George Jones a very amiable young gentleman whose friendship I wish you to cultivate. I shall enclose 4 dollars with which you must buy two umbrellas, cotton umbrellas are cheaper and more lasting. if there should not be money enough you can borrow from Mr Bingham or get him to advance. I hope my Dear children that you will take care of your health and characters, beware of doing a disgraceful action, strictly obey your Teacher and attend to your studies closely, and waste no time recollecting your Father has a large family of Children to provide for—you will see boys no doubt who will have a great deal of money to to waste—but it will not benefit them they would be better without it—take pains with your letters spell well—I know that James is a wild child but you must persuade him to do right and not expose every every little indiscretion of his—you must talk to him & tell him how he must act, he is very young & infirm in health—be sure & let us know if he has any sign of that disease returning—your Father was well when I heard from him—I expect to go home next month early—I shall write you /as/ soon as I get home—My dear sons, I am your affectionate mother

Ann Pettigrew.

Ask Mrs B. if she will please to <have> have your cloaks tucked—they are too long

[*Addressed*] Mr Charles & William Pettigrew,
Hillsborough,
No Carolina.

Ebenezer Pettigrew to Ann Blount Pettigrew UNC

Lake Phelps Jan. 11, 1830

Fearing that business or intruders may prevent me from writing as long a letter to my Dear wife as I wish, I have commenced the day before the mail, though I feel illy able from having been necessarily exposed all the morning to the cold air which is this morning more like winter than any thing I have seen before <this winter> since it came in. I hope it will continue and give a check to the wheat, which was geting too forward. We have had so far a delightfull winter for work. Though we have had very little rain the Lake keeps at such a hight as to saw, and thereby enables me to supply the timber for the new houses that are building. I last thursday evening went to mothers for the purpose of geting some more pine timber for the floor of the new house, (fearing that I had not enough) also some Hickory for rail mals & to smoke the bacon with, which employed me the remainder of the week, and I did not return home untill sunday evening, having stayed as it was quarte/r/ly meeting. I however did not stay at the Chapel long. The house was so much crouded that I did not think proper to go in & before 12 it began to rain; feeling very unwell I returned to mothers: On my return home I was taken, between the two gates in a squall, from the west in which I for a few minutes thought myself in great danger. The limbs flew & the trees bent over the carriage to no small alarm of the horses, but thank providence there was no injury.

Knowing that I had a certain quantity of work to do in a given time, I was up & out on Fryday morning before one could be distinguished ten feet, and went into the woods immediately to look for timber, I returned to breakfast late & then had to wait, I then to please the old Lady had to walk round her fence to see if it wanted mending, and to tell her overseer what to do, from which I returned about 12 compleatly exhausted, and in a conversation with her on my return as compensation for my fatigue was told that I took no interest in the concern. You may be certain that I was not behind in talking. I consider her totally unmanagable. There can be no doubt had it not been for me she at this day would not be worth one dollar. The next day I was also in the woods very early, and returned to breakfast, after which I think I had a chil, succeeded by fever, since which time my old complaint has been more painful, though better today than yesterday. I adhere strictly to the regimen in my former letter. I have hope, but, sometimes am very desponding. My sweet Girl my own pleasures are but a drop to the ocean, when in comparison to one I love so much; I last night heard the clock strike 4, and concluded that I would spend the remainder of the night in contemplating my dear Nancy. There is so little energy in my system that I cannot be kept warm /in bed/ by all the blankets I can put on.

I understand that the old Squires /or young Squires/ ball was an abation, The Doctor who was before anxious that I should go, says now, that he was glad I did not. Doct[r] Lewis came there drunk, & M[r] Dickinson in dancing fell down & put his wrist out of place, I understand it is useless yet. They invited what they would call the grandees from a distance & but few came. It was all hands dance a six handed reel & change partners & dance again. I left at Mothers yesterday The Elder & M[r] Bell, M[rs] Spelman & little girl old M[rs] Forlaw & [Lidy]. Her overseer is really a poor Bitch.

It is with regret I inform you that the Messrs Turners have failed, it is said for 30,000, dollars. I am not surprised, their business was with negroes, and their lenity of sentiment & no doubt of conduct, would in time break any one. I went on thursday to mothers in a flat, and as I passed Dan. Woodleys, William Woodley was there & I missed him, he however went to the lake & next day cut the [saw], & in the evening came to mothers, where he staid untill sunday morning. He was very sick with bilious complain in the Christmas & left one of M[r] Johnstons' overseers dangerously ill. He says th[ere] is no comparison between the health of where he is now & the Lake, the latter is so much to be prefered.

Jan 12. Though your poor old husband has but the remains of a shattered frame he was up this morning at 6 oclock which by refering to the Almanack, you will find is more than an hou[r] before sunrise. I had no fever yesterday, and this morning [fee]l tolerable well, though my pulse cannot b[*torn*] My dearest Girl, Although my frame is a wreck, the energy of my mind & warmth of soul is not in the slightest degree impaired. I have all I ever had.

I learn from Ben that M[r] J. Collins jun & Lady stayed at mothers last night, after an absence of 4 weeks wanting a day. Hogs not killed. Overseer not engaged. &c &c. This [needs] nothing [from /me./]

M[rs] Warrington & our dear little children are quite well and very happy, they are very fond of M[rs] W. & she is alike kind to both of them I believe they slept with her last night.

I am in high hopes of geting a letter today to learn of yours and our dear little boys health in the mean time assure yourself of the unfeigned Love of your Husband

E Pettigrew

Pray excuse this miserable scratch

M[rs] A. B. Pettigrew

[*Addressed*] M[rs] Ann B. Pettigrew
New Bern N.C

Charles Lockhart Pettigrew to Ebenezer Pettigrew UNC

Hillsborough Feb 16 1830

Dear Father

I received your letter last night about 9 oclock the stage coming latter then than usual I suppose on account of the bad weather. I was very sorry to hear that you were unwell so long and sepent your time so lonely I know it is very trying to you who have spent so much of your time there so happily when you contrast them you can look at one with pleasure and the other with regret and I am very glad to hear that you were a greadeal better, and that your overseer suited you so well he is then without dou<gh>/b/t of great service to you since he attends to your business so well I was very glad to hear the negroes behaved so very well which saves you from a great quantity of trouble both corporal and mental which if you had to endure would put you in a fever ever time you were vexed by them you being at present in such a state of health. I received the sum of money which was stated in your letter and was very thankful to for it /and/ for striving hard to send us to school up here decenly. I am at /present/ studying Virgil and smiths arithmetic that being <the> one, of the most improved editions of the time I study that in the place of greek I will soon be through it and will begin geometry. Virgil is very interesting if you get a clear view of the subject. We have tripping in our class which makes the boys very emulous and striving to out do eachother they take the same places in virgil as when they recite <vig> greek and therefore they do not like my taking my p/l/ace in virgil because they say I ought to foot every day because I have nothing to do but to get the virgil but there /they are/ mistaken because all the time they appropriate to greek I get my Arithmetic Mr Bingham wants me to go on as fast as I can. Brother William has joined the polemic sciety which is a very useful institution they have bought some books they have a pretty good little library which the boys who belong to the society use /which/ at their pleasure, it a debateing society and improves the mind very much because they all have to make a speech of their own composition on the subject selected for discussion, it has greatly improved within a few weeks because Mr Bingham has compeled althose thwelve and over that (that being the age they are ad<d>mitted to become regular members of the society) to join Mr Bingham formerly had monitors but the members of the society have formed a law <to> after this manner that ever <person> /boy/ should be reported to the society who did not behave himself discretely shal be fined some sume at their discression they have monitor to report to them, Mr Bingham took this instead of making them give their seals and words to him they would return and consid miself in duty bound to report fathfully, and I shall report for if I do not I shall be telling a story <I> and there fore I think I had better report and not tell a<l>lie which /if I did tell a liy/ would be distressing to my relations though I incur the dis pleasure of a few of my school mates. I have been a little indesposed for the last week brother William has been a little unwell but we are both very well now Mr Bingham will give you a full discription on the next page of Brother James's health

I am you dutiful and affectionate son
Charles L Pettigrew

Ebenezer Pettigrew to James Cathcart Johnston UNC

Lake Phelps March 9, 1830

My dear Sir,

I received your favour of 30 Jan. together with the axes & a quantity of baskets, for all which pl[ease] to accept my sincere thanks. I have no doubt the hoes will come in due time, as my time for ditching is after the crop is over. I set out on the 2nd of Feb. for Newbern to accompany Mrs Pettigrew home. I was caught there in the snow, and found when I arrived that the small Pox was in the place. In consequence of which I had to leave before the snow was off the ground, which made my trip the more disagreeable. The day I left the place I took a violent cold and have been confined several times to the bed & almost entirely to the house ever since. In the mean time my disease before mentioned grew worse & I have submited to two excessively painful opperations, on my urethra. The swelling still continues, though I think I am some better. You will I know say with me that this is serious sort of business, and needs a great share of fortitude. If I had not possessed fortitude or obstinacy like a Bull Dog, to resist the world, the flesh, the Devil & the People / people & every other obstacle that could present itself, I should long since, have sunk under their power; but so long as there is a shot in the locker, I will not give up the ship.

My business is going on better than could be expected I am in a great state of forwardness in the farm particularly when I am expecting to take in 75 Acres of new ground. I expect to begin to plant corn by the 25th and hope to plant 200 Acres. But Alas! If I have to visit Dr Phisic[1] this spring what will become of all these calculations? What is the use of the best constructed steam machinery without fire? All I can say is that I will do my best. I was surprised to learn that the former plantation of Messrs Iredell & Treadwell was in such order. Could any man have chosen more inefficient partners than Mr Iredell did? I have had a return from my shipment to Charleston. The cargo nets me $4.85 cts pr barril.

Mr Edmondston[2] sayd it was much liked & sold for from 4 to 5 cents more in the bushel than any other in market. My wheat looks finely & is out of danger from frost. I have a hope of a great crop. When I left Caledonia[3] last I looked as well as I could at the valey runing I think about Toms house, and from its appearance I would suggest the propriety of examining the ground well before I dug any more on the canal in that quarter. I do not pretend to know anything about, but I recollect you spoke of that vally. I have inquired & heard of no fresh on Roanoak [*River*] this winter since the first, & hope by or before this you are safe with the mill. I confidently expect to receive a visit from you this spring. You need not be afraid of my being from home when you come. If I should go to Philidelphia, you will be advised of in due time. If I go, I hope to be back by the first of may. Johnston has been at the point of death with Croup & then inflamitory fever, he is now toler[ably] recovered. Mrs Pettigrew & the other children who are with me are well, she sends her respects to you, & little Mary sends a kiss, though she would much prefer giving them in Propera Persona, being a kissing little girl. Please to assure yourself of the Esteem & regard of yours sincerely

E Pettigrew

Mr James C. Johnston

N.B. Please to give my compliment to Mr Woodley & tell him I will write him in short time.

[*Addressed*] James C. Johnston Esqr
Caledonea.
Halifax P. office
N. Carolina

---

[1]Philip Syng Physick (1768-1837) was a Philadelphia surgeon noted for his inventions of surgical instruments and procedures. A native of Pennsylvania, he had studied in London and Edinburgh. *DAB*, XIV, 554-555.

[2]Charles Edmondston (1782-1861) was born in Scotland and immigrated to Charleston, South Carolina, where he was a businessman and civic leader. His son Patrick Muir Edmondston married the daughter of Thomas Pollock Devereux (1793-1869), a North Carolina attorney and wealthy plantation owner, in 1846. Crabtree and Patton, *"Journal of a Secesh Lady,"* xi, xiii-xiv, xxi-xxiii.

[3]Caledonia plantation, located in Halifax County, was owned by James C. Johnston.

Ann Blount Pettigrew to Mary Williams Bryan A&H, BRYAN

Lake Phelps March 9th 1830

My Dear Sister,

I suppose you have heard of my arrival home, after suffering many useless apprehensions as to the difficulties we should meet with respecting having left a place infected with the small pox but fortunately we met with no detention, we seemed to excite no fears after we left the town of Washington, we spent a day at Mr Trotters— Mr Pettigrew was confined to the bed half the day, William Blount[1] & a young lady from Washington came to visit the family but seeing our carriage in the yard, they inquired and understood we were there, they immediately turned back home. this will give you an idea of the fear that pervaded the place—at Mr Trotters we were agreeably entertained found M & Mrs Wetherby[2] very clever, Mr[*s*] Wetherby spent 3 months last summer & fall travelling to the North she seems to have seen & recollected of what she did see a good deal, she there learnd to make a centre table, one of simple wood, painted black & covered with interesting prints, then highly varnished and rubbed, and it is really one of the prettiest & most interesting things I ever saw, I have heard them described before, and think them more suitable than Miss Smyth's elegant carved one covered with Albums. but enough of centre tables—

Since my return Henry has been sick with the croup, Johnston has been very ill with the same disease which was very distressing— you have no idea of a child choaking two or three days & taking emeticks all that time, your children are so healthy you have no idea of the trouble of them— Mr Pettigrew has been unwell ever since his return, but notwithstanding will be obliged to attend Bertie Court next week—Lake Phelps looks very pretty—green fields of wheat as far as the eye can reach so luxurient and refreshing to the eyes when every thing else presents the gloomy aspect of winter—we also have green yards and fine gardens— which is not the case in other places. I have not taken a walk, except two morning visits since my return—I have not been off the lot for Mr Pettigrew is so much confined I stay in the house to keep him company—you know walking is the only pleasure in the country— I expect by this time you are willing to close this dull letter—and to relieve you I will conclude by requesting you to give our respects to Mr Bryan and except from Mr P—— the same with my love to the children—

affectionately yours,
Ann Pettigrew

[*Addressed*] Mrs Mary W Bryan,
Newbern,
N Carolina.

[1]This was possibly William Augustus Blount (1792-1867) of Beaufort County, a planter who had been an army officer and a member of the House of Commons. Keith and others, *Blount Papers*, IV, 101n. Blount's first wife, Ann Hawkins Haywood Blount, died in January, 1825. *North Carolina Star* (Raleigh), January 14, 1825.

[2]Thomas Trotter's daughter Ellen (Eleanor, Elena) married the Reverend James Weatherby in June, 1826. *North Carolina Star* (Raleigh), June 30, 1826.

Mary Williams Bryan to Ann Blount Pettigrew A&H, BRYAN

New Bern March 16th 1830

My dear Sister

I received by friday's mail your very acceptable letter of the 9th inst. by which I very much regretted to learn the continued indisposition of Mr Pettigrew, I had entertained the hope that his health would improve as the warm weather approaches, & your dear children too, how distressing it must be to see them labouring under that dreadful disease the croup, of which I know nothing from experience never having had it in my family. My children as you say are very healthy & I thank God for it, for what should I do with so many little ones if they were as sickly as yours? Heaven only knows, for I have my hands full now. William and Mary have been unwell since you left New Bern.

The Washingtonians had many & just fears about the Small-pox for it is a horrible disease, I was very apprehensive about our children taking it, I have had them all vaccinated, they had very good arms & were not made sick at all, a general vaccination has taken place & the small pox entirely disappeared.

From your description of Mrs Wetherby's centre table I think it must be very pretty. I should like to have one myself I imagine she saw many agreeable sights during her northern trip, preachers wives have a glorious life, they are not plagued with the cares of housekeeping like we of the laity, nothing to do but travel about with their husbands living upon the fat of the land— I should be delighted to make a northern tour myself if hard times and a numerous offspring did not prevent me.

I suppose ere this you have heard of the death of our dear & ever to be lamented Bishop [*John Stark Ravenscroft*], poor old man! even his enemies now will be willing to let the grave hide his faults & remember only his virtues and his fervent & exalted piety, our Church has sustained the greatest possible loss & one from which it will be a long time if she ever recovers—last sunday the pulpit desk & gallery were hung with mourning which produced the most lugubrious feelings & most of the congregation wore crape to testify their respect for his memory.

Ma' has been very unwell since you left here, I think she looks much better now, tho' very badly yet—Charles has also been sick, he looks very doleful indeed, I am sometimes distressed to see how very sombre he looks, he says he intends writing as soon as he gets Watson's acc^{t} Yesterday there was an alarm of fire in Ma's neighbourhood but which fortunately was soon discovered and extinguished before any mischief was done it was supposed to be the work of an incendiary. Genl [*Durant*] Hatch appears to be finishing his course on earth, he looks dreadful, has had the jaundice for some time & refuses medical aid, he says he is willing to die, I never saw so perfect a prostration of strength & spirits in so short a time in my life—

Give my love to Aunt Pettigrew, remember me to Mr P. & believe me to be

Your very affectionate Sister
Mary W Bryan.

N.B. My good man is at Court or he would send his respects to you—as you now will have much more leisure on hand than heretofore I [*torn*] to hear frequently from you I will pro[*torn*] as often as I can.

[*Addressed*] Mrs. Ann B. Pettigrew
Cool Spring
Washington County
N.C.

Frederick Biddle Shepard to Ann Blount Pettigrew A&H

Fairfield June 20th [*18*]30—[1]

My dear Sister

I hope you will not be surprised at receiving a letter from me after so long a silence. I have just returned from Phila. where I have been for my old complaint under the care of Dr Chapman.[2]—I have suffered more than you can conceive, not only with inflamation arising from the disease, but from two operations on the ball of my eye. I presume you have heard of my confinement in Norfolk which was the most tedious and irksome three months that I ever experienced.—I sometimes think I am the most unfortunate of our family in every respect.—I am the very beacon of bad luck—It appears to me that wherever I go misfortune awaits me on every side, and I do not recollect ever to have Succeeded in any one undertaking—I do not know whether my failures are to be attributed to a want of energy & industry or whether they have been owing to adventitious circumstances—circumstances over which I could have no control. The great anxiety of some of the family to get me to the western country has been most unfortunate & I attribute my late Sickness to the trip I undertook in Nov. last. My right eye has been so much obscured that it is impossible for me to read the largest print.—In fact I use only one eye. There is another difficulty, which if you are not fatigued with my disaster, I will relate to you.—Previous to my leaving Pasquotank I was involved in a contest that occured during my absence in Tenn: at the plantation. I made an effort to avoid any thing like a personal contest with the man opposed to me, until I had received such abuse as no man of feeling could submit to—If I had appealed to the Law it never would have wiped off the blow I received from the person alluded to aided by two of his negroes.—So I took the Law into my own hands and made preparation for a slight encounter—I was fortunate enough after horse whiping the Master and inflicting certain other uncomfortable chastisement upon him to put him to flight, and he took shelter in his house until I had left for the west, when he sallied out and obtained two writs against me, one for a common assault,—and another of a more serious nature.—I have not given myself to the authorities because I know if the Law is against me, I have the strictest justice on my side throughout the whole transaction.—I am waiting to see William.—

I saw the Biddles in Phila. Mary, Ann, & William made frequent enquiry's after you, I also saw Fanny Lardner—[3]

Fanny looks rather old-timey—They all wished to be remembered to you. Give my love to Mr Pettigrew

Your aff brother
Fredk B Shepard

[*Addressed*] Mrs Ann Pettigrew
Lake Phelps
Tyrrell County

[1]This letter is mounted in the volume containing correspondence for the year 1831 in the Pettigrew Papers, North Carolina Archives.

[2]Nathaniel Chapman (1780-1853), a physician in Philadelphia, was educated at the University of Pennsylvania. He founded the Medical Institute of Philadelphia and served as the first president of the American Medical Association. *CDAB*, 158.

[3]These were cousins of Frederick Biddle Shepard and Nancy Pettigrew.

Ebenezer Pettigrew to William James Bingham A&H

Lake Phelps July 6, 1830

My dear Sir,

Please to get my three dear sons together and communicate this my letter to them in any way you may think best.

Your friend
E Pettigrew

My dearest, sons, Charles, William & James It is with the deepest anguish of heart, I inform you that your dearest Mother is no more, she closed her eyes in death, on the first day of this month at sunrise. She was taken in labour the evening before at sunset, at 20 minutes of 12 oclock she was delivered of a daughter, shortly after which alarming symptoms came on & D[r] Warren was sent for, who had been three day before thrown from his chair & so crippled as not to be able to walk, & but for that untoward event would have been sent for when your dear ma was first taken as I have always done before. Alas the last pulsation of your dearest Mamas heart had ceased to beat about 20 minutes before he arrived. She was taken so ill immediately after the birth as not [to ask] what it was or to say one word of her dear little infant. The seen after your dear mama became so ill beggars all discription. When your fathers greatest exertions were needed, and your dear ma would put her hand to him, his poor feeble frame gave way, & he was obliged to lay down or fall, and after M[rs] B[*r*]ickhouse had made her last effort, she fell prostrate on the floor & lay apparently lifeless for near an hour. The servants in attendance were obliged to be taken from the house that the dear woman should not be roused from her slumbers in death by their cries. O my dear sons your loss is beyond all understanding and your dear father who in his weak & emaciated state of health knows not how to to support it. He is undone for ever. O my dear sons you have lost one of the best of mothers & your dear father one of the kindest & best of wives, She is no more to guide her dear children in their path to manhood, and to hold out the kind hand of Love to your Father. But consider the anguish of your father, when your poor little sister Mary got up in the morning she got a brush and went to keeping the flies off her dear ma, as your brother Henry has frequently done this summer when she would sleep. O my children! My dear children. O my wife, my dearest Lovely Nancy. I am undone forever. I am your afflicted & know you will believe your

affectionate father E. Pettigrew

[*Addressed*] M[r] W J Bingham
Hillborough
N. Carolina

Ebenezer Pettigrew to John Herritage and Mary Williams Bryan UNC

Lake Phelps July 12, 1830

My dear Sir,

Consolation is not for me, my cup is filled to the brim. The parting with my children last winter was difficult, but the separation now from my other four, dear little innocent creatures can add nothing more to my agony. The sun has set forever upon all my comfort in this world. Alas my only stay, my all, is gone forever, and my house is left desolate, nothing remains but the silence of death. My wife! My dearest Nancy! Mrs Warren takes my dear little infant, untill the fall when it will be able to be carried. I have sent my other three little innocents to their dear relations, will you my dear Sir, assist in the distribution of them. All that I can say is, that I wish them to be with their dear relations.

Your afflicted friend
E Pettigrew

over

My dear Sister.

I receivd with an humble heart of gratitude your request to take my dear little children. I cannot be more sensible of any thing, than the part you would exercise towards them. All I can, is that one of the greatest sonsolations I have on earth, that they have such an aunt, and a dear woman in whom no sister could have had more confidence, than my dear Nancy had in her. After consulting our dear Mothers wishes as far as can be, I resign them to you, knowing that they are in the hands of inestimable worth.

I am your afflicted brother
E Pettigrew

[*Addressed*] John H. Bryan Esqr
Newbern

Richard Muse Shepard to Ebenezer Pettigrew A&H

New Bern. July. 17th. 1830.

My dear Brother,

I hasten as soon as I have arrived at the place of destination to inform <of> you of the state of the children's health, and the manner in which the bore the fatigue of travelling. Never has it been my lot to mark so much cheerfulness, and good feeling to exist among so many young, and of course restless children as was evinced by the conduct of yours. Henry and Mary were delighted and every time they saw any cattle houses, or anything of the kind they saw, or fancied they saw some thinking resemblance to objects of the same nature at the Lake. I was apprehensive that the journey would be tiresome, and to prevent that loneliness of feeling that is apt to oppress us I procured from Dr Warren two novels. But of these I had no need for I was so much engaged with the boys and Mary, as to abstract my attention from all other external objects. The journey progressed as you predicted. every body with whom we met sympathized with us, and as far as I could infer, would if necessary have tendered something more substantial than their sympathies. And would it be unjust as well as ungenerous if I passed over in silence of Mr Nichols family at Plymouth. If they had been [their] dearest conexexions they could not have been more tender with them. Every delicacy they could procure (except those you interdicted) were sought after, and everything that could please. were sought with as much eagerness as if it had been for their own offspring. This would have been discreditable to them, if it had been accompanied with an exorbitant charge, but when the old man told me that would exact nothing for the children, I thought that however destitute the higher orders might be of all honourable feeling yet still it was not banished from the world. I have dwelled upon this trifling incident because it is pleasing to notice such deeds, and because it was a manifastation of affection for your children with which it is proper you should be acquainted. Mr. Weatherby you have seen, and I acquainted with the children's health when he saw us last. from that time till now they have enjoyed unvaried good health, and good spirits. Mary has taken up her abod with her aunt, leaving the boys with us. She seems to be pleased with sister's children, and will live very happily. Though now she sometimes cries for her uncle Richard, and wishes him to take her to her papa,—yet—this arises solely from her change of home, and change of companions. Mary, Mama, and Penelope all unite in tendering <their> kind regards to you, and beg me to inform that whatever can be done to contribute to the improuvement, or to advance the happiness of your children shall be performed. Mama is now getting aged, and infirm but will nevertheless do every thing that is requisite for the benefit of Henry and Johns[*t*]on. Her health is much the same as when I left her. Mary Bryan has had a bad fall from a chair, but is now recovering. Charles is sick a bed in Yew York.

Yours Affectionately
R M Shepard

[*Addressed*] Mr E. Pettigrew
Lak Phellps
NC.

Ebenezer Pettigrew to Mary Williams Bryan A&H, BRYAN

New York Aug 24, 1830

My dear Sister

With this you will receive a carriage for our dear little daughters, as well as some other articles in it, also a box of toys for all our dear little children. Pray divide them among them all, share & share alike.

You have before this learned that my stay in Philadelphia was but a day & two nights, and the cause why it was no longer. I expect to leave this for Phil. on the 29th by which time Dr Phisic will have returned. Since I left my Prison I think my general health better. But I cannot feel a wish to be restored to health. The remainder of my journey through life, I view with the utmost horror. My God how can I travil through this wilderness without my dearest dear Nancy. No parent living can have a more tender affection for his children, and no children can have greater claims on a parent than mine But I know they will forgive me when I say that nothing is so desirable to me as death. O Nancy, Nancy how can I live without you? I have been keept alive in this giddy multitude, by being employed in geting the mementos of my dear wife. My God my god how does my heart bleed when I hand to the engraver, to the Printer to the coffinmaker, to the marble factor, these words. Ann Blount Pettigrew died July 1, 1830. I am sometimes fit to say, can it be possible that my dear Love is banished from sight for ever, that I shall never more hear that dear voice, nor feel those tender hands of my dear sweet Nancy, that idol of my Heart. God be merciful to me, O wretch that I am.

Inclosed is the Epitaph of my dear Nancy also of my poor little John. I had it printed that the engraver might not make a mistake on her monument also to give to a few of her friends. I am having a Mahogony case made for my dear Nancys coffin; It will then be /placed/ in a stone case. I have come to the conclusion not /to/ remove my dear wife, I wish when ever I look out while at my prison to be able to see the spot where all my heart is buried. I have come to the determination to remove my Father, Mother, Brother, (and sister Hannah, if it is approved of by her Mother) to the place where my dear dear Nancy sleeps. All these things may seem useless or strange in /the/ eyes of the sordid multitude, but if it gives me a ray of consolation, it is right to do it. No honours which I can pay to the memory of my dear departed Love can be too great. O Nancy how many hours have I spent in beholding you with extacy & delight?

Aug. 25. I have not departed from my manner of living prescribed by Dr Warren at christmas. My God what a reverse /of/ fortune! All the year, because I was restricted, my dear dear wife would have something prepaired for me that was delicate, but now though I sit down to a sumptuous dinner, there is nothing scarcely on it that I can eat. I made my dinner yesterday after waiting for it until 3oclok on Irish patatoes, & squashes, with bread & water. No one cares whether I eat or not. Thus I am to travil through this dreary wilderness, and I am on my fifty sixth day of the journey. It feels to my mind as though as though it was as many years. I can scarcely look back to the begining. It certainly is the longest part of my life On this subject I could dwell forever, my mind is on no other, but I will conclude by sending my affectionate regards to our dear Mother, Mr Bryan, Brothers & sister Penelope. Pray kiss my dear motherles little children for me and believe me your afflicted & affectionate Brother.

E Pettigrew

[*Addressed*] Mrs Mary W. Bryan
Newbern

Ebenezer Pettigrew to Mary Williams Bryan UNC

Philadelphia Sep. 23. 1830

My dear Sister

After filling a small commission this morning from Dr Warren & walking to view the house where my dear, dear, Nancy once lived, a thing I have never failed to do every day I have been in the City, I return to my room to spend the remainder of the morning in answering your kind and affectionate favour of the 13th received last evening on my return from New York. It would seem from my letters that I am all the time in New York. I had been fifteen days with Dr Physick when he said I might be discharged. I then told him that it was my wish to go to N. York before I went to the south; to which he was much pleased as he said he should be pleased to see me after the space of a week. My sole object in visiting N. York again was this: When in that place first I had determined to have taken by the celebrated painter Mr Ingham[1] a Portrait from the minature of my dearest Wife, which I have had set in gold and intend wearing the remainder of my days. Mr I was out of town while I was there, and I left it with Mr Chester[2] to have taken while I returned to Phila. and my last visit to N.Y. /was/ to get that dear representation of my sweet Nancy. But I was still disappointed for Mr I. had not returned. I had to leave it with a promise from Mr Asa Jones[3] that he would take my dear Nancys minature with him to Newbern. I received your dear Husbands favour some time ago. I marked its resoning together with yours of yesterday with a melted heart. They br/e/athe a goodness of soul, a power of reasoning, at the same time a eulogy of that dear dear woman who my heart bleeds for the loss of. Yes I may say with truth. I die dayly. How can I reason myself in to composure? When my reason has left me. I know that I am the Husband of an angel in He/a/ven. I also know that I am on earth, a poor *solitary, forlorn* being, with duties to beform of a most imperious nature, without the power to perform them. O if we both had duties equivalant to all our powers how can *I* now alone, with all my energies gone, do anything I hope I prove my good intentions by my visit to the Doctor by abstinance, from anything that would tend to make /me/ worse or shorten life. Though death of all things would be to me the most desirable. I now promise in the most positive manner, that so far as in my power lyes, I will take every means in my power to prolong my life, which shall devoted to my dear children those sweet pledges of my dear Nancys Love for me. At the same time I must be allowed the privalidge of grieving for one [of] the /most/ lovely, the most amiable, the most worthy in every respect, of women. I had intended to have answered that part of your letter, on my convertion from the world, but my head aches & is so confused that I [can] write no more on the subject now.

I regret to learn of the declining state of health of our dear mother. I fear her sorrows will shorten her days, would to God my claim in this world were no greater & I could see that great enemy of human nature approaching. Please to give my kind regards to her. A part of my disease is better, though I have no expectation of ever being a sound man. I have been quite sick for the week past with violent cold. I expect to leave this for Baltimore /tomorrow/, I shall stay there probably 3 days. I then proceed as fast as I can for my prison. I am very desirous to visit Hills[borough] an Newbern, and shall do so. But in my present [con]fused & agitated state of mind, it is impossible for me to make any arraingments. Br. William left this 4 days ago for Baltimore, I expect to come up with him at Norfolk. Please to remember me affectionately to Mr Bryan & all the family. Kiss my dear little innocents for there father & believe me your afflicted & affectionate Brother

E Pettigrew

Mrs Mary W. Bryan

P.S. Mr Chester wrote the Epitaph of my dear, dear, Nancy.
N.B. Pray excuse this miserable scrawl my head aches fit to split.

[*Addressed*] Mrs Mary W. Bryan
New Bern
North Carolina

[1]The portrait painter Charles Cromwell Ingham (1796-1863) came from Ireland to New York with his family in 1820. He painted "fashionable beauties" and such notables as Lafayette and DeWitt Clinton. *DAB*, IX, 473. Correspondence between Ingham and Ebenezer Pettigrew may be found in the Pettigrew Family Papers, Southern Historical Collection.

[2]S. M. Chester appears to have been a resident of New Bern at one time; this may account for Ebenezer Pettigrew's acquaintance with him. In 1822 he was secretary of the board of the Presbyterian Church in New Bern. *Carolina Centinel* (New Bern), January 26, 1822.

[3]Asa Jones was a merchant from New Bern, according to the announcement of his marriage to Sarah Bryan in the *North Carolina Star* (Raleigh), January 10, 1812.

Thomas Pettigru to Ebenezer Pettigrew A&H

Landover Oct. 7th 1830

Dear Cousin,

Since I had the pleasure of seeing you I have become a man of family I have now a local habitation. I believe I told you I was on a matrimonial course when I left you—I have succeeded to my heart[s] content

The lady I married[1] lived near Georgetown in this State. I have taken up my abode on the same place—She has neither brother sister father or mother, so that I have not increased my connections a great deal—I plant nothing but rice which is the only article grown in the neighbourhood. the gale this year had done us great injury & we shall make sorry crops. I hope yours will be better. Corn with us will find a ready market. I believe you send sometimes to Charleston. The merchant I bot from, told me he had purchased a cargo of yours: from which I judge you have the vessel you were going to build, completed. I shall have to purchase, until I get in the way of raising corn, every year about a thousand bushels—how would you like to send a cargo to Georgetown. the vessel could come to my door. I am now with Father on a visit to the place where I was raised,[2] until I enterd the Navy—he *is* quite well & hearty & desires to be remembered to you. I shall return to Georgetown in 2 or 3 weeks where I hope to hear from you. All your relations in South Carolina are I believe doing as well as people generally. The excitement produced by the tariff has caused your Cousin James L[*ouis Petigru*] who resides in Charleston to offer for the State Senate, not that he wishes the situation, but that he may use his influence to stop the wild notion of nullification from putting the State in a Situation that wd lead to civil war or division[3]—I hope you will approve of such conduct. There are some in this district (Abbeville) who say the Pettigrews were tories during the Revolution. I think this rather complimentary than otherwise for if there was any thing against the name they would not go so far back accusations—but this is as false as any thing that could be said of more recent occurrence. How are all your family? I observed by the papers the loss you have had to bear with. I hope that providence will sustain you in yr affliction & prepare you to receive with resignation the fate which awaits us all—God bless & prosper you my dear Coz is the wish of all your kinfolks in these parts—remember me kindly to aunt [*Mary Lockhart Pettigrew*]—father desires his love to her also

Yours affectionately
T. P—

Direct to me at Georgetown S° Ca

[*Addressed*] Ebenezer Pettigrew Esqr
near Lake Phelps
Tyrrell County
N° Carolina

[1]The lady was Mary Ann LaBruce (1793-1869). She brought "considerable wealth" to the marriage. Carson, *James Louis Petigru*, 182. The couple had two children: Martha (1830-1855), who died unmarried, and James Louis, Jr. (1832-1853), who died by drowning. Martha W. Daniels to Sarah McCulloh Lemmon, February 16, 1983.

[2]The family lived at Badwell, fifteen miles from Abbeville, South Carolina. Carson, *James Louis Petigru*, 14-15.

[3]Although he held no public office after 1830, James Louis Petigru was a leading opponent of John C. Calhoun's program of nullification and secession. *DAB*, XIV, 514-515.

Nathaniel Phelps[1] *to Ebenezer Pettigrew* A&H

Illinoise near Miscipee River [*October 10, 1830*]

Mr E Pettigrew

Dear Sir

I have to inform you that my Helth is not good at Present and have reached within 95 miles of my fathers where I Shall not Stay more than a few days and then return home By the first day of december or there a bout I have [Seen] a grate deal of [*illegible*] on my Jorney Sir I remember my best Respects to and hope thise Lines may find you in good helth I have Seen the buties of the Ohioe and Verry Considerable of fertile Soils of a Luce nature Verry diferent from any Construction that you Can Lay on it without any Rock in it this night I am on the Edge of a [Pocasin] tin miles wide and about as Long and understand that ballance of the way is about the Sam discription of Country it will take me two mutch time to Informe you of all the Perticulars of my Journey and this Country to night but have wrte this to Let you See my friend that I am yet a Living "for man to View the wondrous works of almighty god is grate" with helth & hope I Shall be able to Inform you about Christmash of what I have seen for I have not time this night and have a bad opertunity of writing at all

I have Had tiresome Jorney So far and think that wee are as well off as any Contry So far the greatest drouth that you Ever Saw has Taken Place in all the States that I have Bin in but this and Soile is So good here and Some Rain that they are well off here Excuse this Bad writting my Paper is [Ruented] and no Light to write by that is good here is a grate deal of Sickness in this Part of the World as well as where whe Live all the Springs is gone dry where they never was known to before I must Conclude for want of Light Sir I Remain your affectionate friend &c untill death

Nathaniel Phelps

October 10th 1830—

[*Addressed*] Ebenezer Pettigrew Esqr
Noth Corrolina
Washington County
Col Spring office

---

[1]When Nathaniel (Nathan A.) Phelps died, Ebenezer Pettigrew was named executor of his estate. Other letters pertaining to the estate settlement are located in the Pettigrew Papers at the North Carolina Archives, dated March 18, 1833; May 24, 1833; June 28, 1834; September 9, 1834; November 9, 1834; August 25, 1835; November 24, 1835; December 10, 1835; and April 20, 1836. The last three letters relate to Pettigrew's transfer of duties to John Herritage Bryan upon the former's election to Congress and consequent absence from Tyrrell County.

Phelps left a married daughter, Lethea A. O. Chesson, for whom he named his father, Joseph Phelps of Illinois, as guardian, an illustration of the lowly legal position of women in the 1830s.

Ebenezer Pettigrew to James Cathcart Johnston UNC

Lake Phelps December 5, 1830

My dear Johnston,

This will be handed by Bob, who I have kept untill this time, having found him so good a servant as almost to think him indispensable. I am however, now stationed and have no farther use for him. Yes my dear friend, I have arrived at, and set myself down on the place of my woe.

I had hoped from the comparitive composure of my mind on my return from the North, that my second arrival would be supportable. But my God! My heart bleeds at every artery. I am now living without the hope of one single day of comfort in this world. But I am in it, and while I live, I have most sacred duties to perform, not only to the dead but to the living. I have seven dear and helpless infants, (who to say are dearer to me than my life, would be saying nothing) those dear pledges of the Love of her whome I so much grieve for, who look up only to me their father for protection. Yes those dear little ones of my flesh must be protected so long as their is a pulsation in my heart. Twenty seven years of unremiting attention to my duty cannot easily be eradicated from the mind and my business which has grown up with me, and /is/ identified with me, can be managed almost without thought. My works prove whether I have had energy, but the presant dispensation of providence requires more than energy it demands a renewal of the man, a regeneration. My pleasures are all gone in the world, and I can but live for the duty, which I owe to my children and my friends. Let me give you a picture of the change. The silence of death pervades my house. I am asked to give out something to be cooked. I take my dear wifes basket of keys, I then have to ask where is such & such things, when I go to them I there see the hand of that dear woman. The food is prepaired, I set down to one plate, one knife, one fork; At night I set untill 11, or 12 oclock, I retire to my cell and what are my reflections? There is the Crib, where my dear Wife has nursed her infants and where but five months & one day ago, I expected my last would lie; now vacant. There is the spot where my three other little innocents were wont to lay, and where I have so often got on my knees & kissed them. Now a bare floor. There is the mattress on which this day five months the life blood of my heart ran out. There is the Beadstead on which I am to lay my weary limbs, where my dear dear Nancy lay in death. The silence of death reigns, my house is bolted, and no one breaths its air but myself. You will say that this is a glomy picture of human woe, and that it is a hard life. It is a true picture, and it is hard to live, but it is also true that I am alive. Yes my dear friend I know you will rejoice, when I tell you; I can live & can interest myself in my business, and can say Gods will be done; The Lord gave and the Lord hath taken away blessed be the name of the Lord.

I hope I have always been governed by principle founded on the most mature deliberation. Under every difficulty in this world I have brought philosophy to my aid, but in the present heart rending bereavement it has been no more than a drop of water to a world on fire. That God who governs, and rules the universe, is my stay, that consolation, and hope which the world cannot give, nor take away is mine. I live under a full assurance of being again united to her whome, I so much deplore the loss of. Nothing but such a hope could make me continue to drink of so bitter a draft.

I wrote by the last mail to Mr Woodley asking him to perform the service which I mentioned to you. It will take probably a month if you can spare him. My health is better than when I wrote you last from Hillsboro. I hope yourself & sisters are in the enjoyment of that blessings, Please to give my kind respects to them and believe me your sincere friend

E Pettigrew

James C. Johnston esqr

N.B. When Mr Woodley goes over to Mr Blounts for me I expect to send the remainder of the boards for you in the vessil

E P.

N.B. I was exceedingly gratified with the affectionate conduct towards me and the general good character of my two sons at Hillsboro. Charles & William. No falt to find of poor little James, he is yet a child.

[*Addressed*] James C Johnston Esqr
Hayes

Charles Lockhart Pettigrew to Ebenezer Pettigrew UNC

Hillsborough December 20th 1830

Dear father

I have not writen you since you left <from> this place brother William wrote you about three weeks and he received your letter about a week ago in it you stated your feelings when you entered the house I could very easy imagine them if you had not stated them, because it is so different from what it used to be from being a house of joy and bustle to one of Silence and distress I know the contrast /must/ be very striking to you one who was before that time happy in the company of my dear mother and dear little brothers and sisters but now you are alone in that house I think you may be said to be so because the overseer will be no company to you one who is as much above him as he is above the negroes no one can form an opinion how much you will suffer during the following year the company you will have and composure of mind will be in your library and while you are read religeous books such as the bible and sermons and tracts sunday will be your most pleasant day because your thoughts will be <w>holly engrosed in religion and will not be drawn of by any thing world-ly beca/u/se if you were to think and plan out things to be done <on> during the following week you had as well be haveing them /done/ at that time because your thoughts are entirely taken f/r/om /every/ any religious duty and put upon them it is in some part of the bible a person should on sunday think of nothing but heavenly things it is very s/e/ldom that po/e/ple obey that sentence they think it is no harm to think of worldly things if they do not execute them the sabath in general is too much neglected by every one when it is one of the most religeous duties that can be perfomed and is thought by the majority of poeple to be the most unnessary duty that is and one day in seven not too much to be devoted to the lord on the other hand it is too little poeple generally dislike for the sabath to come if every person around them attends strictly to publick worship and the duties of the sabath when I look back upon the way I used to spend my sabaths I am surprised how I could do it with impunity from our heaven ly father when my dear mother would try to correct me every chance I could get I would slipout among /neg/r/oes/ and play with them and would think it very hard not to be permited to go among them and romp and play with them but my mind is much changed since that time by the late misfor/t/une which happened to our family and I hope for the better I hope I will do those things which my dear mother was so anxous teach me and anticipate her will as when alive and follow it and moreover when I would go to my grandmama's she would wish me to read the bible to her I never would do it with an unwilling heart but I think hereafter I will do it with pleasure. You said in your letter the farm was not going on as well as you would expect it you expect<ed> to raise 15 Hundred barrels of corn this fall I think that is a ver good crop as you was not there it could not be expect Mr Davis would manage as well as you would because he is not so experienced in those matter. There is a report here that the negroes had revolded in <new> Newbern but were soon put down sixty negroes were killed and no<t> White person was killed or wonded the pople in Hillsborough are on their gard there is an intended insurrection of the slaves about christmas in this place all poeple are upon the lookout Mr Bingham is prepared for an attack the poeple have met and formed their plan they have formed twelve companies with about ten in each company a company patrole every night but I do not apprehend <every> /any/ danger. Pleas excuse my bad writing my pen was very bad and I could not make it better We are all well and send our love to you Brother James is well <at> only he has little twiching

P [S] I am your affectionateson

Charles L Pettigrew.

[*Addressed*] Mr E Pettigrew
Cool Spring
Washington Co.
N Carolina

Ebenezer Pettigrew to John Herritage Bryan UNC

Lake Phelps Jan 23, 1831

My dear Sir,

I duely received your kind and consolitary favour of the 2nd Ult. for which please to accept my heartfelt acknoledgments. I know it breaths the language of truth and fortitude, but my dear friend, I have no fortitude on that subject for which I suffer. I loved and always did love after the first three days that I ever saw my dearest dear Nancy, with a perfectly undivided heart; not only when compaired to others of her sex, but to all things and every thing on earth, my acquaintance with her increased (if possible) that Love, aded to that I was as it were secluded from the world, and looked upon her as necessary to my existance. Yes as literally a part of my essential existance. I know that it is unmanly to act as I have done, but if I have shown the man in contending with the difficulties of this world, in resisting and overcoming all the evill propensities, which man is heir too; I hope I shall be forgiven this one weekness, though it even cost me my life. I know that it is the will of God that I should be thus afflicted, and I never cease to pray for submition to his mighty power, and for fortitude to withstand this bereavement, that I may live to protect and defend my poor little dear children in this wicked world. I have the most /perfect/ hope and confidence in the goodness of my Creator, and that /this/ dispensation may be to me a means of everlasting glory, and of meeting my God at the final and great day of <final> account, with that peace which passeth all understanding. I do and always did believe that I must give an account to the Judge of all the earth on that day when the stoutest mens hearts men hearts will tremble, and when they will call on the rocks and mountains to fall on them to hide them from the face of their maker, who will do *right* and will then seperate the good from wicked, with that most awful sentance to the latter. Depart from me /ye/ accursed /to/ the place prepaired for the Devil & his angels.

I have had an opportunity of realising my anticipation of the horrors of a sick bed, and can say that it can be better immagined than I can describe. On Fryday the 14, I was necessary to lay off an avenue through the woods. It was very cold, and began to sleet and snow, and before I got to the house I got a good deal sprinked, which gave me a considerable stiffness of the breast, the second day after I did not intend going out of the house, but after breakfast I was taken, with a very unplesant fullness of the head, (an affection I have had at intervals since Christmas week) and thought I would take a small walk, but before I returned I had walked nine miles, a part of it over an unleviled bank of a ditch & exceedingly ruff. I had a high fever that night, and have been the whole week confined to the house & for the last three days to the bed. I am siting up to day and of course better. My domesticks and overseer are attentive to my wants; but Alas! I want nothing they can give, and that which I do want is never more to console me in this world on a languishing bed. I knew my own disease, was not in eminent dainger, and did not send for the Doctor. The sickest day that I had he was at Mr Collins by invitation to dine as well as myself with Mr Fred Sawyer,[1] but I disliked to abridge his pleasures and /he/ came over at nine oclock at night, and was off again to Mr Cs as soon as he thought they had eat breakfast. Dont be alarmed my dear friends, I am not going to die yet. I shall revive, I shall /be/ a man again, and if my Chrisstian principles do not prevent, I shall grind some people to powder, or in other words let them alone and they will go into thin air, themselves, by that mighty power of evaporation.

Mr Woodley has returned with the corpses of my dear friends The vessil has not yet been able to get up the river with them in consequence of the ice. The coffins were all rotten except poor Hannah. all which I had anticipated and had them made here and carried with them. I received a letter from Hicks & Smith dated the 5 Inst. informing me that the Marble for my dear Nancys grave was done, that a vessil was engaged and that it would be here by /the time/ that letter was. Ten days has passed since that receit, and I have strong fears that the snow storm since that time has cast away the vessil. My anxiety for those articles during the whole winter has been beyond bearing. But I can only sit still, and keep my peace. I receved by yesterdays mail a letter from Richard, I could have wished he had informed me of the health of my poor little children, or our dear Mother Please to give my affectionate regards to her also to Sister Mary and tell <the> Sister M. that a letter will always be gratifiing to me, but I can [make] every allowance for situation. Tell dear little Mary that her Papa is mightily pleased to have so good accounts of her and that when she learns to read he has a pretty little Bible full of pictures for her.

Frederick Shepard has been here. he changed his sulkey at Plymouth for a gig to take in Lieutenant [*Frederick*] Norcom for company. On his return to Plymouth he met with Frederick Sawyer coming to the Lake to visit his friend & acquaintance Mr C. F. Shepard gives him an open letter to me informing me of his visit to Mr C. and wishing me to be attentive to him also. I suppose give him a dinner of[*f*] the head of my dear wifes & his dear sisters coffin. My God! what does he think of? He is more perfectly wreckless than I ever conceived any one could be I think his frolick must end with a pistol. So much for predestination. Please to give my kind regards to all the family and assure yourself of my Gratitude and best feelings for your kindness

E Pettigrew

N.B. Please to tell Lidia her children are all well
N.B. Mr Sawyer did not bring Mr Shepards letter but sent it the second day by Mr C. I read it, (I was then sick) and took no farther notice of it. F. Shepard is of all other<s> men the most mistaken in his friends.

I have writen you a letter of blunders and know not whether you can make any thing of half of it. I know little about /it/ myself. But I did not wish this mail to pas without a letter. I know you will excuse its inaccuracyies

E P.

I will write again soon

[*Addressed*] John H. Bryan Esqr
Newbern
N. Carolina

[1]This may refer to Frederick A. Sawyer, who was the son of Enoch Sawyer. He was attending the University of North Carolina in 1820. He represented Pasquotank County in the state House of Commons in the 1832 session and later moved out of state. Elizabeth Gregory McPherson, "Unpublished Letters from North Carolinians to Polk," *North Carolina Historical Review*, XVII (July, 1940), 251n; Cheney, *North Carolina Government*, 299.

William James Bingham to Ebenezer Pettigrew UNC

Hillsboro', April 10th 1831.

Mr Pettigrew.

My dear Sir—
I am afraid James's disease is not yielding to the doctor's treatment. It is true he is not now, nor has he been for months as much affected as he was while you were here. Still the disease seems to yield but partially. He has never been quite clear of it since its return upon the discontinuance of bathing during the severest part of the winter. Ever since the beginning of December he has been able to hold his book & use his knife & fork well enough. This will serve to show you how much he is affected. He walks without any danger. The indications of disease are principally in his arms: and tho' he can play, eat and button his clothes without inconvenience, yet the symptoms of disease are unequivocal. I do not perceive that his mind is at all affected. He makes very little progress in learning to be sure: but that is easily accounted for on other grounds. Considering his health of paramount importance, I have kept him at home and had him bathed five or six times a day

& encouraged him to take exercise during the intervals. My wife hears him two or three little lessons each day—our aim as to his education being at present very little more than to keep him from losing ground.—Charles & William attend to his bathing, which is so managed as to prevent their losing much time. He is bathed at Sun-rise or a little before, again just before breakfast, a third time in the middle of the forenoon, and a fourth before dinner. In the afternoon he is bathed at three o'clock & at sun-set. His appetite is ravenous. We have to allowance him regularly; and he frequently eludes our vigilance, as well as that of the servants, & gets something to eat out of the kitchen between meals. His voracious appetite, produced no doubt by his disease & the medicine which he daily takes, is, I apprehend, the greatest enemy to his convalescence. You would be astonished at the quantity of stale light bread which he would consume. The D^r^ thought for some time his appetite might be satiated with that without detriment to him, but has found it necessary to prescribe a limit. I hope you will come up at the end of the present session (the last of May) and you can determine better by your own observation what measures should be taken. As to the trouble and anxiety which he occasions, most cheerfully would Eliza and myself undergo all & much more, if his health seemed likely to be restored.

Charles & W^m^ are doing very well. C. is making some progress in Geometry—He will succeed well in that branch. He has gone through Arithmetic in a very thorough manner. W^m^ is too diligent. I am obliged to drive him to exercise. The health of both is good.—William's class has received some accession from the class above; and as these individuals, tho' unable to compete with the class they left, have been over the studies of W^m's^ class, they have rather the advantage.

The number of students is 57.—I am very full of employment. Two of my students—no[*torn*]repared for the Sophomore class in College—assist me with the lower classes. I am negociating with a first rate young man to assist me next session.—I regret to inform you that M^r^ S— my former assistant—is getting along badly with his school.—We are all well. Our children are remarkably thriving.—We regret that your health is still so feeble; but [we] hope that our God will sanctify this & all your afflictions to your best spiritual interests, and then you will be enabled even to rejoice in them.

I am, dear Sir, very respectfully & sincerely yours
W. J. Bingham

[*Addressed*] Mr Ebenezer Pettigrew
Cool Spring P.O—
Washington C^o^
N.C

Thomas Turner to Ebenezer Pettigrew A&H

Plymo NC June 23 1831

My dear Sir,

In the course my interview yesterday with Mr Bryan, I learned from him that you contemplated making your expected trip with our unfortunate son to the north, by way of the sea in some vessel, this summer:—and I come to tell you, That this will not do: at least, that it is my opinion, if you undertake it, you will heartily repent, before the voyage is ended, that you you had not gone by land. I come to tell you also some of the reasons for this opinion.

1st you and your son, will in all probability be sea sick the whole voyage. This sea sickness is the most unpleasant discouraging desponding of diseases. It is besides a very sick disease—; and (remember) it will last the whole voyage.

2d The sea air is a damp atmostphere. This will be a very disagreeable feeling to you: but your son may not perhaps regard it.

3 In this warm weather, you will scarcely find a vessil, free of Chintses cock roaches, bugs—These added to the dirt & filth of most vessels, will be exceedingly disagreeable, if not injurious. It may be injurious by depriving you of rest and pleasure.

4 There is no shade at sea. You can find there, no protection from the sun. The heat of the sun is more intollerable there, than in your fields—If you go below, you are stewed; if you remain on deck you are burnt up.

5 Either of these evils, when it falls upon a man in health, & who withal is used to it, is bad eno, and he can scarcely stand it. What then are you and your son to do, who are not used to any one of them. Think of the sea sickness; the dampness of your clothes & face & hands & that you cant dry them; the chintses, bugs, dirt, filth; the intolerable heat above and below deck; and that these are to be blended all together, & thrown upon you and our little son for 10 days or a fortnight; and then answer me, if there is any advantage in such a voyage to compensate for this amount of human suffering?—I tell you sir, If you undertake that voyage, you will repent it a 1000 times before it ends—And this repentance will be associated with despondency, such an accumulation of ills, added to the sea sickness, will make you look a head with no spirit, competent to endure the whole, with patience for 10 days.

If however you will go that way, then let me recommend, that you take some medicines with you. Coasting vessels are not apt to have them, and you know not, what you may want before the end of the voyage. Opium, I have read, & believe, affords considerable relief to sea sickness. Take some books with you also: for you will need something besides the conversation <in the con> of sea men, to entertain you, in the course of 10 to 20, or 30 days.

Perhaps you will say, the sea air and the sea voyage is recommended for the health of my son—Then, let him in the summer enjoy the sea air in some of the northern ports; say Newport Rhode Island, which I believe to be freer from Bilious diseases than any other sea port in the United States; and in the spring & fall let him take the sea voyage. The weather is then milder.

And now when I come to say Good bye, my heart is full & my head empty and I can only say God bless you Sir, & yours

Fare well
Th. Turner

[*Addressed*] Ebenezer Pettigrew Esquire
Cool Spring
NC

John Herritage Bryan to Ebenezer Pettigrew A&H

New Bern Friday, June 25, 1831

My dear Sir,

We arrived at home today about 3 oClock, without the occurrence of any unpleasant accident.—Your children are very well, Nancy has never looked so well.—

I have not had a return of fever & hope I shall escape it.

The State-House has been burned by the most culpable carelessness in one of the workmen employed in making the roof *fire-proof*. It seems as if our State has been visited by Providence with calamity.—The statue is irreparably injured.—[1]

The portrait has not yet arrived, at least not as far as Mrs Shepard knows.—

Mary sends her love to Mrs Pettigrew and yourself.—

Very truly Yr friend
Jn. H. Bryan

[*Addressed*] E Pettigrew Esqr
Cool Spring
N.C

[1]The State House in Raleigh housed a statue of George Washington by Antonio Canova. The building burned on June 21, 1831, and the statue was damaged beyond repair. Construction of a new Capitol was completed in 1840, and a duplicate of the original Canova statue was placed in the rotunda of the Greek Revival building in 1970. Cheney, *North Carolina Government*, 621-622.

Ebenezer Pettigrew to Charles Lockhart and William Shepard Pettigrew UNC

New York July 27, 1831

My dear Charles,

I received your letter by the mail since my arrival which was 19th Inst. I was much pleased to learn that you were both well and had arrived to your pace of destination in safety. I had a ten days passage and was a good deal fatigued and incommoded on board of the vessil. I am almost too old now to undertake such voyages. I was quite unwell before I left home & am yet a good deal so. James who came with me makes a very good s/a/ilor, when he arrived at this place, he was perfectly free from any symptom of his disease, but it has returned and he is not so well. He is at home at the City Hotel, he called for Ice in his water at dinner as well as any of the other gentlemen. Though he is modest, and by no means pert. He likes Lake Phelps best. I leave this place today and where I shall go I have not yet determined. The wheat sold better than I expected 105 cents pr bushel, but I did not raise a half a crop. My expences are exceeding. My dear Sons, I hope you have entered on your studies, with a determination to accomplish the all important end of acquiring an education, depend upon /it/ if that is not your intention, your poor wretched father, has sacrificed your dear dear Mothers and his own comfort to very little purpose. As soon as I can get James disposed off, if I should not conclude to put myself in hands of Dr Physic again, I shall return to Carolina, this place of amusement has no charmes for me. I am weary of the world, and I can wish to live but for my dear children. O my dear sons let me not live in vain. Let me not pass through this world of sorrow and have it to say at the end, O that I had never been born, for I have no comfort in my children. God is great, and his goodness is equal to his power, he knowest what is best for me, and in him do I put my trust. Tell Mr Bingham that I am much obliged to him for his part of the letter, and that I never cease to pray that God will sanctify the dispensation of his providence to my everlasting happiness. That as to this world I am one of the most wretched men on earth. Give my kind regards to him, and Mrs Bingham and believe me my dear sons your afflicted but ever affectionate father.

E Pettigrew

Masters C. & W. Pettigrew

[*Addressed*] Masters Charles & William Pettigrew
Hillsborough
N. Carolina

Ebenezer Pettigrew to [Richard Muse] Shepard UNC

New York Aug. 20, 1831.

My dear Brother

On the 13th of the month I addressed a letter to Mr Bryan informing him, that on the 11th I had a surgical opperation performed by Dr Bushe[1] of this city. I cannot conceive of an opperation being performed more skillfully and with more success. I was about 45 minutes on the table and 25 under the knife, in which time I suffered the most excrutiating pain. From sympathy my pain came on after I was put to bed and was almost insupportable for an hour <they> it then abated, and was at intervals for about 24 hours, when they left me. To give you an idea of the success of the opperation and my good fortune as Dr Bushe remarks, the wound though nearly three inches long is almost entirely healed, and I was /so/ well that day & [hour] week after, as to put on my cloths (which was the first time) and walk nearly an half mile to the ferry and go over the North river to Hoboken, by & with the advice of the Doctor, as he said, that I might get a few hours of fresh air, which was truely acceptable, for there is none in this City & if possible less in the City Hotel, where I am. I have had every attention I could ask, and I hope to be perfectly restored of that part of my disease in a week. I consider myself very fortunate in determining to apply to Dr Bushe in preference to Dr Physic. I cannot say too much for D^r^ Bs skill, kindness of manner and attention. Previous to my confinement I took poor little James into Connecticut to a Dr Vanderburg,[2] who say he thinks he can cure him, that his disease arrises from an affection of the stomach. If he should not, he, Dr V. advises a voyage or two to Europe, which accords perfectly with my idea, from what I saw of his improvement on the voyage from Carolina. If /I/ have any knowledge a fine family and an amiable woman, <is> Mrs Vanderburg, and her family /are one./ All I am afraid of is that James will exercise his selfrule, though he behaved quite well while with me. He indicated a great deal of mind in all his movements and is not put out. Though there is nothing like forwardness in his general deportment.

Pretty soon after I get perfectly well of the opperation I expect to take <take> passage for Ocacock and then to Beaufort and to Newbern. My object in visiting Beaufort is to contract with a shipcarpenter to build Capt. Dunbar & myself a small schooner for the canal, to Norfolk. I hope by the time you will receive this that our dear Mother will have received the Portrait of my Dear dear Nancy, It was shipped last week. Please to give my Love to our dear

Mother, Brothers & sisters also my dearest dear Children and accept the affectionate regard of your afflicted Brother

E Pettigrew

N.B. I have directed this to Charles in the event of your absence as I have heard some one say that you were expected [here]

---

[1]George Macartney Bushe (1793-1836), a native of Ireland, came to the United States in 1828 as a professor at Rutgers Medical College. He maintained an active surgical practice in New York. Howard A. Kelly and Walter L. Burrage, *Dictionary of American Medical Biography* (New York: D. Appleton and Company, 1928), 180-181.

[2]No further information about Dr. Frederick Vanderburgh has been found.

[Dr.] William C. Warren to Ebenezer Pettigrew A&H

Tyrrell August 29th 1831

My Dear Sir,

I recd by the mail of last Wed. Mr Turner's favour communicating intelligence of your health etc. I am very happy to hear you have submitted to an operation and I hope most sincerely, it has proved entirely successful. The removal of the *Cist* will no doubt relieve your mind of much anxiety as well as your body of some pain—the latter I know you did not regard—Mr. T. informs me, that you bore the operation most heroically. I expected that, as I am aware of your decision & firmness. I should suppose before this you have recovered and I trust it will not be a great while before we shall have the pleasure of seeing you in Carolina—

Capt Dunbar returned a few days after the date of my last letter—all well. The articles sent for me I recd in good order—they are such as we wanted—The *book case* answers extremely well both in size & quality. Accept my best thanks for your kindness & trouble—Capt D. took a cargo of staves down to the *bar*, for Mr Dickinson who was loading a vessel for the West Indies—I was at the Lake two days since & went to your house—Your negroes were all well, though some of them have had mild bilious attacks—Mr [*Doctrine*] Davenport has also been indisposed, but is well again—he has had a dreadful season for ditching, but I believe his industry & perseverance will triumph over the elements.

Mr & Mrs Collins left here last friday for the north—They go through Richmond where they will find Mr. Collins Senr who will accompany them to N. York—

Mrs Warren was very near being killed on Sunday week—She was going to the Chapel, to attend the Sunday School, in Mr Weatherby's double gig, driven by Wm one of the traces broke & she was thrown out with her Infant in her arms—The Infant escaped with a bruize on the head, but Harriat had her arm partially dislocated at the elbow—she is now much better—

We have been much excited here within the last four days, by news of the insurrection in Southampton Va[1] I dont believe the negroes here have entertained any such design—

Mrs Warren begs you to accept her best wishes—Present me very kindly to Mr Turner & assure him of my most friendly consideration—(in great haste)

Your Friend most truly
& affectionately
W. C. Warren

It is very sickly here.

[*Addressed*] Ebenezer Pettigrew Esqr
Care of
Hicks & Smith
New. York

---

[1]A black field hand and lay preacher, Nat Turner, led a band of slaves in an uprising in Southampton County on August 22-23, 1831. The insurgents killed about sixty whites before the militia suppressed the revolt. Nat Turner's Rebellion influenced southern states to strengthen their slave codes and militias. Stephen B. Oates, *The Fires of Jubilee: Nat Turner's Fierce Rebellion* (New York: Harper and Row, 1975; New York: Mentor Books, 1976), 78-112, 164.

Charles Lockhart Pettigrew to Ebenezer Pettigrew UNC

Hillsboro September 19th 1831

Dear Papa

Brother William received your letter of 11th I was very glad to hear that you had recovered and that brother James was well and that he was situated in such a family. but I was very sorry to hear that he was so much hurt by the upseting of the cart and we may thank that God who rules all things that he was not taken from us. The Episcopal minister, Mr Green[1] gave notice that the Bishop[2] would visit Hillsboro about the middle of October; I ask your opinion about joining the church at that time <it> & whether you think it best to join then or not, please write me in your next letter what your opinion on that subject. It is my most ardent wish to join some church and fight under the banner of my lord and redeemer to fight under the banner of him who alone can give comfort to the soul. I have <a> very little prefference between the Presbyterian and the Episcopal churches, the only /difference/ is that my parents are in one, however I shall wait the arrival of your letter so anxiously looked for by me which is to contain such important news. By Religeon dear father we are able to bear up under any affliction whatever we can console our selves for the /loss/ our dear relations, our heavenly father (we know) sends nothing on his children which is not for their own good if he takes away a relation very dear to us it is for our good he does it try our faith or because our affections are to much placed on him. He who has God for his friend <is> has an unspeakable pleasure he is more than any earthly friend he can see into futurity and direct in the path of rectitude and pleasure all those who love and serve him. It would afford me great pleasure to say more on this important subject but paper and time will not allow. I am sorry to say that some of the boys who have empraced that religion which alone maketh rich have already or are <abut> about to fall, (I mean at chapel hill) O if they but knew the pangs they would suffer they would quickly return and that joifully. The celebrated minister which has done so much good throughout this country is again coming through here and then going to Chapel Hill. Not more that a fifth part of Mr Bingham's school are professors of religeon. it is to be hoped that as he comes through here he will impress the word deeply on their hearts so that they may turn from their sinful ways and live. Mr Mac Cever was here the first part of the session and I had the pleasure of his company several times, he has been to our house and knows you, he told me to send his respects to you. I have visited Mrs Scot twice since I left home; the family are all well; Mr Scot had his child christened the other day. There is a great rumor spread about here concerning the insurrection of the slaves, it frighted the poeple very much and it was <be> beleived so firmed beleived by the greater part of them that they formed a company and started off to oppose them but when they got as far a Chapel Hill they found that it was mear-ly <ar> a report; and they not only got the town company but sent Constables to summon men to attend a draft. the report originated <from> from the poeple of Wilmington send-ing to the govenor for arms. The rumor was that the negroes had burnt Wilmington and that a body of four thousand strong were marching to Av/a/resboro. Our /winter/ cloths are wearing out because having not had a ful supply of summer ones we were obliged to wear our winter cloths I ask you if it would not be best for our cloths to be mad at <new> New-bern and sent here by the stage you know that a coat made by a woman cannot set well and their is not a boy /in school/ from a distance who has not a taler made coat and I would not wish to be meaner clad than any of them and the talors charge so much here and the clothe also comes higher and therefore I thought it wold be best to have them sent from Newburn but it makes not much difference as I should submit to your better judgement. I can send my measure down in my next letter to that place. Uncle James [*Shepard*] gets all his cloths there and sent up to him and I suppose it must be cheaper to him please tell me in your next letter what I shall do. We are all very well please write as soon as you receive this

I am your affect/i/onate son
C L Pettigrew

[*Addressed*] Mr E Pettigrew
Newburn
N Carolina

---

[1]William Mercer Green, class of 1818 at the University of North Carolina, was a deacon at St. John's Church, Williamsboro, in 1822 and became rector there in 1823. He moved to Orange County in 1827, serving as rector of St. Matthew's Episcopal Church in Hillsborough until 1836 and then as a professor in the university until 1844. He was elected bishop of Mississippi in 1849 and served until 1887. Battle, *History of the University*, I, 339, 697, 789, 836; *Journal of the Proceedings of the Sixth Annual Convention of the Protestant Episcopal Church in the State of North Carolina . . . 1822* (New Bern: Pasteur & Watson, 1822), 3; *Journal of the Proceedings of the Seventh Annual Convention of the Protestant Episcopal Church in the State of North Carolina . . . 1823* (New Bern: Pasteur & Watson, 1823), 3; *Journal of the Diocesan Convention, 1827*, 3.

[2]Levi Silliman Ives (1797-1867) was elected bishop of North Carolina in 1831, succeeding John Stark Ravenscroft. A controversial figure in later life, he became Roman Catholic and resigned as bishop in 1852. After visiting Rome he returned to New York, where he taught the remaining years of his life. Haywood, *Lives of the Bishops*, 91-139. See also *DAB*, IX, 521-522. The *Whig* (Washington, N.C.), March 12, 1839, and February 20, 1842, published schedules of visitations, including several to Pettigrew's Chapel at Scuppernong and to Lake Phelps.

*Charles Biddle Shepard to [Charles Lockhart and William Shepard Pettigrew]**

A&H

Copy

New Bern, Oct. 1, 1831

My dear Nephews,

You will probably be surprised to receive this letter, but be assured that you have always been objects of lively solicitude to your uncle, tho he rarely has an opportunity to manifest his feelings. You are the children of a woman, who was adorned with every virtue that fallen humanity can attain—of a sister who was tenderly beloved by her relations, and whose untimely death has created a void in their hearts which will never be filled. As offspring of such a person you have, independently of your own qualifications, and youthful years, claims on the kindness &

attention of those who remember her good offices, & esteem her virtues. As a friend, a relative, as the brother of your departed mother, permit me, my dear boys, to ask your serious attention for a very few moments. You have publicly acknowledged yourselves sinners, & have asked the advise of your father relative to your future conduct. It delights me to think that you have begun thus early to love & reverence the Creator. The pleasures of this life too easily satiate the most greedy appetite to be objects of zealous persuit; we obtain them to day & we throw them off to morrow, with disgust & ennui. Those who have been the most steady & persevier-ing in their endeavours after earthly happiness, have at last been compelled to acknowledge the vanity of their wishes, expectations. He who rises early & labours assiduously, will reap the most fruitful harvest, so he that bows before his God in youth & continues steadfast in the faith, will receive the brightest crown of glory in a future world.

But let me beg you to be cautious & circumspect. Many have mistaken the influence of fright for the suggest[io]ns of the spirit: too many have yealded to the whispers of fancy [i]nstead of calling to their aid the power of the understanding. At Chapel Hill, some of those who <possessed> professed to be Christians have returned unto the ranks of the ungodly, & I dare say that they are much worse people now, than before their *conversion*. Why is this? They were excited when they made professions. A guilty conscience will rain specters, which cause the stoutest hearts to quail. The preachers also often seek to arouse the feelings, and thro' them bring a wicked creature to act without referrence to his reason; Talk to a sinner of hell & its horrors, get him to believe himself on the eve of entering that direfull place and he will make any acknowledgements, any promise to escape. But when the excite-ment has subsided, when he feels that he is yet far from the regions of the damned, he will go back to the ways of wickedness. All sudden conversions should be distrusted, enthusiasm & violence [c]annot convince the understanding, and that Religion, which does not have the understanding for its basis, is not a Religion fit for reasonable creatures. My dear boys, when a man is in anger, he is ignorant of what he does or says; as soon as the fit is passed, he feels ashamed of his conduct, & he will scarcely believe that he acted so much like a fool. A similar remark will apply when any other violent passion is operating on the mind. I hope that the Religion which you profess comes from the heart, I hope that it has proceeded from the gradual wo[rk]ings of the mind, & not from a heated & unhealthy immagination. I will /give/ you a test of its purity. If the love of God is always warm in your hearts; if when you lie down to sleep & when you rise to work, you have the same feelings of unabated affection for the Maker; if during the business of the day the trials & vexations of a school boy's life you still remember the Deity & still feel towards him as one should feel to the father who protects & cherishes him, your Religion is a Righteous Religion. But if when alone you forget him, if the persuasions of enthusiastic men, if vehement preachings, if violent revilings of the Devil, are necessary to keep alive the spirit of Religion, be assured that such a religion will never carry you to Heven. Retire to your closit, let no one see you but your Heavenly King, commune with him, examine your heart / heart & ask yourself those questions, Am I a sinner? do I love God? Is he a good God? do I obey him? does my Religion proceed him from gratitude, from filial fear? Am I in a right state of mind to think on so awful a subject? If these questions are answered affirmatively your Religion is a good Religion. But what Church will you join? by all means, the Epis[co]pal. That is the Church of your pious Grandfather & sainted mother. They were wise & virtuous, you are young & inexperienced; and untill you are convinced that they were wrong, you shoud walk in the path which they have made to keep you from wandering.

If my prayers could avail on high, you should have them, my dear Charles & William; but I am too great a sinner to expect that my intercession could benefit any body. I can only wish you happiness & prosperity, both earthly & heavenly.

Ch. Shepard

William A. Turner to [Ebenezer Pettigrew] A&H

New York. Octo 21. 1831.

My Good Sir,

I had the pleasure to receive your letter dated at Newbern 23rd Ulto. by the discourse of the mail and I rejoice that you, not only passed over the deep water safely, but continue in health. I need not now inform you how much I should dread the Sea, but I will say that as I heard the wind whistle by my window during one or two nights of the week which followed your departure I could but reflect upon the dangers which were probably at those moments surrounding you, yet I hoped, as it is common for winds to be violent here, and not extend far to the south, that you were out of their reach.

I am afraid of the Sea; and it always seems to me that when a man ventures upon it, he tacitly challenges and defies the power of his Maker, or, that he is forgetful of his own comparative nothingness. Nevertheless, if I had it as a duty to live upon the waves; I can but believe, that I could become a seaman equal to any common trial. You speak of the heavy winds you experienced, and you seem, while lost in the contemplation of your misfortunes, to consider /their/ attendant gloom, as resembling your broodings over the past. My sympathies in your feelings are as accute as ever, and while I would exclaim how comfortable would be a state of forgetfulness of our misfortunes, it occurs to me in the next breath, how miserable would be the refections which would lead to it as a choice, indeed they would be intolerable. I would rather hug my miseries the more closely to my breast than to forget my affections. If the sympathies of your friends could avail to alleviate your condition, and remove the depression you habitually suffer, your Sea of life would be smooth indeed, and fair would be the breeze that would move you upon it: But, they can not. The Power that gave us life has fixed his veto; He has for his own unquestionable purposes, (and it is to be ardently hoped, and confidently trusted, for our ultimate good,) decreed that Man, while in this world shall mourn.

In your letter I read with sincerest concern, the heart rending cruelties produced by the evil of the whites and blacks living in the same community, and neither sufficiently understanding how to govern.

I coincide with you entirely, in the opinion that much is owing to the bad management experienced by the blacks from the whites. And all know that if the blacks had the ascendancy it would be worse.

Where is the remedy? It is resolvable, after years of reflection upon it, in this. In the promulgation of that principle which is couched in the words. "Do unto others as you would have others to do unto you." and until this shall become universally the rule and conduct of each individual. Peace & happiness will not fix their abodes on earth.

I now come to the part of your letter communiting /the/ unfortunate situation of your son [*Henry*], attacked in the same way that James is. It seemed that you previously had a heavy load of cares; This addition to them is peculiarly distressing. But are you sure you do not do yourself injustice in taking it as an infliction upon you for your faults? Injustice should not be done to oneself any more than to others. and as we can not even peep into the purposes of infinite wisdom, and ought not to question his management of us, it would be a step toward consolation to submit and ascribe it to other designs of Providence than to afflict us for our wrong doings, especially when they are so small and unimportant as to require magnifying greatly to bring them to a mark of compunction.

I sincerely hope he may experience only a momentary duration of the disease and that he may fill, ultimately, the measure of your hopes & expectations of him.

I have now only to add that no change has occurred in my affairs, and that I am still calculating upon working my safety apparattus into use, Some of the best judges of such things, in this city, have declared in its favour. I perceive by some inquiries of the Treasury department in the papers that Congress will shortly have the subject under consideration and if I can bring my plan before their committee fairly, I shall bravely undertake to show its perfect feasibility. As <good> sure a way to get at the upper branches of a tree, as any, is to cut away its trunk & have nothing to support them. So,—as sure a way to prevent explosion is to not have too much fire, & for *itself* to put *itself* out. when *itself* shall become so intense as to endanger *itself* blowing *itself* to atoms in every direction.

I am in good health, and am charged by Mrs. Street to thank you for your complimentary respects, and to reciprocate to you, hers with mine which I assure are as ever, and will be forever, most sincerely felt, & cherished.

Wm. A. Turner

Richard Muse Shepard to Ebenezer Pettigrew UNC

NewBern. Novem 11, 1831

Dear Brother

I regret that I am again compelled by painful, but unavoidable circumstances to remit the intelligence of Henry's increasing danger.—If it had /been/ the ordinary disease, that /has/ par<y>alyzed his energies, and reduced him to a mere autometon, it would perhaps then appear, as if the desire of communicating was superfluous, if not improper.—But in addition to the enormous load of human misery that is inseparable from the nature of his disease, he has been visited by the fever, whose attack is extremely dangerous, if not fatal. As I wish not to inflict unnecessary pain by transmitting exaggerated /intelligence/ so I would not lull you by deceitful representations into a false security.—His danger is very great, and even if he should survive this attack, would not his frame be as shattered, and his constitution so weakened, as to render his cure permanent [*sic*]? It would be needless to say that every attention to restore him to health has been, and will continue to be extended, as long as he remains with us. I would not consent to write this letter untill I was earnestly /requested/ by mother and the rest of the family. believe to be your's truly

R. M. Shepard

[*Addressed*] Mr E. Pettigrew
Cool. Springs
Tyrrell County
N Carolina

Ebenezer Pettigrew to Charles Lockhart and William Shepard Pettigrew UNC

Lake Phelps. Dec. 11, 1831

My dear sons,

When I left Newbern on the 4th I requested your Uncle Charles (which he has no doubt done) to inform you of the death your dear little brother Henry. O! my dear sons your poor Father has had to pass through another heart rending scene, that of witnessing the last agonies of his sweet little dear boy Henry. He was some time in the fall taken with the disease which your brother James had, and was taken with an affection of the breast, accompanied with a fever which did not intermit for thirty five days, at which time it pleased our Almighty father to require his soul. When his disease became dangerous I was sent for, and was with him nineteen days, under the greatest state of hope & dispair. My dear boys, the love which I bear to my children is beyond my language to express, but the mild, condesending, patient and affectionate conduct of my dear Henry bound me to him with cords, that it was more than death to break. But praised be God, I am able to say with sincerity of heart. The Lord gave and the Lord hath taken away, blessed be the name of the Lord. The dear little boy bore his sufferings without a murmur, and would even ask me, when excessively oppressed with fever, if he might put out from under the covering one of his armes, before he would do it. One night while I & Jim [*James Biddle Shepard*] were siting up with, him, about eleven oclock, I was siting by his bed side he told me he wanted Uncle Jim to sit beside him, after Jim was seated, he called me to him & remarked Pa dont you want to go to sleep. Mr Goodman visited him twice and talked to him about his situation, and prayed by him, /in/ all which he acted with that composure which belongs to mature age. After one of Mr G. visits he told me he was glad to hear <my> him talk so. O! my dear sons endeavour to regulate your conduct in this world so that when it /may/ please your blessed Father to call you, you /may/ see your dear dear Mother & little brothers in that world where sorrow is not known, and the tears shall be wiped from every eye. My dear little Henry was in the agonies of death for 4 hours, but retained his senses to the very last, and as long as he could speak he kept calling Pa, but alas I could understand nothing more. Not long before he expired he held up his arm & pointed his finger to his Aunt Pene[*lo*]pe, she went to him but he could not speak, when not long after he resigned his soul to that blessed God who gave it. I brought his pretious remains with me and he is laid with his dear Mother & brothers. My dear sons, by this lamantable occurrance my sorrows are multiplyed but they cannot be increased, my cup was full, and all I can say is blessed be the name of the Lord.

My dear Charles, I receivd your letter on my arrival here. I cannot say how much I was gratified at its contents, My dear sons strive to enter in at the traight gate, and to lay up treasure in heaven where moth nor rust do not corrup, nor theaves do not break though and steal. If your poor sorrowing Father had the wealth of worlds, h[*torn*] would give it all, and would be willing to be turned upon [*torn*] world as naked as he came into it, could he have been brou[*torn*] your age to a sense of his duty to his God & his son our [*torn*]viour Jesus Christ. But blessed be God I have been brought to a knowledge <of my duty towards him> /that/ my redemer liveth and that he shall stand at the latter day upon the earth, and that I shall see God. Mr Collins has returned from the North. He says your Brother James is well, but I regret exceedingly to inform you, that he has behaved very bad. He has been very ungovernable, and cursed the family, refuses to go to sunday school or church. The family he is with, is one among the kindest & best I have ever seen. I wish my dear sons, you would write me oftener by turns. Give my kind regards to M^r^ & Mrs Bingham, and beleve me your afflicted & affectionate father

E Pettigrew

[*Addressed*] Masters Charles & William Pettigrew
Hillsborough
N. Carolina

Agreement between Jesse Spruill and Ebenezer Pettigrew A&H

Dec. 22, 1831

This agreement between E. Pettigrew of the one part and Jessie Spruill of the other part witnesseth, That the Said Jesse Spruill doth agree to attend to the said E Pettigrew's plantation named Belgrade, in the capacity of an Overseer, to be up late & early and obey all the lawfull & reasonable orders of the said E Pettigrew in the year 1832, and the said E Pettigrew doth on his part agree to furnish the said Spruill within said year, four hundred pounds pork, one barrell Herrings, ten gallons Molasses, and meal as he may want. Also at the end of the year for the well performance of his duty the said E Pettigrew doth agree to pay to the said Jesse Spruill the sum of seventy five dollars and if he approves fully of the said Jesse Spruill's conduct, he agrees to give him over and above the sum of seventy five dollars above mentioned, the sum of twenty five dollars. Witness our hands and seals this twenty second day of December 1831.

E Pettigrew (seal)

Jesse Spruil (seal)
his mark

Witness
Doctrine Davenport

John Herritage Bryan to Ebenezer Pettigrew **A&H**

Monday 30 Jany. 1832

My dear Sir,

I wrote you during the first week in this month, since which I have not heard from you.—The children are well—Mary & Nancy are in very good health.—

We have the Bishop now with us, he gives very great satisfaction—he is plain, pious & zealous. Knowing that it would be very agreeable to you to see him at the Lake, I mentioned the subject to him, and he has very kindly consented to go down.—His regular appointment is at Plymo. on Thursday the 16th Feby. He says that he will be at Plymo. on his way to the Lake on the Monday night before, that is the 13th—

You will I have no doubt derive great Comfort and benefit from his Society & conversation.—

Mrs Ives, & one child are with him.—

He requests me to say to you, that you may make an appointment for him to preach at the Chapel (your father's) either Tuesday afternoon or Wednesday morning at lunch <time> hour as you think best, bearing in mind that he is to be in Plymo. to preach at 11 on Thursday the 16th—

You will be able I hope to meet him at Plymo. Monday night, and you had better come in your barouche.

Mrs Bryan is not well—she has a cough which I fear is the commencement of the influenza.—

Mrs Shepard and family are in ordinary health.

Very truly
Yr friend & relative
Jn H Bryan

[*Addressed*] Ebenezer Pettigrew Eq
Cool Spring
N.C

Ebenezer Pettigrew to Charles Lockhart and William Shepard Pettigrew UNC

Charleston S.C., Apr. 2, 1832

My dear sons,

You will be surprised to see this letter dated from this place. I am on my way to visit your Uncle John Shepard, and from thence to the western district of Tennessee, where I hope to be able to effect something with my lands in that place.

I passed through Newbern & stayed eight days with your dear little sisters & brother, they were all well. I received also a letter from Dr Vanderburg who James lives with. He writes me that James is quite recovered from his disease. In truth he gives a very flattering account of him. My dear sons, I was exceeding gratified to learn from Mr Bingham of your good conduct <in the s> with him, but I hope you will not forget everything else but your studies. I have not received from you William since Octber a single letter, and but one from you Charles, and in that you never seemed to recollect your poor dear little /brother/ Henrys death. O that dear little boy. How my heart bleeds when I think of him. But blessed be God he is gone to the arms of his & your dear ever dear Mother. I had wished you alternately to write your father every fortnight, and if you Knew with what axiety I send to the office you would not withhold your pen. With regard to your coming down at the end of the session I have not yet determined. Neither whether you (Charles) will go to College or not. It is of great importance in the event of my death that some one should know something of the plantation. Depend upon that if I were dead you would find yourselves in a very different situation from what you now are. Recollect my dear Charles, that you have got a dear little Sister not yet two years old. Who is her natural Guardian in the event of your fathers death? Her two elder brothers. If they will not come forward, no other person will consider themselves bound. O my dear Charles & William, in the event of my death, watch over, & guard your two dear little innocent sisters. Remember they are the helpless, they are the innocent part of creation, they are the <are the> daughters of your dear dear Mother, who had she lived, would have cherished them as the apple of her eye. Guard over them, watch over them & so protect the dear little innocents, as that when it may please your heavenly /father/ to take them from this world of sorrow they may be found fit to be received into the bosom of <your of> their dear Mother. My dear sons keep up that spirit of vital religion of which you have made a profession.

I am now with all your relations the Pettigrews. I am pleased to say that they are very respectable, and would be a credit to us any where. Remember me affectionately to Mr & Mrs Bingham. and beleive always your affectionate & afflicted father

E Pettigrew

[*Addressed*] Masters Charles & William Pettigrew
Hillborough
North Carolina

Charles Biddle Shepard to Ebenezer Pettigrew A&H

[*New Bern*] July 22d 1832

My dear Brother,

I received your letter a few weeks ago, & was glad that your health was good & that you found <your> the plantation in good order—

I am better in health than when you left New Bern; tho' I still feel weak & prostrate. Lydia's health is very bad; I have tried to persuade her to take a trip to the West, but I am unsuccessful. Mary has recovered from her attack of bilious fever, & I think with little care will be as well as ever—Your children are in excellent health; particularly Johns[*t*]on, who has gone with Mama to Beaufort. Mama has been complaining, & she thought that the sea air might be serviceable—Richard has returned & gone down to Beaufort—Br John staid with us abut a month. I hope that you will not spend all the warm season at the Lake; I think that your health might be benefitted & your spirits refreshed by a little jaunt. To the south I would not go; for I would not unnecissarily expose my self to disease, tho' I might be sure that I should escape A merchant of N. York wrote a letter to Mr Jones, stating that the Cholera had produced a very disastrous effect on the business of the city; many failures had taken place & more were expected. I expect that the population of N.Y. is the most excitable in the Union; Philadelphia is quite calm about the disease, but N.Y. was thrown into alarm & confusion when it first reached the Continent. The reason must be, that the people of the latter city [*illegible*] evil & terrible & I suppose also that it was more liable to suffer in consequence of its immense commerce—therefore more excitement—

Richard was delighted with Louisiana. He thinks of settling in N. Orleans, & I believe that he would make a fortune there, if he could resist the temptations of the city—Quarre? He gives a gloomy account of the lands in Tennesse; he could not sell them at any price & I fear that they will become valueless—My taxes were 64$; I will not pay this sum often, I would prefer to give the lands away—

Lydia joins me in love to you

Believe me your aff Brother
C. Shepard

[*Addressed*] E. Pettigrew Esq
Cool Spring
Washington C.
N.C.

Charles Lockhart Pettigrew to Ebenezer Pettigrew UNC

Chapel-Hill Monday 6th Aust 1832

Dear father

I have entered college and am about to recite my first lesson on ancient geography. I have taken up my board at the same place where uncle James boards and which is /the best place/ in the village it is a very good house and I <board> think I shall board as long as I stay here; Mr Bingham tried to get my board a doctor Caldwell's[1] but his wife[2] being sick <I cou> he could not take me. I am in very good health and have not been sick since I got clear of that coald. It is very healthy here and there are very few people sick, there is a great drought in this part of the contry and it is thought there will not be more than half crops made there has not been /<rain> except/ within a few days a sufficient quantity of rain in a-bout three months.

I <shall ha> have to study very hard but neverthe less I have adopted the plan of not eating much and taking regular exercise we recite three lessons every day one in the morning and another at eleven O clock and a third in the evening, I /have/ but little time to spare. Uncle James is a very hard student he studies nearly all day and very late at night and I am glad to say that he studies to some purpose he about the best scholar in his class and it is very likely that he will speak the latin speach which is a great honour. When I left Hillsborough for Chapel Hill Mr Bingham gave me 80 dollars to bear my expences for the present session and told me if <I> I r/e/quired more he would give it /to/ me, but I feel a diffidence in asking or writting to him for money which I would not feel by applying to you and I being no more his scholar it would be as well for me nex session to get the money from you that is if it accords with your wishes it is now now about ten O clock and I must go to bed and I end my letter by telling you good night please give my love to Grand ma and <and> respects to all my acquaintances

I shall ever your affectionate and dutiful son
Charles L Pettigrew

N.B. I here send you a copy of Mr Gaston's speech[3] before the dielectic and Philanthropic societies. Direct you your letters to Chapel Hill.

[*Addressed*] M^r^ E Pettigrew
Cool Spring
N.C.

---

[1]The Reverend Joseph Caldwell (1773-1835) was born in New Jersey, graduated from Princeton, and studied for the ministry. He became professor of mathematics at the University of North Carolina in 1796. Caldwell was elected by the trustees as the first president of the university in 1804; he resigned in 1812 to devote more time to his studies and teaching and resumed the presidency in 1817. He served until his death and energetically devoted himself to the growth of the university. Powell, *DNCB*, I, 303-304.

[2]Caldwell and his second wife, Helen Hogg Hooper of Hillsborough, were married in 1809. Powell, *DNCB*, I, 303.

[3]In his 1832 commencement address at the university, William Gaston denounced disunion and predicted the eventual abolition of slavery. The speech was regarded as one of his two most exceptional, and it "met with public favor to a most extraordinary degree." Battle, *History of the University*, I, 344.

James Biddle Shepard to [Ebenezer Pettigrew] UNC

[*Chapel Hill*] Saturday August 2/5/th 1832.

Dear Cousin

It is with pleasure that I set down to write you a few lines. I have for a long time intended to write you a letter. I am now in the Junior Class. The tutors hear the Freshman and Sophomore classes and the Professors hear the Junior and Senior classes. As I have nothing more to do with the tutors, we very often visit each other. Frequently I make inquiries concerning Charles, and I am glad to inform you that he stands very good and that he holds a high station with respect to his moral or religious character. I heard from Charles that James had relapsed into his old state. Mr Bingham informs me that William studies quite hard. He is certainly the most ambitious little fellow that I ever heard of, which, I think, is very good, if not carried to an excess, for you know moderation in every particular is preferable. I arrived at Hillsboro on the day after you left in May last. I saw Brother John a few weeks ago. He has gone to Tennessee. His house at Florida was blown up by some means or other, no one knows how. He has some idea of moving from Florida. I suppose you have heard how fatal the cholera has been in Norfolk perhaps more fatal than in Europe according to its population. I am in hopes that it will not reach this part of the state in which I now am, owing to its elevated situation. I hope you will write me as soon as you can and believe me

Yours forever
James B. Shepard

Ebenezer Pettigrew to Mary Williams Bryan UNC

Plymouth Aug 25, 1832

My dear Sister

Yesterday afternoon I received a letter from Dr Vanderburgh /dated the 16th/ giving me a hopeless account of my poor dear James' disease. I give you a copy of his letter.

Since I last wrote you James has experienced some amendment of his disease till last week, when his mouth became suddenly enflamed & his digestive organs much more deranged.

He is now confined to his bed and complains of pain at intervals about the region of the heart which produces a deep flush of the face & indicates the approach of spasms—I am begining to feel anxious for the result—I am still in consultation with Dr Bushe but our united efforts thus far hold no command over the progress of disease.

At the receit of this information you can better immagine my feelings (who know me so well) than I can discribe them & With the advice of Dr Warren I determined once more to see him if alive, and have accordingly set out this morning at 6 oclok. I take the boat at this place at half after 2. and hope if not stoped by Cholera to be at New Milford, Ct. by next thursday. I shall pass through all the infected towns, but have great Reliance on my digestive powers, temperate habits, and the mercy of a Good and patient God. My life is a great burden, but I know it is of the first importance to my poor little dear children that I should live. My health at this time was never better. I will write on my arrival at Connecticut. I feel great solicitude for & wish very much to see my dear little children in your town. Please to kiss them for me Give my affectionate regards to our dear mother your companion and my other friends & believe me your afflicted brother

E Pettigrew

[*Addressed*] Mrs Mary W. Bryan
Newbern
N. Carolina

Ebenezer Pettigrew to Mary Williams Bryan UNC

Lake Phelps Sep 27, 1832

My dear Sister,

I returned to my prison the day before yesterday. I found my dear James, better than when the Doctor wrote but still in a deplorable situation. He is unable to turn himself in bed or to walk a step. He can sit in a chair when taken up, and had improved very much from the time of arrival & leaving. His mind is perfectly unimpaired, and spirits unbroken. He is very much pleased with all the people, and they with him & are exceedingly kind to him. His character stands very high for talent, good humour, Tractibleness &c. The Doctor is satisfied that his disease has been brought on this time by indulgence in eating & that it can <it can> be cured. When he gets on his feet again, (which I /pray/ God will be in a month) the Dr will send him to Europe or some long voyage to sea. He, with myself thinks it the best chance to make a permanent cure. The Doctor as well as myself have not the smallest doubt but that poor James disease was first brought on by eating too much & too rich food. Pray my dear Sister, do not permit my dear little Girls /to/ run the like risk by eating. I fear they have the stomach of my dear dear Nancy their mother. My sufferings now, are as great as my mind can bear, and if they should take the disease I know not what would become of me. On my return I found a letter from Mr Bingham and James Shepard; both which are truely flattering of my two dear sons. No one can have a higher character than Charles. Praised be Almighty God, for directing me to so dear a mother for my children. Oh! that she could have lived to have seen her fruit thus ripen. But blessed be God she is enjoying the fruit of a short but well spent life, and I /am/ left a poor, miserable, disconsolate wretch, that I may repent of my past most awfull sins & prepare for that world where she has gone. But for the mercy of God, who willeth not the death of sinner but that all should turn to him & live, I should /long/ have been plunged into everlasting & irremediless wo.

I regret very much to learn of the loss of Cousin Rachel [*Blount?*], in the death of Cousin Mary. For one who needs so much consolation as myself and who is suffering so keen an anguish, consolation in words cannot be expected. The Lord giveth & the Lord taketh away, blessed be the name of the Lord.

Ann Blount (Nancy) Shepard and Ebenezer Pettigrew were married in 1815. Mrs. Pettigrew spent part of each year at Bonarva on Lake Phelps and part with her family in New Bern, resulting in an extensive correspondence. Photographs of portraits at Mulberry Plantation, Camden, South Carolina, courtesy of Mrs. John H. Daniels.

William Shepard Pettigrew, the second surviving son of Ebenezer and Nancy Pettigrew, was born in 1818. Photograph of a portrait courtesy of Mrs. John H. Daniels.

Ebenezer Pettigrew's daughter Mary Blount Pettigrew lived with the family of her aunt and uncle, Mr. and Mrs. John Herritage Bryan, after the death of her mother in 1830. Photograph of a portrait courtesy of Mrs. John H. Daniels.

Mary Blount Pettigrew, 1750-1786, wife of the Reverend Charles Pettigrew and mother of Ebenezer Pettigrew. Photograph of a portrait by William Williams courtesy of the Museum of Early Southern Decorative Arts, Winston-Salem.

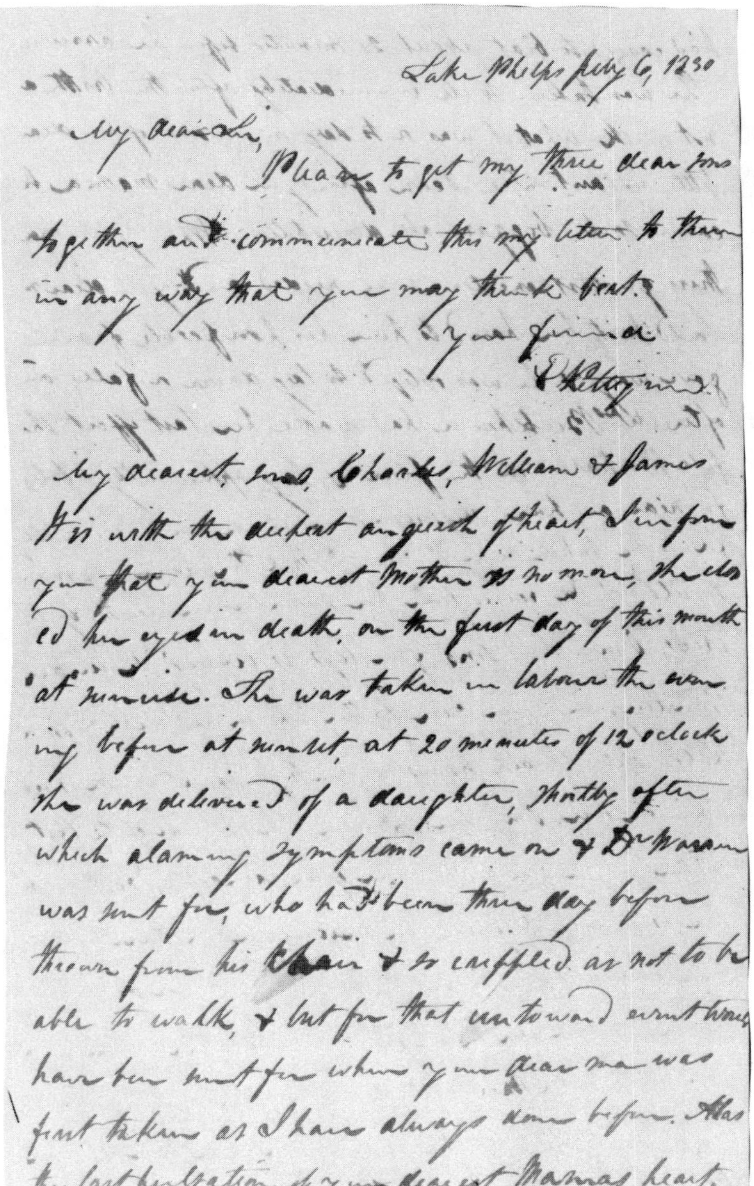
Lake Phelps July 6, 1830

My dear Sir,

Please to get my three dear sons together and communicate this my letter to them in any way that you may think best.

Your friend
E. Pettigrew

My dearest sons, Charles, William & James
It is with the deepest anguish of heart, I inform you that your dearest Mother is no more, she clos ed her eyes in death, on the first day of this month at sunrise. She was taken in labour the even ing before at sunset, at 20 minutes of 12 o'clock she was delivered of a daughter, shortly after which alarming symptoms came on & Dr Warren was sent for, who had been three days before thrown from his chair & so crippled as not to be able to walk, & but for that untoward event would have been sent for when your dear ma was first taken as I have always done before. Alas the last pulsation of your dearest Mamas heart.

Ebenezer Pettigrew wrote this letter to his sons and their schoolmaster, William J. Bingham. A transcription of the document, which is in the Archives, Division of Archives and History, is printed on page 142.

My health was never /better/ than at this time. Distress & anxiety of mind it seems cannot Kill me. I am condemned to live. I passed through all the Cholera towns on the road. I have lost all fear of it & am satisfied from what I can learn that at least ¼ who die of it, die from fear. It is an awful disease. I had at New York, when going to New Millford, the premonotory symptoms, very marked. I sent for Dr Bushe and got the necessary medicine, but did not nead them my system /& habits/ was equivalent to resist the disease. It is at Edenton & what I learned yesterday I suspect it is /in/ Scuppernong. I wish exceedingly to visit you but cannot tell how to do it.

The week previous to my return Dr Warren moved pack & package to Edenton. I have no comment to make on the subject. Mr & Mrs Collins are staying there also at this time. So that I may be considered alone. Perhaps the more weight of that kind I may have to bear, the more energy I may have. There is a Doctor taken Dr W.s place. I have not seen him. I do /not/ care much for any of them, I have at last learned that they are but men, and as mean and ignorent as other men, and little to be depended on.

I hope my dear Sister that you are in health. I regret to learn when at Edenton from a Mr Latimer that you were <des> rather desponding. Let me besseech /you/ to let no such ideas dwell on your mind, nothing can be worse. Our fears kill us. and if they do not they detress & make us miserable. Fear nothing. /That/ God whom you worship is with you, he has promised that he will not leave nor forsake those who serve & put their trust in him. He is able to save all. Therefore fear not.

As respects Cholera, which you must have in Newbern sooner or later, their laws to the contrary notwithstanding, I would advise great temperance in eating, avoiding all fruit & vegetables, also exposure so as to obstruct perperation, with a mind <cool> cool, composed, & fearless. There /are/ great differences of opinion among the Doctors to the North concerning the manner of treating but not as to the manner of living. No doubt great numbers have been killed by them. The great thing, as a Physitian told me, is to attack the premonotary symptoms, that the cramp may not appear.

Please to give my kind regards to Mr Bryan our dear mother, our brothers & sisters & Kiss my dear children for [*torn*] Hoping they are all well, and believe me to be y[our *torn*] affectionate Brother

E Pettigrew

Mrs Mary W. Bryan.

N.B. Pleease to /tell/ Lidia that her three younger children have been sick but they are all at this time perfectly well. My negroes were a good deal sick while I was gone, but by good luck & not management, none of them died & there is not at this time one on the sick list, which is saying a good deal for 70 persons at this season of the year in a mud hole as some think.

E P.

N.B. Octr 1, 1832 I went to the office in full expectation of a letter from some of my friends in Newbern, but alas! there was none. Pray ask some one to write by the next mail. A letter put in the office on Thursday I can get on sunday My poor Old Mother is in usual health, but very dissatisfied & out of mind. Poor me.

E P.

[*Addressed*] Mrs Mary W. Bryan
Newbern
North Carolina

Charles Lockhart Pettigrew to Ebenezer Pettigrew UNC

Chapel-Hill, Nov. 3^{d} 1832

Dear Father.

I received your letter of 28th with much pleasure and was glad to hear that poor brother James had somewhat recovered from the unfortunate state into which, he had at length fallen, and I still hope that there may be a prospect of his recovery, though it should be slow. Your plan of sending him to Europe will no doubt be of great service to him, but worst of it is to get him with a suitable person or persons and they are very hard to be fou/n/d in a ship-crew. however upon the whole he will derive infinite advantage from it. I should wish to know whether the Cholera had commited much distruction among the people over the Sound and the most distinguished <victims> /persons/ that have fallen victims to its rage; it will however soon cross the Sound and ravage our whole country except in those places where it cannot go on account of the thinness of the population. I regret to learn the feeble state of my dear grandma health however her age will not permit her <my> to enjoy the health of youth she has lived a long life having enjoyed both the pleasures and pains of life and it begins to be time for her to think of leaving this world for another: Please give my love and kind regard to her and remind her that I have not forgotten her.

You were on your way from Newbern to Lake Phelps, when you wrote your letter, together with my dear little sisters and brother to visit the place which had given birth to them and had souccoured them in their infancy and the place at which I have spent so many happy hours which never will be equaled again, I fear; and then I suppose they will again be carried to Newbern. I am very sorry to think that the Cholera will prevent my going home in the vacation for I should like to see us all together again after so long a separation but I hope the Cholera will not get their by that time or will have passed by in the meantime I shall try to use my time to the best advantage: and I also shall be as economical as is consistent. this session is all so a more costly session than common, for this being the begin I to supply myself with every thing and also I have to contribute to the raising of a monument over a fellow student who has lately die for I could not refuse as every member of my society has contributed to it and also other expenses. And I shall express my sentiments freely to you know that you will hear them. I am now in the first session of the freshman class and will have three more years and a half to stay before I can graduate and am under the direction of tutors who know comparitively nothing, there I think it would be best for me to go home this vacation and to remain / to remain home during the next session and join my class in in the Sophomore class the reason why I propose this is because the studies are easy and I can get them at home without any assistants and and it would save between <tw> one and <thre> two hundred dollars which is better saved than lost for those reasons I would prefer going home and stay for six months and then we can arrange matters to our mutual satisfaction. I was very much rejoiced to hear that you would come to Chapel Hill the latter part of this month for I should be very glad to see you. Please answer my letter as soon as you can, and believe me to be you most affectionate so[*n*]

Charles L. Pe[ttigrew]

[*Addressed*] Mr Ebenezer Pettigrew
Cool Spring
Washington Co
N. Carolina

William G——[1] *to Nathaniel Phelps* A&H

Jefferson [*Tennessee*] Jan 7th 1833

Dr Sir

This will inform you and all inquiring friends That I am still alive and in good heath. I have no news of mutch importance to give you. Our cotten crops have nearly made a total failure we dont make more than an average of three hundred to the acre. This makes the times distressing to all who are in debt. The Lands and negroes in this section bares high prices Lands in this neighbourhood from ten to twenty Dollars P^{r} acre and negroes in proportion to those prices. Our cotten is only worth two cents in the Seed corn is from Seventy five cents to one dollar P. Barrel. Pork from one fifty to two dollars coffee from twelve to fifteen cents and Sugar from Six to eight cts Pr [pnd]. This is about our times here we have but few nulafyers and they are thought to be strongly mixt with the foul disease of Toryism and I hope that all sutch men and principles will not be treated with any good respects. From true Republicans nulafyers are calculated to sap and destroy this happy and equitable Goverment which stands unrivald in the History of Nations. Destroy this and freedom will groan Under the Yoke of despots and Tyrants. Away then with all sutch principles and thaughts to the nethermost regeons from whence they sprang. For it was the same principle which sprang from selfish disappointment. That made the Devil in disguise creep into the happy Garden under false shape and delusive persuasions. To bring a curse and eturnal ruion upon the thoughtless and happy acupents of that blissful place of abode. Those are reflections that are sufficient. If properly applide to the present crises of our happy Goverment. I will turn if you please to matters of Smaller importance. Tho matters that afford us a gradeal of pleasure. That of conversing with a friend tho at a great distance and hearing from our friends. I want to hear from you so soon as you get this and from the following Familys and persons Uncle Joseph Wynne and family Jerry Wynne and family B. L Hathaway and family. John Whorton and family Asa Alexander and family Mrs Lavina Phelps and family Dempsey Sprewil and family Col Benjamin Tarkenton and family—But Joyce Hathaway that was in perticular. I want to hear from her and that she is doing as well as life can wish. You know how times was once. Give them all My love and best respects. Tell them I would be [*torn*] to receive a letter from any of them when any of [*torn*] take the time to write. I was at old friend [*torn*] the other day they are both in good health tho [*torn*] done a bad business on the Road they have [*torn*] their place to pay their debts and it is barely [*torn*] as it 36 36. I remain your sencer friend [*torn*] time shall close those Earthly seans.

Wm G[*torn*]

Jefferson Lin
Jany 11th

[*Addressed*] Mr Nathaniel Phelps
Cool Springs
Washington County
N. Carolina

[1]The letter is torn.

William Shepard Pettigrew to Ebenezer Pettigrew UNC

Hillsborough 15th of January 1833

Dear Father

With the greatest pleasure I asshure you I commence at this time to write you a fiew lines. In my journy to Hillsboro, several very disagreeale inconveniences happened, for when we arrived at Raleigh all the seats in the stage wer engaged, and so we could not go that day without hiring something, at last we hired a carriage and started<e> for Hillsboro about 4 in the evening, but we had not gone more than 14 miles When the cariage broke down, then we started to Mr Morear's which was about six miles and remained their untill day and then walked to Chapelhill, and their <we> I remain untill Sunday evening when I started to Hillsboro, when we wer within about one mile of Hillsboro, the stage overturned and hurt several of the passengers, particularly an old man who almost had his arn broken, I escaped without the least injury I arrived t this place about 4 Oclock on Monday morning, Mr and Mrs Bingham are very well, very fiew of Mr B scholars have arrived. You must excuse my bad writing for I have a very long and hard lesson to gett to night. Give my best love to Grand Ma and all my friende's and relations.

Believe me your affectionate Sone
William S Pettigrew

[*Addressed*] Mr Ebenezer Pettigrew
Coolspring Postoffie
Washington County
NC.

Sarah Porter Fuller[1] *to Ebenezer Pettigrew* UNC

[*Chowan*] January the 23. 1833

My dear Cousin

It is with great diffidence I address you on <you> the present Occasion, Not that I distrust your affection & generosity, nor that I have ceased to feel that natural & affectionate regard for you which I have ever expressed; nor yet that I have undone or even thought anything to your prejudice, or that could in any manner /render/ me unworthy of your kindness & esteem; but I am afraid you will not be able fully to appreciate my feelings or to judge of my situation—could you do this, I know you would soon have renewed in your bosom that tender regard for my happiness which I am certain you once felt for it. you know me too well, Cousin E to think me a hypocrite; and, I think, I am too well acquainted with you to believe that you will be regardless of professions which nothing but affection could dictate, or that you will turn a deaf ear to complaints which nothing but nec/e/ssity & the helpless condition in which I am placed could draw from me. If it were in the power of my brother Clement to befriend me, I should not be obliged to have recourse to your liberality; but you are aware that he is scarcely able to take care of my mother & himself, & that he is comp/e/lled to appropriate every farthing that he can get ahead of his necessary expences, to the satisfaction of his creditors. I have been obliged to let him have the use of my most valuable negroes to enable me to get provisions for my support, so that with the utmost economy, & the most prudent management of my domestic affairs, I can Scarcely make out to keep myself respectably clothed. in a few years more, when my little negroes shall be large enough to hire out, I hope I shall be able to live better: at this time, they are more expensive than profitable & serve only to increase the difficulties of my life—the <princp> principal reason of my applying to you at the present moment is to beg the favour of you to help me with means of discharging /a debt/ of about 20 Dolls incured for having imprisoned my woman Sarah, for impudence to me & for Violence offered by her to my person. I intended to have sold her, but could not get any thing like her value,: I was of course compelled to submit to the evil of taking her back to my <Servi> Service—you will do me a great kindness by enabling me to pay this charge; & /any/ other assistance you can conveniently render me will be thankfully received & <gratell> gratefully remembered by one who has never ceased to love you—

your affectionate Cousin
Sarah Porter Fuller

Mr E Pettigrew

[1]Sarah Porter Blount Fuller was the daughter of James and Ann Hall Blount and was sister to Clement Hall Blount and Dr. Frederick Blount. She married James B. Fuller. Because her father was brother to Mary Blount Pettigrew, she was first cousin to Ebenezer Pettigrew. Lemmon, *Pettigrew Papers*, I, xvi.

James Biddle Shepard to William Shepard Pettigrew UNC

[*Chapel Hill*] January 26th 1833

Dear William

I received your letter a few days ago, and was sorry to hear that you had so bad a journey from this place to Hillsborough. You mentioned that you never felt so bad as you have since your return to Hillsboro. But I imagine that you have felt little, very little in comparison with what I have. I have tried but in vain to throw off the gloom & melancholy which seems to torture my very existence. I am disturbed in my solitary walks by day, I am haunted in my dreams by night. But at last I have found a remedy. Study, hard, close, persevering industry, alone will assist one. I would advise you to read the life of Dr Goldsmith. You will see that his life was but one continued scene of hardships & privations. Read also his works, particularly his poetical ones & they will dispel all your melancholy. For it has been said with truth that poetry has the power of softening the heart of man. Which we see from the following sentence,

"Say, Heavenly Muse, their youthful fray's rehearse,
Begin, Ye Daughters of Immortal verse.
Exulting rocks have own'd the power of song
And rivers listened as they flow'd along."

Where we see that not only man, but even rocks have own'd the power of song. You are now just (as it were) commencing life. You have every prospect before you & believe me, when I tell you, that I have an interest in your welfare. I hope you will study your books hard & if you have time to read, I would advise you to read the following, as they are the best that I know of in /the/ English Language. The best Historical Works are Rollin, Hume, Goldsmith, Ireland, and a few others. The best poetical works, are Goldsmith, Dryden, Pope, &c, although I by no means advise you to neglect your studies to read any of them. But read them when you are at leisure & have nothing to occupy you. I hope you'll take this advice as coming from one that has a sincere affection for you & who wishes for your good. It always gives me the greatest pleasure to hear from you. You must write me often & write long letters. Give my respects to Mr Bingham & his lady. You must answer this letter immediately, and Believe me,

Your most Affectionate Uncle
James B Shepard

P.S. Be certain to assure Mr Bingham & his Lady of my high respect & esteem,

Your most Affectionate Uncle
James B Shepard

[*Addressed*] Mr William Pettigrew
Hillsborough
N.C.

[Dr.] Frederick Vanderburgh to Ebenezer Pettigrew UNC

New York March 8th 1833

My dear sir

The day before your letter of the 23 Ult reached me, I was advised by my brother that the approach of spring gradually reproduced James's infirmity; & wrote immediately in reply, to have him sent to New York and I am now making enquiries for a suitabl man for him to take a voyage with.—

As soon as he arrives I will inform you of his condition & prospects & as soon as I can find a man, with whom I should be willing to entrust my own child, I shall send him to sea—The finest men & finest ships go to Liverpool & London & I think I should prefer that voyage

Very sincerely your friend
F Vanderburgh

[*Addressed*] E Pettigrew Esqr
Cool Spring
Washington County
N Carolina

Ebenezer Pettigrew to William Shepard Pettigrew UNC

Lake Phelps March 15, 1833

My dear William

I received your letter shortly after your arrival at Hillsboro and was very much pleased to learn after the accidents which had occured to you, that you had nevertheless reached home without any serious injury to you. My son you have need to be thankful to your heavenly father for his kind protection of you, and of all other things you should not forget the author of your being, but pray to him for that guidance through life which will lead to a happy issue into eternity. I would have writen you long since, but my business has been so constant & pressing as /to/ oblige me to neglect almost all my friends. I hope however to /be/ more at leasure in a few weeks, so as to enable me to visit your dear little sisters & brother & Newbern.

Mr [*George*] Jones & your Brother Charles are with me and geting along very well. Charles is attending sufficiently to his studies, and thinks he will be fully prepared for his class, by the time you return from Hillsboro, so as to go with you to the North to see your brother James, and then to accompany you to the Round Hill school,[1] the place which I think of sending you to next. I hope my son, that you do not study to intently, but that you pay that attention which will /be/ sufficient to get your lessons well, and that you will be able to make a respectable entry at the above shool. I have not heard anything by letters from James since you were here, but I am told that he is now perfectly well. I pray God he may continue so. Your poor old Grandmother Pettigrew is tolerable well but exceedingly feble.

My business is progressing very well. I have hardly had a sick person on the land since you left, and my own health was never better. The wheat is very promising & in another week I shall begin to plant corn, for which I am in full readiness. M^r [*Nathaniel*] Brickhouse will begin week after next on a large Barn at Belgrade.

I hope my dear son you conduct yourself with strict propriety to M^r & Mrs Bingham, believe me they are both your friends as they are mine. Give my best respects to them & tell them that I had the pleasure of Judge Norwoods[2] company two days last week He was tolerable well, except one day he walked too far. Mr Jones & your Brother send their love to you & believe me to be your affectionate father

E Pettigrew

N.B. Write me soon, & let me know how you come on

March 17, Mike at your Grandmmas died last. He had been ill ten days. The Doctor as well as all others who saw him believed that he was injured by some of his own misconduct, but he could not be induced to tell any thing.

[*Addressed*] Mr William S. Pettigrew
Hillsborough
North Carolina

---

[1]Round Hill School was a boys' school founded by the historian George Bancroft and Joseph Green Cogswell at Northampton, Massachusetts, in 1823. After eight years Bancroft sold his interest to Cogswell, who was forced to give up the school entirely in 1834 for financial reasons. *DAB*, I, 656. Cogswell then moved to Raleigh, where he became rector of the Episcopal School for Boys. Coon, *North Carolina Schools and Academies*, 537-538.

[2]William Norwood (1767-1842) of Hillsborough served as a superior court judge from 1820 to 1836. Hamilton and Williams, *Graham Papers*, I, 459n.

[Dr.] William C. Warren to Ebenezer Pettigrew UNC

Edenton, 20th April 1833

My Dear Friend—

I have not had the pleasure of receiving a letter from you for some time, though I have frequently heard of you through others—I suppose your business occupies nearly the whole of your time, which is always a valid excuse for neglecting a correspondence of friendship—I however shall be very happy to receive a line from you when you can conveniently write.—

Last week was quite an interesting period here—M^r [*William*] Gaston, M^r [*Gavin*] Hogg & M^r [*James*] Iredell were in attendance on this Court, and all three of them were employed in the suit of Moor[s] against Mr Collins—Mr Gaston made a very fine speech and I thought would certainly gain the cause, but he failed to do so. The jury found for Moor[s], and the case is again carried to the Supreme Court.—Mr Gaston is no doubt one of the first men in the Country. Mr Hogg disappointed me—he has no eloquence, and there is something about him extremely forbidding and unpleasant. Mr Wm Shepard was here also—his health is entirely reestablish^d, and he is another person by it—he is really a very social & agreeable man. He is a candidate for Congress again and will certainly be elected—

I rec^d my due bill by M^r [*Frederick*] Norcom—My collections in Tyrrell have been so slow, that I have not found it convenient to pay you the balance on my note yet. I hope it will not be long before I can liquidate the debt.—

Mrs Warren and our Children are in the enjoyment of very good health—Mrs W. sends her best respects to you, and we both desire to be very kindly remembered to your Mother—

I am very sincerely your friend—
W. C. Warren

P.S. I send you a box of very fine shaving soap You must put a small quantity on your face with your finger & then use the brush—I also send you a very neat pocket knife—both of which, you will receive as marks o[f] friendship—

[*Addressed*] E. Pettigrew Esqr
Lake Phelps

Sarah Porter Fuller to Ebenezer Pettigrew UNC

Chowan May 31. 1833

My Dear Cousin

it is now about a month since I had the pleasure to receive your kind letter with its contents, for which I return you a thousand thanks: I know I ought to have written you sooner, but I have no good accommodation for writing, and if I had, it is a hard duty for me to perform having been so long out of the habit of writing—I hope it will not be long before I shall be so happy as to see you:

Indeed it would give me very great happiness: Do if you ever come near me come and see me; you cannot imagine how much pleasure a visit from you would afford me. Mother and Clement are both well & much engaged—Brother Clement has the prospect of a fine little crop & will make enough to make them comfortable, if no disaster occurs to frustrate his labours, they send their love to you—please to give my love to Aunt Pettigrew accept of my sincere wishes for your health and happiness; and for the prosperity of your dear little children, & believe me /to/ remain your affectionate cousin—

Sarah Porter Fuller

[*Addressed*] Ebenezer Pettigrew Esqr
Tyrrell County
Lake Phelps

Hicks and Smith to Ebenezer Pettigrew A&H

New York June 8th 1833

E Pettigrew Esq

Dear Sir

We enclose your sales of Corn rec^{d} pr Sch^{r} Lady of the Lake netting \$1308 78/100—On taking out the Corn it was discovered after 700 bus. were discharged, that the balance of the Cargo was considerably injured by mould and dampness—The purchaser declined taking any more of it except at a reduction in price, and we eventually induced him to take it at 65¢ pr bushel, except 28 bus which was very much injured, and sold at 25¢ pr bushel—We could have put it in store and had it dried, but the expense on it would have been but little, if anything short of five cents pr bus. and as the mould, could not be got out of it, it would never have brought the price of sound Corn. The damage was caused by the leaking of the vessel, and if the passage had been a long one most of the cargo would have been spoiled—The Captain has had the vessel caulked and he thinks she is now tight—We have shipped the five bbls wine to New Orleans as you directed—We will have the books bound and send them by the next return of the vessel in the amount of J. H. Bryans account \$10.5 11/100 we have charged to you as you directed—We paid on the 1st inst Doctor Vanderberg's order for \$342 95/100 which we have charged to your account—We have procured for you two Terrier Dogs male and female, they are both said to be of a good breed, and to be excellent rat catchers—

The quantity of wheat in market is too small, to admit of an extensive business, North Carolina of good quality would bring

118¢ to 120¢—The first of the new Crop will be much wanted, and will sell well—The price of Corn has declined a little the last few days, North Carolina of the usual quality would bring 66¢ to 67¢—such as yours would bring about 69¢—we enclose a bill of medicines, which we are assured are all of the very best quality—

Yours with respect
Hicks & Smith

[*Addressed*] E Pettigrew Esqr
Cool Spring
N. Carolina

Charles Biddle Shepard to Ebenezer Pettigrew A&H

New Berne June 9th 1833

My dear brother,

I am on the eve of starting for Jones-Court, & therefore shall not be able to write a long letter. Johnstone has been unwell for some time; he is walking about, but he has taken a considerable quantity of physic which has not benefitted him much; his looks too prove that the little fellow is labouring under disease, & he is very fretful, another evidence that he is sick—Mama desired me to give you this information, in order that you might consider whether something can't be done for the improvement of his health; my own opinion is that the child is kept too confined, & that traveling would be of service. I however do not presume to advise. It grieves me to see a boy of so much genius appear to droop at so early a period of life; & I can't help from entertaining the belief that, if he is spared, & proper attention is paid to his education, he will become an extraordinary man—

If you are not too busy, it would be advisable to come over & see Johnstone.

Give our love to George [*L. Jones*]. Tell him that his Sister and myself often think & talk of him—His continued silence is incomprehensible. Mrs Bryan & Mary have gone to the Convention.[1] Mary & Nancy are in excellent health; I have never seen the latter look so well & so beautiful

Give my love to Charles, & believe me your aff. broth[er]

C. Shepard

Mama has been & is now quite sick.

C S.

[*Addressed*] E. Pettigrew Esq.
Cool Spring
Washington Co.

[1]The annual convention of the Protestant Episcopal Diocese of North Carolina in 1833 was held May 29-June 3 in Immanuel Church, Warrenton. *Journal of the Diocesan Convention, 1833*, [1].

Ebenezer Pettigrew to William Shepard Pettigrew UNC

Lake Phelps June 10, 1833

My dear William

Though I hope to see you in the last of this month, I write you a few lines in direction. I wish you to bring with you all the books that are with you of any sort. Your Brother C[*h*]arles says that you can leave Hillsboro on the 20th or 21st of this month, as an examination of you will not take place. You will take the stage for Newbern; be sure you engage your seat in time. You will stay at Newbern with your dear sisters & brother untill Fryday the twenty eighth, when you will take the stage for Plymouth where you will find my Baruch to bring you home.

Give my kind regards to M^{r} and Mrs Bingham & tell Mr B. that I regret very much not having the pleasure of a visit from him, and that I will write him in answer to his last letter in a few weeks. Also ask him to furnish you with as much money as will pay your way home, and let me know my arrears to him & I will send him a <check> draft for it on New York.

My dear Child you are about to leave the place where you have been three years and a half, Pray leave it with good will towards all and a display of those feelings which becomes a Christian. If you have had any unpleasant feeling to any, let them be buried, and carry your resentment no farther. O my son I have to repent to the last day of my life that I have carried my resentments so far, they have been too far, too far. But blessed be God I have conquered my self, and have a firm hope through the mercy of our Heavenly father & merits of a dying Savior that I shall secure that reward which is due to a well spent life. O! my dear son depart not from the faith, but hold to that profession which you /have/ made that you may thereby receive that happy sentence "enter in the joys of thy Lord.

I am your affectionate father
E Pettigrew

[*Addressed*] Mr William S Pettigrew
<Hillsborough> /Cool Spring/
/Washington C^{o}/
N. Carolina

Gorham Dummer Abbott[1] *to Ebenezer Pettigrew* UNC

New-York June 15. 1833. Saturday Evening ½ after 8.

Mr Pettigrew,

Dear Sir,

Last week Dr Vanderburgh laid before me, a proposition respecting a voyage with your son James, across the Atlantic. My situation & circumstances did not allow of my acceptance of it, without previously visiting Boston. Yesterday week, three hours after the decision was made, I left N. York & hastened home, to adjust my engagements & arrange my affairs for a voyage.

I returned this morning, & have been *entirely* engrossed during the day, with the necessary arrangements for departure.

Ever since I called upon James, to have an interview with him, in order to decide the question of several months companionship, I have wished to address myself to you. But the multiplicity of calls upon time & attention, which so sudden an engagement has occasioned, has absolutely forbidden me the opportunity.

Dr V. has doubtless, or will apprise you of all the particulars of the understanding between us. I wish it were in my power, to have more communication with you, than I can possibly have now. The Ship sails tomorrow at 10. A.M. & I am almost completely exhausted with the duties of the day.

I have often before had young persons /for a year/ under my especial supervision & care. But never have I undertaken such a charge, with the same sense of responsibility that accompanies this. The illness of your son, <the> his tender age, the distance & dangers of the voyage, combine to make me feel that it is no ordinary charge, that I have accepted.

Still there are many circumstances, which awaken most pleasing emotions. The amiable character which I hear of your son, & the peculiar disabilities under which he has labored, in efforts to improve the mind, & the many incidents which we may anticipate, calculated to interest & improve us mutually, are sources of expected enjoyment. Besides I hope, that whatever may be the issue of the voyage as to his health, that I may be able to return /him to/ you improved some what at least, in mind & in character.

But a weary head admonishes me, that I must to night be brief. The first opportunity you shall hear from us again, & I hope that every successive communication, I may be permitted to announce good tidings of your absent son.

Meanwhile with sincere wishes for the health & happiness of your family at home, I am very respectfully yours

Gorham D. Abbott

[*Addressed*] E Pettigrew Esqr
Cool Spring
Washington Cty
North Carolina

[1]Gorham Dummer Abbott (1807-1874) was a New England Presbyterian clergyman who became a noted teacher in New Rochelle, New York. James Grant Wilson and John Fiske (eds.), *Appleton's Cyclopedia of American Biography* (New York: D. Appleton and Company, 7 volumes, 1887-1900), I, 6, hereinafter cited as *Appleton's Cyclopedia*; *CDAB*, 1.

Alfred Gardner[1] *to Ebenezer Pettigrew* A&H

Dresden, Tenn. June 19th 1833

My Dear Sir,

Sometime last fall Mr John S. Shepheard was in this county and Settled all the Taxes on your lands and others of your relativs up to the present year—He at the same time appointed me agent for him for the purpose of listing his lands for the Taxes etc. I was also requested by him to do the Same for you and to write you when the mony would be due—I have listed your lands regularly for the present year and The Taxes are now due—Though I am not compelled to hav the mony for some time yet. But believing that you would be glad to know some time in advance that you may be enabled to meet it at leisure I have Therefore given you these lines—

By the request of Esq. John S. I listed all the lands belonging to the connexion—But I do not know where to address William B. and James B. Shepheard—I hope you will inform thim that they had better make arrangements to meet these Taxes Shortly—Mr Charles Shepheard & J. H. Bryan have sent me a draft for their Taxes for the present year. J. S. has also make arrangements. the balance are yet unpaid. I have written to New Orleans to Richd M. [*Shepard*]—

Below I give you the amount of your Taxes at 80 cents pr. hundred acres, and Should any of the other Claimants wish to join you in Sending money They will know how much by making a calculation.

I presume there is no danger in Sending the money by mail—I have been in the habit of receiving from Sundry indivduals and have never yet met with any miscarriage—Though the best way will be to Send me a Check on the U.S.A. Bank at Nashville which will ansure me as good as the money—

Your Taxes are.

Per 1250. @ 80. cts.—	$10.
" 1084—	8.67
1250—	10.00
	28.67

My fees for listing & attention.

One Dollar pr. tract—	3.00
Total—	$31.67

Should you send a draft you can make the exact change. Though if you send the money and can not make the correct amount it can stand over untill next year. You will do well to have your Taxes punctually paid. as reporting land is bad business for the owners—

Very respectfully
Alfred Gardner

Mr E Petigrew.

[*Addressed*] Ebenezer Petigrew Esqr.
Tyrrell Cty
Cool Springs.
N.C.

[*Notation on back by Ebenezer Pettigrew*]

Exchange

35.00 State of North Carolina Lake Phelps [*June, 1833*]

<Please to pay> One day after sight of this my first & only Bill of Exchange of this time and date, pay to Alfred Gardner or order the sum of thirty five dollars, for value received, & place the same with or without further advice to account of

Your Obdt Sevt
E Pettigrew

To
Messer Hick[s] & Smith
New York.

---

[1]The letters indicate that Alfred Gardner was at one time sheriff of Overton County, Tennessee, where the Shepards and Pettigrews owned land. He was engaged as an agent to handle business matters there, as it was located a great distance from Moses E. Cator.

*Ebenezer Pettigrew to Hicks and Smith** A&H

Lake Phelps June 22, 1833

Messrs Hicks & Smith,

Gentlemen

Inclosed is bill of lading of the cargo of Lady of the Lake, Which <cargo> you will please sell to the best advantage. The wheat is inferior, and /I have saved/ but half a crop, which is the case as far as I can learn in all this country. I have sent a sample of that grown at the two plantations. There is 1460 bus of that in the bottom of the bag, the remainder is of that in the upper end. I have a hope it will be the first in market, and there by command a tolerable price. I am sending my son William Pettigrew to Round Hill School, /He arrives in the schooner/ what funds <he> may want at the school you will please to honour the draft of his principle, <and> <and> pay to <him> /William/ the amount necessary for him <when> in going from New York to <the> Round Hill. You will find inclosed <the> samples of cloths. Please to get for me something like them according to the memorandum.* I shall want for the year about 500 Gal molasses. I do not know at what time of the year it is cheapest, I should be glad if you will procure me that quantity at a time when you may think it is at its lowest. *The shirting of which I send you sample is the best & has worn better than any I ever had & cost much less than some other <say 17 cents.> Capt Dunbar procured it for me in 1831

I am Gentlemen
Very Respectfully
E Pettigrew

Memorandum

250 yds Wollen negro cloth
350 Do. Shirting for do do
Molasses according to directions
2 Black Silk Bonnets for old ladies of about 60 year of age & in midling station
1 Ream good letter paper that which I write on is I think too thin

Gorham Dummer Abbott to Ebenezer Pettigrew UNC

Ship South America July 4. 1833.
Lat. 48.°45. Long. 18.°30′

Mr Pettigrew,

Dear Sir,

We have now arrived within a few days sail of Cape Clear. I have some hope that we may speak <some> /a/ vessel<s>, bound to the U. States, & I wish to be ready to embrace the first opportunity of apprising you of the situation & present prospects of your Son.

The first week, after leaving Sandy Hook, James was very sick. He took scarcely any nourishment the whole week. He bore however his long seasoning very manfully, & said he would cheerfully be sick, if it would be the means of restoring his health. Since that time he has been perfectly well, as it respects sea-sickness. His involuntary motions have *very much* diminished & his whole appearance so much improved that it is a matter of daily remark, to almost all our fellow-passengers.

When he first came on board, his movements were so uncontrollable, that I used to assist him, in dressing, <eating [*illegible*]> at table, & indeed in almost all his personal duties. During the first ten days, these symptoms very rapidly diminished. It seemed regularly as his sea-sickness increased & continued, that his limbs came more under his control.

But for the last week, I do not think the improvement has been so great. Yet he dresses himself almost entirely /alone,/, manages his plate, knife & fork, plays with my knife, cutting sticks & amuses himself with twine /about the ship/ & other things quite skilfully. Still the nervous affection, is by no means, entirely removed.

He has a fine appetite, & I have had to reason the case with him, in order to induce him to deny it, cordially & cheerfully, which he has been willing to do.

His tongue indicates that all is not perfectly right, & I have had to be cautious, in the indulgences allowed him at <the> abundant table of our Packet.

He has lately improved very much in spirits & appears to enjoy himself, in a manner which has encouraged me to hope, that a favorable change may be working, that will ultimately remove all traces of his disease. But I have been disappointed in not seeing <more> the change more rapid & complete, for the last week.

I just called James to me & told <me> /him/ that I was going to write to you & asked him what I should say. He desired me to give his love to you all, & to say that he was better.

As it regards the attention, which I have been able to bestow to the improvement of his mind & manners, I find that thus far,

<that> hours of sickness, of rolling waves, & of various other hindrances, have prevented my attempting much towards his mental cultivation. What I do is necessarily <almost solely by> /confined to/ the voice, without books. He has however several times read to me & seems really to *feel* a strong desire to make progress in his studies.

I cannot but sympathise with him, when he manifests as he has done, no little sensibility at the thought, that his education has suffered from his long & distressing illness.

I hoped when I accepted this charge, that I should be able to *do something* to improve his mind & character that would be a source of gratification to me, even should the voyage not effect that cure which was anticipated.

But the most that can be done, will be in the way of conversation, giving him such information as is suited to his age & acquirements. And I have found him already quite an interesting companion in the enquiries which he is often making.

As to the course which I shall pursue, on our arrival at L, I am yet undecided. Our Captain & all the passengers, some of whom have been 14 times across the Atlantic, say that the month of Oct. is by all means, the best fall month for a return. During the hot months of summer the atmosphere on the American shores becomes very much rarified. And ordinarily, the denser atmosphere over the Atlantic, rushes in to restore the equilibrium, in the month of Sept. giving us our September gales. On this account, I should prefer to embark the first of October & thus avoid the boisterous storms, which are often to be encountered in the preceding month.

I might embark the 14 of August, but that would allow us but a very short visit in London, perhaps not more than a week or ten days. To day is the 5th of July & we may be a week in the channel, while we have not yet made Cape Clear.

Did every thing favor it, I <should> think we could spend the intervening time between this & Oct 1st in visiting the scenes of interest, to which we shall soon be near. But I do not see, now, how I shall be able to remain so long in England. And so far as I can tell at present, I shall not remain more than a month or 6 weeks & that will require me to re embark about the 1st of Sept.

Every body tells me, I ought not return to America without peeping at Paris, as it is only a 30 hours trip from London. But if I begin to make excursions it is exceedingly difficult to know which to choose [*torn*] Edinborough, Glasgow, Belfast & Dublin are all within [*torn*] days or a week even (in haste,) from Liverpool. And as it now seems to be out of my power to reconnoitre much, I expect to make our way /from Liverpool/ to London, slowly, to see what we *can* by the way, & after 3 or 4 weeks *there*, to return.

However, you will hear from me again, <on> by the first Packet from London, after our arrival, & should any thing then occur to change my arrangements, I shall appraise you of it.

James is as well to-day as yesterday, he asked me this morning, if I had sent his love to all.

with my regards for the members of your family, I am respectfully yours,

Gorham D. Abbott.

[*Addressed*] Ebenezer Pettigrew Esqr
Cool Spring
Washington County
North Carolina

[*Notation by Dr. Frederick Vanderburgh*]

N York Aug 16th 1833

My dear Sir, I am overwhelmed with business but mean to write you the first opportunity affords Your friend

F. Vanderburgh

William Shepard Pettigrew to Ebenezer Pettigrew UNC

New York 6th July 1833

Dear Father

I arrived at this place <of> on the fourth of July about three Oclock in afternoon, being detained at Ocracok bar five days on account of contrary winds, whare we enjoyed ourselvs in caching and eating fish, and then we had a fair wind untill we came within something like 45 miles of New York, and then We had a verry hard shower and the wind blew from the north untill about 12 O-clock Wednesday neight and then the wind was fair so that we arrived a the time above stated, I was sick but one day, and I think upon the whole stood it verry well, I found the Captain to be a verry fine man nor did I find any fault with the crew. I came <th> to Mr Hik's on the ensueing day, he seamed verry polite /and/ seamed to regret verry much that his family had gon out of the city, which rendered it so that I could not stay at his house, but however I fell in with one of his clerks who is verry polite <ant> and obliging, and boards at a verry good house whare I now reside, the Lady's name is Potter. I have not seen Doctor Vandebourg as /yet/ but espect to go there as soon as I find out his number, I have traversed New York considerably but after all I have seen no <place> spot in it which I like <as well> as well as Lake Phelps, for I have heard so much racket, and seen so many fops struting about the streets that I almost have become tiered of it. I hope that my Dear Grandmother is yet alive but alas /I fear/ it is but a hope, But if she has departed this life, I boath hope and expect she has gon to a better, and if she is yet alive give my sincere and tender love to her and also to brother Charles, on to all my relations.

Remember me to Mr Jones and Mr Davenport and Mrs Hanah.

Believe me most sincerely Your affectionate son
William S Pettigrew

[*Addressed*] Mr Ebenezer Pettigrew
Coolspring Postoffice
Washington County
North, Carolina,

Charles Lockhart Pettigrew to Ebenezer Pettigrew UNC

Chapel-Hill July 17th [*1833*]

My dear father

I thought it best to bring brother Johnston the whole way to Chapel Hill: The first part of the journy he bore very well, but as he was coming from Smithfield to Raleigh he complained several times of being tired and when I came to Raleigh finding the stage very ful for that eveni/n/g and I could not have got a seat had I have tried, so I concluded that it was best to come Chapel-Hill in the barouche than stay there two two or three days and then have a crowded stage. Brother Johnston has behaved himself very well, and whatever I have said has been the law with him, I have had no difficulty to restrain him from eating, <the> he rather acquiesed in <doing> whatever he thought I would like for him to eat, when I came to Raleigh I went to Mr Gyon's [*Guion's Hotel*] but he had no room and then I drove to Mr Cook's and there I staid untill I came away, I found Uncle James [*Shepard*] at Raleigh and he came with me to Chapel-Hill, he has determined not to go to Richmond. It is said that Raleigh never was so ful as it was on the fourth of July. I saw <Mr Iredel> governer Iredel in Rale/i/gh and spoke to him at Mr Cook's steps, he did not know me and he was so much intoxicated that he come very near falling off the steps and when he went away he could not walk the path he went to the assembly of delegates on the rail-road and got up and made some fo/o/lish speech but Jud[*g*]e Badger, to keep him from exposing himself any further and knowing his situation moved an adjournment

Brother Johnston has had very good passages and sometimes his evacuations have been rather too free; I asked him several times while coming up if he wanted to return to Newbern and he universaly answered in the negative yesterday while coming to Chapel Hill he expressed a wish to see his grandma and to day he asked me to let him go<t> to Newbern with Jim and when I told him he must stay here with me he cried to go back and said he did not wish to stay here.

I arrived a this place on saturday from Raleigh and intend Jim to stay to day and start very soon monday morning for home. Mrs Nun's[1] is not altogether the sort of place I could wish it to be; Mrs Nun is disabled by a fall and has but few servants to attend well to the business they have to attend to <so that> and she has no command over them and of course they are lazy so that I fear next session, when I shall be busy, Johnston will not be as well attended to as could be wished, during the vacation that will will not be of so much importance for I can attend to him myself; I think it would be well if grandma would come up here about the end of the vaction, that difficulty would then <be> in a measure disappear. But I will take the utmost care of him and do with him to the best advantage. Another objection, I have, there is a young fellow, an <res> inhabitant of the place, who lives at Mrs Nun's and will be there most of his time whose company I dislike very much for Johnston to keep, and as Johnston next session will be there most of his time it would be impossible for him to be kept from this fellow he would learn him to swear and he would talk every sort of evel conversation before him.

Nevertheless my dear father you may assure yourself that he will /not/ stand in need from my negligence for I consider it to be a sacred duty I owe to My God and you to protect whatever is put in my care to the best of <y> my ability and especially a brother whom I love and would cherish and protect /hin/ in any situation and knowing how he must feel being taken so young from the persons with whom he had been accustomed to live and place as it were among strangers, I hope you will make yourself satisfied if I change his situation in any manner I shall let you know and assign my reasons for so doing. I shall write you write you very often and let you know how we all are. We are quite well Johnston sends his love to you. I shall give Jim $12, which I think will be sufficient give my respects to Mr Jones and Mr Davenport and believe me your

Affectionate son
Charles L Pettigrew

[*Addressed*] Mr E. Pettigrew
Cool-Spring
Washington Co
N. Carolina

[1]Charles refers to the boarding house in Chapel Hill operated for many years by Mrs. Elizabeth Nunn, who died in 1851. Battle, *History of the University*, I, 272, 613-614.

Gorham Dummer Abbott to [Dr.] Frederick Vanderburgh UNC

London. July 17th 1833. 12 Adam St. Adelphi.

Dr Vanderburgh

My Dear Sir,

We <ha> arrived in London Last Saturday evening. Last night I learned that the mail bag for the next packet would be closed to-day. Accordingly I am required to make out a parcel of letters in haste.

James, I am happy to say, is more cheerful & in better spirits than I have known him to be in. But his nervous affection does not entirely disappear. I think he appears *better* however, in all respects. He says he is. Still I find that he is very restless & very evidently muscular motion is not completely within his control.

His tongue is furred, or rather has a little milky coat. Appetite good & his bodily occasions regular, which he says he never used to have so regular before.

We are staying at the Hotel, a sort of retired & private establishment of a widow lady Mrs Wright, in Adam St, Adelphi, a few doors out of the strand.

London is a noisy, smoky, bustling, wicked Babylon. In the morning I generally rise a little more reconciled to prolonging my visit, than I am at night. After the fatigues of the day, I am almost ready to sigh for a speedy return to the quiet & endearing atmosphere of my mother's fireside. What a place is home!

We employ the days variously. James I sometimes set to work writing or drawing. He has succeeded in both of these attempts, much better than I supposed he would. While he spend a part of the forenoon, in some such exercise as this, I am occupied delivering my letters of introduction & attending to sundry private matters. In the afternoon, the time is generally devoted to seeing the Lions.

But it is rather difficult to decide upon the limits of afternoon here. The king often takes breakfast at 6 o'clock in the evening, dinner at 12 at night, of course daylight or sunrise is just about bed-time.—

I have not as yet made any enquiries about the packets. Dr Cox is in Paris. And I have enquired several times, to ascertain when he will return. A gentleman told me, he beleived about the 10th of Septr If so, I shall probably take passage in the same ship.

Perhaps however it is not so.

If possible I shall write to Day, to Mr Pettigrew & enclose in this, as I did my last. You may expect to hear once more before I reembark.—

In the mean time with assurance of my affectionate regard for all your family, I am respectfully your's

Gorham D. Abbott

[*Notation by Dr. Frederick Vanderburgh*]

N.Y. Aug. 26th 1833—

Dear Sir,

I have just recieved this letter from London and forward it to you. I dislocated my wrist last Friday and am unable to write. The rest of the family are as well as usual, and beg to be remembered to you.

Affectionately Your friend,
F. Vanderburgh.

[*Addressed*] <Dr Vanderburgh
New York
N.Y.>

E. Pettigrew Esq.
Cool Spring.
Washington County.
North-Carolina.

Ebenezer Pettigrew to James Cathcart Johnston UNC

Lake Phelps July 22, 1833

My dear Sir,

I received your favour of June 24, at Plymouth on my way to Newbern to visit and to determine what course to take with my poor little Johnston who was in very declining health. It inclosed my note to you, which upon examination, after making the deduction for the purchase of the boards, thirty five dollars & ten dollars freight, for them leaves a balance due you of ninety dollars, which sum I will pay you the first opportunity that may occur I could not make any charge for the threshing machine, It was of no use to me & has been of none to you & therefore is worth nothing, and I hope you know my prin[*ci*]ples too well to think that I would take something for that which was worth nothing.

On the subject of the money due Joseph Blount I should like to pay a small amount on that note say two thousand dollars, the remaining sum I may have, I can probably manage. As regards the increasing my stock of negroes, The multiplication of negroes adds to the managers tro/u/bles, and though I seem to get along with them and my business in general, pretty smoothly, & without much bustle, yet My dear Friend, it is too often with the greatest angush of mind, When I reflect that there is not one ray of hope in this world to counter balance this excessive anxiety of mind, I am fit to sink down in dispair. Not a single individual within my reach that I can in safety deposit an expression. In truth I feel as though I was in the midst of the ocean upon a single plank. How many times has the night which we spent together at Plymouth passed over my mind, and how rejoiced would I be if that meeting could take /place/ even once a month. My dear ever dear Companion was my stay, my earthly all, my solace under every difficulty. My children, bone of my bone & flesh of my flesh the offspring of my dear wife, who are dearer to me than ten thousand lives, and to whome I owe that obligation that can not be removed, call on my constant & unremiting attention to my business, and their interest must not be neglected, but how rejoiced would I be to retire from all kind of business and dwell upon my miseries in this world & conte/m/plate my father in Heaven and the world to come. But why am I thus tormenting my friend? I will end it by an extract from a letter from my dear Nancy after the death of her sister 'No one knows my distress, I communicate it to no one, it is ungenerous to burden others with my distresses, when they have enough of their own to bear'.

In the first part of my letter I mentioned Johnston illness, When I got to Newbern I found him some better so /as/ to be able I thought to travil, I accordingly sent him with his brother Charles who was about returning to Chapel Hill, where I expect he /will/ remain the fall. By the return of the Baruche I received a letter from Charles saying they got up very well that J. was better, that he was very obedient to him, and farthermore giving the most flattering evidence of his duty towards his God & his father, in protecting his brothers & sisters. I can not be led away by my partialities, but if I know an amiable young man, my son Charles is one. You will be certain had I not that opinion I could not have sent an infant of 5 years old with him.

My second son William who had got through at Hillsboro I have sent to Round Hill school, he went in /my/ schooner to New York he has writen me from there where he has my permition to stay a few days. He had a pleasant trip of 13 days in which he was sea sick but one day. He seems to be tired looking at dandeis in N. York. My poor diseased son James sailed in the packet for England on the 16 June under the care of a Revd Mr Abot, who has the first recomdation from Dr Vanderburgh. It is the last hope to restore the poor little fellow to health. My two dear little daughters are in health the younger is thought to be a beautiful child. I think it the

<heal> healthiest I have ever had. The day of my leaving Newbern I gave Mary twenty five cents, /with/ a part of which she bought a ginger cake & gave me when I was about to leave. It is never to be eaten while I live. It is the first present I ever received from one of my children. By the return of the Baruche my son Charles sent me a new book, 'The happiness of the Blessed' by Bishop [*torn*]mant. These presents though small are great to a father [*torn*]

I agree perfectly with your opinion on /the/ subject of the professions & agriculture, also the certain interest in negroes well managed, and of the no value of land in this country without them. I regreted to learn of /the/ great damage by the freshet to your crops & embankments on the river but with your percevierance and unremiting attention they will soon be restored. My corn crop by excessive hard labour was a good one but it is now firing and suffering exceedingly from the drought, & what will be the result I cannot think. My wheat was a half crop. I shiped it the 22nd June, and I learn it sold for 126 cents.

Please to give my kind regards to your Sisters and believe to be your sincere friend

E Pettigrew

James C. Johnston esqr

N.B. Pray do not apologise in future at the length of your letter, but write them longer and as often as convenience will allow. I will not say excuse mine; I know you take an interest in me and mine.

E P.

[*Addressed*] James C. Johnston Esqr
Hayes
Edenton P. Office

Ebenezer Pettigrew to Mary Williams Bryan UNC

Belgrade Aug 4, 1833

My dear sister

I received your obliging favour of the first, today. It found me in sincere sorrow. My dear & poor old Mother expired this morning /at sunrise/ after suffering the most excrutiating torture for 54 days. The last fifteen hours she was in the agonies of death. They are beyond my powers of discription. Mrs Warrington & Mrs Hooker among others were with her they say such a contest with death is entirely beyond what they had ever seen. It is unnecessary for me to express my feelings on the subject. She was the kind affectionate companion of my father, she had acted towards me the part of a mother for 39. years, she had been the kind & tender friend of my dear Nancy, the affectionate grandmother of my children. I can but say I am reconciled to the bereavment from her declining age, and intense suffering from which there <w> seemed no hope of recovery. I am now left entirely alone, and feel it most sensibly, and O! if it was not for <my> the duty which I owe to my dear ever dear children, how rejoiced I would be to have the sentence in my ear. This night thy soul shall be required of thee. O my God how tired I am of the world.

Will Mr Bryan write an Obituary notice for the paper[1] she was 84 years 7 m. & 20 days old. You knew well her character. I would write you a longer letter, but I am by the death of mother made an executor, to her will I am extremly ignorent, and need advice, and expect therefore to be with you on fryday next, when I hope Mr Bryan will be at home. I know you will excuse /the shortness of/ my /letter/ when I tell you that I slept none last, night, that I have been to the Lake & returned, and have but this evening to write [four] letters. Please to remember me affectionately to Mr Bryan brother Charles sister Lydia, and my dear little daughters

& believe me to be your affectionate & afflicted brother
E Pettigrew

Mrs Mary W. Bryan

N.B. My poor old mothers countinance while in the agonies of death was so altered that I could not have known her.

E P.

[*Addressed*] Mrs Mary W. Bryan
Newbern
N.C.

[1]The obituary of Mary Lockhart Pettigrew appeared August 9, 1833, in the *New Bern Spectator*. She was termed a "venerable and estimable lady" who was just and kind and a friend to the poor. Her "lamp was kept constantly trimmed."

William Shepard Pettigrew to Ebenezer Pettigrew UNC

Northampton 10th August 1833

Dear Father

With the greatest pleasure I commence now the pleasant task of writing you a fiew lines. I arrived at this place on 11th July and on the 14th I joined school, I think that this place surpasses any I ever saw in point of beauty, the town is in a vall/e/y surrounded by several beautyfull mountains one of which is something like a mile and a half in height, and every thing seams to exibit the greatest taste, before every house their are beautyfull treas so as to protect them from the sun, the school is situated on a hill <about> at the edge of town, there are four bildings where all the boys stay and Mr Cogswell also with several of the tutors, there are six teachers one for writing, exclusively, one for Mathematicks, one for greek, another for french, another for Latin, one for English, and in short I expect that this school surpasses any in the United states. I have to recite something like five times a day and some of the boys six or seven. I find Mr Cogswell to be a very <f> good man, he keeps us in his room one our every night and three hours on sunday <an> besides going to preaching twice and should their be no preaching we stay in five hours, he never whips the boys, but when they do not know their lessons he detains them after the school is dismissed, and if they misbehave he puts them in the dungeon, in fiew words I like the school very much. I have been very desireous to hear from home on account of Grandma and therefore I would be glad to recieve a letter as quick as pos/si/ble, but I hope that se is well but alo alas I fear in vane, should her life have been spared thus far remember me to her in tender love and regard, also remember me to Mr Jones and Mr Davenport.

Believe me your Affectionate son
Wm S Pettigrew

Direct your letters to Round Hill Nortampton Massachusetts

Charles Lockhart Pettigrew to Ebenezer Pettigrew UNC

Chapel-Hill, August 26th 1833

Dear Father

I received your letter duly and was glad to hear that you did not have a severe attack of sickness. you reverted to the subject of taking care of money I am as careful of it as I can well and I am thus careful of /it, not only/ because you have told me to be so but it would be the hight of impropriety for me to spend it uselessly, but as every person needs caution, I am glad you have given it to me other wise I would very probably be led away, forgeting my duty, and how necessary it was to act judiciously as to those matters; I have got me a coat for $20, 25 it is quite a good one; but I do not wear it yet as my old one lasts me yet very decently; I am quite a hard student I get a mathematical lesson 1/3 of my time and am as good a scollar <of> on it as anyone in the class and on latin and greek I am very nearly as good a scholar as any in the class. I am quite restored to health, and I think will keep it. Dear Father when I think of my dear grandma I can hardly get my mind to assent to what I know to be true, it seems to be almost impossible for such a change to have taken place since my leaving home, it seems to me as if I can see her siting in her own little room and occupying her place in the little circle. I have a very ha/r/d lesson in Demostenes, the hardest greek in college to get this evening and therefore you must excuse my brevity. Brother Johnston is at present at Hillsborough and I have not been there since I wrote you my last letter but I shall go to Hillsboro in a about a week.

I am your ever affectionate son,
Charles L Pettigrew

[*Addressed*] Mr E. Pettigrew
Cool Spring
Washington
N. Carolina

Laurence Chu[r]n and William Watts[1]
to Ebenezer Pettigrew A&H

Williamston Sept. 10. 1833

Dear Sir,

We have a company incorporated to build a Turnpike Road across the Low lands of Roanoke and not willing to commence the undertaking without information from some practical individual as to the probable cost of the work. the Board of Directors have appointed the undersigned a committee to address you: confiding in your knowledge in estimating the costs of such works: to request your views on the subject—The Road will run through land that will soon become solid by embankment and is to be 20 feet wide. Sixty feet will be condemned for the use of the company which is covered with timber—It is proposed to log the sides of the Road and to have Arches about every half quarter of a mile—The Road will be three miles long and will have to be raised five feet upon an average—There will be 17 Arches 20 feet wide and 8 Bridges 30 feet wide upon an average in the whole length—We would be glad to have your estimate for one mile supposing 6 Arches and 2 Bridges and also an estimate of the whole Road according to the foregoing statement—An answer to this as early as will suit your conveneince will confer a particular favor on the Stockholders and very

Much oblige Yr. Most Obt Servts.
Laurence Chu[r]n
Wm Watts

E. Pettigrew

P.S. We omitted to mention that the earth that will be thrown up to make the Road will be good solid ground & as before stated will become *very hard* after embankment—

[*Addressed*] E. Petegrew Esquire
Cool Spring
Washington County

---

[1]William Watts of Williamston, Martin County, is listed in the *1830 Census Index*, 196. Laurence Churn (Chunn) has not been identified.

Ebenezer Pettigrew to William Shepard Pettigrew UNC

Lake Phelps Octr 7, 1833

My dear son

I received your letter of the 7th ult. and am not able to express the pleasure I felt at some of the sentiments it expressed. I hope you will continue to exercise them and increase in your power to do right. If you waste and throw away your time all my labour and the sacrifice of happiness is in vain.

I think you say that your vacation is in November and in the spring, and you are desirous to make an excurtion during the November one. If you should go any where then I could wish you not to stay long, so as to add but very little cost to your present expences. I could wish very much that you would spend a part of your time in learning to write. You say that board is five dollars a week Is it five dollars at all times or only during the vacation. I should like to know. My son I do not wish to cramp in your /ex/spenditures, but it will be necessary to be economical. When you reflect that there are six of you and that every one is every day on expences you will say with me that I have a heavy hand. And you will I know my dear son reflect that you are all to be set up in life to begin above the powers of /the/ rich. Lose no time you are advancing rapidly to manhood, three day ago & you were fifteen, six years more & you must set up for yourself & if I am alive relieve me of a part of this heavy load I am under. My dear William, I am willing to devote my time to my dear children, It /is/ my duty, It is an obligation which cannot be removed untill death and all I ask of my children is to do their duty to themselves. I am informed by last mail that your brother James has returned to New York & quite well and very much improved. I have directed him to be sent immediately to sea again in the hope that it make a permanent cure of him. I also heard from your Brothers up the country and your sisters in Newbern, they were all well. I should like in some of James' stays in N. York that you could go and see him. I have /had/ several attacks of fever this fall but am now tolerable. Mr Collins' family has been <extem> extremely sickly. Mrs C. has been very ill but better & I hope out of danger. It has been an awfully sickly fall, and there has been an incredible number of deaths. There has been a great number of my negroes sick but no deaths. I have been the Physician. Mr Davinport and Mr Brickhouse have not been sick. Which has been greatly to my advantage, for we have all enough to do My business does on as usual. I have made at Belgrade 60,000 Bricks and they were fired on saturday, I begin to sow wheat next week. I make but a half crop of corn from the drought, so you see my son a half crop of wheat and half crop of corn, makes a half loaf. I have got a six feet ditch into the Juniper swamp that was talked of when you were home, but I have been afraid of too much fatigue & have not been there yet. There is some value in it, but how much I cannot tell. It is never well to presume too much. Go on my dear son & /may you/ prepare yourself for usefulness in this life & that happiness which our blessed father has promised in another to those who love & serve him, is the Prayer of your

Affectionate father
E Pettigrew

[*Addressed*] Master William S. Pettigrew
North Hampton
Round Hill school
Mass

*Ebenezer Pettigrew to Laurence Chu[r]n
and William Watts** A&H

Octr 12, 1833

Gentlemen

Yours of the 10 Ult. came to hand in the due course of the mail and should have been answered sooner but for the multiplicity of business, and for the last week <th> attention to the sick. On the subject of your letter. I would say that twenty feet would not be wide enough for two carriages to pass with safety, and if a few accidents should happen for the want of width it might lessen traviling. If the road is twenty feet /wide/ at top it should be thirty at bottom /if 5 ft elevation/. You might put one log at the commencement of the road in a line with it but no more. If loged up to the top <of the> /with/ ordinary timber /it/ would soon rot & fall down, cost a considerable labour in the begining for no use. The bridges on the road (I suppose for the /water in/ freshets to pass,) will cost very little more than the like number of /lineal/ feet of earth, /supposing the timber to be free./ and I will make a calculation of a mile as though it was all earth, supposing the road 30 ft at base, 20 ft at top & 5 ft high. I would suggest the propriety of raising the road above the highest freshets ever know one ft. I know you must be aware of the injury done & the additional cost of repair in the event of the current passing over it. It will be necessary to log up the sluices left for the bridges, that the water passing through [*blotted*] in freshets might not carray away the <beach> /earth/

I think that any tolerable good hand would make of the road two lineal ft in a day which is raising 250 cubit ft of earth. There being 5280 lineal ft in a mile would make 2640 day work which at 26 days to the month would be 101 month & 14 day work <or 304 mnth and 16 days work>, one mile long & 60 ft wide which you will find I think not sufficient width includes /little more than/ 7. acres /& a fraction/ to cut down and clear <for> /for the road &/ will take one month & 12 days making 103 months work to one mile and supposing them to cost with their tools & provision \$15 a month. making for the mile \$1545. p^r mile I estimate hands at \$15 a month, it would be well to get by the year, and I would think <them> they might be had at a less price than 15. There is a considerable art in the use of the spade. Ther may be some error in my calculation as the above has been made in great haste. Any /further/ information which <I may have> /you might want/ on the above subject will be given with great pleasure.

[Dr.] Frederick Vanderburgh to Ebenezer Pettigrew UNC

New York Oct 1833[1]

Dear Sir

I wrote you on Jame's return that he was very week—He had not been on shore more than ten days: when I perceived that he lost in appearance—as well as in strength—

Whether this unfavourable change was owing to his being on shore, or whether, it arose from indulgence in food & the fruits of the Season, I could not tell: but as soon as I saw his strength fail, & the inability increase to hold things in his hand I lost no time in preparing him again for Sea—

I foresaw that a long voyage was indispensible: <oft> yet I did not like to send him where we could not hear from him often—Capt Phillips of the Ship Waverly saild on tuesday for Mobile—from thence to Liverpool—from thence to Mobile—from thence to London & from thence to N York

This will occupy the coming year & we can hear from Ja^{s} on his arrival & departure from every Port—The Ship is of the first Class & belongs to my friend Robt Center & he speaks of Capt Philips in the highest terms—

I told Capt P— that James health was the first object & the second was to employ him as much as was consistent with his health & give him all the instruction & practical information. that would qualify him for <use> future usefulness—He promised on the faith of a Lutheran, that he would put Ja^{s} as his constant companion & treat him in all respects as his own Son—

I have furnished James with clothes & the et ceteras for the Years voyage and given 18 to 20 Volumes of a little library that he will peruse in his leisure hours—

He went off in fine Spirits & promised that you & I should have letters from every Port—I have little doubt that his health will be permanently re-established at Sea—

Knowing your desire to preserve his remains, if he should die abroad & furnished every necessary article & written instructions, to accomplish your wishes—

I drew on your Agent Messrs Hicks & Smith for One hundred dollars more & will give you an account of my steward ship as soon as I have time—

Very sincerely your friend
F Vanderburgh

[*Addressed*] Ebenezer Pettigrew Esqr
Cool Spring
Washington Ct^{y}
North Carolina

[1]A notation in Ebenezer Pettigrew's hand on the outside of this letter indicates that he received it on October 18.

William Shepard Pettigrew to Ebenezer Pettigrew UNC

Round Hill Northampton 21 October 1833

Dear Pa

I received your letter of the 7 instant, and was very glad to hear that you had es-caped telerable well from the fall sickness. You stated that Mr Collins's family had been very sick, which I was very sory to hear, but it was what I expected., I was in hopes that Mr Burnit would recover from his dissease, but brother Charles writes me that he died about a month ago. I have not yet come to a conclusion where I shall go next vacation, but whereever I go I shall be as careful as pos/s/able, as I know it will be both for my good and the good of my brothers, and sisters, and to your satisfaction. You wanted to know if the board was $5 in the vacation only, or in the session, as to that, I do not know but the boys say that is the price both in the session, and in the vacation. You would be astonished to see how different the people at the north, live, from those at the south, at breakfast, we have litebread, and butter, and at dinner, mutten, and py, and at supper litebread and butter, each having three pieces as his allowance, I have not seen a peace of corn bread since I have been in Massachusetts, and but very fiew biscuits. I should like to know you intend Brother James to go whether, in a ship, or in a common schooner, <I> however I expect it would be best for him to go in the Navy where he would be constantly at see, but in the mean time his education would be stoped which would be very bad, as I expect he has gon<e> to school very little. By next August I expect by hard study I will be prepaired for the Sophamore class in Cambridge, but it is imiterial to me whether I go to College or no. for I would equally as live be farming at Belgrade as /be/ any whare else. I have been sick several times since I came here, but am tolerable well, at present. I enjoy myself very well here, and have to study very hard.

I am your affectionate son
William S Pettigrew

[*Addressed*] Mr Ebenezer Pettigrew
Coolspring Postoffice
Washington County
North Carolina

John Herritage Bryan to Ebenezer Pettigrew UNC

New Bern Novr 7. 1833

My dear Sir,

I write merely to inform you that we are all well—Mary & Nancy are in very good health. Charles & Betsey have had very bad colds & we were apprehensive that they had the whooping cough (which is still in town & in our neighbourhood) but our fears have not been realized.—

They have commenced the repairs of the Church and have taken off the shingles of the centre of the roof, and the defect is now visible—the pressure had been lateral & the collar beams were very much strained & the rafters partially split.—

The architect who is from Philad^{a} seems to scientific & sanguine in his opinion that he can repair it at a moderate expense—but not at $500.

The Rev. Mr Freeman[1] is here soliciting subscripns for the Epl. School.—The Bishop returned to N.Y. in consequence of the death of his child & will probably not be in New Bern till Jany.—

Bishop England[2] is here and Sister Penelope is quite happy.—There is no material change in Lydia, she appears to be slowly declining.—

Mary sends her affectionate regard to you.—

Your friend & relative
Jn. H. Bryan

[*Addressed*] Ebenezer Pettigrew Esqr
Cool Spring
N.C.

[1]The Reverend George W. Freeman was at this time rector of Christ Church, Raleigh. *Journal of the Diocesan Convention, 1833*, 3.

[2]Bishop John England (1786-1842) came to the Roman Catholic diocese of South Carolina in 1820. He was very active in missionary work and in parochial education. *DAB*, VI, 161-163. While in New Bern at the time of this letter, he lectured each evening in the Masonic Hall to "crowded and attentive audiences." *Newbern Spectator*, November 1, 1833.

Frederick S. Blount to John Herritage Bryan UNC

Mobile November 7th 1833.—

My dear Brother,[1]

By the mail that will bring you this letter, you will receive a newspaper containing an obituary notice prepared by me for James Pettigrew.—This melancholy event while it would under ordinary circumstances have created most poignant sorrow in the bosom of his Father, must from the distressing nature of the accident by which he was lost to him, carry a double portion of anguish with it.—

I do not know what were the directions given by Cousin Ebenezer to Dr Vanderberg relative to James—but having an oppertunity of inspecting that gentlemans directions to Captain Phillips, I was much surprised that there was no one on board the vessel but the Captain, who could, or would afford him any relief in case of sickness:—He was not provided with a Cabin passage, and eat and slept in the forecastle with the men.—*His duty on board ship was that of a servant in the ladies cabin.*—The clothes which he had with him were furnished by Capt Phillips, and were common sailer clothes—and Captain Phillips informs me, that he was far from being decently clad when these clothes were purchased for him.—

My friend Mr Samuel M Ogden of New York was a passenger on board the Waverly, and states that while the ship was running down the Bahama Banks with the land close aboard James ascended, *unnoticed*, the foremast.—Many passengers had gone aloft to look out,—The first intimation that any one had of James being out of the ship, was his hearing something strike the railing of the ship near the bows, and fall in the water. He passed immediately under the stern, and cried to those who were standing on the deck "Oh! Come."—The vessel was going nine miles an hour.—He states further that he was lying on his back and his legs had the appearance of being broke, <as> he supposes from the fall, as he did not use them.—Every exertion was made by the Captain to save him but they were all in vain.—The boat was lowered and on the spot in ten minutes after the accident occurred—but he was never seen more.—

Such are the outlines of this truly melancholy occurrence—When the ship arrived I accidentally saw on the Bulletin at the exchange, a notice of the loss of a master James *Pettonger*, and on further inquiry discovered that it was James Pettigrew.—

Yesterday I wrote a letter to Cousin Ebenezer informing him of the circumstances—but giving him none of the details contained in this letter.—I fervently wish that he may bear his affliction with resignation and fortitude. It has made me quite sad.—

I found a letter from Mr Gaston to me, had been published at New Haven since my departure from thence.—This was done without my knowledge and consent, and it was with painful regret that I found my Agent there by the advice of his friends, and without any notice to me of his intention, published this letter to vindicate himself from charges made against him by the Abolition Society.—I have written to Mr G. explaining the matter—as he must deem it a gross viola[tion of] confidence which we repose in those with whom we corresp[ond] of publishing our letters without our consent.—The letter in question was left by mistake in a large package of papers relating to the negro, and handed to the Agent at New Haven.—

Our rivers are very low—no produce can come to market and times are rather dull.—I found all my friends in good health and pleased to see me.—So soon as the rivers rise—business will be brisk and every thing active.—I overtook John Shepard and Col. Cadwallader Jones in the Creek Nation, and I expect them here daily.—The Col. proposes purchasing a plantation in the Cane Brake for Allen.[2]—

Remember me affectionately to the family, my love to Sister Mary, and believe me truly & faithfully

Your Brother
Frederic S. Blount

P.S. Will you mention to N. G. Blount that I have not received his papers.—

[*Addressed*] The Honble. John H. Bryan
Newbern
North Carolina

---

[1]Frederick (Frederic) S. Blount and John Herritage Bryan were half-brothers. Lemmon, *Pettigrew Papers*, I, xvi; Miller, "Recollections," 26; Ebenezer Pettigrew to James Cathcart Johnston, February 4, 1822, note, in this volume. Blount migrated to Alabama as a young attorney because he thought that state was more up-and-coming than North Carolina. Johnson, *Ante-Bellum North Carolina*, 37.

[2]Allen Cadwallader Jones, son of Col. Cadwallader Jones, was an 1831 graduate of the University of North Carolina. He went to Alabama, where he served in the state legislature; later he was a colonel in the Confederate army. Battle, *History of the University*, I, 794.

Hicks and Smith to Ebenezer Pettigrew A&H

New York November 15th 1833

E Pettigrew Esqr

Dear Sir

The price of Corn since the date of our last (the 26th ulto) has varied but little, at present it is rather dull, and rates are somewhat lower—North Carolina is worth 64¢ to 66¢ according to quality such as yours, if in prime order, and sound, would bring 72¢—Captain Combs informed us, just before he left here, that you talked of making Juniper Shingles, and would like to know how they sold in this place—The quantity consumed here now, is much less that formerly, in consequence of the almost general use of Slate and Tin for roofing—The present price of three feet shingles is $14½ to $15 per thousand, and for two feet shingles $7½ to $8—The size of the three feet is 31 Inches long 6½ to 7 Inches wide and ¾ of an Inch thick—The size of the Two feet is 24 Inches long, and the same width and thickness as the three feet shingles—We paid on the 4th inst to Mr Cogswell for School expenses of your Son $2.50—on the 5th inst to Doctr Vanderberg $30—and on the same date to your Son William $30, all which sums are charged to your acct—Your Son William left here some days since for Boston, he was in perfect health—

Yours with respect
Hicks & Smith

[*Addressed*] E Pettigrew Esqr.
Cool Spring
Washington County
N.C.

Asa Biggs[1] *to Ebenezer Pettigrew* A&H

Williamston Nov. 28. 1833.

Sir

The last general meeting of the Stockholders of the Williamston & Windsor Turnpike Company were much gratified and derived important information by your letter received through their corresponding committee and it was unaminously Resolved that the thanks of the meeting be tendered you for your esteemed favor—It now becomes my duty as it is a pleasure to communicate the same to you—

The Directors have resolved to let out the Road to the lowest bidder on 16th December next— The Board meets here on 9th Decr for the purpose of deciding upon the plan of the road & to make other necessary arrangements. The Directors and several Stockholders have requested me to communicate the same to you and solicit your attendance if it will suit your convenience—If not before we should be much pleased to see you here on 16th

I should be glad to learn by the return mail that the time appointed will not conflict with any of your arrangements & that we may expect you—

With much respect I am
Yr. obt servt.
Asa Biggs Secretary of the Board of
Directors of W & W T. C.

[*Addressed*] E. Pettigrew esquire
Cool Spring
N.C.

[1]Asa Biggs (1811-1878), a jurist and United States senator (1854), was admitted to the bar in 1831 and practiced law in Williamston. President James Buchanan appointed him a federal judge in 1858. He was a delegate from Martin County to the North Carolina Constitutional Convention of 1835, a delegate to the Secession Convention, and a judge for the Confederate States of America. Powell, *DNCB*, I, 151-152; Henderson, *North Carolina*, II, 202, 223.

Thomas Turner to Ebenezer Pettigrew A&H

Plymo NC Dec 5 1833

Dear Sir

Yours of the 4th is this moment at hand. You say /that/ you wish to go to Williamston on Wednesday 11th; that for this purpose you wish your Carriage to meet you in Washington on tuesday the 10th; that you have already ordered it to meet you in Plymouth on monday the 9th; but that here by your order it would stop to wait for you; and that you would have me send it on to you at Washington in order to take you to Wmston on the day mentioned.

It shall be done precisely as you now direct, unless on the receipt of this you order otherwise.

On tuesday next Cameron's negroes are to be sold by the Sheriff who has taken them under execution, and who will then sell them subject to the deed of trust: that is to say he will satisfy the deed of trust out of the sales, and apply the remainder of moneys to the execution. This I think he has authority to do, and if so, no doubt can arise as to the title which the purchaser will obtain. I mention this to you because I have heard that you would have bid on the negroes had they been sold at Court; and because you can easily reach Plym^{o} /in time for the sale/ by the Stage on tuesday, and then Wmston from Plymouth in your carriage on Wednesday the 11th—

Should you therefore wish me on the receipt of this *not* to send your carriage to Washington on tuesday, I shall let it remain here: If however I receive no letter from you giving that direction, I shall send it as directed in your letter received this day.

One word more as to the deed for the lands you bought belonging to Davenport's heirs—I think you directed that when the deed should be written, it should be given to John D. Bennett that he might get the Coroner to sign it. Having conversed with Bennett and learnt from him that he cannot recommend the Coroner to sign the deed for 4/7 & 1/6 of a 1/7th of a certain tract; having understood from you that you bot the whole estate of the heirs being 4/7^{ths} or more or less; /and/ having written the deed agreeably to your understanding of your purchase; I think it unnecessary to put it into Bennetts hands, as he would not act upon it; and therefore I shall keep it for your return together with the other title papers.

I am very sincerely
yours
Th: Turner

I think the negroes will sell very low; because I do not see that any persons wanting them and having the money are likely to be at the sale. Sale for cash.

[*Notation on back*]

It is important that Mr Pettigrew should receive this letter that he may reply by the return of the mail on Saturday the 7th The P.M. could therefore oblige him & me by sending it as soon as it arrives—

Th: Turner

[*Addressed*] Ebenezer Pettigrew Esq
Newbern NC

Charles Lockhart Pettigrew to Ebenezer Pettigrew UNC

Chapel-Hill Dec 11th 1833

Dear Father

I recieved your letter about two weeks ago, which contained the mournful intelligence of brother James's death; it was quite an unexpected information, for I the rather expected to hear of his entire recovery to health than to recieve the information that he was no more, it is truly distressing to look back and observe the alteration which has taken place within a few years; when I see that there are now only three brothers I feel astonished and hardly know what to think; but it is all for some wise purpose and therefore let us feel resigned, perhaps brother James would never have been a healthy man and might have spent his days without much happiness; according to your wish I communicated the disagreeable intelligence to Mr Bingham. I observed, the other day the death of Uncle Charles's wife,[1] it must have been very distressing to him having gone to Raleigh only a few days before, he is thus early in life deprived of an amiable and affectionate wife, she was a very fine woman and her loss is to be lamented by all her acquaintances. I have recieved frequent letters from brother William this Session his letters generally are very long and quite entertaining, his hand-writing is improving very fast, he now writes quite a decent hand, his diction too is much better than it formerly was; I think upon the whole he seems to have improved himself more within the last six months than I ever knew him in any length of time before. I am in hopes he writes you oftener than he did, In his letters to me he always expressed a wish to keep up a more frequent correspondance I am in hopes he will continue to improve knowing how important time now is. The vacation commenced day before yesterday, I have concluded to spend the greater part of my vacation on chapel-Hill not knowing how you wished me to spend it. I shall study good part of the time having no other way of spending my time but not so much as to render me unfit to go through with the next session. I have recieved my cloack about a month ago and am very much pleased with it, it fits me very neatly. You wished me to give you an account of my money I have at present about $15, which will last me during the vacation, but I shall want money for next session I shall need a certain sum by the first day of the session which is four weeks from this time the sum which I think will be sufficient will be $150 and if /it/ should not be enough I can apply for more but if it should be more than sufficient I can retain it for the next session the best way and the safest way is to send a check on some bank at New York which I can easily sell to the merchant at this place: do not think my dear father that I spent money uselessly, but be assured <of> that I mindful of my own interest, will take care of it. I am in very good heath and be assured of my tender regard for you as a kind parent

Charles L. Pettigrew

[*Addressed*] To Mr E. Pettigrew
Cool Spring
Washington Co
N. Car.

---

[1]This refers to the death of Lydia Jones Shepard.

Ebenezer Pettigrew to George L. Jones A&H

Lake Phelps Dec. 22, 1833. 11^oclock at night

My dear young friend,

An hour ago, I received your fav^r of the 20th I should not write to night, it being sunday, but I am moving the houses at Belgrade, and shall have no time in the morning, and wish to loos no time in reply.

As to Ives' land do not give his price anyhow Let him Keep it and eat it, and as to the other project, do abandon it, and never think of it again.

Consider me the purchaser, and let me beseech you to get your horse and loose no time in starting for the southwest. Do not stay one hour longer than it will take to get in order to start.

If you stay you will have all the difficulties to encounter that I had, and not one near to stay you, and you have not enough of the *devil* in you as I had to stand against all opposition, and therefore you can not succeed, which will mortify you to death, and be *no* less unpleasant to my feelings. The inhabitants of /the/ place you range in will be a dead weight against you and you never can get along. Therefore for my sake for my feelings as a friend, let me beg of you to quit, take your horse and go where no one will care what you do, if it is to cut your throat, and then you will rest upon your own energies, and have no one to paralise them. I say again consider me the owner of your purchase at the price & interest, I am perfectly willing to be the owner. When Charles & William are grown (if the poor boys should live) I will go there and commence opperations. It will give new life to my broken spirits. The funds for your purchase is not just at this time convenient, but a few months and I will be able to meet you. I say again quit the land, and be gone as quick as possible, there is a curse up it. Let it remain a howling wilderness. Quit the country and go to a place where all can exert themselves in there own way and may God Almighty protect you in this world and prepare you for that world when all will enjoy that blessing which is for the rightous, is the prayer of your sincere friend.

E. Pettigrew

N.B. Do not give away the water shovel I sent you by Tom when you start for the west. You can however let Mr. B. take a patern from it. Donot wait, but go, go, go, go.

Mr. George Jones dont hang about but go, go, go. Leave the Land. It is under a curse. It is doomed to be a howling wilderness. I subscribe myself what I always hope to be in this world (not to be shaken by every blast of wind)

Ebenezer Pettigrew

[*Addressed*] Mr George Jones
Newbern
N. Carolina

Charles Lockhart Pettigrew to William Shepard Pettigrew UNC

Chapel-Hill, Jan 1st 1834

My dear brother

Perhaps you will be somewhat astonished when you observe a letter from me knowing that this is the general time of the Chapel-Hill vacation; the vacation commenced on the 14th of Dec and will continue untill the 12th Jan, four weeks, it generally is so cold and disagreeable traveling in the winter vacation and with all the time is so very short for one having to travel so far before they arrive home that taking into consideration all these preventitives I thought it best not to go home. I have spent my vacation on the whole as agreeably as could be supposed, I have been to Hillsborough and made a stay of 3 days and have remained on the hill the remainder part of the time, reading books of different sorts, but have not read any novels, for I think that young /persons/ ought to employ their time re/a/ding some thing better which can afford solid food for the mind; for the mind as the body must (especially while it is in a growing state) have substantial fare to live /on/, and if it does not it soon withers away, and thereby renders it unfit to perform the functions for which it was made, the course of reading which is practiced by most young persons is very injurious to them, they frequently have the habitual practice of reding a little out of one thing and then out of another and not sticking to one thing long enough to know it merits but read untill they get tired and then lay it aside and take up another /and/ so on, every ought to persue a regular course of a reading after they acquire the age of twelve years, or sooner for a good habit can not be acquired at too early an age: Studies ought first to take up our attention and after we have examined our lesson thouroughly then sit down to reading some useful book or the plan /of/ some history: it is necessary also for persons by the time they enter upon the broad expanse of life to have formed some correct stile of writing and conversation, to the acquiring of which the best method is to select some author who stands high in the literary world for poducing the most cocise and at the same time beautiful composition, such as Addison you will find many of his numbers in the Spectator signed C. and also Arch Bishop Tillotson's works are deservedly celebrated for correctness of stile, I have them in reading myself and I think I shall read his entire works and endeavour to form a stile analogous to it. You wish to hear something about the report, I will state it as briefly as possible, no report was read out about the Senior Class but [*James*] Shepard is first though it is thought he will not get the Latin for some of the Faculty will /not/ give concientious votes. The Junior, [*Thomas H.*] Brown and [*Haywood Williams*] Guion first there were 8 persons turned back, three of which were Phis [*John H.*] Watson, [*John L.*] Gay, [*Richard Benbury*] Creecy The Sophomore 4 fi[*r*]st and 7 second among whom was myself. Several recommended to study harder. The Freshmen 2 Emunds and Sims, Enoch [*Sawyer*] did not get <a mite> any thing, /one turned back, Seawell/ perhaps you are astonished to heare of my not being among the first, I was quite an Idle fellow last sesion. You have recieved that Catalogue and Badger's address[1] /I sent you/.

I have not writen you a letter since the death of our poor brother James, but it is truth he is no more, and perhaps it was a blessing to him to have been taken off so soon, and also I suppose you have heard of Uncle Charles' wife, while we have these two instances of human frailty before us it is but sutable for us to consider how liable to be taken from this world at any moment of time, and knowing that, certainly it is the height of wisdom to prepare for that awfull hour, and on the contrary the madness is inconceivable to neglect it, to be careless and seem as if we thought nothing of it. I received a letter from our dear father three or f/o/ur days ago, how much ought we to love and respect him and do every thing in our power to oblige him, for he is now [*torn*] home endeavouring to obtain a comfortable living for [*torn*] and to give us both good educations so as to take our stand among those that have some pretentions to literature. I am in hopes you write to him often, for it must be a great pleasure to him to get letters from his children; for hours pass very heavyly with /him when/ none of us /are/ with him to talk to /him/ and it ought to be a great preasure to us his children to gratify him when it is in our power.

I think you are improving very much in your writing, sp/e/lling and diction. I am in hopes you may continue to improve I am in hopes your letters will be long and interesting and about once every month as I shall write as often as that, I saw G[*aston*]. Wilder[2] at Hillsboro he is quite well

Believe me to be ever affectionate
Charles L Pettigrew

[*Addressed*] To Mr William S. Pettigrew
Round-Hill
Northhampton
Mass.

---

[1]George E. Badger delivered an address before the Dialectic and Philanthropic societies at the University of North Carolina during the 1833 commencement. Battle, *History of the University*, I, 353.

[2]Gaston H. Wilder was a student in Hillsborough at this time. He was an 1838 graduate of the University of North Carolina and later served as a state senator and a Confederate government official. Battle, *History of the University*, I, 441, 796.

*Ebenezer Pettigrew's Tax List** UNC

Tax list of E Pettigrew in Tyrrel County 1834

6850 Acres Land on which I live	[$]15000
38 Black Poles	

Tax list of E Pettigrew in Washington County 1834

187	Acres		on which the dwelling is placed	at $10	$1870..00
41¼	do	bot	of Willoby Phelps	3	125..75
67¼	do	"	of Lewis	2	134..00
4	do	"	of C<harles>aleb Phelps	3	22..00
450	do	"	of S. B. Carraway		2500..00
208	do	"	of S. Davenport		2000..00
28	do	"	of J. J. Phelps		204..00
215	do	"	of Spencer Hall		750..00
62	do	"	My part of Edmond Howell's land		
62	do	"	Where W. F. Davenport lived		357..32
100	do	"	On deep Creek		$795<5>1..07
1424½					

The last pieces of land I perchased of the estate of W. F. Davenport at P sale
10 Black Poles

100	Acres bot of the heirs of Wodsen Spruil	200
1524½		815<5>1..09

Black Polls in Tyrrell County		40
Do	do Washington do	12

Dennis Dozier Ferebee[1] *to William Shepard Pettigrew* UNC

Hillsborough Jan 2d 1834

Esteemed friend

I do now for the second time resume my pen with the intention of addressing you a letter of the following import. As the pen and scrip is the only means in our present situation, to foster and initiate a mutual correspondance between us, to keep from receding and slumbering those affections of amicable and scholastic attachments towards *you*, and the cotemporary /students/ of this institution. I expect you think I have forgotten you, by my neglecting to write; but I assure you I have not had time, I have had to attend to lessons in my own class, and keep up with the class above, on the greek grammar, but though the intervening space between us is broad, yet, I assure you my esteemed friend, the respect which I have for you, draws my heart near to thee. How often does thy deportments which were left behind you, represent itself to me, and even while thinking on them I think I see your visage. But let me not waste my time on these encomiums which I have no doubt are manifest to you. I will in the next place give you the melancholy inlligence, that at the last examination at Chapel Hill, there was about twenty students turned back, (or using the school boys tech/n/ical term for it, glystered;) there was but two, out, of the class that left here last June among this number, they were Charles Nelms, & Sidney Smith. I believe I mentioned to you in my other epistle, that George Polk[2] had been suspended from Chapel Hill, for blowing a trumpet after nine—o-clock. I herd that his father was very angry with him indeed, and put him out in the country under a peasant, to study mathematicks for two months; that being the time of his temporary cessation and at the end of it he returned to college again. There is very little news stiring in town, though business appears to /be/ brisk, and health as usual, good. I believe they are doing very little at the legislature; but I don't know <that> whether that is necessary to mention, for you know that is ordinarirly the case. A day or two after the sitting of the legislature, it was supposed they would adjourn and go to Fayetteville, on the account of the smallpock there; there is now two cases of it <there>, and I am very sure they will have several more. They are about a school in Raleigh, which I am very sure will be better for scholars in some respect than Chapel Hill. The buildings are now commenced and will be carried on very brisk, though I know not what time they will have them done. The statehouse appears to go on very slow; they are now at the top of the first windows; it is thought by most persons that when it is done, it will be one of the most magnificent /buildings/ any where south of the of the Potomach river.[3] Gaston Wilder informed me to-day, that he had received your last letter, and will answer it shortly; he is now (as well as myself) enjoying all the pleasures of a social and agreeable life, as far as a scholar is permitted. I believe he and myself are the only two, of the number of those, that were here when you were, that remain here this vacation; we spend our time mostly in hunting Mr Price has got married, and has brought his wife to Hillsborough, <he> her visage I assure you is very homely; but I am informed she is very accomplished indeed, and indeed I inform you, she has one of the most magnificent voices, that nature ever bestowed upon a female. This lady in question, is far inferiour as to her beauty, to that one whose very name is so melodious to you; but she will be shortly where you may see her cheeks, which are more beautiful than the rose, and her eyes, which I anticipate you think, even excelles the Gazelles, in beauty, and brilliancy. Do not think these adulations which I anticipate you have concerning that lady, to be reciprocal to me, for I assure you that there is one whom I think, is as handsome as Venus as graceful Juno and as stately as Minerva; whom she be, I shall not pretend to tell thee; but do not fear it to be you procus. Your dear has left here, and has gone to Edenton; she will in the course of a few weeks, leave there, and go to New Haven. But I have now spent enough time, paper, and ink, about foolishness, for [*torn*] afraid I shall tire out your patience with my heedless and <and> insipid letter. You will, (by excusing my numerous mistakes and responding to this immediately) do me a very great favour.

I am with respect and esteem
your dear friend
D. D. Ferebee

[*Addressed*] Mr Wm Pettigrew
Roundhill
Northhampton
Massachusetts

[1]Dennis Dozier Ferebee of Currituck County graduated from the University of North Carolina in 1839. He later served several terms in the state legislature, was a delegate to both the Secession Convention and the Constitutional Convention of 1865, and was a colonel of cavalry in the Confederate army. Battle, *History of the University*, I, 459, 796. This letter indicates that he had been a schoolmate of William Shepard Pettigrew at Hillsborough Academy. Other letters from Ferebee not included in this volume may be found in the Pettigrew Family Papers, UNC.

[2]George Washington Polk was the son of Col. William Polk (1758-1834). He also had been a schoolmate of William Shepard Pettigrew at Hillsborough Academy. Paul H. Bergeron (ed.), "My Brother's Keeper: William H. Polk Goes to School," *North Carolina Historical Review*, XLIV (April, 1967), 190n, 192, 192n, 197n.

[3]Construction of the new state Capitol began in 1833. The building, designed by Ithiel Town and David Paton, did become known as a fine example of Greek Revival architecture. Lefler and Newsome, *North Carolina*, 352.

Ebenezer Pettigrew to William Shepard Pettigrew UNC

City Hotel New York Feb, 16, 1834

My dear William,

Some time in the last month, I received a letter from you as well as Mr Cogswell that the school at Round Hill was breaking up, and I determined to go and see you, accordingly I set out on the last of that month, but have been unable to get any farther than this place from bad health, where I shall stay untill you arrive which you will do as soon as you can possibly square up your matters at Round Hill. With regard to your matras [*mattress*], you must do with it the best you can. If it could be conveyed without much cost to New York, Mr Hicks would then send it without any to Carolina. My son you will leave nothing at Round Hill, such as book, trunks, /or/ cloths but bring them down with you.

My dear Son, of all things leave no debts behind but let the smallest ones be paid. Call on Mr Cogswell /who/ will have I suppose a surplus as the se/s/cion will close so much before its usual time. You will bring Mr Cooswell account settled in full & any surplus funds, and if none Mr Hicks will settle the remainder when Mr C. comes to the City which will be before he goes to North Carolina.

I got Mr Hicks to write to /Mr/ C. yesterday the purport of this letter, & I should have written you at the same time but was prevented. I send you a duplicate of this letter by the next mail least this might miss carry. Believe me to be with sincere Love and affection your father

E Pettigrew

N.B. When you arrive at the City, come direct to the City Hotel & enquire at the bar for Mr Pettigrew.

Receipt for Payment for Pigs UNC

March 14th 1834.

Recd of Ebenezer Pettigrew (by the hand of Henry Alexander) three Dollars in full payment, of a sow and sum pigs, which I say, that your man Bill killed, and also in full Debs, Dues, and Demand; of kind and sorts up to this Date Given under my hand

Nancy a spruill

Saml C Patrick

Ebenezer Pettigrew to John Herritage Bryan UNC

Lake Phelps March 29, 1834

My dear Sir,

I receivd your favour of the 12th Feb. on my return from the North. It contained information respecting my dear little Nancys cough which I was very desirous to know while I was gone. I would have liked to have been informed how the disease was with your children, several of whome I think I learned from Sister Marys letter had it, also how Francis' cough was. In my leasure or without leasure hours these questions enter my mind. I regret to learn that Sister Mary is low spirited. I fear the burden of so large a family is too great for any spirits, but she must & I know will bring Christianity to her aid. She must recollect that she yet has with her all her dear offspring, they have been spared to her by a kind providence. While I am writing of large families it reminds me that I have two fat beaves, one or both of which I think of sending to my dear friends in Newbern, they will leave without something occurs, about the 7th next month. I do not know whether they are out of season or not, but I know that about this /time/ fresh provision is scarce. I have no one with me but the overseer & one dear son, we are by the nature of the case bound to live hard. One of my great punishments is to direct what is to /be/ prepared for the next meal. I do not know how far I am right in withholding from my house hold (not the necessaries of life but) the little luxuries; I am for my self willing to mortify the flesh, to any extent.

My dear son William is with me, he has grown exceedingly, in stature and I think as much in mind & deportment. In truth he gives me no trouble, and of coarse a great deal of consolation. When in New York I sent to the Miss Mary's a writing desk a piece, tell the dear little girls that the old man expects to receive a letter from them writen on those desks, before long.

I am glad to learn that you have matched Jackson (not old General Jackson; for his match is not to be found in this world) but the horse Jackson, I hope Sister Mary will ride in more safety without which there is no <safety> comfort. It would be impossible to sell Clay in this county. Money is awfully scarce in /this/ quarter, and I know not what the class who live by <this> geting shingles will do for bread, there is no doubt but they will suffer exceedingly.

I could wish <to> very much to visit you but my time is very much occupied with my necessary business. It would have given me great pleasure to have been with you at the time you mention, but there seems a fatality attending the Bishop and myself geting together. In our moving through this world more than a half dozen times have we been in the same town & not seen each other. It is the farthest from my wishes to avoid him. I have yet some affection of the head occasionally & particularly when excited, from any cause. I can feal it in a measurable degree by a half dozen signs with mental affection to produce them. I avoid even language which will *excite*, as much as possible. I am now under medicine which the Doctor says will undoubtedly relieve. That or company has relieved me in a great degree, so that for days I /have/ none of it. I regret that our banks are so backward in geting into opperation, but they could not have commenced in a worse time. Had it not been for the present state of things, I think I should have <my> subscribed for a small amount, but if I can now hold on I shall do well. If ever a debt /of gratitude/ was paid in this world, the people of the United States have paid their debt to General Jackson.

I hope Sister Marys health is better and that your self & Children are in that enjoyment, Please to remember me affectionately to her and all my dear friends with you &

Believe me sincerely & truely
your friend & relative
E Pettigrew

John H. Bryan esqr

[*Addressed*] John H. Bryan Esqr
Newbern
North Carolina

Mary Blount Shepard to Ebenezer Pettigrew UNC

New Bern April 14. 1834.

My dear son

Pompey arrived with the beeves last Friday and I am exceedingly obliged to you for mine. I was quite sick and confined to my room when they came but am better to day, Johnston is in better health than I have ever seen him, he had an attack of croup about six weeks ago which left him with a cough for a short time, the rest of us are tolerable well except Mary who has been unwell for sometime and I fear her health and constitution are gone, Penelope also has been sick a greater part of the winter, you express a wish for me to visit you this spring but it will be out of my power to do so, Mary expects to be confined every day and I cannot think of leaving her at this time, she is very low-spirited and has taken up a notion that she will never get up again.

I wish very much to go /to/ the convention in May if I can, Charles left here three weeks ago for New York and when he will return I do not know.

Mr [*John M.*] Roberts gave me 40 D 25 Cts of your money and I paid Mr Pasteur[1] for your paper as you requested, I sent Mr Roberts a very fine peice of the beef with your respects and sent a good many of my acquaintances (not friends for they are scarce) a piece.

You are so kind & make me so many presents I do not know how I shall repay your kindness, I shall be very glad to see you & William whenever you can leave home. I have kept Pompey to day to put away my beef & shall start him to morrow which will be the 15 of the month. Penelope joins me in love to you and William and believe me

your affectionate mother
Mary Shepard

[*Addressed*] Mr Ebenezer Pettigrew
Lake Phelps,
Tyrrel county.

[1]Probably this was John I. Pasteur, an owner and editor of the *Carolina Sentinel* in New Bern. Miller, "Recollections," 57.

Charles Lockhart Pettigrew to Ebenezer Pettigrew UNC

Chapel-Hill April 16th 1834

Dear Father.

I received your letter, dated at home, a few days since; I was sorry to learn of your indisposition, it certainly must be very troublesome to you. You mentioned that brother William had come home, and was very much improved in size, manners and disposition. I am in hopes he will continue to improve; I know from his letters to me he has gained considerable knowledge, his hand writing had become tolerable his diction and spelling much better than it was formerly. I have purchased this mare, as you have found out, she is one of the best animals I ever saw, I went to Hillsborough last saturday on her, and when we got there, although we rode a pretty good gait, she did not exhibit the least appearance of being tired; to be candid about it, I do not expect you, at first, will like my bargain, but when she is tried she will prove herself, she is one of the easiest and best saddle horses I ever saw, so that I almost wish she could remain so, she has plenty of spirits, and when I ride I never pretend to use either whip or spur, she is of good blood her sire being the "Irish man" I saw the <her> horse is quite a good looking animal, I have understood that this mare is swift-footed. I gave a hundred and 90 dollars for her and to be kept in the village untill june, and to be at my service when ever I wish to ride, I had an offer to sell her the<r> other day, the gentleman offered 75 $ and a horse of his own which horse he has since sold for $75, but I concluded I had rather keep the mare than part <whi> with her even for that price. Mr Bingham at Hillsboro passed sentence on her and said I had give a good price but she was a fine animal, she is six years old this spring, she is peculiarly valuable to me having to ride so far next vaction; I am in hopes you will be pleased with her when she has a fair trial.

I have just received your letter of the 14th I have received several letters from you since you left home for the no/r/th and my reason for not writing then was that I did not know where to direct my letters, about <a> a week and a half since I received brother William's letter stating your return home; and intended to write home in about the usual time after having received yours. In your letter before the last you spoke of brother William's coming to college next june <and> wishing me to send him a catalogue of studies, I shall send him one with this letter, his class will then be entering the sopomore year and he of course will stand for that class, the Faculty have some notion of raising the standard of studies, and therefore I would advise him to attend diligently to <me> them, for I should dislike /for/ him to be rejected: Also with respect to /a/ room I have at present a very fine one thought by some to the best in college and we can room together very well, for as you remarked in one of your letters "a two fold cord is stronger than one" my health is as good now as it ever was, My dear Father I am in hopes you will not in the least suppose my affection for you is cooling or that I have become callous to the many benefits I have received at your hand, give my love to brother William and tell him

I shall write him in about a fortnight and be <su> assured that I still remain dutiful

Charles L Pettigrew

[*Addressed*] Mr E. Pettigrew Esq
Cool Spring
Tyrrel
N.C.

Charles Lockhart Pettigrew
to William Shepard Pettigrew UNC

Chapel Hill May 1834

Dear brother

I expect father has received my last letter some time since and now I shall attempt to answer your letter, I hope you will have no more cause to complain of my not writing, at least when I do write I shall endeavour to give you a full letter, though I shall take care not to be so long as to trouble you with reading. In your letter, you gave me a cursory recital of your journey home ward from the north, I wish<ed> you<r> had delt more in particulars, and <have> had given me a minute detail of circumstances as they presented themselves to your astonished view; perhaps it might afford me that pleasure which you speak of as having reaped; in the latter part of your letter you spoke of your health by saying "it was as usual" now if I had have been in the habit of receiving letters from you I might have then know how to have understood you, and such an expression would have been allowable, therefore you will please to explain how it usually is and then I shall have the satisfaction of thouroughly knowing you exact state.

You expect to come here next session and join college, I would advise you to apply yourself diligently the short time you remain home, and for this reason because I fear unless you are a good <schl> scholar you will not be able to enter the sophomore class; the faculty and trustees have determined to advance the standard of studies, that is to make the entrance into college more difficult in asmuch as they will have to know more and so also with every other class, for that reason those who enter the sophomore will have to be well versed in the studies. I sent you a catalogue the other day of the studies which I am in hopes you will persue exactly; in the second session you find algebra the distance to which classes generally go is through the article on Quadratic equations. I should be very sorry if you were not to get in I would advise you to study very hard so as to be sure, for in your not being ad<d>mited you would not only feel yourself but also subject your <self> friends and relations to the same bad feeling; however I hope you will be ad<d>mited it will depend with <your self> yourself. It is universally the case that almost all who come to college, when they first arrive on the hill and join their class, seem to be fully determined to study hard <finally> and for what? why this is the reason they hope to speak the "latin"[1] when they graduate indeed I say these <who> are but few, who come here; without pretentions for the "Latin": in one year how many drop off and become idle lazy and a perfect pest to college, in the <the> begin/n/ing of the sophomore year there are not more than 6 out of a class of 35, see what an awful decrease the forths have given out the idea and become spendthrifts sots and every thing that is disgraceful, in the commencement of the junior how many do we find then that hold out there may be 4 and in the senior not more than one or two. thus I have given you a history of fellows running for the Latin: you /can/ now very easily guess by what sort of a principal they are actuated, and how evanesent it is. Let us look <us> into the principal itself giving it a candid and minute examination without bias either to one side or the other being guided by truth in our investigation: the fact of running for the "Latin" comes under the head of ambition, that is a desire to excell others and why? to be above them and have the pleasure of looking down upon your inferiors, not a desire to be more thorough scholars than they are and to have improved time better than they have, Oh no, but a mere desire to be said to be superior to them, if they were all miserably bad scholars, the latin man would only care to be a little above, if they knew nothing about the studies they had been over he would content himself to know /only/ so much about them that is the studies as to give him a superior place: Now I put the question what sort of a man would you suppose him to be who is governed by such motives? it does not require a moment's time to answer, he must have a domineering spirit and one which would go to any lengths to gratify it's sordid and unbounded ambition <who with out> ruled alone by interest without any regard to the rules of justice and right whenever they came in contact with it. Perhaps you would here be ready to say and do you really believe that every /latin/ man is influenced by such motives? I answer most assuredly in the negative at the same time using an old but pert adige, "there are exceptions to all general rules" yes there are some who are pressing after that mark <who> that are as honerable as any men to be found in the whole country, but the majority of them are as dark and revengeful as the grave, men so entirely devoted to their own interest that they neglect every thing in stead of that. You might here be ready to say <your> according to your doctrine a person must study only enough to stand respectably, I answer no that it is the duty of every person while at college to attend to his duties well; I am very far from saying that every person who speaks the latin makes it the object of his persute his chief aim, no, no, many a person has spoken the first speach, who has made knowledge and literature his aim and I say that ought to be the way a man should act.

Continuing the same subject the next question I would ask is whether a person making the latin the end of all his cares and toils in the end: is as thorough a sc/h/olar as he who only makes it object to learn; the former is not influenced by any love for literature and therefore he does not persue it with that intense interest which he ought to; he confines himself to get those parts well on which he supposes he will the taken up and those question alone which he thinks will be asked; but how does the latter conduct himself [what] sort of a course does he adopt, one entirely different? yes [*torn*] urged to his studies by a love for them and an ardent wish to make himself of the several subjects on which they treat, he does not confine himself to the particular parts on which he may be taken but gets the whole of it he not only solves the questions which may be asked but also every other one connected with the subject at what conclusion do you now arrive? most certainly this, that the first one is a man entirely superficial without having the least solidity not to be depended /on/ in any thing which requires knowledge and that the latter is a man of great depth and soundness one to be depended on <and under> in any circumstaces with which he has ever become acquainted. I wish time would allow me to finish my remarks but I hope you will consider them well and frame you conduct accordingly I am at present very well; give /my/ love to Father and be assured of my affection for yourself

Charles L Pettigrew

[*Addressed*] Mr William S Pettigrew
Cool Spring
Washington Co
N C.

---

[1]The delivery of the Latin salutatory was the highest honor given to a member of the graduating class at the university.

William Woodley to Ebenezer Pettigrew A&H

Edenton 3rd May 1834

Mr E. Pettigrew,

Dear Sir

Last winter during my stay at Mr Harrisons, I was going to the Lake but heard that you was gone to the north and Mr Davenport was in the Shingle /Swamp/ geting Shingles and there was no white person at your house—on your returne from the north, I heard you was in Plymouth—I went to town the next morning to See you there but you had Set out for the Lake in the morning before I got there—and two days after that—I Received a letter from Mr Johnston Requesting me to go over and See him that he might give me Some directions about his work before he returned up the river—Mr Johnston Set me to geting Timber with his hands to Build a house for a Steam Mill—Mr Johnston was well when he left home—and he is not yet returned—

Dear Sir, though I am some distance from you and do not see you often, yet I allways keep in remembrance the good advice and business you have given to me—that got me out of debt—it was by your kindness and Recommendation, that got me into Mr Johnstons employ—and I Shall allways feal greatfull and give to you my Sincere thanks for your goodness—if I can get time to leave Mr Johnstons work this Summer I will come to See you if I am alive and well—and bring with me the Pinion pattorn—I am Sorrow it has been neglected so long—if you Should want it before—Please to inform me and I will Send it to you—my health is reasonably good at this time—and I hope you will have the Pleasure to inform me that your Self Sons and Daughters are all in good health—and I remain yours etc.

Most Respectfully
W. Woodley

[*Addressed*] Ebenezer Pettigrew Esqr
Cool Spring Post office
Washington County
N.C.

Thomas Trotter to Ebenezer Pettigrew UNC

Prospect Hill May 17th 1834

Dear Friend

Your favour of April 4th I received with pleasure I was going to write to you when I was informed by S[*noad B.*]. Carraway that you had gone to the Northard, I also should wrote you some days after receiving your letter had not Mr Bryan told me he expected you here at the Convention, he was here and expected to have seen you, had you been here you would been amused, to me it put me on Mind of St Bartholemews fair in London, there was about 25 Carriages constantly parading the Streets, some times whites & sometimes Blacks & some times empty those who had Carriages would neither go to Church or Visit for 200 Yards, but must have a Carriage, in the time of worship, after carrying the owners to Church, the Carriages were occupied in carrying Whites & Blacks a pleasuring round Towen untill sermon was over when they than waited at Church for the Nobility, there was a great many people here, and a great part paid attention to divine service, <and> and a good many did not, but appeared as if they came to a frolik of eating & drinking, on saturday night they were putting the Town to right, by taking the head boards or stones from the Graves & putting against peoples doors & saying the burial of the dead, such bad behaviour was disgracefull. I am glad it was not done by the Citisons of Washington, there are wild Characters, every where & they ought to be stayd at home, there were a great many respectable people here, from Raleigh, Faytteville, Wilmington, Halifax, Tarborough, Greenville, Newbern & Edenton &c &c. there never was the like here before, & I believe the People spared no pains to treat them well, what was done in Church I cannot tell as I did not go there, some people spoke in favour of the abilitys of the Clergy.

I am exceedingly sorry that you was taken so strongly with the headach did the Physition, give you any information what to do if it should return as it seemed to be so singular a Case, it would be well for you to know, should it return, to be prepared for an attack, as it is generally very sudden, and you are often without Company, I was Glad to be informed by you that you had brought home your Son William, which will Yield you much comfort and pleasure by his Company, I was happy to hear that he has made such good progress in his learning, I hope you and him will enjoy good health after so much fatigue in bad health also.

In your Visit to Washington you did not say that you saw old Hickery and his Kitchen Cabinet, if you had you might well said they were the greatest Scoundrels could be produced in the United States.

It is reported in Newspapers that /they/ want to go to Warr with France for them not complying with the Treaty for their Spoliations with us[1] if that is the case we shall want the deposits, we shall want a National Bank also, for their favorite Banks have no credit abroad. I expect they will be persuaded what to do, I am sorry for the French refusing to comply with the Treaty on my own Account,

I expected to have got part of Burbank Claim in August next, and should have tryed to sold the Ballance, which would releaved me of my difficultys, which must now continue some monts longer for the French Government a Great part is in favor of it, /of our Claim/ and our real government intends to push for a compliance of it. Mr Adams speech in Congress wishes to make the French government comply to the Treaty.

The Season here with us is remarkably dry, What corn is up does not grow, and there has been a great deal killed by the frost, Cottin has been in light ground entirely killed down, and what has stood in general is much injured, there is many people would plant over if they had seed, Vegetation seems to be entirely at a stand. Turpentine makers suffers, the trees does / does not yield the turpentine it is so dry, My wheat is much Injured first by the wett and now the drowth causes the heads to be very short, and a good deal of lace Cheat in it, it is now beginning to turn, My oats has been also much injured by the wett & now dry weather. I never saw so much wet at one time before as we had in April my low ground was nearly all covered, yet if it seasonable I hope to make a good Crop of Corn, all kind of produce are low here Corn is \$3 by the quantity. there is but little in Market, what comes is from up the river there is none from Matamuskeet this season they made such bad crops last season, and navel stores are low also, there is no money stirring, Jackson has the whole blame, even the Lumber from the steam mill meets no cash contracts, our fishers has been very unprofitable this season Herrings are scarce at <\$50> \$4.50 a Barrel.

I observe you are making great improvements on Belgrade, there is nothing like it as I expect you intend it for one of your Children, your experience in bulding & planing, will be done cheaper & better than they could do it.

in the death of Col^{o} Tarkinton his Estate cannot be more embarassed than I expected, I am in hopes it is more healthy in your neighborhood than it has been.

I have injoyed very good heath since I saw you. Mrs Trotter has been very sick Elena is gone with Mr Weatherby to Alabama much against her inclination and ours

I am much distressed in my mind in my family affairs as well, with Burbank affairs, my two son in laws are at enmity against each other, for which shall have the largest share of what property I have left, I will write you fully on this next letter as also my other concerns, there is no person I can reveal my thoughts to so well as to you, Mrs Trotter has recovered her health so as to be about, she joins me in comp^{ts} to you and William hoping your health will continue

I remain Dear Friend Affectionatly Yours
Thomas Trotter

[*Addressed*] Eben^{r} Pettigrew esq^{r}
Lake Phelps
Tyrrel County

[1]In 1831 the United States had concluded a treaty to secure settlement of more than 12 million dollars in claims against France that arose mainly from the confiscation of American shipping between 1806 and 1810. When France failed to comply with the treaty, the threat of war arose. With British mediation in 1836, the dispute was resolved diplomatically. Wayne Andrews (ed.), *Concise Dictionary of American History* (New York: Charles Scribner's Sons, 1962), 385-386, hereinafter cited as *CDAH*; Henry Blumenthal, *France and the United States: Their Diplomatic Relations, 1789-1914* (Chapel Hill: University of North Carolina Press, 1970), 44.

Hicks Smith and Company to Ebenezer Pettigrew A&H

New York June 24th 1834

E Pettigrew Esq

Dear Sir

We enclose your sales of cargo p^{r} the Lady of the Lake netting \$133$^{56/100}$ to your credit, and also bill of articles sent by the same vessel amounting to \$430$^{38/100}$—we paid to Capt Dunbar on your account \$150—the freight and carting of the wine is \$3, and the cost of binding the "American Farmer" is \$1.—We find that there is very little negro cloth in market, and most of that is inferior. and as the supplies for the Fall will arrive by the return of your vessel, we thought it better to wait until then, when we shall be able to do better—we have some doubt, whether the best Blankets now sent, are not too good, for the purpose you want them, we should like to know how you like them, as the information may be of service to us in future purchases—we will have the Harness made in time to send by the next Trip, and will give the maker particular charge as to the quality of the Leather—The quality of your Corn was very good, and it brought about 5$^{¢}$ pr bushel more, than the ordinary quality from your State, the price of the latter being about 61$^{¢}$—The supplies of this article continue to be quite light, but the price of whiskey, and other Kinds of Grain are so low, that it will be difficult for the price of corn, to advance materially—The growing crop of wheat in the northern and western sections of this State are very promising both as to the quantity and quality, and it is the opinion of Dealers in flour that unless some foreign demand should take place prices will be low it is probable that the first new wheat in market, will bring about \$1$^{12/100}$ and that subsequent arrivals will go for something less—Red oak Hhd Staves $20—white oak do $33

Yours with respect
Hicks Smith & Co

[*Addressed*] E Pettigrew Esq[r]
Cool Spring
Washington County
N. Carolina

John Herritage Bryan to Ebenezer Pettigrew UNC

New Bern July 3. 1834

My dear Sir,

I returned from Raleigh last Saturday night and found all well here—two or three of the children (Mary Pettigrew & Charles particularly) look rather puny, and M[rs] B. thinks that a trip to Beaufort would be of great service to them.

Our family seems destined to trouble—James Shepard the day after commencement, caned Hayw[d] Guion for having used Some *vulgar* language respecting—whom would you think? Mary W Bryan!!! the sister of your departed wife.—

We have had the town during my absence /very much excited/ on account of a fight between some of Dixon's apprentices /on one side/—and Alex: & Herritage Blount and a son of W[m] Street[1] on the other; in the course of which, Herritage stabbed two of the apprentices one of them dangerously.—they have since recovered.

Johnston & Nancy are in very good health, and I am pleased to inform you that *here* Johnston behaves very well, and is easily managed.--

You allude in your letter to Penelope, to a letter to M[rs] Bryan—this she has *not* received.—

I heard nothing new in Raleigh, I saw the Bishop, his health was so indifferent that he did not preach.—M[r] Hogg returned in fine health, but in a day or two after his return, had a very violent attack of Vertigo & fell prostrate.—

The Episcopal School seems to have made a very fair start—they have about 50 students in the whole, about 30 of which are boarders.

Penelope says that the last of this month will be time enough for her to leave here for Hillsbo.—

Our town is full of idle, discontented people, whose vicious appetites seem to crave scandal for their daily food, the place is hardly fit for an honest man to live in; & the country seems to be so impoverished as to afford no business worth pursuing.—The times seem to be evil indeed.—I should like very much to hear some good news—it would be a rarity.—

Mary & Penelope desire to be affectionately presented to you.—

Very truly
yr friend & relation
Jn H. Bryan

[*Addressed*] E Pettigrew Esqr
Cool Spring
N.C

[1]Alexander Clement Hall Blount (1816-1912) was a son of Dr. Frederick Blount; possibly Herritage Blount was, also. The other participant mentioned was a son of William R. Street and his wife, née Saunders. Powell, *DNCB*, I, 178; Miller, "Recollections," 46. Alexander Blount married Julia Elizabeth Washington (1824-1888) on October 26, 1843, and settled in Florida. Parish Register of Christ Church, New Bern, Marriages, 138; Hamilton and Williams, *Graham Papers*, VII, 602n.

[Dr.] Frederick Vanderburgh to Ebenezer Pettigrew UNC

New York 4th Aug 1834

My dear friend

I have taken the liberty to send by your Lady of the Lake another horse power & threshg machine which you may keep or sell as you like—It runs with less power than the other & threshes faster & as clean.

Your overseer will know how to put it in motion— Would it not be easier for you to thresh your wheat in the field & afterwards throw the straw into your yard or leave it where it is for manure— the Dutch farmers of Maryland do so & save all their wheat by spreading 60 or 70 yds of Canvass about the machine.

If rain comes up they throw the straw over the wheat. that keeps it dry—after threshg they put this hor[*se*] power to a wheel on their farming mill & clean it all on the spot—You will perceive that half the multiplying power is on the machine & half on the horse power so that the power can be applied to various uses. The teeth in the machine is a little longer & the throat layer for the passage of the straw that enables it to thresh faster than the other

I can easily fit a horse power by your model if you want it; but you can thresh with the one you have with the machine 100 ft above the power if you wish—It is ascertained by experiment that the longer the strap, the easier the machine runs & you can thresh easier with your power on the ground & machine in the 2d or 3d story than to have them close together

I wish when your schooner returns you would throw the big wheel of the first horse power on board & let me put it in right order—the wedge that holds it on the shaft is iron & it wants 2 more wedges fitted in—I sent a cold chisel & some wedges to cut new key seats & put in new wedges but we had better do it here—

My family are all at Saratoga & I am living a Bachelors life—. Give my respects to your Son & believe me sincerely your friend [*torn*]

F. Vanderburgh

[*Addressed*] E Pettigrew Eqr
Cool Spring
Washington County
North Carolina

Ebenezer Pettigrew to William Shepard Pettigrew UNC

Lake Phelps Aug 29, 1834

My Dear William

I received your letter of the 16th by the last mail, and although you wrote in great haste and it was pretty much of a scribble yet I was very glad to receive it, hoping you will take more pains when you get settled down & quiet at your studies. You did not say what class you joined. The faculty rejecting you on Arithmatic was a little surprising, but I should take no notice of it. It is a sufficient lesson for you, to know that you must be circumspect or worse will come of it. They have the power and the majority of what is called the higher class will go with them, no matter what they do, to the great prejudice & sometimes ruin of a boy, and I would advise you & I now enjoin it on you to deport yourself towards them *all* with the strictest propriety, obeying the laws in all things, and thereby you force them into justice. I fear they would be pleased to have an opportunity to disgrace one of my sons, from the dislike Mr Cal[*d*]well has to their father; but my dear give them not that pleasure and that tryumph over your poor forlorn Father. Let him rise into notice through the excellence of his children, and everything depends on you two older sons conduct in the outset in life. Therefore my dear son as you value your poor disconsolate Fathers little remaining comfort, & the happiness & prosperity of your younger brother & dear little innocent sisters, let your conduct be mild & orderly, attentive to your studies and thereby laying up a stock of information for future life, which will put you above the frowns of /the/ proud & self sufficient part of the community. My son, let me insist on your not reading novels, they will inevitably destroy your taste for every thing else, and be assured they are as infatuating is ardent spirits.

I am going on as usual. Mr Davinport returned in due time from N. York, in good spirits but he soon got in the dumps. He has been nearby ever since at Belgrade ditching; all which ditches I shall have compleated next week. Mr Tarkenton will nearly compleat two of the house chimneys this week. He would have been farther forward but he was two weeks at the Lake pilering the smoke house & horse stable which was settling very much from the roting of the blocks.

I have purchased Jordan Phelps land at one thousand dollars, so that I shall now be able to square up on that side. I am diging a five feet ditch on the side of the Poplar neck road to Doughs & Claytons so that no water can remain in those back grou/n/ds a day. The wheat netted above a fraction over 95 cents and in loading the schooner again I found that I own enough /corn/ to load her. Mr Hicks wrote me that it would be worth 70 cents. the Captain has sailed 16 days but I fear the head winds have been against him. Though the wheat neted more than I expected & the corn should command the price above, yet the thousand dollars /I have to pay for the land/ with other expences will leave me but enough to go through the year. My dear sons I am making great /exertions &/ sacrifises for your interest let me ask of you to make some for your selves. I am doing my duty to you let me ask of you to do your to yourselves, and let me say this to you which never forget, be united, Love one another. A two fold cord is not easily broken. without unity you must fall. Tell Brother Charles I should like to get a line from him & to know whether he paid <my> & has he paid my E.P. [*Episcopal*] school subscription. also has he got from N[*ew Bern*]. to C. Hill.

I received a letter from little Mary two mails ago she <was> expressed great pleasure at seeing her brothers how did her brothers feel towards them.

Your uncle Frederick was with me last week our conversation produced a good deal of excitement in me & my head has suffered a good deal. I have been some unwell this week and find that from the past weeks excitement that I cannot take Qinine without its deranging my head so as to make unable to walk. It is a grand remedy for fall diseases & I regret very much not to be able to use it. It is very healthy so far, as far as I know not a sick one on the list here or at Belgrade. Mr Griffisth has been sick with bilious fever at Mr Haughtons for the last 12 days. He has been very ill & the T/h/ompson remedies came near killing him. He has now employed Dr Lewis. Dr. H[*ardison*].[1] held up while Mr C. was here & I understand promised a thorough reform, but that /day/ week Mr C. <lef> left he got uncommonly drunk. 'Sic transit gloria mundi.'

May God Almighty bless you my dear sons I the prayer of your [*illegible*] Father

E Pettigrew

[*Addressed*] Mr William S Pettigrew
Chapel Hill
N. Carolina

[1]Dr. Hardy Hardison was a delegate from the Cool Spring district to the Whig convention held April 8, 1842, in Raleigh. *Whig* (Washington, N.C.), March 23, 1842, April 13, 1842. Other delegates included William Shepard Pettigrew, Josiah Collins III, and Doctrine Davenport.

Charles Lockhart Pettigrew to Ebenezer Pettigrew UNC

Chapel Hill Aug 30 [*1834*]

Dear father

I expect that you have received a letter from brother William before this. I arrived at Newburn without injury and what is very extraordinary I was not sick at all during my ride untill I arrived within about 6 miles of Newburn, it being night then, it could hardly have been expected that I should have escaped all the bad effects of riding at once. I remained in Newburn untill Wednesday when I took the stage for Raleigh and had as pleasant a ride there a<nd>s I had enjoyed before have to ride very little in the night; however there is one <subject> circumstance which I had almost forgotten to mention, that is after I had gone about 12 miles from Newburn the stage b/r/oke down, but that was /misfortune/ soon remedied by putting a rail under the injured side thus we proceeded to Raleigh nevertheless we proceeded without any father danger I arrived at C.H. the morning after the session had begun but brother William had preserved my room and by that means I was no <losser> looser. I had the draft cashed, you were so kind to give me, at the Newburn at ½ per ct making the amount I received about $848.25. Mr Bryan told me I could have it cashed there and was so kind as to go with me to the bank, I was ignorant that I should have to pay percentage <untl> untill the casher Mr Guion[1] <to> said he would negotiate it ½ perct at that time having the draft in his hand. I wrote to Mr [*George W.*] Freeman soon after I arrived here, not having been able to see him in Raleigh, <I> according to your direction informing him that I had so much money at my command subject to his order, he /wrote me/ in about a week ordering the money to him by mail, and thus expressing himself in one part which I shall quote verbum ve/r/bo "In the name of the School committee I desire, through you, to tender our thankful acknowledgements to your father for his liberality, in thus anticipating the several installments on his subscription—particularly at this time when the institution is so much in want of funds." I intend sending the money to him this evening by mail, and shall have a witness to see me put <it in the> the money in a letter <at the> in the presence of the post master the responsibility will then cease from my hands; he will send me a receipt on his recieving <my> the money. I would lengthen my letter but in consequence of business which I had necessarily to perform I shall have to conclude my letter. Brother William has been quite unwell with a cold, but owing to a very sudden change in the weather he has had some slight chills and fever I am in hopes with care and attention he will soon recover; I have been and am yet quite well, believe me your

affectionate son
Charles L Pettigrew

[*Addressed*] Mr E. Pettigrew
Cool-Spring
Washington Co
N.C.

---

[1]John W. Guion was cashier at the Bank of New Bern. Miller, "Recollections," 35.

William Biddle Shepard to Ebenezer Pettigrew A&H

Alexandria D.C.— Augt 31st 1834

My Dear Sir,

Having concluded after what may well be called deliberation, that I had no great deal of time to spare if I ever intended to commit matrimony, I am about to venture upon that often tried experiment.—I am engaged to be married to a lady of this town Miss Charlotte Cazenove, the ceremony will take place about the middle of October next, and I should be much pleased if you could witness the ceremony. I am somewhat afraid you will not believe in the reality of the event unless you are an eye witness, in fact I am hardly myself convinced it is a fact.—I am well aware that there is little inducement in a simple ceremony of marriage to bring you from Carolina here, but if your business will admit of it, I should be much pleased to see you, and to introduce you to my intended.—The event will take place somewhere about the middle of October, the precise day is not yet definitely fixed.—

Yours truly
Wm. B. Shepard

[*Addressed*] Ebenezer Pettigrew Esqr
Cool Spring
Washington County
N. Carolina

Ebenezer Pettigrew to Mary Williams Bryan A&H, BRYAN

Lake Phelps Sep 25, 1834

My dear Sister,

I received your kind favour of the 11th with great pleasure, I regret to learn of Mr Bryans indisposition, but from the tenor of your letter expect it was of short continuance. When ever the Quinine will put a stop to the fever, and restore obstructed perspiration, the cure is almost certain. It was with very great pleasure I learned of yours (I presume) and the health of your dear little family. My dear little Mary being so very thin, I hope is no evidence of bad health. I hope Heritage Blount & poor old Mrs Furlow are before this recovered. I regret to see in the last paper the death of one of Judge Donalds [*Donnell's*][1] children. And it is with great sorrow I learn by your letter of the sickness of our dear relatives in Hillsboro; the mail previous I learned by letter from Charles Pettigrew that his brother William was sick & from his letter I apprehend bilious fever, which I consider a very dangerous disease in the up country. Poor sister Penelope I fear is not long for this world. This is an opinion I have had for some time. May God in his infinite mercy prepare her for that which he has made for the righteous in his kingdom.

It was with great pleasure I received your opinion of my dear two sons. I scarcely ever look at them without thinking of their dear ever dear Mother. Though not like her, I view them as her representitives once as part of her, which gives to me such sensations as I am unable to describe. They are promising boys and I have great hope in them. Since they left, I have had a lonely time. My overseers, workmen, and a forigner, who though an examplary man, has no conversation either religious or worldly and is therefore as company a Blank & in the way so far as preventing me from going to Belgrade and staying as long as my business requires; to which place the greater part of my opperations are going on. People have acquired an opinion that I have a great deal of judgment in business, and also a great deal of money and everything else, and you wo/u/ld be astonished to learn how many applications I have for every thing I have got. Were I not to resist with firmness which I thank God belongs to me; I should have nothing in a year at my command. I have no perticular referance to any one person. The applications are far & near. But my dear Sister, I know who I am pledged to protect, and defend. I know that, that which my dear, dear, Nancy sacrificed so much for, it not mine, but to manage for her dear children. I know also that I am bound in duty to those dear children to hand down to them a character unsullied for virtue, honesty, truth & sobriety, and that I am bound not to bring a blush to their cheaks for any <of> leading vices; and by Gods help I will go on to the end of /my/ pilgrimage. As for cringing and bowing and accepting the fawning of every one who has become sensible of my wealth, I cannot, I will not. Not because I am offended with them. No I am not at war in my heart with any one, but I have a bad opinion of many and do not wish anything to do with them. If they are great I wish them to be so and I do not wish them to impart any of it to me; I get along very well without it. The time has gone by when these things could gratify me, My *sun* has set, and I am now traviling a lonely, dark, road under a firm hope of being again united in sweet converse to a dear ever dear wife when the night shall close and were it not the duty which I owe to my dear children & few friends, with composure would I close my eyes on this world forever; but I must fill my course, and rejoice to know that I can say with truth. My blessed Father, thy will & not mine be done.

You some time back understood of the injury done to my leg, and that it was well, as I thought; but about a fortneight ago, I felt a sharp sting within & at the place where the injury was, which I took no immediate notice of but it continued to hurt for some days and when I looked at it, I observed the swelling on the shin, and I have assertaind that it is no more nor less than an Aneurism. It is necessary to keep my leg bandaged; and then it is troublesome & somewhat <troublesome> painfull. But for the soundness of my system I should apprehend great danger, and perhaps a spedey termination of life. It may /be/ necessary to have an opperation and perhaps an amputation before there is a cure, but time will tell more about it. My general health was never better, nor was I ever fater. The fall continues healthy, little or no sickness & what there is easily removed. Please to tell Lidia that her children are all well & that I wish she could see her children, & that I could see mine. I received a letter from W[*illiam*]. B[*iddle*]. S[*hepard*]. inviting me to his weding. I thanked him & declined, by saying I should be as much at a loss at a weding at Washington as /at/ Fidlers green. Frederick [*Shepard*] has at last been to see me, and stayed six days. He is F. B. Shepard yet, but he seemed to feel much more at the forlorn state of the place than he did when here the winter after these things began. Please to give my kind regards to Mr Bryan, and my love to the dear little children and believe me to be your affctionate Brother

E Pettigrew

M[rs] M. Bryan

[*Addressed*] M[rs] John H. Bryan
Newbern
N. Carolina

---

[1]John R. Donnell (1791-1864), a lawyer in Craven County, served as a superior court judge from 1819 until 1836. Keith and others, *Blount Papers*, IV, 372n.

Ebenezer Pettigrew to William Shepard Pettigrew UNC

Lake Phelps Nov. 15, 1834

My dear William

I have received letters from you & also Charles, and two weeks ago answered partially them in a letter addressed to Charles. I was then very sick from a cold which I had taken, from which I have pretty well recovered except at intervals a bad cough. I regret the cough the more as I expect to leave on the 20th for the North. My leg is no better and I have no hope of its recovery without surgical aid, and what that aid will be is unknown to me. At this time I think my life in danger /from/ hemorage. My dear Sons, it is uncertain whether I shall ever return, and I am prepaired for the worst, but live under a firm hope in the Love of God and that his will is right My sons I feel very great interest in the turn you may take in the commencement of life. One will lead to honour, ease and comfort through life, while the other will lead to disgrace, misery and endless wo in this and the next world. My dear sons weigh well your first acts in life, and never forget that any improper or disgracfull act, will not only attach disgrace to you & your dear brothers & little sisters (who depend on you for their future advancement in life) but will disgrace your dear Mother and father in their *graves*. My dear Sons rather honour them while they are no longer on this earth to add to that of /which/ they had so great a share while here below. Remember this age in which you will live is an eventfull one and /an/ age of letters & improvement, and I beseech you my dear sons loose not that opportunity to make yourselves equal to your fellows. Remember my dear sons, the sacrifices which your dear ever dear Mother made for your advancement and what your father has made and is yet willing to make, and be not prodigal of the little which <I> We have gathered for you, which with negligen<t>ce & prodigality will vanish before you think of it, leaving you in a merciless world without any thing. May God of his infinite mercy impress upon your hearts & minds a love of him, a duty to him which will lead to his blessing and your wellfare & happiness in this and the next world. My dear Sons do not forget in your prayers to your blessed father in heaven to petion for the safe recovery of your father on earth, and that he may be restored once more to the protection of his dear, dear, children. My sons, your father is not afraid to die and but for his dear children would he be <afraid> reluctant to die, but those dear little ones of your dear Mother he is willing to live for, his whole sould is devoted to their advancement and comfort, in this & the next world.

I am afraid my dear William from some remarks of your Grandma [*Shepard*], that you are very tired of Chapel Hill. I know it is a tiresome place, and lonesome, but my son you go for a certain object, which object is of the first consequence, and without it you will alway feel the want in an emenent degree. Therefore I hope you will submit to all the privations of the situation and lay in a stock of information which will be your greatest comfort in life. Pray my son avoid reading novels, but spend your leasure hours in acquiring usefull knowledge. Though it may appear a long time to the end of your stay, it will be over. Recollect my sons, your father is hard at work for you and that his experience will do more than you can do yet. I have at last got all the lines around the Belgrade plantation pretty well established, and have raised about 250 barils corn there, the stable will be done next week. The [Dewing] house wants about a weeks work to finish it: it will then be painted. Mr Brickhouse will then proceed with the hands to geting timber to add 40 ft more to the barn, and when that is done there will be house room enough for 15 mules & 5 yoke oxen, 2500 <& 2500> barrils corn & 2500 bus. wheat. My crop at the Lake was a good one but there was not enough ground planted for much corn. I finised gathering yesterday the crop is about 1100 barrils. I have sown 100 acres of wheat at the lake & about 44 at Belgrade, so you see my sons my income [must] be small for a year to come. I have got at the Lake [*torn*] broke for corn and shall begin to break at Belgrade Monday Mr Brickhouse & Mr Davinport get along very well, but Mr Hathaway is a poor creature. it is probable I shall not employ him next year. Mr B. & Davenport send their compliments to you. You see my dear sons by my latter information that I am in the full tide of successfull experement, go on & do likewise, and let me intreat you, to let Brotherly Love prevail a two fold cord is not easily broken. Love one another my dear children. Go on and be what your father has not had it in his power to be. Farewell, alway Farewell my dear son & may God Almighty bless you is the prayer of your affect. Father

E Pettigrew

N.B. My dear Charles I will write you shortly after my arrival in New York. Farewell

[*Addressed*] Mr William S. Pettigrew
Chapel Hill
North Carolina

Ebenezer Pettigrew to Mary Williams Bryan UNC

New York Dec 8, 1834

My dear Sister,

It seems as though I would inundate your home with letters, but this is one of business as well as Friendship. Shortly after my arrival I understood this was the time to purchase match horses, and determined to buy for myself a pair, and knowing that you had but one, and him (though a good stage horse), no one ought to try to get a fellow to, I determined to try and get a pair of good family ones for you. I accordingly attended the auction with my friend Dr Vanderburgh where there was to be sold such a pair & bought them. After keeping them two days I found them [the veryest] cheats & returned them. In the mean time I bought for myself a good pair at private sale. My mind still intent upon a pair for you, I bought another, of what the Doctor who drove /them/ says an excellent pair of family horses who travil alike as much as any pair he ever drove. I went to the Norfolk Packet and ordered four stalls and they were to go on board the next day. In five hours after I had bought & paid for the two match, one of mine was taken sick & was expected to die all night, the next day a doubtfull case totally unfit to be shipped, but your pair was shipped & they will I fear be made sailors of today. My sick horse is today out of danger, & they will go in the next packet, five days from the first. I should have left tomorrow morning but I wish the horses gone first, /that/ I may me/e/t them at Norfolk to make arraingments to get them on. You will say that I have been a good /deal/ pl/a/gued, and so I have but It has not produced a ruffle in my countenace, this is but moonshine and must [hapin] in passing through life. Even my leg is but a trifle although it has become by two much walking very sensitive & sometimes painfull, so much so that on saturday having spent the evening at Mr Kents, which is the upper part of the City I could not have walked to the City Hotel a distance of two miles in two hours if atall & for the first time I acknoledged my dependance on an omnibus. I am however geting along very chearily taking my Christmas, a little before the usual time I have more acquantance, more social intercourse, [*torn*] have it in my power to have, in this City, than in all the towns in my native state. Here I stand amongst my acquaintance as a clever, worthy man, my company seems to be acceptable, & I am asked to call in without reserve, which I do, but O! Horrable I leave without reserve on Saterday next for N. Carolina, and to be as sullen as a [Possum]. I am thankfull for this little spell of recreation, and am willing to go and serve my dear, dear Children & friends, without whome I am nothing. Afer Christmas I discharge one of overseers to take his place which I hope will be an evidence that N. York has not run me carazy. I know what I am, and never can forget while there is a pulsation /in my heart,/ in any place no matter how entertaining my dear ever dear Nancy; I thank my Blessed God, every day for that angellic gift, that dear woman, and that he has impressed on my heart a knowledge of his goodness & mercy to me a *poor wicked sinner*.

My dear Sister, I have used up all my money in this place. Will you ask Mr Bryan if it is perfectly convenient for him to have paid to Charles & William for them both two hundred & fifty dollars but if it is not perfectly convenient he will write me upon the receit of this, to Cool Spring P.O. I think I can sell <his the> Clay, to the Stage contracter, but, in the mean time he may try what he can get & inform me I will send the horses as before agreed on to Washington. Please to give my Affectionate regard to [*torn*] Mother & tell her that in the purchase of the [four] horses I had an eye to her visit in the spring and that I can never *forget* that she gave birth to her who was dearer to me than all the world beside. Please give my Love to my dear children & all my dear friends of the family & believe me

your affectionate Brother
E Pettigrew

Mrs J. H. Bryan

N.B. Excuse this hurried letter. I had been up to see my sick horse & have had no more time before the mail came for this day.

N.B. I go with Mr [*S. M.*] Chester to night to the Opera for the first time I saw to day the Chinese Cady[*?*] a stupid thing.

[*Addressed*] Mrs John H. Bryan
Newbern
N. Carolina

Samuel Latham[1] *to Ebenezer Pettigrew* A&H

Washington Tuesday 16h Decr 1834

(private)

Dear Sir,

You will probably receive at the same time with this, a letter from the committee of five appointed by the District Convention to inform you of your nomination by said convention & soliciting your compliance and an answer.[2]

The undersigned a member of the committee & the only member having any acquaintance with yourself takes the liberty of making a suggestion to you concerning your answer. The opposition in the District tho unanamous in a general abhorrence of the acts and pretensions of the Administration generally, yet differ upon many minor subjects of policy & constitutional law. You will therefore perceive (& this is the suggestion deemed important) that a prudent reply on your part will avoid as much as possible any topic which may disturb the unanimity now prevailing among our friends, indeed will avoid any unnecessary committal of any sort. The topics deemed most dangerous are Internal Improvements & the Bank.

I hope Sir you will excuse the liberty I have taken I am actuated by the deep interest I feel in the approaching Election. I have always supported Dr [*Thomas H.*] Hall but cannot do so longer he adheres too closely to the slaveish doctrines of the administration. In conclusion Sir let me hope you will not decline but rather that you will unite with us in redeeming from disgrace the District in which we live. I pledge myself (as far as my feeble aid will go to Elect you) that no exertion on my part shall be wanting to accomplish that object.

Your friend
Saml Latham

[*Addressed*] Mr Ebenr Pettigrew Esqr
Lake Phelps
Via Colspring Post Office
Washington County

---

[1]Samuel Latham married Mary Ann Trotter, daughter of Thomas Trotter, at the home of the latter on December 13, 1821. Parish Register of Christ Church, New Bern, Marriages, 128.

[2]News of the Whig campaign for Congress may be found in extant issues of the *Whig*, published by H. D. Machen in Washington, North Carolina. A headline in the issue for August 1, 1835, reads "Old Rip Wide Awake." For additional information on the Whig party in North Carolina see Arthur Charles Cole, *The Whig Party in the South* (Washington: American Historical Association, 1913), 80-81, hereinafter cited as Cole, *Whig Party in the South*.

See also William S. Hoffman, "John Branch and the Origins of the Whig Party in North Carolina," *North Carolina Historical Review*, XXXV (July, 1958), 299-309, and Max R. Williams, "The Foundations of the Whig Party in North Carolina: A Synthesis and a Modest Proposal," *North Carolina Historical Review*, XLVII (April, 1970), 115-129. Cole names George E. Badger, William A. Graham, Willie P. Mangum, Thomas L. Clingman, Edward Stanly, and Kenneth Rayner as leaders.

Joseph Ramsey and Samuel Hardison[1] *to Ebenezer Pettigrew* A&H

[*December 23, 1834*]

At a Meeting of the Citizens of Plymouth and its vicinity at the Court House on the 23d inst, <called> for the purpose of nominating a suitable person to represent this District in the next Congress—Samuel Hardison Esq was called to the Chair & Joseph Ramsey was appointed Secretary—

On Motion made & seconded, the following committee was chosen to draw up resolutions (viz) Joseph C Norcom,[2] John B Beasley & John D. Bennett and the said committee having reported the following resolutions they were unanimously adopted

1st Resolved—That we concur with the convention which assembled at Washington on the 15h inst in the nomination of Ebenezer Pettigrew Esq as a suitable person to represent the 3d Congressional District in the next Congress—

2D That knowing Mr Pettigrew to be a man of talents & unimpeachable character & believing him to be of firm & approved political principles & a man in whom we can confide, we do the more cheerfully enter into the above resolution

3D Resolved that George Nichols, John B. Beasley, John D. Bennett, J. C Norcom & Benj Maitland be appointed a Committee to wait on Mr Pettigrew and request his acceptance of the nomination of said Convention, and in the event of his declining the nomination, that they have authority to confer with Committees or delegates from the other Counties comprising the said District to fix on some other proper person in his stead

On Motion made & seconded—Resolved that the proceedings of this meeting be published in the Washington Whig, and that a Copy be sent to Richard Bonner,[3] President of the Convention—

(signed) Joseph Ramsey Secretary
(signed) Saml Hardison *Chair*man

Decem 23d 1834—

[1]Samuel Hardison was a member of the House of Commons from Washington County in the 1832 and 1833 sessions of the General Assembly. Cheney, *North Carolina Government*, 299, 301. No information about Joseph Ramsey other than that in this letter has been located.

[2]Joseph C. Norcom was a delegate from Washington County to the Constitutional Convention of 1835 and served in the House of Commons from the same county in the General Assembly of 1842. Cheney, *North Carolina Government*, 312, 818.

[3]Richard H. Bonner served in the House of Commons from Beaufort County in the 1831 and 1832 state legislatures and was a member of the Constitutional Convention of 1835 from the same county. Cheney, *North Carolina Government*, 296, 298, 817.

Ebenezer Pettigrew to William Shepard Pettigrew UNC

Lake Phelps Jan 23, 1835

My dear Sons,

I wrote to you a few days before I left for Newbern to visit your dear little sisters & brother. I had a very cold & disagreeable ride there and it was excessivly cold while there. I found your sister Mary & Johnston better but they are both very thin & look badly. Poor little Mary has scurf I fear a tetter worm in her head & has to have her hair taken off & wear /a/ greasy cap.

You have I found receivd the $250 which I requested M[r] Bryan to send you, I have since requested him to send you 100$ more which will make out the 350 which I understood from you was necessary. I hope & believe you will be prudent & carefull with it, for money is geting at a low eb having so many calls & perticularly at Belgrade, as all my work & expenditures are there now, when at home.

I have at last consented to become a Candidate for Congress. Nothing of my life has plagued me so much to decide, for generally & some of the most important affairs of my life have been decided in five minutes /—but this has taken five weeks./ I am aware of the trouble & turmoil, but it was not for me to resist the call of so numerous a body. I would advise you to be very circumspect in all your remarks, for every word will be caught. Nothing I desire so much as quiet, secluded life, but this next six months will be the very opposit. My business is in a very snug way & I suppose with M[r] Davinports attention can get along. There has been the deepest snow here that /has/ fallen for fifty years; at any rate deeper than I have ever seen. There are various opinions at to depth from 14 to 18 inch. eight is the deepest I ever measured.

Charles I observe in your two last letters a remark which seems to convey an idea that you & William did not live in the same room. I hope for the character of the thing you have not divided & taken seperate rooms, also the cost, for you two can sit by one fire as well as two & also sleep in one bed, and if you have taken seperate establishments it is a sign you have two much money, and that your tempers are not what they aught to be for Christians, but I will make this remark, you had better seperate than quarril, but if you had the right spirit you would not disagree. I wish to know in the next after this. What I said in my last to you Charles was all in joke about geting married, I hope your good sense will teach you not to think of a family untill you are not only settled but will settled in life. Do not make to much calculations from me for it is probable I shall spend the best part of my estate in raising my children & in my own indulgences. My sons I had expected an account of your expences for the last half year according to your promise.

My son William I had been looking for a letter untill I fear you have forgotten the old man. You aught not to forget him at any rate while he is thinking so much about you, I hope you have not forgotten him so soon; I should have expected a letter would have been quite entertaining after your return from visiting Raleigh particularly during the session of the Legislature. I should liked to have heard how you went through your examination & how you get along in general, for I know not when I /did/ get a letter from you. We are geting along chearily at Belgrade. All the lumber is got and in the yard for the addition to the machine pens or Barn and Mr Brickhouse has begun to frame. Mr Davenport has inclosed all the deaded woods with fence; he has since plouging all the ground for the next corn field cut down 45 acres of new ground & rooted half of it for ploughing, so you see there is no idleness in my establishment. Mr Collins spent the night with me two nights ago, and several times remarked how fortunate my two sons were in having a father in the full vigor of life at the time when they were about to take the stage. My dear Sons if you are fortunate in such a Father let me beseech, let me pray, to my sons to let their Father be /equelly/ fortunate in such sons. Rem/em/ber my sons that a two fold cord is not easily broken, and always bear in mind all [my] hopes in this world is <my> in my dear children and if they [bring] my gray hairs with sorrow to the grave I have lived in vain. My health is as good as it ever was but my leg is not well nor I suppose ever will be, but I am able to get along without much pain, but I fear I never shall be able to walk as I have done. I think your Uncle Bryan & aunt Mary are beginning to feel considerable anxiety to know what to do with all their sons; your aunt remarked to me you have no difficulty to know what to do or provide for your sons, her remark led me to think she had unequivocally changed her mind as respects farming. Ah! my sons I had to work up a steep hill against the current, but all now give up that I was right, and because I have forced them into the belief from my success, which seems to be more generally known than I had any idea of. My dear Sons go on and do likewise & believe in your fathers opinions as well as in his Love & affection to his children

E Pettigrew

[*Addressed*] Mr William S. Pettigrew
Chapel Hill
N. Carolina

Ebenezer Pettigrew to James Cathcart Johnston UNC

Lake Phelps Ap. 5, 1835

My dear friend,

From time to time have I determined to answer your very flattering favour of last fall, but have as often been prevented by various causes. It is not a call to Congress or the marked attentions of my friends in visiting the district canvassing for that place, that can make *me* forget the expretions in that letter. No my friend, they know nothing of me but common report, and I view their good opinions of me as but a bubble compaired to your expretions, and it was more than gratifying to read them from the pen of one whose good opinion I value above all others of my acquaintance. I am a poor miserable creature, & have & am now suffering all the anguish of heart which the human system is able to bear, but I have alway had a duty to perform in this life, and when ever my afflictions would give me life to perform them I have done so, regardless of all things that might haras or embarras me. Nothing is more desirable to me than seclusion & retirement from the world, but from a sense of duty & *nothing else*, I have now entered into the greatest turmoil that it appears any man can get, and what is more awful than all & every other part, the *drinking*, which seems as necessary to success as to be a citizen of the state. I have been two months on the business & have four more when I hope to be done forever. I have laid my hand to the plough & nothing shall be wanting on my part. My motto is Stimulate, Fulminate, depricate, & go on at any rate. I stop at nothing, Wine, Brandy whisky & if necessary Yankey Rum sweetened with molasses & stired with my finger. My health was never better & though I was in different parts of the district in all the bad weather since Christmas I was not made sick. It seems I cannot die, unless /by/ my own wicked hand & I hope my God in his goodness will give me grace that such an idea may never enter my immagination. You will ask why did I get into such a difficulty. My answer, I knew not how to refuse so great & respectable a call, espetially when I had no doubt of success. My prospect is as good as it ever was, & I have made friends wherever I have gone, for I not only know how to take a drink, but I know how to shake hands with & talk to all sorts of men. I have from my place of residence been assotiated with them & have no difficulty in ingratiating myself. I have no doubt of geting a majority in five out of the six counties, & shall not lose more than five votes in Tyrrell & twenty in Washington, & unless something turns up that cannot be forseen the Doctor [*Thomas H. Hall*] must stay at home. It is not yet declared that he is a candidate. I leave this day week for an eight weeks cruise through the district. Being a man of business you will say, what becomes of your farms in all this time. It is in perfect order on the Lake as well as that in Scuppernong, and managed by the overseer which I have had for four years, and one of the smartest & most deserving men in his station in the Union.

My wheat is much injured by the frost & cannot produce more than two thirds of a crop. I am under good way in corn planting, & nothing to do but plant. I am going for a pretty large crop this year.

I wrote to Dr Vanderburgh soon after my return when I saw you respecting your threshing machine & received an answer the other day, that it was done, but that he had mislaid my letter & could not tell where to send it. I have written him twice since & in bothe times directed him so that I think there can be no doubt of your geting it in time.

To satisfy you that my present electioneering engagements have not paralised my opperations at home, I will give you an account of my opperations at my place in Scupperno/n/g which is called Belgrade. I finished since Christmas a stable two stories 34. by 60 ft. I built a barn last year 40 by 40 ft two stories I am now adding to it 40 ft more in length, which will be compleat by harvest. The dwelling of my father is moved to were my buildings are now, & well fited up & I have all the necessary out houses on the place. Just as I finished (place) our old preacher came in & I was obliged to go with him to Mr Collins, & hear him talk weltch to the negroes O what [*torn*] boar. This morning business has driven all my ideas from my head, and I must conclude by sending my kind regards to your sisters & beging you to assure your self of the sincere Esteem & Regard of your friend

E Pettigrew

James C. Johnston esqr.

N.B. Please to write to me soon, & will you oblige me so far as to visit me as soon after the Congretional canvass is over as you can. I shall /not/ leave home <after> this fall but to carry my younger son to Hillboro & see my two sons at Chapel Hill Charles will graduate in June year but I think of taking him home at Christmas. What is a graduation at Chapel Hill worth? An ounce of moonshine.

Ever yours
E P.

[*Addressed*] James C Johnston Esqr
Hayes
Edenton Post office

Charles Petigru to John Gough and Jane Gibert Petigru North UNC

Appalachicola Arsenal
Chattahoochie—Fla: April 29th, 1835

Dear North and Dear Sister—

—for I am going to write to you both <got> together—I am here enjoying the luxuries of command—My word there is none to gainsay—I am almost as absolute as Robinson Crusoe—but I am not like <Robert> /Robinson/ on a desert Island—but in the heart of a town—an incorporated town of which <in a certain> /indeed/ I am myself the heart—and Uncle Sam's cash, expended /thro' me/ in erecting the arsenal here, the blood—I am the head too—for I govern and direct the arsenal and the operations of the arsenal contro/u/l in a mighty degree the destinie of the town—I am the foot too <I am the foot> for the town cannot get along without me—are you not surprised to hear of my being so great a man!—Indeed I shall very soon, in good earnest, "creep into a good opinion of myself"—I have been here a fortnight—have been all the time very busy except about 3 days that I was at Tallahassee on business and took occasion to go & see my friends the Writ family—who reside now some 26 miles therefrom—Those three days were with some exceptions, very pleasant days—the other two weeks have been much of business—I am coming to be very much of a business man—This is almost as wonderful a <change> /transformation/ <and> as my metamorphis into a great man—I have not yet been able quite to see daylight thro' all my predecessors accounts—but begin to see the state of things, &c. around me clear & distinct enough—

The Appalachicola is a mile off—It is a beautiful river—The arsenal is on the top of monstrous hill—where it has no business—The Chattahoochie & Flint Rivers unite to form the Appalachicola two miles above or thereabouts—So you may just stick a pin into my locality—on the east side of the Appalachicola—a mile from it—two miles from the river Chattahoochie /near Musquito Creek,/—& in and making a large portion of the town of Chattahoochie—which is a town not half so big as its name is long. In directing your letters leave out the name of the asenal altogether—Direct to Chattahoochie Florida—That will be a direction long enough—and there will be danger, if you write Appalachicola, of <its> /the letter's/ going down to the Bay & town—150 miles off—To Tallahassee is 50 miles—There is said to be a fine society there—there ought to be for the town is not much for looks or size or business—

The country is much of it poor, & <more> /more/ of it rich than is generally Known [*I*] think—It is now filling up & incr[ea]sing in wealth—The <Forbes> decission [*torn*] the Forbes' claim will do the territory much good and will be the making of many lawyers—For there is litigation <enough> concerned in that matter to the amount 2 million of Dollars—I am writing with a head aching—partly from a bad cold—the worst I ever had—& partly from having been so long over my table—

Write to me and believe me
Your affectionate Brother
Charles Petigru

[*Addressed*] John G. North Esqr.
Georgetown
So: Carolina

[Charles Lockhart Pettigrew to Ebenezer Pettigrew] UNC

University May 26th 183[*5*]

Dear Father

Very probably my letter will not find you at home, as you, I suppose, have not yet completed your electioneering campaign. I am much gratified to learn that your success is apparent, and your prospects so very fair: Mr A Henderson, who came from Edenton but a few days since, says that the general expectation is no other than that you will beat Mr Hall at least 500 votes; such large success is more than I could in my fondest expectations have looked for, and the more especially, as Mr Hall has been going to congress for many years, will the honor of /being/ so far superior be considered uncommon. I was informed by a gentleman immediately from Halifax Co. that the last heard of /you/ was that you were in Washington and that succeed. very well in electioneering: the same gentleman informed me that you were nominated for the state-convention <and> but said, he had not heard whether you had excepted the nomination and consented become a candidate for that high place of honor. While speaking of the convention you may willing to hear who are from this county; the 2 persons elected are Drs Smith[1] and Montgmery.[2] Judge Ruffin[3] who was a candidate was the 5th man on the list. Thus we see that those who are the most worthy are the most neglected by the people. I fear much that this body when assembled will not be much superior if at all to the state legislature. I have not received a letter from you in some time I hope you will write me one soon and tell me what you wish me to do. I suppose as you will be very busy it will be better for us not to go down although it would afford me great pleasure to see you, and also the <offered> sum of money to go down and come up will be considerable for us both therefore it will be best for us to stay. Some money will be necessary for us at commencement and also during the vacation, some is generally necessary at commencement, and as I am one of the speakers and and of course be more prominent, I shall however be economical I suppose $75 will be sufficient for us untill next session. To show you the character we sustain for being punctial in money matters, this very morning I was with gentleman in the village with other students, this gentleman was post-master and tavern-keeper he told them he hoped they would [*get*] a letter with money, but at the same time remarking that "Mr Pettigrew never wants money his father sends to him by hundreds" thus you see how we are regarded and how thankful ought we to be to you who enables us to sustain so fair a reputation. I will soon have time to give you a more particular account. The Commencement will be on the 25 of June I must ask you to excuse the latter part of this letter as I am afraid the mail will be too quick for m[*torn*] his love to yo[u] [*torn*]

Af[*torn*]

---

[1]James Strudwick Smith (1790-1859), a physician in Orange County, had served in Congress as a Democrat, 1817-1821. He represented Hillsborough in the state House of Commons in the 1821 session and was a delegate to the constitutional convention held in 1835. *Biographical Directory of Congress*, 1618.

[2]William Montgomery (1789-1844), also an Orange County physician, was a state senator, 1824-1828 and 1829-1835. He sat in the Constitutional Convention of 1835 and as a Democrat in the United States House of Representatives, 1835-1841. *Biographical Directory of Congress*, 1347; Cheney, *North Carolina Government*, 288-289, 301-302, 817.

[3]Thomas Ruffin (1787-1870) graduated from Princeton in 1805 and established a law practice in Hillsborough in 1809. He served in the state House of Commons and as a superior court judge before becoming a justice on the North Carolina Supreme Court. He served from 1829 to 1852; he was chief justice from 1833. Ruffin achieved a wide reputation as a constitutional lawyer and a judge. Ashe, *Biographical History*, V, 350-359.

Ebenezer Pettigrew to William Shepard Pettigrew UNC

Belgrade June 23, 1835

My dear Sons

I addressed a letter to you about a fortnight ago in which I sent you a draft for $100 on Mr Hicks New York & which I hope you have received before this. In that letter I advised you not to come down the country for reasons then given, but one stronger than all in this part is the measels which has been very fatal & William you have not had it. I hope my sons you will spend your vacation profitably, & prudently.

I am now harvesting at this place & expect this day to go to the Lake to commence. It is quite late this year & not good, but I hope to get a half a crop. The corn is very likely.

Mr Davinport was married on the 11, & his wife is [*illegible*] here, she seems to be a modest well disposed woman & I hope they will do well. If you Judge Norwood's family & Mr Bingham in the course of the vacation give my kind regards to them. My dear sons God Almighty bless you

E Pettigrew

[*Addressed*] Mr William S Pettigrew
Chapel Hill
N. Carolina

Charles Lockhart Pettigrew to Ebenezer Pettigrew UNC

University Aug 1st 1835

Dear Father

Your letter from Plymouth was duly received a few days since. You stated that you had then commenced the last tour you would make before the termination of the contest; I hope you /will/ come off ultimately victorious and your efforts will be crowned with the greatest success you could have wished. I have frequent opportunities from persons passing and those who have connexions /in the low country/ of hearing from you and of the prospect of your election, the opinion that I have always expressed is that you will beat Mr Hall 500 votes.

I have frequently seen communications in the "Tarboro Press" against you, and in one which I saw the other day it was stated that you had said you knew nothing about the land question: this assertion is I suppose false. In this part of the country there seems to be no one opposed to it even the warmest supporters of General Jackson do no dare to defend his conduct in vetoing that bill All the candidates to a man condemn his conduct. I was very glad to learn that your corn-crop was so fine and exhibited the appearance of a plentiful harvest. You have had no opportunity of leaning that I had to deliver an oration on the 4th of July at Chapel-Hill by choice to the meeting that appointed me: the performance of which duty I accepted and discharged <to> Although I had but a short time to prepare in. I composed my speech in one day. I held a high standing in my class in the last report the were only 3 placed before me. I am now a member of the senior or highest class in college, and will stand higher of course as the seniors are the oldest, the most advanced, and the most respected. You informed me in your letter of Mr Beasley's intention to send his son Joe to college he has since arrived and appears to be a boy of good intelect and great application to business, I have procured a room for him and will pay particular attention to him.[1] I will also tell you the amount of money for the next session about $375 /<for Brother>/ will se/r/ve us untill the end of next session $200 for myself and $175 /for Brother/ as he has to get no books but can use the books I had, and I have to get the books for the senior year. I have no doubt but you will be astonished at my sending for so large a sum but I can assure that I have been and will be economical <an> as an instace of this I have not had a breast-pin since I have been a member of college when others have one and two and some half a dozen my only reason for not buying one <was not> is not <is> to spend money: at commencement I was one of the speakers and as all the others had them I borowed and it was the same case <frequently> last year. I have never bought a glass of wine since I have been a member of the institution which has now been three years. You are thought to be rich here for one member of <of> college told me that he heard that you could make an income of $25,000 a year if you would exert yourself much. Be assured that I will as I can without incuring the character of being stingy my dear Father I have always been sensible that you will supply your children with the necessary funds for their education and it will always be a source gratitude to me that I have such a father. I hope in less than a year to graduate and come home and try how hard it is to make a living: I will then have a good education and it will devolve on me to make something or nothing of myself. I feel confident of your election and hope to see it officially announced in a few days.

Believe me dear Father
ever affectionate
Charles L Pettigrew

Brother sends his love to you
The session will on 6th of August again commence

[*Addressed*] Mr E. Pettigrew Esq
Cool Spring
Washington Co
N.C.

---

[1]Battle, *History of the University*, does not list a Joseph Beasley as having attended the university.

Ebenezer Pettigrew to William Shepard Pettigrew UNC

Plymouth Aug 3, 1835

My dear Sons

I am just returning from the elections whic <is> are all over except Tyrrel. All the banks not heard from and I am now ahead a few votes, and Tyrrel will give almost if not quite a unanimous vote so that my majority will be between 5 & 600 votes. My sons this is an exceeding honour and let it be a lesson for you. Nothing could have given me success but my character which I had been making for thirty years, & which my dear sons stands against the world. But my dear boys dont pride yourself altogether on the character of your father, you have one also to make & do not forget that by your conduct you can loose the one your father may give you in a very short time. Pray do not forget that you must make your own character by puting the finishing hand to it. The last three weeks has [*blotted*] the most awfull tryal & the hardest work I ever did. but it is over & my labours have been crowned with sucess. Do not boast of it; it is enough that I have succeeded.

You will receive a [*torn*] on the other page for $250.[1] (Economy my sons) I w[ill en]deavour to see some time in this fall. I [*torn*] the latter part of the campaign astonishing [*torn*]alth was even better I hope you are [*torn*] [G]od almighty bless y[ou] [*torn*] [pra]yer of your [*torn*] father

E Pettigrew

[*Addressed*] William S. Pettigrew
Chapel Hill
North Carolina

---

[1]A draft was often written, in a form similar to that of a modern check, on the top or bottom half of a letter. The recipient then cut it off like a coupon and negotiated it. Several letters in the Pettigrew Family Papers at the Southern Historical Collection have clipped pages for this reason.

Moses E. Cator to Ebenezer Pettigrew A&H

Williamson County 14 Aug 1835

My Dear Friend

You will be informed by this that I am Still in the land amongst the living you have No doubt previous to this Seen by the papers the Dreadful effect of the Cholera in this Section of Country it has Truly been awful and alarming Maney of our Valuable Citizens have fallen Victims to it and have gone to Eternity. I had a Verrey Severe attackt with it about the first of July the Docktor who attended me as well as all of my friends who Saw me Despaired of my Recovery and indeed I had But little hope of it my Self But Contrarey to all of our expectation Devine Providence has again Raised me up and in a great Measure Restored me to Helth I am as yet Verrey weak and feable But think I am a gaining as fast as Could be expected being of an advanced age after being Redused So Verrey low. I Sincerely hope these limes may find you and your family in perfect Helth. it has been So long Since I wrote to you or Received a letter from you that I have almost forgotten who wrote last But Rather think it was your Self in which you Stated that your Self or one of your Sons would Visit this part of the Country at a time Spesifyed in Said letter in Consequence of which I have looked in Vain for a long time past The Tax on your land in Dwyer County have Been Regularly paid. I Sent Two Dollars last year to Mr Davis and never heard from him untill a fiew days past when I Received a letter from him with the Sheriffs Receipt inclosed for $2.88 which Ballance I Shall immediately Send to him and also the Money for this years Tax presuming it will be the Same for this year as it was last. I immajine you have heard of the Constitution of our State Being amended in Consequence of which after this year we Shall have to pay Taxes agreeable to Valuation So that if your lands out hear are of But litle Value in Course your Tax will be light . . . under our old Constitution the most inferior land in the State was Taxed as high as the most Valuable which I have always thought unjust as there is Such a great Contrast in the Valuation of land in this State

If my Helth will admit this faul I intend going to the District and if I Cannot Sell your land in Dwyer to employ Some person whom I think may be depended upon to attend to your land for you. I Know this will be a Considerable undertaking for me. But I Shall take my time for it perhaps not Travel more than 25 Miles a day. when we devided Said land the Compass we had was not to be depended upon. Mr John Miller who was present at the time who also is a worthy Respectable Man promised us that he would git a good Compass and Run the devideing lines Between you and Davis and

Johnston this Buiseness I also wish to See too I am well asured in my mind if Said land Could be Sold even on a long Credit So that the money Could be Sure it would be much more to your interest than to let it Remain as it is espesially as you live at so great a distance from it if I Should go down this faul I will do the Best in my power for your Interst and write you immediately on my Return Home. we have had a Remarkably wet Summer our Corn and wheat Crops are Verry good—I am doubtful our Cotton Crops will not be Verry good oweing to So much wet weather

I have a Reputed daughter who lives on Second Creek[1] who I understand is Maried to a man by the name of Levin Davis. I wish them poor Creatures to Come out to this Country. I have lately purchased 450 acrees of land in this County which I intend for them people if they will Move to it and if they Could Come out it would be in my power to asist them Verry much Such as firnishing of them with provision Stock to begin with &c that is if they Should Come while I am liveing the land Lays on lick Creek about 10 Miles from franklin and near the Barrons altho this land is well Timbered on the 50 acres Tract there is a Considerable Clearin a Comfortable Cabin &c &c a familey are now liveing on Said place it is true the greater part of Said land are thin But I think it far Superior to the Second Creek land. will you be So Kind Some time hence as to Ride over and See what prospect there is for their git out hear I Realey fear the prospect is Verrey gloomey for I expect they are Quite Illiterate and ignorant in so much that I fear they would never find the way out hear unless they had Some person to pilot them. please to try to find out their true Situation and inform me in your next my Reason for explaining the above to you is that you may tell them the whole Circumstance of the Buiseness and of my intention.

To Conclude my long Epistle I am as ever your Readey friend and well wisher untill Death

Moses E. Cator

P S please to present my love to all inquiring friends and accept the Same your Self

[*Addressed*] E. Pettigrew Esquire
Cool Spring P office
N. Carolina

---

[1]Second Creek is located in Tyrrell County. Powell, *North Carolina Gazetteer*, 444.

William Biddle Shepard to Ebenezer Pettigrew A&H

Alexandria Sept 20th 1835

My Dear Sir

I have intended for some time past to write to you, but I have hitheto been prevented by the sickness of Mrs Shepard who has been confined to her bed for two months past.—Her indisposition has settled down into chills and fevers which adhered to her so pertinaceously that I almost despair of her getting rid of them during the winter.

I suppose you are quite recovered from the fatigues of your campaign, I was myself in the commencement of my career generally, all the fall and winter recruiting from the love frolics, I was obliged to take among the people. I presume you were not aware of the great labour necessary to convince the sovereign people of a very few and very plain matters, which it is indispensable they should know.—

I would like very much to mess with you next winter and if you have no objection I will engage a room for you at the same house where I lodge—There is always some difficulty at the commencement of a Congress to secure good quarters. I being on the Spot earlier than you may like to leave home, will if you say so, look out for lodgings for both of us. It is my intention if Mrs Shepard's health improves sufficiently to carry her to Newbern this fall; should her health not permit her to travel I shall go alone I hope I may see you on my route.—

Yours sincerely
Wm B. Shepard

[*Addressed*] Ebenezer Pettigrew Esqr
Cool Spring
Washington County
No Carolina

Bryan and Maitland to Ebenezer Pettigrew[1] UNC

New York, October 1st 1835.

E. Pettigrew Esqr

Dear Sir

We beg leave to inform you that we have established a House in this City for the transaction of COMMISSION BUSINESS, under the firm of JOHN S. BRYAN & CO., to be conducted by John S. Bryan.

We tender you our services, and should you intrust any business to our care, we will endeavour to give satisfaction.

The business at Plymouth, N.C. will be continued as heretofore, under the firm of BRYAN & MAITLAND, and will be conducted by Benjamin Maitland.

Very respectfully,
Your most obedient servants,
Jno. S. Bryan
Benj Maitland

JOHN S. BRYAN will sign Jno. S. Bryan &C°

BENJAMIN MAITLAND John S. Bryan &C°

[*Addressed*] E. Pettigrew Esq
Cool Spring
N Ca

---

[1]This document is a printed form letter, with the date, addresses, salutation, and signatures in handwriting.

William Biddle Shepard to Ebenezer Pettigrew A&H

Alexandria D.C. Oct 8th 1835

My Dear Sir

I received your letter a few days ago and on yesterday I went to Washington to enquire of Gadsby at what price you could procure two rooms.—

His charge is five dollars a day I did not make any engagement with him thinking the price exorbitant and more than you would be willing to pay.—I think you will find a private boarding house preferable to a hotel on many accounts, the hours of meals at the Hotels are not arranged to suit members, and as to being alone, you can be as retired, as you please in a boarding house. I shall leave this place tomorrow for Newbern & expect to be absent about three weeks, on my return I will engage room at Gadsby's if you think proper.—I have received an offer for all the land near Memphis at 2½ dolls per acre, are you disposed to sell? I think the offer a very good one and that it is the interest of the heirs to accept it.—There are many squatters on the land, they are continually buying it for the taxes, and in a few years they will contrive to get it, or envolve us in a lawsuit that will cost more than the land is worth—Let me know your determination that I may communicate it to the person who wishes to purchase.

Yours truly
W B Shepard

[*Addressed*] E Pettigrew Esqr
Cool Spring
North Carolina

Charles Lockhart Pettigrew to Ebenezer Pettigrew UNC

University Oct 11th 1835

Dear father

It is more than probable that you have heard from me more than once since you left this place if not concerning my health and state of mind at least of my relative standing in college.

The /trusstees/ passed a law that the parents of each student should be informed of the manner he was conducting himself in the institution. As to the relative number of each member of the class little confidence can be placed in them, for it is very difficult to distinguish between men nearly equal, and also the teacher is biassed sometimes in favour of one to the disparagement of another. The time is now at hand when the members of the senior class have to make each an original speech. I have prepared mine with considerable diligence, and hope to acquit /myself/ with credit: much is generally expected from them. The subject which I have chosen for my theme is emigration to the west. Almost the whole population in some parts of the state seem to be going to the west. Many who have made crops of corn <are> during the present year are making arrangements to sell and have an opportunity of of moving off as quick as possible. One gentleman living about 10 or 15 miles from this place and wishing to dispose of his crop of corn to give him an opportunity of leaving the state, could not sell at 75 cents a bbl which shows the great abundance of crops in this section of the country. I expe/c/t corn will be very cheap and will bearly compensate the expense and trouble in producing it. And not only is the corn-crop abundant but also the other kinds of products cotton (says a gentleman who has travelled all through /the south/ purposely to know the state of the crop) never was more abundant and no season seems to have been more advantageous to its cultivation than the present. I should suppose therefore that it would be more advantageous to sell early. I saw elder Carson a few days ago he looked the same as he did when I first saw him at home, he was here attending at a <camp> camp-meeting, he informed me that he would be down <ho> in our part of the country in the fall. He is quite a good preacher and is a man of sound intellect. I received those monumental inscriptions that you sent me by the return stage. I have not as yet seen Mr Bingham <ano> but will hand him one of them /when I do/. I have a bad cold such an one as may prevent my speaking otherwise I am in good health, brother William is well and sends his love to you I hope my dear father that you have enjoyed good he/a/lth through the sickly season I should be very glad to hear from you soon and I beg you to recive the grateful affection of a dutiful son

Charles L Pettigrew

[*Addressed*] Mr E. Pettigrew Esq
Cool Spring
Washington Co
N.C.

Richard Benbury Creecy[1] *to William Shepard Pettigrew* UNC

Edenton. Oct. 16th 1835.

Dear Billy:—

Upon my return from the coast, a short time since, I found in the office the letter which you did me the favour to address me. It had been in the office for some time before my arrival, which explains the reason of it's having been so long unanswered.—The eastern coast of North Carolina, is an isolated situation, cut off from the mainland <in> by all regular communication, which renders them totally unacquainted with the circumstances and events which agitate the public mind away from home. They live on the barren sand and subsist on the products of fishing and the chase.—The portion of my time which I spent on the coast was quite agreeable from the novelty of the scenes by which I was surrounded. The manners & customs of the poeple and the general state of society was such as I had never before witnessed—and excited in my mind / mind some surprise, which nevertheless afforded considerable amusement. You see mankind in the primative state of society before they have been checked by the refinements of civilized society or have felt the influence of education. They are as wild and untrameled & untaught as the beasts that bound over their native sand hills. And I must confess that I find as much to admire in the character of these untaught men as I do in the character of those among whom education has shed her benign influence, and artificial regulations have marked out the pathway of rectitude. They are hospitable generous & humane, almost to a fault—and act upon that great & pure moral precept that we should do unto others as we would they should do unto us.—I remained among them during the whole of our sickly season and returned with very favourable impressions of the country & its / its inhabitants.

I also found in the Office, on my return a letter from Charles which I wish you would inform him, I will soon reply to. I also recieved a communication from a committee of the Society—for which I beg you will make my acknowledgments & assure the society that I will soon reply to it.—

Your sincere friend
Richd. B. Creecy

[*Addressed*] Mr Wm S. Pettigrew
Student
Chapel Hill
N.C.

---

[1]Richard Benbury Creecy (1813-1908), author and newspaper editor, was born near Edenton. After graduating from the University of North Carolina in 1835, he passed the bar and settled in Elizabeth City, where he practiced law and then became a planter on the estate of his father-in-law, Edmund Perkins. In 1872 he began publishing a newspaper, the *Economist*, which was anti-Republican and anti-carpetbagger. He wrote a number of historical pieces, including some for Samuel A. Ashe's *Biographical History of North Carolina*, one of which was the sketch of his friend William Biddle Shepard. Creecy was a lifelong Episcopalian. Powell, *DNCB*, I, 460-461; Battle, *History of the University*, I, 422, 795.

Willis F. Riddick[1] *to Ebenezer Pettigrew* UNC

Sunsbury, Oct. 27th 1835.

Hon. Ebenezer Pettigrew

Dear Sir,

Your kind and friendly letter of the 29th ultimo. (enclosing three small volumes: two of which, contain Copies of "*Epitaphs* in the *Grave Yard* at *Bonarva Lake Phelps*," and the other one contains a copy of the "last *Advice* of the *Rev. Charles Pettigrew* to *his sons*;") has been duly received;—And all of which, I accept of, with pleasure and gratitude.—I have been benefitted by reading them.— I have made my little nephews read them.—I have loaned them to Samuel R. Harrell, son of Mr. Noah Harrell, to read; and I intend to keep them while I live; and if I leave a Son, I will bequeath to him "the *last Advice of a Father to his Sons*;" as an inheritance more worthy of his acceptance, than "*much money*."

The remaining four Barrels of Brandy, were sent in time, to go over in the next Boat.—I hope you have received the whole in Safety. I shall expect to See you, at our *Old Cottage* as you go on to Washington City.—Please use your influence to keep the Hon. Wm B. Shepard in the District, as our Representative. I hope to see you again. Soon. I feel much indebted to you; and therefore

I am with much esteem,
Yours respectfully, &c.
Willis F. Riddick.

[*Addressed*] Hon. Ebenezer Pettigrew.
Cool Spring,
Washington County,
N° Carolina

[1]Willis Riddick represented Perquimans County in the North Carolina House of Commons in 1805, 1806, and 1807 and was a member of the state Senate from the same county in every session from 1808 to 1829 except that of 1822. Cheney, *North Carolina Government*, 250, 252, 254, 256, 258, 260, 262, 263, 265, 267, 269, 270, 272, 274, 276, 278, 281, 283, 285, 287, 289, 291, 292.

*Ebenezer Pettigrew to Major Samuel Latham** A&H

Lake Phelps Nov. 2, 1835

My dear Sir,

The time is fast approaching when I must leave my solitary home, and a place in which I have spent so many days of close, and unremitting attention to agricultural persuits for an entire new field, and certainly no man ever entered the Hall of Congress with less confidence; but I commence my new station with clean hands and a pure heart and most fervantly pray that I may retire from it with at least the approbation of a majority of my fellow citizens; nothing can embitter my last day more than their disapproval of my course, but I flatter myself that I shall be judged with an indugent eyes by at least a majority, and consider my errors to be of the head. I know I am poor creature. Since my return from visiting my dear children I have been busily engaged picking up the scattered pieces which an almost entire absence from my affairs had produced.

It is a vain task to contemplate with composure my absence from my business and friends seven months, and in all that time pent up in a city, but as I am a fatallist I can but be reconciled to what may be.

I understand that Dr Hall has appeared quite reconciled to his defeat and says that if he was to be he had rather it was myself than any one else, and farther he has told his friends that I am a safe man. If all that is from the bottom of his heart, (which I have no right to doubt) he has very much my respect and I do, as I have before done regret to have given him so much mortification, while I at the same time think most sincerely that the Doctor had gone long enough if not too long.

About the middle of the month I expect to pass through Washington to visit my dear little children for a few days & on other private business at Newbern. I have been trying to so arrange it that I could spend between a stage at Washington but I think it will be impracticable and I shall be constrained to pass through. I should be very glad however to see you if it was but for a moment and I will inform Mr Wiswel when I shall return back from Newbern, at which time I shall [be] glad to inquire. I regret exceedingly to see the death of my friend Mr. Oliver; Poor man I thought he promised to live as long as any of the rest of us. But in the midst of life we are in death

Will you have the goodness with some of my other friends in Beaufort County to give me the names of all those persons and their post office to whom I should send documents. I have made a similar request to Mr H. S. Clark[1] of Loghouse.

Agreeable to my expectation we had some early frost but since it has been warm, and the most unaccountable spell of N.C. weather that I have seen, which makes a miserable business of gathering corn & sowing wheat. a business I am now in the midst of, and I suspect it is not very good for picking out cotton. Hoping you are geting along well and to your satisfaction I will endeavor by sending my kind regards to Mrs Latham. Make my best respects to all my friends of your acquaintance and assure yourself of my Esteem & Regard

E Pettigrew

Maj. S. Latham

[1]This might refer to Henry S. Clark, who represented Beaufort County in the North Carolina House of Commons from 1832 to 1836 and served in the United States House of Representatives, 1845-1847. Cheney, *North Carolina Government*, 298, 302, 304, 685.

Charles Lockhart Pettigrew to Ebenezer Pettigrew UNC

University Nov 7th 1835

Dear father

Brother William received your letter containing the bill of $100 without any delay or any hindrance. The sum will be more than will /be/ needed for this session, but as you remarked the surplus can remain to lessen the sum necessary to be sent at the commencement of next session. I have now but a few more months to remain on the hill and will not require a sum much larger than I have hitherto had. You of course have recived letters from the faculty concerning our relative standing in our respective classes, whether it be good or bad; I hope that my general position has been such as to please you and entirely fair. I should be much gratified to learn from you in you letters what my number has been in my several studies so as to know whether it is as good as I expect it to be and whether I should apply my self with greater diligence. There has been a much greater amount of studying in college since this plan has been adopted, as all wish a good account to be sent to their parents and friends. It would /be/ a gratification and more than probably a permanent good to have an account of what the faculty /consider/ us in our college duties.

Mr C. Burgwyn[1] met with quite a severe accident yesterday: he with four other young gentlemen went partridge-hunting and when in the act of shooting a bird one of them shot Mr B. the bird having flown between him and the one shoting—his injury is not very serious, but it has made quite sick, he rec/e/ived two shot the one in his nose in the place where it joins the face and the other in the extreme corner of this eye. That kind of hunting where they shoot entirely on the wing is quite dangerous and more especially when there are several in company; the animation is so great, and so great quickness is necessary, that they never look what they are about or who is in danger, the bird is the only object that attracts attention. I have dear father received nothing very deffinite with respect to the place where I shall spend my vacation. Some month ago I recived a letter from James Shepard in which he said that grandma expressed great joy at the prospect of seeing us this winter.—It would doubtless be a source of /the/ greatest pleasure to spend it in Newburn, when I should have an opportunity of seeing my relations and my dear little brother and sisters. But I am inclined to ask you for another destiny, for a very good reason. My teeth are in a very bad condition, I have but few teeth that are not decaying; all my jaw-teeth are rotting and m/an/y of them so far that I shall have to lose them and my front teeth have also commenced, and the decay proceeds so fast, that I really fear, unless something is done quickly, nothing can be done The more rubbing them with a brush, makes the bleed every morning Therefore I assume it as position that something is necessary to be done. The dentists in this part of the country are quacks and frequently do more harm than good. By going a little farther North I may come a-cross one that is a good one. The sum of money it will take to go from here to Baltimore /is/ $22,50 this account I saw the merchant make out, who had been from here there only a month ago; and from thence to Washington <[*illegible*] with> but little additional expense will be incurred. It would take $12 to go from here <home> /to Newburn/ and to home $21. So that it will cost but little more to go to Baltimore than to go home, where I might meet with a first rate dentist. My dear father I write this as the honest conviction of my heart for my own good, and not because I wish [to] go for the purpose of having a fine jaunt and of say[ing] I have been to Baltimore or Washington, I have, I am glad to say, no such silly axiety; silly because it is childish. For my own part, if it were not to see my relations, and but for the reasons just given, I had infinitely rather remain on C. Hill. But not withstanding these reason of the calmest kind I submit myself entirely to your better judgement and without pressing the matter further and will cherfully do as you say. and I would not even now have suggested the plan I proposed had I not been influenced by the firmest conviction of my mind after tho<u>rough consideration that the small sum spent now will be of incalculable value hereafter, and that if that sum is now withheld in a short time the desired object could not be obtain even with 20 times the amount. We are both well. Brother William sends his love to you and believe me to be <ver> /ever/ dutiful and affectionate

Charles L Pettigrew

Please answer this letter soon

C P

[*Addressed*] Mr E. Pettigrew Esq
Cool-Spring
Washington Co
N Carolina

---

[1]The only Burgwyn who has been identified as a university student at the time this letter was written is Hasel (Hazell) Witherspoon Burgwyn of Hillsborough. Battle, *History of the University*, I, 433, 796.

James Louis Petigru to Ebenezer Pettigrew UNC

Charleston 25 Novr 1835

Dear Ebenezer,

You will receive this letter by the hands of my friend and school fellow Mr Grayson,[1] to whom I have been long and faithfully attached.—Your friend Shocco Jones[2] told me last summer that the Nullifiers in your district all voted for you, and I infer from that, that there is no danger in introducing a nullifier to you—and I gratify my feelings in making you acquainted with a gentleman of the greatest worth, without apprehending any shock to your steadfast union principles.—Wishing you a pleasant season and hoping to here from you sometimes I am Dear Ebenezer

Your friend & cousin
J. L Petigru

---

[1]Perhaps Petigru referred to William John Grayson (1788-1863); both men graduated from South Carolina College in 1809. Grayson, an attorney, served as a Whig in the United States House of Representatives, 1833-1837. *Biographical Directory of Congress*, 969.

[2]Joseph Seawell Jones (ca. 1808-1855) of Shocco Springs, Warren County, was a North Carolina historian, a man of fashion, a noted duellist, and a prankster. Some time after the date of this letter he moved to Mississippi, where he spent the remaining years of his life. Marshall DeLancey Haywood, *Builders of the Old North State*, edited by Sarah McCulloh Lemmon (Raleigh: Privately printed, 1968), 179-183, hereinafter cited as Haywood, *Builders of the Old North State*. Shocco Springs was a popular resort for many years. Johnson, *Ante-Bellum North Carolina*, 188.

Ebenezer Pettigrew to Mary Williams Bryan UNC

Washington City Dec. 9, 1835

My dear Sister,

I received your favor of the 3rd yesterday and have but time to say that I received Mr Bryans letter as I left Plymouth and gave Jim the necessary orders respecting my dear dear Nancys Piano, which was that Ben should take it to you as soon as he returned & rested. I hope you have it by this. I directed Jim to take all the music out, if he has not you will be so good as to take care of it as I wish all my dear wifes music to be saved untill her dear daughters are grown.

You see by the date of my letter that I am in Washington and I now am writing you this letter at my desk in the H. of R. more at home than you could immagine for poor forlorn me, but I have no home and consequenly every place has been for the last five years a home. I am strange to the world & <every> no one is a stranger to me. I find I am not the meanest man in this house. But believe me I think I am a poor creature. I am yet at <the> Browns Hotel, but expect to join a mess tomorrow. William Shepard & Gov. Kent[1] for two of it.

I think Parties will run high, and I shall be a doubtfull character in the eyes of men. You know I am a mighty independent man when I sit out.

We begin to die very soon. Senator Smith[2] of Connecticut was put away yesterday and I learn from a Doctor, that Kain[3] the Senator from Illinois is at the point of death & he has no hope of him. I took a violent cold on the way, and have had a bad cough, but it is wearing out. The weather has been cold & I am told that north and west of this there is plenty of snow. Nothing has been done yet and we expect to adjourn from Thursday to Monday, happy times, good pay & nothing to do yet. Genl Speight[4] has been confined to his room for the last two day with indisposition. I think he is more unwell than his friend Dr [*William*] Mongomery did but he is the doctor & *must be right*. William says that Mrs S[*hepard*]. is under the direction of a Physician from Baltimore, & she is very much oppressed with his medicines she is no better, perhaps a little better today. Do write frequently & let me know how you are, for this place can never impair my memory. I am perfectly satisfyed why persons are so anxious to get to the white house. but I have not time to tell now. Please to see that the Spectator is directed to this place. May God Almighty have mercy on me & bless you all is the prayer of your affct. Brother

E Pettigrew

---

[1]Joseph Kent (1779-1837) was governor of Maryland, 1826-1829. A supporter of Henry Clay, he was elected to the United States Senate in 1833, where he was serving at the time of his death. *DAB*, X, 347-348.

[2]Nathan Smith (1770-1835) served in the United States Senate from 1833 until December 6, 1835, the date of his death. *Biographical Directory of Congress*, 1621-1622.

[3]Elias Kent Kane (1794-1835) served in the United States Senate from 1825 until December 12, 1835, the date of his death. *Biographical Directory of Congress*, 1143.

[4]Jesse Speight, a Whig from Greene County, was in Congress at this time. He was succeeded in the next term by Charles Biddle Shepard. Cheney, *North Carolina Government*, 680.

Doctrine and Mary Davenport to Ebenezer Pettigrew A&H

Belgrade December 18th, 1835

Dear Friend,

I received your favour A few days since and was sorry to hear that you was unwell but I am in hopes that you will soon recover from your cold I have got popler neck broke up and I expect it wil take me About four days to finish at Belgrade breaking up ground I am at this time having the staulks caryed from the new ground to the old ground and it is enugh to very the pattience of Jobe I have burnt the bricks and I think they have burnt betr than eny I have ever seen burnt About here and I do not think their is 2 thousand but what is good bricks I examined the corn to day and found it awl kept well the hogs are very good I do not think I shal have any pork to by the hogs at Belgrade are very good I think some of them wil go to two hundred Mr Newberry has fixt at his old mill and has gone to grinding himself he sent over some corn and it was not fit to grind one/half of it was rat tails and I sent him word if he did not send better corn I wod not grind it is not fit to feed the sows and pigs and thank god I have got clear of one truble Ben and Lydia has arived at home safe now I have sent him back with the Pianno he told me that your little Children was awl well Dr Bell will not be mareead this side of Chrismas

I remain your sincier friend
Doctrin Davenport

Dear Friend,

I receved your preasent with A greate deale of pleasure I was sory to hear that you was unwell and was a thousand times Ablige to you for it. Mr Pettigrew you have more than I could expect from eny person I could not expect what you have done for me from a Father I fear that you have put your self to two much trouble for me Mr Pettigrew they have bin great calculations made at the Lake since you left by Mrs Sam Spruil and Miss Caroline bateman they went to take A look at the lake since you left Mrs Spruil say that you have two Daughter and she has two sons they can mary when old enough and her orther Daugher can mary Mr William Pettigrew and live at Belgrade and Miss Caroline mary Mr Charles Pettigrew and live at the Lake Miss Caroline says that she will like to live at the Lake very well

I remain your sincier friend
Mary M Davenport

[*Addressed*] Hon. E Pettigrew
H R
Washington City
D.C.

Ebenezer Pettigrew to John Herritage Bryan UNC

Washington City Dec 20, 1835

My dear Sir,

I received your favour in due course of the mail and am very much obliged for your attention to my business. I hope all /will/ be got straight. Agreeable to your request I called at the office of the Intelligencer and paid the sum according to the receit inclosed.

Lidias reluctance to leave Newbern and my poor dear little Nancys distress at her going, has given me a great deal of sorrow & distress, and I do wish I knew what was right to do as respects Lidia, she deserves a great deal from my hands, but how I am to treat her except as a favorite slave, I know not, and I think there is no other treatment that will give her so much real composure through life, as for happiness ther is none in this world.

Frederick Shepard, & Charles Pettigrew are here, and I suppose will stay some days more to see the fashions of the city.

I am located at a boarding house on the Avenue about half way from Gadsbys to the Capital. It is a good house, and a good mess, among them are brother W. when in the City, Gov. Kent & Mr Goldsborough[1] of the Senate.

Frederick, tells me to say, that he was on his way to the promised land but /he/ is so bound up with ice as not to be able to go farther,

& I think will return to his wife & child for this winter at least.

I have not yet seen Mrs W. S. Poor woman from what I can learn she is evidently no better, and I am of the opinion gradually sinking into the grave.

So far I am geting along tolerably composed; I find they are not all great men that are here. On Fryday last there was a petition from Massachussets presented for the abolition of Slavery in the district, which produced a great deal of angry debate, and such words as I thought might bring on a fight. The animation or ranting was equal to any of mine on the plantation. I believe the subject of abolition will be in the House of Representitives, like a fire brand in a powder house., <de> Depend upon it, it is a dangerous question to discuss in that house, though I am decidedly in favour of having the subject fully argued, let the consequences be what they might. We may by that means know what we have to depend on.

I have a bad cold which I took geting here and am now labouring under a very disagreeable head ache, which renders me a part of the time unfit for anything. Had my health permited I should this evening gone with Fredrick & Charles to Alexandria.

We have had it very cold, and disagreeable since I have been here, and I apprehend a cold miserable winter, and as much pleasure as if I was in the penatentiary, but it will go in a life time. I have called on the President & Judge White[2] & no more I am invited to an evening Party at the Presidents on the 24th, but I think of going down to Baltimore that evening to be out of the way of the mirth on Christmas. Christmas /day/ has been the very opposit of mirth to me for the /last/ six. I have not since the year 1829 inclusive either eat or drank, on that day nor do I ever believe I shall while I live. I would to God that the past year had been spent in such a way as to justify my conscience in going to the Lords table, but mercifull God I have thought too little of those eternal affairs to venture. If my present situation had been of my own seeking, I should be obliged to die, but I hope God will have mercy on me and continue to strive with poor wicked me.

Please to make my kind regards to Sister Mary the dear children, and all my other friends, and accept assurances of my sincere Esteem & Regard

E Pettigrew

John H. Bryan Esqr

---

[1]Robert Henry Goldsborough (1779-1836) was a Whig senator from Maryland. He died on October 5, 1836. *Biographical Directory of Congress*, 954.

[2]Hugh Lawson White (1773-1840), a senator from Tennessee, was the southern conservative choice for the presidency over Martin Van Buren but did not receive the Whig party nomination. *Biographical Directory of Congress*, 1804; Cole, *Whig Party in the South*, 39-44.

John Herritage Bryan to Ebenezer Pettigrew A&H

New Bern Dec. 28. 1835.

My dear Sir,

I recd. yours of the [*blank*] by last Ral^{h} [*Raleigh*] mail—we are all truly concerned to learn that William's wife is so low & sympathize with him in his affliction.—We are all very well—William P. is here & seems quite sedate & contented.—<The> I shall leave here for the Sup^{me} Co. about the 1st Jany. and shall be absent about 10 days.—Mary Pettigrew learns her music very well—Nancy seems now quite reconciled to the absence of Lydia—she is learning very prettily & quite fast enough.—

Alex: Gaston[1] & wife have sold their Mattamuskeet plant^{n} for $17,500, he talks of going to Tenn.

All the children wish to subscribe to the Washington monument[2]—I will send you their subscriptions written by & *with* the hand of each of them in due time.—I am obliged to you for the doccuments you send me occasionally—

Your friend & relation
Jn. H. Bryan

The piano arrived without injury.

[*Addressed*] Hon: E Pettigrew
H of R
Washington City

---

[1]Alexander Gaston, the son of William Gaston, represented Hyde County in the Constitutional Convention of 1835. He was a major general of the state militia. Gaston eventually moved to Burke County. Ashe, *Biographical History*, VII, 114.

[2]The Washington National Monument Society was formed in 1833 to raise funds for the erection of the monument presently in Washington, D.C. The cornerstone was laid in 1848 and the monument was completed in 1884. *World Book Encyclopedia* (1978 edition), XXI, 86.

Charles Lockhart Pettigrew and Ebenezer Pettigrew to William Shepard Pettigrew UNC

Washington City Dec 30 1835

Dear Brother

I at length have commenced writing you a letter, doubtless you have been expecting one for a long time, and have wondered why I delay so long the reason is most plain and evident for in Washington no one has time to do any necessary business the time slips off from morning untill night and no one can tell how it passes, it is spent very agreeably, although one could wish more profitably: In the morning we rise late and when seated at the dinner table we need not expect to rise before the twilight begins to glow around us. I was quite agreeably entertained by a few remarks which flowed mellifluent from the lips of our great American orator H[*enry*]. Clay, his words were few, but they carried the feelings to whatsoever part they tended: his manner the /most/ affable and enticing, the tones of his well modulated voice representing fitly the sentiments they were intended to convey. In truth to have duly appreciated his manly eloquence it would have been necessary to have heard <of heard> him. Washington is quite an active and lively place. The President gave a large party at which *I* had the honor to be present; Governor Cass[1] will give one soon. I shall be able to communicate <to> with you more intelligibly when I see you Give my love to Grandma my uncles and Aunt and also tell my little brother and sisters that I often think of them

Your Brother
Charles L Pettigrew

I left my letter open for father to write some in but he says he can not now he sends his love to you and all his relations

Charles L Pettigrew

My dear Son,

I had told brother Charles that I could not come up to write, but the company broke from Dinner about six oclock and I got up stair in time to take a peep at his letter & write these few lines. Brother Charles has writen a real Shepard letter. I am my dear William as tired of this place and legislating as I ever was with any business in my life, but I am going ahead with my usual energy and am trying to make myself conspicuous & to do something for the honour of the nation. I was invited to Presidents party but that night I went to Baltimore, that I might in Christmas times indulge the gloomy habit of my soul. I go tomorrow night to Gov. Cass, and Mrs Cass party. May God bless you my dear William

E Pettigrew

[*Addressed*] Mr William Pettigrew
<Newbern> /Chapel Hill/
N. Carolina

[1] Lewis Cass (1782-1866) had served as governor of Michigan Territory, 1813-1831. He was secretary of war under President Andrew Jackson from 1831 to 1836. Later Cass was minister to France, a United States senator, and secretary of state under President James Buchanan. *DAB*, III, 563.

Joshua S. Swift[1] *to Ebenezer Pettigrew* A&H

Raleigh Jan 9th 1836.

Dear Sir

Having an opportunity I cheerfully embrace it to inform you of the passage of your bill through both Houses. It simply empowers you to build a bridge with a draw, and compels you or your associates to keep the Bridge in repair according to the existing law on the subject. There is a penalty amount to the bill of fifty Dollars should it sustain any injury or damage by any individual— We have agreed to adjourn on next Saturday but it is out of the question the most important business is now before the Legislature

The surplus revenue & the bill to incorporate the Charleston & Cincinatti railroad company with banking privileges—which has passed the Senate

The Legislature is nearly through with the revised code & the election of all the Officers of the State except one Judge. Moses Bailey, Heath, & W. C. Stanly are in nomination Stanly it is supposed will be withdrawn if he is I fear for Bailey. I believe that it is admitted by all that this session has been distinguished for its political & party feelings—I had no idea of the extent that those feelings were frequently carried I lament exceedingly that you have any idea of withdrawing into private life, though I must admit that your view of the subject is both right and powerful I do most truly appreciate your sacrifices, which are as great or greater than these of any person and full well do I know how revolting the life is to one of your habits & pursuits. I have conversed with several gentlemen from the District who are exceedingly anxious that you should continue. I should be very much gratified myself were you to run, but I leave it all entirely with yourself knowing that whatever <deciss> course you pursue will be the correct one. I should like to hear how you are, you wrote me before that you were unwell. I hope that you have recovered. Please accept my respects &c.

With respect and esteem yours &c. &c.
Joshua S. Swift

Hon. E Pettigrew

N.B. I took the liberty of sending you a discourse delivered by the Rev. Mr. Freeman of this place on the duties of master and servant.

Very &c.
J. S. Swift

[*Addressed*] Hon. Ebenezer Pettigrew.
Washington City.
D. Columbia.

[1]Joshua S. Swift served in the North Carolina House of Commons from Washington County, 1836-1837. Cheney, *North Carolina Government*, 308.

Ebenezer Pettigrew to James Cathcart Johnston UNC

[*January 15, 1836*]

Washington City Jan 15, 1836, 8 oclock and I have just retired from the Tea & dinner table, having set down to the dinner table at half past 4 oclock. Good Lord deliver me from this body of bustle, confusion fashion & sin, and forgetfullness of him who made me and has protected me to this day; and do you think My dear Friend, that I have forgoten you? I answer no, for I have from time to time intended to write to you but a multiplicity of everything & not least; necessary correspondence has prevented. I repeat again No, May dear friend this mind of mine can never forget days gone by. I thank my God it never can, and that my recollections will go down with me to the grave. Although I seem to be enjoying the present, my mind dwells & lives upon the past. But you will say enough of this, and so will I & quit.

You no doubt see from the papers what that most *magnanimous* & I may almost say rowdy body the House of Representitives are doing, which is as near nothing as any thing can be. This is called the calm deliberative assembly of the whole nation. Mercy defend me. A body with a few exceptions composed of all sorts of men. Why my dear sir before I came here I thought I should be the smallest of the small, but without flatery I now think no such thing. My self esteem has I hope been moderately small, but to think *that* I must have not one particle. I am accommodating myself to my situation and geting along chearily, exercising all the prudence in talking and acting which is in my power, but my friends tell me /I am/ in a good deal of danger. I cannot feel fear and when a dog growls I feel like I want to kick him.

I did not get in at Gadsby's the extortionate wretch by his charge forbid it, and I think I am much better situated even if it were the same price. Our mess is composed of the Senators from Maryland, and three representitives of that State & Mr Shepard, who poor fellow does not stay with us more than his duties demand. Mrs Shepard being at her fathers (Alexandia) in I fear the last stage of consumption. Mans joys are of but short duration in this poor, miserable scurvy world. The two Senators & one of the House are fine jovial men I make the fourth. I have been since I came and was at the time of my coming some what indisposed, but I am now in as good health as I ever was. It would seem as if nothing could kill me but bullets or dirks.

Any thing, no matter what, will excite the house and bring forth the most violent ranting & raving, called speeches, but the most exciting subjects that will be before the house this session are the Abolition & Ohio & Michigan Boundry, and they are really so. I can compare an abolition petition presented to the house to a firebrand thrown into a powder magazine and socner or later and probably sooner than many are aware will blow up this Union The French war[1] seems to be at an end, though I did not for a moment think that this congress would declare war or any restrictive measures. Mr Barton[2] has arrived and though nothing official to congress, has been given, nor anything to the public from the administration yet I was confidentially informed yesterday <who was> by a member who was told by one deep in the secrets that there would be no war, nor the least probability of one. It is said there is a great deal of party action here, but I take no part in it yet and have not seen any reason. I have and think shall take the liberty of voting as I think right. I think I discover a good deal of distance from some of the red hot partisans, but poor devils, it has no more effect on my feelings than the power of a Hackman, many of whome are probably as good as they are. O with what disgust do I look at some of those would be great men, and how perfectly is the mistery solved, why men would leave their wives & families and their little interest at home that they might be in Congress. To be called the *Honourable*, to /be/ waited on by white men, to be bowed to in the most humble and in many instances in the sicofantic manner, to be invited to the partis of the first man of the nation, the President, and then by the heads of departments, in truth to be courted in all sorts of ways, and finally to exchange their miserable filthy Yankey rum, & whiskey which most of them swill at home, for their Madeira wine &c and their fine dinners whch the eight dollars allows is enough make a great many leave everything for.

This is the patrotism which actuates most of our public men. When I set down to write I had no idea of all this philipic against the imperfection of man. and will have done after ask my pardon. Prices of all sort of Provisions are high and I see no probability of their being lower. In truth there are good times for planters and I hope from the crop of corn which I gathered before I left home to be able to sink a portion of my debt with you.

I regreted that my business prevented my leaving home a day or two sooner that I might have visited you on the way to this place. I hope to see you at this place before the end of the winter, when I think you may make out to spend a week or two tolerably pleasantly if not profitably. Please to /make/ my best respects to the Ladies and assure yourself of the Esteem & regard of your friend

E Pettigrew

Excuse this miserable scrawl believe me I am perfectly sober but full of impetuousity & mistake

James C. Johnston esqr

N.B. Give my compliments to Mr Woodley and tell him I am going on here in the same way I did on the Plantation. Right ahead

[*Addressed*] James C. Johnston Esqr
Edenton
N. Carolina.

[1]At this time the dispute between the United States and France concerning spoliation claims was at a critical stage. See Thomas Trotter to Ebenezer Pettigrew, May 17, 1834, note, in this volume.

[2]Thomas Pennant Barton (1803-1869) was a United States diplomat who lived in France and served as charge d'affaires during the negotiations of spoliation claims in 1835 and 1836. Barton also acquired a large collection of rare books. *Who Was Who in America: Historical Volume, 1607-1896* (Chicago: Marquis Who's Who, revised edition, 1967), 112.

Doctrine Davenport to Ebenezer Pettigrew A&H

Belgray Jan. 17, 1836

Dear Friend

I recived your letter and nothing give me and Mary so much pleasure as to hear from you every thing is A going on as well as I could expect it continers wet last eaveing we had A litle snow which was A bout two inches deep rain folowed it which melted it it is now mild and pleasent we have had one good weake of weather since Christmas in seaven day we have roled logs of forty acars of ground which I defy North [Amerca] to beater we have not got the lodgs eny of them burnt yit have ben so weet I have got the pine thicket cut down at the howel place I have got A bout six hundread barrels of corn nubed I was at Mr Wood[*l*]eys to day and saw his corn I do not think he will have more than one hundread barrels to sell. Bill have behaved him self very well and have bin great assistance to me old Charles is no earthly A count he have disobade my orders he and Jim both at this time the famialey is awl healthey and strong now I give you the nuse of scuperlong and woful nuse it is I am sorry to inform you that the small pox is in this neighborhood in the neighborhood of John Houghton so says Dr Bell and Dr Seavis their was A gentlemon from Elizabeth city which brought it here he came her with it her and had it so litely that he did not no what it was his buisness was to keep store at the wood place their was three men that was in his company and awl three caught it gid Lamb has dide with it nemine [*Nehemiah*]

Norman expecting to dy with it Mathews felp [*Phelps*] expecting him to dy with it the people have no kind of prudence they have gone far and ner to see them their is no doubt in one faughtnit their will be fifty cases of it in the county god have mercy [u]pun us pray advise with me what is the best corse to persue I am determin to make my people awl stay at home I intend for Mary and my self to stay in the chimney corner I have talked to the negros and told them the consquence it is my and Marys sincier prare that we may see you once more nothing wold give us so much as to have one hours chat with you we look out in our lonesome hours to see if you are comeing but we no it is in vain but we pray to that god that rules the heavens and the earth that we may see you one more Mr Stubs Daughter Nancy was taken sicke the orther night and when they waked in the morning they found her dead and no one knew any thing about it until they went in the rome next morning on the 15 day of this month Piner blowed Zack Bonds brains out he is taken and putin Plymth jail the lode went in at his eye and went out at the back part of his head so you see Mr Pettigrew the people are wors her then they are at the city washinton Dr Bell met with A bad accdent he got one of his best beds burnt up his negro woman went in after [*illegible*] and carlessley tutced fir to the bed and had liked to burnt the house up Dr Bell at this time has gon up the sound to get married and expect to bring his lady down in A day or two Mary sinds her love to you

I remain your sincier freind
Doctrin Davenport

NB <I have rote> I have wrote A letter every mail and please to let me no if you reciv one every mail I recved A letter from William Pettigrew he is well please to write me as soon as you get this letter

[*Addressed*] Hon E Pettigrew
H of R
Washington
City

John Herritage Bryan to Ebenezer Pettigrew A&H

New Bern Jany. 19. 1836

My dear Sir,

I wrote you from Raleigh & hope you received my letter in due time.—

We are all well—Mr. Hawks[1] has taken charge of the Griffin School & our daughters now go to Miss Allen in the Academy.—

It appears that our section of the State will not be benefited by the distribution of the surplus by our legislature—the state of things here & the prospect never were more gloomy.—

I have been strongly urged by Judge Cameron[2] to remove to Raleigh—the advantages in rearing the children in a healthy country & in good society are very strong inducements.—

Things here I fear will become worse & worse, and as the girls grow up their associations will be more & more important.

I believe that Mrs Shepard has made up her mind to remove with James [*Biddle Shepard*]. She could not live without him & he is willing to fix himself in Raleigh which will no doubt fix her residence there—

You must not however let this be known as coming from me; as you know she likes secrets.

I think it very probable that I shall remove to Raleigh; tho' I should have to make a great sacrifice in property & business—but the health of Mrs B & the family would no doubt be much benefited.—

I am much obliged to you for purchasing the book for me, I have not yet received it.—Our mails are in a very confused state.—

If we conclude to remove to Raleigh, it wd. be better probably to have the family there by next summer.—

Mrs Bryan sends her affectionate regards. Mary will write shortly.—

Yrs truly
Jn. H. Bryan

[*Addressed*] [To/] of The Hon:
E Pettigrew
Ho. of Repr.
Washington

---

[1]This may refer to Cicero Stephens Hawks of New Bern, who graduated from the University of North Carolina in 1830. He later moved to New York, and in 1844 he was elected bishop of the Protestant Episcopal Church of Missouri. Battle, *History of the University*, I, 325, 793; *Appleton's Cyclopedia*, III, 122.

[2]This probably refers to Duncan Cameron (1777-1853), an attorney who had served at one time as a superior court judge. He had also sat in both houses of the state legislature and was president of the State Bank of North Carolina, clerk of the state supreme court, and a member of the board of internal improvements. Cameron was one of the largest plantation owners in the South. He lived at Fairntosh and in Raleigh. Powell, *DNCB*, I, 311.

Doctrine Davenport to Ebenezer Pettigrew A&H

Belgrade Janu 24, 1836

Dear Friend

I recived you favour and it give me and Mary great pleasure and satisfaction to hear from you at this time every thing is agoing on as well as I could expect Awl the famialey is in very good health at this time it is very wet the water in the Lake is five feet and continues to rise the bee tree is stil sunke in water I have had but one good weake of weather since Chrismas last eavening we had the heavest rain that I have seen in twelve months the hole face of the earth is sunke in water at this time I am nubing corn at the Lake I can do nothing else I shal finish nubing corn in A bout three day more I have finished roleing logs I have roled logs of eaighty acars of land in A bout 15 day with sixteen hands so you see Mr Pettigrew that I am A hole hog man rain or shine I have not bin able to start A plough since Christmas I have got my sawing nearley awl done at the Lake I shal finish in A bout A weake more I have got pomp and Jerry sawing out her and Hary and sam hewing those men which rold logs their shose Mr Pettigrew is giveing out may I not give them A norther pare I thinke they are deserveing of them they have not worked like men they have worked like horses I can say Mr Pettigrew you no the corse I have stucke to them excepting one or two the negrose have behaved very well Tom Bell Sam and Hary sends their compliments to you I recived A letter from Provedence last mail stateing that corne was was one doller and five sents A bushes and none in market I recived A letter from you Mr Pettigrew stateing some articals in which you send to Mary and Mary says she is A thousan times Ablige to you it is more than she could expect from A father she cannot express her thankes by wordes please to write me when you wish A lode of corn shipt now I give you the nuse of scupernong Mr felpes is dead with the small pox their is three or four more cases of it Dr Bell is married and brought his lady down Mary has bin in her company and is very much pleased wither they are very fashingible they dine at two and set until four and drinke tea half after eaight and set until A leaven for my part Mr Pettigrew I am out of the scrape their is no one can teach him except Mr Collinse he has broyed every thing he can bory ande I expect he wil send over after the [methene] [*machine?*] house and stables next I thinke it is anorther Dr Warren. Mary wente over to prepare the super ande it come one to raine and she had to walke home in the raine his horses ande brush [*barouche*] doing nothing Joeseph Tarkenton laste thursday night was married to jentla armstrong General Batemane hirs Mr Alexandria and gives him two hundred ande fiftey dollers Mary now sendes you A peace of the Dr wedding cake of her one [*own*] make Mary sendes her kind and affectionate love to you I remaine your sincier friende

Doctrin Davenport

[*Addressed*] Hon. E Pettigrew
H. R.
Washington City

Ebenezer Pettigrew to John Herritage Bryan UNC

Washington Jan 27, 1836

My dear Sir,

I receivd your favour of 22nd today and took no time in answering it, which is the 54th since I came to this place. I attended to the business mentioned in your letter without delay and wrote Mr Blount on the 15th and you will please to give my love to my dear little Mary and tell her that I answered her favour on the 14th. I think Genl McKey is a keen hand at a bargain. If I can promote Young Streets wishes it will be done. Genl <Speight> Speight was taken sick the first week of the session and was not in the house often, about a fortneight ago he left for N.C. and I understand he will not be back before the first of March. I send you today the document asked and one on the legacy to the City. I am glad to learn that your Bank declares so good a dividend, but we are geting into a bad state with our currency, Banks are multiplying to such a degree that in less than five years there will be a greater flood of paper than was ever known, and if we should have a French war, I know not what will become of us, so perfectly defenceless as we are on the whole coast. On that subject I have not had the least idea that we should have a war untill within ten days, but since that time my opinion has been changing, though not in the secrets, and to strengthen my apprehention, Mr C. C. Cambeling[1] in a speech today on Mr J. Q Adams' resolution to enquire into the cause of the loss of the appro<pro>priation bill for fortifications on the last day of the last session of Congress remarked 'that peace & war with France w<as>ere so equally balanced that a feather would turn the scale. You are at liberty to hand this extract to the Spectator

William S. went this afternoon to Alexandria; I will mention your request to him. Last week they thought Mrs S a little better but this week not so well. I cannot see how it is possible for the poor dear woman ever to recover, and I consider the case next to entirely hopeless. Mr S. bears his situation with great firmness.

My health is at this time perfectly good, but on that subject and my opinion of Congress & & I must refer you to brother Charles' letter of the 26th The debate continued all this day on Mr A. resolution, and there are not less than fifteen that have speeches on hand for that subject. Three full days have already been spent and but four have yet spoken. I cannot but think that if our constituants could but be here and see what we spend our time at, the Hall would be very soon emptied. We have had a great deal of bad weather since the year set in; not less than ten snows & the ground is now covered and the slays driving as if old satan was after the people, to the great injury & distress of the horses. I regret to learn that Poor Johnston is so thin and puny. I very much fear that he will not be raised, and /all/ I can say is, God's will be done.

I am pleased to understand that you are all except Poor Johnston in good health, I pray you may continue so. Please to make my kind regards to sister Mary, and all other of my friends, and tell them that though I am in this crazy place, and am going with the multitude old friends & days gone by cannot nor shall not ever be forgoten by me.

Sincerely & truely your friend & relation
E Pettigrew

John H. Bryan

N.B. I feared before I came to this place I should be one amongst the poorest members in the house, but tis without flattery to myself I think no such thing, but all that is no compliment. Many are poor indeed, and in more ways than one or two.

You see the indian war[2] is like to be a serious affair, yesterday the house appropriated five hundred thousand dollars more to carry on the war with the poor miserable, persecuted, and oppressed wretches. My heart bleeds when I think how those poor wretches have been dealt with from the cupidity of the whites. This nation must be visited for such offences to God. Nothing do I believe more certainly than that the Almighty will reward good & punish evil, as well in nations as in individuals. I have been to two parties (Gov. Cass') and quit; there is too great a squese for me, and what I call gentlemen are too scarce at them for me. My God how many here are in disguise.

Tell sister Mary that though a poor wicked sinner, I keep the bible & prayer book on my writing table, and that I must read it through before I leave this City. I take this not as a task but as a duty & pleasure.

E P.

[*January*] 28 P.S. I am sick this morning. I shall always be glad to hear from you & any of my friends. Please to make my respects to my friend Mr Robarts.

[*Addressed*] John H. Bryan esqr
Newbern
N. Carolina

---

[1]Churchill Caldom Cambreleng (1786-1862) of New York City was born in Washington, North Carolina. A businessman, he served in the United States House of Representatives from 1821 to 1839 and later was minister to Russia. *Biographical Directory of Congress*, 651.

[2]There were two Seminole Indian wars in Florida, in 1816-1818 and 1835-1842. The first resulted in the cession of East Florida by Spain to the United States. The second involved the removal of hostile Indian groups from the area. It has been called "the fiercest war waged against the American Indians." It cost 1500 lives and 20 million dollars. *CDAH*, 474; *Encyclopedia Americana* (1977 edition), XXIV, 540.

Ebenezer Pettigrew to James Cathcart Johnston UNC

Washington Jan 30, 1836

My dear friend,

I received your favour of the 17th on the 26th and should have answered it on the following day as it made an enquiry on business but was too much indisposed. Today I am better. On the subject of your enquiry respecting Mr J. C[*ollins?*][junr]. The property cannot be worth less than 50 thousand dollars, and I have not the least reason to think that it is incumbered by any acts of his and if not by him, no other, than his fathers life estate which he (the Father) will not I think relinquish in life. I think a debt of 10 thosd cannot be better secured. I will however make one remark respecting the present and approaching state of the money market. The U.S. Bank is put down I think forever, and no other will rise on its ruins. In the room of that Bank a number of the States, (and all will follow the example) are chartering Banks, to an enormous amount, and I think for the want of that U.S.B. as a check, upon their issues, there will in less than five years be twice if not ten times the amount of Bank paper in circulation that was two years ago. In consequence of the averice of the stock holders of those enormous state banks; /&/ knowing the power that a U.S.B. would have to regulate them and bring them /with/in due bounds, there will be keept up a most violent and determined hostility, to such a *monster*. It will be to the interest of those stock holders in the state banks to keep up a hue & cry against anything of that sort by the nation, in as much as it would be so *monstrous Big*, and they will not be found wanting in dishonesty to blind the eyes of the multitude, and to make any misrepresentation, that would answer their purpose. O! tempora O! mores. I think we have now in the price of almost every article, an evidence of the increase of circulating medium, and I fear that we are only at the begining. I deplore it, and had rather pay my debt at $2. pr bbl. for corn than that, that should take place which I fear will, so great a derangement of our circulating medium

For my opinion of the H.R. &c. I refer you to my former letter of the 15th My time is very much occupyed as you have been informed by that letter, but if it will possibly permit I shall be pleased to give you my ideas of men and things, though permit me to say that I cannot believe for a moment that /they/ are intitled to that confidence which you express. I hope they will however be given at all times with virtuous boldness.

Mr [*John Quincy*] Adams' course since I entered this hall had disgusted and in truth displeased me very much with him so as to cut that acquaintance which I sought the first day of the session. You have no doubt seen the debate on his resolution to appoint a committee to enquire into the cause of the bill for the appropriation for Fortifications being lost /the/ last day of the last session. Mr A. followed the resolution with a violent speech of more than an hour in which he wished to say exceeding sevier things of members of the Senate, but was as often called to order, it being contrary to a rule that one branch of C. should make in debate personal allusion to the members of the other, but he remarked it had been said by a member else where that he would not vote for that bill if the enemy were at the /door of the/ Capital, 'and but one step more to join the enemy and batten down these walls'. The allusion was to Mr Webster. Mr A, sits not far from me, and when he began to speek a great many members left their seats & stood near that they might hear. It was in vain that the speaker called to order & asked gentlemen to take their seats, but when that remark was made, I was thunder struck. There was not less that fifty claping of hands by the members. & I learned pr Mr Shepard from another quarter hissing. The speaker rose and called to order with great apparent indignation as well as other members remarking that they had never seen such disorder in that house before. My God! says I to myself, is this the calm deliberative body of the United states, is this the Congress the H.R. that in all probability /are/ to decide in a few weeks on the question of peace or war, with one of the most powerfull nations of Europe, in which there will be spilled oceans of human blood, & millions of treasure, will /be/ spent. Four days, and better have already been taken in speaking on the subject, one of them Mr Hardin[1] of Keny. who is a man of good strong mind but not one degree removed from a savage, in which speech he handled Mr Adams roughly, but the speech made on the same side on thursday last by Mr Evans[2] of Maine was a closer. Mr Evans is not middle aged yet but /is/ said to be one of the most talented men in the house. His argumentitive, calm manner, and equally so in his concluding and personal remarks to & of Mr Adams, touching on his vehemence, his desertion of his friends, &c &c &c disarmed all my resentment towards the poor old man (who set but a short distance from him and would now & then nod his head at the speaker) and I could with difficulty restrain my tears to see so great a man in information, & in the honours of his country, bring himself down to a seat in that house, and then enter into all sort of contests and lay himself liable deservedly to such a reprimand as I never before heard or thought of. Poor old man! he was always wrong, but I have no idea (& it is an opinion <only> /which I soon formed & which is/ strenghened by observation) but /that/ his mind has failed by age & to use my common expretion he is deranged; and I fear though never a good /man/ I feel exceedingly for him, I never can again feel dislike, I never will war with the dead. He rose on saturday and made a few remarks as bitter & as venomous as a tiger hoping the previous question would not be put on his resolution without giving him an opportunity of answering some of those vials of wrath that had been poured upon him. He cannot answer that speech but if my vote will give it, he shall have the opportunity /if it but in satisfaction to an old man./. The old man quailed, and look wretched under that speech and I again repeat Poor old man, though all the truth, it would I thought make the most obdurate heart feel for him, but such is man I found many who did not.

I shall be glad to give you my ideas of the men who are before the Union as leading men if my time will possibly pemit You see by my letter of the 15th that Congress hall & this crazy place could /not/ make me forget my friends whom I had left behind, but my dear friend legislation and judging legislators is very foreign from my occupation. My God! what vicissitudes there has been in various times of my life. For 27 years I was employed in matters of fact cuting down trees and diging ditches, in which there could be no deception For 4½ years, I have been employed moving over the country without business, and as it were with home, and every place my home, a poor miserable mortal, and but for the firm hope /in/ another and a better world could not stay, wishing for nothing so much as total seclusion from the world. For the last year ending yesterday I have been entirely employed in words, hard at work with /or rather in/ words, and that now is my daily employ, and when it is to end god only knows. The first is the life which I should prefer and shall with my last breath deplore my being taken from it, but I am reconciled or /will/ try and make myself so to all the dispensations of providence. All this is not my seeking, though it may be my falt. I cannot but believe had I not been a misserable wicked sinner my Almighty Father would not have thus afflicted me, for I not only believe that he deprived me of all my comfort in this world that I might be brought to a sense of my duty towards him, but that my call to this place is a punishment for my sins, but pray let me stop this. I began this letter yesterday; when I had writen a page I was taken away and finish today. I had a sevier pain last evening in my great toe joint (which /is/ no more nor less than gout) and today I have been quite sick and barely able to finish this letter in time for the office, which I hope you /will/ excuse the interlineations &c of. Though I am now where the sole employ is letter writing, backing documents, and words, most of them without knowledge <are the> I am very deficient. My life has been spent in a more substanial way, a matter of fact business. I <shall be> would advise you to read those speeches on Mr A's resolution. I shall be glad to receive a letter from you, and also expect you at this place before the winter ends. All is snow here, about 12 since Christmas

Please to make my best respects to the Ladies and assure yourself of sincere Esteem & regard of your friend

E Pettigrew

James C. Johnston esqr.

[*Addressed*] James C. Johnston esqr
Edenton
North Carolina

[1]Benjamin Hardin (1784-1852), a Kentucky attorney, had been a member of the legislature in that state. He served in Congress 1815-1817, 1819-1823, and 1833-1837. Hardin was also secretary of state of Kentucky. *Biographical Directory of Congress*, 1005.

[2]George Evans (1797-1867) was an attorney who served in the Maine state legislature. He sat in the United States House of Representatives from 1829 to 1841 and in the Senate from 1841 to 1847. Later he was attorney general of Maine. *Biographical Directory of Congress*, 868.

Ebenezer Pettigrew to William Shepard Pettigrew UNC

Washington City Feb. 18, 1836

My dear Son William

I received your favour of Jan 31st about a fortnight after its date. I had been expecting to receive a line from you for some time, having had a great deal of anxiety with regard to your trip from Newbern to Chapel Hill in that inclement season and extreme bad weather for the season. I was also anxious to learn of the health of your brother Charles who had informed me that he was sick. But you did not mention the trip nor your Brother Charles' name and I have to presume.

My son I was not a little surprised to read in your letter the expression of your being hard run for money, when I have been so liberal with you & your brother. Believe me each of you have had more money spent on you yearly than was ever spent on your father in all the education he had. If any fathers conscience is clear on the allowance and conduct to his sons your father is. I know /that/ you both know, that I tell the truth when I say that I have given you both more money at all times than you have said you could make out with, and I have sent you more money almost in every instance than you have writen for. Be assured if you ever have a family you will be assured of my liberal treatment of you both. Though now near two years ago I requested of you both to keep an account of your expenditures, it has not been done and I have passed it by without scarcly a word. My son what will be your pecuniary situation if the abolitionists can effect their object, a thing I very much apprehend will take place much sooner than people are aware of. My dear son you /have/ so far forgoten your fathers kindness to you that you neglected to acknowledge the two presents which he sent you by your brother Charles, and farther at the ending of your letter to acknowledge yourself as his son. I will give you the end of your letter. 'Brother Charles gave me <me> the sum which you directed him to deliver at his arrival & I likewise received the draft from Mr Bryan, for both of which favours I feel very grateful'

Will. S. Pettigrew

I suppose I must submit to be forgoten but I hope that my God will not forget *me* and I pray God, which I never neglect to do in all my petitions, that he will not forget my dear children, the dear offspring of my dear ever dear wife & your most excellent Mother.

I have been a good deal unwell with a complaint which I have been free from for a number of years, and for the last week the fullness of my head has been excessive so as to apprehend appoplexy. By the course which I have adopted I am some what relieved. This of all other places is the coldest and the most heartless. No one cares for the well, the sick, the dying, or the dead, and of all places & employments this is to me the most awful, and how I am to remain here 5 months longer I cannot think. The cold is intence and I have suffered with it very much, but as my life has been & is to continue on of trouble & slavery I forbare to complain.

I received a letter about three weeks ago from Mr Davenport informing me that there were about 50 cases of small pox within five miles of Belgrade and some within a / a mile. I should have been there before this but there is no geting along for the ice, which is a foot thick, as soon as it is possible I shall go there my health permiting. If the disease should get among the negroes or should

M[r] Davenport take it, it will make small receits from the the Plantation.

My dear son Charles, I expected to have had another letter from you concerning your heath. You have been inquired for by a number, & I have been requested to give complements to you when I write.

May God Almighty bless you my dear sons is the sincere prayer of your affectionate father

E Pettigrew

[*Addressed*] M[r] William Shepard Pettigrew
Chapel Hill
Noth Carolina

Ebenezer Pettigrew to William Shepard Pettigrew A&H

Washington March 31, 1836

My dear Son,

On my return from visiting Scuppernong I found your favour of the 2nd inst. My dear William it gave me great pleasure, and in so many words, it was fully satisfactory on all points, and all I have to ask of my dear children is not to forget their *only* remaining parent, a *parent* who has no words to express his affection & Love for his children, and who never forgets them for a day no not for an hour. I have been interrupted. Ap. 1—

I returned to this miserable place on the 18th after being gone 16 days. It was with as much reluctance as if I was going to Jail. It is a place of great labour, and fatigue, and a miserable climate. The manner of life, the employment, and the climate is breaking down my health most rapidly, and if the next winter session should be as distressing as this has & promises to be my health will be gone. It is also such a species of slavery to the body and to my constituants, as you have no idea of & such as I pray God a son will have descretion enough, with the advice of his father founded on his experience, as never to get into. I hope my sons I am not to be heard for my much speaking, and I will have done. I sent you a Globe paper yesterday giving an account of saturday nights work on the contested election with some remarks on the envelop, and will say nothing more. But depend upon it my son your father has got into the worst scrape he ever was in by accepting a seat in this rowdy establishment.

When the house will break up is altogether uncertain. I shall vote for the earlyest day. Nothing has yet been done.

When I got to Scuppernong the Small pox was in a mile of Belgrade but I learn that it has abated; the necessary steps were

taken to prevent its geting to Belgrade & I hope it will not spread.
It has been in Scuppernong an extreme wet winter and the Lake is full & running over in every direction. My shore is pretty safe but Mr Collins has & will suffer very much. Mr C. was at the Lake a few days while I was the only time since November. My dear sons that will not do for interest. It was not the way your father made his estate and if he your father had not the best overseer, it would not be the way that he would keep it. Mr Davenport has done a great deal as much as I could do at any time. He has cleared this winter at Belgrade eighty acres of ground & it is ready to plant.

I sowed the wheat this fall unusually thick, and though it has been a killing winter it is thick enough, and when I was there looked promising. I believe I sowed about 170. acres at both places. I think it promises a good price, in the summer. Corn is not as high as I expected, but it will rise. The hard winter upon animals has made a great use of corn never theless, I have a good quantity for sale, which I hope will keep on going & in two years pay my debt to Mr. J[*ohnston*]. I do not think my pay here will more than pay my expenses, which may seem strange to you. I mark every cent and shall be able to tell what has gone with it.

With my benedection I will end, May God almighty Bless you my dear sons.

E Pettigrew

Write me often

[*Addressed*] Mr William S. Pettigrew
Chapel Hill
North Carolina

Peter Evans[1] *to Ebenezer Pettigrew* UNC

Sparta April 4th 1836

My Dear Sir:

I have not had the pleasure of a personal interview, or to receve a letter from you since you were at my House in July. I should very much like to visit Washington—this spring if my business was not so urgent, as to require every moment of my time.—I can assure you—I was as much gratified at your success—, as you possibly could be: I hope & trust, it will be a lasting defeat. There can be no doubt, provided no exceptions can be taken to your votes—and—as far as I have examined them—they have been such, as I would have given in every case. I should go against the abolitionist in every shape & form: it is a vital question with the south—and it is down right impudence in those fellows, to meddle with us and our slaves: I should not be able to keep my temper on subject, when that question was agitated:—the south will have to form a confederacy & go against the north in all political & pecuniary matters this will be the most effectual way to bring those fellows to their senses.—The south ought to cut off all moneyed opperations, with the north;—we can soon bring them to terms in this way.—

The south, is too much divided—to effect any great object But this will not be the case as soon as we can get clear of G[l] Jackson: woe be unto his successor, if he attemps to pursue his course.—I think you must have a dry time of it, with those abolition petitions—it is enough to wear out the patience of a southern man—to witness the baseness of the Van Buren party in congress—they have sufferd severely in their feelings—if they have any; for the oposition have skewered them fore & aft. there certainly never was a more corrupt party in any Government. We are apt in every thing we try to learn—I am now of the opinion this very question, sooner or later, will be the cause of a separation of the states.—The south seems to be preparing for the event. these railroads will have a good effect in uniting the southern people together it will throw their Interest very much together & this is the way to keep the people united—I like to see those works going on in the south.—It is my opinion negro property will soon become of very little value—there will be the devil to play in the southern states in the course of two or three years—with the negroes—I feel very much like getting clear of mine this fall—I expect my son George to be in Washington in the course of a few days, on his way home—have taken the liberty to inclose a letter to him in this epistle to you Will you do me the favour to hand it to him on his arrival—and say to him I have requested you to caution him against falling into the company of the sons of the officers of the government & members of congress—who have nothing to do—but to spend money—foolishly & wastfully—I am told there are very many young men of this discription in your place—& George is not proof against temptation—He would take it kindly from you—His object in coming by is to see M[r] Webster who has promised to receive him as a law student. I should be much gratified to hear from you—

Yours very respectfully
Peter Evans

[*Addressed*] Honourable Ebenezer Pettigrew
Washington City

[1]Peter Evans in 1829 was a partner in the Edgecombe Manufacturing Company, capitalized at 200 thousand dollars to manufacture cotton, flax, and hemp. Ashe, *History of North Carolina*, II, 317. For information on early cotton manufacturing in the state see Diffee W. Standard and Richard W. Griffin,

"The Cotton Textile Industry in Ante-Bellum North Carolina," *North Carolina Historical Review*, XXXIV (January, April, 1957), 15-35, 131-164, hereinafter cited as Standard and Griffin, "Cotton Textile Industry."

David M. Sargent[1] *to Ebenezer Pettigrew*[2] A&H

[*Tillatoba, Mississippi, April 12, 1836*]

My Dear Friend

I am at last, here, & partially settled. We had a tedious journey of about nine weeks. I could do nothing at the sale of public land at Pontotoc in Jany last. And I have, like many others, settled on land belonging to the U States. I however purchased some improvements a man had made upon it, who expects to <expects> obtain <to> a right by preemption & in that case is to convey to me when he will be entitled to an additional sum, or in case of no preemption law I shall have to purchase the public sales whenever it comes into market. It is on a gore of land lying between the Choctaw & Chickasaw nations of Indians & is in dispute by those tribes, it probably will not come into market before that dispute is settled, but should it be offered for sale this year I shall be greatly obliged if you will inform me of it as soon practicable. I have not settled on the most fertile lands to be found here, but I believe it to be very fine of the kind i.e. high rolling land—such I choose for a healthy situation. I am well pleased, in some respects with this place, it is the finest place for raising hogs I ever saw, Cattle do well, & it is a good Cotton & Corn country but it is not without its disadvantages & inconveniences and, judging from what I have seen, I will say, taking it as a whole (the north part of this State) it has been greatly overa<r>ted—there are large quantities of inferior land, some of which is mountainous, a great deal of is extreemly broken & much of it swampy, & the greatest part of it affords the worst of roads All ride on horseback here & I think they are doomed to do so untill great improvements are are made. There are, however, some tracts of very fine land The river bottoms are destined to become the most fertile & valuable land in the State if inundation does not prevent if, but they are bound to be sickly; there is an immence quantity of land or swamp of this descreption, between this place & the Mississippi River

I have now traveled a long road & have seen som desirable plantations, or I should say many, but I have seen none that would bear any comparison with your splendid Plantation at Lake Phelps, nor yet with Bellgrade, such propperty would certainly be held in high estimation any where, but when situated on a navigable river within fifty miles of the Ocean & in a County affording the best roads in the Universe it ought, certainly to be held above all price

I am entirely without papers or information of any kind, foreign or domestic, not having seen but two or three papers that were printed this year, I thot to have ordered my papers to be sent here but I found that the great irregularity of the mails would prevent my receiving many before I should leave for the eastward, & did not order them, I think, however now that I shall not return, that is, leave untill June.

Please to inform /me/ if any thing unusual is going on and particularly, anthing relating to land matters where I am If it would not be too much trouble, be pleased to send me two or three papers that you have read.

The 16th Section in Township 22 Range 1 West of the Meridian line, in the Choctaw nation will be offered for sale in June probably, or perhaps late in May under the following circumstances, as I have understood them. In the first place all 16th Sections are reserved or allowed the State or county for some purpos, probably for Schools, the Trustees or propper authorities are going to sell this one pursueant to law /or/ orders, & some Speculator /has/ laid a Float or claim of a similar discreption upon it Will you be so kind as to ask the Attorney General or some other person possing informamtion to be depended upon, whether this sale will convey a good title? & inform me as soon as you conveniently can? This section said to be a very valuable one & it is expected to sell low

It is understood here that the late edition of Floats are defeated (a good thing, if so,) but the one spoken of above, is probably of a former class

With great respect Sir

Your Obt Servant
D M Sargent

Hon E Pettigrew

Tillatoba, Talahatchie County, Mississippi, April 12th 1836.

[*Addressed*] Honorable Ebenr Pettigrew
Member of Congress
Washington
D.C

---

[1]In 1830 David M. Sargent was a resident of Tyrrell County. *1830 Census Index*, 164.

[2]This letter is one of several in this volume that illustrate the westward movement during the 1830s. Census figures show that between 1830 and 1840 the population of both Tyrrell and Washington counties declined. Cheney, *North Carolina Government*, 1290, 1304.

Ebenezer Pettigrew to James Cathcart Johnston UNC

Washington City April 24, 1836

My dear friend

Your favor of the 8th March came to hand in due time as well as yours of Ap 19th yesterday. In not answering yours of the 8th ult before this I should reproach myself and you might think me neglectfull of /a/ duty to my best friend, but for the reasons which follow. Shortly, the second day after my return I was taken sick, and though able to attend with the exception of a few days to the House, yet I continued to decline with that rapidity which brought me to think that without a change I was not much longer for this world. With my bad health, my spirits declined and were exceedingly depressed. Out of health & a spirit to do anything but the most imperious calls, I continued untill last week, by which time I found my room fast filling with all manner of trash, goten together for my constituents. I mean documents, speeches, newspapers, &c &c &c. The franking & directing of which is an excessive labour, when carried to /the/ extent which I am going. I paid the sum which I recived in your letter the day after I recived it and could have acknowleded it in so many words, but waited untill I should be able to say all that my capacity & time will allow.

It is no joke. I really did think that time was about to end with me in this world. And blessed be God; I viewed it with all that composure with which I would a picture. That great enemy of human nature has lost all its terrors in my breast. I consider it no enemy of mine. I contemplate it with pleasure. I long to /be/ gone. For the sake of my *dear dear* children I regret that I do. But O! I so much desire for rest from this wicked world. I however will be resigned to the will of a kind & indulgent Providence. All is for the best, and I have found it so, after I have passed over it without a single exception. It is well that I am afflicted. God will do with me as he thinks best, and I should not have been here had it not been his will. After going home in March and remaining a few days, with what reluctance did I return to this place. I felt as if I would have given anything to have remained at my solitary but peacefull home, to have taken those lonely walks, to rest at the siting places, and whether walking or siting to be permited to contemplate in solitude the busy but happy hours & days *gone, gone, gone*, never to return. Fate has ordered otherwise and it must be right. Pray excuse this melancholy strain. It was not /in/ my power to stop sooner.

You naturally would wish to know something about this place and the people that are in it, and though I think I know a great deal about them I know not where to begin. In the first place I doubt the political honesty of a large majority on both & all sides Ambition and all the bad passions /that man is heir to/ are <the> prevailing at this place to its highest degree, and how a government can stand, with such spirits in the ins and the outs, I cannot conceive. The abolition concerns, with the mean & contemptable looking Pinkney[1] at their head seems to sleep and I think it doubtfull whether he will report this session, and if he does it will be a milk & water one. No such looking man can make any other. There was a memorial introduced the other day from Pensyvania asking of Congress to prohibit slavery in Arkansas before admission into the union. It knocked up a real brease, and only stoped by the hour coming for something else. It is highly probable there are a majority of Abolitionists in the house. I have no doubt, that if we do not fall to pieces from corruption too soon, the subject of slavery will dissove this union. I agree with you that the southerners have managed the matter badly, there has been no /general/ concert, every one acts in his own way and makes defence as he thinks best, while the opposition are a unit. That north & north western coolness will always govern this country, whether united or divided. I do not deserve the credit of your receiving My Preston speech I have not the Honour of an acquaintance with /that/ Gentleman.[2] The winter was so bad that I could visit but very little, if I had had time; withall I had not time, and since my return I have been a great part of the time too unwell, and aded to that it takes at least six introductions for most of / of the very great men to know small little ones. You know I am a retiring man. You would be astonished to see how persons here are influencd by party and what slight acts either way will produce a go by or a smile. These things have not the slighest effect on my mind. I assure you I am not under /the/ slightest mortification. I am perfectly indifferent to the movements of I may say all. If any feeling is produced, it is that of pity, to both sides. I feell most perfectly independant in my actions, and I cannot make a partisan. There has been not much done yet and I fear not much will be done. There is a strong effort making to use as much of the revenue as possible, and it is the /opinion that/ the surplus will not be disposed of this session. The Florida war is geting along badly & I understand the President complains very much of the management.

I send you by this mail a Speech of Secretary Cass, a speech of Chilton Allen,[3] one of Mr Wise,[4] and one of Mr Bell,[5] the [*torn*] speaker of the house, and who I think is one of the most [*torn*]tified men here. He is trying to work up hill, but it is do/u/btfull whether he will not go lower. He is thought to be one of the most talented men in the house but I see no influence of his. Mr Wise has lost a good of influence by violence. The two candidates for the Vice Presidency who are in our house, I think are poor creatures for great men, or to fill high & responsible stations. There seems to be no other opinion than that the election of President will go to the house of Representitives.

My dear friend I expect to pay you four thousand dollars of the debt which I owe you, by the first day of September and you can make arraingments to that effect.

Please to make my best respects to the Ladies and assure yourself of the Esteem of your friend

E Pettigrew

James C. Johnston esqr

N.B. among other evils I am troubled with an affection of the eyes which prevents my writing or reading as much as I would.
I inclose your Gales & Seatons receit.

[*Addressed*] James C. Johnston esqr
Edenton
N. Carolina

---

[1]Henry Laurens Pinckney (1794-1863), a South Carolina attorney and newspaper editor, served as a Democrat in the United States House of Representatives, 1833-1837. *Biographical Directory of Congress*, 1460.

[2]This probably refers to William Campbell Preston (1794-1860) of South Carolina. A Calhoun nullifier, he was a lawyer and state legislator and sat in the United States Senate from 1833 to 1842. *Biographical Directory of Congress*, 1481.

[3]Chilton Allan (1786-1858) was a Democratic representative from Kentucky, 1831-1837. Allan was also an attorney and a state legislator. *Biographical Directory of Congress*, 468.

[4]Henry Alexander Wise (1806-1876) of Virginia sat in Congress from 1833 to 1844 and was at various times a Whig and a Democrat. Later governor of Virginia and a Confederate general, he was a "tactless and unduly aggressive" defender of southern rights. *DAB*, XX, 423-425; *Biographical Directory of Congress*, 1838.

[5]John Bell (1797-1869) of Tennessee, a lawyer, was a Democrat and then a Whig. He sat in the House of Representatives, 1827-1841, and was Speaker, 1834-1835. He later served as secretary of war and as a United States senator from 1847 to 1859. The Constitutional Union party candidate for president in 1860, Bell was defeated by Abraham Lincoln. *Biographical Directory of Congress*, 539.

Ebenezer Pettigrew to John Herritage Bryan A&H, BRYAN

H.R. April 27, 1836

My dear Sir,

I received your favour of Ap 20, yesterday and with great regret learned of the indisposition of our Mother [*Mary Blount Shepard*]. I should suppose that a trip to the Virginia Springs would be a much better visit for her health than the north. In her bad health she will find the bustle of a northern tour very disagreeable, and I fear disgusting.

My health has been very bad and I had some doubts whether my time was not coming, but disease has left me & I now have health enough to attend to my duties & to be in comfort. In consequence of my bad health my documents &c &c had accumulated to such an extent as to keep me at extreme close & hard work, the hardest I have had in ten years. I am sometimes so tired of this place as to be almost fit to take French leave, but Fate has placed me here and I will not complain. I hope that the character I shall be able to give to public life will prevent my sons from ever permiting themselves from being put into such a difficulty in time to come, which I pray God to guard them from.

I am very glad to learn that the Phelps affair is closed, and am much obliged for the part which you have taken. I am not fit to undertake the business of any but my own.

All kinds of provisions are alike high at this place. I know nothing here is not high unless it might be wives, who, from the number candidates I would think cheap. But thank God I am only a listener and & looker on, on that subject as well as with the wine & strong drink. I take a small quantity of stimulant each day, but am perfectly disgusted with excess. I have in truth come very nearly down to my Lake habbits, in eating, drinking & *visiting*. I am not wanting in attention to my business, and am as content in my room as elsewhere.

Party runs high and I frequenty observe frowns or smiles according to my votes, but they are all alike to me. I can not make a partizan. I can do no other than act under my best conviction. I am not dependent on any one for anything here as long as Uncle Sam honours my drafts. I see plainly that I shall alway be the same thing. The Globe of today has pronounced me a White man & a nullifier.[1] If the party could establish me the latter in my district a reelection would be over, a thing very desirable to them I suppose, but God knows that if I have a wish in the world greater than another it is to end my Congretional life on the 4 March 1837, and I could assure the corrupt Globe that he may withold his lies from me & keep them /for/ other objects. The poor corrupt wretch has not yet produced any excitement in my breast. I am rejoiced at your report of my dear little daughters health & improvement, if it is possible to increase my feelings of affection & love for those dear representives of my *dear* ever *dear Nancy* I know that it will be. I sent Mary 2 little spoons envoloped in a document [per] her Uncle Charles which I suppose was miscarryed. I will bring her some when I come.

Please to give my kind & affectionate regard to sister Mary & all my friends in your town, and believe me to be sincerely your friend & relation

E Pettigrew

John H. Bryan esq^r

I will quit as I am writing under the voice of Eli More the Fanny Wright member from New York[2] on the subject or in favor of the labouring class in New York. If it /is/ in the papers I will send it to you

[*Addressed*] John H. Bryan esqr
Newbern
N. Carolina

---

[1]An article on the third page of the *Globe* (Washington, D.C.), April 28, 1836, lists Ebenezer Pettigrew among supporters of Hugh Lawson White and also as a nullifier.

[2]Ely Moore (1798-1861) was a representative who served in Congress as a Democrat from 1835 to 1839. He studied medicine and edited a newspaper prior to his election. *Biographical Directory of Congress*, 1350.

To call him the "Fanny Wright member" was to label him radical. Frances (Fanny) Wright (1795-1852) was a free thinker and a social reformer. *CDAB*, 1256.

John Herritage Bryan to Ebenezer Pettigrew A&H

New Bern May 23. 1836—

My dear Sir,

We have not heard from you for some weeks, but I suppose you are now very much occupied with the business of the House.

Our [*diocesan*] convention was but thinly attended owing to the rumor of the small pox and bad weather.—We had at our house however Mr Davis of Wilmington & M^r E L Winslow of Fayetteville, with his mother & a Miss King.—

Mary Pettigrew & Nancy are very well Johnston has been sick again & Dr Boyd had to give him calomel—he is up again, but looks badly.—Charles Pettigrew is expected I believe in the next stage.—Mrs Shepard's health is very feeble, she expects to leave here on her journey tomorrow week; she will probably spend a week in Pasquotank—I think it is probable that she will go to the Fauquir Springs, where she is very desirous that Mrs Bryan should join her, as soon as she can conveniently leave home—but whether that will ever be is doubtful.—I should be very willing & desirous that Mrs B. should take a little trip—for she needs it & is anxious to do so—but what to do with all the children is the question.—If she *does* go, it would probably be the middle or last of June, before she could leave here.

I returned from Wayne C[*ounty*]. Court the other day & learned that a negro boy of yours by the name of Jess had been seen about here, & next morning I spoke to an officer to have him taken—but he has not yet caught him.—

We have had another case of small pox—it occurred on Friday or Saturday.—

Mrs Bryan desires to be affectionately remembered by you [*illegible*]

Very truly
Yr friend relative
Jn. H. Bryan

[*Addressed*] The Hon. E. Pettigrew
H.R.
Washington City
[To/]

Ebenezer Pettigrew to John Herritage Bryan A&H, BRYAN

H.R. June 17, 1836.

My dear Sir,

Your favours of May 23, & June 6th came safe to hand. The letter to Slye or Hall was given a safe conveyance by one of the clerks.

I regret exceedingly, in truth it was with great sorrow that I learned that it was apprehended, your little Octavia has choria. I most sincerely hope it will be found not so. I never think of the disease without shuddering and my soul sinks within me, and how many hours have I spent thinking or fearing that some one of my dear younger children might take the disease.

I am very much obliged by your attention to my business. Demps is a durty dog & I should not care if he was to die.

The house has at last come to the determination to quit or scatter on the 4th July and no one is more rejoyced at the emancipation from this body of sin &c, &c, &c &c, &c &c than I am. My energy is entirely paralised, and though fatter & in <in> good health to all appearances yet without strength to put on my cloths with/out/ resting, and the mind as much affeced as the body. The Lord have mercy on the poor wretch who is condemned to spend his time here. I had almost as lieve go with /a/ son to his grave as to see him in my situation.

You will see by the papers that we had a continued session of 25 hours, in which there was some sharp words between Mr Bynum &

Mr Jennefer of Maryland, which enventuatd in a duell on tuesday morning last.[1] Six shot was exchanged without effect and they shook hands and quit.

I shall be very much pleased to learn of Sister Mary taking a trip to some of the watering places hoping it might give health & some little recreation & relaxation from the constant scene at Newbern and should be much pleased that Mary Pettigrew could go, but I fear that she will be too many when she takes those other children that ought to go.

I could wish to know whether my note in the bank of Newbern could be renewed or whether it would be expected to be paid up. My reasons are simply these for the questions. My first cargo of corn was shipped to New York & sold on a credit. The proceeds will be due on the 11th of August. The next cargo was ordered to Boston & to be sold for cash. The head winds delayed the vessil so long at sea that it was thought by the Captain prudent after having the cargo in 20 days to run into New York, and there the cargo was found to be hot & in such a state as to make it necessary that it should be stored, and consequently nothing can be realised from it yet. The remain/in/g corn I have direted not to be shipped untill my return. also my wheat, which (though the likelyest crop I have had for years) I am informed by my overseer has been very much injured by the 15 days rain at the very time when wheat wants none. The partial but much more total destruction of the wheat crop as far as I have heard from all parts of country which information is extensive has given every reason to suppose that wheat will be high when that information is realised, and I am hesitating whether I will /not/ hold my wheat over to the spring It must pay good interest, if I am not more mistaken than I ever was.

Mrs Shepard & James have not made their appearance here yet. It is probable that will take place some time in next week. William Shepard says he is tired out, and would be crazy in month more at this miserable place. Please to tell Mary Pettigrew that I sent her & her sister Mary [*sic*] some songs two or three months ago. I have also sent a number of documents to you & brother Charles & have had some anxiety to know whether they were received.

I shall be pleased to receive a letter in answer to this as soon as convenient. which you will please to direct to Cool Spring No. Ca.

With affectionate regards to Sister Mary & the dear children Please to assure yourself of my

sincere esteem & Regard
E Pettigrew

John H. [Bry]an esq

[*Addressed*] John H. Bryan esqr
Newbern
North Carolina

[1] Jesse Atherton Bynum was challenged to a duel by Daniel Jenifer. After the opponents fired six shots each with "no harm done" the duel concluded. *New Bern Spectator*, June 24, 1836.

Bynum (1797-1868) served in Congress from North Carolina as a Democrat, 1833-1841. He later moved to Louisiana. *Biographical Directory of Congress*, 642. Bynum was once called "that nuisance in the political world . . . turbulent and unbridled." Moore, *History of North Carolina*, I, 490.

Jenifer (1791-1855) served as a National Republican representative from Maryland, 1831-1833 and 1835-1841. *Biographical Directory of Congress*, 1119.

Richard S. Sims[1] *to William Shepard Pettigrew* UNC

Union College N. York July 22nd 1836—

Dear William.

Since now we are separated, and no longer permitted to enjoy, within the precincts of the same Alma mater, that deep flow of soul—that sweet communion of congenial feeling, which has heretofore characterised our intercourse, and rendered hallowed a thousand scenes of undying recollection, I know of no better means than the pen and the post office afford, to repair, even in a slight degree, the regretted but necessary eruption of that enjoyment. We have a great variety of character exhibitted in college out of so large a number of students. There are some here who write poetry, wear whiskers and swear fluently, and on every afternoon of a fair day may be seen walking the streets of Schenectady, puffing away at the butt end of a Spanish segar, and talking wisely of the politicks of the day. There is also another portion, the summit of whose ambition is to stand at the head of the merit roll; and therefore use all means fair and foul to accomplish the object of their wishes. Again there is a third order, who are excited to high and noble exertions not by present distinctions or college honours—You could scarcely offer them a more direct insult, than to spread out before them such paltry motives. They cast their eyes forward, and gather motives from the future; have referen/ce/ to the high and glorious rewards of a useful life, which meet their view on the one hand, and the disgrace of a mind grovelling in ignorance and darkness which presents itself on the other. They know well that the petty distinctions and honours of college, are the glittering toys which are held up for the purpose of coaxing a few grown up children to study their lessons, and whose little minds are incapable of appreciating the force of nobler and loftier motives. They admire the honour and dignity of that student, who, trampling with scorn on all these little distinctions, explores the depths of science from a relish of its beauties; who acts from the deep conviction, that his mightiest efforts are necessary for success, and that glory has woven her choicest garland for the brow of him who gives up the golden years of his existence, to the pursuit of literature. Such men as these are destined to be ornaments of society, and to be remembered with gratitude, when the whole tribe of college wits shall have vanished like the insects of a day. You mentioned in your last that Wilder was sadly disappointed in his expectation of being elected representative. This exactly illustrates a rule Wm S— we have often talked over together and applied to the different characters in college Viz. that plans may be formed and great diligence employed to put them in exicution—but unless the foundations of exertion be laid in honourable and noble motives, all the superstructures will fall and crumble into dust, and like "the baseless fabrick of a vision leave scarce a wreck behind." Commencement will be here on the 27th of this month, after which we shall have a vacation of six weeks. We are expecting a fine time at commencement as there will probably be two or three hundred ladies up from N. York & Albany, and some from Saratoga Springs besides those that reside in Schenectady. I expect to remain here and at Saratoga Springs together during the vacation, as the distance is too great for me to think of going home. I want you to answer this letter as soon as convenient after you receive it, and write me all the news about your commencement and also the report of the several classes.

My respects to all enquiring friends.

I am with the greatest respect and esteem

your sincere friend and humble Servant.
Richard S. Sims

[*Addressed*] Mr. William S. Pettigrew
Chapel Hill
North Carolina

[1]Richard S. Sims may be the student named Sims mentioned in Charles Lockhart Pettigrew to William Shepard Pettigrew, January 1, 1834, in this volume. Possibly he attended Hillsborough Academy with William Shepard Pettigrew.

James Alfred Pearce[1] *to Ebenezer Pettigrew* A&H

Chestertown [*Maryland*] Augs 2d 1836

My Dear Sir,

<Wh> I do not know that I gave you any intimation of my intention to inflict a letter upon you, occasionally; but I have persuaded myself, that you will not be sorry to hear from me. It was impossible for me to part from a mess, with whom I have been so pleasurably associated for seven months, without feelings of regret; or to avoid recurring, frequently, to the recollection of them.

You will not, I am sure, suspect me of any affectation when I say that, besides this, a desire to give you some evidence of the regard, which our familiar intercourse for so long a <period> session has ripened into the most sincere esteem, prompts me to interrupt your quiet at Lake Phelps. If this be not a good reason to give, it is the only one; for there is nothing else on which I could build up a letter at present. In my retired way of life there is nothing happening of any interest to persons at a distance—scandal is plenty; but that we ought to leave to the ladies tea table, where they say there is a prescriptive right for that sort of talk: and a discourse upon politicks, unless very unlike most of those we heard last winter, you would probably postpone for a dose of epecachuana. If I were to indulge in the strain most congenial to my present mood, I should give you a fit of the blues, for I am well nigh hipped myself. My family are almost all sick. My Aunt has had a hemorrhage of the lungs.—My cousin, a young man living with me, has been laid up by a rheumatic affection Mrs Pearce is unwell a I am grumpy myself. My little daughter is the only one of the family not out of sorts.—But these are only temporary evils, which a little cupping and bleeding, a sulphur bath, and a dose of rhubarb may cure. But the *consumption of the purse* which afflicts the most of my fellow citizens what shall cure?—I am satisfied that the county in which I reside will not yield wheat enough for the fall sowing—The hard winter, the fly, and then the scab have ruined all our crops—The best farms will not yield 3 for 1; and in many instances, within my knowledge, the crops have not given ½ a bushel for one. It is even worse with the rye growers, and the corn promises no better. The long rains in May and June, followed by a drought of nearly six weeks duration, and [*illegible*] is not yet terminated, have scalded and burnt the growing corn, so that many farmers will not make more than enough for their own consumption. These are our only staples, and when they *all fail*, general embarrassment must ensue—a French traveller, Volney,[2] I think, predicted that this country, in the course of time, would become liable to famine, and great earthquakes. This prediction seems likely to be verified in part, and if the sins of the people and the Government recieve an exact retribution, I do not know that we shall not have the whole prophecy fulfilled.—

I found my professional business gave me a great deal of trouble when I returned to my office. It was up hill work, and now I am impatient to get off on my western trip. Perhaps I may reach our frontier states, in time to see old Granny Gaines,[3] and the Mexicans clapper claw one another. [H]is march to Nacogdoches is a most extraordinary and improper step, prompted by no other motive, whatever may be professed, but a disposition to assist the Texians

I have very little respect for the Mexican character, and I abhor the conduct of their commanders, in massacreing their prisoners;

but as between Mexico and the US good faith ought to be preserved, in spite of our sympathies.
Our treaty stipulations have not been enforced as they should have been—the violation of them has been winked at, and now, I suppose, we are about to interfere openly.

This "infamous thirst of gold" is the well spring of all Texian patriotism, and of the most of our sympathy. It is a vile world, and wags wickedly—

Present me to your son if he be with you—Mrs Pearce desires me to present her kindest regard to you— For myself. accept the assurance of the

sincere esteem with which I am yrs
Jas Alfred Pearce

[*Addressed*] For.
The. Honble. E. Pettigrew
M.C.
Coole Spring
Washington Cy
N. Carolina

[1]James Alfred Pearce (1805-1862), a Whig, served in the House of Representatives from Maryland, 1835-1843, and then in the United States Senate, 1843-1862. He was a man of broad cultural interests who formed "warm and deep friendships." *DAB*, XIV, 352-353.

[2]Constantin Francois de Chasseboeuf, Comte de Volney (1757-1820), was a French scholar who wrote about his travels. *Webster's Biographical Dictionary*, 1528.

[3]Pearce might refer to Edmund Pendleton Gaines (1777-1849), who had participated in various Indian wars and was commander of the western department of the army. *CDAB*, 323.

Receipt for Bill Paid to New Bern Jailer UNC

[*August 5, 1836*]

Mr E Petegrew

1836	To David Lewis	Dr
June 7	for 20 Days Jail fees of Negro Man Gi[*illegible*] @ 4/	$8.00
	Blankets 20 days @ 2½ pr day	.50
	Reward for Apprehending him	10.00
	Receieving and Discharging 6/	.60
		$19.10

Recd payment Augt 5th 1836

David Lewis

Charles Lockhart Pettigrew to Ebenezer Pettigrew UNC

New York August 9th 1836

Dear Father

I am now about to leave this place to proceed up the Hudson river, and write you some thing with respect to my future plans. I shall go to Niagara and then down lake Ontario and the St Lawrence to Montreal, I shall also visit Boston. I arrived in Philadelphia on saturday about 2 Oclock after I left Plymouth. I remained there a day and made some inquires about Grandma—fortunately as soon as landed and went to the Mansion House I met Joe. S. Jones who gave me some information as to where Grandma boarded: I called there and found that she had left the city about a week since for Newport. I immediately repaired to New York at which I am at present but shall leave in the morning I have concluded not to go to New Haven. I was much astonished to find that captain Dunbar had come into port, I saw him at Mr Bryan's office: he says that as soon as he got out of the bar the winds began to blow from the south he therefore could not proceed and moreover he had heard from vessels immediately from that port that corn was /very low/ he then determined to go to Providence, but after he he had proceeded a days voyage the wi/n/de came round to the north <again> again and looked as if it would stay there at least a week, to proceed was impossible so he concluded that he would try to get to <Boston> the south. He there went back untill he came to the bar when to his astonishment the wind changed again. He at length /reached/ this port on Friday last. The corn sold for 96 cts and on the same morning Mr Bryan got a letter from [*John*] Williams[1] Charleston saying that corn was worth from 68 to 82 cts. Capt Dunbar attributes the fall of corn in Charleston to the fact that the northerly wind carried so many vessels there. I have not been able to assertain the price of corn in Providence. I have bought me a watch and key for $145 a very nice one indeed; I shall <endeavour>, dear father, <to> keep it as a memento of /your/ affection, and always endeavour to act worthy of that affection. I have also bought some cloths. I drew upon Mr Bryan for $[4]00,00 which I think will be sufficient. I will write you again <this> soon

Your affectionate son
Charles L Pettigrew

Mr & Mrs Collins are here and quite well I dined with them at Mrs Riggs' to day.

Capt Dunbar will take home all the articles except the negro /cloth/ which may be delay<ed> because Mr Bryan says he is expecting a very superior article. The axes come as near as they could be got, I went with Mr Bryan to look for them and these were the best that could be found, the axes were all too light about 5¼ and 5½: these are from 6 to 7 pounds each

[*Addressed*] Hon E. Pettigrew
Cool Spring
Washington Co
N. Ca.

---

[1]John Williams, apparently a native of Baltimore, was a commission merchant in Charleston, South Carolina, who marketed Ebenezer Pettigrew's corn to nearby rice planters and retailers. He seems not to have sold goods to Pettigrew but to have deposited his credit as directed to other agents, several times to banks in Baltimore.

Charles Lockhart Pettigrew
to William Shepard Pettigrew UNC

Niagara falls Aug 20th 1836

Dear brother

You will perceive from the head of my letter that I have at length arrived at the far-famed falls of Niagara—the wonder of the world; and I must tell you that I am highly gratified; so far from being disappointed I think that they are worth a journey from North Carolina, and that the man who has never seen them has some thing in reserve which will one day afford him the greatest pleasure;

I was at Saratoga a few days observing the forms and fassions of the day; their were there about 2,000 people and they of all sorts and descriptions; every one seemed disposed to exhibit <th> him or her self to the best advantage; only a few invalids were there I suppose it was too gay; for each week there were 3 balls and 3 hops (perhaps you dont under stand that word it means an<d> inferior ball) so that sunday was the only night in the 7 that all was quiet. We had music at our meals; A band was engaged by 3 of the public houses which staid at each of the houses two days in the week and played when ever it was wanted.

I saw Dick Simms <as> when I passed through Schenectady for Saratoga; he seemed very glad to see me. I took him by supprise I arrived at schenectady at night and went early next morning to see him, when I got to his boarding house I went to his room and /he/ was in bed and was only a woke by the noise at his door, he is very well pleased with /his/ situation. I bought me a fine gold watch in New-York for $145. I am very tired walking about the falls and climbing the banks of the river which are very high and steep. You must excuse the short ness of this letter for I know you expect a longer one but it is the only time that I /have/ touched pen /to paper/ except when I wrote to father from New-York, and my hand is so unsteady I can hardly write. I will write again soon. You can direct your letter to Boston if you will write sufficiently early for your letter to get there by the 1st of Oct at which time I leave that place. I go<t> to Montreal to morrow then to Quebec thence to Burlington thence to Boston. I am on the British side of the falls in Canada

Your affectionate brother
Charles L Pettigrew

Charles Lockhart Pettigrew to Ebenezer Pettigrew UNC

Quebec Sept 5th 1836

Dear Father

I have at length arrived at this place from which I shall make the best of my way home: it begins to be a little cold here, and indeed it ought to be <a>so far North; <a> there have been several frosts although I believe none of them very severe. I wrote you from Niagara falls, which I left the day after the date of my letter; I came down the lake in a very pleasant boat, I stoped a night at Toronto the capital of Upper Canada and the residence of the governor of that province; fortunately for myself the lake was very very smooth the day and night that I was in it, there was scarcely a wave to be seen, so that I was not the least sick, I was also very comfortably situated in my passage down the river St Lawrence, the scenery on this river is remarkably beautiful and attractive. I was very much disappointed in Montreal, the streets are narrow and verry dirty It is indeed not worth going to see except to gratify one's curiosity I found, when I reached Montreal that uncle Frederick and his lady had left that place only two days on their way home, also general Bl[*o*]unt & his family left at the same time. From Montreal I proceeded immediately to Quebec and arrived here on <Saturday> Sunday night week. I will relate to you a little circumstance which perhaps may may be /as/ amusing to you as it was fortunate to myself. As I was coming from Montreal to this place I was conversing with a gentleman and in the course of my remarks to told him that I saw in one of the papers that Graham[1] had been returned to Congress by a majority of about 1,000, he went away and brought up another gentleman who asked me was I very certain of that, I told him I was and gave him my authority and moreover <tho> told him that it was more than probable that the whole state would go against the little magician; We of course entered into /an/ argument with respect to the merits of the respective candidates, and I gave him my reasons for not prefering Mr Van Buren and what I thought of the party at <w>Washington; I would assert such and such things upon the authority of the papers and he would deny saying that he was there at the time; he finally told me that he was a member of Congress and knew what he said to be so. I was perfectly astonished and asked his pardon for being so positive as I would not put my knowled[*ge*] of the political state of the country in comparason to his since it was his duty to study it. We became acquainted and he treated me very politely while he remained and introduced me to several of his relations and acquaintances in Quebec. So that I feel very <gratefu> grateful to him for his politeness. His name is Dudley Farlin[2] /of New York/; he is a complete Jackson Van Buren man but I believe sincere in his choice of a president.

I met with <w>a young gentleman, who is taking the Northern tour, having been but a short time from France; he intends also next spring visiting most of the towns /in the South west/ but will spend the winter in some part of the United States. We became acquainted </with him/> at Quebec and he, wishing to get a more thorough knowledge of our language than he has, intends spending the winter with some person who can speak it well; he speaks French well and fluently having been educated in France. He offers to teach me the language if I will but allow him to reside with me in order that he may from hearing me speak, improve himself in English. I myself much approve of the measure as it will be my only opportunity of leaning a tongue /with/ which most educated persons are now acquainte[d.] It will [n]ot prevent me from attending to my business as I can devot[e] the eve[nings] after I return to the house to that study; they are very long and we[ll] afford ample time: The presence of this gentleman will be no inconvenience to <me as> you as you will be at Washington. I informed him that I would let him know at Norfolk wither my engagements would permit me to learn the language at that time. I shall dear father make my arrangements so as to reach that place by the 15th Oct I shall there-fore expect an answer from you on that subject at that place I submit to your better judgement altho I hope it m/a/y approve of my wishes, for I can assure you it shall not interupt my business. I am very anxious father to hear from you to know how you are and whether you have escaped the fall diseases. I hope I shall find a letter in the Boston post office when I reach that place. I wish very much to hear from home and my relations. Give my respects to Mr & Mrs Davenport and Mr Brickhouse

Your affetionate son
Charles L Pettigrew

I wish the 20th Oct to come quickly
I leave /in/ a day or two for Boston and shall carry my letter and have it mailed there as I shall have to pay the British government and it may be delayed if I put it in here

C. P.

[*Addressed*] Hon. E. Pettigrew
Cool-Spring
Washington Co.
North Carolina.

---

[1]James Graham (1793-1851), a Whig, was an attorney in Rutherford County who had sat in the state legislature and in the United States House of Representatives, 1833-1835. His election to the Twenty-fourth Congress was contested by David Newlands and a new election was held. Charles Pettigrew's letter refers to this election. Graham subsequently served until 1843 and again in 1845-1847. *Biographical Directory of Congress*, 964; Cheney, *North Carolina Government*, 745.

[2]Dudley Farlin (1777-1837), a Democrat, had been a presidential elector on the Jackson-Van Buren ticket in 1832 and served in Congress, 1835-1837. *Biographical Directory of Congress*, 875.

Peter Evans to Ebenezer Pettigrew A&H

Sparta Septr 6th 1836

Ebenezer Pettigrew Esqr:

My Dear Sir:

I am at present, on a short visit to this place & have some leisure moments, that I can spare to the addressing of you a few lines.—I will here tender you my many thanks for your attention to me, in forwarding me, so many valuable documents.—I find some of them very interesting, on many subjects that concerns the planters.—

You must have had a tiresome session of it—and I expect there never has been one, better calculated to disgust a man of your nice feelings—But, let me tell you; the *bubble is bursted* & we shall not have the like again soon—those base scroundrels—have been told their own so well, by [Wise], and others; and there is now a split in the [pa]rty—So the people can have time to pause & see what has been done by their public agents—& the old chief, will soon lose his influence & without *that phantom* they will not be able to move an inch.—as was anticipated by all of the thinking whigs—you now see, when it is left to Van Buran, He will go to the walls—He has no claims upon the earth—or the people, for any favour: He has never studied their interest in a single act of his life: his whole life has been made up on taking care of himself, at the expense of friends &

foes; and it is the most astonishing thing to me, that any southern man, can for a moment—think of supporting such a man: every act of his life has been against Southern interest—I now am firmly of the belief, he has no chance of reaching the presidency:—Virginia will profit from the late course of NC. & I hope will decide against him & if she does, his fate is sealed. I feel sorry to hear you express so much dislike to your situation in Congress, and hope you will not think of declining tendering your services to the district, untill we can get some man to take your place that can carry the vote of the district against such a base party—for I do not believe there ever was a baser party, formed in any civilized government.—is it not strange /that/ the people have suffered them to go to such lengths: the party, would not have given up the surplus [revenue]—But, from pure fear of their constituants; the people began to speak a language, that they could not misunderstand—& they became alarmed: it did not proceed from honesty.—they know after Genl Jackson, retired—they could not sustain themselves under Van Buren—& those that had some regard for honesty, were afraid to continue in that course any longer.—Their conduct was so [*illegible*]ably exposed by the whig party—that they became alarmed—& turned: for base men, are always cowardly. I never have known a party to receve such a drubbing; & old Jackson will make my words true; that he [would] ruin the government & go out disgraced:—see the course, he is pursuing in Tennessee; what a Humilleating reflection it is, to see such a man engaged in such dishonourable business—& how severely he will feel the effects of such conduct, when he retires into private life—and can hear & feel what the people think of his administration. you must not think of giving up the ship yet, & let me advise you, not to express you disgust too freely to every body—your enemies will use it against you—as the people will not hear any thing like a slight: they cannot bear to hear, their agents, complain—of their situation:—they think there is no man but ought to think himself—highly honoured, to be placed in your situation—according to my judgment, I think your course, has been entirely unexceptionable—& if you do not injure your self—by using thoughtless expressions—you will have but little trouble to keep down any man they can start—I have never heard of any of the party, taking any exceptions to any of your votes on any thing you have done—whilest in Congress—and you owe it to your self, to your district & to *your country*, to hold on untill some suitable person can be fixed on to take your place; and this cannot be done for these 3 years to come. They speak of running [*illegible*] Wilson;[1] He is their best chance, & you will beat him, at least, 1000 votes—and after he is put down—the party will separate & we then can have matters arranged to suit our views—

I would like very much for you to visit me at Egypt in Chatham County. I can only promise you a plenty to eat, & the sight of a pretty farm—with a good crop on it—It is a healthy section of the state—& if you can spare the time—you had as well come up & visit as you will see many of your [*illegible*] who will be glad to see you—& at Pittsbo—you can spend some time very pleasantly—there is good society in that place in the summer. If you cannot come up, write me—& let me hear how your crops are in Tyrrell & Washington—we shall not make more than half the corn we did last year in this county & the cotton, do not promise much more than the corn—should it be an early fall—we shall not make half cotton crop,—direct your letters to—Haywood Chatham County.—

very sincerely & truly
your ob^{t} sv^{t}
Peter Evans

[*Addressed*] To the Honourable
Ebenezer Pettigrew
Cool Spring Post office
Washington County NC

---

[1]The candidate was a prominent Democrat, Louis D. Wilson (1789-1847) of Edgecombe County. A longtime member of the General Assembly who sat in the Constitutional Convention of 1835, Wilson later died of disease while serving as an officer in the Mexican War. Alan D. Watson, *Edgecombe County: A Brief History* (Raleigh: Division of Archives and History, Department of Cultural Resources, 1979), 33-35; R. D. W. Connor, *North Carolina: Rebuilding an Ancient Commonwealth, 1584-1925* (1929; reprint edition, Spartanburg, South Carolina: Reprint Company, 2 volumes, 1973), I, 571-572.

Charles Lockhart Pettigrew to William Shepard Pettigrew UNC

Lake Phelps Oct 26th 1836

Dear brother

I have at length arrived home and glad to have a quiet rest from travel: there is nothing that will not after so long a time produce satiety and to an ordinary mind the continual change of traveling is as wearisome after a while as the most monotinous uniformity. I was much pleased with my jaunt and I hope that it will prove to me a source of great advantage.

I received your kind letter at Boston and was much surprised at its contents: I intended to have answered it in Philadelphia but was prevented by not staying at that place as long as I expected. I should have <m> been much gratified if you <could> ha<ve>d graduated, but as I wrote father, according to your statement it was all for the best; I hope however that you may well improve the remainder of your time at College which is but short.

You doubtless wish to know how I have proceeded in my journey, since I left Niagara falls. From this place I went to Lake Ontario and took the steam-boat to Toronto the capital of Upper Canada, from thence I continued down the lake stop<p>ing at several towns on the margine; I continued down the river st Lawrence to Montreal; the scenery of this river is most beautiful and it has deservedly been the theme of many a beautiful description. I was not much pleased with Montreal, the streets are very narrow and disagreeable and in many instances the side walks are so contracted that two persons can with difficulty walk abreast. There are about forty thousand inhabitants in this place. I next visited Quebec, about 180 miles below Montreal; this city is complete walled around, (I mean all the city proper). The city proper is situated on the top of a hill <about> between 2 and 3 hundred feet high; a large proportion /of the business/ is done with out the walls in What is called the lower town. The views about Quebec are more beautiful than any in any other part of America, and from the top of the citidel you can see for many miles all around, immediately around the city, the country is thickly inhabited <which gives a> and the houses are all painted white which /is/ a beautiful addition to the general pearance of the country. I was on the celebrated plains of Abraham during a most splendid /review/ of <the> /three/ British regiments in full dress, stood on the spot where the great Wolfe fell <was /saw/> was near the place where the galant Montgomery was killed when attacking the citidel and saw the position of the cannon that shot him. From Quebec I passed thro the lower part of Canada and Maine; I stopped at most of the towns in M. I then continued on to Boston to Providence, Hertford, New Haven and then to New York again.

When I got home I found father very ill with a bilious fever but I am glad to say he soon recovered. I hope his journey will not have any bad effect upon him.

I wish you would send me [*by*] father my college diploma and the seal to my society diploma, also, since You are not studying French I should like if you could spare them, that you would send me your Dufief. I hope dear brother that you will write me frequently, and let us act as we ought to act and as I feel forgeting any unkind expression that may ever have passed between us, for we should all be of a forgiving disposition as we hope to be forgiven.

Father will give you this letter

I am your affetionate brother
Charles L. Pettigrew

[*Addressed*] Mr William S. Pettigrew
Chapel Hill

James Johnston Pettigrew to Ebenezer Pettigrew UNC

Lake Phelps Dec 6 1836

My Dear Father

I hope you have arrived safe in Washington and you have not been stoped by the cold weather D[r] Bell going to move to Plymouth next week and he says that I will be cured in a week or so, brother Charles had a little cold but he has got well of it, M[r] Davenport sends his respetcs to you. the farm is doing pretty smart brother Charles went to preaching and left me home, brother Charles saw M[rs] Haughton and she invited him to stay 2 or 3 days. M[r] Collins has arriveed. we had a verry hard rain the Night before last but not as to stop the ploughers.

brother Charles got a long verry well but with one whom he had to whip he thinks he will do better, I am verry <muc> much pleased that musket which you sent me they are a great many ducks the lake as well as squirrils in the woods, we are done gathering corn all but the beetree feild, we have <done> /killed/ another beef yesterday evening, brother Charles rode his mare out to belgrade last week, they are a plenty of birds in the field, brother Charles let me shoot twice at a hawk but did not kill him with his shot gun brother Charles says that he try and shoot some duks with my musket brother Charles sends his love to you

Your affectionate son
James Johnston Pettigrew

[*Addressed*] Hon. E. Pettigrew
H.R.
City of Washington

*Ebenezer Pettigrew to Josiah Collins** A&H

Copy

Washington City Dec 7, 1836

My dear Sir

I rise (12 oclk) from a sick bed to write you on the subject which we had been talking &c &c. I had taken cold before I left Carolina, which has continued to increase and last night I was much inconvenenced by fever, head ache & a slight pain in my breast. I am better now, but shall not go out today as the air is cold & damp.

Genl. Jackson is in a very feble state & I think it highly probable will not see the end of his term, but I hope he will, in as much as I want no parade of funerals, nor of any other sort while I am here and farthermore it will cost the nation a million of dollars. Even a funeral of one of us poor devils, costs five thousand.

On the subject of a Partnership in the silk culture[1] with you. I have concluded to unite with you provided the sum which I can now advance without being too much cramped, will suit your convenience at this time. I can draw on New York for seven hundred dollars & I have a note of Doctor Warrens on which there are upwards of three hundred dollars due, which sum I suppose he would pay on presentment & would have paid long before this had he not forgotten its existance. These two amounts will make, say one thousand dollars and I may receive some money due by the County and in the county by individuals when I return home. I expect after six months to be in funds for any sum that the concern may call for on my part unless something may turn up over which I can have no control. I should now be above the present demand but my mother in her last will left to my son Charles a legacy to be paid him when he arrived at age & I had told him previous to my conversation with you that the money arising from the sale of my wheat should be paid to him.

On the receit of this you will please to write to me your conclusions and if you should think proper to form a partnership, you will take the necessary steps to that effect.

This is a most extravagant place. As one evidence, I am paying $15 a week board. I am with the same gentlemen (except poor Mr Goldsborough) who formed the mess last year. In the same house & room, so that it seems more like home; a home I hope never to claim after the 4th March next.

We are going to the devil & I have not vanity enough to think for a moment that I can put a stop to the journey one hour, and therefore cannot see any reason for my sacrifising all the *little* the *very little* composure which has fallen to my lot in my later days.

With my best respect to Mrs Collins

I am your friend & obd^t^ srvt.
E Pettigrew

Josiah Collins [Jr.] Esqr

[1]The enthusiasm for silk culture swept North Carolina and other southern states after 1828 for two decades. The species of mulberry tree known as *Morus multicaulis* was extensively cultivated at this time. Unfortunately, the speculation in trees overshadowed the production of silk itself and eventually there was a collapse of the boom, with orchards of dead mulberry trees standing where once there had been budding hopes. Ashe, *History of North Carolina*, II, 387; William F. Leggett, *The Story of Silk* (New York: Lifetime Editions, 1949), 332-336. The *Newbern Spectator*, October 4, 1839, carried advertisements for *Morus multicaulis* trees and silkworm eggs for sale.

Charles Lockhart Pettigrew to Ebenezer Pettigrew UNC

Lake Pheps Dec 14th 1836

My dear Father

We have had some very cold weather since I last wrote you, but I hope that you have not experienced any ill effect from it; the snow was as deep as ever I remember to have seen it, however notwithstanding the great fall, the snow melted very rapidly the two first days then there came a rain which completely cleared the ground of its white coat.

Mr Davenport killed the hoggs on the day after the snow, there were 55 of them and they /made/ an average of a fraction <of> /over/ 152 apiece they were fine looking, one of them went as high as 257 and there was one that weighed 54. Also on the same day he killed 4 beeves which weighed somewhat more than 1300 weight, there is one more <f> beef to kill. Old Charles attended to the fat and brought in not but a little over two barrells, and Mr Davenport and myself concluded that he has kept back a considerable portion of it, he however protests his innocence so that we concluded to let you see it and determine for yourself whether it is all there since you know how much ought to come from hoggs so fat.

Mr Davenport has <done> finished plowing one half of the Bee tree field and there only remains the middle and the other half of the Beetree. he also has a little more than half of the field before the house plowed.

I have rather a bad account to give of your corn-sheller Mr Brickhouse and Mr Davenport were trying the machine by hand on Sunday last when one of the wheels of the power <broak> broke, Mr Davenport s/a/ys it is the smallest wheel that there is, for I have not seen it since /the/ accident: moreover Mr D. informed me that whenever there were a good /many/ ears in, the band would slip, so that I suppose you will have to get a chain-band. Mr D. says he does not like it and swears that he can eat the corn as fast as it can shell it. However pa before I write you again I will see Mr Brickhouse and know all about /it/ and write you what he thinks best to be done, and what is really the matter with it.

Mr Davenport has recieved a new <case> /instance/ of provocation from Mr Dempsey Spruill. The evening that Mr D. was done with the hogs he sent most of the forces to Belgrade as there was nothing here to do: as the hands were going along Mr S. looked at them and saw Arthur and says to him you are the d——m scoundrel that stole my hogs and your master has brought you up to it, and with that Mr S. run after him <un> but the negro ran into the swamp and thus saved himself: this is the tale that Arthur and Mack tells. Mr D. says that on sunday last he Mr Brickhouse and Mr Woodley were riding along the road and that they were abusing

Mr S. when lo they came across Mr S. laying /in weight/ as Mr D. says, to catch his negros and whip them, that Mr S. heard all they /is/ said but stood and grinned and looked as mean as a man could look. I think that in as much as you have hired Mr D.'s negro he is yours for the time being and that your negros ought certainly to be able to go about your business. I being in your place here feel myself bound to protect your property from the aggressions of other men. So that if it meets with your approbation I will speak to Mr Spruill about it and also the case of Jeff. And if he sh/o/uld continue so to act notwithstand what I will tell him I would ask you how then to act or what redress to take.

16th Dec

Mr Davenport recievd a note from Mr Halsey purporting that the articles which you sent had arrived, and this morning I have sent for them. I am very much obliged to you f[or] them. I also sent to Columbia for 2 bushels of coarse salt suppos[i]ng that [*torn*] would not be enough. I have also the intelligence to [commu]nicate to you that Mr L. D. Wilson has some time since declared himself a candidate whether you oppose or not. Mr Davenport as well as myself are very anxious to know whether this has wrought any change in your views. I myself would greatly prefer your not coming out since it affords you no pleasure and the winters are attended with great danger to your health; withal if you were not to drink it might cost you your election after much effort. The people will immediately say that since you had got to Congress your had become too proud to drink with them You<r> are aware by this time of Dr Bell's intention to leave us, but he says he will come down from Plymouth to see Johnston untill he is perfectly recovered he is improving there are no appearances on his hands and the sores on his body (which are 3 or 4) looked much deadened I think that he must be entirely free. /in a mo/u/nth/ Johnston wished me to give his love to you Mr Dav[e]nport his also and believe me your affectionate son

Charles L Pettigrew

Please give my love to Uncle William and my best respects to Gov Kent and Mr Pearce

[*Addressed*] Hon E. Pettigrew H.R.
City of
Washington

*Ebenezer Pettigrew to Dempsey Spruill** A&H

Copy to Dempsey Spruill

[*Washington, D.C.*] Dec 26, 1836

Sir,

In a letter from my son I have been informed of an act of yours, which I think it my duty to take notice of, it being the second & is satisfactory evidence to me of your unfriendly desposition to me. The first act is Your driving Jeff away from your house because he had been sent by M[r] Davenport with a message which M[r] Davenport was induced to send to Capt Dudley from the anxiety I had expressed /to him/ to get my flats which I had hired to Captain Dudley in time for the delivery of my wheat. The next is your late attack on Arther when passing between my two plantations. In the first place I wish you to understand that I have hired Arther from his master M[r] Davenport and while I have him hired he is mine. And, really things have come to a fine pass that I cannot send a message to a man at your house because my words pass from the mouth of M[r] Davenport to the negro who delivers the message and that my negroes can not pass along the road by your house from one plantation to the other without your attemping to beat them. Sir I shall consider these acts as intended for me because I have not joined with you in your venom towards M[r] Davenport and I shall not put up with such any more.

In the name of common sense are you so full of bitterness towards M[r] Davenport that you cannot see a poor slave that calls him master, but of which slave I am now the master without wishing to beat him. If that is your nature & desposition you must certainly be one of the most malignant men on earth and if you continue to indulge in such a temper there is no telling what you will not get to before you end your few remaining days in this world according to the ordinary <course of nature> length of human life. I have not taken part in your quarrel with M[r] Davenport except <to> in endeavouring to restrain his feelings, but perhaps that is my offense to you & the cause of your conduct, but Be assured that neither you nor any other person living in any way whatever can induce me to join against the innocent. No sir I am the last man living who would say guilty without there being guilt, and it was idle and foolish you at first to expect it, you ought to have known me better than to have hoped for such a thing.

I am not desirous that there should be any intercourse between yours & mine and you are perfectly <willing> welcome to drive away any & all of my negroes & every other person who may be a part of my household from any part of your premises, but Sir, they must be permited to pass along the common highway unmolested

& without interruption on ther good behaviour, and let me ask of you to read and recollect this letter for I say again, that I will /not/ put up with any /more/ arbitary acts from you in any shape. I am your &c

E Pettigrew

but believe me it is the last of my wishes to get in to difficulty with you, & I will <to> avoid them in all honourable ways, but without the slightest submission.

William Shepard Pettigrew to Ebenezer Pettigrew UNC

University of N. Carolina Jan. 12th 1837

Dear Pa

Knowing your anxiety to hear from me I take the first opportunity after my arrival to write.

My journey between Washington and Fredricksburg though not very pleasant was as much so as could be expected when you consider what the road generally is, the ground was frosen hard and we traveled quite safely with the exception of one upset, but by which no one had the misfortune of being hurt. The rest of my trip was safe. I was sorry to find after arriving at Raleigh that Uncle Bryan <an> had left together with Uncle James [*Shepard*] who had obtained his county court license. The bundle and letter I gave to Mr Guion to be sent to Newbern by the earliest opportunity.

In conclusion I will mention a high compliment which a gentleman who traveled in company from Washington told me he heard passed on you in that City by a distinguished man. "That you were too honest a man to be in Congress". Hoping at the same time that you would again be a candidate.

Please remember me to all who inquire, and particularly to Gov. Kent I am very well.

Believe me your
affectionate son
William S. Pettigrew

[*Addressed*] Hon E. Pettigrew
H.R.
Washington City

Ebenezer Pettigrew to John Herritage Bryan UNC

Washington Jan 14, 1837

My dear Sir,

I received your favour of the 5th about five ago and am much obliged to you for the contents. The die is cast. My letter declining a reelection is in the hands of the Printer & I expect will be sent out in all of next week. Confound this place altogether, but I find one other reason for declining.—which is that I am becoming more partizan, and am acquiring in spite of my exertions to the contrary a most unpleasant feeling towards the dishonest part of Congress, so much so that if I had no other reason it would be sufficient that I should quit. You know how imprudent I am in speaking of those who I think are scoundrals or that I dislike. God help us! I think there are in Congress as much dishonesty as among the same number of people in any part of the United States. The expunging resolutions will pass. I heard yesterday a most eloquent speech from Mr [*William Campbell*] Preston on the subject and one of the most violent replys from Rives.[1] R's words were very violent but his gestures & manner much more so, repeatedly shaking his fist in the most grog shop manner at Preston. It was very near <eque> equal to the house of R. and old John Adams. I thought Mr Preston made a very happy reply. I expect they will be in the Intelegencer. If so I would recommend the perusal of them to you. [*Thomas Hart*] Benton has as much the command of the Senate as you have of your office and the only hope the country can have of geting out from /the powers of/ this wretched party <in power> is a collision between Benton & Rives, as it is confidently asserted that they are both looking for the Presidency and hate each other. I fear this /is/ a vain hope for I apprehend the common rule will not apply in this case among these uncommon S——. that when rogues fall out, honest men come to their rights

The chairman of the Committee of ways & means has brought forth a bill to reduce the Tariff which will meet with violent opposition; and what will be the result no one can tell. At any rate I suspect it will consume the greater part of the session to the exclusion of the claim for French spoliations and some other important subjects.

So far there has been but few documents, what there has been I have sent you not long since. I mentioned to Wm B. S. your message about Frederick S's debt who says that he has as much as he can do to pay his own debts, and that he thinks Frederick will be able to pay to you the debt which he owes you next year after he makes a crop. Mr W. B. S. farther requests me to say to you that he would be glad if you would write him in answer to several letters which he has lately writen to you. Commidore, Biddle[2] is here on a court marshal and is staying in our mess.

I am glad to inform you that my health is improving for which I give credit to ante smoking & ante stimulating but I look badly and much broke, however that is nothing to me, so long as I have energy of mind and body. It is with great pleasure that I count up the weeks as they pass away, and look with great anxiety to the time when I shall be again as free as I was two years ago. It is said that the new elected Senator from Virginia is about to be off. There is a good deal of disease among the members, but none that I know very seriously ill except the one above mentioned. We have had a small fall of snow & it is quite cold.

I direct this letter to Newbern supposing from your remark /when/ with you that you will have left Raleigh before this can reach that place.

I hope you are well and that you have born the travil at this enclement seson without much suffering. Also that sister Mary & children are all well. Please to make my kind regards to her & all the children as well as my friends else where & believe me your friend & relation

E Pettigrew

[*Addressed*] John H. Bryan esqr
Newbern
North Carolina

---

[1]William Cabell Rives (1792-1868) of Virginia, a Whig, was a lawyer who had served in the state legislature. He was a member of the United States House of Representatives, 1823-1829, and of the Senate, 1832-1834, 1836-1839, and 1841-1845. *Biographical Directory of Congress*, 1524.

[2]James Biddle (1783-1848) of Philadelphia was a naval officer who held many important commands at sea. He was a brother of Nicholas Biddle. *CDAB*, 72.

Edward Stanly to Ebenezer Pettigrew A&H

Washington [*North Carolina*] Jany: 16th 1837

My Dear Sir,

Your letter of the 20 Ult: was received some time since, and would have been answered earlier, but I thought you had better have a resting spell, and not receive letters too fast, I know your duties in this particular are onerous, and the calls upon your time frequent and constant.—I am much indebted to your kindness for the information you sent me relative to the Missouri lands. I have been trying for the last three or four years to ascertain something upon this subject, but have been unsuccessful until now. Will you oblige me by presenting my grateful acknowledgments to Mr Harrison for his kindness, and tell him I shall follow his advice as to the Illinois lands, and without accident shall go there this ensuing summer.— As the next thing now to be done is,—to prevent these lands now redeemable, from being sold again, I must trouble you further; Will you ascertain from Mr Harrison whether there is any danger that the lands will be sold this year, and how I shall proceed to redeem them? If there is no immediate danger of their being sold. I will not trespass farther on your kindness or on his, but should the laws of Missouri, demand their sale before July or August next, Can you assist me farther in preventing this by advancing for me the requisite sum, or telling me how I can get funds to the proper place?—I have no means except through you, of procuring any information, as to the regulations of the land matters in the West. You know at Washington City, I could not find out anything, and now *land* is insight. I intend to keep a steady look out, until I reach the object in view.

I fear with you our country's affairs are in a most horrible condition,—but we must not despair. I still hope after Jackson is dead, and the reptiles who have crawled into power during his reign, will have lost his influence, that the eyes of a deluded people will be opened, and all things come right again.—I do not wish the death of Andrew Jackson or any other living creature, but I believe the County will lose nothing by it, and if he is alive on the 4th March next, I wish the people of Beaufort, to celebrate his retirement with "bonfires and illuminations" and to have a day of public prayer, to thank heaven, his reign is over, and pray, to arest the evils so justly apprehended from his successor.—Was there ever a parcel of greater fools and knaves, that those who now control our financial matters?—but I will write no more on these subjects,—you know more of them than I, and the more I think of them the more exasperated I feel.—

I hope you may be successful in your attempts, to procure an appropriation for another dredge boat—the operations of the one that was burnt I learn were of material service, and bid fair to do much more. Poor North Carolina. I hope her luck will take a turn, but there is very little prospect of it.—

I regret to hear your health is bad,—but I am not surprised at it; to be confined as much as you are, to see the workings of the dirty tools of party, to be thrown so continually among such a parcel of Rowdies, and many of those *Hon*: Representatives are, to witness the base sycophancy by which they have crawled, and are crawling into power, is enough to sicken any independent gentleman, who has any regard for decency, or ever felt one throb of patriotism.—But Do not despair There still be seven thousand, "who have not bowed the knee to Baal".—If it be possible, you must serve another term. I know this is contray to your wishes, but the political integrity of the district depends upon it; if you are a candidate, it seems to be generally understood, there will be no opposition, but if you withdraw, it will be "confusion more confounded" Our friend Toole[1] is *anxious* to offer, but I fear he would be badly beaten, and this seems to be the better opinion.—I have made a poor return for your favor in writing you so much nonsense, but excuse it, it was not done with "malice aforethought."—again, present my respects to Mr Harrison and accept the good wishes of your friend

Edw. Stanly

[*Addressed*] Hon: Ebenezer Pettigrew
House of Representatives
Washington City

[1]This may have been Henry Toole, who represented Pitt County in the North Carolina House of Commons in the 1831 session. Cheney, *North Carolina Government*, 297.

Ebenezer Pettigrew to William Shepard Pettigrew A&H

Washington Jan 20, 1837

My dear Son

I received your letter of the 13th with great pleasure, in as much as it informed me of your safe arrival at home. I should have liked <to> you had informed me what became of & how you got along with your /double barrel/ firelock.

Just praise is no flattery my son & knowing your nature to dispondency, it is with pleasure that I inform you, that the enquiries for you, & how you got along, and the remarks of your appearance & deportment by the mess, particularly Mrs Byard[1] & Miss Catherine were really gratifying. Mrs B. expressed a great deal of feeling for your sufferings in consequence of the coldness of the weather. Oh my dear Son continue to deserve that commendation by that only course which will insure your happiness in this world & in that to come. I enclose Mr Websters card, left for you the day you left. Now my dear son do not let the above have any improper weight in your mind. Take this with you from me & that it is my settled opinion from observation; that this is a most heartless place, *Nothing* but self is the order of the day here, and no one ought to believe anything which he hears without first taking all the circumstances into consideration and even then he may be most egrediously mistaken.

With this I send you my letter declining a candidacy again for Congress. I cannot express to you my pleasure at coming to that determination and that I had the firmness to resist all importunities to the contrary. I would rather be gibbeted than spend two more sessions here. I am much obliged to the Gentleman of this place who ever he may be. for <this> the good opinion expressed of me. If I deserve it now, I fear I should not at the end of another term. This place is enough to corrupt the devil in /one/ way or /an/other.

We are going on in the old way, but little doing and not much of that done to the advantage of the country. I look forward to the end of the next forty two days with great anxiety and pleasure.

My dear son I look back with great pleasure at the gratification & I hope pleasure which you received in <visiting> your visit to this and I hope you are satisfyed that the necessary sum expended in that visit was advanced as free as water by your father, but to give you an idea how money can go, I will for your satisfaction give you a statement of it. as follows.

Traveling to this place $30-00. pr. short Boots. $3.50—	$33-50
pr Gloves $1.00— 3 pr. stockings 1.55— Stock 1-50. Cash $10.—	14-05
Theater $1.00— Washing 55— Blanket 1-25—	2-80
Three weeks board at 13-00— $39-00 Traveling [home] $40—	79-00
	$129-35

My dear Son. I will again say it is money well spent. & I am gratified as much as you are and all I ask of you is do not be waistful & make unnecessary expenditures.

In conversation when here you asked me if I was willing for you to study Kents commentaries. and I gave you an indefinate answer. I now say that I wish you to study them, and as for the cost of the book It is well worth it for the library at home.

I got a letter two day ago from Mr Davenport dated Jan 5th in which he sends his & Mrs Ds compliments to you & that he will write you in a short time. He further informs me that your Brother Charles is sick at which I am very uneasy. I have not received a letter from Charls since 24 Dec. My health had continued to improve untill /within/ a few days, when I am declining from this miserable way of living say dining at five o clock With a blessing this next forty two days shall be the last of such suffering.

And now my dear son I will conclude this letter by wishing you to write often & may God Almighty Bless you is the prayer

of your affect. father
E Pettigrew

Mr W. S. Pettigrew

N.B. I am now very unwell

[*Addressed*] M^{r} W^{m} S Pettigrew
Chapel Hill
North Carolina

---

[1]This probably refers to the wife of Richard Henry Bayard (1796-1868), a United States senator from Delaware. Bayard practiced law and served in the Senate, 1836-1839 and 1841-1845. *Biographical Directory of Congress*, 528.

John F. Hughes[1] *to Ebenezer Pettigrew* A&H

Sparta N Ca Feby 3rd 1837

Hon E Petigrew

Dr Sir.

Your circular letter, dated "Washington City Jany 10th 1837", addressed to your constituents of this Congressional District, announcing your withdrawal as a candidate, for their suffrages, to the next Congress of the US, has been rec^{d} by me, in common with your other friends and constituents in this vicinity, and altho' my personal acquaintance with you, is extremely limited, I avail myself of the first <occasion> opportunity, to express my unfeigned regrets on the occasion and to assure you that, should you retire from /the/ strife of a political life, you will bear with you into retirement the thanks and best wishes of the *Whigs* of this Congressional District,—

I do not know of any period in our national history, so pregnant with coming events, and which cast their *shadows* with such ominous import, as the present—indeed, the *moral* of political life, seems to be fast sinking into the vortex of imbecility and depravity, and I am inclined to the opinion that this Republic, has passed its meridian splendour and now going down in corruption, amidst its own rays of glory,

Never did Egypt, when under the dominion of famine and the locust, experience a more deadly scourge, than this far famed Country, is now suffering from those political leaches, who are preying upon the vitals of our mangled Constitution, and who are daily and hourly making inroads, upon the integrity and virtue of our national character—

Did you know, (surely you do) that nothing in this wide world, so much resembles truth as falsehood—virtue as vice, then nothing in this wide world, resembles a corrupt Government more than an overflowing Treasury and irresponsible Agents—When I see those political maggots, fairly at work on the *marrow bones* of the Republic, I feel, as you very forcibly expressed at the conclusion of your Circular, "a disgust and indignation which I want language to express".

Mr Van Buren, has promised to follow in the footsteps of his predecessor, so we may expect more travelling

"Over ruts and ridges
And wooden bridges,
Made of planks
In open ranks,"

Be that as it may, I pray you to present the complements of a stranger, to those vigelent sentinels on <the> our "Watch Tower of Liberty," Messrs Peyton[2] and [*Henry Alexander*] Wise of the House of Reps and accept for yourself assurances of my distinguished consideration,

Your most Obdt Svt
Jno F Hughes

[*Addressed*] Hon E. Petigrew
House of Reps
Washington City

---

[1]John F. Hughes has not been identified. However, Sparta was undoubtedly the community later called Old Sparta in Edgecombe County on the Tar River. Powell, *North Carolina Gazetteer*, 363.

Other letters expressing sentiments similar to those given here were omitted from this volume but may be found in the Pettigrew collections at the North Carolina Archives and the Southern Historical Collection.

[2]Balie Peyton (1803-1878), an attorney, represented Tennessee in Congress as a Whig, 1833-1837. *Biographical Directory of Congress*, 1450-1451.

Invoice for Purchases by Ebenezer Pettigrew UNC

Baltimore Feb 7th 1837

Hon E Pettigrew

Bot of J. S. Eastman

1 oz	Early York	Cabbage	Seed	25
1 ″	Philadelphia	do	″	25
1 ″	Early Battersea	do	″	25
1 ″	drumhead Savoy	do	″	50
1 ″	Flat Dutch	do	″	50
2 ″	Early turnip	Beet	″	25

2 "	Long Blood	do	"	25
1 "	long orange	carrot	"	12½
2 "	fine sugar	Parsnip	"	25
2 papers	Early frame	peas	"	25
2 oz	long Scarlet	radish	"	25
2 "	white turnip rooted	do	"	25
1 "	yellow turnip rooted	do	"	12½
1 "	Early Bush	Squash—	do	12½
1 "	cocoa nut	do	"	12½
1 "	long green	do	"	12½
1 "	Early cabb	Lettuce		12½
1 paper	Large Lima	Beans		12½
1 "	red Speckled Valentine	do		12½
				$4.25

Rec^d payment

J. S. Eastman
Per Y. N. TURNER

Charles Lockhart Pettigrew to Ebenezer Pettigrew UNC

Lake Phelps Feb 16th 1837

Dear Father

In my letter last week I informed you that Johnston was quite well, and I am happy to say that he continues to improve in health, and is now perfectly well. But it is quite the contrary with myself I seem to improve very little, if at all, my cold and cough still continue to be troublesome, and I cannot tell when to expect it to get better. They are prevalent about the country and I understand from /Plymouth/ that many cases have proved fatal.

In your letter to me in which you enclosed the letter to Captain S. Spruill, you requested me to carry it to his house; but learning that he had gone to Charleston I concluded I would await his return; but he has not yet returned and some fears begin to be entertained that he is lost, he has not been heard of since he left the Bar A captain who went out with him says there was a considerable gale soon after they went out, he went to Charleston and had a considerable amount of replairs /done/ on his own vessel which delayed him sometime, but still he /neither/ heard nor saw any thing of him. I much fear that he has been blown somewhere entirely out of his reconing for I understand he is ignorant of navigation or been lost.

Mr Davenport is conducting the business with his usual expedition, although my being so unwell has prevented me from going to Belgrade very lately.

Mr Brickhouse arrived here on monday last and I was sorry to learn from him that you were unwell; I hope however you will soon recover

The mails are now in /so/ disordered a condition that perhaps this will be the only letter that will certainly reach you before you leave for home so that I will mention some things that I should be glad if you would please procure for me. vis some stuff for Pantaloons as I have but the pair you got for me before you left for every day wear, my other every day ones have become old and unfit for wear. Day's Mathematics which I suppose you forgot to send me: also since I <have plan> intend to plant the /Sugar/ Beet<s so that> I would like to know something def<f>inite about it which I can learn from Chaptal's work on the Sugar-Beet and the Report of the Philadelphia Sugar-Beet Society: I should be glad if you you would procure them for me. Further Lidia, although she had as much of the Bed-Ticking as the others who had it says it is not enough and wants more over long sleves. I told her I would write to you and if you thought proper when /you returned/ you would bring some more, she wants 2 or 3 yards more. Johnston wants a little book of Tales, and request me to ask you to bring him something of the kind, he is much obliged to you for his candy and sends his love to you

Believe me your dutiful son
Charles L Pettigrew

[*Addressed*] Hon. E. Pettigrew
City of
Washington

Richard Hines to Ebenezer Pettigrew A&H

Hermitage Near Sparta 16th Febry: 1837

Dear Sir,

Absence from home and other engagements have prevented my writing you much longer than I wished or intended. Although I have been a silent I have by no means been an inatentive or uninterested spectator of the sayings and doings at Washington. Much as I regreat it truth compels me to say I look upon the Constatutional existance of our Government as at an end, for we are already under the absolute will and controul of one man, and that man a malicious, vindictive, despot, false and corrupt to the very hearts core in the whole administration of the Government for the last few years at least. Who knows no law but his own will, whether that be to make M. V. B. president or R. H. Whitney /pass for/ an honest man—I pray God to forgive me for the part I had in his elevation. I will try and sin no more. If there was any doubt of the correctness of my conclusions before, I think the Presidents recent letter to Mr Wise, Whitneys' conduct before one committee, and answer to another, Mr Adam's (Oh! how has the mighty fallen.) on the subject /of/ abolition and the slaves. And last though not least the Presidents letter to Mr Calhoun the most vindictive malicious unconstitutional production that ever emenated from the heart of any citizen of this once happy country. Would seam to leave no doubt of their correctness. I see no hope for the south but to put her self at once upon her own rightes—the sooner the better.

I envy not the feelings of the southern friends of the administration just now. I must confess I have had some hopes from Mr Van Burin but begin to dispair for him—he even disposed it would be next to impossable to place the affairs of the goverment as they were—

Your few but warm friends in this part of the Country very much regreat the necessity you found yourself under of declining a reelection, which I am very certain you could have obtained without difficulty. I believe without opposition. Knowing as I do the climate of Washington your constatution and habits of life, I must confess I was not surprised, however much I regreated your determination. The administration party here I believe are determined to drop Dr Hall. Genl Wilson will be their candidate. The Whigs will probably have a convention at Washington [*North Carolina*] nominate their candidate. Who he will be is uncertain.

Mr [*Peter*] Evans has sold his plantation near me & forty of his negros and will remove permenantly to Chatham in a few weeks. he was here yesterday and requested to be affectionately remembered to you. We are very anxious to have a view behind the scene, the ondits &.c. about the new cabinet at Washington, and your opinion of the present and probable coming state of our Government. Please send me the reports of the investigating committees.

Very respectfully & truly your
Obt: Servt:
Richd: Hines

John F. Hughes Esqr. near Sparta was one of your warmest friends in this neighborhood.

[*Addressed*] Hon: E. Petigrew
Washington
D.C.

Ebenezer Pettigrew to Edward Bishop Dudley and James W[est] Bryan[1]* UNC

Copy to <D> Govr Duldy

Washington City Feb 27, 1837

Sir,

I have received your letter of the 20th Inst. and had also received one from James W. Bryan esqr dated the 26th Ult. on the subject to which yours is relating. To the letter of Mr Bryan I directed an answer & in his absence from Newbern to Mr John H. Bryan dated 13th Instant. The sub<ject>stance of which letter is as follows.

No one can feel more interest in the improvment of the State of N. Carolina than myself, having long since made up my mind to continue in it the remainder of my life and also willing that my children shall after me, under a very firm belief (if we would think so) that there is not a State in union which has greater /natural/ advantages than that we life in.

The day was when nothing could have been so congenial to my nature & wishes as to have been offered that which is now proposed in your letter. I was a perfect enthusiast <i> on the subject. For twenty seven years I had a fixed & never changing eye to the object for which I set out, and as a private individual, with very limited means, did a great deal; and from my long experience in draining swamp lands, <my unremiting habit of atention to /that/ business> my fondness for it, aded to my unremiting habit of attention to business, did believe that I could have done justice to the State. But <alas>! those days are gone by. My <measurable /in a great degree/> retirement <from> in a great degree from those active & to me pleasing <duties> employments for now nearly seven years, together with my advancing age has very much impaired my energies & nothing at this time is so desirable as to be retired from the bustle & busy scenes of life, with some small interest to occupy my attention, which I can retire from & attend to at pleasure In truth my servitude at this most miserable of places which unfits a man for any other place but this after a few years stay at it, has worn me out in both mind & body, more than ten years /of/ ditching in the swamps of N. Carolina, and at this time I am not fit for anything but to lay by & repair damages, if there is enough soundness to be worth repair.

To do my duty in whatever station I may be placed /as far as in my power lies/ whether in /this/ rowdy & disorderly body the H. of Representitives, & this most corrupt & corruping place, or in the swamps of N. Carolina (from the former I most sincerely thank my God I am about to be released) I hope will alway be a governing principle with me, & one of the great consolations which I shall have when about to close my eyes on this world forever. But to do my duty in the offer proposed in your letter at my time of life & with my present habits <of care & melancholy> would I fear be impossible & while I feel highly honoured by the request in your letter <to accept> & the advice of a number of my friends to accept /knowing myself better/ I am constrained to decline it.

I have the honour to be your Obdt Sevt
E Pettigrew

Copy to James W. Bryan

My dear Sir,

But two days ago I received yours of Jan 26. I went on Saturday the 4th to Baltimore on a little business and was there sick several days and on returning two Locomotives, one of which I was drawn by meet on the road and we were brought to full stop. Both were unable to proceed farther, and in truth ours /& our/ forward car <and> were literally demolished. This disaster detained me a day longer.—As to the subject of your letter. No one can feel more interest in the improvement of the state of N. Ca. than myself, and the day was when nothing could have been so congenial to my nature & wishes as to have been offered that which is now proposed in your letter. I was a perfect enthusiast on the subject, and did think I could do justice to the state in that business, from my long experience, my habits of attention to <business> it, aded to my fondness for it, but alas! that is gone by. My misfortune which is not nor never can be obliterated from mind & consequently my measurable retirement from those active & to me pleasing duties, <together with my advancing age> for now near seven years together with my advancing age has very much impaired my energies, and nothing now is so desirable as to be removed from the bustle & busy scenes of life with some small interest to occupy my attention, from which I can retire & attend to at pleasure. To you my dear Sir, I will say, it was truly said, 'When such friends part the survivor dies.'

To accept of the Commission proposed & to do my duty in that office & to do my duty in whatever station I may be placed whether in Congress or in the swamps of North Carolina fighting musquitoes & yellow flies (the latter place I should greatly prefer) will I hope be one of the great consolations I shall have when I come to leave this world, But to do my duty in the business proposed at my time of life & with my /present/ habits would be I fear impossible and while I feel highly honoured by the request am constrained to decline it.

I am with great respect your obdt Servt
E Pettigrew

[1]James West Bryan (1805-1864) of New Bern, brother to John Herritage Bryan, was an attorney. A Whig, he represented Carteret County in the North Carolina Senate, 1835-1836. Powell, *DNCB*, I, 255.

John Williams to Ebenezer Pettigrew UNC

Charleston Feby 2<9>8, 1837

Hon^{e} E. Pettigrew

Dear Sir,

I am this moment in rec^{t} of your valued favour of the 22^{d} Inst. contents Note^{d} I am still of the Same opinion that corn will continue at & above $1. Through the Season both north & south, if your /corn/ is white it will I think be good in this market for more than $1. The last sale but a few days since of skinners white corn I made @ 117¢ and have no doubt but I shall obtain from 112 to 117. for all there corn ship^{d} in future. If you wish me to contract for your corn in this market I think I can do So @ 112¢ to be deliv^{d} between this and the last of May, nor should I be anxious to contract at that price, This is however only my opinion which I do not urge in opposition to your better Judgement. I have sold within the last two weeks 40,000 Bushels corn from 103. to 107¢ Prime white is still in demand @108. to 115¢ I have now on the way from your state 30,000 Bushels and would advise you not to ship Just now. I think it better to defer for about 30 days, in the mean time will keep you advis^{d} of the market, and if you can forward to Mess Bryan & Maitland of Plymouth N Ca a small sample of your corn for them to forward me I could then advise you with more correctness, and certainty, if white I have no doubt but it will command the rise of $1 in this market ship^{d} between this and the first June—

Your frd
John Williams

N.B. The Lady of the Lake was abandon^{d} at Sea on the 15^{h} Jany. and should the crew have reach^{d} home I will thank you to have the protest noted & Extended if not previously done and forward me to enable me to collect the Insurance on the cargo of corn—I can not do this untill I received the protest

J W

2 oclock

Since writing the above I have seen all the corn Dealers, and am now offerd for your corn 115¢ to be deliv^{d} between this and the last of June—if you therefore wish me to ingage it at that price I will do

So on rec[t] of your answers—you will therefore write me forthwith, should you conclude the purchaser wishes one cargo ship[d] as soon as you can make it convenient—

Your frd
John Williams

[*Addressed*] Hon[e] E. Pettigrew
Cool Spring P. office
Washington County
North Carolina

Invoice of Medicines for Ebenezer Pettigrew UNC

[*March 6, 1837*]

E. Petigrew Esq[r] of North Carolina

Bo[t] of Rob[t] H. Coleman & Co
N[o] 133 Market St.
Balt[o] March 6. 1837.

[2] oz Paregoric and Phial	$ 25
1 oz Calomel and Phial	25
1 Box Refined Liquorice	12½
½ [lb] Blistering Ointment 75 Jar 12½	88
2 boxes Seidlitz Powders at 50	1 00
[lb i] Flour Sulphur	25
6 bottles Pure Quinine 1 oz. each at 225	13.50
[lb ii] *Best* Lima Bark at 150	3 00
¼ Yard Adhesive Plaster	25
½ Doz. Large botts. best Castor Oil	3 50
1 box Regnaults Paste	50
Box &porterage	62½
	$24.13

Rec[d] payment

Rob. H. Coleman & Co

Nathan A. Brickhouse[1] *to [William Shepard Pettigrew]* UNC

Columbia Tyrrel County March the 17th 1837

Dr Sir

I received your faviour of the 19th January and was glad to here from you. I was not at home when your letter come. the last week in

January I left for Baltimore at which place I arrived Safe and from their to washington City to See the capital of the Nation and Congress in Sesion. i Saw them both and was pleased to See the Sight but what give me more pleasure then any thing else was to Meet My olde and good friende your father I found him in rather bad health he went to Baltimore with me and Staid too days with me then he left for Fredrick but was Sum better. and I Done my business and set out for home the next day which was the 9th of February I got home without delay or accident your father got home the 10th Inst. and was verry feeble but was not confind but was weake I hope he will Soon recrute which he will. The Object of my going to the North was to get a Steme Enjoine for to work at Columbia to Saw and grind which object I accomplished the Enjoine is 30 horse power, to work 18 Saws and 2 run of mill Stones 5 feet diametore I contracted for the Enjoine Mill Stones and mishenery and all the millright work in order for opperation for 7000 dollars except the buildings and Brickwork which we do our Selves the Mill is to be in opperation by the 20th of November acording to contract

The partners is Charles L Pettigrew Joseph Halsey Joseph Brickhouse and My Self we are now ingaged in making purchises of Lands and Timber for the mill the whole amount of Cappital which we Shal have to Expende will be about 12.000 dollars. we have helde a meeting in Tyrrel County and apointed Deligates to attende a convention at washington N C the 1 Monday in May to Nominate M[r] Collins to fill the place in congress of your father.

I must Come to a Close

yours with Respect
Nathan A Brickhouse

[1]Nathan A. Brickhouse served as postmaster at Columbia, Tyrrell County, and was subscription agent for the *Whig*. *Whig* (Washington, N.C.), October 6, 1841. In 1830, a Nathaniel Brickhouse lived in Caswell County. *1830 Census Index*, 21.

Ebenezer Pettigrew to William Shepard Pettigrew A&H

[*April 1, 1837*]

My Dear Son

On my return from Newbern yesterday I received your letter of March 11th—I regret very much that it was [*not*] answered sooner on account of the request in it. I had intended to write you from Newbern for the purpose of sending you the above draft, thinking that you would begin to need money, but deferred it from day to day untill it was passed by. However I hope you nor my credit has not yet failed for this short time but I wish you to ask no more credit than is not to be avoided.

My object in visiting Newbern so shortly after my return from Washington was in consequence of a letter informing that your dear little Nancy had St. Vitus' dance. When I arrived I found the dear little creature unable to walk a step at which I know my dear William it is unnecessary for me to express my sensation. It is enough to say that it is enough to Kill me. I am however happy to inform you that she was much better before I left. so as to feed herself and to walk about without inconvenience, & I pray God will recover. Both your dear little sisters had, had the measells, but were well.

My health is better but yet not well. Your brother Charles is well & very busily engaged with the farm Davenport having been very sick with the Influenza which has prevailed, to the death of a great many persons in all parts of this country. In truth this has been the sickliest winter & more death than has been known for twenty. All the familys black & white have been sick, & most of them very sick, but blessed be God none have have died. Mr Davenport & Child I found quite sick & Poor Johnston was taken sick after my arrival at home yesterday, I hope he will not be sick much. Your brother Charles & Johnston & Mr Davenport desire to be affectionately remembered to you, & say that they have been looking & would be glad to receive a letter from and you will be so good as to acknowledge the receit of this draft that I may know you have got it. I hope my dear, dear, son that you have too much respect for yourself & love for your poor destressed father & brothers & sisters to engage in the disgraceful conduct you mention.

Your affect & [*illegible*] father
E Pettigrew

[*Addressed*] M^r^ W^m^ S Pettigrew
Chapel Hill
North Carolina

John Williams to Ebenezer Pettigrew UNC

Charleston April 17th 1837

E. Pettigrew Esq

Dear Sir

Our market is glutted with corn and would advise you not to ship *this way*. The sudden decline North and New Orleans have causd it to be pressd on this Market, and to such extent that it is impossible to effect Sales hardly at *any price*—The many failures all round us North & South East & West, have caus[d] many to take place here. Business is nearly or entirely suspended, confidence destroy[d] Banks have stop[d] discounting even the best of business paper at short time. The produce of the country rapidly declining and where it will stop, who can tell, from all around us we hear of failures, and the efforts have been made by Mr Biddle & the U.S. Bank—such aid as has been extended, up to the present, seems to have very little /effect/,—certainly has given no relief, I fear the commercial (or it should be call[d]) the shaving imporium, N.Y. is too *rotten*, to be aided by the means tried—& brought to a final cure—The vice of *stock Gambling* in that city has so superseded the legitimate business of trade and commerce that I fear the community *there*, must undergo a strong purgation, in the opperation of which many will die—commercialy—I now begin to fear for the Banks, what can sustain them *under existing circumstances*, cotton down to 7 & 9.[c] this the main spring of produce having its effect on every other article of trade & product of the world. I say again when will these things come to an end, *I fear when too Late*, do not ship any corn this way—

your frd
John Williams

[*Addressed*] Mr. E. Pettigrew
Lake Phelps
cool Spring P. Office
Wasington County
N[o] C[a]

Mary Williams Bryan to Ebenezer Pettigrew UNC

New Bern April 19. 1837—

My dear Brother

I am very happy to inform you that dear little Nancy has improved very much, she looks well & lively & that nervous affection has worn off I may say entirely, for I have not perceived it in several days,—whether she will continue so God only knows I trust she will—Last friday was a week ago she was quite nervous all day & a little so the next day & it was slightly perceptible for several days after—her physician has not seen her since you left, she has been with the exception of the time I mention gradually improving without the aid of medicine

I don't know how to advise you about taking her to a more salubrious climate for the summer, you must judge of that yourself, you understand her disease much better than I do—I should suppose that by having her constitution strengthened by change of climate she would be better able to resist any future attack she might have—

Mr Bryan is again absent, he rec^{d} a letter last week from Judge Cameron stating that we could not get the house we expected & that he knows of none that we could get—so that our moving to Raleigh for this year at least is abandoned. I mention this because you know when you were here we talked of it, & I thought perhaps that moving there would be all that would be desirable for Nancy, it being much he/a/lthier than this place.—

Ma' & family are tolerably well—I have been suffering very much for the last fortnight with influenza, I still have a bad cough tho' it is now much better—it has been worse than any I ever had before—

Lydia has been unwell almost ever since you left, she has now a swelled face & suffered very much with tooth ache & jaw ache, I am apprehensive her face will rise—

Mary and Nancy send their love to Pa' & brothers, Nancy thinks she can hem Pa' a handkerchief now— Remember me to Charles & Johns[*t*]on & believe me

Your affectionate Sister
Mary W Bryan.—

[*Addressed*] Hon. E. Pettigrew
Cool Spring
N. Carolina

John Baptist Beasley to Ebenezer Pettigrew A&H

Vicksburg [*Mississippi*] 4th May 1837

Dear Sir

I should think that I had not discharged my duty did I not drop you a line on the subject of these fair famed regions To undertake, an opinion, in general it would require more space, than can be found within the compass of this sheet. I therefore, will only submit a few remarks with my opinions on certain matters that have come under my observation since I have been here, and <will> leave the ballance to the judgment of others. It would be needless for me to tell you of the great advantage my money would have been to me. had I have brought it. but Haughton Boardman & Nobles failure has nailed me to the Counter. This act, of my own folly, can never be erased from my memory. It was an unfortunate step indeed and criminal in M^{r} H in the highest decree. as he knows where I was bound and must have seen 30 days ahead. He has written me upon the subject. says that my money is in no danger and that they will resume in 10 days

If this could be done, I should suffer but little, but I am perfectly satisfied, that under the great disordered state of money matters their expectations will fail. consequently I shall have to remain in great suspence until I receive intelligence of the certainty of things one way or the other. I must stop at this place until this news reaches me for this information, I have written with a candid and unaffected reply and I am daily looking for an answer I have been thus candid with them, in order to know how to regulate my conduct and movements

This is a place of immense business and in a rapid state of improvement, even beyond the calculation of any man that is not an eye witness, the buildings that have been, and will be compleated, within the present year, will not cost less than a Million of Dollars, and where the money is to come from to pay for them I am entirely at a loss to know. As the Banks in this place will not discount upon no terms whatever. they are bound to take this step for preservation alone as there is at least $60000 drawn in specie every 14 days & The necessary consequence will be, that a fall in every species of property will, and must take place Negroes can be bought here for cash on better terms than with us. likewise provisions of every description. But the most fatal error, under which the people of this place are labouring, is to be found in their demands for rents, and if persisted in must impede the speedy prosperity of the place as I am confident men of reason and judgment, would prefer hazarding almost any alternative rather than locating upon such unfavourable and unpropitious terms.

Any House in this place similar to mine would command $1500 per annum and in like proportion, down to a Hovel, store commands from 1000 to 2500 single rooms. now any man of reason & responsibility will but in a case of extreme necessity submit to such a state of things. As to myself No mortal on earth with all the plausible means he could use. could ever reconcile me to come into such measures. And unless I could get a permanent foothold and that upon reasonable terms I am bound by a sense of duty I owe myself and family to look for prospects in a more favourable region. Real estate in this place that sold last fall on 1 2 &3 Years credit @ $10.000 sold for cash at public auction this week during Court for $2000. I should have bought it If I had have known it. It rents for $900. this was reasonable enough. Young likely house maids & men sold from 675 to 785 either would have sold here on a credit last fall from 1500 to 2000. but such is the scarcity of money that nothing will command much. If I had have had mine I could have doubled it (without any possible danger of loss in 12 /mo/ but there is a fate that attends all mankind and when his prospects appear to him most bright and clear, an unfortunate cloud suddenly surrounds him. And thus I am bound to conclude I am now at the zenith of my glory. fate has decreed it, and I most cheerfully submit. under a full assurance that all things are designed by the great Creator for some more lasting and permanent good. I therefore shall persue the even tenour of my way, and await with patience the final result of my folly for it was most assuredly a folly indeed, but let the circumstance sink in oblivion could it have only operated upon myself alone, I could have borne it cheerfully. but to know that it must affect them in whom I venerate beyond price, is a mortification to me beyond measure And although my money may again be returned to the last farthing. The mortification under which I have laboured from the disappointment can never, no never, be healed. and will justly be remembered by me as long as I have an existence

Had the news have come to my ears before my departure, it would have been a mere bubble in comparison to the effect it had upon me at this remote distance from the bosom of my family, (and I may say Land of strangers) They may brook it if they choose and can act with me in like manners but I do assure them they shall find me to the end as unbending as the mastiff oak and no satisfaction will answer until the last cent is paid. I am now with William Norcom who with Fred [*Norcom*] appears to be doing a fair business all of which and families are well, I presume Mr Alexander will have left before this reaches you. I hope he may not be disappointed in his imaginary views of these represented regions of bliss

Real estate sells in this place higher than in the City of Newyork there are many acres of unimproved lots been sold here as high as 20,000 Dollars and which will cost 5000 more, to level the hills before a suitable place can be made to set a respectable building up There is one Gentleman here building 16 Houses that will cost when compleated $12,000, each, and which he calculated to sell the [insueing] fall at 25000 each but as all operations here are and have been carried on upon the credit system. These hard time has compelled him to abandon them. and the workmen has quit and gone home. without their pay and will no doubt be seriously injured as the lots were under mortgage for the purchase money. there are many operations of this kind here and a man hardly knows when he can make a safe contract

I took a stroll to look at the speculations made by Benjamin Halsey of Halifax. He (agreed) to pay $19500 for 2 lots a part of which sum he paid in cash say $3500. which sum I consider the full value of both lots, but I can get no one here to agree with me in opinion. but I will venture to say that at a call sale this would not commad 5000 and I would agree to bet that sum of it.

We shall see in the course of 18 months how things go on here. I think if I could get myself comfortably located here I should with a great deal of pleasure do so. but under the present circumstances. I cannot do so. Wm Norcom is about to put up 11 houses the frames are now here already mortised and fitted one of which he says that I may have at cost and will give me ground to put it on. which is more than I could ask. But the location does not suit me and unless I can suit myself I will not come to the place. I can hire my negroes out here for $30 pr month the year round and women @ $20. but every species of labour is as high in proportion and at certain times they are high to criminality. The vegetation here are the same as in our state but spring earlier and as abundantly I see plenty of white clover in the woods 8 inches high at this time and as to the fertility of the soil there is no doubt even in the uneven land. the only advantages I can see is in the climate and ease of cultivation.

I shall consider well before I take a certain start. Eno M Hassell has bettered himself much I think his and the land around him is as good as any I have seen since. I advised his brother to come out forthwith and buy the tract adjoining Hassell as the price was $3 per acre 50 of which I would not give for the whole of Second [Creek]

My mind has undergone no change since I last saw you taking every thing in a general mass and giving true ballances, every thing here depends upon the success in speculation many of which will fall in the general wreck of ruin. that must take place with in the next 18 months. Then will be the time for money to be used to the best profitable advantage and I shall use my efforts to return and come prepared to mingle in the strife. If I can meet with any success at home neither can the Banks or the next crop avert the calamity. there are not less than 3 Millions of Dollars to be collected here and where specie daily is demanded from the Banks for all its paper & this money must be raised in cash. I am well and can but hope you may be in the enjoyment of the same blessing

Yours Truly
J B Beasley

E Pettigrew Esq

[*Addressed*] Ebenezer Pettigrew Esqr
Washington County
No Ca
Cool Spring P.O.

Charles Lockhart Pettigrew to Ebenezer Pettigrew UNC

Newbern May 26th 1837

Dear Father

I arrived in this place on Tuesday last and will leave to morrow with my sisters. I left Plymouth in company with Judge Toomer,[1] <and> who continued with me untill we arrived in Raleigh. From Raleigh I continued to Chapel Hill on the next day, brother William is in good health and is willing to remain in Hillsboro during the fall. I left $100.00 with him which he said would be enough untill september or some where about that time. In the evening of the next day it rained so I could [*not*] go to H. untill the next morning. On that day Johnston complained of being unwell, Dr Webb[2] was passing by the hotel and I concluded to call him in; he said he had a slight fever, but gave him no medicine the next day he was so well that I thought I might leave him Accordingly <on the next day> I left for Newbern. I gave Mr Bingham $100 for the use of Johnston and selected a place for my sisters. I am very much pleased with the place I could not have got a better Mrs Waters is the name of the lady who takes them she has a very small family and I think will attend to them well she does not wish a servant and I think /it is/ as well, not to send Lidia.

The family are all well here Mary and Ann look as well as I ever saw them, Ann looks in exceedingly fine health. There seems to be little reason to expect a return of her disease Aunt Mary says she is willing that Lidia should go home: Lidia herself is very desirous to go home to see her children and Aunt Mary says she does not like to detain her. I think that she will need her, because uncle Charles is going to send his servant with Fred up the country and she will thus loose too servants from the family. I therefore write you to let you know in order that you may do for the best. I leave Newbern for Hillsboro to morrow morning I cannot tell at what time I shall be able to get home, but it will be as soon as possible

I will take the barouche; Grandma and the family send their love to you

Your affectionate son
Charles L Pettigrew

Johnston is of course at Mrs Norwood's; the blank Bills of lading are procured [*torn*]

[*Addressed*] Hon. E. Pettigrew
Cool-spring
Washington Co
N. Carolina

[1]John Duncan Toomer, class of 1802 at the University of North Carolina, was judge of the superior and supreme courts of North Carolina. He was a university trustee in 1821. Battle, *History of the University*, I, 168, 279-280.

[2]James Webb (1774-1855) was a noted pioneer physician of Hillsborough. After studying at Jefferson Medical College, University of Pennsylvania, he established himself as a physician and merchant. He was a member of the board of trustees of the Hillsborough Academy from 1804 through at least 1839, serving as guardian for many boys, boarding some in his home, and sometimes assuming their financial responsibility. He was also an instigator and "patron" of the Burwell Female School in Hillsborough, where Mary Pettigrew and Mary Bryan studied. Mary Clare Engstrom, manuscript sketch of Webb for publication in projected volume of Powell, *DNCB*.

Partnership Agreement UNC

[*May 31, 1837*]

Whereas Ebenezer Pettigrew and Josiah Collins Jun[r] have entered into Co-partnership for the purpose of cultivating silk and whereas such culture is to be at the joint expense of both parties equally, both as it regards Investments in Land or Stock—Therefore, this is to certify, that in the event of Death or Accident to either party, before the necessary completion of the papers of Co-partnership, that the purchase of Lands or Stock is to be settled at the mutual cost of both parties, and this paper writing is to be held and deemed conclusive of such obligation, so to settle on the part of both Said parties. And to the faithful fulfillment of the foregoing agreement, we bind ourselves each severally to the other, our heirs, executors, administrators, assigns, in the Sum of Four Thousand Dollars under our hands & seals this 31st May 1837

E Pettigrew seal

Josiah Collins *Jun[r]* seal

John Williams to Ebenezer Pettigrew UNC

Charleston June 29—1837

Hon[l] E Pettigrew

Dear Sir

The Schr E. Hardy not yet arrivd and have this effected Insurance on your corn valued @ $2,000 @ 1 pr ct premium, in doing so I may have done wrong as you do not order Insurance, but supposing you might possible overlook[d] it, and not knowing whether it is your wish or not I preferd acting on the prudent side

The navigation as you know about Ocracock is a very dangerous one and within the Past 3 months, 7 cargoes of corn have been lost there bound to this place, and the North. If I have done contrary to your wish and custom it will I assure you afford me pleasure not to make charge of premium in the Sales should the vessel arrive Safe—Our market is nearly bare of corn and hope to obtain a good price for yours on arrival say 125. to 128.¢ the stock now on hand does not exceed 5000 Bushels.

The demand and price must continue fair through the balance of the season as much will be wanted by Government for the Indian War—

in haste
Your frd
John Williams

[*Addressed*] Hon[l] E Pettigrew
Cool Spring P. Office
Washington County
N[o] C[a]

John Herritage Bryan to Ebenezer Pettigrew A&H

New Bern July 5 1837—

My dear Sir,

I returned from Raleigh a few days since; during my absence, I went to Chapel Hill & attended commencement there—I was with William he was well & said he sh[d] go to Hillsb[o]—in a few days—I heard from the girls, they were very well; I sh'd have been much pleased to see them, but was indebted to a friend for a seat in his carriage to the Hill, & had to return with him—the stages were much crowded.—

I purchased M[r] Badger's residence in Raleigh, it is about 400 yds N.E. of the State ho: & near M[rs] Polk's.—The lot is an entire square containing 2 acres & has a great many conveniences—the water is excellent & the situation very healthy.—I am entitled to the possession on the 1st of Jany. next & we wish to move in in Jany, if conveniently practicable.—I am to give $5000. in instalments, to be secured by notes with good security—Will you do me the favour to sign with me?—You will be able to visit us very conveniently by steam boat & rail road.—

Charles [*Shepard*] is absent on an electioneering tour, He hesitated long about coming out, & I fear came out rather late.—

William [*Shepard*] did not settle the estate while here, nor make any payment on account—He stated that his funds were in stocks & he could not sell unless at a great sacrifice.—

Mrs Shepard has determined to move to Ralh if she can get a house—James Shepard has already gone there, to commence a circuit.—

We are all tolerably well—Charles & Octavia have had fever—& Mrs Shepard is complaining.—

Mrs Bryan begs to be affectionately remembered, to you & Charles

Very truly
yr friend relative
Jn. H. Bryan

P.S I enclose the notes for my purchase—the town [*New Bern*] property was divided when Wm was here and the ground on Craven Street below the Merchant's Bank, nearly opposite the brick stores, was divided between, Mary & your children.—

[*Addressed*] Hon: E. Pettigrew
Cool Spring
N.C

John James Pearson[1] *to Ebenezer Pettigrew* UNC

Mercer Penna July 9th 1837

My dear friend

Your very kind letter of the 22nd May arived safely early in June and gave me many mixed sensations of grief and joy—grief at the picture you draw of the desolation of your feelings and your once hapy home, feelings which you doubtless have heretofore found it impossible to eradicate or overcome, joy at your finding your family in health except your little favorite daughter who I hope is long ere this enjoying that same best boon of providence 'good health.'—I fear from your statements last winter as well as the descriptions in your letter that your location is too unhealthy, that much of the sickness endured by your family has arisen from your local position, if so I should rather abandon your fine fertile lands and rich meadows and take up my abode on the sandy pine covered hills of North Carolina,—yea! even of Nova Scotia, than abide there the season through. the anual attacks of bilious fever must undermine even the strongest constitution, how much then must the gradually forming system and feble bodies of children suffer from such an anual affliction, persons raised in sickly vicinities are subject to attacks such as you speak of your daughter suffering from and in some parts of our country particularly on the gulf of Mexico probably not one fourth of the children are raised to manhood. I sincerely rejoice with you at the returning health of your daughter and hope you will take the course proposed of sending her from your beautiful but I fear sickly plantation and pleasant lake to the more healthful atmosphere of the mountains. If you desire to perfectly restore your own health and that of your family I would beg leave to suggest a voyage or journey to the north this summer and in that case if you could be induced to visit our great western lakes your humble servant might promise himself the pleasure of once more meeting one who from a comparative short acquaintance he hopes to make a long and steadfast friend, in fact nothing would give me more sincere and heartfelt pleasure than to have you located for a few weeks of our healthy cool & pleasant summer beneath my humble roof—M[rs] Pearson would also greet you as a most welcome guest her feelings being strongly enlisted in your favor by my previous description and those impressions greatly strengthened by reading your letter which you might almost certainly have known I would show her—should you ever be induced to visit our poor northern slave hating region of Pennsylvania take this as a standing invitation, most truly, cordially, and sincerely given. The subject of abolition is now rarely spoken of in this country the people having something of more immediate interest to engage their attention, having troubles of their own they now cease to trouble their neighbors or take on themselves the immaginary troubles of the negroes. I say immaginary because even the abolitionists with us will generally admit that so far as respects animal comforts the slave is better off than the free negro or poor white, but they have not liberty!! "liberty the best boon of good to man" and poor fools they immagine the slave spends his day of labor and night of sleepless sorrow pining for liberty, a feeling he never possessd, a blessing he never enjoyed & is totally incapable of realizing—their idea of liberty is the same as that of the newly imported Irishman who knocked down the first man he met and swor he was in a free country & had a right to do as he pleased. *their liberty is mere licensiousness*—miserable indeed will be their situation and that of the whites whose lot is cast amongst them the day they are emancipated—the abolition fever has not infected more than one tenth man or woman in Penn[a] but I am sorry to find it rather increasing & extending in New England—the intelligent and well informed in all parts of the United states are opposed to it but we all know they constitute but a small portion of the great mass—the time may and probably will soon come when it will be made a political question in many of the non slaveholding states. in Pennsylvania the attachment to the union is such that so long as the people are or can be satisfied the peace of the country will be endangered by any action of congress on the subject the party will always be weak. one session in congress will convince any man both of the danger, folly, & impropriety of agitating the subject. I think the next congress will be less trouble than we were, they will have sufficient real ills to remedy & will probably abstain from meddling with immaginary ones.—what they will do for the relief of the country it is impossible for me to say or even conjecture—party pride will prevent the Jackson men from coming out like men acknowledging their errors and admitting the *old roman* the *greatest* & *best*, did not know all things, that he showed more of the general than the statesman in destroying the U.S. bank, for disguise it as we will, atribute the failure & universal bankruptcy of the country to what we may the destruction of that institution was the remote yet certain cause of all the present embarressments. had it been suffered to flourish the thousands of state banks with their millions of notes would never have existed—without them there would have been none of the overtrading which the administration now complains causes the distress and the whole business of the country would have progressed in the same smooth rational and safe manner it did from 1824 till 1834 a time of unexampled prospertity in the U.S.—but the bubble has burst and already the knaves and fools who caused it are endeavoring to turn public odium from themselves and throw it onto that very instituon which was one principal cause of <their> our prosperity, the cry here is that if Penn[a] had not chartered the U.S. bank the other banks could have continued a specie redemption of their paper in addition the gold humbug is taking vastly with our simpletons, they contend the whole business of the country could readily be done with gold & silver, that bank paper is useless and a mere scheme of fraud—and that had the U.S. bank continued as in 1832 our currency would have been no better than it now is—that general Jackson would have introduced a specie currency and was taking rapid measures to bring it about by causing heavy importations from abroad, as the French indemnity &c &c now we all know that at the time of that importation bills on France were worth three to five per cent advance and the persons who were to receive the money beged to have it remain there but it was imported at considerable expense which with the premium lost occasioned a clear loss of at least six per cent to the poor d——ls who were before receiving about 33 per cent on their <losses> claims, but what of that if General Jackson could say to the poor cajoled fools of the U. States 'that he had caused the indemnity to be imported in *specie*' and now to cap the climax they are paid not with a draft on France worth now 5 per cent but on a *deposit* bank not worth a *d——n*!—one of Jackson & Reubens pets!—but this is a subject on which I should never write as I run wild and never know when to cease. in fact I agree with you that this country had better have paid General J. $25,000,000. than to have elected him president. I go further—it would have been better for the U. States that New Orleans had been burnt & pilaged by the british than to have had such a curse on us for the last eight years. the pecuniary loss to the country would have been less and our beloved constitution would have been spared the many rude shocks & wounds it has received, wounds which in the end will probably cause its death unless the party in power can be displaced and the presidents be overruled and by the universal voice of public opinion utterly and forever condemned—but I can rejoice with you that so far as respects myself I stand out of the reach of pecuniary dificulties. I cannot even loose but must make by the present embarrasments. they bring a rich harvest to the sickel of the practising lawyer. we have the misfortune to live on the vices, follies & losses of mankind. I have so managed as to become in a manner independent—that is—what is so considered in a poor country—and you know all things are by comparison—twenty thousand dollars here is a greater fortune than an hundred thousand in the cities—the embarrasments greatly increase my business, in fact I have latterly had so much to do that it has prevented a more prompt answer to your letter which is my only apology for leaving it so long but if I do not soon come to a close you will be sorry I had not been busyer, left it longer, or omitted it alltogether! as I have inflicted a prety great task on you to read it. You must not for a moment suppose from the above that I rejoice in the misfortunes of my fellow citizens as afording me the means of bettering my pecuniary situation, God forbid! I feel just as does the humane physician in times of general sickness and would most cheerfully forego the advantage of making money that others might suffer less—all my regret is that the supporters of the 'greatest & best' are not the sole sufferers—but unfortunately the generals blessings like the rains of heaven fall alike on the just and the unjust, on friends & enemies—in fact his enemies suffer most as his friends in Penn^a^ are generally composed of that class who have nothing to loose, many of the wealthy & respectable formerly belonged to his party but have long since forsaken him & his nuisances—his letter in reply to Judge [*Hugh Lawson*] White which I have just read caps the climax of his lies and iniquity, but the credulous fools of this country will believe his word in preference to Judge Whits oath, so goes the world—if a man can get his name up he may lie with impunity.—

But I have again got on the never ending topic and must break off.

Mrs Pearson altho a total stranger sends her respects to you. I hope to hear from you again when at leisure and believe me sincerely your friend.

Jno J. Pearson

Hon E. Pettigrew

N.B. A word as to the weather & crops—we have had continued rain with not more than one days intermission for six weeks, our farmers have rarely got their corn worked the first time, we plant last of May our wheat crops look bad, if dry weather does not soon come will fill badly and harvest will not begin before the first of August, nearly a month later than usual.

[*Addressed*] Hon Ebenezer Pettigrew M.C.
Coolspring Washington County
North Carolina

---

[1]John James Pearson (1800-1888), an attorney and later a judge, served as a Whig member of Congress from Pennsylvania, December, 1836, to March, 1837. *Biographical Directory of Congress*, 1437.

William A. Dickinson[1] *to Ebenezer Pettigrew* A&H

East Wetumpka 21. July 1837.

Hon: E: Pettigrew

Dear Sir

Since I had the pleasure of seeing you at Lake Phelps I have enjoyed good health, trusting this will find you and your family all well.

I left Coolspring on 10th May via Norfolk to Mobile in 14 days. from Charleston to Augusta I saw no good Land. Augusta to La Grainge thro: Georgia & part of Florida to Pensacolla from thence to Mobile. Augusta looks well & Trades considerable from Augusta to Pensacolla I saw no good Land, poor high white sandy piney Land. the Country around Pensacolla is covered with scruby pines & sand as white as silver, but a very pleasant and healthy place. Mobile as a Commercial City stands in a good situation and looks well. it is cool in summer in consequence of a breeze from the Bay every day, but I found every thing in the way of trade extremely dull. Goods selling in many instances at less than first cost, I stayed at Mobile 1 month when I met Mr Douglas from N. Orleans so I made up my mind to go to the Wetumpka's up the Alabama River, distance 350 Miles, [*by*] Steam Boat, This town contains the rise of twothousand Inhabitants. it is divided into three parts. West. East & North, Wetumpka, east & west are divided by the Fallas [*falls?*] of the head of the Alabama River, by a very fine Bridge of 900 feet, supported by piers about 90 feet from the bed of the river, the west side is more level than the east & north towns. it being surrounded by high hills and deep gullies, there is an extensive view from the top of the highest as far as the eye can reach upon the whole it is the prettiest place I have seen in all my travells, this being the head of navigation all the merchandise from the interior flows thro: this place, there are no good land nigher this plance than 20 miles, as I have been here only a few weeks I do not pretend to in this to give you a satisfactory account of the place, only the situation as far as regards its locality is very advantageously chosen, both as regards health, and trade, this river is navigable from Mobile to this place at all times of the year and entirely free from danger in its navigation. I can go from this place to New Orleans in 4[½] days at an expense of 35 Dollars: upon the whole I am at present well satisfied with this place, we have a market every morning for Beff. Fish. Poultry etc. etc., corn is selling @ 1½ $ pr Bushell. Flower 8¢ p lb. Green Oats 3$ p 100 lbs Bacon 16 & 18¾. Sugar 12½. Coffee 18¾. Rents for stores range at 250 to 1,000 p annum. there now building about 10, or 15, New Store Houses, all of Brick of the very best description. I have to pay 240$ a year for a small place. Boarding 2$ p Day. I board myself it does not cost me more than 8 Dollars p mo & I live better than I do at the Teverns. for the present I have given you all the News. ("no say I pay 10 Dols. for Town Tax. & 4 Dols for State Tax"). I should like to know if the post office business is fully settled, and how Hardy H: Phelps gits on in the Office. If you have any opportunity in sending to Coolspring please let my wife know that I am well. give my kind remembrance to Mr Charles Pettigrew. Mrs D. Davenport & Mr Davenport

When I left Plymouth I thought I would go thro: Washington & pay for the Whig N: Paper, but not going that way I was prevented from doing so. shall be glad to hear how all the elections are going on in N.C. shall be truly happy to hear from you soon the crops looks well, principally corn, the weather very warm. I suppose it is so with you, I now thank you for your kind friendship. wishing you & your family health & happiness, and am

Dear Sir
Yours very Respectfully
William A: Dickinson

address
W. A. Dickinson
East Wetumpka
Alabama

[*Addressed*] Hon: Ebenezer Pettigrew
Coolspring
N.C.

[1]William A. Dickinson was postmaster at Plymouth until he left to better his fortune, first in Pennsylvania and then in Alabama. This letter is another illustration of the westward movement. Dickinson's letters to Ebenezer Pettigrew from Pennsylvania have been omitted from this volume; they are at the Southern Historical Collection.

William Shepard Pettigrew to Ebenezer Pettigrew UNC

Chapel Hill August 28th 1837

Dear Pa

You will no doubt be surprised to receive a letter so soon after the one I sent the other day. I am sorry I did not let the other letter contain the object of this. The merchants are going on to the North some time next month, and as I will need some money before I leave here, it would be best to send the draft immediately in order that they may cash it, for if it were to come after they leave I would find it difficult, I fear, to get it cashed on Chapel Hill. It will take about forty or forty five dollars to square me off entirely, supposing that I remain here until the middle of October. I hope you will not think I have been extravagant I assure /you/ I have been any thing else but that. I have been as careful as I could be. And as I am now about to come home and close my school-boy expenses forever. I can say with truth I have not spent one dollar since my first arrival on the Hill which I do not sincerely believe was well laid out. I have recovered from my cold. I hope you and brother Charles are in good health. Please give my love to brother Charles.

Your affectionate son
Will S Pettigrew

[*Addressed*] Hon E Pettigrew
Cool Spring
Washington Co
N. Carolina

James Alfred Pearce to Ebenezer Pettigrew A&H

Washington Sept 6th 1837.

My Dear Sir

I reached this place the day before Congress met and have already fixed myself in a pleasant mess and at a most capital house.—Mrs Dyers opposite the old General P Office and next door to that cold blooded scoundrel Amos Kendall.[1] The house is small but very comfortable—the rooms spacious though few and exquisitely *neat*. We have two parlours four chambers and a small spare room for a friend—and the Mess, Bayard, Milligan, Philips, & myself *control* the house.—Won't you come see us? If nay, will you be glad to see me?—for I have talked with Charles Shepard and partly agreed to make an incursion into the Dismal when the sickly season shall be over. In this too I am *serious*

When the Session is a little more advanced I shall take occasion to tell you my views of men and things.—This morning after writing the above I went to the House and after a Session of 4 hours we succeeded in electing a printer to the House—Blair and Rives[2] are ousted and the Editor of the Madisonian is elected by the votes of 90 whigs and 22 or 23 conservatives. Gales and Seaton[3] will do the printing. For Allen[4] is not prepared to it as yet. This is a great point gained. The defeat of the Globe is a rebuke the spirit of levelling and disorganization throughout the land—especially, coming, as it does, from a H. of Representatives which had just elected an administration Speaker. I do not however anticipate any benefit from the meeting of Congress—I mean any immediate remedy for the evils of a depreciated currency and a depressed commerce. I saw M Frederick Sheppard today as also his brother in congress and W B. S who is now in Alexandria I expected to dine with me to day but the bad weather has prevented his coming up I suppose—

Patton[5] Garland[6] Legare[7] of SC and some of the New Yorkers <members of> with the 3 Illinois men make up the body of conservatives Nick [*Nicholas*] Biddle has a brother[8] in Congress who moved a resolution to day that is likely to open the fountains of the great deep of debate—if so it will be long before the talking will cease and action commence—

Present me to yr. Sons, and believe me very sincerely

Yr frd
J A Pearce

[*Addressed*] Hon. E. Pettigrew
Cool Spring
Washington Cy
N Carolina

---

[1]Amos Kendall (1789-1869), a journalist, was Andrew Jackson's postmaster general and an able member of the administration. He was instrumental in bringing Francis P. Blair to Washington to start the *Globe*, a partisan Democratic paper. *DAB*, X, 325-327.

[2]John Cook Rives (1795-1864) was Francis P. Blair's partner in the management of the *Globe*. He also reported debates in *The Congressional Globe* from 1833 to 1864. *CDAB*, 869.

[3]Joseph Gales, Jr. (1786-1860), and William Winston Seaton (1785-1866) were publishers of the *National Intelligencer*. They reported congressional debates

and published the *Annals of Congress* (1834-1856) and the *American State Papers* (1832-1861). *CDAB*, 324, 930.

[4]Thomas Allen (1813-1882) established the *Madisonian* in Washington in 1837. He was printer to the House of Representatives from 1837 to 1839, then acted as printer to the Senate until 1842. Allen served in Congress as a Democrat from Missouri, March 4, 1881-April 8, 1882. *Biographical Directory of Congress*, 473.

[5]John Mercer Patton (1797-1858) served in the House of Representatives as a Democrat from Virginia from 1830 to 1838. *Biographical Directory of Congress*, 1434.

[6]James Garland (1791-1885) represented Virginia in Congress as a Democrat, 1835-1841. *Biographical Directory of Congress*, 930.

[7]Hugh Swinton Legaré (1797-1843) was a Union Democrat from South Carolina who sat in the House of Representatives, 1837-1839. *Biographical Directory of Congress*, 1209.

[8]Richard Biddle (1796-1847) served in Congress as a Whig from Pennsylvania, 1837-1840. *Biographical Directory of Congress*, 551.

Charles Lockhart Pettigrew to William Shepard Pettigrew UNC

Lake Phelps Oct 9th 1837

My dear brother

I received your letter by the last mail and forthwith proceed to answer the enquiry when you will come home. I commence by telling you that Pa left Lake Phelps on last Saturday morning for the City of New York where he will be detained a few days on business vis purchasing some articles for Mr Davenport and himself and will proceed immediately to Hillsborough. He expects to reach home with you Mary Johnnston and Nancy about the last of October or the first of November so you may hold yourself in readiness about a fortnight from the date of this letter. Pa will pass through Newbern but his stay there will be short. You doubtless feel some anxiety to be at home. Things move on here in the old Style except that now and then a refractory negro has to be taken care of alias put in irons. Your man Gabe has become quite incorrigable and was sent to me the other day from Belgrade to be ironed: which I accordingly did. You must allow me to say I am much obliged to you for your description of commencement and I am much pleased to see my "Alma Mater" on the improving list. I hope she will continue to improve. Hooper[1] has accepted an appointment in S. Carolina I believe.

You mention Miss Penelope Skinner and her admirers; I learn that her conduct has not been without censure in her affair with Standin. I pretend myself to know nothing about the case and there is but little confidence to be placed in the flying reports we catch about the country. I read the greater part of your letter to Pa and from your mentioning the names of only two of Miss P's admirers he felt desirous to ask if you were not one of them. I told /him/ I could not inform him, he could better ascertain by asking you when he saw you

You mention the name of Sam Sawyer[2] I think he seems to be taking rather an ambiguous part in Congress during the present session, I have not examined his votes particularly, but he seems to be very often opposed to the whigs.

You wish to know whether Nash[3] is under any obligation to visit me this winter. You give me the first information of the fact that Nash will be in Edenton during the winter and I am not aware that he intends to come to our side of the Sound at all.

You will be much pleased when you see Mr Davenport's residence it is <a> small but comfortable and very roomy for its capacity he has it painted very neatly and the plastering is done /in/ a very good style. He will be very well situated when he goes home to live

I shall see you before you can answer this letter

truly your brother
Chas L. Pettigrew

P.S. You would much oblige me by giving my best respects to Mr & Mrs Bingham and request Mr Bingham to be so good as to send me by you a /parcel/ of his finest Carrot and Parsnip seed. I should be glad if you could get as many as he has to spare.

[*Addressed*] For Mr William S. Pettigrew
Hillsborough
Orange Co
N. Carolina

---

[1]William Hooper (1792-1876) taught ancient languages at the University of North Carolina. An Episcopal clergyman, he became Baptist in 1831 and in 1838 left the university to become professor of theology at Furman, a Baptist college in South Carolina. In later years he was connected with Wake Forest College and Chowan Female Institute, both North Carolina Baptist institutions. Battle, *History of the University*, I, 436-438.

[2]Samuel Tredwell Sawyer (1800-1865) of Edenton was the son of Dr. Matthias E. Sawyer. He served as a Whig in the House of Representatives for the 1837-1839 session. *Biographical Directory of Congress*, 1565; Cheney, *North Carolina Government*, 680. Sawyer appears to have been hotheaded. In 1828 he wrote a letter to Dr. James A. Norcom apologizing for an undescribed affront. A notation by Norcom reads: "Letters of this kind are rare; but they are far more honourable than a thousand victories gained by treachery or the sword!!" Samuel T. Sawyer to Dr. James Norcom, July 2, 1828, Private Collections, Dr. James Norcom Papers, PC 73, North Carolina Archives.

[3]Possibly this was Henry Kollock Nash (1817-1897) of Hillsborough, a member of Charles Lockhart Pettigrew's class (1836) at the university. Nash was a member of the state House of Commons in the 1842 legislative session. Hamilton and Williams, *Graham Papers*, VII, 617n.

Charles Lockhart Pettigrew to Ebenezer Pettigrew UNC

Lake Phelps Oct 26 1837

My dear father

I write to communicate rather bad news—the Select Cap[t] Etheridge so far from arriving at New York before you got there, came into the mouth of the river on Friday last with her cargo damaged. Cap[t] Owens came up saturday to inform me of the fact, and learn what should be done, the vessel he said had sprung her mast and that the hull leaked so that it required the pump to be going half the time to free her of water. I upon consulting M[r] Davenport thought it best to have it spread in the barn at Belgrade, and accordingly order the vessel to the landing, saying that it would be taken out as soon as she arrived there. <Mr Davenport> The hands went out <with the hands> on Sunday morning <and> but the wind being ahead M[r] Davenport concluded to return the same evening. The vessel got to the landing on Wednesday morning and the corn was to taken out that day. M[r] Davenport says that about 300 bushels cannot be reshiped but the rest will bear it when it becomes perfectly cool. It seems Cap[t] Etheridge <when> went over the bar on Friday of the General Muster but seeing the gale in prospect he concluded to come back, he says that it was mere chance that the vessel was not lost; he could see nothing and was following another vessel that struck but drawing less water he went clear. He thinks that she could not have lived out the storm at see: as it is Cap[t] Owens says she will have to be taken up and repaired, which will cost him $100. This is quite an unexpected loss but I suppose it cannot be helped.

But I have still something else to write of interest. I received /to day/ a message from M[r] Newberry that there was a mad dog there from the country, he had not killed him but /he/ was in the woods between M[r] Collins' and your canal. I have ordered our dogs to be confined and will keep a strict watch for him as well as on M[r] C.'s dogs. They might do a great deal of mischeif by biting hogs mules and cattle and even negroes. I learn that two children have been bitten by <them> those in the country. numbers of hogs have been destroyed, and it is a fact it seems that what ever eats of an animal dying of madness will have the same disease. I shall take /care/, if possible, that we sustain no injury from them

Mr D. goes to Edenton <to morrow> for Mrs D. tomorrow and expects to return on saturday. Notwithstanding all hindrance M[r] Davenport is about even with the commencement of the vineyard sowing wheat and has gather through to long-wood except forty rows. The corn still gathers light and is much shrunk. I am tolerably well at present please give my love to my Grandma brothers and sisters and relations in Newbern and believe me your

affec^{ate} son
Chas L Pettigrew

[*Addressed*] Hon E. Pettigrew
Newbern
N. Car—

John M. Ashurst[1] *to William Shepard Pettigrew* UNC

Milledgeville. Ga—Nov. 11th 1837—

My Dear Friend,

Your favour of last month came safely to hand: & was joyfully received. I am sorry that I can write nothing that would interest you. It may seem strange to you too that I should have nothing to communicate of note, & at Milledgeville too, where at least it is said, are the reputed talents of Ga, But it is true. Our legislature is in session, *as usual, doing nothing.* Notwithstanding we have elected a State Rights Governor, yet our legislature is contrould by *soap tailism.* The elections for Judges have been against us. But I think the shackles are fast falling from the hands of the nominal Union party. They, who are honest in their political tenets, are opening their eyes to the truth. They see or begin to see, the deception which has been thrown before them to lull them into toleration of federalism. Many who before worshiped at the shrine of Schley,[2] Fort[3] & Co. begin to doubt the infalibility of their leaders—I do not wish to speak in terms of disrespect of a majority of the people of my native state, but am compelled to tell the truth. You know what ignorance reigned at one time in No Ca. legislature. You can recollect when the powers & offices of that state were vested in the hands of those, who could not even define the nature of their constitution. So it is with us now. We have Judges & Soliciters who could not make out bill in a plain case of assault & battery—men who however honest in their intentions are incapable of doing justice to the laws which they construe.

Our mutual friend Mr Lewis[4] is acting as secratary to the Governor. Sam Blake is practising law in the middle circuit. And could not my friend William lend his name to Georgia? Nothing would afford me more peasure than to <see> welcome you to the state of my nativity. The inducements are great. You intend to cultivate the soil, Here we have in some sections a fruitful earth & salubrious climate combined. A romantic country where the imagination may play at will. Citizens generous & noble. Should you delight in the sport of the field, here the stag can be chased or as the veritable Crockett has it you may overtake any kind of wild varmints

I have not yet selected a partner to share with me the joys & distresses of life—I thought at one time I had found the being of my hearts desire—Young, beutiful accomplished & artless. I was deceived—*she was a woman.* And without foreswearing the sex, I can say, that at least it is my intention now of enjoying the comforts of single blessedness—My notions may change My resolutions may vanish before the bewitching glance of a bright pair eyes.—I am not infallible.

I shall remain here about a week, when I shall return home, to eatonton, Write to me upon the reception of this—& believe me as ever

your sincere Friend
John M Ashurst

To—
Wm S. Pettigrew

[*Addressed*] Wm S. Pettigrew, Esqr
Cool Spring
Washington Co—
N. Ca

[1]Ashurst, a classmate of William Shepard Pettigrew at the University of North Carolina, was a native Georgian and later became solicitor general of that state. Battle, *History of the University*, I, 796.

[2]William Schley (1786-1858) served in the Georgia House of Representatives in 1830, in Congress as a Democrat from 1833 to 1835, and as governor of Georgia, 1835-1837. *Biographical Directory of Congress*, 1568.

[3]Tomlinson Fort (1787-1859) sat in the Georgia House of Representatives, 1818-1826, and as a Democrat in Congress, 1827-1829. *Biographical Directory of Congress*, 906.

[4]David W. Lewis of Georgia was in the same class as William Shepard Pettigrew at the University of North Carolina but did not graduate. Later he was a member of the Confederate States Congress from Georgia. Battle, *History of the University*, I, 796.

William A. Dickinson to Ebenezer Pettigrew A&H

East Wetumpka [*Alabama*] 18th Decr 1837

E. Pettegrew Esqr

Dear Sir

I have for a long time been looking for a letter from you. I wrote on the 21st July—since that time I have frequently heard of you. Mr

Douglas is at this place, he told me that he saw you in New York. I was glad to hear that you was well. I hope this will reach you safe and find you & your family all well. I like this place, and am sorry that I did not steer my course this way a year or two ago. I think If I keep my health. I now stand a fair chance of doing very well, I am so far engaged in business as will by & by answer my expectations at present we have no reason to complain as business is gitting better and a good deal now doing, this town is well situated for becoming of some importance, five years ago there were only a few Log Houses. it now contains nigh 4,000 Inhabitants with a number of good & large Brick Buildings being erected

Mr Douglas has brought a large assortment of Merchandise to this place and is selling considerable no doubt but he will do well

I send you a Newspaper by which you will see the present prices of this market. I see Corn still mantains its price at the north. I was sorry to hear of the storm having done so much damage I hope you did not suffer much at Lake Phelps as was at first anticipated, I hope tobe able to visit North Carolina in about six months <o>if in good health, when I shall be happy to see you, and will try hard to make you a return for your abundent kindness but you know I made nothing at Coolspring & since I have been at a considerable outlay so it will take some time and perseverance to git ahead again. but nothing shall be wanting on my part to try hard for it.

Give my respects to Mr Charles Pettigrew Mr D. Davenport, hoping that he and Mrs D. & children are well. We have had a very long continuation of Dry warm weather it is now cold with a few bitting frosts—shall be exceedinly happy to hear from you my best wishes for your continuation of good health and many returns of the season.

Very Respectfully
Dear Sir,
Your obdt Sevt
W: A: Dickinson

[*Addressed*] Ebenezer Pettegrew Esqr
Lake Phelps
Cool Spring
North Carolina

Charles Biddle Shepard to Ebenezer Pettigrew A&H

Washington 19th Decr 1837.

My dear Mr Pettigrew,

I have received your letter and am very glad to hear that Charles will pay Mother a visit at Christmas; I hope that he will stay as long as possible, for I have no doubt that he will find it a pleasant trip & I know that it will be very agreeable to his Grandmother—

The House has not yet got under way (to use a nautical phrase) but the abolitionist are on the alert and have already commence to agitate both branches of Congress. Clay & Calho[*u*]n had a most interesting discussion on Monday on this subject—& Tuesday next is the day fixed on to to discuss a memorial sent here from the Legislature of Vermont (passed unanimously) You know that I have long entertained the opinion that these fellows ought to be permitted to go as far they wish, and [thus] then the South will know what to expect, & may then look to their own resources—

I have said & now say that we are deceived, that we know not what these men are doing, and I am determined to let the people know (as far as I can) what they must expect from this Govenment.

Old Adams abused us last week in the foulest terms--the Southerns (like Jack) became very hot but the matter was laid on the table—contrary to my opinion, for I wish to know the whole truth—& not to be cajoled by those who wish to keep our trade & yet violate our rights.

At this moment Hade of Vermont is spouting about abolition—He is a poor devil & deserves nothing harsher than contempt—but I fear that some fool will rise, & rant abut Southern chivalry when coolness is all important—

Can you continue to get me a dozen bottles of the best Scuppernong? & can you have it sent to me at Alexandria (care of A. C. Cazenove)? Write me & I will endeaver to correspond regularly as I can—I would send you documents, but I suppose that your representative is very attentive—

Very truly & affectionately
Your brthr
Ch Shepard

[*Addressed*] To
The Hon. E. Pettigrew
Cool. Spring
Washington Co
NC

Ebenezer Pettigrew's Tax List UNC

Tax list of E Pettigrew in Tyrrel Co. 1838

6850 Acres of Land valued by the assors in the year 1837 at	$21212..00
40 Black Polls	

Tax list of E Pettigrew in Washington Co. 1838

1573 Acres of Land valued by the Assors in the year 1837 at $8000..00
12 Black Polls

Charles Pettigrew 1 white Poll in Tyrrel Co

William Biddle Shepard to Ebenezer Pettigrew A&H

Eliz. City, Jany 15th 1838

My Dear Sir

I returned a few days ago from a long and disagreeable journey through the Southwestern country. Of the very great capacity of that country for planting advantageously I am fully satisfied. I have never seen any Country where the earth produced every thing put into it, with so great abundance and at so little expenditure of labour as the middle part of Alabama. It is as different a country from Georgia or South Carolina as you can well conceive.

With all these advantages however, I found the planters generally embarrassed, from their thoughtless extravagance and their great want of any thing like economy. The people in that section have been very much like drunkards who have been for some time revelling under very great excitement but have at length recovered from their delirium and have found that they have wasted in a debauch what would have lasted an ordinary life for a series of years. As regards our location in Alabama, it is a very advantageous one, & if well managed it must ultimately prove advantageous, I have had however sundry misgivings & much anxiety about Fred's [*Frederick Shepard*] movements, he is beyond all sort of doubt the hardest man to keep in the traces I have ever met with, he seems to have forgotten that industry and attention to business are indispensable requisites for success in all situations. We have made a pretty good crop but not as good a one as we might have made if the owner had not trusted too much to the overseer, under all circumstances however I think it better than could have been done in Camden.—

The fatigue and anxiety I incurred during the last summer and fall, have very materially affected my health, I have been for several months past very much troubled with a sickness of the stomack which usually attacks me in the afternoon and lasts sometimes for one or two hours and is attended with loss of appetite. In the fore part of the day I feel pretty well but as night approaches my stomack seems to give way and I cannot eat any thing without a disposition to vomit. Having great reliance on your judgment in such matters I would be glad if you would give me your opinion on this subject. A physician here tells me it is a nervous irritability of the stomack and advises me to be cupped, having however a great aversion to unusual remedies I have not as yet adopted his advice.—

I suppose you donot feel any regrets at not being in Washington this winter, I have been so constantly moving about and altogether so unsettled that I have not paid any attention to the proceedings of that august body. I see however they are at the old subject of abolition.

Remember me to Charles & William who I suppose are both with you and believe me

Yours truly
W B Shepard

[*Addressed*] Hon
E. Pettigrew
Cool Spring
Washington County
North Carolina

Albert Gallatin Hubbird[1] *to William Shepard Pettigrew* UNC

Chapel Hill Feb. 12th 1838

Dear Friend:

I have really forgotten which of us promised to write first & have delayed writing thus long in expectation of getting a letter from you But as it seems you are either in the same dilemma with myself or for some other cause are backward in commencing our promised correspondence I have thought proper to begin it myself You must not suspect me of indifference towards you, for you ought to know me too well to suppose for a moment that I could /ever/ forget one with whom I have spent many of the happiest moments of my life Indeed the remembrance of old friends is to me a Source of the sweetest though of melancholy pleasure It frequently conjures up reveries of the most pleasing nature amid severer occupations, & <at times> often I throw aside my books to indulge in the luxury of roaming in fancy over bright scenes of the past, I wish you were back here to share in our enjoyments. The number of students this session is about the same I believe as when you were here Several of your old acquaintances however have left Burke,[2] Edmunds, Peebles, Nixon & others. But their places have been supplied by new comers and our Society, I believe, is still as large as ever. Mr

Hooper took leave of us the first of the session in a handsome valedictory address When published I will send you a copy of it I don't know yet who will deliver the next annual address Judge /Nash/[3] has been elected & written to, but has not been heard from Mr McQueen[4] is still here & in fine spirits. He occupies the house which Blake[5] formerly had, & lives as secluded & solitary as a hermit. He seldom comes to college but on Society evenings. He sends you his respects & says he will write to you soon. There will be but little celebration here on the 22nd We held a meeting some time since to elect an orator for the occasion & Judge Owens was elected, but declined. The two Societies have passed resolutions that their representatives hereafter shall declaim their own compositions. It is not known who will be ours, *Clement*[6] & *Pharr*[7] are both eager candidates It is very assuring to hear Clement talk on the subject I asked him some time since, if he would appear on the stage under the appointment of the faculty to speek a 'funny'? He seemed very indignant at the question. I believe he has the vanity to think he will be a representative. Quite an amusing scence occurred in the hall at a late meeting. During the progress of the debate which had rather begun to flag, Clement who had been sitting for some time a silent spectator suddenly rose, on the question being called for. & exclaimed in a passion that he was not going to sit there and see certain members keep the floor all night & he not say any thing himself He then proceded to speak something on the question when he said he believed he'd conclude by relating an anecdote He then commenced tellin[g] [*torn*] anecdote when the President (Hase) told him he was not on the subject. Clement replied that his anecdote did have a bearing on the question & that he would not be stopped unconstitutionally On being suffered to proceed he went on very slowly as if he had forgotten the thread of his story when the house beginning to laugh & the President being vexed at his nonsense ordered him to take his seat. Clement obeyed but before doing so <he> stood & stared the P. in the face, presenting a most ludicrous appearance. He & the P—— have since settled it amicably I have made these personal allusions in confidence merely to afford you amusement. You must answer this letter immediately. Dennis [*Ferebee*], & many more send you their respects,

Yours truly
Albert G Hubbird

[*Addressed*] Mr William S Pettigrew
Cool Springs
Washington County
N. Carolina

[1]Albert Gallatin Hubbird, from Leesburg, was an 1838 graduate of the University of North Carolina. Later he was named to the first list of county escheators for the county of Carteret. Battle, *History of the University*, I, 622, 796.

[2]James M. Burke was a student at the University of North Carolina in 1837 and, like William Shepard Pettigrew, was a member of the Philanthropic Society. He died in 1840. Battle, *History of the University*, I, 433, 511.

[3]Frederick Nash (1781-1858), an attorney in Hillsborough, served in the state legislature and was a superior court judge from 1818 to 1826 and from 1836 to 1844. He sat on the state supreme court, 1844-1858, and was chief justice after 1852. *CDAB*, 720.

[4]Hugh McQueen lived in Chapel Hill in 1836. Apparently an eccentric, he published the *Columbian Repository* at that time. Battle comments on "the unfortunate habits of the otherwise gifted editor." Battle, *History of the University*, I, 377. In an address at the university in 1839, McQueen deplored the lack of cultural development in the state. Once again in 1840 he attempted to publish a magazine, this one to be called the *Emerald*, but no copies are known to exist. Henderson, *North Carolina*, II, 672, 709.

[5]Samuel Richardson Blake graduated from the University of North Carolina in 1834 and served as a tutor there, 1834-1835. Battle, *History of the University*, I, 421, 795.

[6]This might refer to R. Alexander Clement of Franklin, Virginia, an 1840 graduate of the University of North Carolina. Battle, *History of the University*, I, 797.

[7]Walter W. Pharr of Cabarrus County received a degree from the university in 1840. Battle, *History of the University*, I, 471.

John Herritage Bryan to Ebenezer Pettigrew UNC

Raleigh Feb. 27. '38

My dear sir

We arrived here last Saturday night after a most fatiguing journey, rendered more disagreeable by the severity of the weather, but thank God, we have all arrived safely.—Mrs. B. had as you may well suppose many & great anxieties for the children, she has something of the rheumatism in the head & shoulders, occasioned by sleeping in cold bed rooms with the glass out of the windows

About half of our furniture is still at Waynesboro.—We find our place a very handsome one but it is small for our family, but may be added to in convenient time.—

Mrs B. says she should be glad to see you & the children as soon as convenient.—

Mrs Shepard appears anxious to come up & I should [*not*] be surprised if she comes in 4 or 5 weeks. Mary desires to be kindly remembered—and sends her love to the children.—

Present my Respects & good wishes to Charles & Wm—

Very truly & respy
yr friend
Jn. H. Bryan

[*Addressed*] E Pettigrew Esq
Cool Spring
Washington Co
N.C

Ebenezer Pettigrew to Mary Williams Bryan UNC

Lake Phelps April 2, 1838

My dear Sister,

I have been for a long time wishing to write you but the affection of my eyes in the first instance and since that such a constant attention to business as to cause me to defer it untill now.

My dear Mary received your kind & affectionate letter mail before last. It found us all well, though in this country it has been exceeding sickly and at no season since I have known the country so many deaths. It is a new disease. I think somewhat like the [old] plague. I hope it will disappear with warm weather.

It gave me great pleasure to learn from Mr B's as well as your letter that you had got to your new home without accident or any thing to regret but *so much* fatigue & trouble. I pray God it may be to your general interest & benefit.

We are all /now & have been through the winter/ in good health. Charles & William have taken hold like they should, if atall. The two dear little Girls & Johnston are deporting themselves very well, but learning nothing, none of us having time to attend to them. I begin to grow very anxious to get them away & expect to set for Raleigh between the 15th & 20 of this month with them. I fear by going at this time (for I cannot defer it longer neither can I stay long) I shall not have the pleasure of seeing Mr Bryan.

My eyes admonish me that I must quit and I will conclude by presenting mine together with the Love of my dear children to you & your dear children and believe me to be

your affectionate Brother
E Pettigrew

Mrs John H. Bryan

[*Addressed*] Mrs John H. Bryan
Raleigh
N. Ca

Alfred Gardner to Ebenezer Pettigrew UNC

Oakland [*Tennessee*] 22nd May 1838

Dear Sir.

I received yours a few days since, stating that you thought as your interest in the Loose Hatcher lands was small you thought It advisable to sell, I think you are correct in This opinion—Since I wrote you last I have visited the land and found it had been sold for taxes and several years due upon it—fortunately however I was in time to redeem it—which I done and have it now clear of incumbrance

All the Legatees but J S. & R. M Shepard & youself have parted with their interest. and four of the shares have been set apart to those who purchased from the residue of the heirs—The Commissionrs appointed to divide the land gave one grant to the applicants under the order leaving the other to yourself & the others just mentioned and one share sold by Charles Shepard, for which the <applic> purchaser (Mr White I think) has not yet applied, which makes your int & J S. & R M.s the three fourths of the grant

I found the land of a good quality, though broken and heavy timbered, and surrounded by swamps, being bounded south by the Hatcher & North by big Creek—

If It were situated only five or six miles south of the river it would command a good price but where it is its dull sale, I think I can sell it perhaps this fall as soon as the embarrassments in pecuniary matters shall subside which I hope will not last long.

The last Legislature of Tennessee chartered a new State Bank which will commence business in a few days. and although I am not an advocate for Banks in general yet I think the new Bank will commence on a good footing and will measureably relieve the people of the state—

I think you had better send me a power of attorney, The manner of authenticating which you will see by reffernce to an act of Congress, I think of 1804, so that I might sell at any time should an oppertunity offer, I have a power from R M. Shepard & have written to J S. for one

I suppose you own ⅛ of Penelope Shepard lands. I do not know what the administrator Mr. C Shepard intends doing with it. Though my advice would be to sell it and divide the proceeds for the land could not be divided conveniently and I think could be sold for a fair price all together. About this you can consult the adm & Legatees, and should they conclude to Sell I will attend to it on reasonable terms—

very Respectfully your obt & humb. Svt
Alfred Gardner

[*Addressed*] E Petegrew Esqr
Lake Phelps

John Herritage Bryan to Ebenezer Pettigrew UNC

Raleigh May 28, 1838

My dear sir,

I am just about leaving hence for Johnston County Court, but delay a moment to inform you that I have rec^{d} from John Williams of Chaston, a check on U.S. B^{k} Philad^{a} for $1000. which I hold subject to your order.—

I regretted very much not seeing you when you bro't the girls—but hope you or Chas or W^{m} will come up this summer—Mrs Shepard is getting pleased with Ral^{h}—and the horses have become quite gentle again.—The girls are very well and are going to school to Miss Betsey Haywood, and are I believe making fair progress.—We expect in the course of the summer to have a teacher for young ladies.—Gov: Iredell talks very strongly of going to Mobile.—

Judge Dick[1] requested me last fall to beg the favour of you to let him have a bbl of Scup^{g} wine—& the other day repeated the request.—

Remember me kindly to Chas & W^{m}—Mary Pettigrew has a letter for you in a course of preparation

Mrs B. offers her affectionate regard to you all.

Very truly & respy yr friend & relation.
Jn. H. Bryan

[*Addressed*] E Pettigrew Esq
Cool Spring
Washington County
N^{o} Ca

---

[1]John M. Dick of Guilford County was a superior court judge from 1835 until his death in 1861. Cheney, *North Carolina Government*, 361, 370.

Edward Stanly to Ebenezer Pettigrew A&H

House of Reps: May 30th 1838—

My Dear Sir,

Your favor of the 18th Inst: was received a few days since, and has given me much pleasure.

I am gratified to learn that what I said has met your approbation, and that you think the 'Connecticut nightingale', deserved even more.[1] Your opinion of this cold blooded—(blood fearing,) viper is correct. He is a v[*er*]y chivalrous gentleman, when I had *alluded* to him, disrespectfully, as he thought he could put on a swaggering air of defiance, to a 'dagger of both,' as he said; but when I made a *direct* personal attack upon him, he slunk away like a whipt hound.—I think he is better behaved since.—

I should not have made any speech at all, but for the silly argument, that the reference of petitions to a committee, gave that Committee the power, to report a bill granting the prayer of the petitioners.—I could not stand that.—it was akin to abolitionism, and I thought I was discharging my duty, in dissenting from it.—

The duel affair seems to have passed off, the party became rather sick of that before it was finished—beaten even in Cilley's own district. I sincerely sympathised with Greaves, but after he had been so imprudent as to carry Webb's note I think with you, he was forced to act as he did.[2]

Poor Cilly was mistaken, he was rushing madly on, and unfortunately had bad advisers.—[*Jesse Atherton*] Bynum, Duncan & such cattle as friends!—What could the poor man expect, with such counsellors?—

I delivered your message to Greaves & Wise,[3] they beg me, to make their respects to you, and are glad that you still remember them.—Charles Shepard is quite well; There was a report in circulation a week or two ago, that he was paying his addresses to Miss Singleton of So: Ca: but I believe it was a report started or encouraged by the friends of the young lady herself, to seek her triumph merely.—He denies it.—

Your friend Mr Pearce of Maryland sits near me, and frequently mentions you in terms of affectionate respect. I have begged him to visit you, to go and see you at home, to see your farm, of which I have given him a most glowing description. As far as I can learn, every gentleman of your acquaintance here, entertains a high respect for you, and Pearce says he wishes you were with him, that you might together abuse these "subtreasury Jackson van-Buren men."—

We have had some hopes that Wood*bug*[4] (as the French call him,) would resign,—but poor Devil, he is afraid to go, and knows he will get into deeper and deeper mire, if he stays.—Like the ass, between the two stacks of fodder,—though he has feathered his nest pretty well, out of Uncle Sam's stack I suspect.—You know he is appointed Judge of a Supreme Court in N. Hampshire.—

The more I think of these rascals, the more I hate them.—and the more I write, the more I have to write about them. To discuss the characters of such men, as you mention in your last,—is like shingling anew an old house.—every old shingle you tore off.

shows another place which wants mending.—We have talked about adjourning early in July. The banks still have hopes of carrying the sub-treasury scheme.—It is rumoured here that our friend [*Samuel Tredwell*] Sawyer will probably support the Bill.—I can hardly believe it, but his remaining affection—for the Nullifiers may lead him astray, unless some of our friends in his district, write to him, and express their opposition to it. However I mention this not to be told to others, unless you can confide it, in such a manner, as to operate upon him, without injuring him, either in public estimation, or in the opinion of any friend.—The Van Buren men, hope to carry it by one or two votes. It is possible our fears may be unnecessarily alarmed—but these fellows many of them—New Yorkers & conservatives want money, and the administration wants votes.—

My respects to your son—I wish I was sitting in your porch, looking on the glad waters' of Lake Phelps, and listening to the gentle sighing of the summer breeze, through your sycamores, for a few hours,—how much more delightful than the yelping of these hounds of party.

Very truly yours
Edw. Stanly

[*Addressed*] Hon: Eb: Pettigrew
Cool Spring
Washington County
No: Ca:

---

[1]This probably refers to Isaac Toucey (1796-1869), a Democratic representative from Connecticut. He later served in President James K. Polk's cabinet, as a United States senator, and as secretary of the navy. *Biographical Directory of Congress*, 1722. Toucey chaired a committee on duelling, which reported to the House. Stanly spoke against it and verbally delivered "a bolt of keen, bitter irony and sarcasm" and "defeated" Toucey. *Newbern Spectator*, May 11, 1838.

[2]Congressmen William Jordan Graves (1805-1848), a Whig from Kentucky, and Jonathan Cilley (1802-1838), a Jacksonian Democrat from Maine, engaged in a duel on February 24, 1838, and Cilley was killed. *Biographical Directory of Congress*, 692, 967; *DAB*, XX, 423-425. Webb remains unidentified.

[3]Henry Alexander Wise was a second in the duel between Graves and Cilley. Although both were southerners, Stanly and Wise clashed more than once. An extensive account of a near duel between the two may be found in the *Whig* (Washington, N.C.), May 11, May 25, June 1, and June 22, 1843.

[4]Levi Woodbury (1789-1851) was governor of New Hampshire in 1823 and 1824. He sat in the United States Senate as a Democrat, 1825-1831 and 1841-1845, and served as secretary of the navy, 1831-1834, and secretary of the treasury, 1834-1841. He declined the judgeship mentioned in this letter. Woodbury supported President Andrew Jackson's bank policies and favored Martin Van Buren's independent treasury system, under which the federal government would deposit funds in regional treasury offices instead of banks. *CDAB*, 1247-1248; *Biographical Directory of Congress*, 1845.

Charles Biddle Shepard to Ebenezer Pettigrew A&H

Washington, June 2, 1838

My dear Mr Pettigrew,

I have received from Br. W^m a check on the Bank for Penelope's legacy, amounting to \$5100-\$5200 (I do not recollect which), to one ninth part of which your children are entitled—Charles & W^m are of age & they can receive their share—the others must have a guardian to take possession of theirs. If Charles & William will make you their attorny to receive, & you will be appointed guardian for the others, I will send you a check for the whole amount—

We are going on shortly, & I am almost tired to death—Yesterday we had a *real fight* in the *House* between Bell of Tenn. and Turney[1] one of his colleagues. The Speaker took the chair from the Chairman of the Committee & the members seperated the combatants. So we go on. What next, can't be predicted. The House *merely* required an *apology*; & things went on as if nothing had happend.—

My love to the boys—

Very affectionately
Yrs.
Charles Shepard

[*Addressed*] E. Pettigrew Esq
Cool Spring
Washington Co
N.C.

[1]Hopkins Lacy Turney (1797-1857) served as a Democratic Congressman, 1837-1843, and sat in the United States Senate from 1845 to 1851. *Biographical Directory of Congress*, 1734.

Thomas P. Williams to Ebenezer Pettigrew UNC

Charleston June 19, 1838

Hon^l E. Pettigrue

Dear Sir

Your favour of the 8th Ins^t came to hand yesterday, and agreeable to your request I have handed over to our Mayor \$100 for the sufferes by the late fire in our city,[1] as a donation for you. I now send you inclosed Bank check. on New York for \$400 for which I had to pay 3 pr cent prem: and above you have my draft on Hardy & Bro^s of Norfolk for 300\$.—My Bro M^r J Williams is absent for a few days on a visit to N.C I expect him by the 30th Ins^t—

Vy Truly.
T. P. Williams

John Herritage Bryan of New Bern and Raleigh, a lawyer, married Ann Blount Shepard Pettigrew's sister Mary Williams Shepard. Photograph of a portrait from the North Carolina Collection, University of North Carolina Library, Chapel Hill.

William Biddle Shepard, brother-in-law to Ebenezer Pettigrew, was a lawyer, planter, banker, and politician. Engraving from Samuel A. Ashe and others (eds.), *Biographical History of North Carolina: From Colonial Times to the Present* (Greensboro: Charles L. Van Noppen, 8 volumes, 1905-1917), VII, facing 421.

Charlotte Cazenove (1812-1836) of Alexandria, Virginia, the first wife of William Biddle Shepard. Photograph of a portrait from Laura MacMillan (comp.), *The North Carolina Portrait Index, 1700-1860* (Chapel Hill: University of North Carolina Press, 1963), 208.

William Biddle Shepard married Anne Daves Collins, daughter of Josiah Collins II, in 1843. Photograph of a portrait from MacMillan, *North Carolina Portrait Index*, 209.

William James Bingham (1802-1866) operated the highly regarded preparatory school in Hillsborough attended by Ebenezer's sons. Engraving from Ashe, *Biographical History*, VI, facing 69.

James Cathcart Johnston of Hayes Plantation, Edenton, was a close friend of Ebenezer Pettigrew, and the two exchanged lengthy letters. Photograph of a lithograph from the files of the Division of Archives and History.

Josiah Collins II, a merchant and planter, lived in Edenton and at Somerset, the plantation neighboring Bonarva. Photograph of a portrait from the files of the Division of Archives and History.

Whig leader Edward Stanly filled the seat in Congress vacated by Ebenezer Pettigrew in 1837. Stanly served as military governor of North Carolina for a time during the Civil War. Photograph from the North Carolina Collection.

[*Addressed*] Hon^{l} E. Pettigrue
Cool Spring
Washington County
North Carolina

---

[1] A detailed description of the Charleston fire of April 27, 1838, extracted from the *Southern Patriot,* is reprinted in the *New Bern Spectator*, May 4, 1838, under the heading "Destructive and Awful Conflagration."

Ebenezer Pettigrew to James Alfred Pearce A&H

Lake Phelps June 29, 1838

My dear Sir,

Ever since the commencement of the session I have been wishing to write you, but in December I took cold in my eyes which rendered me unable to write or read almost the whole winter I could not form any idea before of the imm[*en*]se /importance/ the use of the eye is to human life. Since the recovery of my sight I have been engaged so as to defer writing from mail to mail untill now. Although nothing in the way of a letter could have been more desirable than from you, I know too well the labours of Congress to expect one from you, and it must be a more wretched place than when I was there.

I observe you have given out dueling & gone to fisting it. A gentlemanly act for Honble members of Congress. I have no respect for Mr Bell & Turney, I do not know, and should only have said fight on boys, Hell was not made for dogs. I regret that Mr Mercer[1] will engage the house with endeavoring to prevent their fighting. If a dozen or two were allowed to kill each other, they would endeavor to act the gentleman so as to give no farther offence in debate. What a miserable pack. Thank God I am free from them.

Was there ever such a vilinous, corrupt, & crazy scheme to ruin the country as the Sub Treasury one. Poor Mr Calhoun! I pitty him from my heart, and when /I see his/ name in the list of votes, my refections on poor fallen man are beyond my power of expresion. What in the name of common sence is his mind? Is he crazy? or what is the matter with him. To read in the list: viz. Benton,[2] [Beirne],[3] *Calhoun*, Niles,[4] Strange[5] &c., Why I would hesitate before I would vote with such D——d corrupt witches, if they were right. At least I should respect my judgment. But there are a few Van Buren men who either from fear of their constituants or disposition will sometimes <to> do right and I think that the confounded bill will be lost in the house. I look forward with delight to the close of Jacksons administration carryed out by that FOX

Van Buren. I suppose you intend to sit all the year so as to have but two sessions. I see our friend Steel[6] will be in nomination for governor. If he wishes (& I hope he does) I hope he will be elected. But let me drop politicks. I know you are tired to death with them. I should /have/ been very glad to have received a visit from you & do /not/ dispair of that pleasure yet. I am much obliged for the documents I observed Mrs R's remarks of Mr Jenefer's eye. I hope he will make his forture by his union with Mrs McK. Give my best respects to him /& tell him/ not to let the present oportunity pass unimproved.

I have been for the last ten days closely engaged in harvest, and up to today (which is very threatening) I have had fine weather. The crop is a good one though not equal to what I have had. My corn is good & would have been surpassing, but for two excessive storms of rain & wind which we harvested in this month but it is so likely that I should be very glad to share it to you. And now lastly in my letter but first in my mind. I express that of mine as well as /that of/ my two sons extreme regret at the unfortunate death of our most worthy friend Gov. [*Joseph*] Kent. We knew no man of so kind feelings & no man who deserves to live longer in /the/ hearts of his friends. To me here in solitude & seclusion he will never be forgotten no never can, but I suppose in /the/ bustle & confusion at Washington where was the theatre of his action & usefulness he is by this scarcely thought off, but when some of those heartless beings at Washington need his services. O man what a *beast* thou art? Please to make my respects to his successor, Mr Shepard & Mr Stanly. And now my friend make my kind regards to Mrs Pearce hoping that herself & your daughter are well & that when you get home you will write me. Believe me your frnd

E Pettigrew

Hon. J. A. Pearce

N.B. On reading this to W. P. he adviced me to strike out the D——d but I am a plain man.

[*Addressed*] Honble James A. Pearce
H.R.
Washington City

---

[1]This might refer to Charles Fenton Mercer (1778-1858), a Democrat from Virginia who served in the House of Representatives, 1817-1839. *Biographical Directory of Congress*, 1320-1321.

[2]Thomas Hart Benton (1782-1858) of Missouri, a Democrat, served in the United States Senate, 1821-1851, and in the House of Representatives, 1853-1855. *Biographical Directory of Congress*, 546.

[3]Andrew Beirne (1771-1845), a native of Ireland, was a Van Buren Democrat from Virgina who sat in Congress from 1837 to 1841. *Biographical Directory of Congress*, 536.

[4]John Milton Niles (1787-1856) of Connecticut was a Democratic member of the United States Senate, 1835-1839. He served as postmaster general under President Martin Van Buren, 1840-1841, and then served again in the Senate, 1843-1849. *Biographical Directory of Congress*, 1390.

[5]Robert Strange (1796-1854) was a Fayetteville attorney who served in the United States Senate as a Democrat from 1836 to 1840. *Biographical Directory of Congress*, 1667.

[6]John Nevett Steele (1796-1853), a Whig, was an unsuccessful candidate for governor of Maryland in 1838. An attorney, he had served in Congress and in the state legislature. *Biographical Directory of Congress*, 1648.

Thomas Turner to Ebenezer Pettigrew UNC

Plymo NC July 14 1838

Dear Sir

I had the pleasure to see your son Charles the other evening as he passed through this place. I was glad too to see he was in such good health. I regretted to hear from him that you suspected you had had a touch of the gout in your toes. I hope you mistake the disease. Your son passed on from Plymouth /in the steam Boat/ at about half past 10 of the evening of his arrival. <in the steam Boat.> He brought me the Memoirs of Kotzebue[1] which I had given you to read. This is precisely like you; Punctual in all things. But if you thought I wished any punctuality here, or so soon a return of the book, or even any return at all, you mistake me. Men in different circumstances, differently educated, and of different habits, will act differently even when they are *equally afflicted* by the *same causes*. The only resemblance which I noticed between you and Kotzebue was in the loss of the same personal relation, the deep affliction, and the everlasting grief and lamentation expressed with the same force and tenderness. But his grief forced him into one line of conduct, and yours you into another, in which there was no resemblance. I recommended you to read the book merely because I wished you to have some as deeply afflicted, and from the same cause as yourself, to cry with you, and to say, "Severe and grievious as it is, we cannot, we will not forego nor forget the grief of the grave." It is seldom a man can have a companion in his tears. I thought you would find one in Kotzebue.

My brother [*Dr. William A. Turner*] and I were to come to see you. Let me tell how that intention now lies; and how it was overcome for the time. You & Mr Collins had gone to Newbern. We were to /make our/ visit shortly after your return. My brother seized upon the time of your absence on that trip, to visit Salmon Creek and Windsor; intending to return and go to the Lake. On the day of his arrival at Windsor, although he had not then determined to settle there; he was called to two patients. One a poor whiteman with his guts in his bag as low as his knees, as large as his hat, of 6 to 8 years standing.—In half an hour the man's guts <was> were secured in his body by a truss; where they still are.—Several other attempts had been made, as I have heard, to keep them up in that manner by that means, but had failed; the trusses which had been applied could not be made to fit. The one my brother applied, did not fit /at first/; but he made it fit, by a little twisting and turning and hammering and padding. The other patient was a negro some ten miles off. He visited him 4 times, got him up, /and/ left him for a week to visit Doctor Henderson at Edenton. At the end of the week the negro was taken down again and in 10 days died. My brother had also one or two other calls which being a confidential nature, I know nothing of them. He was at Windsor on this visit some 8 or 10 days. He was much urged to settle there; the prospect was, if he did, he would go at once into as much practice as he could do.—His reception at Windsor by every body was very warm, cordial, and gratifying. I could not explain it here and do it half the justice it would merit. He was so pressed, *that, all things considered*, he felt that he ought to <do so> settle there, and so he determined. Having come to this determination, it was impossible that he should not see the Crisis he was in.—The sickly season approaching; he without a horse, gig, harness, medicines, shop, servant; the vacancy occasioned by Dr Haywood's death then filling up; people then in the act of determining what physician they should employ; Gilliam & Johnson, physicians, having entered into Copartnership, and being themselves honourable, liberal, generous gentlemen, besides good physicians,—to compete with them was not /an/ undertaking to be disregarded, nor one in which success might be hoped for, without instant action with a great deal of attention, industry, perseverance, and zeal. Gilliam had been for 2 or 3 years already settled there; Johnson had been settled there only for a month or two. The persons who had formerly employed Haywood, had not yet had occasion to employ any one in his room: Their custom was on the eve of being bestowed; and it was necessary to be in the way if one would get a share of it.—So my brother /considered that he ought/ to settle there; to give out for the present his visits to you & others; He did so; and from that time to this he has had as much as he can do.[2]—I am Dear Sir

Your faithful & obliged &
affectionate friend
Th: Turner

[*Addressed*] Ebenezer Pettigrew Esqre
Cool Spring
N.C.

[1]August Friedrich Ferdinand von Kotzebue (1761-1819) was a German playwright and satirist. This probably refers to his *Mein Literarischer Lebenslauf* (1796), published in London in 1830 as *Sketch of the Life and Literary Career of August von Kotzebue.* Stanley J. Kunitz and Vineta Colby (eds.), *European Authors, 1000-1900: A Biographical Dictionary of European Literature* (New York: H. W. Wilson Company, 1967), 500-501.

[2]Upon the death of Dr. William A. Turner, William Darden Valentine of Winton gave a detailed description of him, with comments on his brother Thomas. In a diary entry dated June 23, 1854, Valentine praised the doctor's scientific comprehension, saying that he was rather unpopular among physicians but was too benevolent to the poor for his own good. Valentine noted that Thomas Turner "was imbued with much literary acquirements and was interesting in the social circles, by his elegant conversation." Diary of William Darden Valentine, Southern Historical Collection.

Ebenezer Pettigrew to James Johnston Pettigrew UNC

Lake Phelps July 16, 1838

My dear Johnston,

I received your letter /of/ June 18th in due time, and was very glad to learn that you were geting along well with your studies and that you were in good health, but regreted very much to find that you were not so well pleased with the place you were at. I regret it the more because I know, if I have a friend in the world who is a sincere one to me and my children it is Mr Bingham. He has proven it beyond doubt in all instances, and no one is now more sensible of it than your brother William, who once thought that Mr Bingham hated him, and it was with great difficulty that Mr Bingham or myself could put up with his notions. I know my dear Johnston that you will in time think with your brothers William & Charles & your father that except your father Mr Bingham was the best friend you ever had and I there/fore/ cannot think of your leaving where you are for any place but your fathers. I know as well my dear son that Mr Bingham has a great regard for you as I can know anything and believe me my dear Johnston that if you will conduct yourself in a propper manner (as you are well able to do) that he & Mrs Bingham will treat you with all the kindness that you could ask.

We had two floods of rain in June which injured the corn some but the seasons have been good since and my corn looks well. I sent a load of wheat for New York last week. It was the best I ever raised but once.

Mr & Mrs Davenport are well, also Mr & Mrs Collins & children. They have an expectation of spending the fall or a greater part of it on the Lake. It is now tolerable healthy, but I fear as the fall advances it will be very sickly. Your brother Charles left last saturday the 14th for old Point comfort.[1] His health was so feble that I could not risk him here any longer. Your brother William will join him in about ten days. They have some idea of going to Ohio & where then is not determined. William is yet well. My health has been very declining untill about a fortnight or three weeks, when I have become quite restored & think with Mr Davenports assistance that I shall manage the business this fall & not be sick much. I had ten days ago a marked & distinct case of the Gout. It was entirely across my toes.

Give my Love to your sisters, Grand ma, & Aunt & Uncle Bryan & all your little cousins & believe me my dear son your affectionate & loving father

E Pettigrew

Mr J. Johnston Pettigrew

July 20 N.B. I began /this/ letter because I had time but tomorrow is mail day & I will close it.

Thinking you might be a little scant of cash I have taken the liberty to inclose you a five dollar bill, to pay your postage &c &c—I hope you will take no offence at it. My son be a good boy. and give your father no trouble except for your health.

E P.

[*Addressed*] Mr J. Johnston Pettigrew
Raleigh
N. Carolina

[1]Old Point Comfort was a fashionable resort in Virginia. James A. Padgett (ed.), "The Life of Alfred Mordecai, As Related by Himself," *North Carolina Historical Review*, XXII (January, 1945), 85.

Ebenezer Pettigrew to James Cathcart Johnston UNC

Lake Phelps July 16. 1838

My dear friend

With very great pleasure I received yours of the 12th Inst. I had been anxious to hear from you which I had not untill Mr Woodley who was at Belgrade about a fortneight /ago,/ informed me that you had just come from Pasquotank & was well. You need not at any time be afraid of the length of your letters, the longer the more acceptable because more entertaining. & interesting.

As for the conventional report, I have not seen it, nor have I much expectation of being favoured with one in the regular way. It is highly probable that I am not considered one of the chosen few. The mercy of God and the constitution of the country has made me free, & how long it will last is very doubtfull, but I am determined while I have that privalege, to exercise it to a rational extent. The exercise of that liberty is not so agreeable to those who wish to govern & consequently I am rather excluded from a full participation. In truth I wish it to be so. It was necessarily so that it might be known how much I would bear. That course of conduct which I had to take no doubt gave great dissatisfaction to the little officiate [*Edward N. Forbes*][1] at this place, who is very much flattered, and I think vain. In consequence of which I think he seemed at various times to act towards me indignantly as I am sure he felt. This course of conduct from him brought a like course from me. From my feelings of disaprobation to the things that be, it may be possible that my opinions may in part be in error, but I think I am correct in my conclusions. From what I can learn from the negroes there is very little religion in the case. There are but twenty on the Lake /that profess./ Three at my place & seventeen at the other. My three are much as they have been for a number of years before. It is said that some of the seventeen are very corrupt in their moral conduct. That <they> /negroes/ in general behave better, do their work better and that there is less stealing at my neighbours, there is no doubt, but I account for it in a very different way. Viz. The owner has now been longer with them, and they fare /in food/ much better; (so much so that there is no complaint) /they have more leasure time given them/ & do their work with more ability and less punishment, and are in a better humor. This I believe is the true cause of that change, and not the preaching or praying in the least degree. But it will always pass for that benign influence of religion, and so let it be. I shall never give myself any trouble to correct the opinion. Be assured that religion among the mass of negroes who profess, is nothing more than a humbug.

When the thing was first in agitation Mr C. proposed to me to take an active part, but I told him I did not believe in the efficacy of preaching to negroes & would never contribute a cent for that purpose, because I had made it a rule never to undertake that which I could not do, but at the same time I was willing to support a minister in scuppernong, or assist in supporting one. This is all I know on the subject of Lake religion among the blacks, and it is what I do believe. I am taking the best course (a distant one) to get along with the little officiate but I wish he may not be so imprudent as to conduct himself so offensively towards me as to draw or force from me that line of conduct which may do him harm and be used to my greatest possible disadvantage. I promise to avoid it if possible without my honour shall be at hazard. But I cannot bear long with a vain upstart, let his cloth be what it may. I do not like to call in question the general conduct either agricultural, or religious of my neighbours, but I think I could improve both in a degree. Since writing, by accident I learn that since the first of march, there /has/ died on the place thirteen horses & mules, & the other animals are exceedingly exha/u/sted. It is said by some that they died of distemper, but others say it is ploughing I have heard no mention of the occurrance from the whites. About four weeks ago, my son Charles was in Mr /C.s/ field & the overseer then talked as well as the principle had at other times of the great quantity of ground ploughed to the horse say 3 or 3½ Acres /a day/. I, when told it, said that I was considered to have as good team as any one, & I had no knowledge of geting quite two Acres to the plough, and that /they/ did as much as I was willing they should, & that if they did do this great work, it /was/ impossible they could stand it and they must die. This is the result. With but a word of comment. Though I do not boast of much religion, I am not willing that any thing living shall labour unto death or shall have its days shortened an hour for my agrandizment or ease. I know not how many ministers it would be required of a man to support, to cover such offences towards the great giver of all good. You will observe by the first part of my letter that no apology was necessary for your remarks or enquiry. You can give me no offence, unless you intend it, and that your own mind will tell you. I will now quit the Paradise subject.

I shipped a load of wheat on the 12th It was the heaviest wheat I ever raised but once & so much heavier than corn that the Captain who was but loaded with 2500 bushels corn could take but 2225 of wheat. I am glad to find that your crop was so fine & that the seed which I furnished you promises to be an acquisition not only to you but to that section of country. All I regret about it is, that it has my name. There is no man in the world who can be more averse to ostentation than myself, if I have done any good I cannot fail to receive my reward, whether the world knows it or not. O my dear friend! what can equal an approving mind? Whilst I know that I am a poor miserable, wicked sinner and live but <through> /from/ the hope of peace, through the mercy of God, and merrits of a Saviour, yet I am contious of having endeavoured to the utmost of my ability to do my duty in that station which it has pleased him to call me, and to do all the good I can to my fellow being. I would to God it were in my power to do more. We are all poor miserable creatures in this world by the general laws of nature (I can truly say so of myself) and I am not willing to add one pang that can be avoided, but on the contratry to increase the sum of human comfort as much as in my power lies. It is with /these/ sentiments that I endeavour to be reconciled to my fate and though it is to me a hard task, I can but ask myself why should I not? Have I not the representitives of that earthly all of my comforts. Five children who give me no distress but for their health & comfort in this world. Can that /man/ live who is more thankfull to his Creator than I am? for those dear children, and <that> I can say with truth, of the two who have arrived to manhood. I have no fear or uneasiness in trusting them out of my sight or influence. Whether these things are from nature or education it is not necessary to enquire. It is the work of God and blessed be his name. Charles' heath declined to rapidly, that I feard to let him stay, and he left on the 14th for Old point comfort, there to remain untill his brother William joins him which I expect will be on sunday the 29th Williams health appears yet good. He has not been exposed, this summer, having lived at Belgrade to keep house where my overseer attended to the farm. It has been different with poor Charles. He has be unremiting in attention to the Lake farm and it has broke him down It is his first summers exposure, and he may become seasoned to it, but I have strong fears.

When the boys get together I expect they will go to Ohio and in that region, to New York. They are hence under no limit, but to be prudent and act like Gentlemen and not to forget their Mother who is in her silent grave and their father who yet lives to take care of their interest, while he expects them to be laying up a stock of health and information for future usefullness.

Ah! my friend! When the dream of life has passed away what will it avail if we leave no traces of usefullness behind?

By my last letters from Raleigh my two little Girls & boy were in health & my little boy Johnston was down there with his grandmother, during the Hillsborough vacation. Mr Bingham writes that he learns well & is very docile. He boards with Mr Bingham.

Taking my crop of corn together It is likely and having a larger one than ever before I have a hope of having a considerable quantity to ship but it is now suffering now very much from drought. The part of the field called the Bee Tree & the <sava> savanna has been nearly ruined by the rains in June; I have become satisfied that if the savanna is laid sufficiently dry it will be excelent corn land, and have come to the determination to did [*dig*] another canal to the south east of my others & paralel with them which will certainly effect the object. It will drain effectually the Bee Tree field and put in a state of improvement about one thousand acres more savanna. I have satisfied my sons & negroes of the general advantage of the work & they are quite enthusiatic on it. I expect to plant a less crop of corn next year & to attend to the canal in person. I hope to live to finish it, which I shall consider the closing act of importance in my life.

Since commencing this letter time has passed to August the third. William left last week, which with the lameness of my overseer from spr/a/ining his ankle the whole business devolves on me and this week has been a particularly <a> heavy one, in consequence of cleaning out my canals. Though the weather has been intencely hot, I have been with the hands from day light to night. Eating my meals on the canal &. My health is perfecly good and I never stood it better. After this job I shall get the remainder of my wheat in order in hopes of the vessils return shortly to take it. I am aware that the price will fall, but we must abide by the loss.

I have now writen you a long and confused letter. (Letters are not my occupation) and I hope you will do with it as you requested me of yours, which I shall comply with so far as the first sheet, (the excesseanable part) to day.

My dear friend, I observe your kind & friendly observations on the subject of my debt, & your indulgent remarks. From your indulgence & my perfect confidence in it I have had no sort of uneasiness, but the time has arrived when it ought to be paid & when it will give me no inconvenience to commence it, you will accordingly receive a check inclosed for twenty two hundred & one dollars & twenty three cents. which you will please to place to my credit. I hope to be able shortly to send you a draft on New York for something like two thousd seven or eight hundred dollars so as to make the payment $5,000. My next payment will depend on my sales of produce, for though I have loaned out $5000, it would be impossible to command at this time one hundred, if ever.

I shall always be glad to hear from you my friend. In the mean time please to assure yourself of my sincere esteem & Regard

E Pettigrew

James C. Johnston esqr

[*Addressed*] James C. Johnston Esqr
Hays
Edenton Post office

---

[1]Three Episcopal clergymen served Pettigrew's Chapel and the Lake Phelps area as missionaries between 1835 and 1843: David Griffith, 1835; Edward N. Forbes, 1836-1840; and Charles Aldis, 1841-1843. In 1843 Aldis was succeeded by W. B. Otis, missionary to Plymouth and "parts adjacent," and in 1844 John S. Kidney was named minister of Pettigrew's Chapel and Lake Scuppernong. Forbes went to Lincolnton, North Carolina, after leaving Lake Phelps, and both he and Aldis left the state after 1843. *Journal of the Diocesan Convention, 1835*, 3; *Journal of the Diocesan Convention, 1836*, 3; *Journal of the Diocesan Convention, 1841*, 3; *Journal of the Proceedings of the Twenty-Sixth Annual Convention of the Protestant Episcopal Church in the State of North Carolina . . . 1842* (Fayetteville: Edward J. Hale, 1842), 3, hereinafter cited as *Journal of the Diocesan Convention, 1842*; *Journal of the Twenty-Seventh Annual Convention of the Protestant Episcopal Church in the State of North Carolina . . . 1843* (Fayetteville: Edward J. Hale, 1843), 3, hereinafter cited as *Journal of the Diocesan Convention, 1843*; *Journal of the Diocesan Convention, 1844*, 3.

Charles Lockhart Pettigrew to Ebenezer Pettigrew UNC

Portsmouth 16th July 1838

My dear Father

I arrived in this place on Sunday evening by the portsmouth cars, without any thing material having happened. The sound was slightly rough on Saturday night just before entering Edenton bay and as a matter of course I was sick but I soon got over it and went to bed and had a fine nap. This morning the boat left for "Old Point" while I was in the counting house of Messrs Hardy & Brothers so that I shall not be able to leave for that place before to morrow morning (Tuesday)

But from what I can learn I shall not meet with much comfort during the fortnight that I propose to remain there

The <palc> place, I hear, is much crowded and the accommodations are but scanty. I shall hope for the best.

Mr [*John*] Williams of Charleston S.C. is at present in Norfolk, I was introduced to him this morning <by> /at/ Messrs Hardy & Brothers'. he has been absent from Charleston about a week and will leave this place for Balt. on Wednesday next.

I am much pleased with the appearance of your commission merchants in this place as well as Charleston; they seem to be clever men and to have an assiduity that will certainly ensure success. They all asked very kindly after your health.

I have much improved in my he/a/lth since I left home; I now have a good appetite and <fell> /feel/ quite strong. I shall in a short time be perfectly well. The Crawford-House Portsmouth is my present abode, I have a large cool room entirely to my self; there being but little company in the house.

The hair brush which I had laid on the drawers to put in my trunk, I came off and left, we shall need one and brother William had better bring it when he comes on, it would also be well for him to take with him a half a quire of paper for writing we shall stand in need of it when we wish to write.

The draft you gave was cashed this morning by the Messrs H. I found $15 amply sufficient to bring me from Plymouth here. I have nothing more to write at present

Blieve me your affate son

Chas L Pettigrew

[*Addressed*] E Pettigrew Esq
Cool Spring
N. Carolina

William Shepard Pettigrew to Ebenezer Pettigrew UNC

Baltimore August 4th 1838

Dear Pa

On Monday morning last, the day we wrote you, we went from Norfolk to Old Point We reached the latter place about 11 Oclock, the weather was quite oppressive at the Point, but I was glad to discover that it was not near as much so there, as at Norfolk, the Thermometer has been as high as a hundred and two. On Monday evening we went into the Fort, it is a splendid work; well garisoned, it must be almost impregnable. The soldiers live in rooms made under the embankment, they must be very comfortable dwellings in the Winter, but uncomfortable in Summer. On Thursday the 2d of August we arrived at this place, at 1 we went to Mr Hilberg's, and engaged a suit of clothes a piece, they are to be done this evening; his charge will be a hundred and four dollars. Brother Charles paid your iron bill this morning, it amounted to twenty two dollars and twenty five cents. Baltimore seems to be in a flourishing condition. I think they have the finest horses I ever saw. On yesterday we went to Mr Belman's to see his Durham cattle, we saw a bull which the keaper said would weigh if he were fat 3000 lb, he had several cows which would weigh more than our work oxen, and calves that he would not take less than five hundred dollars for. We shall leave tomorrow morning for Harper's Ferry, where we will remain about two weeks, please write to Winchester a village near the Ferry (I should have said we will spend about two weeks in the neighborhood of Harpers Ferry instead of at the Ferry itself, as it is said to be unhealthy some seasons). We are well and hope you are enjoying the same blessing.

Believe me your affectionate son
Will S Pettigrew

P.S. We join in love to you.

Charles Lockhart Pettigrew to Ebenezer Pettigrew UNC

Winchester Va. Aug 13 1838

My dear Father

We wish very much to hear from home as well to know whether it is perfectly healthy as to learn the prospect of the corn crop in that part of our state.

The corn crops from Baltimore to this place looked a w[e]ek since entirely ruined by the drought: the under leaves of the stalk were completely dead, and the others withered to the top. So <bad is> discouraging is the prospect that many farmers are debating whether they had not better make fodder of their whole fields. In walking into the suburbs of Winchester yesterday evening <wte> we observed that the cattle and hogs were actually turned into a field of corn. The papers /give/ so <extended> /alarming/ an account abt. the great extent of the drought that I think that it is more than probable that corn will be equal inprice to what it was last year. An ol[d] farmer remarked in our presen[ce] the other day that the prospect must be truly distressing to a farmer with alarge number of negroes.

From Baltimere we came to Harper's ferry passing through the rich section of Ma/r/yland about frederic city. The ferry, (where the Potomac passes thro the blue ridge) is a most splendid sight; it /is/ well worth a place in the journal of a traveller. We are at present in what is generally called the richest section of Virginia. But altho it stands so high and its reputation has extended so far, it is not equal in my opinion to the lands in our immediate neighbourhood. There may be a small portion on the Shenandoah river equal to it. A farmer informed me that the soil was from 2 to 3 feet deep in many places.

We hope you<r> are not suffer[i]ng from want of rain like they have b[e]en in this section of the state. If you have there is a prospect that we may be hard run for bread. But on Saturday last they had a most destructive rain here: it came too late for the corne and did a great deal of damage by carrying away mill dams fences etc. We shall proceed from this place immediately to Lexington Ky and th[e]nce to Cincinnati Ohio so that you will please dir[e]ct to us at the latter place. Brother William sends his love to you We are well.

your affectionate son
Chas L. Pettigrew

[*Addressed*] E. Pettigrew Esq
Cool Spring
Washington
N.C.

Ebenezer Pettigrew to John Herritage Bryan UNC

Belgrade Aug 24, 1838

My dear Sir,

Your favour of 12th came to hand by the last mail, and I take a little interval from attention to business to write a few lines. My occupation to business was never more intence & I am happy to say my health never better, nor energies more alive at any time of my life. The gout is very marked in finger joints.

The drought is very searis in all this part of the country, & my crop must be shortened nearly one half.

I am pleased to learn that you are about to get a good female teacher for our daughters It is of the first consequence. Please to tell my dear little Nancy that it was with unutterable pleasure I received her first letter. I hope now she has begun she will often write her poor old disconsolate father, who loves her more than life.

I received the pamphlet you were so good as to send me, and a certain part I read with perfect astonishment, although my mind was prepaired for something of the kind. My God how can we blame those political lyars when we read so much error & misrepresentation in so sacred a place, as I think is in that.

I will with pleasure attend to your request respecting Mr Washington.

Some time in the first of July I addressed a letter to J. Johnston Pettigrew at Raleigh but not to the care of any person. I received one from Johnston by the last mail in which he does not acknowledge the receit of that one. I inclosed five dollars in the letter to Johnston, & have strong reason to believe it was suppressed at Cool Spring office, on the receit of this will you please to make the necessary enquiry at your office. About the same time I inclosed twenty dollars to Edenton on important business, have written again and can get no answer. I fear it has gone the same way. Johnston seemed to be dissatisfied with his place at Hillsboro, & that letter was to opperate on his mind in favor.

And now my dear Sir make my kin[d] regards to Sister Mary, my dear little girls & my other dear friends & believe me sincerely

Your friend & Relation
E Pettigrew

John H. Bryan esqr

turn over

N.B. You will naturally ask what on earth am I so busy about. I am taking down a pretty stout house at the Lake & carrying it to Belgrade, I am building two others there also replastering the house & fiting it up against Williams return. And I am cuting the avenue for a canal from the Lake plantation though the dismal, which will be near seven miles long, which with all the minutia of business you will say gives me very little time for company. I find I cannot die, I have suffered a thousand mental deaths, have no doubt of suffering as many /corporeal/ with this gout as well as my mental anguish, which never can be removed but by death, & I wish to put my life to the best account, hoping that a mercifull God, will have compassion on /poor/ *me* through the merrits & mediation of a blessed savior

E P.

[*Addressed*] John H. Bryan Esqr
Raleigh
N. Carolina

*William Shepard Pettigrew to Ebenezer Pettigrew** UNC

Copy

Lexington, Ky, Sep. 5, 1838.

My dear Father

We were glad to learn, by your favour of the 15th Ult, that your health was good, & that the corn was not more seriously affected by drought. In the portion of Virginia & Maryland through which we passed the crops must have sustained an injury of three fourths; the prospect in Pennsylvania is but little better; & in Ohio & Kentucky, they are also seriously impaired.

We traveled from Harpers Ferry to Winchester in company with Gov. Kent's widow & daughter. This we were not aware of at the time, but discovered it on the Register at Taylor's Hotel. The Governor's son was also in company.

The scenery, while crossing the Alleghenies, is most beautiful. Among other things, the "Hanging Rock" is worth seeing; it <is> rises between one & two hundred feet perpendicularly.

In the State of Ohio, there is much equality existing between the Whites & Negroes. It is not uncommon, in small towns, to see the latter sitting in a bar-room in company with the former, & drinking water at the bar; they are also seen playing in the street with boys of corresponding years. An old gentleman in Va. informed us that he was some years since in Ohio, when, at breakfast, he was conducted to a room, in which he found a negro seated at the table where he was to sit; the gentleman declined eating, whereupon he negro was offended, & remarked he was not his inferior, & was disposed to attack him, the old /gentleman/, however, drew his pistol, & the African thought it prudent to retreat.

We arrived here on Friday last. There was a dinner given, on the 29 ult., to the President & Directors of the Charleston & Cincinati Rail Road, who met in Lexington on the 27th Gen. Hayne, of S:C.,[1] (the Pres.) is said to have delivered an eloquent speech.

The cattle Fair commenced here this morning, & will continue for three days. On the first, cattle will be exhibited; on the second, horses; on the third, mules. There was a yoke of oxen shown, this morning, that must have weighed 5000 lbs. Those gaining the prize are rewarded with a silver cup, varying in value, according to the animal. For a bull beyond three years, its value is $30.; under that age, $12. Messrs [*Henry*] Clay, Crittenden,[2] & Hayne were at the Fair. Gen. H. is a fine looking man. I saw Gov. Poindexter,[3] on Saturday last. He walks with difficulty. Lexington is surrounded by many beautiful residences. Ashland is situated a mile from the City. The shady groves are beautiful. We called on Mr C[*lay*].; but he was not at home.

I regreted to learn by yours that Pompey was dying.

In a few days, we shall leave for Cincinati, by way of Louisville.

Please direct your next to Albany N.Y. Brother Charles joins me in love to you.

Believe me, your affectionate son,

William S. Pettigrew.

E. Pettigrew Esq.

[*Addressed*] Ebenezer Pettigrew Esq.
Cool Spring
N. Carolina.

---

[1]Robert Young Hayne (1791-1839) was at this time president of the projected Louisville, Cincinnati, and Charleston Railroad. He had been a United States senator and governor of South Carolina. *DAB*, VIII, 456-459.

[2]John Jordan Crittenden (1787-1836), an attorney from Kentucky, was a United States senator, 1817-1819, 1835-1841, 1842-1848, and 1855-1861. He also served as United States attorney general, as governor of Kentucky, and in the United States House of Representatives. *Biographical Directory of Congress*, 754-755.

[3]George Poindexter (1779-1855) had represented Mississippi in Congress and had served as governor of that state. At this time he was practicing law in Lexington, Kentucky. *Biographical Directory of Congress*, 1466.

Henry Alexander[1] *to Ebenezer Pettigrew* A&H

Somerville [*Tennessee*] Septr 5th 1838.

Dear Sir

In complyance with your Request I consider it my Dute to write you, all Though nothing of importance has occurred since I left you,

I arived here on the 11th of August I found my son well and all my negros, no axedence had happened. Durin my abstence, I had one of the hotess times out here that I ever Did see, Charles Blunt came out with me we Suffered a grate Deale with the heat, my negros behaved well on the way out, my horse <my horse> performed well, The Drouth has been and is now verry Suver in this Part of the Country. The farmers think that the crops are Injured half in this part of the Country

South of this in north Miss^{i} they think more than half North of this crops are better, the Opinion is that thair will be grain anuff for the cosumption of the Country but it has caused provishons to be high now (and I Exspect it will continue so through the next year) baken is worth at this time 15 cts per lbs Corn $3. to 3.50 per barel, flower from 8 to 10 $ per Barel. The Price of laber and the price of Negros, are no higher than thay wore when I Saw you, negros are worth but little more here than thay /are/ with you after Ducting the Exspence of moving them and the Diference of Discount in money

I have hired out Camberidge for a Month at $16.66 and Emanuel. at $10. I Exspect my son James up from Lau^{a} about 20th Ins^{t} if he should not come I shall Go Down thair soon after that time I understand that negros is higher in Lau^{a} than thay are here, but how much < but how much> I am not abel to tell you for I have not Rec^{d} Letter from James on that subject.

I have land offered me all most Ever Day but I have not bough any yet, and I cannot tell you when I Shall, for my present impression is that I can make more by hirin out my negros than I can by farming when taking in to consideration the hight Prices Provishions must be next year. There is a grat Deale of buying and Selling Gowin on out here in this country, but a large propotion is Dun on Cr. which I consider a bad bisness at this time, and I cannot alow my Self to Engage in wile Speculations, We have a Branch Bank of the State here in this Place, But her notes may only be cauld post nots. for thay are on C^{r} of Twelve Month /and/ with out In^{t} but this figticus way of Dowing bisness has no influence on me. This Bank has cause Rale Estate to wrise here from 10 to 15 per cts. (I am in hopes that Ma[ne] you had of is Dowing will) I will write you again Soon as I have Something worth Comuncating Please write me, of you well fare and all the Prticelers of your Part of the country, on the Recpt of, for it all ways Gratifiing to here from old N.C. you Please to present my Respect to Charles & Wm Pettigrew & your other Children to M^{r} & Mrs Collins /and Mr Forbs/ to M^{r} & Mrs Davenport and all inquring frends—

I have been some sick since I saw you but nothing serious, my ancles have hurt me some since I saw you, but my helth is Good at this time as it was when I left you my Sons are both in Good helth, when I hered from James Jessee is keeping books at this time in the house of Armor Lake & Smith (of this place) my negros are all well.

Jesse send his Respts to you & you Sons; and said he should be Glad to here from them & you

I cannot close this letter without and Exspreshion of my fealing to wards you, there is no man living that I love more than you, your fealing to wards me are of the fines kind and I know it, you have my best wishis both for your helth and Prosperity, Oh my Dear frend, if the Sentence of the law, of God Should be Prenounce against us, So that we cannot meet again in this world. I Pray God that we may meet, on the Banks of Eturnel Deliverance, where Parting is no more,

with the hiest Respet. I Remain you Ob Ser[t]
Henry Alexander

E. Pettigrew Esq[r]

[*Addressed*] Ebenezer Pettigrew Esqr.
Cool Spring
North Carolina

---

[1]Henry Alexander of Tyrrell County was sheriff at one time. See Ebenezer Pettigrew to John Herritage Bryan, April 18, 1826, in this volume. He joined the emigration to the West. Several other letters from him are included in this volume.

*Ebenezer Pettigrew to Alfred Gardner** A&H

Lake Phelps Sep[r] 12, 1838

Alfred Gardner esqr

D[r] Sir

I received yours of May 22nd, & agreeable to your advice & my opinion have inclosed to you a power to sell the lands on L[uzee] Hatcher which my children became heir to by ther Mother; I also thought it advisable to include in the power the small parcel which they became heir to by the death of their aunt Penelope S. which you will please to sell with the other, charging me commissions as customary for the same. That of M[rs] Pettigrew I have agreed to give to you the one half the purchase money, you paying all expences that may accrue agreeable to my letter of Nov. 23, 1837. I leave it to your entire discretion as to credit &&, in the sale, as I wish the most made of it that can be reasonably done

With regard to my land on the Obion, I should like to know if there are any settlers on it & whether the timber is protected from pillage. I could wish it protected if possible & no more settlers than would be possetively to my interest, but all this I have no doubt you will have a particular eye to.

I shall be glad to hear from you on the receit of this, In the mein time I am Respectfully

Your Obd^{t} Sv^{t}
E Pettigrew

Charles Lockhart Pettigrew to Ebenezer Pettigrew UNC

Cincinnati Ohio Sept 14th 1838

My dear Pa

You will perceive by the date of this letter that we have at length arrived at the place where /we/ were to receive your next letter. We however are much disappointed that there is none in the office awaiting us. Your letter would certainly have had time to arrive had you written it immediately upon the reception of my letter from Winchester. it must therefore have miscarried and I fear will not arrive. We have been at this place since the evening of the 12th and will remain untill tomorrow hoping that a letter may yet <be> arrive before we leave.

Brother Will. wrote you from Lexington Ky give an account of the places we passed thro untill we arrived <at that> there. We left Lexington on Sunday evening and reached Frankfort the same evening a distance of 28 miles. The town of Frankfort has only about 2 thousand inhabitants, it has some good <bui> buildings, a state house, courthouse, State's prison, in it. Senator Crittenden resides in Frankfort in a plain brick building. On the next day we continued our journey to Louisville 52 miles farther. It is a much larger place than I expected to find it. It is very nearly as large at Cincinnati having about 30 thousand inhabitants. The hotels seem to be the largest and finest buildings in Louisville. They are erecting a very large and handsome court house. We came from Louisville to Cin. /in/ the steamer Lily.

The weather still continues very dry but /the/ season of the year is rather late for it be hot. We hope that you have at least received one advantage from the dry weather, that of having a healty fall; for all the stagnent water must certainly have disappeared during the drouth I understand that south west has [*been*] remarkably healthy brother Will wishes to write a few /lines/[1] and I must therefore close

Believe me your aff^{ate} Son
Chas L Pettigrew

[*Addressed*] Mr Ebenezer Pettigrew
Cool Spring
Washington Co
North Carolina

[1]The portion of the letter by William, if indeed written, is missing.

Ebenezer Pettigrew to William Shepard Pettigrew UNC

Lake Phelps Sep 19, 1838

My Dear sons

I wrote to you directed to Winchester & to Cincinnati as you requested, but have recvd no letter from you since the Winchester one. From a sevier storm we have had, I have received no letters by the last mail. The season advancing I shall direct this to New York, but you will not return to this place before the 20th proximo if as soon. We have up to this time had it remarkably healthy but the storm gave us a great deal of rain some say as much as the August one of 1837, but it did not rais the Lake more than eight inches & could not be as much. however the river was between 2 & 3 ft on the road, the Bee Tree canal overflown & every swamp & hole as full as it /could/ hold, which waters must become stagnant so far as they pond and it is not by any means too late to be sickly & today looks more like the kind of weather to produce bilious fever than any one I have seen this fall. The corn was much blown down & broken off in the storm. I am having it picked up, & find far more that ought to come in than is sufficient for the hogs & horses. The crop is a short one any how. I am carpentering, Bricklaing, & plastering at Belgrade also widening the main /ditch/ from the swamp which together with some other ditches & other work will I fear employ me untill time to gather corn & sow wheat, more particularly if we have much bilious fever to finish the fall with. I have got up the fatening hogs both here & at Belgade & I regret to say they are a poor looking set.

I have come to this place today to have more cloths & shoes cut out, & to see how the other little work goes on. So you will see that I have not spent an idle fall. In truth my exertions are so great & my capacity for it that negroes & whites are surprised. I am glad it has so happened that a certain man /as well as all other men/ may be convinced at the wind up, that I have not lost my energy in the least degree, & that in my business I am an independant man. You had better while in New York get some garden seeds particularly Parsly seed. Enquire of the prospect of Clover seed. By the last mail I wrote to Mr Hilberg for a pair of pantaloons & vest. Informing him that you would call & get them & pay for them, which you will do, if he has not sent them by some coaster to Columbia.

Sep 28. I did not send this letter because I did not get one by the mail. I sent to Plymouth on Monday last and got your two letters from Lexington & Cinninati. I am glad to find you are well. Nothing new here, but extremely wet & disagreeable. My son William As to /the/ side board, such a one as Mr Davenports will do, his cost I think fifty dollars, such a one will probably cost more by 10 pr Ct You may get a wash stand of moderate size basin & pitcher. & such chairs as you like & think will suit.

The rains have deranged my business & I am in a real bother & will quit by assuring you my dear sons of the regard & sincere affection of y father

E Pettigrew

N.B. My health is still good but worry[*torn*] albut to death with negros, whites & wett weather

[*Addressed*] Mr William S. Pettigrew
Care of Messrs John S Bryan & Co
New York

*Ebenezer Pettigrew to John Williams** A&H

Lake Phelps Sep 22, 1838

Dr Sir

Your favour of the 4th inst. came duly to hand. I find all right. I observe that this cargo although a long time in the vessel and as given measure gives as it is the first or second, but barely sold out, and nine bushels of that charged to the captain. I will mearly remark, that it is probable your opinion of the Captain's honesty is a little [——ing]. I am prepared to suffer from trick and dishonesty. On the subject of guaranteeing my sales, I am willing to stand my own not doubting but that you will never sell to any except those whom you believe to be perfectly safe and if there should be a failure when I have received the amount, I shall at all time be ready to refund.

You will please to place my remaining funds in your hands in some safe house in Baltimore either Bank or private. Perhaps one of the Banks might be best, but I leave it to your discretion. And please to accept my sincere thanks for your attention to my business, and assure your self of the

Esteem of your friend
E. Pettigrew

N.B. I am about to buy a vessel in partnership with Captain Joseph Spruill to carry away my crops in future

Joseph A. Spruill[1] *to Ebenezer Pettigrew* A&H

October the 1 1838

Mr Petegrew

sir after the most dissagreeble voige I ever made for to bee a safe one I have <I have> returnd home at last I have a frieght but it wont pay /much/ for it is to go to so many plases Edenton plimmouth and hertford but it was the best I could dwo I had the half bshel of wheat weigh it we/i/gh the /same/ as you made it I cant acunt for it falling short in weight I have made such along voige I had to draw /more/ mony than I expected I drew an you seventy five dollars I hope it will bee right with you if I Should live I make it right when I git clear of my freight I shall proseed to E city and take the vessel on the ways and fix her for the winter I wish you would right to me at E city and say when you want me to load for you say as long a time as you can to dwo Justice to yourself for this will bee plenty work this winter but sir /when/ you want me say the word and I will cum as quick as I can. the storms has tare the vessels up very bad I pass five racks from New york to Ocracoke leas and this found them /in/ piles fromwhat I can hear the stormes has done more damage than enny storm has don for twenty years to vessels I was in the first one and had it very bad. when I left New yak wheat was worth $2 per bushel corn $1.18 ct per bush pork $27 per barrel the war and tar of a mans teeth is somthing in these days I find it so

I am respectfully yours
Joseph A Spruill

I got over the bar the 28 of sept and got up to the mashes just as the last storme begun and rode it out I have not heard from it but expect it has done a greatdeal of damage for it was very bad this is /the/ third one and I hope the last for if thier is many more thir will bee no vessels left

J A Spruill

[*Addressed*] Mr. E Petegrew
Coolspring

---

[1]As indicated in the preceding letter, Captain Joseph A. Spruill was partner to Ebenezer Pettigrew in ownership of a cargo vessel.

William Shepard Pettigrew to Ebenezer Pettigrew A&H

City of New York October 7th 1838

Dear Pa

Your favor of the 19th came to hand yesterday morning. We were glad to learn you were well and hope this will find you /still/ enjoying the same blessing. We arrived here on Tuesday last from Albany or I should have said from West Point, as we arrived there from Albany on Monday evening and remained until four Oclock, Tuesday P.M. In trave[l]ing from Cincinati to Sandusky City (the latter is the port we started from for Buffalo, situated on the upper end of Lake Erie) the roads were very dusty, as we generally found them throughout the whole west, this prevented our journey from being as comfortable as it otherwise would. The country we passed through was flourishing, though not more so than Kentucky. We passed within eight miles of the Hon Mr Whittlesey's,[1] he is said to be very wealthy. I suppose you know he has declined being a candidate for Congress, the Whig candidate who it is thought will succeed him is the gentleman Senator Benton had brought to the bar of the Senate when the expunging resolution was passed. We remained in Buffalo something over a day and then left for Niagara Falls. We also went on the Canada side of the Falls; there are stationed there, about a hundred English troops. They are fine looking soldiers; larger I think than the American soldiers, if those few I saw in Buffalo are specimens. There are sentinels on the Canada side of the ferry across Niagara river, who make every person that comes over tell his name and his business. Shortly before we went Lord Durham[2] was there with his me[n]. He rented the whole of one of the hotels I was told his expenses were a hundred pounds daily. I thought the Canadians eyed us rather cautiously. I declin/ed/ going to Montreal as the season was too far advanced for the jaunt to be a pleasant one and also as I wished to see the western part of New York, and particularly the small Lakes in the western and centeral parts. I must confess I was a good deal surprised to find that Ohio was so nearly equal to the western part of New York in cleared land. At Rochester I saw Mr Granger.[3] He resides at Canandagua, I saw his residence as I passed through. It is a handsome one. This state has suffered scarcely any from the drought. Wheat was selling at Rochester for $2, but this was caused by the report that the crops in England were bad, when that report was corrected the price soon fell. Mr Bryan thinks it is fortunate your wheat came when it did, instead of when the price was so high, as, in all likelihood, /the vessel/ would have been out in the storm, had the wheat been in market at the latter time. Mr Collins is expected in the City on Tuesday, he has been in New Jersey for some days with the Rigses: we have not seen him. I was sorry to hear of Mr Houser's death. Your propesy came true; you said you, expected one of the family would die before the fall closed. I heard at Mr Bryan's the other night that Mrs H. had a family of children in New York; their situation will be a lamentable one. I am sorry the corn was injured by the storm, but it is to be hoped you will make up in price, what you lose in quantity. I purchased the carpet yesterday for $1 and three cents a yard & 2 rugs for $7 and 50 /¢/, & a dozzen chairs for $19. I hope I have not purchased better articles than you wished. I think I can get a very good sideboard for $45, & 2 shades for $3 & 50/¢/. Brother C. purchased the garden seed. As the crop is short, we have concluded not to get the saddles. The bedstead you said I might get can also be easyly dispensed with. I enquired at 2 places this morning about clover seed—one said they sold red clover seed at 31¼ cen/ts/ a pound, & white at 37½;—the other, the red at 25 & the white at 31¼. The first said it bid fair to be higher. I will learn further of Mr Bryan when I see him.

We go to Philadelphia Wednesday morning, please direct your next there. Please give my respects to M^{r} & Mrs Daven/port/ We are well and join in love to you.

Your affectionate son,
Will: S Pettigrew

[*Addressed*] M^{r} E Pettigrew
Cool Spring
Washington Co
North Carolina

[1]Elisha Whittlesey (1783-1863), of Canfield, Ohio, served in Congress from 1823 to 1838. He was a founder of the Whig party. *Biographical Directory of Congress*, 1810.

[2]John George Lambton, first earl of Durham (1792-1840), was governor general and lord high commissioner in Canada. *Webster's Biographical Dictionary*, 852.

[3]Francis Granger (1792-1868), of Canandaigua, New York, was a Whig who served in Congress, 1835-1837, 1839-1841, and 1841-1843. *Biographical Directory of Congress*, 966.

Charles Lockhart Pettigrew to Ebenezer Pettigrew UNC

Philadelphia Oct 14th 1838

My dear Father

We have at length arrived in this place thus far on our way home. We left New York last friday after brother William had purchased the articles for the house at Belgrade.

Your letter stated that we should not come before the 20th of the present month, we much regretted that we should not be able to reach home earlier; but agreeably to your directions we will arrange our coming so as to reach Plymouth on Saturday night and go home on sunday the 21st. We are <quite> quite tired out with traveling and gladly welcome the time when we shall again be still.

We saw Mr & Mrs Collins who reached New York on Tuesday before we left on Friday Tey were both well as also their children. They both agree in saying that my excursion has improved my health very much. Mr C. says he never saw Me look better in his life. Brother William they say has not gained much in flesh, but is about as <weh> when he left home.

Under—standing that the co/u/ntry has not become sickly since the rains we have concluded to come home thus early after the time proposed by you; and the principal object of this letter is to /request you to/ send up on Saturday to Plymouth that we may return on Sunday.

While in New York we made several attempts to see Mr Riggs but failed he was absent in the country. Mr Riggs called on us also but we had changed our quarters and we failed to see him Brother William sends his love to you and we both hope to see you well on sunday next. Your affate son

Chas L. Pettigrew

I have your watch from N. York, /and/ shall call for you cloths in Baltimore

Henry Alexander to Ebenezer Pettigrew A&H

Somerville Tennessee November 5th 1838

E. Pettigrew Esqr

Dear Sir

I returned from Louisiana a few days ago, I am not so well pleased as I expected I find that the country is sickly and not very good society, the Land is rich, but they ask enormous prices for it, say from $40 to 80 per acre, when I arrived at New Carthage I was some what astonished to find James so pale and look so unhealthy. but they informed me that he looked healthy for that country. he intends remaining thire until next March he will then come up into Tennessee. I examined the Land uppon the Lakes and Bioes [*bayous*] & I found it to be verry rich, the cotton is from 6 to 8 feet in height. I was informed by some of the most honest farmers that a Bale of Cotton pr acre was considered an avaridged crop. the crops are good this year (and they said it would not avarige more than a Bale) Six to Seven acres are calculated to the hand. It is a good corn country but they pay no attention to that crop. I visited La with the intention of settling in that State, Since I have explored it (nearly to) my satisfaction, uppon due consideration I have come to the conclusion not to settle in that country, in the first place it is sickly and without society and in the second place the price of Land is beyond its intrinsic value, negro men are worth from $800. to 1000, women 600 to 750, but few sales at these prices, they are worth in this place men from $700 to 800 women from 500. to 600. it is thought by some that they will be lower, I carried down to Lousiana Cambridge and Emanuel and have hired them until next March. Cambridge @ $25. and Emanuel @ $\$12^{50}/_{100}$ pr month. and directed James to Sell them at the expiration of the time they are hired, they are not to return here, I find that your advice in relation to them is verry correct for no confidince can be placed in either of them,

I sill remain undetermined what course I shall persue for the next year but think it probable that I shall hire my hands, I am satisfied that more can be made by hiring that farming (at the present). I have made no purchase and it is uncertain where I shall, for I believe that Land must be lower, the present state of the currency forbids a man making a large purchase, and I entertain a belief that by a delay I shall sustain no injury, it is certain that the currency of the country must be regulated before the price of property is settled, if I should purchase this fall it will be a small place and in the vicinity of Memphis. I expect to attend the Public Land sales on the first Monday in January at Pontotoc Mississippi—I rec^{d} a letter from Mr Beasley a few days ago which informed me that Joseph W. Tarkinton obtained a Judgment against [*me*].[1] for $110. and the costs amounted to $\$53.^{94}/_{100}$ as to the Judgment I do not mind it but dislike for such men as him and Heath to get any thing out of me. he has now don all that is in his power, and the next turn is mine. I have no doubt but Justice will overtake him in the bitterness of his Soul. I have two things which consolate me, I know my friends will not forsake me, and I shall this year make more money than the plantation is worth. I am pleased to learn that it is healthy and that you have good crops in Tyrrell, It is has been verry healthy in the District this season, and the crops are some better than was expected. Corn is worth $\$2^{50}/_{100}$, to $2^{75}/_{100}$ pr Bbl Flour $8 to 9. Pork is expected to be heigh, cotton is selling from 8 to 8½¢ pr lb. The Circuit Court of this County has been in session for two weeks and will not adjourn until the middle or latter part of this week there is 365 cases on the Trial Docket, and 250 on the Appearance, their is Judgments taken to the amount of $120,000, and their is about $30,000 more to take, '(this looks like squally times') The Jones charged with the murder of Co^{l} Edward Ward was not tried at the last Circuit Court of Shelby County. I am in tolerable health. Jesse and the rest of my family are in good health, Jesse sends his respects to you and sons, and all inquiring friends,

You will please present my respects to your Sons, Mr Forbes, Mr & Mrs Collins, Mr & Mrs Doctrine Davenport and all inquiring friends, and assure yourself of my best wishes

With respect I remain your
friend and obt & St.
Henry Alexander

P.S. I wrote you in August and I have not herd from you, You will please write me on the receipt of this letter

H A

[*Addressed*] E. Pettigrew Esqr
Cool Spring
Tyrrell County
North, Carolina

[1]The dispute between Tarkinton and Alexander originated sometime after 1830, this particular action beginning in 1834 when Tarkinton attempted to eject Alexander from a tract of land in Tyrrell County. The land originally had belonged to Benjamin Tarkinton, and after his death it was sold to Ebenezer Pettigrew by a former sheriff to satisfy debts. Ebenezer in turn sold it to Henry Alexander. With appeals, the case continued to the state supreme court in 1836 and apparently went up again in 1839, although the record is incomplete. *Joseph W. Tarkinton* v. *Henry Alexander*, 19 N.C. 87-97 (1836). See also John Herritage Bryan to Ebenezer Pettigrew, January 28, 1840, in this volume.

James Alfred Pearce to Ebenezer Pettigrew A&H

Chestertown [*Maryland*] Nov. 20. 1838

My Dear Sir

I should be ashamed of the date of this letter if I had not been more constantly and labouriously engaged since the rising of congress than I recollect to have been ever before. My professional business has been arduous and private affairs of my own and of female relatives dependant upon me have completely engrossed my leisure. Yet I might have answered yr last acceptable letter which I have just read again with satisfaction. Shall I tell you why?—Because you speak out what you think with perfect freedom and don't correct according to those "Sober second "thoughts" which are very well when a man is going to make a bargain but only mar a letter from one friend to another. You see I set myself upon a perfect equality with you disregarding the twenty years difference in our ages and writing as if you were a youngster or I were a venerable seigner of fifty. I assure you that you have had many of my kindest thoughts since I rec[d] y[r] letter and that M[rs] Pearce and myself frequently talk over the scenes in which you bore a part—I was on the point of going to see you last April when in Norfolk but my sister who was under my charge detained me so long that I had to hurry on to Washington and thence to one of my Courts which sat early in May—Whenever I can get an opportunity however I intend to inflict a visitation on you—You have seen that our friend [*John Nevett*] Steele was defeated. It was a result I always feared. The Whigs were quarreling every where in the State with one another and the expenditures of our legislation for internal improvements which have been heavy and in several instances very injudicious were all charged (injustly however) to our account. In addition to this the cry of "reform" was raised by the demagogues *out* of power and the cognizant were dr[iven] off from us by proposals to *elect all officers* of the state including the Judiciary System people. Steeles friends were much mortified and disappointed. I spent a day or two with him in July when he did not anticipate a defeat.

Calhoun is a radically selfish politician. He has hedged as the Jackeys' say once too often and every one now sees how shameless and selfish a great man can be when his own advancement becomes the sole subject of his ambition. His political adversaries will have no trouble in killing him off—He is one of those politicians who die like the scorpion of their own sting. The Election in New York has nipped the second bloom of hope for the administration but it is really difficult now to place any reliance on the steadiness of public sentiment. The leaders of party are generally too much like Knickerbock[er] patriots whose first care is for themselves though after that is satisfied they are willing enough to look after the countrys welfare. "Get money" or "get office" seem to be the cardinal doctrines of these men whom we call statesmen and a term in Congress seems either to disgust or to corrupt the really patriotic. My party wish me to run again and I believe I could be reelected but I mean to imitate y[r] example and retire before I can be charged with the political taint which is so common—

Every body in this part of the world is crazy about the silk culture. I am a member of a silk company in this place incorporated last winter—We have *cleared* $10.000 this year by the sale of morus multicaulis—have purchased a farm and are about to erect a cocoonery &c. and to return to the stock holders their original investment. This success has turned the heads of my fellow citizens and almost every one has purchased cuttings and planted a mulberry orchard. The thing has been speculated on until I fear much loss will ensue but in the end it will benefit the country as I doubt not from the experiments made we can raise silk worms and make silk as cheap as they do in Europe or Asia—and a new branch of industry is needed for a people who have worn out their lands by the careless cultivation of wheat corn and tobacco

The poor old Governor [*Joseph Kent*] is not forgotten by me—indeed he left many friends who will long cherish his memory

His debts were large owing to his Southern speculation but I understand there will be 80. or $90.000 nett for his family. Mrs Kent is living at Alexandria—I have another daughter about 9 months old—Charlotte we call her—My Eldest who is 6 years old is learning French under my tuition and promises to be a good scholar. Mrs Pearce is well and desires me to present her regards to you and say she will be very glad to greet you in her own house.

Remember me to y^{r} sons and when they travel north encourage them to cross the Chesapeake to Chestertown. Why can't you come yrself?

It would be a great pleasure to me to have a visit from you—Don't let a long interval pass between this letter & yr reply and believe me

vry truly
yr friend
J. A. Pearce

[*Addressed*] Hon. E. Pettigrew
Cool Spring
Washington Cy
N. Carolina

Ebenezer Pettigrew to James Alfred Pearce A&H

Belgrade Jan 14, 1839

My dear Sir,

I received with great pleasure in the tedious conveyance of the mail your favour of Nov 20. I assure you I did not intend to retaliate on you by leting so much time pass before it was answered, but a great press of business, not such as yours in letters, but, in logs, in mud, in ditches, in ploughs in sowing wheat, in gathering corn, in making & repairing fences, in truth in all things belonging to two tolerably well regulated farms has delayed it untill now. To give you an evidence of my constant intention <to> to be punctual; your letter has not been out of my pocket untill now.

It is too much my character to say & write what I think, and I am now too old to change my disposition however desirable it may be, and I am in your last much flattered by your giving that imprudence (as I call it) the name of candor. My familiar conduct toward those with whom I am intimate, always produce a like familiarity either in young or old, rich or poor. It is the only way that I can get along. Put me on my reserve and a more starched being cannot be found. I hope you /will/ act toward me /no other/ than as an equal in social intercourses. /In all/ other ways I will knock under. If our friend Steel wanted the office of Governor, I regret that he was not elected. For my own Part the honors or emolumnts of office is a mere farce a perfect blank compaired with the fatigues, and troubles attendant on them. There is no act of my life that I commend myself more for tha<t>n that of resisting a reelection. But It is doubtfull how much credit I am entitled to for that when I was perfectly certain, that I could /not/ live another Congress. To that [honour] I would say that death has no terrors for me, in as much as this world has no pleasures. But on this subject I will stop. I know I commit an offen[se] to my maker in uttering the least complaint. Providence has blessed me with five children. The world says they are promising, and I as a father am obliged to think so likewise. My two oldest Charles & William who you have seen are at my two places attending to their respective duties, and I am as closely employed counciling and supervising their acts. They give me no trouble, but to instruct them in the way they should go. But with all these blessings a *void*, a *space*, yes my dear Sir, a *wide space*, has been made in my domestic circle, which can never be closed, and which will embitter my days to the last hour. Grat God! What a man I am to be writing to a member of Congress at the City Washington of my domestic trobles of eight years standing.

I congratulate you on an acqusition to your family & the promise of your little girls.

I am largely engaged in morus muticaulis. You probably remember of hearing me talk on the silk partnership. It has resulted in having at this time in stock (Mr Collins & mself) forty thousand, trees 2 & 3 years old, which we expect to sell this spring. We have already sold about six thousand dollas worth. It is probable that a number will be sent to Baltimore for sale in proper time for seting. Thi sucess has not made me much. I rely mostly on my exertions of thirty five year back they are slow but to me have been sure.

I should be much pleased to visit you & Mrs Pearce. I receive her kind remembrance with great pleasure. Please when you write to her make mine, and tell her that I hope to see her once more before I go hence, but that I have so much work carved out for myself to do that I know not how to leave home. I hope to have the pleasure of seeing you at my quarters this spring. If you will give me time by notice of it I will send a conveyance for you /to/ Plymouth the stage line. You will think just before you get to my place that you are near the jumping off plac[e] Do'nt be uneasy you shall not jump off. I hope my brother Charles Shepard joining the Van Buren party will not prevent your visiting me with him. My paper is full & my head empty and I will quit. My sons desire to be remembered to you and Please to assure yourself of /my/ sincere Esteem & Regard

E Pettigrew

Hon J. A. Pearce

[*Addressed*] Hon. James A. Pearce
H.R.
Washington City

Ebenezer Pettigrew to Hardy and Brothers A&H

Jan 15, 1839 Belgrade near Cool Spring

Messers Hardy & Brothers

Gentlemen,

I am now making a few staves, and have engaged a vessil to take two loads (she carries between 7 & 8000.) The Captain promises to be here & take the first load about the 25 or 28. of the month I give him a high freight, for his engaging to take a back load of Oyster shells say 600 bus & if convenint 700. The object of this letter is to ask of you to be so good as to procure the shells in time so that there shall be no delay of the vessil & no disappointment in my geting them. I wish to try the effect of shells on a particular piece of land, and am willing to give for good ones the market price & if not /to/ be got at that, a little higher.

I am Gentlemen very

Respectfully your obdt Srv^{t}
E Pettigrew

N.B. I shall be glad to hear from you on the receit of this

E P.

[*Addressed*] Messrs Hardy & Brothers
Norfolk
Va.

Ebenezer Pettigrew to John Herritage Bryan UNC

Belgrade Jan 18, 1839

My dear Sir,

Ever since my return from Raleigh I have wanted to write you & you will naturally wonder when I say that I have been too much engaged untill now. It is true that I have two agents, my two sons (my overseer having left at Christmas) and they are disposed to do every thing that I could wish or ask, yet they are unexperienced, particularly William, who only commenced any direction of the plantation on New Years day, and therefore needs a great deal of my advice. I cannot speak it /with/ too much gratitude to my Creator, that they give me no earthy trouble in their conduct in any & in all respects. I have the strongest hope through the blessing and protection of an all wise providence that these things are for life. Charles is more at home in the business having attended to it last year, but William bends his whole mind, as well as body to it & cannot fail to succeed health & life lasting. When occasion requires it he eats his dinner at the work with the labourers.

We have had a most m[iser]able wet & disagreeable winter so far. But one whole week of good weather since it set in. My corn gathered better than I expected, and I think I have guessed well in sowing as large a crop of wheat as I shall be able to harvest for from the last advises from England it must be very high in all next year, as all counts untill the first of the next crop gets to market.

I have received the account of the movements <of> of the convention & the Legislature on the subject of internal improvement. It is all well, & I could wish that the most of that resolved on would be put in execution I hope that *some* of it will. I am and expect ever to be a citizen of N. Carolina & would say if you will not improve that part of it in which I live, do go to work & improve it some where. But there seems to be some hope that my immediate section will get a share of consideration. There is a great deal of wealth on the waters of Albemarle Sound and its tributaries but I fear the holders of it are close calculators & will not subscribe the sum requisit for the aid of the state. However I hope for the best. There is but one objection in my mind to the work, which is, in the evant of a seperation from the North, (a thing that must take place and I fear sooner than is generally thought) we shall be more exposed to their depredations than if they came in to the south of Cape Hataras. That however will not govern my actions. Three or even two millions of dollars would not be too much <to> for the state to borrow *if it was judiciously employed*, but I observe some of the States are geting most heavily in debt, & it might be well for us to be a little more cautious & learn how to use money before we borrow too much. But on calm reflection where is the use of /all/

this public & private improvement of the country? Not twenty five years will have passed away before this happy, happy, but div[id]ed country will be drenched in human blood and the butcheries if possible will be more horrable than even Spain at this time. We are unworthy of that inestimable blessing which God has given us for fifty years, and we are or will be given up to the free exercise of all the bad passions that man is heir to, and perhaps no set of people on earth ever possessed more bad passions & carried them to a greater height than the American. For the proof of this latter assertion but take a retrospective view of them for the last ten years. Look at those *vitious* Yankeys pulling down convents, and marching into a peacable country & butchering the inhabitants for plunder & on the other side the /half horse half aligator/ southerners going into another for the same perpose, &c, &c, &c &c &c &c

We have sold of the morus multicaulis about $6,000 worth, they are yet in demand at two cents a bud my partner who has all the correspondence on the subj[ect] is very sanguine of realising all that we had expeted. We shall probably have to ship a considerable number to Baltimore.

My sons including the little squire are all well as likewise myself. They join me in Love to their Aunt & Uncle, Sisters & cousins, & believe me to be sincerely your friend & relation.

E Pettigrew

John H. Bryan esqr

Jan 21st

N.B. I have been blessed with health for the last year & up to this time both in my white & black family, but it is exceeding sickly around me and awfully so in the lower part of the county. The disease is called by the Doctors Epidemic Influenza Whole families will be sick at a time. The disease frequenly attacks the brain & the patient /is/ raving for two or three days before he dies. In others, strong & healthy persons are well in the afternoon and dead before day. I learn that <two of> Col. McCless lost two negroes with it the week before he got home and yesterday <he> sent for the Doctor. Himself and all his family were attacked. I was told yesterday by the Doctor that coming from the lower part of the country he meet three coffins.

E P.

[*Addressed*] John H. Bryan Esqr
Raleigh
N. Carolina

Thomas Turner to Ebenezer Pettigrew A&H

Raleigh NC Feb 5, [*18*]'39

Dear sir:

I have been in this place several days—I came via Black Water, Weldon, Gaston Henderson, to Raleigh—: on Railroad, to Henderson, in the stage to Raleigh, 50 miles, all night. I brought with me the multicaulis in three small boxes.

I did not find it necessary in order to ascertain that I could not sell them, to let it be known that I had them. For conversation concerning was brief enough of itself, and it seldom closed without mention price, and demand—

The demand I found to be small, and the price 3 Cents per bud—but three cents per bud for only small quantities.

Not finding the price higher, nor the demand greater I did not offer for sale those that I had—

I found a parcel selling here at 3 Cents, that were already sprouted and growing. The sprouts were green and very tender, and about ¼ to a ½ inch long. I suspect a good many of them must perish with cold—: for only a very few can be kept in a cellar or other place out of the frost; whereas the gentleman was buying 9000—But he was buying not for himself but for a man in Guilford County. I suspect he would not have bought such for himself.

Finding the price no more than 3 Cents, and that the demand would not sell all that I have at that price under several weeks, I go to Hillsborough to day—and expect thence to go farther—

I am a good deal discouraged—and begin to think I shall not do anything to be pleased with—. I shall leave the buds in Raleigh—and if I should want them, shall provide for them to be sent to me—

At this place I called on Mrs Shepard—there I saw Mrs Bryan, Mr J H Bryan, their daughter Mary and your daughter Mary. I also saw Mr James Shepard the day before in the street. He had gone to one of his Courts when I called on his mother. Your daughter is in good health, and said your daughter Nancy was in good health also. They send their love to you. If I come via this place on my return, I shall call to see them again—

Please make this letter known to Mr Collins

Your most affectionate friend & hum ser
Th: Turner

[*Addressed*] Ebenezer Pettegrew Esq
Cool Spring
Washington Co
N.C.

William A. Dickinson to Ebenezer Pettigrew A&H

Wetumpka City Ala 7 Feby 1839

Dear Sir

Your very Kind letter of the 5th Octo. 1838. containing the grape seed, come safe to hand, I thank you for your attention to the grape seed,

It afforded me much pleashure to learn that you & your family was all well. I arrived here with my family all in good health after being on the road about 43 days, one of my Horses was sick 14 ds: and the wagon I had at Plymouth was constantly breaking down, these things so taking place was the cause of our being so long on the road, I found all things here on my arrival in good order, I would have written you sooner but having met with an accident last Decr in getting my fingers very much bruised as completely disabled me from writting It unfortunately happened to be my second & third fingers on my right hand, they are far from being well and at this time I only can write with difficulty, [bend] of my third finger I am affraid I shall loose the use of it at all events it will be a long time before it gitts well,

I am exceedingly sorry to learn that you had so much wet soon after I left, we had rain on the other side of Tarboro & at Fayetteville it blew a hurricun for three days, and raised the Creeks very much so that we crossed them with difficulty & danger, I am sorry that provisions are so high in Washington Co—I observe what you say about the Raceing affair, on the road towards the Canal, It appears that bad times do not stop those expensive & time wasting follies,

I am informed by Mr Hardy H Phelps that there has been considerable number of Deaths, I am sorry to hear of Alexander H. Davenport, I told him often that he thought himself too much of a Man, how uncertain are we in all things,

Our buseness season will be over in about two months, this winter has fallen far short of the quantity of buseness transactions here Compared with last Winter, you will observe that the Banks in this state have resumed Speicie payments, This place is now a City & the State Penitentiary is to be buit here, it is supposed in a year or two that the New State House will be buit here, since last Nov. up to this day the weather has been exceadingly cold some rain & Stow during the Winter but barely enough rain to keep the River in good Boating order, I send you a Wetumpka Paper by this days mail in which you will see the City Laws.

I hope this will find you all in good health as my family & self are well, give my respects to Mr Charles & Mr William Pettigrew. Mr Doctrn Davenport & Daniel Woodly. Corn here from 25-31¼¢. Bush at the Plantation. Cotten 12-13½¢ p w, Pork $8. p 100w Beff 4-6¢ p w.

Fodder 1$ p w. I will continue from time to time to send you a News Paper.

Shall be very happy to hear from you at all times, tell Mr Phelps I got his letter safe will write him soon, trusting this will find you in good health. and am Dear Sir

Yours very Respectfully
William A. Dickinson

[*Addressed*] Ebenezer Pettigrew Esqr.
Coolspring
N.C.

James Johnston Pettigrew to [Mary Blount Pettigrew] UNC

Lake Phelps Feb. 25th 1839

Dear sister

I take this opportunity to write to you. Par went out to belgrade last night. Par shiped a load of staves to Norfolk some week or two ago. As we were coming down home; Par carried me off to Pourtsmouth, intending to carry me to Gosport to see the navy yard: but it rained the next day. In the morning par went over to Norfolk and Bought me a book named "the sayings and doings of Sam Slick of Slicsville"; in the evening we went to the navyyrd. We first went to the "Pensylvania" a ship of the line which 60 feet long in the stern post and 144 guns because we counted them, I believe guns has two n instead of one, it drew 30 ft water and /has/ four decks, "she is a reele noble craft I tell you, that's a fact; I was right smart ryled that I did not stay longer on the deck on that are mortal great ship" be the foloing ships and frigates were there Delaware Constitution, Brandy Wine Java Guerrie North carolina and several others Then there was the drydock and the machinery to pum[p] the water out. and two ships building a <large> large Establishment to build boats in and another to make masts in and sheares; and a large blacksmithshop—Mr Collins of Edenton is dead. Pa [&] brother Charles joins me in sending our love to you, grandma Aunt Mary and all the children, we are all well.

I am your
affectionate brother
J. Johnston Pettigrew

Griffin and Gaskins to Josiah Collins and Ebenezer Pettigrew A&H

Eliz City April 19th 1839

Mess. Collins & Petigrew

Gent.

We have been informed that you have for Sale the Morus Multicaulus trees or buds—if this be true you will confer a favour by informing us of it by maile as soon as convenient—also your prices and we will remit to you the amt. of money for which we wish to invest in the mulbury tree—if you have but few to sell you will much oblige us if you will only spare 20 or $25—worth—we have sent to Norfolk [bu]t could not obtain them there—but have been informed that there are some /buds/ in Baltimore, but hering that you have them we think they must be fresher and better.—

Your attention to the above will much oblige

Your Respectfully
Griffin & Gaskins

[*Addressed*] Mess. Collins & Petigrew
Lake Phelps
Tyrrell Co.
N. Caroli[na]

John Herritage Bryan to Ebenezer Pettigrew UNC

Raleigh May 15. 1839—

My dear Sir,

I recd at Washington your letter directed to that place apprizing me that Mr Williams would transmit a drft. for $1.000. which he has done & it came to hand by last night's mail:—It is very true that you do not & cannot over estimate Mrs B's affection & care of your children; but it is no less true (& we both appreciate it highly) that you avail yourself of every opportunity of making known your gratitude & kindness by every mode of compensation:—

Mrs B. has been quite sick for two or three days She suffers much from dyspepsia & head ache—She was in bed for two days.—

Mary & Nancy are both very well:—We were much disappointed that none of you could come up to the Conventn

Mrs Shepard is over head & ears in repairing & fixing & gives herself a great deal of trouble—but it can't be helped.—

Our house proceeds but slowly—I fear that Mr Martindale has committed the error against which you cautioned him of undertaking too many jobs at the same time.—

I have had a very poor circuit, the business in New Bern is generally of a trifling character & if it were not for my connections with the place I believe, I sh[d] not go there.—

Our rail road, it is expected, or hoped will be completed in the fall, but I apprehend that my investment there will be substantially a loss—It will cost nearly twice as much as was estimated & of course can't produce much of a div[d] the expenses will be very great, of stocking it & keeping it in repair.—

I understand that Frank [*Francis Theodore Bryan*] will probably take the first honor in his class solus [*alone*];—

M[rs] B says that Mary P. will write you next week & sends her affectionate remembrance & regard to you & Charls & W[m] to which I will add my own:—

Very truly & Respy
yr friend & relative
Jn. H. Bryan

[*Addressed*] E. Pettigrew Esq[r]
Cool Spring
N.C

Henry Alexander to Ebenezer Pettigrew A&H

Sumerville Tenn. June 11th 1839.

My Dear Sir

Yours faver of the 5 Janary came to hand the 4 of Feb[r], for which I am verry much obliged. I owe you apology for not ansterining of yours Sooner But the Truth is the best apology, at the time I Receved yours I had nothing new worth your attention (and it is all most the case now) I had Just thin at that time made up my mind to visit Florida, and thought then that I would write you whle thair but did not, I Returned to this place about 10 Days Scince found Jesse and the family all well. James went with me to Florida.

I traveled Down through Alabama when I Got To Florida. I thin went to Mariana and from thair to Quincy, and from thair to Tallahassa, and made a Small Stay in that naberhood. we could not visit East Florida, for the Seminole Indians. still continued thair hosstilities and Commited Some Deperdations while we wre thair, The lands Round Tallahassa are sellining high it is verry Broken and washis badly. and in a shorest time will become poor, in the naberhood of Quincy the land is also broken and washis badly, and will soon be poor. on the Apalachicola River, thair is but little good land and what thair is overflows therefore I consider it of but little value. The land in the nabrhood of Marianna it is more level but not Rich, the Good land in Florida lies in smals parcels, on Nabarhoods from 10 to 15 Miles Distince, Some of Which is level and some hammack land, you will then travel Sometimes 10 to 20 and 30 miles through a poor piney Country before you come to any land worth Cultivating there is verry little of the land that has any Clay at all, a large proportion of the land has a Sandy foundation, interspurse with Rotten limestone, from Marianna to St. Joseph. is 93 Miles through a poor piney Country which is Good for nothing as to farming, thair Good land is Sillining, I think for Twice its value from $10 to 30. per acre, thair land will not on and Average perduece more than half a bale of Cotten to and acre, of Corn about 20 to 25 bushels per acre. I cannot beleave that Country to be helthy, But the inhabence Say it is helthy, they are verry anxious to see people moving in thair Thair Money afairs were in Rather a bad State when I was thair. Negro men was Rating from $900. to 1100. women $600. 800. but no Sales while I was thair. I will here stop this subject, and will say to you that I shall not move to Florida for I think it of less value than any Country that I Ever visited, I fell in with agrate many of my N. Carolina acquiantinces while in Florida I have not yet purched land, thair is a grate Deal of land in market, I intend to buy this Sommer, or Fall, I think better Bargans can be bought now than has been since I have been in the Country. The corps at this time are likily all over the South & west Country,

I learn that my Sute against Tarkington went against me at Tyrrell Superior Court,[1] and that Judge Give a new trial and moved it /to/ Edenten, thair I hope I shall Get Justice if I Should not I have Directed it to be Taken to the Supreame Court, if I cannot beet at law I will then Return to North Carolina and try the Court of Equity. for I never intend to Give it up, (I am Mighty fraid that Jos. Tarkenton Boylen will bust before we can have it Determined) The Money in Miss^{i} is in a Derange State <mo[re] of> the money is at a Discount from 10 to 45 per Cts. The land is now selling low in Miss^{i} but it is a verry hard matter to Get a Good title, Richard Wood and famley have move from Taxas. back to the wistern Districk

In louisiana last Feb^{r} I Sold man Cambridge, Emanul I still keep. my helth at this time is Good. (but I am alittle Sifer [*stiffer?*] from the Rheumatism) James & Jesse are Both in Good helth, Thay send thair Best Respcts to you & sons

you will Please present my Respcts to Chs. W^{m} & your other children, to Mr Forbes Mr D. Davenport & lady M^{r} & Mrs Collins. and all inquiring frends, and accept for youself my Best wishes both for you helth and Prosperity

with Sincere Esteem your frind
Henry Alexander

E. Pettigrew Esqr.

N.B. Please let me here from you

H. A.

[*Addressed*] Ebenezer Pettigrew Esqr
Cool Spring
Washington County
N. Carolina

[1]Tyrrell County court records for this year are missing.

William James Bingham to Ebenezer Pettigrew UNC

Hillsboro'—July 1st 1839—

Dear Sir;

I was sorry to learn by a letter from William to Johnston that you had been dangerously ill, & tho' free from disease at the date of his letter, still feeble. I hope you will soon recover your wonted strength.

I suppose J. has sent you his certificate of progress & deportment. The exceptions in deportment, tho' represented in their true character as 'unimportant,' may nevertheless occasion uneasiness, as their specific nature was not explained: and therefore I avail myself of the first leisure moment to relieve you. One was beating on a bench in the Acad'y with sticks, in imitation of a drummer, not in school hours however. As the act had recently been strictly forbidden, and some boys punished for it, it was the less excusable. He was drumming *softly however*, & did not expect to be heard; nor would he have been, had not I stepped into the Acad'y unexpectedly. On this ground I excused him from punishment, but thought it necessary for his good to make the exception in his certificate.—The other consisted in putting on a mannish air. (the only time he has dared to do so, & I don't think he will dare /to/ repeat it)—It happened a fortnight ago that a gentleman stepped in without Mrs B's knowledge, after she had gone into the dining room. We were very soon summoned to dinner, and an additional plate not being put on the table, Johnston, on coming to the door & seeing no seat provided for him, marched off to the Acad'y, leaving <word> instructions with one of my little daughters in case he should be inquird for, to say, that he had gone to the Acad'y, as there was no chair at the table for him. The waiter soon made arrangements, and went to call him, when my little daughter appeared, & in all simplicity, reported his message. I ordered him back from the Acad'y, & made him take his seat & eat his dinner, intending after that operation to switch him. He was so deeply mortified however & ashamed, that I let him off with a lecture, and his promise never to assume another air while under my charge.

These things tho', to be regretted, are not such as justly to produce serious uneasiness.—Time & judicious management will set all right.—Boys are much more of men now-a-days, than when you & I were boys. This is the fault of the *age* & *the government*, especially domestic and family government. So general is the error, that even when a parent brings up his children under the old regime, they catch the contagion from intercourse with other children.—Johnston thinks a long-tailed coat is much cooler this hot weather, than a sound jacket, & begs his tailoress to tell me that all the little boys wear frock coats, & persuade me to get one for him, but by no means to let me know that he desires it. So I told her to make him a *sunday-long-tail or frock*.

I expect to go bag & baggage in a day or two, on a visit to my sister, twelve miles in the country, to spend a few days. I have made arrangements with Mr Jo. Norwood[1] to take J. & delegated all necessary authority to him. To his judicious control & paternal care I entrust J. with all confidence.

Mrs B. requests her kind regards to Charles, Wm and yourself. Please present me affectionately to the boys, and believe me as ever

Your friend & obed't ser't
W. J. Bingham

P.S. I apprehend no serious difficulty in Johnston's management, and have no doubt of his making a good scholar. We are all very well.—Wheat crops in some instances much injured by the bug, but generally good. Corn crops very promising.—I wrote you soon after Wm was here.

[*Addressed*] Hon. E. Pettigrew.
Cool Spring
Washington Co.
N.C.—

[1]This probably refers to John Wall Norwood (1802-1885) of Hillsborough, an attorney. Hamilton and Williams, *Graham Papers*, VII, 617n.

W[ilson] B. Hodges to Ebenezer Pettigrew A&H

Belmont Hyde County July 27th, 1839

Dear Sir,

The election for a member of Congress is over with us, in this County; believing you would like to hear the result; and as it will be acceptable generally, to the friends of Mr [*Edward*] Stanly in your quarter, I address you. I have been at a great many elections, but never before, have I witnessed, such a warmly contested one, as ours at Germanton. I got in the Village early in the morning. two handsome flags, with Stanly and Liberty hoisted—a fine dinner was prepared, and a plenty of the *ardent*, set out—(we *the people* of Hyde, would not suffer the little, "Conquerer" to be at any expense.) after the Polls was opened, the Hall gentry, began to rave curse and threaten. I took my station, at the ballot box—determined, to see that there was no foul play. I kept my station until the Poll was closed. the patint democrats, were routed—they beat a retreat; and a considerable number of them, were found lying along the road—while the friends of Stanly returned to their homes rejoicing—We have heard from all the elections in this County, except the banks. Stanlys' majority is 368—[*Thomas H.*] Hall cannot get more than four or five /votes/ at the Banks. Stanly will get enough, to make his majority at least 500. You may be certain that Old Hyde has given Stanly 500 majority:

I hope that Tyrrell and Washington may have done and will do as well. I should be glad to hear from You. we are all well, accept my best wishes for your health and happiness and believe me yours truly

W. B. Hodges

Polls in Hyde as far as heard from.

	Stanly	*Hall*
Germanton	82	23
Clarks Mills	9	26
North Lake	46	4
Swan Quarter	86	8
Lake Landing	225	19
	448	80
	80	
	368 Majority for Stanly.	

exclusive of two elections on the Banks. where Hall cannot get more than 5

[*Addressed*] Honbl. Ebenezer Pettigrew
Cool Spring P. Office
Washington County
No Ca

Charles Lockhart Pettigrew to Ebenezer Pettigrew UNC

Baltimore Wednesday 21st Aug 1839

My dear Father

I arrived here from Washington on yesterday evening having passed thro Petersburg [&] Richmond.

This morning I called on Mr [*J. S.*] Eastman and delivered your letter and also paid him the $35 for the fan he says he will have the other done in about 3 weeks I told him to make it in every respect like the one sent. He seemed to be much gratified that you were so <much> /well/ pleased with the other I also this morning called at Hilburgh's shop and engaged your over coat, and also one for myself. they will cost $40 each he showed me the Beaver cloth which his son said you looked at when you were here. I called on Mr [*John*] Trimble and enquired about the corn sheller he paid $50 for the patern and $2 for boxing and varnishing. The casting weighed 301 lb he paid for that $15.05 and 25 to drayage making the cost $67.30. I also have been to see Mr Wheeler and told him you wished the lower gears to 3½ wide joining the pot 3 in long, and the hole to commence [up] an inch from the pot. the upper ones I told him trim a little from the buly at the end. I showed him with my hand; I think he cannot make a mistake. I have bought 100 lb of Tobacco the cheapest that could be had. it is much higher, 18 cts, than we talked of. There was some 15 cts but it was considerably inferior. I also purchase the hair matrass its cost is $25. I purchased <them> both these articles with the advise of Mr Trimble. The price of Red clover seed is $10 a bushel. White is 37½ cts per pound. I let you know the price so that should you wish to purchase at those rates you could write to Mr Trimble. With respects clover seed it is a biennial plant and will not seed the first year. The [*clover*] was almost entirely killed last year so there will not be a full crop of seed untill the next year. There will be some seed in market but it is thought it will not decline much in price. I should have left here this evening but I am compelled untill Friday Evening Mr Hilburgh says he can not get it done before that time.

I have visited Petersburg & Richmond and made all the necessary inquiries with respect to lumber. they will be good markets. I stoped at Washington part of a day. I find it a very dull article in both <those pla> that place and Baltimore. I think my jaunt will be attended with considerable advantage. I have not had to take Dr Lewis's Medicine I am gaining in weight. Dear father you or brother W. will plase write me at New York so I may get it as I return I am afraid I shall not be home as soon as I expected please give my love to Brother William.

I remain your affate son
Charles L. Pettigrew

[*Addressed*] E. Pettigrew Esq
Cool Spring
Washington Co
N Carolina

Ebenezer Pettigrew to James Johnston Pettigrew UNC

Lake Phelps Sep 2, 1839

My dear Johnston,

I have not received a letter from you for a long time, not since the one in which you wrote me that Mr Bingham was going to whip you that day. I was very sorry to learn my dear son that a boy who could learn his lesson so easily should still do something that would subject him to correction. You think that Mr Bingham is geting more strict, but my son you are mistaken you are geting more self willed, and do not know it, and will not believe it when you are told so by others. I know that Mr Bingham loves you Johnston, and that he /is/ anxious to overlook little errors as far as he consistantly can, but to let a boy have his own way, is to ruin him forever and what I never could allow in my children. Look at your brothers Charles & William, how strictly they obey. Do you think they would be so if they <had> had been allowed to do their own way. No by no means. Look at other young men who have been permited to do as they think proper. Where are they. Gone and going to distruction as fast as they can to the sorrow & missery of their parents. My dear son recollect your parents, recollect your poor Ma in her grave, and pray do not disgrace her in her silent grave, but let /her/ rest in peace.

Your brother Charles went to the north about three weeks ago, upon business of the mill, his health was declining when he started, but, in two letters he has written since he left, he says he is improving. Your brother William is well, and at Belgrade.

We had a dreadfull storm on the 29th Ult. which has overflowed & tore every thing to pieces.[1] The greater part of the Lake corn is under water and the water in /the/ Lake 6 ft. 3½ inch high. It is almost ready to run over at all places. The water in Scuppernong river is from 3½ to 4 ft high in the swamp. The Virginia Hodges left the mouth of the river right before for New York, and I fear could not get there in time to escape the storm & if she did not, the Lord knows what has become of her. Lost I fear.

My health is now good, and I hope to visit you in Octr or Nov. but I am mortally busy. I hope my dear little Johnston you are in good health and geting along like a good boy should with the approbation of all around you.

Believe me to be your affectionate
father
E Pettigrew

Mr J. Johnston Pettigrew

[*Addressed*] Mr J. Johnston Pettigrew
Hillsborough
N. Carolina

[1]Usually in late August or September hurricanes battered the low country of eastern North Carolina. Many references to them are scattered throughout this volume. Two especially severe storms are referred to in the *Whig* (Washington, N.C.), July 27 and August 31, 1843. The first one flooded the head of Pungo River, while in the second one eight ships were lost at Ocracoke Bar.

Ebenezer Pettigrew to Mary Williams Bryan A&H, BRYAN

Belgrade Octr 1, 1839

My dear Sister,

I have been for months intending to write you, but some how or other, I will not say unaccountably, (for I can account for the apparent neglect) I have not written to you untill now, and at this time I have been out at daylight & have only time to say a few words before the mail passes.

I regret exceedingly My dear sister to learn of your continued indisposition, but I hope & pray that it will wear out after a time and that you will be restored to perfect health.

My health is now and has been for some time good, also Charles & William are well. In truth there is little or [*no*] sickness in my establishment, though a good deal is about me.

Charles came from the north about a fortneight ago, much improved in health. His business there was on the Steem mill & to get a man to repair my mill at the Lake.

We have had a desperate storm which has done a great deal of injury to the standing timber & corn.

It is with great sorrow that I cannot stay more with you & my dear little daughters, nothing could give me so much pleasure than to spend more much more time with you all, but really I am so much involved in business that I cannot see the time to go any where th positive business does not call. All this attention is /not/ req from any want of attention from my sons, they do all I war or ask, of them but we are all busy, and as much so as

I hope in five years more to get things so arranged as to be able to quit, and be at leasure. when I will spend not only weeks but months with you. I am begining to-day to sow wheat and hope to be able to visit you & my dear little girls in the last of this month or first of next.

I suppose Mr Bryan is on the circuit, when at home make my kind regards to him, our Mother & all the children. to which my /sons/ request as well as yourself, and please to assure yourself of the affectionate regards

of your brother
E Pettigrew

Mrs Mary W. Bryan

[*Addressed*] Mrs John H. Bryan
Raleigh
No Ca

James Louis Petigru to Ebenezer Pettigrew UNC

Charleston 29 Octr 1839

Dear Cousin,

This letter is to introduce my friend Mr Edmondson[1] one of our first merchants and a gentleman for whom I have a very great regard—As he proposes to go into your country I hope that he will have the opportunity of bringing me some account of you as an eyewitness--and any attentions that you may pay him will give me the greatest satisfaction.

It would be a great pleasure to see you again in Charleston, but one that I am afraid we will have to wait for a long time, unless you will forego something of that attachment to home that has characterized you a long time—When my wife and I were in Baltimore a year ago we had such a serious intention of reproaching you with your neglect that nothing but our ill health prevented us from changing our route in search of you—I am Dear Coz

Yours truly
J L Petigru

[*Addressed*] The Honble
E. Pettigrew
Tyrrel County
North Carolina

[1] A notation on the outside of this letter indicates that "C. Edmondson Esqr" delivered it. The bearer may have been Charles Edmondston.

William James Bingham to Ebenezer Pettigrew UNC

Hillsboro'—Nov[r] 4th 1839—

My dear Sir;

Johnston's health has been uniformly good; and he is doing *well* both in his studies and his deportment.

I made him put on his flannil when the cool weather <appr> commenced, and had *proper* shoes made for him. His winter clothes would have been made long ago, but for his own neglect. They have been in the seamstress's hand some time however, and are probably done. The weather has been such that he did not need them.

My family are all well. M[rs] B. & my brother unite with me in kind regards to Charles, William & yourself.

The session will end on the 6th of Dec[r] & the next will begin on the 6th of Jan'y. This is done to meet the alteration at Chapel Hill.

Every thing has been quiet & orderly since the rebellion.[1] First & last I have dismissed twenty, & still have ninety six. We are very much relieved by getting rid of the disorderly spirits.

In haste Yours truly
W. J. Bingham

[*Addressed*] Hon. E. Pettigrew
Cool Spring
Washington Co—
N.C—

[1]In September, 1839, a group of larger students, led by Alexander Croom, conspired to challenge the authority of William J. Bingham at his academy by force. The plot was detected and an armed confrontation took place between Bingham and Croom. Bingham was victorious with no shots having been fired. On September 13 the trustees met, commended Bingham, and expelled all known conspirators. Printed letter, September 16, 1839, Pettigrew Family Papers, Southern Historical Collection.

James Cathcart Johnston to William Shepard Pettigrew UNC

Hays. 15th Nov[r] 1839.

M[r] William Pettigrew

Dear Sir

I send by your Father a small bundle of Strawberry vines which may supply any loss you have sustain[d] in those you had set out, they are taken from some I got from New York last spring and may be very good or may be a Humbug I know not /which/—the New Yorkers are great humbuggers—that you may talk learned about them I send you the fine names of the different kinds, which are put up seperately and designated by /a/ stick in each bunch with notches correspondinding to the N°—

with great regard
your friend
Ja. C. Johnston.

N° 1. Large Early Scarlet
2 Melon. (very [fine])
3 Bishop Orange
4 Bostock or Willington
5 Knight's narrow leaf
6 Nairns Scarlet
7 Elton Ludling, large
8 Downton late
9. New Black Musk [Hawthorn]
10. Faulkner's Scarlet.

[*Addressed*] Mr William Pettigrew
Belgrade

Edmund Ruffin[1] *to Ebenezer Pettigrew* UNC

Petersburg [*Virginia*] Nov. 28. 1839

Dear Sir

I avail myself of the earliest time after my reaching home (to day) to urge upon you a request that was omitted, in the very short visit which I made you, among the many other things which I would have said, & the greater number which I should have liked to have heard from you,—because we were so straitened for *time*. My request is, that what I had not time to hear you *tell* in words, that you will communicate in writing for the Far. Reg.; & without meaning to limit your subjects, or to restrain your pen, & wishing to receive from you any communication & on any subject which you may be willing to give, I will state that what I especially desire, & what I think would be especially interesting, is a narrative & descriptive statement of your remarkable labour & successful improvements in your draining & cultivation, from the beginning to the end. This statement would be appropriately accompanied by such accounts of the swamp & lake, & the /most/ remarkable circumstance & changes of both, together with whatever was connected therewith or having a bearing thereon, in the agricultural condition of the adjacet part of the country. If you will confer this favor on me & on my readers, you will probably at the same time do good to your country, & promote improvement by draining, by the striking manner in which your views of /the/ swamp & <its> the benefit of its improvement will be presented. I am prepared in advance with your answer & objection to this—the same which keeps concealed & useless so much of the exciting knowledge of men of the most practical knowledge—that is, that writing for the public has not been your habit, & that no task is more irksome to one of your mode of life. But I pay no respect to such ground of denial, except so far as it affects your pleasure or convenience, on which I am unwilling to press or intrude. But sir, as to *ability*, if you will merely write as you *talk*, & of the same things, your manner & your matter will be fully satisfactory. I hope you will not disappoint my wishes.

I shall get into my next No. part of my own /recently formed & crude/ views on the general subject—& will send you (in advance of the suceeding No.) the <proof> sheets, as printed, of the concluding part. As a matter of course, I must have comitted many mistakes & shown a stranger's ignorance. This, as well as my request to you, will afford you means for your better account, & any material errors into which I may fall, I beg you to refer to, & to correct. I shall take the liberty of stating my request to you now urged, & my hope that it may be complied with.

Knowing by experience the trouble of *shipping* any small articles by a person not in that kind of business, I spoke to Mr Boyle about sending to me the wine, should Mr C. Pettigrew succeed in procuring it for me. Mr B. can send anything delivered to him in a few weeks to City Point. This is merely mentioned to save some of the trouble which I put on your son, but nothing has been done to interfere with any other arrangement which he may prefer.

With respect & esteem
Yours &c
Ed: Ruffin

[*Addressed*] Ebenezer Pettigrew esqr
Cool Spring
Washington County
N.C.

---

[1]Edmund Ruffin (1794-1865) was a noted Virginia agriculturist and publisher who founded the *Farmer's Register* in 1833. In his work entitled *Agricultural, Geological, and Descriptive Sketches of Lower North Carolina, and the Similar Adjacent Lands* (Raleigh, 1861), 233-234, Ruffin described the Collins canal from "Lake Scuppernong" to the river, adding that "Mr. E. Pettigrew" built a fifteen-foot-wide canal later. Interesting descriptions of the lands around the lake may be found on pages 194, 195, 198, 237, and 238.

Proslavery and secessionist, Edmund Ruffin fired the first shot at Fort Sumter in 1861 and committed suicide upon the fall of the Confederacy. *DAB*, XVI, 214-216.

[Bishop] Levi Silliman Ives to Ebenezer Pettigrew UNC

The Lake Nov 29th 1839

My dear Sir,

I regret, that, being under the necessity of going to day to Edenton & not being sufficiently well to make the additional exertion of a visit to Belgrade as I had inted, I shall not be able to see you till the spring: When, D[*eo*]. V[*olente*]. I hope to have the privalege of at least a day or two with you, to enjoy your society, & look over the papers of your venerated Father.[1]

Please present my kind regards to your son William, &

believe me
very truly
Your friend
L. S Ives

E. Pettigrew Esquire

[*Addressed*] The Hon,
E. Pettigrew
Belgrade
Washington Co.
N.C.

[1]Levi S. Ives was at this time bishop of the Episcopal Diocese of North Carolina. In 1794 the Reverend Charles Pettigrew had become the first person elected to that position, although he was never consecrated. Lemmon, *Pettigrew Papers*, I, xv, 133. The papers of Charles Pettigrew are published in the first volume of this series.

James Johnston Pettigrew to Ebenezer Pettigrew UNC

Raleigh Decr 31st 1839

Dear Father

As I have not written to you in a long while, I take the opportunity to write as [more] as I can. I have not receieved a letter fro[m] home in a long time, and I begin to feel anxious about your health. I came down here on the third day since the session broke up as Mr Bingham said that he was afraid to trust me in a crowd of boys so I had to wait a day or two. It has been extremely bad weather since you left Hillsboro' between then and the time I came away it was <one> one continued spell of bad weathe it snowed and almost incessantly the streets were perfect mud puddle; but it has been better down here at Raleigh; there has been one snow that laid on the gound five or six days it is snowing hard now which is the second time it has snowed; to say the least it has been very cold and is likely to continue so. I stay at grandmar's with uncle James. I have seen all the wonders of <rawleigh> Raleigh and I think it will rise when the railroad is finished and all that it lacks of being finished is the iron being laid, they are building a depot and Mr. Garnet[1] thinks it will be finished in february. Give my love to my brothers. We are all well and Gradmar sends her respects,

and beleive me to Your affectionate son
J. Johnston Pettigrew

[*Addressed*] Ebenezer Pettigrew Esq.
Cool-Spring
Tyrrel county
N.C.

---

[1]Charles F. M. Garnett was chief engineer for construction of the Raleigh and Gaston Railroad, which opened to Raleigh on March 21, 1840. John Gilbert and Grady Jefferys, *Crossties through Carolina: The Story of North Carolina's Early Day Railroads* (Raleigh: Helios Press, 1969), 24.

Francis Theodore Bryan to Ebenezer Pettigrew UNC

C. Hill Jan 4th 1840

Dear Uncle

I arrived safe in Raleigh on Monday after I left Belgrade and found all the family pretty well. We had a heavy fall of snow on Saturday evening which we feared would hinder the cars from travelling but it was washed off before morning by the rain. We spent quite a merry Christmas in Raleigh. Sister Mary Pettigrew received your letter before I left Raleigh. She is very well and Nancy & Johns[*t*]on also. Johns[*t*]on intended to come to Chapel Hill with me in Father's barouche, but the weather was /so bad/ we concluded it would be better to come in the public conveyance. He went to Hillsboro' yesterday. Grandma was in pretty good health when I left.

I was very much pleased with my visit to the Lake and am very thankful to you for your kindness to me in carrying me down and also cousins Charles & William.

The Raleigh & Gaston rail-road is expected to be done by the first of March when there will be a great ball in the capitol, planks being placed in the Commons Hall for that purpose There is not much news here only that it is expec- that college duties will not commence to-morrow the greatest part of students being delayed by the snow.

Give my love to cousin Charles and cousin William.

Your affectionate nephew
F. T. Bryan

[*Addressed*] Hon E. Pettigrew
Cool-Spring
Washington Co.
N. Ca.

*Ebenezer Pettigrew to Edmund Ruffin** UNC

Copy

Lake Phelps Jan 6th 1840

Dr Sir

I received your favor of Nov 28th together with several pamphlets which you were so good as to send me, in their due time. You will please to accept my thanks for them. When you first published Johnston on draining I got ten copies and presented them to various of my friends. The one on Milaria I read when it first made its appearance in the Register with great interest. I thought I knew every word of it to be true, from long observation and suffering, from the ignorance of those facts in early time, but for more than twenty five years I have been fully convinced of the gr/e/at cause of most of our sickness in this country (stagnant water and mud exposed to a hot fall sun) and have spared no labour or cost in my power to avoid them. One of the strong reasons for moving my house at Belgrade from my Father's location was to get it farther from the Scuppernong river swamp, and though it was but two hundred and fifty yards I have no doubt of having long since been remunerated for the cost in the health of my people, though it has been but six years. it is a work which ought to be in the house of every man who lives in the low country, or bilious feaver region of our country. I hold the right of property inviolable except in cases of life and death, but were I living in the neighborhood of a *mill pond* I shoul/d/ consider the right of property in it no more than that of a tame Bear who was devouring my child. To calmly sit by and see all ones children, & dear companion as pale as corpses, in a short time violent disease and after watching, with the utmost anxiety to follow to the grave those dear objects of your love, perhaps one after the other until all are gone, and to know that all those heart rending sufferings arise from the milaria of the various mill ponds in your neighborhood must evince a degree of forbearance beyond christian, and an obduracy of heart in the owner of mills, almost equal to that of cold blooded murder. If I know anything that would induce me to accept the dictatorship of a country it would be that of having the power to constrain the inhabita/nts/ in the bilious fever region to remove all stagnant waters from it, and to keep all arrable land in the fall covered with vegitation & thereby sheltered from the power or influence of the sun.

You request me to give you in a series of Letters an accou/nt/ of my operations in the swamp for the last thirty six years. I will not say what many might, that it would be of no use, because I think it probable some few might be benefited. But a part of my experience is that which the young of this day, have no idea of, *Labor* and *Privation* of comforts. Their education and habits are entirely at variance with it. No my dear Sir the fashionable life of this day will never ditch and clear a swamp but I can tell you what it will do. It will very soon spend the proceeds from one that is ditched and cleared, unless they are very great.

If I could spend my information on paper as easily as I can /my ideas/ on a swamp, I could soon do what you want; but that is not my habit, and therefore would be gr/e/at labour; withall I am admonished that my time is growing to a close. I have other greater & more important duties to perform if it be possible before I go hence and therefore am bound for the present to decline doing that which it would give me so much pleasure to do. Write what I have seen, & done & thought. For in the early and middle part of my life, being poor and a farmer of the swamp, I was not allowed to enter that society which I *vainly* thought I was entitled to, and solitude and seclusion was the consequence, which resulted in a great deal of my time spent in thought of men and things, looking at them as through a spy glass at a great distance. I hav/e/ not had reason to change my impressions then made. I sat down this day week to write this lette/r/ but was taken with an ague which continued 12 hours & an affection of the brain that very much endangered my life. I am better but quite feeble, with some affection of the liver, which is the first time from my feeling that I ever knew I had a liver.

Please assure yourself of my Esteem
E Pettigrew

Edmund Ruffin Esq

John Herritage Bryan to Ebenezer Pettigrew A&H

Raleigh Jany. 28th 1840

My dear sir,

I am happy to inform you that yesterday about 5 oClock in the morning, Mary gave birth to a daughter & is now doing tolerably well.—

The family are all well; your daughters are in excellent health, Mary P. never was in as good health, I think as she now is.—

We hope to get them at school by the spring; the weather has been so inclement during this season, that they could hardly have attended school with much regularity.—

The Supreme Co. have decided the case of Alexander v Tarkinton in favour of my client & I have written to Mr Beasley informing him of it. I shd like to know who are Tarkinton's heirs, as it may be necessary (for the benefit of the sureties) to issue a Sci: fa: to them to subject the land.—

My best wishes to Charles & William—Mary desires to be affecty remembered by all of you Mrs Shepard has just completed the painting of her house & it looks very well.—

Augustine Sheppard[1] is spoken of, as the new Judge in Saunders[2] place.—

The Bishop has been a good deal unwell & is threatened with hernia, which wd be a dreadful inconvenience—but I hope that as his general health improves the danger will be removed—

Very truly yr friend relati[ve]
Jn. H. Bryan

[*Addressed*] E Pettigrew Esqr
Cool Spring
N.C

---

[1]Augustine Henry Shepperd (1792-1864), an attorney, represented Stokes County in the North Carolina House of Commons from 1822 until 1827, then served in Congress nine sessions between 1827 and 1851. Cheney, *North Carolina Government*, 281, 282, 284, 286, 288, 677, 678, 679, 680, 683, 686; *Biographical Directory of Congress*, 1592.

[2]Romulus Mitchell Saunders (1791-1867), an attorney from Caswell County, had served in the North Carolina General Assembly as a representative, senator, and Speaker of the House of Commons. He was state attorney general before being elected a superior court judge in 1835. In 1840 he received the Democratic nomination for governor and was defeated by the Whig candidate, John Motley Morehead. Ashe, *Biographical History*, III, 386-389.

Thomas Emory[1] *to Ebenezer Pettigrew* A&H

Poplar Grove near Centreville [*Maryland*] Feb 1. 1840.

Dear Sir,

I have <recently> read an acct of your vicinity recently in the farmers Register, and it has created a great desire to see your place & Mr Collins', if I ever should get withn striking distance—Like yourself my taste is for fine lands and *fine improvements* upon them, & where these are united to a well regulated & excellent neighbourhood society as you have, nothig can be more delightful in the, '*land of liberty*' or elsewhere, in this world.

I know that you live in the region of the North Carolina long leaf yellow pine, and also of the pitch pine—from the kindness of the growth of all other varieties of the pine I am satisfied these would also thrive here and I am anxious to introduce them.

May I therefore ask the favour that you will have me a small parcel of the seed of each of these varieties collected for me and sent by the first conveyance to the care of Wm R. Stuart Commission merchant, Bowleys Wharf Baltimore. or if it is too late to gather the seed could you hire some one in the neighborhood of the woodlands take me up a given number of seedling or two year old plants of the two varieties & put them up in a sort of crate—so that the trees crate & freight to Baltimore when they reach there shall not cost me more than 20 dollars.

I have had a great deal of experience in transplanting ever greens, and I have found it necessary that each plant be taken up with a spade by four cuts including a ball of earth and as much of the tap root as as possible.— There is another rule with regard to pine trees—They live well if tak<ing>en up before the bud pushes—badly afterwards—The bud pushes somewhat in length the first start of vegetating weather either in Feby or March, consequently they require to be taken up <before> very soon after the frost is out of the ground in Winter. I suppose it is so with you now—day before yesterday it was *nearly out here*—But the wind changed & it is again locked up, and last night we had a fall of snow a foot deep & it is still falling.

If you can with perfect convenience to yourself hire some one to do either of the above Jobs for me & transmit his draft along with the seed or the plants you will much oblige me, and it would afford me much pleasure to render you a similar service here if you should ever require it—How did you progress in the collection of your debt in Balt.— I hope when you come there again on this or other business I shall have the pleasure of seeing you here.

Very Resply Dr Sir Yr Obt Servt
Tho: Emory

[*Addressed*] The Hon. Ebenezer Pettigrew
near
Plymouth
North Carolina

---

[1]No additional information has been found on Thomas Emory.

Margaret Pettigrew to James Louis Petigru[1]* UNC

[*Ireland March 1, 1840*]

My dear Cousin James,

Your letter of Novbr 1835 has remained so long unanswered that you have no doubt supposed it never would be replied to, I received it just after a dangerous illness, the dregs of which appeared to settle upon my lungs and my medical attendants thought it advisable to remove me to a warmer climate than any Ireland could afford, accordingly I was obliged to emigrate and thank the Lord after two years very delicate health I gradually recruited and I have for the last two years been in general very well, by the time I had returned to Ireland your letter had so long lain unnoticed that I hardly then knew how to begin. An opportunity now offers that encouraged me to take up my pen and venture however late to address you: A Servant who has lived six years with us is now going to America, and if he does not find employment in New York, means to proceed to Charleston; he wishes for some introduction and I immediately thought I would take the liberty of recommending him to your notice and make him the bearer of my letter. If you could do anything to forward his interests I should feel obliged, his name is Ricd Curran, he is a very good inside servant, very honest and sober, and I think in a respectable gentleman's family would give satisfaction. If he proceeds to Charleston he will deliver this letter to you himself and be able to tell you all about your Irish cousins and if he stop in New York I shall desire him to send it to you by post. I felt greatly gratified by your nice long letter and the account you kindly gave me of all the other branches of your family, I assure your I have quite a feeling of relationship for you all but I believe for you particularly as my first correspondent, and I hope you will allow me the pleasure of again hearing from you soon; and pray don't begin 'Madame" remember I am your cousin and write to me as such, or I shall feel offended. I was glad that my letter afforded you any satisfactory information on your family history, I cannot give you <any> /much/ information as to why our coat of arms are red scotch, I have understood that our family were originally french but remaining some time both in Scotland and England ere they came to Ireland it is thought probable that the Scotch orthography was adopted by them instead of the french, besides I have heard that my great great Grandmother was of Scotch descend and patriotically attached /to/ the land of her forefathers. In this way the name may have become Scotch and therefore had assigned to it the same arms as the Scotch family, there was something about the name having become changed, but I really don't know what the tradition was and all the old members of the family are gone who might have been able to tell something about it. During my long absence I believe our coat of arms was sent to you by a young friend of mine, notwithstanding I shall seal this letter with the family seal which you can examine. My family; now reduced to myself, 3 nephews and two nieces, are Episcopalians my dear brothers when living were the same and in politics were high tory, for myself I am not politician, and the dear boys are too young to favor any party, and trust when older / and trust when older they will learn their politics from the Bible; you will perhaps think this a strange sentiment and begin to suspect I am a methodist indeed I am, what the gay world generally honor with the appelation though I belong not to the Wesleyan Society, but Episcopalians if a little stricter than their neighbours are often classed with Methodists, nor have I any objection to be so classed, they are a body of people I greatly esteem and respect and I often attend their ministry. You will be glad to [*know*] your cousins here are all enjoying excellent health save one whose very slight indisposition will I trust be of no consequence. My eldest nephew is now at a classical school in training for the University, and his two younger brothers are at a preparatory school. My eldest niece is also at school they all promise to be amiable in their dispositions and I trust will turn out useful and respectable members of society but here we must not be too sanguine many promising appearances have only mocked and disappointed the hopes they have raised. It is rather the fashion now for you transatlantic folk to visit Europe and our british isles why should not some of your family cross the waters? believe me I should feel glad to see any of its members in Erin go Bragh, I rather think I shall never visit your shores but it might be, some of the young people may and if they do I should feel anxious they should see and know you this however is a distant anticipation—I would again request to hear from you when you have leisure to write me a long letter. I must now conclude this hasty scrawl I beg my kind remembrances to Mrs Pettigru and to your sisters if they will accept of it. Believe me Dr cousin with sincere good wishes for your present and eternal happiness

I remain very truly yours
Margaret Pettigrew

March 1st 1840.

[1]Internal evidence indicates that the letter writer was a Pettigrew relative in Ireland. Apparently this copy was made by a member of the South Carolina Pettigrew family and is noted as having been copied in Charleston in 1846.

Ebenezer Pettigrew to James Johnston Pettigrew UNC

Belgrade March 24, 1840

My dear son,

I received your letter of the 3rd Instant by the last mail, and take the succeeding one to answer it, as you appear so anxious to hear from home. I was glad to learn that your health has been good with exception<.> /of two days./ The winter has been a very bad one here both from wet & cold.

I regret that Mr Bingham has found it necessary to flog you, but my dear son it must be for your good, and for cause. I know Mr Binghams feelings toward you too well, to ever think that he could give you a lick with a switch or chide you without a sufficient cause from you, and I pray you my dear son to act in all things up to your duty, that you may avoid correction of any sort. I know you have the capacity to do it. and I hope you have the will.

I am very glad to learn from your letter that you are boarding at so good a house, I hope you will conduct yourself in it, and to the family so as to be equally thought of by them.

I have received an invitation to your uncle Charles Shepard's weding to Miss Mary Donald [*Donnell*], but both your brothers & mself are too busy to go. I understand your sister Mary has gone to it with your grandma.

I have been the greater part of the winter in very low health, but am now tolerably recovered Your brothers & myself are all as much engaged as we can be. I have got workmen /from Baltimore/ to repare the race and machinery at the Lake which was bound to be done this spring. Your brother Charles has taken the direction of the steam mill at Columbia, which takes half of his time and gives me a great deal more to do at the Lake.

Your brothers Charles & William are in health they desire their Love to you & wish you to write them. Give my best respects to Mr & Mrs Bingham and assure yourself my dear Johnston of sincere affection of your father

E Pettigrew

Mr J. Johnston Pettigrew

N.B. Mr Daniel Woodlys wife died the first of December & [*he*] is to be married to Mr Robarts Winnes daughter next thursday. E P

Miss Sally Francis was well the oth[er d]ay

[*Addressed*] M[r] Ja. Johnston Pettigrew
Hillsborough
N. Carolina

Mary Williams Bryan to Ebenezer Pettigrew A&H

Raleigh April 20th 1840—

My dear Brother

I was very happy to learn by your letter of the 13 inst. recd night before last that you had recovered your health and feel much gratified by the pleasure you express at my recovery—I have indeed suffered greatly since I saw you but by the blessing of God I am permitted again to walk abroad & enjoy the works of his creation, at this most delightful season of the year all Nature seems teeming with joy & gladness—

I think you should not complain if you can walk eight miles a day, I am almost out of breath by walking even to the Church which is the farthest & almost the only one I have taken since you left here—

I regret exceedingly that you cannot spare the time to make us a visit for a two-fold reason, the first is a desire to enjoy your society & the second that you should see more of your daughters and assist by your counsel and parental authority in moulding their characters to your wishes—We have but a short time to live in this world & why should we make such slaves of ourselves? Our children will be neither wiser better happier nor more grateful for it—the experience of the world teaches us that children seldom regard the sacrifices of their parents.— I am also very anxious that the Marys should be at a good school, before Miss Whitwell resigned (knowing there was not a good school here for girls as far advanced) I requested Brother William to enquire & let me know about the schools in Washington City & Georgetown, he did so, I showed you the letter &c and I thought that you & Mr Bryan concluded that it would be better to keep them here another year attending to their studies & then send them to Washington during the Summer session—I don't think that they could stand the cold of a northern winter, for altho' M B has more strength of constitution that M Pettigrew she has not as much prudence & care and consequently would be liable to suffer

I hoped there would be a good school here before this but I believe there is no prospect of it at present.

If you think it better for Mary to go to Hillsboro' I am perfectly willing Mrs Burrell's is said to be a good school but whether it is worthy of its reputation I do not know—it is the same school Mary & Nancy went to the summer they were in Hillsboro' I thought they learned very little then—Brother John's daughters are at Salem [*Academy*] I should think that was far better than Hillsboro' I imagine the health & morals of the girls are better attended to there—It would be better for you to come up & see us & we will talk it all over & determine what to do if I could leave home as easily as you can I should be very glad to make a visit to you at the Lake—

I have been looking for Ma' for several days but she has not yet come—Mr Bryan left home last friday for the S. Courts of Craven & Beaufort after which his circuit will be over, I hope Lydia got home safe & found her children well—

Our family are all well at present, I & several of the children had the prevailing cold attended with hoarseness and sore throat Nancy escaped & is in very fine health she & Betsey go to Miss Betsey Haywood; I hasten'd to answer your letter & hope that it may induce you to steal a few weeks from your business & make us a visit—last week the Rail Road directers gave the Citizens a ride as far as Wake Forrest depot 15 miles Mr Bryan & I went & took with us Mary Nancy Betsey Charles & Octavia we were much pleased.

Give my love to Charles & William & believe me to be with sentiments of the most sincere regard & esteem

Your affectionate Sister
Mary W Bryan

[*Addressed*] Hon[ble] E. Pettigrew
Cool-Spring
Washington County
N.C.

Jane Gibert Petigru North to Jane Caroline North UNC

Badwell [*South Carolina*] April 23rd [*1840*]

My dear Carey—

This day month I hope to despatch Andrew to Aiken to bring you and Jany and our cousin James to Badwell—I do not mean to write you but one more letter until then—but Mary and Mary will keep up the usual intercourse—Mary C wished to write today to Mother, but I told her to many letters from a dull house at the same time was bad policy, so she has defered it—your letter of the 6th inst— raised my burdened spirits for I must believe your assertion, and your last of the 12th was very pleasant—how often have I pictured the dear party—consisting of those two precious sisters and all the young folk so dear to me, until I almost lose consciousness of my distance, and think think I hear and see them—That is a pleasure not likely to be mine for a long long time if ever again—I trust dear little Adele did not continue long indisposed, and is now well again—and that all things have gone well with you—and that the clerical dinner and the agricultural party were both successful—I was gratified indeed to find that you acquitted yourself to the satisfaction of your kind friends at the musical party—the only return we can make for un[encum]bered acts of kindness from those dear to us, is to be as agreeable as our circumstances or our talents enable us to be—say to Mrs Pinckney I never think of Pee Dee but I remember her with pleasure—in short my love to her—I wonder if you have seen Miss Pringle I wonder also if you have had as uncommon a week of weather in the low country as we have had here—a regular snowstorm on sunday the 15th and frost every succeeding night till saturday—I have had many pangs on account of my wheat, and walked over it the third time this morning, and have decided not to have it cut down to feed the horses on as many persons are doing—I think it will make a little, and corn is so scarce that even a little will be a help--every /thing/ that could be killed in the garden is dead, but I see a few [sat*illegible*]ing peaches but it is doubtful if they reach maturity—Minnies chickens do not do well either whether the frost bit the eggs I cannot tell, but they do not hatch—the only flourishing things at this time are my goslings, and they incur the malediction of Aunt May because next to pigs they are the most detestable of creatures—and you know nothing lives under a ban long, so I expect them to die—Today is mild again but it will be some time before vegetation recovers what it lost and the corn begin to show along the rows again—Andrew went to Hamburg last week and got me some groceries, coffee sugar—molasses salt—the horses look tolerable after their trip and Mary wishes to go the last of the week to see the Wa[dlanes]—she will stay only a day with them—poor dear she is not doing much—she has the North indolence, and the Petigru idleness to contend with so what can we expect—just nothing—I long to get you home again dear child—but if your uncle Jim North were to ask you to spend the summer with him at Norfolk I should say embrace the opportunity—It does, or ought to do every one good to see a little of the world, and it would be selfish in me to prevent your going *were* he to *ask you*—Tell Lou—her page reminded me as much of her friend Miss Martha as of herself—and I hope she will write me soon again—unfortunately I had nine chemises made before her communication came—but will have the petticoats and drawers done for her—and send them when Andrew goes to Aiken— I hope she will have a pleasant and useful sum[mer] with her Aunts—and prepare herself for a useful part in life—is Joe at Matanza too—or is it only Ben and Louis that you designate the boys—My influenza is well—my eyes dim—my head murky—so you will not regret that I am compelled to use one of Mary's small sheets and thereby give you a short letter—my dearest love to your Aunts—kindest remembrance to yr Uncle[1] and embrace the children—Mary had intended going to Edgefield when Andrew goes for you, but as the Butlers will be about that scheme is dropped—I want her to make up her green frock, but she says she will wait till you bring the fashions—is not that *range*—Well! we shall content us—Every day now will diminish the month between us—your affectionate Mamma—

Jane G North

[*Addressed*] Miss J. Caroline North
Care of R F W— Allston
Georgetown
S° Carolina

[1]Robert Francis Withers Allston (1801-1864) was a South Carolina rice planter and governor of the state. He was noted for his application of engineering principles to rice culture. His plantation, located in Georgetown County, was known as Matanzas, but in 1853 the name was changed to Chicora Wood. In 1832 Allston married Adele Petigru, sister to James Louis Petigru of Charleston. *DAB*, I, 223-224; Rogers, *Georgetown County*, 276.

Jane Caroline North, daughter of the widowed Jane Petigru North, another sister, was reared partially by her Aunt Adele and Uncle Allston. Mrs. Allston called her "Carie" and disapproved of her "sojourning on the beach" while young Adele, the Allstons' daughter, studied music. Rogers, *Georgetown County*, 270, 314.

Certificate of Appointment UNC

[*April 27, 1840*]

State of North Carolina.

Tyrrel County.

This may certify, that, at a Public meeting, held at the Court House in Columbia, on the 27th of April 1840, William S. Pettigrew was appointed a Delegate, to represent this County in the "Whig Young mens convention" to be held in Baltimore in May next.

H[*ezekiah*]. G. Spruill Chairman[1]

[1]Washington (and Tyrrell) County Whigs who were active during this period included, in addition to William Shepard Pettigrew, Josiah Collins, Ashbury

Norman, Dr. Hardy Hardison, Doctrine Davenport, and Noah M. Phelps, all named delegates to attend the 1842 state convention, and Gen. Hezekiah G. Spruill, Samuel Newbury, Absalom Davenport, William D. Davenport, John Nicholls, John B. Chesson, William L. Chesson, and Nathaniel Beckwith. *Whig* (Washington, N.C.), March 23, 1842. The issue of April 13, 1842, carried an article on actions by the convention.

The Whig party had held its first statewide political convention in North Carolina in 1839. Henderson, *North Carolina*, II, 124.

John Herritage Bryan to Ebenezer Pettigrew A&H

Washington [*North Carolina*] Apl. 29. 1840

My dear sir,

I had hoped to have heard from you at this place, either by letter or some person who might be at Court from your County:—

I feel anxious upon the subject of the education of the two elder girls of our family, in which I know you participate,—if you could conveniently come up this spring & have a consultation with Mrs B. we might probably fix upon some school that would be suitable & advantageous to them—Miss Mercer's School in Va. & Bishop Doane's[1] School near Burlington in New Jersey are both well spoken of: It might be advisable for them afte going to one of these schools to spend a few months in obtaining the ornamental branches &c.—

I have been annoyed by the easterly winds of NewBern & here, which have made me feel very uncomfortable, tho' I have kept up & attended to my business.—

Mrs Shepard & Mary left NewBern on the 20th & I heard of them within a few miles of Raleigh, by Judge Saunders; they say in NewBern that Mary has improvd very much in health & otherwise.—

The Candidates (for the Governor's chair) addressed the people here on Monday in the Methodist Church, their addresses consumed a great deal of time:—M^r^ [*John Motley*] Morehead seemed to give much satisfaction to his friends & Gen: [*Romulus M.*] Saunders was also much lauded by his—I think M. has the more popular talent.—*

I have found cash both here & at New Bern scarce beyond all former precedent—the Country Courts are better than the town.—

The Bishop is here, but did not preach either here or at NewBern on account of his health, I fear, he never will be a sound man.—

The Demo^s^ had a convention here on Monday & nominated W. L. Kennedy[2] as their Elector.—

I have heard *confidentially* of Richard Shepard, by a gentleman from New Orleans & he represents him as in a very bad way & says if his debts are not paid, he cannot be saved.—

I have not heard from Wm Shepard, since his return from Alaba. & do not know what arrangement of his affairs, Fredk has made.— My kind regards to Charles & William.

Very truly yr friend relative
Jn. H. Bryan

*I think Morehead will certainly be elected.[3]

[*Addressed*] E Pettigrew Eq
Cool Spring
N.C

---

[1]This is probably a reference to George Washington Doane (1799-1859), who had been Episcopal bishop of New Jersey since 1832. He was also rector of St. Mary's Church in Burlington, New Jersey. *CDAB*, 238.

[2]This may have been the William L. Kennedy who represented Beaufort County in the 1833 legislature. Cheney, *North Carolina Government*, 300.

[3]Morehead defeated Saunders by a vote of 44,484 to 35,903 in the gubernatorial election. Cheney, *North Carolina Government*, 1397.

Ebenezer Pettigrew to Mary Williams Bryan A&H, BRYAN

Belgrade May 5, 1840

My dear Sister

I received your favour of the 20th April by the last mail, and was exceedingly gratifyed to find that your health was entirely restored. I hope that it may now continue to a good old age.

I would most gladly accept of your invitation to spend some time with you this spring; not alone for the purpose of being with my dear daughters, (a duty which I owe them) but for the pleasure of the visit, and to have my mind & body relaxed from the continued stretch of business. I know that at my time of life, particularly when spent in such a press of business, it is time to retire & spend the remaining days in contemplating what I have done and the place to which I must before long retire, but alas! I am now more involved in my business than I ever was, not because my sons do not do their duty, but the business is greater, and more to do, more particularly this year. If I were to do any thing with an expectation of gratitude in return I should do very little if any thing, but a sense of duty has governed my actions, and while I seem to neglect my dear little girls, I am endeavouring to provide for the future comfort of my my children, and to finish my plan of business. If I were to be governed by my feelings I would not be from them any one month at a time.

I weell recollect the little my daughters learned when at Hillsborough, and have no sort of preference for the place or Mrs Burrills school, and leave it entirely with you to do with my dear Mary as you think best. It would /be/ very likely best for her to remain <& untill> this summer or untill I come up which I fear cannot be untill the fall, and let her spend next year in finishing her education. In the mean time she can be learning music, & dancing. &c Please to give my Love to my daughters. Make my best respects, Mr Bryan & the children also our Mother, who I suppose has arrived at home by this, I hope safe & sound & Believe me to be with much Esteem & regard

your affectionate Brother
E Pettigrew

Mrs Mary W. Bryan.

N.B. Please to excuse this miserable scratch. I am in a great hurry. Charles is at the Lake and William has gone to Baltimore to the con / <the> convention. They are well. While writing I think it would be best that Mary should not go to Hillborough. It must be a poor concern.
Pray how does Mr Martindale come on in his multifarious buildings.

E P.

God Bless you & yours

[*Addressed*] Mrs John H. Bryan
Raleigh
N. Carolina

Ebenezer Pettigrew to John Baptist Beasley A&H

Belgrade May 11, 1840

Dr Sir,

This will be handed to you by Jim who goes up for William. He will also hand you several other letters, I will be much obliged to you if you will put them in the office, & pay the postage on the one to the Cashier of the Union Bank, Baltimore. Will you also have the goodness to go to /the/ Clerks office and get the order to lay out the road which I have made from my field to the Davis road. The order was passed more than a year ago, & I wish it that the Sheriff may get a jury this week to condemn the land & that I thereby may return it to court next week. Send the order by Jim.

My health has not been good this past week I hope you are all well, Please to make my best respects to Mr Alexander, Mrs Beasley & family and believe me your fd & relative

E Pettigrew

John Beasley esqr

[*Addressed*] John Beasley esqr
Plymouth
N. Ca

John Herritage Bryan to Ebenezer Pettigrew A&H

Raleigh June 2 1840—

My dear Sir,

My laborious circuit is just over, having closed at Smithfield last week—I went from there to Fayetteville to attend a meeting of the stockholders of the Rockfish Man: Co.[1]—I visited the Factory which is about 7 miles below Fayetteville:—It is situated on a never failing & abundant stream, with a fall of near 30 feet & in a very healthy region, the water is very good: The main wheel is 28 feet in diameter, the building is 175 ft. by 50—the first story is built of rock.— The machinery is of the most approved model, & was procured from the [Matteawan] Co. of New York—We have only 14 stockholders & owe for the machinery.— I wish you could see the factory, it is calculated for about 4400 spindles, and is expected to make about 3500 yards of cotton cloth per day.—

We have sent the Marys to M^rs^ Le Mesurier,[2] to learn music, & while there they recite French & Latin to M^r^ Le M^r^ they also review their Geography & English studies & attend to Arithmetic & writing. They remain until about 1 ^o^Clk & are under the immediate charge & care of M^rs^ Le M. who is a genteel & excellent woman.—They as well as the rest of the family are very well.—

Mrs Shepard has been quite sick for a week, but is recovering.—The girls are learning to ride, and seem very fond of it.—

I rec'd your letter directed to me at Wash^n^ as well as your last to this place and am very glad to learn that your health & spirits sustain you in your labours--I think however that it w^d^ be well if you can to provide some good stock for the girls, as the income of a plant^er^ as you know as well or better than most people, depends upon actual residence & personal attention—

Mrs Bryan sends her affectionate regard & love to you & her nephews—Give them my regards, I hope it may be convenient for some of you to be here at the festival on the 10th—

Very truly & respy yr friend &c
Jn H Bryan

[*Addressed*] E Pettigrew
Cool Spring

---

[1]The Rock Fish Manufacturing Company succeeded the Phoenix Mill, which was the first cotton mill in Fayetteville and had been built in 1836. The Rock Fish mill proved very successful. Standard and Griffin, "Cotton Textile Industry," 143-144.

[2]Mrs Le Messurier gave piano lessons in Raleigh, and her husband, Peter, conducted a male academy. Coon, *North Carolina Schools and Academies*, 496, 567.

Mary Blount Pettigrew to William Shepard Pettigrew UNC

[*Raleigh*] June the 20th 1840.

Dear brother,

I have been expecting a letter from you, as I wrote you last. Several of the smaller children are a little sick. Ma is quite sick, and had a chill and fever yesterday. There were a crowd of people here at the festival. They had two balls and a dinner. We went to both the balls, and had an elegant supper. Two of the cakes had the capitol on them, and two others the.—rail road cars. We danced in the senate chamber in the ca/p/itol and had the supper in the passage down stairs. There are two beautiful/l/ chandeliers one in the commons hall and the other in the senate-chamber, which, were lighted. We have had vacation for the last two weeks, and will begin school again on monday. I was very sorry to hear, from Mr Allen a gentleman who dined here during the festival, that Pa was sick at plymouth court, but I hope he is well again. We have had a great deal of rain lately, but it is very warm and the sun is very bright to day. Sister Nancy is well and sends her love to you all. Give my love to Pa and brother Charles. I suppose you are very busy reaping wheat just now, I hope you will make a plentiful crop. Do write to me soon, for I have not heard from you in a long time.

Your affectionate Sister,
Mary B Pettigrew.

Ma' sends her respects to you.

[*Addressed*] Mr William S. Pettigrew.
Cool Spring.
N.C.

Indenture of Ebenezer Pettigrew to William Shepard Pettigrew UNC

[*June 22, 1840*]

I am bound to William S. Pettigrew for one sixth of the nett proceeds of my Plantations from the first day January 1839, also two hundred dollars pr year fr the above date for his attention to my Belgrade plantation, untill I make a division of my estate

E Pettigrew

June 22, 1840

Indenture of Ebenezer Pettigrew to Charles Lockhart Pettigrew UNC

[*June 22, 1840*]

I /am/ bound to Charles L. Pettigrew for one sixth of the <clear> /nett/ income of my Plantations from the first day of January 1836—also two hundred dollars per year from the above date for his attention to my Lake Plantation untill I make a division of my Estate

E Pettigrew

June 22, 1840

James Johnston Pettigrew to Ebenezer Pettigrew UNC

Hillsboro' June 23^{d} 1840

Dear Father

I feel myself compelled to write to write to you to inform, you that Mr Bingham came here yesterday morning <fe> before breakfast and whipped several boys, and me among the rest on the supposition of playing cards and whipped me worse than the rest. I am bruised a great deal and the blood has been cut out of me and I am very sore all over. I think that I have been treated very ill, and I am very tired of this place and Mr Bingham also. I think he has whipped me unjustly. We have had a very hard rain to day and I ex[pec]t some more tomorrow. It is rather muddy up here and there is nothing to amuse a person with the session will begin on the sixteenth of July, being six weeks two days <old> long. Please write to me soon. Give my love to my brothers and sisters.

Beleive me to be your affectionate son

J. Johnston Pettigrew

[*Addressed*] Hon. Ebenezer Pettigrew
Cool Spring
N. Carolina

*Ebenezer Pettigrew to John Herritage Bryan** UNC

Lake Phelps June 24, 1840

My dear Sir

I received your favour of the 2nd by the mail of the 10th also a ticket to the Raleigh entertainment. It was quite too late in the afternoon to get to it, though we have such facilities of traviling. However we were much obliged for the consideration.

Your letter found me recovering from a few weeks spell of affection of the head attended with great debility & incapacity to attend to any thing without great exertion, and on saturday night last I was awoke with a most violent cramp of one leg in which attack I alarmed the whole land, for help, after it had left me and I was about to send away the attendants I was taken as bad in the other leg, which continued as long. I could not have lived through the night with it. In truth it is awfull to /be/ waked in the middle of the night in the most excrutiating pain, with, not a soul in reach of you. I suppose this attack arose from my attending to the hands picking up wheat from dinner to night in which I was much fatigued. I observe my phisical & mental energy is rapidly on the decline, and if my work was finished I should not care how fast, but I have got to put a finishing hand to all my work if possible.

I am very glad to learn that you are all in health and that the girls are doing well. I hope our mother is by this time recovered from the indisposition you mention. Please to make my best respects to her.

I have today finished the harvest, and do not recollect to have ever raked so miserable a crop both for quality & quantity (except when entirely taken by frost) It is worse than the crop of 1836.

I observe your remarks respecting the factory, and I know that farming is a slow way to accumulate wealth, and without strict attention there is /no/ accumulation, yet it is miserable to place your money in stocks equally wretchedly ma/na/ged, without the power to get it out or check the evil. I have a sample before my eyes. Charles Pettigrews steam mill at Columbia, in which he had to take half the interest & then take the management or be inevitably ruined, which occupies half of his time, greatly to his inconvenience & much against his will.

I however have not the means to take stock of any kind at the present, for short crops & low prices give but small sums to the farmer for all his toil, labors. The morus multicaulis speculation, from the villiny of the methodist preacher to whome we sold, has not given anything yet, and it is uncertain when it will, though I think it a safe investment. A grist mill within three miles of Baltemore. I do not like the name. Woodberry mills.

Mrs Collins asked me the other day if Sister Mary wanted a Governess, & said that a Mr Stoughton, who is now a private teacher to their children, has a sister to the south, and that he Mr S. is about to study divinity perhaps with Bishop Ives, and would like to be near his sister. Mr S. has not seen his sister for some time and therefore could not recommend her fully. I merely de[liver] the message as received. If I had time [I] should like to spend two or three weeks with you after corn is hilled, to see if it would recruit me a little. We have had it generally wet for the last eight months, It is about to turn of dry, & I expect a dry fall & a sickly one, but I have stood too many to fear them.

Please /make/ my kind regards & that of my sons to Sister Mary, & the dear children, accept the same for your self and believe me to be sincerely your friend and relative

E Pettigrew

John H. Bryan esqr

N.B. I expect those visionary engeneirs have a design to drain our Lake, to /the/ ruin of us & no benefit to any.

[*Addressed*] John H. Bryan esqr
Raleigh
N. Carolina

Ebenezer Pettigrew to James Johnston Pettigrew UNC

Belgrade July 12,th 1840

My dear son

I received your letter of June the 25th [*sic*] by the last mail and agreeable to your request I answer it soon. I not only feel the utmost regret & mortification, but most perfect astonishment at the subject of it.

Can you for a moment think that I will tolerate card playing or would even excuse /excuse/ Mr Bingham in overlooking in a son of mine such an offence? Do you not think that you had better have been learning to write than playing cards? for so miserablee writing I have never received in a letter except in your little sister Nancys first letter two years ago. Could I bring my mind to think it, I should have believed you half drunk when you wrote it, for playing cards & drunkenness go hand in hand. In concluding your letter you send your Love to your brothers and sisters. Where did you direct your letter to me? I answer Cool Spring, & your sisters are at Raleigh, within thirty eight miles of you; and I expect you would have asked me leave to have gone to see them in the vacation if it had not been for your plan /of/ card playing &c &c in that spare time. Pray how old are you? Only twelve years the 4th of July (this month.)

Let me tell you, I fear your bad & selfwilled nature is developing itself very young, and if there is not a check put to it early there is no knowing to what extent it will lead you. Nature has done a great deal for you, but what will it avail if your evil propensities are not conquered, and I could not expect any more peace of mind in this world if I were to neglect that duty. You say you are tired of that place and Mr Bingham also. Where do you wish to go? Be assured I shall never send you to a place where there is less government or discipline, and if I take you home I do not think you will much better your situation.

In conclusion, I have sacrifised every thing that was & is dear to me for my children and let me beseech you in the language of a father who loves his children far more than his life to so conduct yourself as to let him have some little comfort in his declining years, and do not bring your fathers gray hairs with sorrow to the grave.

Believe me to be your affectionate father

E Pettigrew

Mr J. Johnston Pettigrew

[*Addressed*] Mr J. Johnston Pettigrew
Hillsborough
N. Ca

William A. Dickinson to Ebenezer Pettigrew A&H

Bentonville Ala 26th July 1840

E. Pettegrew Esqr

Dear Sir

It is now a considerable time since I received, or have written to you, but on my part you must excuse me on the grounds that I had nothing of any emport to comunicate to you, but from the very goodness you have at all and in every instance been pleased to shew to me, at all times and on all occassions. I stand deep in your debt, not only for the very pomptness you gave me, but for your generosity in extenssion, it would be useless for me to enter into anything like a tale of craving your indulgence as regards pecunary matters, but merely to state to you that at present I am unable to forward the needfull, but as soon as I can, I will do so. It would be useless for me to give you a History of the times since I last addressd you on the 7th Feby 1839 from Wetumpka, you are a close observer of the Times both as regards Governments & commerce, not to see how the murchants have been brought to the back ground, I set out here with a determination to labour hard, and hard have I laboured with the full expectation of making something, but I have been <badly> severely disappointed, and am sorry to say now that I shall after three years, be or become just as I was, But at the end of this year I shall be able to forward you a remittance, I do not wish you to loose that respect and confidence that has subsisted between us for years. and If I have offended in any; <you> all I have to say is to ask your pardon. I am now thinking of gitting some Land at Government price, and there and then sittle on it, I have not heard from you and your family for some time, only by Uriah Chesson who seems very much pleased with this Country, It afforded me much pleasure to learn that you and your family were all well, and you know that it would give me very great pleasure to hear from you, give my kind respects to all your family, my wife and family enjoys good heath & wee wish you and yours every thing on this earth that may be conducivie toyour happiness and belive me

Dear Sir Yours Respectfully
William A. Dickinson

[*Addressed*] Ebenezer Pettegrew Esqr
Coolspring P:O:
N.C.

*Ebenezer Pettigrew's Tax List** UNC

[*July 29, 1840*]

1840
Tax List of E Pettigrew in Washington County

1216 Acres of Land included in Charles Phelps' survey & Plot in 1835, after deducting that sold to David Clayton say 84 Ac
150 Acres adjoining Called the Miles Spruill place
36 bought of Dillins Hines
65 ″ of D. W. Sargant & J. J. Phelps, called the Charles Phelps Land

3½	bot of Calib Phelps	
48¼	do do do	
1518¾	Acres called Belgrade valued	$8000.00
1518¾		
97	Acres bought of Charles Bateman	
46¾	do " " Jerremiah Phelps	
143¾	Ac. called Q[aushepom]po & valued @	859.99
1662½		8859.99
	1 White Poll W. S. Pettigrew	
	22 Black do	

Tax List of E Pettigrew in Tyrrell County

6850	Acres Land valued by the assessors in 1837	$21212.
	1 White Poll Charles L. Pettigrew	
	32 Black do	

The above is a copy of E P. Tax list in 1840 taken July 29, 1840

John Herritage Bryan to Ebenezer Pettigrew A&H

Raleigh Sept. 20. 1840

My dear sir,

I reached home last night from Edgecombe & found all well: I was prevailed upon to attend a grand barbecue at the Falls of Tar river & made them a speech which seemed to be acceptable.

Mr Iredell & S. B Spruill /& Col. Long/ also addressed the company—there were about 500 present.—

I hope you & one or both of your sons will be up here on the 5th of next month as I expect you would be much amused, if not otherwise benefited.—

Mrs B. feels very uneasy about Charles, as he left, looking very badly.—

There has been considerable alarm in Craven on account of a supposed conspiracy of the negroes, and from what I learn they had been talking about it. It is a terrible state of things especially for the female portion of the community, to be subjected to such horrible apprehensions.—I understand that it is quite sickly in NewBern; it is becoming so on Tar river.—

I heard by a passenger in the Cars this afternoon that Maine had gone *against* the admn if so their case is more hopeless than I had supposed, Van Buren never had any personal popularity of any account, and the force of Jacksonism is well nigh spent.—It is supposed that there will be 10,000 or more people here on the 5th which will be an imposing sight in our country, or at least in our State.—

I saw Dr Williams of Pitt on the 13th inst—the old gentleman I fear cannot remain with us much longer—he has a paralytic affection of the chin which he fears will seize upon his throat & suffocate him.—

Your children are very well & send their love to you & wish to see you on or before the 5th: Mrs B. desires to be affectionately remembered by you & her nephews—My regards to them.

Very truly yr friend relative
Jn H Bryan

Mr Hines & family are here & will remain 'till about the 15th Oct.

[*Addressed*] E Pettigrew Esq
Cool Spring
N.C

*Ebenezer Pettigrew to Moses E. Cator** UNC

Lake Phelps Sep 22, 1840

My dear Sir,

Two mails ago I received a letter from Messrs Bryan & Maitland New York informing me that they had received from you eighty dollars & 36/00 to be placed to my credit which is the final payment on the land which I have sold you in Tennessee, & inclosed you will find my deed for the same, which I hope will arrive safe & in due time. You will observe that I had prepaired the Deed last spring but according to request did not send it then nor untill the remaining sum for the land was paid.

We are geting along in this country in old stile. Produce low & money scarce & very little probabality of its being much more plenty. However we have some hope that the election of Genl. Harrison to the Presidency will give a start to business, & give more confidence, but we have got in to such a state of financial derangement that I fear nothing but time can effect full relief. Our crops of wheat were not good but the price is but eighty cents pr bus. Corn crops are not generally good, from too much rain, but in this immediate neighbourhood they are fair. I do not expect it will be more than two dollars a barril. These prices will pay but few debts contracted in high times, & know not what some people are to do with their debts. You would naturally think that we were flowing with money when I inform you that <land> /woodland/ in Scuppernong has sold at twenty dollars an acre, or that we were multiplying so as to make land scarce. Neither is the fact.

My two sons are yet with me, one at the Lake & the other at my place in Scuppernong, & are very attentive to their business. Their healths <are> stand the climate pretty well. For my age I stand fatigue tolerable well. We have had three falls as healthy in Scuppernong as in the mountains & this so far is not seriously sickly. And now my friend hoping you & yours are in the enjoyment<s> of the blessings of a kind providence I subscribe myself truely your friend

E Petti/g/rew

William Biddle Shepard to Ebenezer Pettigrew A&H

Raleigh Sept 28th 1840

My Dear Sir

You are aware that at our next session of the Legislature it will become necessary to choose two United States Senators. Many persons of course are desirous of being chosen and among that number your humble servant.[1] I have been informed that if I could muster a tolerable number of friends from the Eastern section of the State, I could be chosen. I know of no one that could be of more service to me than yourself, if you would take the trouble, which would be very little. [*George*] Badger is making great exertions to be chosen & I suppose will endeavour through his relative [*Edward*] Stanly[2] to procure the votes of the members from his district. You would oblige me very much if you would use your influence with the members from Tyrrell & Washington & such other persons from that district as you can influence. My position is an unlucky one, Charles' political course[3] is used against me as if I could control it or had any thing to do with it. And I have no doubt from what I have heard Stanly would take great pleasure in defeating me. I feel however very confident that if I can secure 15 or 20 Eastern votes I can be elected very easily. Your assistance together with Charles & William's In speaking on this subject to your members will be of great use to me.

I arrived in this town a few days ago, & I find these Raleigh fellows who are for settling matters in their own way are very much disposed to take upon themselves to say who shall be senators and who not. So that if the members should arrive here without any predilections on this subject, great exertions will probably made to prejudice them against me.—

Your children & all your friends here are very well, I have been confined with the bilious fever but I am convalescent
Remember me to Charles & William

Yours truly
W B Shepard

[*Addressed*] Ebenezer Pettigrew Esqr
Cool Spring
Wash: County
North Carolina

---

[1]William A. Graham and Willie P. Mangum, both Whigs from Orange County, were elected senators by the legislature. Cheney, *North Carolina Government*, 681.

[2]Badger was cousin to John Stanly, Edward Stanly's father. Hamilton and Williams, *Graham Papers*, VII, 164.

[3]William Biddle Shepard and Charles Biddle Shepard were more active politically than Ebenezer Pettigrew. All three were Whigs until 1838, when Charles defected to the Democratic party.

William Shepard had served in Congress from 1829 to 1837 as a National Republican. His chief interest in the National Republican party (later a component of the Whig party) was its support for the Bank of the United States and its opposition to President Andrew Jackson's policy against renewal of the bank's charter. William also favored passage of the Maysville Road bill over Jackson's veto. He declined to run for Congress in 1837, but during 1838-1840 and again during 1848-1850 he served in the North Carolina Senate as a Whig. While there he supported state participation in railroad building.

As this letter indicates, William ran for election to the United States Senate in 1840, but the Whigs from western North Carolina did not support him. When he charged them with ignoring the east, Thomas L. Clingman "read him out of the party." Shepard's response "was very able and exceedingly caustic." In 1850 Shepard authored a minority report from the Joint Committee on Slavery of the North Carolina General Assembly in which he deplored the Compromise of 1850 and supported the right of secession. *Biographical Directory of Congress*, 1591; William K. Boyd, *History of North Carolina: The Federal Period, 1783-1860* (Chicago and New York: Lewis Publishing Company, 1919), 173, 175, 183, 231-232; J. G. de Roulhac Hamilton, *Party Politics in North Carolina, 1835-1860* (Chapel Hill: University of North Carolina Press, 1916), 31, 75, hereinafter cited as Hamilton, *Party Politics in North Carolina*; Clarence Clifford Norton, *The Democratic Party in Ante-Bellum North Carolina, 1835-1861* (Chapel Hill: University of North Carolina Press, 1930), 115-116, hereinafter cited as Norton, *Democratic Party in Ante-Bellum North Carolina*.

Charles Shepard served two terms in Congress: 1837-1839 as a Whig and 1839-1841 as a Democrat. William deplored Charles's defection to the Democrats, fearing it might hurt his own chances of election to the state Senate and his campaign for the United States Senate.

Charles's election district supported him regardless of his party label. However, another defector from the Whigs to the Democrats, Samuel Tredwell Sawyer of Edenton, did not fare as well. Sawyer was defeated in his bid for reelection to Congress for the 1839-1841 session by one of the state's Whig leaders, Kenneth Rayner.

North Carolina Democrats at this time lacked leaders of as high caliber as the Whig leaders, although a number of young men showed political promise. Among these was Charles Shepard, mentioned as a possible candidate for the

United States Senate in 1840. However, his death in 1843 ended his career. *Biographical Directory of Congress*, 1591; Hamilton, *Party Politics in North Carolina*, 55, 70; Norton, *Democratic Party in Ante-Bellum North Carolina*, 80.

James Biddle Shepard, the youngest brother, entered politics as Democratic candidate for governor in 1846, joining Charles in breaking the Whig tradition of the family. An "orator of ability," he canvassed the state enthusiastically but lost to William A. Graham, who was elected to a second term. In 1852 James Shepard seems to have been supported by a group of Whigs as well as Democrats for the nomination to the United States Senate, but James C. Dobbin of Fayetteville received it instead. Norton, *Democratic Party in Ante-Bellum North Carolina*, 151-152, 246n.

In sharp contrast Ebenezer Pettigrew adhered steadfastly to Whig principles his entire life, although he retired from public service after 1837. After the 1835 campaign in which Pettigrew defeated Dr. Thomas H. Hall for a seat in the United States House of Representatives, the prominent Democrat Romulus M. Saunders wrote Vice-President Martin Van Buren: "For Congress we have lost Dr. Hall. . . . Pettigrew is a gentleman. . . . One or both of the Shepards might have been beaten. . . ." Norton, *Democratic Party in Ante-Bellum North Carolina*, 70.

William Shepard Pettigrew to Augustus H. Roby[1]* UNC

Copy

Belgrade, Oct. 12, 1840

Dear Roby

It has been so long since I heard from you, that, unless I soon look you up again, there will be danger of your escaping entirely from me. You Western people a[re] such wanderers that the delightfulness of the section of country in which you reside is but little indication of the permanence of your abode.

I feel much attached to the correspondence which exists between myself and a few friends that I have chosen: they appear to be of a more reliable material that the most of mankind. The constancy of their regard, I am quite sure, cannot be shaken by the chilling influence of absence.

In May last I attended the "young men's Convention" at Baltimore. The representatives were present from every part of the Union, & the assembly was so numerous that no voice could extend over it. Consequently, two stands were erected, the one being occupied by such men as Clay, Webster, [*William C.*] Preston & Hofman;[2] the other by men of a secondary reputation, such as [*Henry A.*] Wise, McMahan [*John V. L. McMahon*] (the President of the Convention), and others. There was no ordinary exhibition of eloquence:—[*John J.*] Crittenden's remarks, on Monday night from the steps of Reverdy Johnson's[3] house, were extremely beautiful.

McQueen, Holly, A. G. Proctor, Randolph,[4] and several others, of your acquaintances, were members of the Convention. McQueen also spoke. I regret you were not with us: but perhaps you are a Calhoun man. If so, I can only say, I admire the ability of your leader, but his political course is so erratic as to prevent my advocating him for the office to which he aspires.

The funeral of the delegate who was murdered[5] occurred while I was in Baltimore, which I attended. I also contributed my quota to his surviving family. The sum raised amounted to $10000; which, no doubt, placed his children in more affluent circumstances than they ever would have attained had he lived. Proctor was married last Spring. If Miss Cornelia have become Mrs Roby, please present her my regards.

Sincerely, your friend,
William S. Pettigrew.

Mr A. H. Roby.

[*Addressed*] Mr Augustus H. Roby
Somerville
North Alabama.

---

[1]Five Roby families lived in Lincoln and Iredell counties, and one in Surry County, according to the *1830 Census Index*, 160. Augustus may have been a member of one of these families.

[2]Josiah Ogden Hoffman (1793-1856), an attorney from New York, sat in Congress as a Whig, 1837-1841. *Biographical Directory of Congress*, 1064.

[3]Reverdy Johnson (1796-1876) of Baltimore practiced law at this time and served in the United States Senate as a Whig, 1845-1849. Later he was United States attorney general and sat in the Senate as a Democrat, 1863-1868. *Biographical Directory of Congress*, 1129.

[4]Some of these people may have been school friends of William Shepard Pettigrew. Battle, *History of the University*, I, 796, names George Stanly Holley, who graduated from the University of North Carolina in 1837 and became a lawyer, and Albert G. Procter, a member of the class of 1838 (Pettigrew's class), who served in the state House of Commons.

[5]At the Young Men's Whig Convention delegate Thomas H. Laughlin, a carpenter of Baltimore, was killed during a procession on the first day. The members adopted a resolution to contribute to the bereaved family, and the convention adjourned to attend the funeral. *Newbern Spectator*, May 23, 1840. The *Spectator* of May 16, 1840, carried an account of the meeting's first day.

John Trimble[1] to Ebenezer Pettigrew A&H

Baltimore 10th mo [1]7th 1840

E. Pettigrew

Esteemed friend.

Thy esteemed favour of the 17 August was recieved on the 2d Inst an earlier acknowledgment of which has been prevented by indisposition.

Captain Caroon[2] delivered me the Box of Hams which I accept with pleasure, and acknowledge with thanks as a pleasing evidence of thy friendly attention and regard: we have tried some of those cured in the common way and find them excellent: and I anticipate much pleasure from a trial of those cured according to the reciepe of Govr Cass.

please have the goodness to convey my respects to thy sons Charles and William. my sons Joseph and James also desire to present their respects to thyself and thy sons.

With esteem and regard I remain

very respectfully thy friend
Jno Trimble

[*Addressed*] Ebenezer Pettigrew
Cool Spring
Tyrel County
North Carolina

---

[1]John Trimble, a Quaker, was a commission merchant in Baltimore from whom Ebenezer Pettigrew purchased. Pettigrew does not appear to have sold his cargoes in Baltimore very frequently, but he did much buying there.

[2]Two Caroon family heads, James and Thomas, lived in Tyrrell County, according to the *1820 Federal Census*, LII, 4, 5.

Ebenezer Pettigrew to William Shepard Pettigrew UNC

Baltimore Octr 28, 1840

My dear son

I arrived at this place on sunday morning /&/ lay by that day & mond/a/y morning directly after breakfast started on the business I came for. It was wretchedly cold & the wind blew hard, and the consequence was I took a bad cold, and am now labouring with cold & fever so as to be barely able to keep up.

I expect to leave this on saturday next & to be at Plymouth on monday night. It is probable I shall bring with me a pair of horses, though I see none that I like much. Will you send this letter to your Brother Charles, or if Jim is with you send him up with the mules & Baruche to Plymouth on monday that I may come down on Tuesday. It will be well to send some one with him to bring the horses down, if I get them, let them take [*torn*] a saddle & bridle.

The delay which has been made by my indisposition has determined me to return home before I go to Raleigh, withall I have been exceedingly uneasy for your healths since I left and have applyed repeatedly at the Post office for letters though I had no hope of geting any

Make my respects to M^r & Mrs Davenport and believe me my sons to be your affectionate father

E Pettigrew

N.B. I send this letter inclosed to Mr Beasley that he may get Mr Nichols to send it express to Belgrade

[*Addressed*] Mr Wm S. Pettigrew
Belgrade

Bill of Sale to Ebenezer Pettigrew UNC

Baltimore October 31. 1840 Rec^d of Mr E. Pettigrew Three hundred and fifty dollars for a pair of Bay. horses. seven years old last spring warranted sound and gentle in harness. which I purchased of Heny Dukeheart

$350

for Saml C. Owings
Saml OMoal^l

Richard S. Sims to William Shepard Pettigrew UNC

Brunswick Co. V^a Nov. 18th 1840

Dear Friend

Your letter dated the 30th of sep. came to hand a few days ago, after some delay in the different post-offices of the county. I was very glad indeed to hear from you and to learn that you were unwilling entirely to loose your old friend and associate. The high regard I entertained for you and your brother Charles while we were at college together, has not in the least deminished by time; but on the contrary must ever increase so long as your actions are influenced by as honourable motives as they were then.

The spring after I saw you and your Brother in Philadelphia I graduated and returned to Brunswick, and immediately commenced the practice of medicine in my native county and neighbourhood; and up /to/ the present, have obtained quite an extensive and profitable practice. I suppose you have settled down to hard study in politicks—This will hardly suit you I think Wm S. You will have to Sacrifice too much of the honest high-minded man, to be an *honest politician.* A little after the time you were in Baltimore, I passed through that place on my way to Philadelphia, not however for the purpose of attending a political caucus, but on private business. About that time I should have been glad to have caught you in Baltimore, and given you a lecture.

Last thursday night the 12th of this month was the time appointed for the celebration of J. E. Crichton's[1] nuptials. He was to have been married to miss Petteway of Southampton Virginia— and if nothing prevented he was made as happy as a new bride can make a man.

James has located himself at Jerusalem in Southampton. He is in partnership with an old physician and I hear is doing quite a good practice. But he is like he used to be at C. Hill, has use for a great deal of pocket change.

Give my best respects to your brother Charles, and also to any of my old friends you may chance to meet with.

With great respect your friend
Richd S. Sims

P.S. Direct your letters hereafter to Powelton Brunswick Co. Virginia

R. S. S.

[*Addressed*] Mr William S. Pettigrew
Cool Spring
Washington Co.
N. Carolina

[1]James E. Crichton of Brunswick, Virginia, was a graduate of the University of North Carolina in the class of 1836. Battle, *History of the University*, I, 427-428.

Hardy and Brothers to Ebenezer Pettigrew A&H

Norfolk, Va 23. Nov. 1840—

E. Pettigrew, Esq—

Dear Sir,

On the 20. inst. we shipped for your account, all the articles enumerated in the annexed bill, with the Box dry Goods you bought of Messrs Paul & Pegram, pr Sch. Columbia, Capt. Brickhouse, and made B/Ldg to Mr. Chs L. Pettigrew, at the Mills, near Columbia, as directed, with request to receive the Goods subject to your order—

We also annex statement of your a/ct as it now stands on our Books shewing balance in our favour of seven dollars & sixty-nine cents, which, if you find correct, please pay at some *convenient* time.

The molasses remained so long, we had to pay an additional month storage—The Pork is better than we intended to send you, but since your order has been in hand, we could find no other *prime* but what was too inferior, and we feared to send you the Sour Butts mentioned by our W. [I]. H. The Raisins are good, and the Figs also, for *Malaga*—No *Smyrna* have yet been recd The Apples too are not so good as we desired to send—but the best in market at the time.

The prospects for corn seem to look rather worse, than otherwise—The markets North & South are *very* low, and our friends will not encourage shipts even at the present low rates—Sales here today at 45¢ for very prime parcels—and some old cubby weavel at 40¢ Cotton is doing better—sales at 9¢ for fair qlty new—And to embrace all descriptions we quote 7½ or 10¢

Yrs Respy, Sir, Yr frds & Sts
Hardy & Brothers

[*Addressed*] Hon: E. Pettigrew
Cool Spring
Washington County No Ca—

Mr E Pettigrew

To Hardy & Brothers Dr

for 1 Hhd Molasses 111-9—102 Gals	@28¢	$ 28.56
4 Bbls prime pork	$14	56.00
2 Ames No 2 Spades	1.25	2.50
3 Half Boxs New Raisins	1⅝	4.88
1 Box Malaga Figs 38-4—34 lbs	8¢	2.72
2 Bbls Apples	2.50	5.00
25 lbs Soft Shell Almonds 17c Box-12c		4.37
Cash paid Hustis for 1 doz Grub Hoes		18.00
do paid Seabury for 1 pr Shoes for Self		3 50
1 Cork Sole		50
1 pr Shoes 11 Inch long for Servant		1.13
1 do do 10 ″ for Woman		1.12
1 do ″ 14 Extra		1.20
12 do 4 ea no 8.9-10	@112½	13 50
1 Mo Storage on Hhd molasses		25
Drayage & Wharfage		69
Coms 2½ pr ct—143 23/100		3.58
		$147.50

Norfolk 20. Nov. 1840—

E. Pettigrew, Esq—In a/ct with Hardy & Bros.

1840		Dr.	Cr.
Octr 23	By his Dft on Bryan & Maitland, N. Yk		300 00
"	" Premium on Same at 2½%		7 50
"	To Cash Self	50 00	
"	" Do Paid Paul & Pegram's Bill	117 69	
Nov. 20	" Bill Sundries, herewith,	147 50	
"	By balance due H & Brs		7 69
		$315 19	315 19
"	To Balance brot down	$ 7 69	

P.S. We have seen Mr. Bryan—and he cannot say what the 4 RailRoad Car wheels & axile will cost exactly—for the size you want—but thinks about sixty-five dollars—He has no pattern for such, which adds much to the cost.

H & Brs

William Shepard Pettigrew to Ebenezer Pettigrew A&H

Belgrade Nov 30th 1840

Dear Pa

I think it doubtful whether this will reach Raleigh previous to your leaving. but nevertheless as it is but little labour to write a letter and much pleasure to receive one I will run the risk of your getting it. Brother Charles wrote you by Mr Collins which I suppose you have received. I was not at the Lake when it was written, I left Sunday evening. Mr C—— expected to start for Raleigh Monday. We have had some rains since you left, but brother Charles will finish br/e/aking up tomorrow, when the force will come here. The new ground at the Lake has gathered well. I have not asked brother C—— since he completed the gathering what the product was, but he said soon after he commenced it was ten barrels to the acre thus far. The product of the crop at Belgrade is nine barrels per acre; this is Mr Davenport/'s/ and my estimate from the quantity in the barn, saying 40 feet square one foot deep contain 144 barrels.

I received the mail after you left a letter from Mr Beasley, dated Nov 18th saying the H Spruil land sold for $1475 he becoming the purchaser, Dempsy Spruil ran it to $1474. I learn Dempsy says he is rejoiced he did not purchase at that price; that he bid so high because he became excited. He bought a negro afterwards with some of his money. Brother Charles returned from Columbia Saturday evening, he underst/ood/ there that Mr Beasley was very ill, that he was alive and no more, he had sent a boat for Dr Norcom and two negro men were drowned, one was his own, I presume they were drowned in going to Edenton not in returning. I should regret his death very much. The Bishop has arrived at the Lake. I was at Mr Rigs' the other day, he is snugly fixed. I went on the Sound side in search of peas. H. Lewis and John Newberry had some but would not take less than fifty cents. I have purchased none. A pretty story that a bushel of peas are worth more than a bushel of corn a season like this. Newberry & Lewis said they would sooner feed them to their hogs than take less than 50¢.

Jerry's child who was sick before you left is yet in a bad way: otherwise all are well. One or another of Mr Davenports family have been sick ever since you left: Major has just returned from there, he says Mrs Davenport is quite sick, little Mary has also been sick but /is/ well enough to be out /to-day/. Mr D. was here on Saturday he was complaining, he was also here yesterday and was pretty well: he is makin/g/ staves. Had they known I intended writing you, they would have sent their respects. Mr Cook is putting up Mr D's mill, he wished him to pay him two dollars & a half per day. Mr Davenport told him two dollars was as much as he could think of. I think one dollar fifty cents is enough for any workman we can employ in these two counties at the present price of corn, unless it be a head workman at the steam-mill, or in repairing your mills or Mr Collins'.

If Brother Charles knew I was writing he would send his love, when I saw him I had not made up my mind to <write> Please remember me to /Sister/ Mary, Nancy, and the family. Tell Mary I received her letter and will soon answer it.

I remain your affectionate son
William S Pettigrew

[*Addressed*] E. Pettigrew Esq
Raleigh
N Carolina

Ebenezer Pettigrew to Mary Williams Bryan A&H, BRYAN

Lake Phelps Dec 29, 1840

My dear Sister

Christmas is over (blessed be the Lord) and tomorrow we go to work. My three sons have been with me since the day commenced and I have not seen the inside /of/ any house but my own yet. We are all tolerable well and I believe clothed in our right minds. Johnston behaves well & is perfectly tractable, but it is impossible to be without trouble in this world and no one need expect it. Charles is about to leave the Lake for the steem mill at Columbia. I regret it extremely for a great many reasons, and I believe he does also, but it must be so, whether for good or for evil nothing but time can tell. I have great fears, that no good can come of it. I have at all times given my advice yes the advice of a father, with kindness, and affection, but /now/ it seems this is the best that can be done. You know as well as I do and better to, that the males of the family cannot be advised, and must and /will/ go their own way. Charles regrets I understand very much that he did not at first & from time to time take my advice, but now matters are in a way that it is almost necessary that he should take this last step, for a year. Had it not been for my purse he would have been before this time exceedingly mortified by having what little was given him by his Grandma taken from him, and then called on for sums which he would have no means of paying. Do not believe I upbraid him in the least. On the contrary I do every thing in my power to support his spirits, by every assistance he wants.

The debts of the country are truely alarming, and prices of produce ruinously low, and still negroes hire higher than they were ever know before Mine from 100 to 125 dollars and on Christmas day a common corn field hand, not superior to twenty that I have, was hired by a farmer for one hundred & fifty one dollars. The labour of the mill is carried on entirely by hired hand, which makes it still worse for Charles, and the state of subordination is such that no negroe hesitates a moment to tell a man that he does not chose to live with that he wo'unt live with him and take the woods on first occasion & to catch him is out of the case. Thus ends the chapter.

I should be glad to know what news from Mrs Bushard's school also how the young ladies come /on/ in their studies, music, sewing & neting stockings. and if they are prepairing not their bodies but their minds for that finishing hand to their education. I hope they, and you all have had a merry christmas, & happy new year and that you will have many succeeding ones; For my part I desire nothing but the absence of misery. I want no change in me untill death, untill I am laid in /the/ silent tomb beside that *dear ever dear woman* from whome I have been seperated now ten & a half years. / years. Yes my dear sister, twelve christmasses have passed away with no mirth in my mind. On the contrary, with fasting & calm meditation on things past present & to come. Blessed God! it is pleasant to enumerate the years gone, because it tells of a less number to come. O if it were not the duty which I owe to the dear children of my Nancy how glad I should be to retire to that place where the wicked cease from troubling & the weary are at rest. Thus ends the second chapter.

My sons had been in my absence very busily employed & all things have gone well & a great deal done. William has nothing like speculation in his mind, but just to stick on the plantation where he is & make the most of it. They all three join me kind regards to yourself & Mr Brian their sisters & cousins and please to assure yourself of the much esteem & regard of your affect. Brother

E Pettigrew

Mrs Mary W. Bryan.

N.B. Please to give my love to my dear daughters and tell them that I will write them each a letter in a few mails.

E P.

P.S. Do not believe by the tenor of this letter that I am in fit of melancholy. I am as calm as the cradled infant.

E P.

[*Addressed*] Mrs John H. Bryan
Raleigh
N. Carolina

Henry Alexander to Ebenezer Pettigrew A&H

Tenn. Fayette Co. Somerville Jany 6th 1841.

Dear sir

I have delayed writing you much longer than I entended. But the Truth is the best apolegee, I was at the Sale of the Fort Pickning lots. which took place on the 19. 20 & 21 of Nov. I thire meet with a Sever axidence. on 21st Nov. the last day of the Sale, I was on horseback attending the Sale, when another horse kick at mine and mist him, and hit my Right leg, about 4 Inches below the knee, The cork of the Shou went to the bone, and laid the bone nakud for one Inch in lenth half Inch in breadth, the bone was not broken, but the Docr thought it fractered, It give me gratt pain in Deed, I could not sleep for 4 days and nights, In fact it had like to coust me my life. But I thank God I am nerely Restored to Good helth again, I am without pain or fiver, and the wound is Cured to a place not larger than a 12½ /Cts/ peace and I can begin to attend to my my busness again

The Fourt Pickning lots Sold high lots. 27. feet. frunt, 65. feet. back on main Street & on the Corners brought $1500. The back lots wore larger, the lots Sold from the above named price down to $300. Thair was Thirteen acres Sold which brought $125,000. This Town lies 2 Miles blow Memphis. It is high Bluff level ground, and a buteful location for a Town—

The Wine you Sent me arived the last of Octr Safe and in good ordor, Several Gentlemen have drink of it, and say, it is as good wine as ever they tasted. I entend to keep it, and not Sell it, For I tell them that is was made in North Carolina and the C^o I lived in and by the hand of my frend.

After I left Plymouth I had a long trip of 47 day. to this place owing to a grate Deal of Rain & bad Roads, The negros behaved well, I had no axidents only the horse I Bought of Mr Hufman became blind, and when I arived here, I found all well Mr E. long who came out with me. had the ague & fever and was quight Sick for 4 or 5 weeks, but he is now in Good helth, and has ingaged to oversee this year for Mr Durant Hattch, at $20 per month, /he said/ pleace let his father hear from Him—I saw him to Day

I have Rented a place this year, 1½ miles from Memphis, about 30 ares fit for Cultivation, I shall hire out my hands again this year, I Sent my hands down last week I exspet to make Memphis or that naberhood my home Negro men N° 1 is worth $550 to 650 women N° 1 $450 to 500 Boys and Girles in Equel portion, Cash, They Sell Some high on Cr Corn $1.50 to 2.00 pork $3.00 to 3.50 per hundred lbs Cotten 8 to 8¼ cets. ever body is looking out for better times, but I can ashoure you that money is perty Scarse, there is a grate deale of Land in markett, but fue Buyers I think that good bargains may be bought in land this year for Cash—

Poplation of this County 21,500 No. of Bails of Cotten in this Co last year was 31,400—

I Rec^d letter not long Since /from my Daughter/[1] which informed me that Mr Beasley had been Dangresly Sick. which [*illegible*] I have truley Regrate but I am in hopes that he has Recovered before this as he was on the mend when She wrote

My famley are all well, my Sons both injoy the best of helth, and they Send thair best Respets to you and yours Sons you will please prsent my Resp^ts to you Sons C. & W^m & and the Rest of your Children to M^r & Mrs Davenport and all inquiring frends and ashoure youself of my best wishes both for your helth & prsperity untile Death

Henry Alexander

E. Pettigrew Esqr.

N.B. Please write me as often as covenant & and also your Sons. you will direct your letters to Memphis Tenn. I shall leave here to morrow morning for Memphis the Distence is 42 Miles

H A

[*Addressed*] E. Pettigrew Esq
Cool Spring
Tyrrell County
North Carolina

[1]His daughter was probably Mary Alexander Beasley. See Ann Blount Pettigrew to Mary Williams Bryan, February 19, [1828], in this volume.

Mary Williams Bryan to Ebenezer Pettigrew A&H

Raleigh Jany 22nd 1841.

My dear Brother

I received your letter in due time by which I was glad to learn that you had safely arrived at home & found things going on well—I did not hear from Mrs Henderson[1] respecting the school untill last week & now make some extracts from her letter to Brother William "She says Miss Breschard will be happy to receive your nieces at the time mentioned in your letter"—In another part of her letter she says "Please say to your Sister, that it will afford me much pleasure to be serviceable in any respect to your nieces & I hope she will not hesitate to call upon me whenever she thinks I can be useful to them—I would recommend their coming immediately to our house, when they reach the City, as it will be less trying to them than to go immediately among so many strangers—I have no hesitation in saying that I believe she will be able to confide them to the care of Miss Breschard with as much confidence as she could repose in any stranger, I have always found her kind & conscientious in the discharge of her duties, and my girls are warmly attached to her—Say to Mrs Bryan also that Miss Breschard attends much to the comfort of her boarders who are less exposed than is common in most boarding schools—They have a large stove in the entry a pipe from which passes into the wash room which is thereby quite comfortable—If Mrs Bryan wishes any further information in regard to the school now or at any other time, say to her I beg she will herself write to me, that it would be to me far from unpleasant or troublesome to relieve any anxiety she might feel or to convey any information she may desire. I hope she will not consider me a stranger, but one somewhat connected with her & which connection I hope will ever be preserved—Whilst memory lasts, I can never forget the one who formed it & for her sake & yours I highly estimate it—"

Now from these extracts, you will be enabled to form some opinion of the lady to whom we shall entrust our girls, & of Mrs Henderson's kindness toward us—We have the girls now with Dr

[*Richard Sharpe*] Mason, whom you very well know, & where I shall continue them 'till they go on to Washington City—his daughter Martha who is about Mary's age has been educated entirely at home, her father continues her studies, & has consented to instruct our girls with her every morning—Mrs Mason instructs Nancy & Betsy with her younger daughter Sally they take no others—I am very much pleased with their progress, they are compelled to study much more than ever, indeed they have scarcely an idle moment, the larger girls have to study late & early to prepare their lessons, they are reading Sallust & pay much attention to Arithmetic.—

We see the sun to day which is very cheering after nearly three weeks of dreadful weather of rain snow & sleet. We learn from New Bern that Mrs Cha[ls] Shepard has a daughter, it is dreadfully sickly there with scarlet fever mumps & small-pox.—Mrs Snell (formerly Miss Tillman) whom you knew, died about a fortnight since with small-pox she took it from her son who carried it there in a vessel, he recovered, but another son who was married in New Bern took the disease & before he was aware of having it, spread it in different parts of the town, he has since died with it.

Mr Bryan is quite unwell to-day indeed he has been very unwell ever since the commencement of the bad weather. The rest of the family are well. I was very sorry to learn thro' Mary's letter that you had been unwell I hope however that you have recovered before this Mr Bryan unites with me in love to you & your sons—I am glad to learn that Johnston is a good boy for I could not love him if he were not dutiful & obedient to his father

Ma' & family are tolerably well

Your aff. Sister
Mary W Bryan.

The girls send their love to all.—

[*Addressed*] E Pettigrew Esq
Cool Spring
N.C

[1]Mrs. Henderson was sister to William Biddle Shepard's first wife, Charlotte Cazenove. She had two daughters attending Miss Breschard's school in Washington, D.C. Ebenezer Pettigrew to James Cathcart Johnston, May 17, 1841, in this volume.

Ebenezer Pettigrew to William Shepard Pettigrew[1] UNC

Lake Phelps Feb. 18, 1841

My dear son

I have sent Jef with some tripe. will you send some of it to M[rs] Davenport with my compliments. I have told Jeff tc change the carts, but bring the same body that he carries back.

Will you send me the two 1½ /inch/ planks that Jim picked out, he says they are in the machine shed. also ten, inch planks that are about the machine house, & ten pounds of ten penny nails by the return of the cart.

If it is convenient suppose you come in this evening. Johnston joins me in love to you we are as usual.

Your affct father
E Pettigrew

It looks like bad weather if you come give out food enough

[*Addressed*] M[r] William Pettigrew
Belgrade

---

[1]This note and the following one are included as examples of daily communication on plantations.

William Shepard Pettigrew to Ebenezer Pettigrew UNC

Belgrade Feb 18th 1841

My Dear Pa.

Your note of this morning came to hand, and I have sent by Jeff the plank & nails and changed the cart wheels.

I was very much obliged to you for the tripe & have sent half of it to M[rs] D. I have not heard from her since Tuesday.

I am obliged to you, I will go in to the Lake this evening.

I am glad you & Johnston are well. Please remember me to him and assure yourself of the best wishes of your

affectionate son
William S Pettigrew

[*Addressed*] E. Pettigrew Esq
Lake Phelps

John Baptist Beasley to Ebenezer Pettigrew UNC

Plymo 29th March 1841

E. Pettigrew Esq

Dear Sir,

Inasmuch as I shall leave this place for the West on monday next, I have thought it advisable to drop you a line before I start in relation to our private matters.

The deed for the Hardy Spruill Land I shall execute and leave with J C Norcom. The ballance due you, on the dft, sent me, by John Williams I have requested C L Pettigrew to pay you as soon as he collects S S Simmons & Co. debts due me. I regret that I did not advise Charles the time I contemplated leaving. If I had have done this Simmons would in all probability have paid his notes early enough for the money to have reached me by this days mail

It however makes no material difference as Charles can hand over the money to you and you can bring it up to May Court and hand it to (either) my wife or Joseph C Norcom. I must confess, <myself,> that the time I have set for starting happens much earlier in the month of Apl than I imagined to myself. I thought it would be about the 10, but it happens on the 4. and I have prepared accordingly, arranged all my matters and see at present nothing to detain me. and as I have it to do. the sooner I get through with it the better. as I am under the impression this visit will finally fix my determination upon the Western fever.

I saw Mr Conner on his return, he has a very favourable opinion of it, how men differ, I never yet saw the devil out there, I presume he is rich in imagination, well I have no objection to his enjoying his own opinion I am sure, but one thing he ought to consider, that what he gave did not belong to him and hardly ever will, and that all these fine farms belonged to somebody else I presume nevertheless, a narrative of his travels, will prove very interesting to Miss C[*aroline Bateman*]. and may act powerfully on / on her nervous system and ultimately produce a great and salutary reaction. If a description of the Western world from an eyewitness & close observer of things, would be listened to by the Old General [*Bateman*], with great patience and would have its weight in the scales of love, I have no doubt but his trip to the west will be the means of making his calling and Election sure in that particular case (provided nevertheless, that the old General is not too far gone to listen)

There is nothing new. The fishermen are nearly all doing well in the shad line Herrings has not yet come very plenty. I was on a visit a week ago to Windsor with my wife to see my cousin Ryans,

They are not slow in [Show] they [went] it cripple while I staid (7 days) They will visit us on my return. I expect I shall have to kill my Horse or be out done. I must nevertheless say <I> we have never been treated more kindly in our lives & shall deem it a pleasure to return such civilities—Dave Ryan is doing well, I learn that Marcus is somewhat embarrassed. *He* has a very agreeable & smart wife and if any injury overtakes them it will not be her fault. after all Windsor is the place for Carriages everybody who can get one does so. dont walk a foot in that place. though you can take a cat by the tail & from the Centre sling him all round Town. There are 4 classes of society in the place My wife when you see her will grade them down. I was so busy about other matters. I could not listen to classes, and do not know which one I belonged to. Martha is little unwell, all the rest are alive in health give my best respects to the boys & accept youself my best wishes

J B Beasley

E Pettigrew Esqr

[*Addressed*] Ebenezer Pettegrew Esqr
Cool Spring

Edward Stanly to Ebenezer Pettigrew A&H

Washington [*North Carolina*] April 12th 1841

My Dear sir;

I send you by this mail, several copies of a short circular, which I thought it best to write, that the people might have information of the time of the election. I find many persons in this county, are not informed of the time.—

I start to-day for Pitt County, where I shall remain only a few days, and after I return, I thought of coming down and paying you & Mr Collins a visit.—Unless I visit lake Phelps, before I return, I shall feel as if I had neglected part of my duty, and lost one of the few enjoyments of my electioneering. I love to look on it's placid waters, to hear the gentle breeze, sifting through the sycamore trees,—to hear the rippling waves, as they beat on the shore, and to contemplate the difference, between the delightful sounds there, and the noisy confusion, and wretched discord, of the House of Representatives. If I thought that a kind Providence, had destined that I should hereafter have a retreat so desirable to the heart of a reasonable man, I could cheerfully tolerate the many inconveniences, and troubles, incident to public life.—

But—"man never *is*, but always *to be* blest."—I might repine, if my present wishes were gratified.—So, I will be content, if possible.—

You have no doubt heard of the death of General Harrison.—Alas, how uncertain is human existence! How unstable, are enjoyments in this world!—I called to see him, the day before I left Washington,—he was quite well, in fine spirits, and happy in the hope of being able to run his country. No one can foresee, all the consequences of this national calamity. I have great confidence in [*Vice-President John*] Tyler, and his Cabinet: though I fear his opinions, are too much like those of the Virginia 98, & 99 abstractionists.[1] We must hope for the best.

I do not hear yet of any *regular* opposition, but from some signs, hereabouts, I have very strong ground for suspecting, a strong vote on election day. It will not do for our friend, therefore, to rest idle in the belief, that all is safe. Locofocoism, never slumbers.—It is the very spirit of evil, and ought always to be watched.—

I have strong hopes of our gaining two or three members of congress. Char's Shephard has declined, and Washington[2] is likely to be elected without opposition. Fisher[3] declines, we shall have a Whig there.—[*William*] Montgomery, Connor[4] & Hill,[5] & our *beauty*, Jesse [*Bynum*], declines also.—In Montgomery's,[6] Hill's,[7] and Bynums'[8] districts we stand a chance of gaining. Rayner,[9] I presume will have no opposition. I trust during the next congress, to make a beginning, with our great work, on our coast. After having had a share, in the good work of defeating VanBuren, I have nothing ahead, to stimulate me to exertion, but the hope of doing something, for our sea <coast> coast. Should I be successful, in having my name connected with such a work, if it is completed, I shall feel more proud than if I had fought a battle, or conquered an Empire.—I go, to Congress next time, (*if* I go), with the words of Harrison, in one of his battles.—"one fire more, and the day is our's."

I shall try and be with you, before the 20th Inst: at what particular time I cannot say.

Present my best respects to your sons, to Doctrine Davenport, and other neighbors, who may ask for me.—

The Sheriff ought to be reminded of his duty to advertise, and appoint inspectors. As there is no court to sit, before the election, the Sheriff must appoint.—

Very truly your's
Edw. Stanly

Hon: E. Pettigrew
Cool Spring
N.C.

[*Addressed*] Hon: E. Pettigrew
Cool Spring
Washington County
No: Ca:

---

[1]Stanly referred to supporters of the Virginia and Kentucky resolutions, passed by the legislatures of those states in 1798 and 1799. In response to the alien and sedition laws enacted by the Federalist Congress, the resolutions held that individual states had the right to judge the constitutionality of actions by the federal government and declared the laws unconstitutional. During the nineteenth century, southern states'-rights advocates used the principles proposed by these resolutions. Richard B. Morris (ed.), *Encyclopedia of American History* (New York: Harper and Row, Publishers, revised edition, 1965), 130, hereinafter cited as Morris, *Encyclopedia of American History*.

[2]William Henry Washington (1813-1860), a Whig of New Bern, replaced Shepard, who was a Democrat. A lawyer, Washington served one term and afterward sat in the North Carolina General Assembly. *Biographical Directory of Congress*, 1781; Cheney, *North Carolina Government*, 681.

[3]Charles Fisher (1789-1849), a Whig from Rowan County, had served in the state legislature and in Congress, 1819-1821 and 1839-1841. His seat was filled by Abraham Rencher (1798-1883), a Democrat from Chatham County. *Biographical Directory of Congress*, 889; Cheney, *North Carolina Government*, 683.

[4]Henry William Connor (1793-1866) of Iredell County served in Congress as a Democrat from 1821 to 1841. *Biographical Directory of Congress*, 730.

[5]John Hill (1797-1861) represented Stokes County in the General Assembly before he served in the United States House of Representatives as a Democrat, 1839-1841. *Biographical Directory of Congress*, 1053.

[6]Montgomery was replaced by Democrat Romulus M. Saunders of Wake County. Saunders served in Congress until 1845 and later was minister to Spain and a superior court judge. Cheney, *North Carolina Government*, 683; *Biographical Directory of Congress*, 1563-1564.

[7]Augustine H. Shepperd, a Whig from Stokes County, filled the seat vacated by Hill. Cheney, *North Carolina Government*, 683.

[8]Another Democrat, John Reeves Jones Daniel (1802-1868) of Halifax, was elected to Bynum's seat. A lawyer and former state legislator and attorney general, Daniel served in Congress until 1853. Cheney, *North Carolina Government*, 683; *Biographical Directory of Congress*, 775.

[9]Kenneth Rayner (1808-1884) was an attorney in Hertford County. A member of the state House of Commons in 1835, 1836, 1846, 1848, and 1850, he sat in Congress as a Whig from 1839 to 1845. Later he served as solicitor of the United States Treasury. *Biographical Directory of Congress*, 1501.

John Baptist Beasley to Ebenezer Pettigrew A&H

Vicksburgh April 28th 1841

E. Pettegrew Esq[r]

Dear Sir

I reached this place on the 21st Inst. & concluded, I would take a little time, to rest, think, & look into matters and things before I wrote you

I found the Norcoms, *familes* & Joseph all well. but the affairs of the State, in a most wretched & deplorable condition in regard to its money matters *every* man, almost, will tell you he is insolvent. while. he at the same time has a plantation & negroes and driving in his coach & 4, and the consequence is, that no business is done upon credit but for *cash* alone, and this cash, is in the notes of the suspended Banks of Orleans, which may not, intrinsically, be worth more, /than/ the Bank paper of the State, Thus it is that N Orleans money finds its way to all the States bordering on the Miss and its tributaries.

All these evils may be traced to the bad system of Laws for this State. In the first place no man can be held to bail. So when he is sued if it should not be convenient for him to pay. He can run away with his property. or If he does not feel inclined to take this course and wish to remain he can (In case of a sale upon him) get his wife to purchase and the property becomes hers and cannot be reached by any creditor. The people here disregard being sued as they can get two or 3 crops before Judgment as the suits are so numerous. that many are left over for the succeeding term. and in the event of a Judgt then the Valuation law operates which is equal to 1½ to 2 years longer. So you see at once the difficulty attending matters of this sort. There is nevertheless in this State many honourable men most of whom are determined if possible to get the State out of her difficulties and seems to be almost the common sentiment that the State will pay her Bonds sold by the Various Banks.

The next legislature will take the proper steps to accomplish this object. the last one. levied a Tax that will amount to $1000000 which is to meet the expences of the government, and pay off state scrip, which scrip is now selling in this place for 60 cents in the Dollar. I have concluded to invest $5000 in this scip if I can get it a 50 or .55 This investment will not only be profitable. but a perfectly safe transaction In making a purchase, of this kind, I can either fund the scrip at an interest of 5 pr ct pay able in 2 & 4 years or can wait without interest one year or 2 and get the cash for the whole at once. If I had $50,000 cash I could more than double it in 5 years without the least possibility of a loss; many persons would say the could make more money on the same amount of cash but past experience tells me that one certainty is worth more than 10 chances in any kind of speculative business and I have found by adhering to this rule as my standard that I have moved slowly but safe in almost every transaction and that while others with better beginnings than myself have dwindled down to a state of insolvency. I therefore, have always found my judment sufficient to prevent my being led into speculations from the impressions of others and I yet rely upon it

I did not stop at Memphis on my way down shall go up the last of this month. Joseph is in one of the first houses in this place, with far better prospects ahead than it was ever my lot to have in the beginning, with these prospects he is dissatisfied and dreams & fancies to himself that this is too small a place for a man of his genius to figure in. his determination therefore Is to locate in a city. that will afford him ample scope so N Orleans is the desired spot, & to N Orleans must he go. So a man, is a man, shirt, or no shirt. & a sheep sometimes may kill a Butcher, I have said all I could to him upon the subject and now say amen

I had the pleasure of seeing J R Crecy a few days ago. he gave me a *luxuriant* squeeze of the hand, and dolefully asked me the state of finances. I answered rather in a bad state. I have not seen him since he lives in a Brick house /@/ $400 a year with a plenty of servants and always says he is in want of bread. *you know him*

The Norcoms are doing well. Fred is now worth 40,000 and in a few years must double that sum even under the worst prospects.

Very respectfully
J B Beasly

[*Addressed*] Ebenezer Pettegrew Esq[r]
Cool Spring P.O.
N Carolina

Ebenezer Pettigrew to James Cathcart Johnston UNC

Belgrade May 17, 1841

My dear friend

I passed by Edenton on my way home on Wednesday the 12th and was very desirous to stop and stay with you two days, for I had a great deal to say to you, but my long absence forbid it, having stayed much over my appointed time, and after having lengthened that time my horses had been staying at Plymouth two days. It was with great exertion that I proceeded on my way when I saw you on horse back on the side of /the/ bay, but I have almost always made my feelings give way for business and in this case I was constrained to carry it out. I had intended before I left home to have given you an answer to your last letter, but bad health & bad weather & a press of business obliged me to defer it. My health has been very bad all winter untill I left and if any thing it has been worse while gone. My general health is declining, and I took a bad cold early on the way, with a most violent cough, which confined me sometimes to the bed, and at all times it was great labor to get along & do that little business which I had to do.

The object of my visit on leaving home, was to carry my eldest daughter Mary Pettigrew & Mrs Bryans eldest daughter to a highly recommended school at Washington City. A Miss Brishard is the principle. The Girls are under the Guardianship of Mrs Henderson, the sister of William Shephards wife & the wife of Col. Henderson of Marines. Mrs Henderson is a most estimable woman & has two daughters going to the school. I propose for Mary P. to stay there six months & no longer, whether for good or for evil God only knows. I have got the risk to run. She is at this time mild, affectionate, diffident, sensitive & very unobtrusive. Perhaps it may give her some confidence. A portion of which is very necessary in this world. The arrangement was made last fall and with a view to avoid a session of Congress, but I missed it, an extra session being called. I stayed at Washington but a day & a half in which time I called on the President, Secretary of the Navy & (Postmaster General on business.) The President looks very much emaciated and so much altered from the time I before saw him (five years) that I hardly knew. I asked him if Wise was not crazy, he said no, that he was a good whig & that all was right with him. I wish it may be so with both of them. [*George*] Badger looks in fine health & I might say spirits, & says he is determined to keep his temper. As far I can hear from all quarters he is a very popular appointment. I wish he may continue so. I thought he intimated, that he intended to stick on. On my way from Raleigh to Washington City I came by Norfolk & Baltimore having business at those two places. While at Norfolk I took the Girls to the Navy Yard, and through the politeness of the officer, Capt Skinner commander we were carried to the Pensylvania lying in the stream and entirely through the ship, greatly to the gratification of the Girls. The fatigue of which & going to the dry dock made me very sick the remainder of the day. Badger expressed his pleasure at learning of our polite treatment.

While at Baltimore I ordered some corn sheller nuts cast according to the altered patern & have directed two of them to be sent to Messrs Hardy & Brothers for you and have informed them in person of it with a request that they wait your direction of them. The only alternation is the lengthing the under /or lower/ teeth so that the nut does not need to be raised so much to shell clean The one I have put up takes in more corn, shells perfectly clean & does not break the cobs as much.

On my arrival at home I found my carpenter out of work & wanting direction as the work I have him at, is puting the crooked steght [*straight*]. I found my son William who has the whole charge geting along very well & much farther ahead than I could have hoped taking into the account the extreme bad weather. He is in fine health & I thank God acquiring a good or sufficient share of confidence in himself, a thing I fear'd at one time he never would. Charles has had fever & ague but is now pretty well he was with me yesterday & seems to be in good spirits with an assurance of not loosing by the mill this year.

I believe I wrote you that I had taken Johnston home to mend his morrals or in other words to learn to be commanded. It has so far succeeded most perfectly and he does not hesitate to express a surprise at the state of his mind before he came to me. He is now as mild as his sister Mary, & as easily controaled. His health is much improved. In truth he has improved in every way, unless it may be in lattin. I think there is a strong probability that we may have a sickly fall & I think of sending him to Mr Bingham at that time, /but/ to stay, the next winter with me if alive. I do not know that it will possibly /be/ in power to visit you before harvest, but I will ask the question, do you expect to leave before that time? I insist you will not alter one hour as it is very uncertain what I can do. For one thing (being entirely unable to attend to business) I wish to adjust & put to rights all my accounts before harvest.

Charles, knowing my intention to write today with William & Johnston who are with me desire their kind regards to you. Please to make mine to Miss Helen Mrs Treadwell & the other Ladies of your family and assure yourself of sincere Esteem & Regard of your friend

E Pettigrew

James C. Johnston esqr

N.B. I think a coolness is taking place between Mr C. & William P. (I make no comment)

Mary Blount Pettigrew to Mary Williams Bryan A&H, BRYAN

[*Washington, D.C.*] May 27th 1841.

My dear Mother,

We were very glad to receive your's & William's letters. They were sent up to us by Mrs Henderson. I had intended to write to you last saturday week, but I was at Mrs Henderson's, and she was writing so I did not think it worth while for me to write. I suppose you have received her's by this time. I understood you to say, on the morning we started, that once a week was often enough, but if you wish it we will try and write oftener. We are well settled now, at the school. We study "astronomy," "arithmetic" and "composition, I am in the second class french and sister Mary in the first, she also studies "arnot's physics." I will tell you in my next what french books I study as I have not all my french studies yet I suppose. Mrs Henderson is exceedingly kind to us, and does every thing she can for us. We like the school very much and find Miss Breschard kind and I think her well qualified to have the care of girls. We are obliged to take up speaking french this week. We were not examined atall, she asked us what we studied before and put us in what she thought could study. We are going to Mrs Henderson's saturday to stay until<l> monday.

The girls can only go out every other saturday, which they call "visiting saturday," The other one the have to stay in the school, In the evening they go on the avenue with a teacher and do all their shopping and then they go to the market house and get candies, cakes and all such things. I shall be very glad to see Mrs Badger and Kate.[1] I hope she will go to our school. Poor Mr Octavius—Cazinove died last wendesday and was buried on friday. Mrs Henderson was down there at the time of his death. She had gone to the Virginia convention which sat <th> in Alexandria last week. There were one hundred ministers and a great crowd of people. I have not seen Mrs Henderson since her brother's death. I expect they are resigned, for the girls say he was prepared and it was best. He was sick three years. Give mine and Mary's love to Father, Grandma' and all the family kiss little Charlotte and Isabel for me and dont let them forget me. Teach Charlotte to call my name when she begins to talk. We have a great deal to do.

Believe me your aff' daughter
M. B. Pettigrew.

To Mrs Mary W Bryan.

[*Addressed*] Mrs John H Bryan
Raleigh
N.C.

---

[1]George Badger's first wife, Rebecca Turner, died in 1824, and he married Mary Polk in 1826. Their daughter Catherine was born in 1827; another daughter, Sarah, was born in 1833. Mary Polk Badger died in 1834, and in 1836 Badger married Delia Haywood Williams, a widow, by whom he had seven children. Powell, *DNCB*, I, 80.

Ebenezer Pettigrew to James Cathcart Johnston UNC

Belgrade June 7, 1841

My dear friend,

I received your favour by the last mail and take the first mail in return to answer it. However anxious I am to visit you I should not be willing to prevent you from attending to your distant business. But as matters are progressing it would be now out of my power at the time I expected to visit you. The wheat when I wrote you looked late & I did not expect to commence harvest much if any before the twenty first but from the drought or dry weather we have since it is advancing rapidly, & I now think we may begin on the fourteenth. I could now cut in patches with safety. The wheat in scuppernong & I have seen most of it is I think very good. Sufficiently thick & with very good heads. Taking it altogether the best we have had, and I think too far advanced to be lessened by the last enemy, rust. I have a neighbour who I learn intends to begin harvest today. I was at a neighbours home last week, & he carried me around his wheat. It contained between 40 & 50 acres. I am satisfied that 30 acres of it are good for 20 bushels to the acre & a good deal of it 25 if not more. The crop of wheat has quadrupled in the last eight years I cannot but flatter myself that my wheat farming at this place, shipping the peoples little crops in my vessil & best of all giving them all the nett proceeds in cash at their doors, has been a great means of increasing the crop. It gave me a great deal of trouble to take their little parcels, but if it has done the good I hope it has I am amply rewarded. But after all this & I suppose two times more, I am a miserable creature not worth the notice of the great unless I will go the whole figure in *church*. I thank my God that there is one country in the world in which religious liberty is established & that I live in it. May it continue as long as the earth bears a plant or the sea rolls its waves. I have a good deal to say to you on that subject which is as well not said in a letter. Some things ought to be enforced but I have trouble enough of my own, & shall not engage in any fresh one. All I ask now is to be let alone, whether well & able to attend to my business, sick, dying, or *dead*. I want no cold, heartlessness to <look> close my eyes or look at my dead body. I have a sufficiency of poor white persons /around me/ who can do those offices with sorrow in their souls & if they are not at hand, I know I have a sufficiency of Negroes who can do those things for me, while the big tear of sorrow will be roaling down their cheaks. I judge from past observation. Pray excuse this digression from farming. It is my nature to run of into the clouds at times.

My corn crop is very backward & from taking in too large a piece of new ground we have had a scuffle to get out of the weeds & gras, but with close attention we shall be able pretty well to do it in this week. But for this dry spell we should have been sevierly in the [*illegible*]. William attends to it from daylight till dark the /whole/ week. These long days and the hot sun is puting him to his best. I fear the fatigue of harvest. The two last, from my fatigue I had the [cramp] to an awfull degree, and from what I have read since I fear that it was something of the tetanus of warm climates. I will do all I can at the same time using the necessary prudence. I can form no idea of what will be the price of wheat. My *most excellent* correspondent writes nothing to me on the subject. I suppose low. The rise of corn was to me entirely unexpected. I believed it would decline instead of rise as the season advanced. In consequence of that opinion I shipped early all I had (about 1000 barrils) & got the lowest price. These things cannot be helped. How this cold season may act upon the corn & grass north I cannot yet learn, but if it should not be injurious & our season should after this be favourable corn will decline again, at all events not advance much more. But if the season north should / should be like that of 1816 then we may look for good prices. However the immense quantity of bread stuffs raised in the northwestern states which can not come to market with the present low prices would be forced into market with high prices in immence quantities & keep the price in a degree lower than in 1817. I should be glad to see a little advance in bread stuffs & a steady demand. But we must take the world as it exists. Its a ruff one in deed but thank God I am geting through it pretty fast.

Never did I know or experince such a winter & spring but now it is geting on the other extreme and I should not be surprised if it is for a time as dry as it has been wet. I never knew the Lake to continue as it did all winter above high water.

Charles Pettigrew is yet driving along at the mill, doing more than has been done before perhaps making both ends meet. He has had fever & ague, aded to that a piece of scantling fell on his foot, which is now tolerably recovered. I was to see him last week. It is hot enough in the mill yard & in the little house he stays to kill a snake. O what an awfull place to have a bilious fever in. I was very much gratified to find in your letter an approval of my course with my children. Let me say to you my dear friend, that I value no persons judgment so much as yours. I wish this winter that my daughter Mary shall stay with me but I am at a loss to know how we are to get along Our society is a strange one. I confess I know not how to manage it, particularly when I have to give advice to the opposite sex. I fear I shall have to submit to a winters seperation from /my/ daughters. My poor little Mary is exceedingly affectionate & deserves to stay with her father & brothers.

Johnston is very mild & managable. He perfectly astonished me the other day. I had been making a long talk to William & Johnston on the subject of parents permiting their children to go to distruction /&/ giving a number of cases. After geting through I took Johnston to walk; & after a little silence he began with this. Pa I think you have salved me from *distruction* by taking me home & I think now I can hold out at Mr Binghams till November & if you will take me back next winter & spring, I shall then be able to get along. I intend sending him to Hisborough to avoid the sickly season. I know, to you, no comment on the forgoing is necessary.

On the last subject of your letter I have no language to express myself. All I need say My dear friend is, that when I read it the tear of deep regret & sorrow passed in my eyes.

Charles was with me yesterday & desired me with /William/ & Johnston to make their best respects to you. Please to make mine to Miss Helen & the other Ladies of your family and assure yourself of sincere Esteem & Regard of your friend

E Pettigrew

James C. Johnston esqr

N.B. I suppose last week has been a great on[*e*] in Edenton, & this & a part of next is to be a great one <in> on the Lake. Good God what is to be the result of all these things. I must be the rock of Giberalter not be battered or frowned down, but blessed be God for his mercies I have been forty years making my defences, & I think am prepaired to make a desperate resistance. I fear fanaticism is taking a desprate hold of some persons. E P.

[*Addressed*] James C. Johnston esqr
Hayes
Edenton P. Office

Hardy and Brothers to Ebenezer Pettigrew A&H

Norfolk, V^{a} 13. July 1841

E. Pettigrew, Esq—

DearSir,

Your favour of the 28. Ult— did not reach us till the morning of the 10. inst— an unaccountable delay, from some cause— We have spoken to our grocers, who trade & have dealings with the craftsmen from your section—and they have promised to let us know of any oppty that may offer of sending you the shoes ordered— We shall also, keep a good lookout ourselves, and send them by the first oppty.

Have made enquiry as to the expense at Old Point, and find the prices vary so much, (according to the *location*, *size*, and *condition* of the *rooms*) that it would be impossible to name a price, that would be more than a guess—We think the lowest board your neighbour could obtain there for himself & wife, in *comfortable quarters*, would be 75$ p^{r} month— and if *he* was absent half the time it would make no difference in the price. Since the first of June Old Point has been crowded with company, & will no doubt continue crowded during this month & next—The season being short, the proprietors say they are compel[d] to charge high prices—While Old Point is perhaps one of the most desireable & delightful resorts in this country for the man of health & pleasure, it does seem to us liable to many & great objections as a place of resort for the *invalid*—The continual crowded state of the Hotel—the small rooms, the *company*—the frequent cool (if not damp) East wind—and above all, the difficulty of procuring *good* water—This of course in confidence—we regret to learn Sir, that your own health is not good—If you could spend one or two months in Norfolk under our *Homeopathic* practice—taking the sea air in Boats that leave & return almost every day, as the weather & your feelings might invite—We think you might return home *perfectly* restored. And we think your neighbours wife would derive more benefit from this practice, remaining in Norfolk; than she would by a long visit to Old Point, or the Springs—

Corn continues scarse & in demand, sales at 65¢ but think it may recede a little when we are better supplied—which will probably be after the Farmers are done "billing—".

Weare Sir
Very Respy
Yrfrds & Sts
Hardy & Brothers

[*Addressed*] Hon. E. Pettigrew
Cool-Spring
Washington County
N[o] Ca—

John Herritage Bryan to Ebenezer Pettigrew UNC

Raleigh July 18 1841

My dear Sir

Johnston arrived here Friday night the (10th), we saw him yesterday, he has improved I think by his sojourn at the Lake: He left yesterday in the Stage.—

I was much concerned to learn that your health was so bad; I think it is time that you should indulge, or at last spare yourself; we hoped that you would have been able to come up & spend as much time as you could spare with us and still hope that you may be able to do so:—

We have no news here of importance, or at least none that I hear but I stay so much at home that I do not collect the floating rumors; I have been confined too very much to the Supreme Co. which has been sitting since the middle of June.

Tho I have had rather more business than usual the Court has been very unproductive of cash.—

Nancy & Betsy go to Miss Mellish & they seem to improve more than they have done since they have been here—they go to dancing school every Saturday & to Church every Sunday where they have to recite Catechism &c so that their time is fully occupied:—

I saw the Bishop last friday, he was lately from Washington & went with M[rs] Badger to see the girls, he said they were looking very well, I suppose you hear from them occasionally & they give you an account of their doings &c.—

The Mechanics here have been incorporated & celebrated their anniversary by a Speech & a dinner. James Shepard was their orator:— Any institution which is calculated to devote & improve the mechanic arts in our Country is very desirable; but I fear that some of the members of this Society are more actuated by the Spirit of the "Trade unions" of the northern cities; than by a desire for improvement; that is, to do as little work as they can, & to get more than it's worth:—

It may tend also to excite a bitter feeling against those whom they term aristocrats & I fear will:— I suspect that James will embark in politicks.—

I wish Charles' Steam instrument was in our Rockfish Co, that is upon the supposition <that> (which I believe) that the Company will do well: He would be enabled also, to live in a healthy region.—

The Gov[r] seems to be very much pleased with the Swamp lands: while down there, Major Jno. Clark of Pungo, put in a claim to some 400 acres said to be very valuable—& the Gov[r] & he agreed to refer the question to me, upon examination I think I shall decide in favour of M[r] Clark who has the law on his side.—

I mention this as it seems to confirm your notion that individuals would be forced to claim a good deal of their lands.—

Nancy is very well & sends her love & says she will write shortly.—

Mrs. B desires to be affectionately remembered by you & her nephews: My regards to them—

Very truly
Yr friend & relative
Jn. H. Bryan

[*Addressed*] E. Pettigrew Esq
Cool Spring
N.C

James Johnston Pettigrew to Ebenezer Pettigrew UNC

Hillsboro July the 20th 1841

Dear Pa,

I arrived up here yesterday morming about 9 o'clock. I am very well now, but at washington I was very costive and was so all the way up until I came to Raleigh. Grandma and all my relations were very well. I saw Mr Bingham yesterday morning at church and spoke to him and found that he was very well and all his family. In coming up from Raleigh I met with Mr Tunstall who introduced himself to me as being a relation of yours. We spent two at Washington but Halsey hired a gig and went up to tarboro' two days before I did and which trip cost him five or six dollars more than it did me. When he got to tarboro' he went about in the night air and also went in the water and in consequnce of which was taken sick but has got well and is up here now. He behaved himself very well in the first part of the [*trip*] to me but between Raleigh and here he became disagreable both to me and every body else with his cursing and noise. He drank pretty frely on the road and there was a man who came along with us from tarboro' named Elliott, the stage contractor, who more than once tried to persuade me to take a drink. At Raleigh in the night just after we had arrived he told me that it would make me feel like a man *and when I got up in the morning I feel like something*. The corn looks very bad I think all the way along, and there has been a great drought up here which has killed all the corn nearly. Give my love to Brother Charles and Brother William, and Beleive me to be

Your affectionate son
J. Johnston Pettigrew

[*Addressed*] E. Pettigrew
Cool spring
N. Carolina

Mary Blount Pettigrew to John Herritage Bryan A&H, BRYAN

Washington [*D.C.*] July 23d 1841.

My dear Father,

As you desired me I have resolved to write you this morning. It is vacation now and we are almost entirely alone, the girls all having left except two who are to leave to day. We are to stay here with Miss Breschard until she goes to the north, which will be in about two weeks, and then we will go to Mrs Henderson's. Miss B— intends hearing us recite our french lessons every day while she is here and we will practice two or three hours so that it will be as improving as if in school. The exhibition was on monday when the best compositions were read and the rewards distributed; the medal in the second class composition was given to Miss Thornton from Kentucky and in the third to Miss Clark from New York. Miss B— is very much pleased with Mary. We had a very pleasant ball on wednesday night with good music and dancing which you know are very neccessary to render one so. There were very few persons whom I knew none except those with whom I have become acquainted since I have been here. We sat up until between one and two o-clock. Miss B— exerted herself very much to make the girls happy and I believe succeeded for they all seemed to enjoy themselves; she is much beloved by her schoolars.

We went yesterday evening to see some celebrated paintings, by different artists brought here for sale, there was one among them taken from the "Vicar of Wakefield" in which there was a child that reminded me so much of dear little Isabel, it looked so innocent. Tell William he must write to me, that I intend to answer his last, but he ought not to wait for an answer because we have so much more to do than he has and so many more letters to write.

I found I knew nothing at all about music when I began to take lessons with this teacher, and I think that Betsy and Nancy had better not take at all than take from Mrs Lucas or Mrs LaMesura[ier] for I dont believe they know much more about teaching than the children themselves; they dont even begin right, and Mrs. Badger seems to think the same. The weather is extremely warm. Mary joins me in love to you, Ma', Grand Ma' and all the family. Give my best love to Nancy, Isabel, and Charlotte.

And believe me ever your
truly aff' daughter M. B. P.

[*Addressed*] John H Bryan Esq.
Raliegh
N.C.

William James Bingham to Ebenezer Pettigrew UNC

[*Hillsborough, August 17, 1841*]

My dear Sir;

Yours of the 12th inst. covering a check for $100. was rec'd this morning (17th Aug.) and Johnston's portion was read to him, to which he made his usual resigned & submissive response "Yes, Sir." He says he never sold any of his clothes, but that he did not take care of them. The latter fact indeed has been regular ground of quarrel between him & me. I have got him one pair of pantaloons,

& I believe one jacket since he came up. With all the clothes he has had, & he has certainly been liberally supplied, it has been next to impossible to keep him decent, in consequence of his carelessness. He is doing very well in his studies, & also in his deportment both at home & at the Academy. I rather incline to think you are too despairing of Johnston. I know his failings; but I can't but think he will surpass your expectations. I hope you will enjoy the satisfaction of seeing him a much more considerate & practical man, than you seem now to anticipate. May your life be prolonged to witness such a consummation. For your children's sake I think your summers ought to be spent either at the North or in the back country. I hope you will not return to the Lake before hard frost.—What if you visit the several watering places in V'a—& return in the Fall by way of Hillsboro'?—

Johnston handed me $6.12½/100— on his arrival, which he said was all he had left, having suffered some detention on the road. He arrived on the 19th ult; and I directed him to write you immediately, & wrote you myself a week or ten days after.

I am truly glad to learn that your health improves so much by travel.

My family are well—except the hooping cough—the three youngest have it—The others had it some years ago. The health of the school is perfect: tho' it is reported that the scarlet fever is in town. Dr Webb says there have been two or three cases of what he calls scarletina—a mild type of scarlet fever, but nothing to excite alarm.

The number of scholars is 85.—

Mrs B. & my brother join in kind regards, your

sincere friend & obedt ser't
W. J. Bingham

P.S.—I will do my utmost to make Johnston careful of his clothes, & will follow your instructions in reference to further supplies.

[*Addressed*] Hon. E. Pettigrew
Winchester
Virginia

Ebenezer Pettigrew to William Shepard Pettigrew UNC

Direct your next to Winchester

Baltimore Aug. 19 1841

My dear Son

I received your favor of the 9th Inst. and was *very very* glad to find all things right, & well I pray God you all may continue well. Pray let me beseach you all to take care of your selves.

We came yesterday from Washington (Mr Johnston is yet with us & expects to to go with us to Winchester today) My health is improved beyond any thing as well as Mrs Davenports that you could think, but I had one very sick night of vomiting at Wahsington & was as weak at death in the morning but soon got over it. I am as cautious as ever in my eating, but not so much so in my walking, which I think was the cause of the sick night. My desperate costiveness is /just/ gone of & my bowils are now at this time & for two or 3 day right. Mrs Davenport is as I before said, but yesterday we left Washington at 6 in the morning & it was cold, & she thought after we got to this place had a chill, however she was better soon & went out in the afternoon /with/ a very respectable Lady a standing boarder in the house shoping and says she is well this morning. She sends her complements to you and Charles & desires her Love to her husband and children & asks him to keep them for her. Tell Mr Davenport, that the Lady above spoken of has taken a great fancy to Mrs D. and that she was treated by Mr Stanly with great atention & politeness as well as all others who she came in contact with & that Mr Stanly has fully paid his debt to him in his atention to his wife, as well as to me in his attentions to me & Mr Johnston who is very much pleased with him. He thinks him a fine fellow. Dr [*Mathew*] Page & the Miss C[*ollins*]. arrived here last night. Mrs D. was introduced in our rooms to Mr Clay, Drank tea at Col Hendersons & in truth has been in high snuff. But more of this when she gets home.

As respects the sowing corn seed I will write you again. Charles is to have some of the negroe cloth he can take if he thinks proper the [inferior] you speak of or the other. I see about the shoes. Captain Coran [*Caroon?*] will take on his return a Black Buckskin & Chester boar (which Mr [Bashorn] says he thinks the best bread) with him he is for Belgrade also 200 wt Brimstone & salpeter, two whips & my old umbrella & Mrs Ds old bonnet to the care of Charles. I have also bought a bull eight months old at one hundred & fifty dollars to be delivered in November. I have also <bout> bought the 24 mules of Mr Clay at $90 a piece they are to be delivered to you at Belgrade. in some time next month & at your infor<mation to>ming me of that fact the money is to be deposited in Baltimore. The sale is if the mules are not sold which Mr Clay is confident is not so. They are to be as good mules as are in Kentucky & /sent/ by a confidential person that will not change them. Would it not /be/ well to fence up the piece of ground at Belgrade we talked of as a pasture for them. It seems to be not doubted that corn will be high, would it not be well to salve all the fodder that you can for those 24 mules & get Mr Davenport to begin to get off some of our inferior ones. I could have bought at this place mules at $65 but they were shaped much like Joe also I saw a drove at Washington at $75 <but> of better looking but not to my expectation. The note for the Woodberry Mills was in bank & all was right.

And now my dear son make my kind regards to Mr D. & all who ask after me and my sin[*ce*]re Love to your brother Charles &

believe me your affect. father
E Pettigrew

N.B. Mr J. says if Miss C. had been in company he should not.

[*Addressed*] William S Pettigrew Esqr
Cool Spring
N. Carolina

William A. Dickinson to Ebenezer Pettigrew A&H

Hillabie [*Alabama*] 4th Septr 1841

E. Pettigrew Esqr Lake Phelps.

Dear Sir

It is now a considerable time since I had this pleasure of writting, or hearing from you, in my last letter to you I stated that by the end of 1840. I would be able to send you the amount of money you was so kind as to loan me, but alace my fond and anticipated calculations are completely defeated, I will go on and tell you how I am situated, when at Wetumpka I was doing very well, but unfortunately I sold to a House there 2,400 Dolls worth of goods one part cash & the balance 6 & 9 mos: some of the parties died insolvent and the others that were or are still alive are also insolvent, leaving a balance of 1,200 Dolls. due me with now 3 years intrest, totaly & *Te, Totaly, lost*, soon after that I went to Benton County & had a store doing business as is usual in the country on a credit, that has also proved a failure owing to so many bad debts at Wetumpka of large amts. and also at Benton, during the two years of my stay at Benton, seeing the coming storm (I entered a tract of Land in the Hillabies in Talladaga County, a year ago,) for the purpose of going to it & retire entirely from merchandising, as I believe 8 out of every 10 engaged in it has failed and will fail in the very fluctuating situation of the country. I am now still in debt to the amount of from 4 to 5 Thousand Dolls. and all I have now left is this Land 160 acres in the wild woods, with a small stock of a few hogs & milch cows &c, I shall have all my bread stuffs to buy for an other year, as I only came here last April and have since then been clearing and fixing a Log cabin to live in which is not yet finished I have almost worked myself down, as I now begin to feel a good deal of stiffness, I am very much afraid that I will have a hard time of it next year, as I hardly see how I shall be able to obtain provisions enough untill I can git something out of the Land, this is my true & real situation, I feel deeply sunk when I think how independant I have passed my former and by gone days, I now have to beg. and offer you as a payment or security for payment a mortgage, or a Deed for this Land, with a consideration to give me time to pay you with intrest the amt: due you, by your acceptance of a mortgage or Deed, it would secure your pay at a future day. as I fully expect my creditors will be down on me, and there will be no help, I can give you a Deed and have it registered in Talledaga this to Lay subject to your pleasure, as yours is a debt of a delicate nature, not being mercantile.

The grape seed you sent me never came up. as I was too long in putting them in the ground, this soil & climate is hily calculated for the growth of the vine as the woods are full of the small bunch grape, I wish you to forward me some more seed as you did before & I will put them in the ground on their arrival. I may if I live and keep my health be able to make some wine, as also peach brandy as the Trees produce abundantly of the best quality I have ever seen, I may in time raise a little silk as my family are growing up they could soon be able to attend to it, trusting this will find you & your family all well, self and family are in good health, we are frequently talking of old N.C. and all our old acquaintances, please write soon & send me some grap seed, which will much oblige, tell H. H. P [*Hardy H. Phelps?*] that I will write him soon, by your early attention to the above contents of this letter will oblige Dear Sir

Your very Obd[t] Svt.
W[m] A Dickinson

[*Addressed*] E. Pettegrew Esq[r]
Lake Phelps
Coolspring P. Office
N: Carolina

Ebenezer Pettigrew to William Shepard Pettigrew UNC

Winchester Sep 5, 1841

My dear son

I receivd your favour of the 31st ult. last night as well & M[rs] Davenport, M[r] Davenports. We are rejoiced to lern that you are all so well, hoping that little Johnstons sickness will be of sort duration. It is with great regret that I learn of /the/ accident at the Steam mill as well for the loss of so much to the mill & of the poor fellows life. And with M[rs] D. I regret the difficuties at M[r]

Davenports and at his children leaving where I thought they would stay the fall. Tell Mr D. to make the best of it & exercise all his christian fortitude. With respect to the ditches through the ponds in the deaded ground. I wish I had mentioned to you to run them (as you of course will do) paralel with /the/ head ditch /of the Poplar neck field/ but directly through the best place to drain the ponds, without any respect to their being equal distance from each other. At the begining I suppose it will /be/ necessary for them to be as deep as the poplar neck ditch to drain the ponds & consequently ought to /be/ 5 or 6 ft wide; above the ponds 3 ft would be wide enough & 2½ deep enough. Your suggestion with respect to the ditch & fence through the Barn fie[*l*]d in your postscrip is right. The ditch ought to be in the field of course. I had expected a letter at this place before this from Mr Clay informing me certainly respecting his mules, but have had none. I did not expect you to sell any but the disabled ones that could be of no use to us, such as Gammel & Godfry untill we are in possession of Mr C's. They will be 2 year old last spring & consequently fit to work half the day at the begining. But we have not got them yet & it is a good rule not to through out dirty water before you get clean if you must have water. I went with Mr Johnston as far as Frederick on the 23rd & by him wrote to your brother Charles & /on/ my return wrote to you. In which I informed you that I had had a very bad night & that it would take me a week to get back, which was true, for the last two or three days I have been pretty well but yesterday in the middle of the day I rode on horseback to a little town 7&½ miles off to see a threshing machine establishment, which made there & back 15 miles & I have not been so well since. I was not so much tired as heated & my bowels have been a little disturbed today.

Mrs Davenport has very much improved in health flesh & appearance but complains of a pain in her side when she walks, which I think is either the splean or the liver. I did not hear her say anything about it untill she came here. She says there is a hard place in her side. Every day confirms me in the opinion that her trip has been of the first consequence to her. she is much surprised to learn from her husbands letter that he has recived only one letter from her when she has writen three. The last by Mr Johnston. She desires her Love to Mr Davenport & best respects to you & Charles.

We expect to leave here tomorrow morning for Harpers ferry & the next day to Baltimore, and we could then wish that anything would justify our keeping on.

No rain here & everything burnt up. Pastures look deplorable & animals generally lean. Wheat taken at the mills as $1.25. & no prospect of a decline. Corn will start at 80 cents because there is little or none to sell. It has been excessively hot at this place. I think more oppressive than with us. In truth this is a hot hollow & not very desirable to stay at. I think /it/ is likely when we get to Baltimore I shall go again to Washington City & see Mr Clay. Mrs Davenport has formed acquaintance at Barnums with some ladies of the house, (the Old mans daughter Mrs McGlocklin /for one/) and spends her time very agreably there. She has not received but the letter last night. She farther requests me to ask you to request Mr Davenport not discharge Miss Nancy because there cannot be such another got. I would also say to him that bad as she may be, he very well recollects how difficult it was get any one worth a straw. And now my son make my Love to your brother Charles, Mr Davenport, Dr Lewis & all inquiring frnds and believe me your affectionat father

E Pettigrew

N.B. Take care of yourselves. Direct your letters to Baltimore in future. I am very glad at your expretions respecting Jos. Beasley.

[*Addressed*] William S. Pettigrew Esqr
Cool Spring
N. Carolina

James B. Clay[1] *to William Shepard Pettigrew* A&H

Ashland [*Kentucky*] Sept 15th 1841

Mr Wm S Pettigrew

Dr Sir—

According to instructions from my father—I start to day twenty four mules, under charge of Mr [W]eimar, with directions to deliver them to you—They were purchased by your father, from mine in Washington—I hope they may reach you in good condition—

I am Respy &c &c
James B Clay

[*Addressed*] Mr Wm S. Pettigrew—
Tyrrel County
NC—

---

[1]James Brown Clay (1817-1864) was a son of Henry Clay. He practiced law with his father in Lexington, Kentucky. Later he served in the United States House of Representatives as a Democrat, 1857-1859. *Biographical Directory of Congress*, 704.

Ebenezer Pettigrew to James Cathcart Johnston UNC

Baltimore Sep 15, 1841

My dear friend

I returned to this place (after staying at H. Ferry a day) on the tuesday the 7th to dinner. I had not received a letter from Mr Clay & went to Washington in the morning of wednesday to see him as well as see the row which I expected on the sending into /the/ house Captain Tylers second veto message.[1] I expected to return to Baltimore at night, but that all absorbing place keept me untill fryday night. I will not give you the political part of Congress because you have seen it correctly reported in the Inteligencer. At the reading of the veto message all <w> continued silent & orderly in the house & galleries & it was made the order of the day /for/ fryday, & I walked into the library & ask for Jacobs report, had not got my hand in the book before some one came in & said there had been a fight in the house at which I put down the book & went in. When I got there [*Henry A.*] Wise was making his apology, order being restored. W. I thought & confirmed by Mr [*James*] Graham looked very much mortified, for [*Edward*] Stanly gave him three licks before they were parted & was geting him down under the desk. After Wise set down Stanly rose & made his explanation with as much coolness as I now write. He in a few minutes came to the bar & I spoke to him. He was as unagitated as when in his own parlor. In truth I never saw nor could I have conceived anything like it. He is spoken of here in the highest terms for his course & particularly his last remarks on the subject of sensure. I dined on thursday at Mr [*George*] Badgers with Mr Clay, Mr Talmage, Mr Speaker of the H.R.[2] They talked freely & jocosely about the cabinet going out[3] & seemed quite unconcerned about it. Mr Ewin[4] & Crittenden[5] came in before we got from the table. You have seen the result of the veto ere this. I had Bennets letter writer pointed out to me. It is said he is at home at the White house & upon terms of strict intimacy /with the two private scretaries/ & therefore knows all the secrets of the President.

I always thaught that Tyler was a miserable poor looking creature for a great man, but my Physiognomy does not quite reach him. The other edition of the President brought the message into the H. of R. I could not find out whether it was first or second. I leave you to the papers for the remainder of the Proceedings of Congress.

I have observed that I came to this place on fryday night, on saturday and sunday was suffering a good deal with head ache & did not go out but very little. Monday evening went to see Mr T. Williams & regret to say his conduct was very marked indifferent.

It made me serious, but not to behave improperly & I set a good while, he attending to his business at intervals. I have but one word to say on this subject & that is That I wish gentlemen would not treat me with such attentions as to justify them in expecting more from me that I have the power or will to give in return. I am alway doing my best, but on the subject of visiting I can not keep /up with/ & meet the expectations of others.

There was an overwhelming meeting in /the/ City last night to pass resolutions to invite Mr Clay to visit this place, & a committee from this visit him today

My health is again restored & I am gaining in health /strength,/ also <Mrs> Mrs Davenport continues to improve & may be said to be well & we are waiting the return of the season to go home.

My dear friend on my return from Was[hing]ton on the 8th I found your favour of the 4th. Its contents gave me great pleasure except that you were still labouring under cold, from which I hope & trust you are before this restored. I do most sincerely wish that you could but have known how your affairs were going in that you might have stayed with us till october. Nothing could have been more gratifying, but I can say with truth that I was sincerly thankfull for so much.

Letters from home up to the 8th Inst inform me that things & going on well & best of all, it is healthy. Charles at the steam mill has meet with the misfortune to have one of the hands drowned, which makes a loss of $650. They insuring the life of all they hire. Thus you see my friend the misfortune of not taking advice. But I say nothing in finding falt. On the contrary am as mild as possible, for fear of worse consequences. I showed that part of your letter in praise of Barnums Hotel to the old man, which was very gratifying, Your political remarks are the most cutting & the very best that can be made. I do wish that they could be put in a paper as an extract from a private letter from the South or N. Carolina if you please. No names mentioned, What do you say.

There was yesterday a smash up at the depot of this place. Two Gentlemen belonging to Pensylvania went down to see there friends off & stood between the office & the railroad just at the gate where there was no room; <I> /one/ a large fat man had his breast so mashed as to break nearly all the bones about it, & the doctor says must die, the other who stays at this house & is here now was squesed so tight about his hips &c as to prevent his walking or moving but will recover, but I suppose the great misfortune with him is that a dimond brest-pin costing $500 was dislodged from his breast, & in the bustle picked up by a boy & borne of so quick that he cannot be recognized. I saw & talked with Mr Southard[6] last night he hoped Mr Clay would not come this way, & other of his express the same opinion. I forgot to tell you about the mules. Mr

Clay informed me that he had receivd a letter from his son & that they were not as fat as could be wished, but in good flesh. They would leave on the 15th this month & expected to be at Belgrade on or by the 10th Octr So that business is fixed. I have said I called monday to see Mr T. Williams, yesterday /morning/ I called to see Mrs W. she had gone to ride. I left my card for Mr & Mrs ——— but no call last night from Mr ——— How difficult it is to keep out of scrapes. I have several invitations on hand now. I have a great mind to cut the whole. All I care for in a place like this is slang away to any one I come up to & then go ahead to the next. I give a fig for any other intercourse in a heartless city as they all are.

I forgot to mention to you that I say W. Shepard the other day at Washington. I have seen two others [ones] at this place, in Barnums passage. And they all swear without reserve, that a certain conduct is very strange and that it is there opinion that he is determined to monopolise both. It was nuts to me. I now think the Gentlemans leaving the parlor so suddenly, was because he saw me. Bow. bow! Mrs Davenport desires her best respects to you, Please to make mine to Miss Helen & the other Ladies & believe me your sincere friend

E Pettigrew

N.B. If I had thought I had so much to say I would have taken a whole instead of half sheet of paper; but must now quit this miserable scratch, which please to excuse.

E P.

[*Addressed*] James C. Johnston esqr
Edenton
N. Carolina

---

[1]In August and September, 1841, President John Tyler vetoed two bills introduced in Congress by the Whigs. The bills would have established a national bank, with branch offices in the states. Morris, *Encyclopedia of American History*, 184.

[2]The Speaker at this time was John White (1802-1845) of Kentucky. A Whig, White served in Congress from 1835 to 1845. *Biographical Directory of Congress*, 1804.

[3]President Tyler's Whig cabinet, except for Secretary of State Daniel Webster, resigned on September 11, two days after Tyler vetoed the second bank bill. Morris, *Encyclopedia of American History*, 184-185.

[4]Thomas Ewing (1789-1871) of Ohio was secretary of the treasury. He sat in the Senate as a Whig, 1831-1837. Later he served as secretary of the interior (1849-1850) and again in the Senate. *Biographical Directory of Congress*, 872.

[5]John J. Crittenden was attorney general at this time. *Biographical Directory of Congress*, 755.

[6]This may refer to Samuel Lewis Southard (1787-1842) from New Jersey. He sat in the Senate as a Whig from 1833 until his death and was president pro tempore at the time of this letter. Prior to this time he was a judge, held several cabinet posts, and served as both attorney general and governor of New Jersey. *Biographical Directory of Congress*, 1633.

Francis Theodore Bryan to William Shepard Pettigrew UNC

Chapel Hill, Oct 17th 1841

Dear Cousin

I received your interesting letter last week & will *now* endeavor to answer it as I was then so much engaged upon Gov Swain[1] & studies that I could not well before this time. I do not recollect that you requested me to send you a catalogue of the books of the Philanthropic Society. I have looked about and asked some of the oldest members about them but I could neither find the catalogues nor any one who could tell me anything of them, they say that there were no catalogues printed that they knew of. I would write you off one from the *one* belonging to the Society, but that it is so large & after it was done there would be no way of getting it to you. However if you still wish for one I will take great pleasure in obliging you in this or any other particular I will send you a catalogue of the members of both, the Dialectic & the Philanthropic Societies.

You say that you wish me to obtain the first distinction in my class & to graduate with it. I do not know whether I shall graduate with it or not. I have got it ever since I joined college & I believe I stand about as I ever did. The only thing which I dislike is the speaking which is made part of a senior's business. I shall have to speak at the end of this session as I have never accustomed myself "to speak in public on the stage" I do /not/ know how I shall come off. I think though that if I make a tolerably good show that I shall not be discontented. That is some six weeks off, so I shall not bother myself about it yet.

I heard of Mr McQueen the other day by Benton Utley who had been to Raleigh to attend Court there. He was very well and as Benton said had distinguished himself on a recent trial. I saw him myself last vacation & we had some chat together.

Prof Roberts[2] has been quite sick for the last week or ten days with a bilious fever which he contracted when in the low country. He has just recovered but is still very weak. I have a talk now & then with him about things which he has seen in his travels. He is very communicative & interesting indeed & seems to take great pleasure in relating incidents of his travels.

The Phi Society does not get on as well as I could wish. Some foolish creatures have tried to create a division amongst the members for their own purposes I suppose. The parties were so excited that in one instance the consequence of a very trifling turning of a chair was a regular fist & scull set-to & it would have ended in something more serious had /not/ the Faculty separated them as both of them had arms about them. Both of the combatants were dismissed next day on account of the arms. One was an Alabamian & the other a Tenneseean.

I received a letter from Washington City last week from Sister, She and Sister M. Pettigrew were both well & seemed to like the school very well. I believe it is nearly time for them to return home & I shall be very glad to see them again after so long an absence. I heard not long ago from Raleigh and was sorry to learn that Father had been quite sick but he has now almost wholly recovered & had gone to Wayne Court. All the rest of the family were well. Grandma had some notion of going to Newbern after the cold weather set in. I suppose you have heard that it was very sickly there this fall, thirteen deaths occurred in one day. I believe the health of your part of the country has been pretty good.

I should be very glad if you could make it convenient to come up the country next summer to our commencement. You will hardly be able to recognize the place I expect so many improvements have been made even since I have been a student. I should also be very glad to see Uncle Pettigrew & Cousin Charles here. Remember me to them if you please.

with great respect I remain your affectionate cousin
Frans. T. Bryan

[*Addressed*] William S. Pettigrew Esqr
Cool-Spring
Washington Co—
N. Ca

[1]David Lowry Swain (1801-1868), a Whig, had been governor of North Carolina, 1832-1835. He had also been a superior court judge and a member of the state House of Commons. Swain served as president of the University of North Carolina from 1835 until shortly before his death. *DAB*, XVIII, 230-231.

[2]John J. Roberts was professor of French at the university in 1841 and 1842. An 1838 graduate, he had studied for two years in France. Roberts became an Episcopal minister and served as principal of schools for girls in Massachusetts and New York City. Battle, *History of the University*, I, 440, 474, 475, 796.

John Herritage Bryan to Ebenezer Pettigrew UNC

NewBern Oct. 28. 1841

My dear sir,

Your letter of the 18th inst. was forwarded to me here, from Ralh.

I am truly sorry to learn that your disease has returned upon you.— Had you not even now come up & stay a while with us before you go on to Washington.

We have concluded to let Mary come home with you in Nov[r] when you bring Mary P.— We had tho'[t] a little of letting her remain, but M[rs] B. has decided on her return with Mary P.—She fears the climate besides other reasons.—

I am glad to learn that your sons have retained their health & hope that Charles' steam is rising & doing well.

I am obliged by your sympathy for my sickness, but I do not know well how to quit Pitt & Edgecombe Courts.—

They have had a dreadful fall here M[r] M[c]Rae told me the other day that 150 white & black had died since June.— M[rs] Emery (daughter of M[rs] Vail) was buried this afternoon.—

I expect to be at Washington next week & to return from there to Ral[h]; I have had slight fever since I have been here but not to interrupt my attention to business.— We have just tried a famous libel suit of D[r] Saml. Dudley agst Thomas Robertson of Portsm[o] which has fagged me very much; it has occupied two days—my client Dudley got a verdict for 225 $.[1] He formerly lived in Plymo.—

I had feared that Tyler had upset & spoiled our mess of pottage.— It is very provoking after so long an agony to be compelled to fight all our battles over again.— I suppose you have heard of the deaths of Gov[r] Owen[2] & W. B Meares.[3]—

My kind regards to Charles & W[m]—

very truly yr friend & relation
Jn. H. Bryan

I forgot to mention that on the 9th of this mo. Mary had a fine boy & is doing very well.

[*Addressed*] E. Pettigrew Esq
Cool Spring
N.C

---

[1]Craven County court records for 1841 are missing.

[2]John Owen (1787-1841) of Bladen County died on October 9 at the home of Henry A. London in Pittsboro. He had been governor of North Carolina, 1828-1830. A Whig, he served as president of the National Whig Convention in 1839. The *Newbern Spectator* carried an obituary on October 18, 1841. Crabtree, *North Carolina Governors*, 76-77; Ashe, *Biographical History*, VIII, 400-401.

[3]This was probably William B. Meares of Wilmington, an attorney who served in the state House of Commons in 1818 and 1819 and in the state Senate in 1828-1829, 1830-1831, and 1833-1834. Moore, *History of North Carolina*, I, 493; Cheney, *North Carolina Government*, 274, 275, 291, 294, 300.

Henry Clay to Ebenezer Pettigrew A&H

Ashland [*Kentucky*] 10th Nov. 1841

My Dear Sir

I received your favor of the 19th Ulto. A few days before its arrival, Mr. Weimar reached home and informed me of the safe delivery of Twenty three of the mules, one having died on the way. I am extremely happy to learn, both from your letter and through Mr. Weimar, that you are pleased with them. As you had purchased without previously seeing them, I felt very solicitous on that point. If you will have them worked lightly and fed well the approaching winter, I think that you will afterwards find that they will work better and wear longer than any lot of mules you have ever had. The black mules are chiefly the get of a Poitou Jack that I imported from France; the two light bays mentioned in your letter were, I believe, the get of a Jack, owned also by me, that was produced by a Maltese Jack and a Jennette descended from the Knight of Malta, the property of Genl Washington.

I cannot think of availing myself of your liberal offer to bear one half or the entire loss of the mule that died. My stipulation was to deliver the mules to you, and the loss must therefore be mine. The Twenty three mules at $90 each produce $2070 from which deduct $50, advanced by you to Mr Weimar, and there remains a balance of $2020. Under the authority contained in your letter, I have this day drawn a check for $2020 on the Farmers and Planters Bank of Baltimore.

With high respect I am Your friend & obt Servt
H. Clay

E. Pettigrew Esq

P.S. I transmitted a letter under cover to Mr. Stanley for you, and one by mail. Of course they will now require no answer.

H. C.

[*Addressed*] E. Pettigrew Esq.
Belgrade.
Washington County,
Cool Spring P.O.
North Carolina

Thomas Turner to Ebenezer Pettigrew UNC

Windsor NC Nov 20 1841

Dear Sir—

In January last I made a deed of trust to John B Beasley for your benefit, conveying my interest in Mrs White's estate to pay you the money which you loaned to me in 1832 & 1833 and the interest /thereon/, and if any remainder, to pay for the Morus Multicaulis.—

At that time, (as indeed ever since,) the chief value of the estate lay in six negroes then and now in my possession in Plymouth. But the negroes were at that time involved in a suit in Equity wherein Pettijohn & Wm White were claiming them as belonging to Wm White deceasd's estate, and I as belong to his widow Mrs White's estate. If Pettijohn & Wm White had recovered, the negroes would have gone to Wm White's children, and I should have <had> got nothing. But if I recovered the negroes would go to Mrs White's legatees of whom I am one for a third, subject to the payment of her debts, about $800 to $900, or less.

The suit terminated /this summer/ agreeably to my expectations, and I recovered the negroes by a decree of the Supreme Court: so that all dispute about the right and title to them is ended.

And now at November County Court at Plymouth, I obtained an order for the sale of them to pay /Mrs White's/ debts and make division of the remainder among her legatees. The order is that the negroes, after advertising according to law, be sold at a credit of six and twelve months.

I shall advertise to sell them separately, and then all together; with right /reserved/ in myself to choose which set of bidders shall be the purchaser.—I shall so advertise because in the first place the law will require that they be sold separately, and in the next place because I wish to sell them all to one person so as not to separate Mother & children; hoping that some person, (yourself for instance,) will give one dollar more for the whole than the aggregate amount of the separate sales.—

The negroes are as follows—:

1 Hannah the mother aged about 36 to 40.
2 Wilson a boy aged about 10 to 11
3 John a boy aged about 8 to 9
4 A girl aged 5 to 6
5 A girl aged 3 to 4
6 A girl aged 1 to 2

These negroes are healthy. Here are 5 of 11 children the woman has had; the other 6 having been sold; not one of whom (so far as I ever heard) is dead. They are also on the side of father and mother of excellent temper and character. The woman has had but the one husband; he but the one wife; they have always lived peaceably together, and were never separated until Decm 1840. They have never been whipped or even scolded except so far as an old woman could scold them, so far as I ever heard.—; but have always been obedient and faithful and always at home, and at peace in the neighborhood.—

I am anxious for you to buy them, and this for several reasons; 1st my share of the purchase money will remain in your hands; 2d the credit is a long one; 3d the negroes are of that quality which time will increase in value faster than 10 P Cent on the purchase of them; 4th I wish you to see that they sell for their value, or if they sell for less, then I prefer you to have them at less than any other person; 5 I should be very sorry to separate them, or to sell them to a person likely soon to separate them; and 6thly I am anxious they should have a good home.

I shall wait to hear from you before I advertise the sale of them; as I will fix in the advertisement that day for the sale on which it will suit your convenience to be in Plymouth, where the sale /will/ be made.

I have not yet mentioned, as I ought to do, that one of the negroes (John) is yet involved in a suit, another suit, between Pettijohn & myself, (myself as executer of Mrs White,) which suit is in Plymouth superior Court, and that I shall wait the event of that suit before I sell him. In the mean time I shall keep possession of him, and shall let him go with the purchaser of his mother; if I like the purchaser when I know him, subject to my recall on the termination of the suit.

My paper is out. My health has been mighty bad all the fall, but I am recovering. My brother has been several times very sick this fall, but recovered soon, and has been and is now much engaged in his profession. I hope you and your sons and daughters at home and abroad have had, & have now, good health. You and they have my best wishes, and I am my dear friend truly yours

Th: Turner

[*Addressed*] Ebenezer Pettigrew Esq
Cool Spring P.O.
Washington Co
NC

Ebenezer Pettigrew to William Shepard Pettigrew UNC

Norfolk Nov. 21, 1841

My dear son,

I got down to Mr Johnstons plantation on Wednesday the day we left Edenton & one of his horses died in a short time after our arrival of grubs or cholic. On fryday we took the stage for this place & we leave tonight for Baltimore. Mr Johnston goes for the purpose of geting another pair of horses as he is on foot & there are none to be had at this place. I found Captain Dunbar here on his way home, and learned from him that the Bull had gone on by Capt. Bowen. I got a parcel of things at this place & have sent them by him to the care of your brother Charles. You had better send a cart for them as soon as you learn of their arrival. Among the articles is a barril of Oysters for Mr or rather Mrs Davinport. She will send you some. I would advise you as well as her & Mr D. to eat them cautiously. Tell them to pour salt water to them to prevent their spoiling. They cost like all the world. Tell Mr or Mrs Davenport that I got some cotton warp at this place & they can have some if they want. We have had a very little rain since I left I learn that there was a good deal of rain & some snow at Baltimore last week. You cant be too carefull of fire. If Mr William Norman should come before I return put him in the little room on the matrass at once or you cant move him after. Let Jim drive the horses as often as is <positively> necessary to keep them /positively/ gentle. It looks much like rain now & I think will rain today.

I learn that Mr Forbs has kicked up a dust sevier where he has gone which is Linconton.

We were told yesterday that one of the best corn dealing houses at this place had bargained for a mans crop say 1000 barrils to be delivered in January at seventy cents. It is yellow & of a good quality and it is the opinion that the article will not be low. so that our small crop will be of more value at at last. I found Godfry here geting a store of goods so you see there will no lack of stores in Scuppernong. Give my love to your Brother Charles & Respects to Mr & Mrs Davenport and believe me to be your affectionate father

E Pettigrew

N.B. my health continues much as when I left.

[*Addressed*] William S. Pettigrew esqr
Cool Spring
North Carolina

William James Bingham to Ebenezer Pettigrew UNC

Hillsboro' Dec'r 1st 1841.—

My dear Sir,

I rec'd your letter this morning, & gave Johnston instructions to be ready for to-morrow's stage. On the 27th ult. I forwarded my acc't to Cool Spring, showing a balance of $25 7¼/100 due me, to which add $\$3^{78}/_{100}$—expenses to Raleigh & postage since, making a total of $28.85¼/100

You will perceive from J's certificate, as also from the letter accompanying my acc't, that he has done admirably in his studies. His deportment too, both at home & at school, has been exemplary. I have had to find fault with him but once; and that for getting a suit of clothes without order, & indeed contrary to instructions; for which I punished him, as stated in my letter of the 27th ult.

You desire my ideas of J. in general, together with any suggestions as to what may be best to do with him?

Well, he has the capacity *to be* & *to do what he pleases*. He has not only the capacity but *the inclination* to be a scholar; and unless some malign influence should come over him, he cannot fail in that. He is inclined to think & act for himself, i.e. he has an independent turn of mind—a very valuable trait of character, when properly chastened by correct moral & religious sentiment—Yet he submits very readily to lawful authority. A more submissive & docile pupil no teacher could desire: yet it is necessary he should feel the *justice* as well as the *weight* of the authority exercised over him. His character, standing & success in life depend more on *moral* than *intellectual* influences, more on the *heart* than on the *head*. With such schooling in morals & common practical sense as his brothers & yourself will give him, I augur well for him.—

He will be able, in one year from next June, to make the acquisitions necessary to a creditable admission into college, even if he should do very little with his books next session.

In haste,
Yours, very truly,
W. J. Bingham

Hon. E. Pettigrew

P.S. On the other leaf you will find a rec't.

$28.85¼/100— Rec'd of Ebenezer Pettigrew twenty eight dollars, eighty five cents, in full of acc't for son Johnston at the Hillsboro' Academy.

W. J. Bingham

Dec'r 1st 1841.—

[*Addressed*] Hon. E. Pettigrew
Raleigh
N.C—

Ebenezer Pettigrew to James Cathcart Johnston UNC

Belgrade Dec 21, 1841

My dear friend

Your favour of the 6th found my home before my self, which was not untill the 13th. I regreted to learn of your inconveniences in returning home but they were nothing compaired /to/ mine with the children. I could not get from Washington City untill saturday at 12 M. and after a most miserable going in stages, cars, & omnibus between one set of cars to another, we got to breakfast on sunday morning to [Gas]ton, that place we left in about two hours (no boddy being in a hurry God help them) the clouds appearing like nothing but snow. Twelve /or 13/ passengers in the car & attached to us nine burthen cars, yes sir as I live nine burthen cars to drag up the country to god knows where. Well we went draging along and in about an hour the snow began to fall in uncommon quantity we holding on to our burthen untill we could go no longer & the conductor droped out some & continuing to drop out, untill the middle of /the/ afternoon when the snow was between 6, & 8 Inch deep & we alone could not go one inch & there we were in the middle of a deep cut 3½ miles from the Warren depot without anything to eat. The conductor took it afoot to this depot and just at night the agent came with a waggon & carryall to take to his house as many as would go. So I & my girls The Hon. Mr Rainer [*Kenneth Rayner*] & three other Gentlemen took out leaving five Ladies & the Hon. John Jones Reives Daniel [*John Reeves Jones Daniel*] who fetched up the next evening at night. The people were kind as they could be. They had no butter nor milk for the good woman said that her husband had a cow but she was inconvenient she sold her. The dwelling was a one room log house with a bed in it which the good woman gave up to the girls & went up the loft where there was another good woman & /her husband/ boarders & the husbands went with us men to the depot room where we stowed in all sorts of stile on the floor with dogs & tame raccoons, I had the Hon. Mr R. for my bed fellow who complained of being very sore in the morning & became quite wolfish as he said at intervals through the next day. Such times & circumstances are a stimulous to the gloom of my soul and if there is any time when I rise superior to my self it is then. I threw over us my big buffeloe skin & I know not when I had a better nights rest, rose perfectly refreshed next morning & such a day of mirth, cracking jokes & talking I hardly ever had, several of the travilers said they should remember that day before any other. In the middle of the day the Bishop & his Lady drove up to take passage but did not stay long /as we could not tell when we should leave that place./ I believe he had been to Warrington to settle a crime. Con affair between the Revd Mr

Backhouse & one of his congregation a married woman & confirmed this year. It was said at the depot that Backhouse was at night to /be/ tar & feathered & rode on a rail and this reaching his ears he thought proper to take out & after demanding an investigation thought it prudent to slope out for the south perhaps Texas, taking french leave of the whole concern. It is said to be a plain case in which there can /be/ no doubt & that his conduct for six months & after he was informed that he was suspected was most bear faced. It is a groaning affair among the bretheren at Raleigh I leave this affair to itself & return to our trip. At dark on monday night the cars & locomotives met from all places & after supper we left the Warren depot for Raleigh, where we arrived after 3 in the morning. There was not more than four inches of snow at that place & had there been no delay on the way & had we not taken that miserable burthen train we should have reached Raleigh in time. No road can ever prosper under such management. People will only travil it where they can go no other way.

After I got to Raleigh there was some bad weather & I determined not to leave untill a week in the mean time my daughter Mary was taken with a cold accompanied with fever & I began to fear greater delay, but it passed off & we left after a softening of the weather on the 9th in the stage for Tarborough & a more miserable trip I never did have traviling at the rate 3½ miles an hour, we were nineteen hours on the road in the smallest & worst stage in the United States. With myself & my three children we had not room to move in one way nor the other. I was so sore the next day that I could hardly move & have been quite sick since with cold & cough & yesterday was confined the greater part of the day with a severe affection of the head.

I found all things going on well & a great deal had been done. There is no mistake in William Pettigrew when he puts his head. Charles will return home after Christmas.

I find by your letter that you found at the half way house my old enemy the plate of butter that persecuted me so much the little time I was with it. I will bet that if it is not thrown to the dogs it may be put on the table every day from the time I saw it last & it will not be a fourth gone when I see it again, if years should elapse. The Lord preserve me from most of the North Carolina taverns, & I call myself a very plain eater too. I had a great deal of anxiety to learn how your creatures went that you got at Baltimore. I have seen Mr Davenport since his return from Edenton. He is quite delighted with your treatment of him. He is I think as good as the Bank for any engagement he may make. I consider myself bound for any bond that he may sign to you.

Mr Davenport brought to me Mr Con[s] account & the money in full for the corn shellers. In the account I find you have bought one.

You had better get a new nut for the pot. It will shell faster, I will send the one from here to Elizabeth City soon after Christmas.

If it is possibly in my power should Genl [*Thomas?*] Emory visit me I will let you know it, but can you not pay me & my five children a visit after every thing gets settled down in to a quiet which generally succeeds the excitement of Christmas, I assure you no visit could be more acceptable to them all, you know I need not speak of *my self*.

To prevent all unpleasant feelings that might be, I did not present your highly valued present to my dear daughter Mary untill our arrival at home. She requests me to present her kind regards to you & to say to you that she has not words to express her sincere thanks for it & your so flattering a rememberance of her.

While at Raleigh I met at Mr Bryans the Hon. Mr [*William H.*] Washington on his way to Washington City & while there I read to him your last political letter, the next day after Mr [*George*] Badger & Mr [*Richard*] Hines called to see us & while they were talking politically Mr Washington asked me to read to those gentlemen your letter, which I was not willing after some importunity to decline. You have no idea of the extasy they were thrown in at the reading, particularly Mr Badger & the high compliments paid to it with an earnest request that it could be extracted in the paper. I remarked that the last of the letter in reply to a former letter would show the ties by which I was bound. They & particularly Mr B. beged me to make [more] sincere the request for liberty to publish, which I now do as not only from them but myself. I do not believe that any thing can come out in the next five years (politically) that will be read with more avidity than the political part of those two letters. And now my dear friend I have writen you all sorts of a letter, please to pardon its imperfections for I cannot transcribe it & do not know that any study would better arrange it by me and will therefore conclude by making my three little childrens best respect to you who are around where I write, & mine to Miss Helen & the other Ladies of your family & believe me sincerely &

truely your friend
E Pettigrew

James C. Johnston esqr

N.B. Not knowing that I should see Mr Davenport before he left for Edenton I left the six boxes of Grays ointment at Mr Nichols Plymouth to be sent over in the boat to the Post Office where I suppose you would get it in the earliest time. I could find no agent in Washington City to Pleasants' paper, & wrote from Raleigh to Mr Stanly on the subject.

Mr Davenport handed me the corn taken from your hopper which you sent to me by him The second guess I was right. It is all in character. My God what a decline in the third generation What would the fourth be? What a nation such a set would make What nation would they be like unto? none that I know on earth.

I also felt quite axious the day we left Baltimore to stay another night for the purpose of seeing Genl Emory but I knew my time was short & it was lucky I lost no time for it would have been dreadfull to have been caught <there> in Washington City in the snow. I no not when I should have got home

E P.

[*Addressed*] James C. Johnston Esqr
Hayes
Edenton P. Office

Thomas Turner to Ebenezer Pettigrew A&H

Windsor NC Dec 28 '41

Dear sir

I received last evening your kind letter of the 20th.— I was very glad to hear from you and your sons and daughters, and especially to hear that they are with you. I know that you are exceedingly happy in them, and they in you. I am also glad to hear that your neice Miss Bryan is with you and them. Earth I should suppose could add little to the happiness of one with your success in such company; and I hope this happiness will long continue without anything to mar it. I wish I could be with you; especially do I wish that my brother could— But so it is that neither of us can. I am greatly gratified to read that you have lately had your health better than usual, and I hope it is the promise that your life shall be spun out to the longest span. A merry christmas and a happy /new/ year, and many returns of both, I pray may be the lot of all and each of you—

As for my brother and myself; but first of him. He had every now and then through August September and October pretty severe fits of the ague and fever; but he speedily recovered from each attack, and went to his work again. His practice was constant and laborious—For one time he did not go /regularly/ to bed to sleep for twelve days and nights, and at several /other/ times he was up two or three days and nights together; catching sleep as he could in the chairs and on benches. One would think this practice would be profitable; and so indeed it appears on the books. But when we come to gather it in, we find but little of it. The poor cannot pay, and the rich are dilatory and not easy to suit.—The season is now healthy, and practice is slacker than it was: yet no day passes over that some ailing person does not call or send for relief: so that the Doctor has no relaxation unless he will take it whether or not from the demands that are made upon him. This my brother cannot yet do, our circumstances are so bad and oppressive. It is said in some old books "that the Gods delight to see an honest man struggling with adversity." If they still have a taste of this kind, they may find what pleasure they please by looking down upon my brother; though I could /wish/ them that pleasure by beholding some other object.—

As for me; the sickness of last fall, worked me harder, and lower, and kept me down longer than any other I ever had. My constitution at last however prevailed, and now I am in good health again. But (shall I say it?) I am very low spirited, almost discouraged by the present state of my affairs and the aspect they bear to the future. However, Time will run on, and will take me with him—I shall not die till my time comes; and so, it is best, if I could, to live virtuously and happy until then;—and if I cannot live prosperously, why submit, and make the best of my fate.—

I am very sorry you decline purchasing the negroes. I wished to get them a good home—and as you own negroes, I was desirous you should have /these also/, because chiefly of their good temper and character, and because they will increase in value every day.—

Adieu my friend. I shall never think of you without regretting that I am moved from Plymouth—You will please remember me with great affection to those you have around you and believe that I am truly & sincerely Your

friend & hum sevt
Th: Turner.

My brother who has the greatest regard for is now 14 miles from home

[*Addressed*] Ebenezer Pettigrew Esq
Cool Spring
Washington County
N Carolina

John Herritage Bryan to Ebenezer Pettigrew UNC

Raleigh Jany. 1. 1842

My dear Sir,

I recd. your letter advising me of your arrival & was sorry to learn that you had such a disagreeable journey.—I feared that the staging between this place & Tarboro' was very bad, but it seems you had in its worst form:—The failure of the land sale, will I apprehend, injure the cause of Int[l] improvement. and places that ought to be patronized will suffer in consequence.—

A few days after you left Mary Bryan was taken with the prevailing cold & suffered from it for a few days.—M[rs] B. has been unwell for two or three days & has kept her bed today.—Old M[rs] Brickell is quite sick.—M[r] Smedes[1] whom the Bishop wishes to take charge of the School, has arrived, but merely for the present on a visit of examination & survey &c, I have not learned yet, how he likes the prospect.—

A gang of thieves broke into my carriage house about 6 nights ago & stole my saddle & some other things—they were runaway negroes; two of them have since been apprehended; they were surprized in the woods & were armed with rifles.—

I understand that the Rev: M[r] Goodman is at Wash[n] City seeking for an office.—

The Supreme Co. is now in session, but there is an unusually small number of new suits, the hard times seem to repress the spirit of litigation, as well as other kinds of spirit.—

Tell Mary P. that John D Hawkins Esq[2] gave a great Christmas frolick which lasted several days, Mary Bryan & Alex[r] Blount were among the guests; they had a great deal of dancing & good cheer, there were about 150 persons in attendance.—

The Rev. M[r] M[c]Rae of NewBern, took tea with us yesterday eveng. he said that he expected to leave NewBern this year,[3] he assigned the unhealthiness of the summer & fall as the cause.—

M[rs] B says she hopes you & Mary will take good care of Nancy; she says that Mary has left several articles of clothing which she thinks she ought to have carried.—

M[rs] B. & Mary send their love to you & the girls *& boys*: Remember me kindly to Chas W[m].

Very truly Yr friend & relation
Jn. H. Bryan

Mary recd. a letter from Anne Henderson in which she said that Mary Lee was very sick with the scarlet fever, at Miss Breschard's school—Anne had recd Mary P's letter

[*Addressed*] E Pettigrew Esqr
Cool Spring
N.C

---

[1]The Reverend Aldert Smedes became principal of St. Mary's School for girls. Battle, *History of the University*, I, 644.

[2]This was probably the John D. Hawkins (1781-1858) who owned a large plantation in Franklin County. A Democrat, Hawkins was a state senator and a strong advocate of railroads. Ashe, *Biographical History*, V, 160-162.

[3]Cameron F. McRae, rector of Christ Church, New Bern, did indeed leave to go to Emmanuel Church in Warrenton. *Journal of the Diocesan Convention, 1841*, 3; *Journal of the Diocesan Convention, 1842*, 3. He resigned for "private and domestic reasons." Carraway, *Crown of Life*, 147-148.

Stevens S. Conner[1] *to Ebenezer Pettigrew* UNC

Livingston Sumter C[o] *Ala.* 2[d] Jany 1842

Hon Eben[r] Pettigrew

Dear sir,

Before I left N.C. I promised to write you after I had been here long enough to see something of the country. I will now attempt to do so.

I must confess I am not as well pleased with this *State* as when I was here last winter I have had a much better oppertunity of seeing and knowing what has and can be done. every thing here [is p]redicated upon cotton and it seems that [all] business is done with a reference to that article, the Lands are very fine as good as any man could wish for—on the banks of the Rivers and in the *cane breaks* & [Perarea] Land but still there has been a failure in the last three crops—of about one half. in addition to that the prices is extreemly low & now ranges in Mobile from 7 to 10 cents pr lb, only about 200 Bags has been sold at the last price, the Planter is subjected to the heaviest expenses here I ever have known it takes one in every ten to pay the freights commissions & Bagging &c—and a fair average for a hand is five bags of 500 lbs each to make, Some planters with a small force has made as high as ten bags to the hand but when one is found to do that under the most favourable circumstances twenty will be found who have not made *four*—and the prospect is that cotton will still go lower as the increase is more than the consumption, I would say to any friend if they are comfortably situated in North Carolina & are doing a fair businss *stay there* and be content, I will be oblige[d] to You to say to Mr Davenport, that [I] was in an error in my views about the Cotton Country. it Costs a great sum to get comfortably fixed here, and then then expectations are seldom realized, we have sold a fair proportion<s> of our goods as we are told by those who are in business here, be pleased to make my best respects to Mess Charles & William Pettigrew, and accept for Youself and them the best wishes of

Your friend & Obdt. servant
S. S. Conner

---

[1]Stevens S. Conner had bought *morus multicaulis* buds from Ebenezer Pettigrew and Josiah Collins in 1839. Account of Stevens S. Conner, January-March, 1839, Pettigrew Family Papers, Southern Historical Collection.

*[Ebenezer Pettigrew to William James Bingham]** UNC

Lake Phelps Jan 5, 1842

My dear Sir,

I receivd your favour by Johnston on his arrival at Raleigh and forthwith according to my letter previous, deposited in the Cape Fear branch Bank twenty nine dollars to your credit & subject to your draft, it being the amount due on your account with me & which sum I presume you have received before this.

I was much pleased to learn from your letter the character which Johnston had acquired. He seems yet to confirm that character but still there is a degree of self will about him that I am determined to put down if it was to the keeping him at home /untill he is grown/ & under my spetial eye to that time. I am determined he shall not take that early start of most of his maternal uncles, if I live, which early start has in my opinion nearly if not entirely destroyed all their usefullness. I was astonished to see in the account his half subscription to the New York Herald. I know if you had had any idea of the paper, you would have thrown ten times the amount of the subscription in the fire. Of all the vilinous papers & the corrupt fellow who publishes it in the United States they are the most so, & I have been induced to take it for the money articles & foreign news, which are important to my business, which news & articls most of the other papers are to abominable lazy to get & even to publish. As one of a thousand evidences of the corruption of the paper, look at Maddam Rastals of her powders to make as she says married women miscarry, sent to any part of the United States in packages by mail at $5 a paper. You will please on the receit of this look at the paper & put Johnstons half in the fire or do in any other way with it that you may think best. I had for myself determined not to take it anymore after the present subscription & should by no means have continued it up to this time but for the reason above.

I also regret Johnston joining the temperance society. I fear it will in time make a drunkard of him. All societies are in my opinion for persons of mature age to join who have some settled opinions & minors are to be governed by those persons of mature age and there is the excelence of your school. You will govern, and that is the reason why I have valued it so highly. So far as I know of Johnston he seems constitutionally sober & no good can arrive to him from his pledging his honour not to taste another drop of any thing stimulating. I have never known any one yet that had not tasted any thing stimulating who if they ever tasted stimulants for the first time after they were twenty five, did not life in drunkenness.

It was entirely accidental that I discovered what Johnston had done. I some times invite my sons to drink but had not said any thing on that subject to him, since his return home, but one day I took a glass of old rum & water & remarking the mildness of it offered to him to taste, when he refused in so singular a manner that his sister says why Johnston you have not joined the temprance society, when he replied yes & [*incomplete*]

William James Bingham to Ebenezer Pettigrew UNC

Hillsboro.' Jan'y 10th 1842.

My dear Sir;

I had the pleasure to receive your letter this morning. You judged rightly that I was not aware of the exceptionable moral character of the Herald. I objected to subscribing for the paper without knowing its character; but the prompt response, 'Pa takes it,' removed my scruples at once: so for once you see my confidence in your judgment & good principles betrayed me into an error. So you are, innocently I admit, 'particeps criminis'. My impression was that Bennett[1] was editor; but this impression was removed by your being a subscriber. Johnston may have been governed in his selection by your example. He did not seem to know that he was to spend the vacation at home, & inquired whether you had written me on the subject. On very many subjects you & I coincide in opinion: but while we agree perfectly in our ideas of the horrible nature of intemperance, we differ in regard to the best mode of arresting that tremendous evil. You think me ultra, & I think you behind the age. Nevertheless you may regard me more *ultra* than I really am. When my little boys consulted me on the subject of signing the "Washington pledge," I uniformly referred them to their parents for advice before doing so. To young men I opposed no obstacle. I do not remember whether Johnston consulted me or not;

(I incline to think he did not) but if he did, I am very sure he was referred to you. If you desire it I will have his name stricken off, of which fact you can inform him. I have not had the slightest reason to suspect him of drinking since his return. On the contrary, I am satisfied that he did not.

I believe that the appetite for intoxicating drinks is an *artificial appetite*, easily acquired by *occasional indulgence*, & especially by *stated, daily indulgence*. I consider no boy, or young man, safe, who takes a *daily drink*. *Total abstinence* is a perfect safeguard, perhaps *the only perfect safeguard*. The sooner a youth begins to taste, the earlier will he *form the appetite*, & the sooner & the more deeply will the desire & love of stimulants become incorporated into his constitution. While total abstinence is *the only remedy* for drunkards, it is, to say the least, *safe* for all. I do not refer to the medicinal use; nor do I by any means admit that the use of spirits is a crime per se. This doctrine I repudiate as fanatical. The former I defend on the ground of expediency. I shall urge no child of mine, before capable of judging for himself, to join a Tem. Society; but should he incline to do so, I shall not forbid it.—I never knew my father to taste spirits but once, and then by mistake, for water. He taught his children to regard every intoxicating drink as dangerous, & kept none in his house. You Know my habits on this subject. Every child of his is as thorough-going as myself. There is this advantage in taking a decided stand while young—viz—One escapes all importunity on the part of his companions to drink. It is no longer an open question. By the grace of God I am resolved that no child of mine shall ever be able to plead his father's example for tasting any intoxicating liquor.—But enough on this topic.—Viewing man in his most comprehensive relations, I consider the *sincere Christian* the only man on earth to be envied. Confining our views to this life, the independent farmer is the only man I could envy. Did I dare, I would devote myself to agriculture. Three considerations forbid. First. It is the imperative duty of every man to use the talents God has given him for the benefit of his species; & if I have any talent, I believe it is to manage boys, & to beat into their heads the little I know myself. 2ndly I can do a better part by my family in the Academy, than on a farm. 3rdly Farming involves—in the South at least—the control of a larger negro force than I am [*torn*] to command.—Should my school go down, most cheerfully, nay joyously, would I fall back on my little farm: for this would obviate the first & second difficulty. Should Providence spare my life, & continue my bodily & mental health, I expect to teach, precisely where I am, for at least twenty years to come. I would not exchange my berth for any professor's chair in the Union, were it in my power to do so. I aspire to no higher round of the literary ladder. I am one of the very few who can honestly say they are contented with their condition.

I sent a check (a few days ago) to a friend in Raleigh for $28 85¼/100. He drew $29.—& the little balance is set to your credit.—I shall forthwith order the discontinuance of the Weekly Herald, leaving the editor to refund or retain the money at his pleasure.

The school opens pretty fairly.—Judge it, no worse, rather better indeed than when I wrote you last. My family well. Mrs B's kind regards to yourself & all your children; Anna's & Robina's to Mary & Nancy. I suppose Mary is nearly or quite grown. Ann grows *distressingly* fast, tho' I am happy to say her mind keeps pace with her body. Please present my affectionate regards to Charles, William, Johnston, Mary & Nancy, and assure yourself of my unabated respect & friendship.

W. J. Bingham

You will not think me an enthusiast in agriculture when I tell you I have not set foot on my farm but twice since I sowed the wheat which you were kind enough to send me—Sept'r 28th.—more than three months ago. It looked very promising six weeks ago.—I sowed two heads of the California wheat in my garden, but expect little from it. I suspected at the time it was a humbug. I have bought another capital hand—have my complement now—two regular field hands being my maximum. So far my hands do not require overseeing. Excuse this long, prosing letter. I shall be happy to hear from you or the boys, provided you do not pay the postage of the letters.

[*Addressed*] Hon. E. Pettigrew
Cool Spring
Washington Co.
N.C—

[1]James Gordon Bennett (1795-1872), publisher of the *New York Herald*, started the successful newspaper in 1835. *CDAB*, 67-68.

*Ebenezer Pettigrew to William James Bingham** UNC

[*Lake Phelps, January 22, 1842*]

My Dear Sir,

I regret to learn by the papers of the death of Judge [*William*] Norwood. Poor old gentleman; I trust & believe he has made a happy entrance into that blessed world where there will be no more sorrow, no more trouble, no more death, but all be joy & everlasting blessedness. His bereaved family & friends cannot mourn as one without hope.

I received your favour of the 10th ult. in the cour[*s*]e of the mail, and in the greater part of it we seem to agree & I will only make a few remarks in reply to it; least it might be erroneously thought, that I am advocating a use of ardent spirits in such a manner as might lead to excess, which is the least of my thought. I have never lived in a house where any one used stimulant to excess, nor do I believe that I could continue in one of that descrition long. No one can have a greater horror of deep drinking & drunkenness than I have. My inclination until a few years led to a free use of stimulants; & I have learned that a considerable number of my father's family incline to free living. I have drank occasionnally up to this time, was /not/ intoxicated until the age of twenty-five & but two or three tim/es/ since, but I was always under law, which I made for myself, & I thank my blessed creator that I am verging close to the end of life with perfect sobriety & although I have not in any restrained my to sons, they have arrived at their present age with perfect temperance. Wine was little drank in my fathers time, therefore little came to his share, being always too poor to buy it. I have often h<eard>/eard/ him say that he never was in the least intoxicated, & that did not beleive that he ever drank more than two gallons of spirits in any one year I had a brother who alas! deid in his twenty-first year who, not restrained from drik, was as temperate as my father. So you observe, my dear sir, the difference of our fathers as to themselves and their children, and the same end is attained: all are passing through life perfectly temperate, I was in my twenty-fifth year when my father died & from my fourteenth year, with the exception of about 18 mon[ths] lived with and not far from him until his death. I well remembered his example & precept, & was of the opinion that he was as near wright as poor frail human nature could be. I was from home when he was taken for death & fearing that I would not arrive in time my mother said to him, "is there any thing you wish to say to ebenezer," his reply was, "no, I have talked a great deal to him in my life & when I am dead he will remember it." I arrived before his dissolution, & the principal remark he made to me was, "take care of your mother," my reply to which was, "if I do not may I die the death of the wicked." She was my stepmother & lived under my protection 26 years; and her last words of approbation were, two night, before, her death is a consolation which the world cannot take away, I am sorry to say that I had all the evil propensities which flesh is heir to, and cannot have gone through life as well (but alas awfully imperfect) without that earthly guide through the mercy of a kind providence. Johnston says he did not consult you & he is I fear too much of a sheppard [*Shepard*] to consult his father therfore he did as the impulse of the moment directed him. I will by no means use my authority to have his name stricken off, least if he become a drunkard some 25 years to come it may be laid to my door. I will leave him to himself, for good or evil, I will now thank you for the *great compliment* which you paid me in telling that I am behind the age. I consider it a great compliment, it is my boast that I am of that past age, the age of my father, & I am with all my power exerting myself to keep & raise my children in that past age, & I pray God they may continue in it to their life's end. To be called a gentleman of the old school is my pride, I then rank with those great & good men who have been gathered to their fathers, & have scarcely left any equal behind. Why sir what is the character of the<re> present age, I know you two well for me to answer the question, but I will say it is only nessessary to look into any newspaper to be disgusted with the present age, and for the aged to I am glad I was not born in this age <T> thank god my time is closing. Why, sir, in my early day the name of speculator was a reproach, but in this day to take all the money from a Bank yes, a fellow using all the money put in his hand is but a spec/ulator/ & this gentleman who has brought to beggary thousands of widows & children passes through the country with as much assurance & more importance than the faithful servant, and Why?, because he has given dinners & entertainments to the great & rich of this age. This is truly the age of faitlessness, sycophancy, & insurbordination, and may god protect my children from its baneful influence, I herewith inclose an extract from a sermon taken from the Newbern paper of Jan. 15, 1842 and which I think is precisely in point. I will correct an error which you seem to have fallen into, that I think you are ultra, Whatever others may think it never was my opinion: flogging in your school, is behind the age; and for which I put a double value on it, Where there is flogging (with your temperance) there is order & government, without which a school is worth nothing, & if I were not to send Johnston to your school, I should close his education abroad. I will mention another evidence of your being of my age. You expect to teach school for a living. & up to the time of your retiring from business. So it was in my day. Teachers continued to the end of theirs days', but alas! in these days the schoolroom is but a stepping stone to quacking in the professions. In conclusion: societies, in general, are too fanatical, & arbitrary for my republican nature, & I avoid them, & I will advise my children to enter them with the greatest caution. I am glad to learn of the health of Mrs Bingham and children. Charles & Johnston & Mary & Nancy are with me, they are and have been all well. Mary and Nancy send their best respects to Mrs B., Anna & Robina, To which please to add that of Charles & Johnston & as well as Myself, & accept the same for yourself, & assure yourself of my sincere frendship,

E. Pettigrew

W. J. B. William has arrived, and joins us in his best respects. E. P.

William James Bingham to Ebenezer Pettigrew UNC

Hillsboro'—March 8th 1842.

My dear Sir;

I was much gratified by the receipt of your long letter, and still more so by its perusal. As we agree on so many points, I think we may well *agree to differ* on the single subject of Temperance Societies. Had you witnessed the wondrous effects, I had almost said the *miracles*, wrought by the W.T.S.—Maniacs restored to their right minds—the lion changed into the lamb,—the vulture into the dove,—the care-stricken wife assuming a cheerfulness unknown for years,—hungry & ragged children well fed & clothed, whatever might be your views of the principles by which such effects were produced, I know your benevolent heart would rejoice in the results & pray for the permanence of the reformation.—In reference to 'gentlemen' aye & ladies too, 'of the old school,' my sentiments accord perfectly with your own: but you do me too much honor in ranking me with men whose character I revere, & whose manners and conduct I would fain emulate. I do most cordially despise the arrogant pretensions, the coxcomical airs, the foolish extravagance, the luxurious indolence, and above all the affected contempt of honest labor, which characterize so many of our modern *would-be-gentlemen. Our* fathers taught *us* better. I deplore with you the degeneracy of the times,—the corruption of morals,—the loss of ancient integrity,—the decay of ancient virtue. But I must not inflict an essay on you.—

The family are all much comforted by the confident hope that the venerable Judge Norwood has exchanged the pains & sorrows of earth for the happiness & peace of heaven.—

Now, my dear Sir, having great confidence as well in your friendship as your soundness of judgment, I desire, in a *confidential* way, to ask your views & counsel in reference to a matter, which may be of much consequence to my family, & of course to myself.—In the family arrangements consequent upon Judge N's death, I may possibly, at the end of the year, remove to Jno. N's present residence, & he to the old mansion. To rear my boys *out of town* has always been a darling project of mine. The distance from the Academy would not be too great; & my assistants boarding in town would obviate the evils of my being out of it. I w'd also be much more convenient to my little farm. But now comes the important subject of inquiry & advice. In the event of moving I think of changing the character of my school from a *public* to a *private* one; limiting the number to twenty four; building a school house, employing one able assistant; M^r Jo. Norwood, who lives from two to three hundred yards from John's, boarding all the boys, & becoming along with me responsible for their moral government. The boys to be prepared, if parents desire it, for advanced classes in college, say for the junior.—Now several grave questions arise. Can I thus discharge as well my duties as a member of the community? If so, Can I get the requisite number of scholars at such a price as to remunerate my toil? For I should labor, if possible, harder than I now do; and my large & growing family requires that my income should not be diminished, but rather increased. The fact is, as I grow older, tho' I do not feel less willing to labor, and am not conscious of any decay in my capacity either to teach or to govern, but on the contrary think that practice has improved my powers in both respects, yet I do feel the moral responsibility for so large a number growing more oppressive & onerous, especially as they are *scattered* over so large a surface, as to make it impossible [*torn*] exercise, by day & by night, the vigilance, which [*torn*] indispensable to preserve them /from/ evil. I have given you a mere outline of the project. The details could not be fully entered into in the compass of a sheet. These I must leave you to imagine.—As the event of removal even is doubtful, & the change of plan not a necessary consequence of a change of residence, you will perceive the reason of my requesting you to regard the matter as confidential.

Please remember me kindly to all your sons & daughters (in which Mrs B. & the children w'd join me, if aware of my writing, but they are all in bed) and assure yourself of the unabated esteem & regard of your friend

W. J. Bingham

I have written in much haste, & at a late hour. You will excuse any blunders or omissions. The scheme does not contemplate that Mr N. should have any thing to do with the teaching—Buildings to be all *between* & in full view of both.

[*Addressed*] Hon. E. Pettigrew
Cool Spring
Washington Co.
N.C.—

John Baptist Beasley to Ebenezer Pettigrew A&H

Plymo 30th March 1842

E Pettegrew Esq[r]

D Sir

M[r] A [*Henry Alexander*] not being here at this time, & fearful he might not return to night from Edenton, have thought it advisable to open your letter directed to him. In order that it might be noticed

He as well as myself will always have due respect to your advice and opinions in general believing that they are at all times entitled to a friendy consideration and deserve respect

I myself however, being tolerably well skilled in financial matters, rather feel inclined to kick at the sentence of condemnation you have passed upon my Bank Stock. I cannot consent that it shall be put upon the same footing with the rotten institutions of other states. well knowing it to be equal, if not superior to any Bank stock in the Union. This is an undoubted fact, and its currency abroad has had less variation in N York than any s or western state paper in the union and still stands higher at the present my stock will now sell for 97½ & I will not take it. & you will say why, because it has depreciated less in value, than any other species of property in the country It is therefore better than and besides it is always cash when I wish to use it. I therefore, when it becomes necessary can avail myself of any bargain that may turn to my advantage, corn negroes & lands have fallen much more in value than this Bank stock, In a word it is now & will continue always to be good except fires & thieves destroy it

This matter however does not disturb my mind the *100*dreth part as much as our national matters they trouble me beyond comprehension at moments I spend a hopeful thought, that the theatened storm will blow over, but my reccollection hurries me back to take a look of seriousness to the many combinations of circumstances detailed in your letter & I must say that I am ready to acknowledge that our country is in a deplorable condition, & If we shall avoid a war, Genl [*Lewis*] Cass Is deserving his countrys everlasting gratitude for rousing the Frenchmen into action, but for this circumstance alone Briton would have still contended for all the slaves being liberated in Cuba, that have been brought in the Island since 1820 in violation of treaty with spain, but as it is Britain has now withdrawn her demand. If she had have succeeded in this, her next philanthropic step can be easily judged. these are the things that baffles my Judgment all others are at present of minor consideration when brough in contact with them. I hope however that we may yet ward of these melancholy and impending evils without either injury to us or the nation

As to money, dont talk about it if it was not for what few herrings & shad on the River we should have no money at all If you need any you can have it is worth 3 pr ct a month on Baltimo[re.] Jim has offered to sell me Squire Charles I cant buy I am well horsed now. Kept a horse 8 months and rode twice. He is out for his victuals & clothes & Corn does me more good I saw M[r] Johnson here a few days ago we agreed in opinion as it regards the movements of England we are all well & send you all our best respects I hear nothing from the S West but a state of Bankruptcy

very respectfully yr Obt St
J B Beasley

[*Addressed*] Ebenezer Pettegrew Esq[r]
Belgrade

Carmichael, Fairbanks and Company to Ebenezer Pettigrew UNC

26 Wall St, New York, Apl. 15, 1842

E. Pettigrew Esqr

Sir

Your favour of Mar 23[d] to Edtr of Tory Whig is at hand and in answer we enclose copy of Report on Machines by Committee from Our Institute—The cost of a machine for canal purposes would be about $5000 to $7000 and easily changed to an upland machine—The machines are particularly advantageous in Canals, inasmuch as while excavating they at same time if necessary deposit alternately from side to side leaving the breadth of the cut and embankments proportionate to the radius of the sweep made by the crane and vibration of the chain by which the shovel is suspended which will give a canal of ten to forty feet in width as may be desired according to size of Crane—If the Excavation is in dry and firm soil and where the water is kept out, the upland machines require no alteration and are adapted to immediate use; but if in swamp or marsh where the contrary is the case the machine is nescissarily placed in a boat or scow performing her work in the same manner as in the latter case and will excavate to any required depth proportionate to the size of crane the ordinary machines from four to Eight ft. They are easily kept in repair and having worked them on our own contracts with most perfect success we are satisfied of their superiority over every other mode—they taken down, moved and put up, with about same time, facility & expense of the ordinary locomotive enjines—and twenty Dolls per day is an ample sum for interest, fuel, mens wages, "wear & tear" of machinery, which will keep them constantly renewed and perfect for a series of years—

In conclusion we would recommend your visiting New York as suggested, inasmuch as we have two machines at work in Brooklyn where you can witness their opperation and receve all explanation relative to their application for your purposes, as well as terms for using the same—

Respectfully
Yours etc
Carmichael Fairbanks & Co

P.S. As the machines are within twenty minutes of our office one day will be all time necessary to detain you here — Office No 7 Second Story 26 Wall St

[*Addressed*] E. Pettigrew Esqr
Barnums Hotel
Baltimore
Md—

[The Reverend] Charles Aldis to Ebenezer Pettigrew UNC

Somerset Place, April 16th 1842.

My dear Sir,

I cannot sufficiently express to you the pain which I have felt in reading your note just received—I had entirely misunderstood the Bishop in relation to the Conversation with you, of which you speak. I had supposed the matter in question to have been fully settled and that you had expressed your willingness to accept the office of Senior Warden of the Church—an idea which I now find to have been entirely unwarranted.

I do not for a moment doubt the weight and importance which you attach to the subject nor that you are conscientiously assured of your duty in the matter and permit me to add my conviction, Sir, that you would act *in every case*, in such way as appeared to you correct—But will you allow me in the most respectful <way> manner to suggest, whether you may not have viewed the subject in a *mistaken* light? You are anxious to escape *responsibility*—but is that a *possible* thing? especially for one placed as you are Sir, in a station of Commanding influence?

If you take part with the Church, by becoming a prominent officer in it, you lend the weight of your *name* to forward the interests of an institution which you yourself profess (and I most heartily believe you) to regard with "the most profound respect and veneration"—If, on the contrary, you withdraw yourself from all concern with the Church, what *must* be the effect of such withdrawal upon the people of this country with whom as you must be aware, your influence is *very great*?

May I then request you to reconsider the matter before giving us a final answer?—I am quite sure that you desire to do that which is right—will you forgive me then, if I have perhaps too boldly ventured to suggest that your view of this matter may be mistaken? I should ill discharge my duty as well to the Church as to yourself, did I forbear thus plainly to express my own opinion, upon a Subject connected as I conceive this to be, with the welfare of *both*. And trusting that you will receive it in the spirit in which it is given, I am Dear Sir

With the utmost respect & esteem Yours.
Charles Aldis

E. Pettigrew Esq[r]
Bonarva

[*Addressed*] Ebenezer Pettigrew Esq[r]
Bonarva

Ebenezer Pettigrew to James Cathcart Johnston UNC

April 18, 1842 Lake Phelps

My dear friend,

With great pleasure I received your favour of the 14 ult. & I carry this answer to it with me as far as Plymouth on my way with Mary to school again. I was much gratified to learn that I had not given you either displeasure or mortification in showing your letters. Be assured it was the least of my wish, and that they were spoken of in the highest terms. I do not know (upon cool reflection) whether your reason is not a good one that you do not wish any thing you say or do to go to the public. I can say with you (though I do not know that you do say so) that the world is <not> not worthy of it, and if you will allow *me* to make the expression I do not think the world is worthy of either of us, and I now almost regret that I ever cared enough about it, to do more than scratch an area of earth merely to get bread enough to sustain my nature untill that power that sent me here that thought proper to take me away. I always did feel a great contempt for the world in general & I fear before I die (which I hope will not be long first) I shall dispise it. Which ever way I cast my eyes, which ever way I move I see something to condemn and whatever move is made to me by Church or State it is with sinister motives. No candor, no honesty, no plain open dealing, no nothing but a constant effort of man to overreach man. The Almighty God has created thousand of worlds and surely this must be the Hell of all of them, for all the devils are here, at least there are as many devils in this world as any thousand worlds ought to have. You may perhaps think from the forgoing remarks that some new developments have taken place. I will say that something is alway opening to my view but nothing very particular, but as you /very/ properly said the world is out of joint, yes the whole world has got or alway had the devil in it and I could wish if it can get no better that the end was come. I am as ready for the day of judgment as I ever shall or expect to be.

From the bursting expression of opinion I fear you may think I am in a difficulty with some of my children and /must/ remark that my sons are sober, attentive, and idustrious as I would wish them to be, & my daughters are discreet, affectionate & perfectly advisable, and if I would ask any more of them /than/ they give it would be unreasonable. I have not had a jar with them (except Johnston when he first came) the whole winter, neither have they as I believe had a spar with each other. There has not been a fever nor any sickness since they got together, & I have as much composure of mind as one of Gods poor imperfect being can have. But I am declining, in strength, in health, & in mind, & it is time I had left the world. I have had time enough in it, am tired looking at it and am willing to close my eyes on it forever & forever Amen.

I am at present in some little difficulty with the church. When Bishop Ives was here he made a strong appeal to me to consent to be senior warden of the church in Scuppernong, /which/ after several refusals I told him that all I could say was that I would consider on the subject & give M^r^ [*Charles*] Aldis an answer. The next sunday notice was given requesting the friends of the church to meet on the first monday of May to appoint a vestry & organise a church & a week after I understood that Mr Aldis should say that I had consented to be senior warden &c &c. and last week I addressed a letter to Mr A. informing him that I had given the subject in conversation with Bishop Ives, a calm consideration and had thought but to decline it, to which I today received an answer of the most regreting sort and beging me to reflect again on the subject. Telling me that there was /great/ responsability on me which I could not remove, that I have great influence with the people of this county, & if I withdraw they cannot be induced to come forward & join the church. So you see my dear friend I am again fairly at points with the church, and all, I fear, because I will /not/ come forward and do a certain thing that a certain man & another little understrapper may have the credit of doing in five years what it was thought never could be done, & old Pil Garlic may go to the devil then for /all/ they care. I know that it is to ring through the state that I promised to accept the appointment & that I have falsified my word, & I mean to say very little about it, but I now call God to witness that I gave the Bishop no reason to think any such think than the bare word, that the most I could say on the subject was that I would agree to think on <The subject> it and give Mr Aldis an answer.

I had prepaired an answer to Mr Aldis' letter, but no answer was particularly requested; I am advised not to send it & have therefore concluded to take the advice, but to give you my sentiments on the subject I will insert a copy, as follows.

Bonarva Ap 18, 1842

My dear Sir,

I have received your letter of the 16th and regret exceedingly that the conversation between Bishop Ives and myself has been misunderstood. It shows the disadvantage of oral instead of writen communications. The suggestions made in your letter I receive as writen with a christian spirit. I have always been sensible of the great responsability I was under to the world and more particularly to my children and have endeavered as much as in my power lay to set good examples in it & to them and to bring <them> up my children in the fear & admonition of the Lord. It is now nearly half a century since I have been an intimate observer of all that has passed and I recollect a great deal and am constrained to say that to attempt to christianise the community by any new act of mine is what I cannot undertake, withall there is certainly a great mistake of opinion as respects the influence which I have in the community at large as well as among those professing christianity. My observation justifies the remark. From my present feelings I am constrained to ask of the world to let me be quiet the few remaining days which I have to stay in it, & which I trust are about to be numbered.

Please to assure yourself of my sincere respect & good will

E Pettigrew

This idea I know will suggest itself to you My dear Friend, that I am the link between the sinners & christians, & the gentlemen & the vagabonds. I will cease.

I have filled one sheat and will begin another, My health is & has been declining for a month. I think I am threatened with inflamation of the intestines & have to quit all stimulants, from the pain which they give, I have also to quit eating meat but to a limited extent, so that my time in this world is becoming very tiresome. Did you ever see such a season? no frost no mater from what point the compass the wind may blow, neither do I expect one to do injury, for the ground is now too warm to allow a freze I think. Wheat still continues to look promising & to head well. As for the Lake wheat I think the prospect equal to anything I ever had even in former days, & Belgrade as good as I have had at that place, but there is a month yet before harvest & I will promise myself nothing from that quarter. The corn is coming on finely, was planted in good order & good time & at least we make a good begining. We have been a little too dry untill the <har> two last days, when we had a fall of rain sufficient & I fear will be too much for the wheat, for it is about to be in blossom. The interval between planting & working out the corn will be spent in the new canal which seems to be the all absorbing object, almost to the exclusion of every thing else. I have made another shipment of corn to Charleston & have a prospect of seventy five cents. I have an opinion that corn will be in demand if not higher as the season advances. There is certainly not as much on the seaboard as was thought nor enough to supply the demand.

You wish to know what the is the price of the corn sheller and ointment. I regret that you are so particular, but I will answer. The first is twenty dollars & the latter three dollars.

I am sorry to learn of the death of Mr Palmer on his own account as well as on account of its increasing your labours. Poor man I did not think when I saw him that was so soon to be numbered with the dead. Pray did his neighbor Blount who was so sick when we were there die or get well?

I hope your new horses meet your fullest expectation.

I was much relieved at the payments which your letter gave me on my note, for I had thought I owed twice the amount, & had been casting in my mind how it was to be paid. I hope to go a great way towards sinking the debt with the present crop. The times are very doubtfull, but with me it is all important, in as much as dead or alive I intend to divide off after the present crop. The present state of things will not do for me & I must change them, so that all may know what is theirs.

My sons & daughters desire their kind regards to you Please to make mine to Miss Helen & the other Lades of your family and assure yourself of the sincere Esteem

and regard of friend
E. Pettigrew

James C. Johnston esqr

N.B. On the subject in your letter respecting the miserable state of the country and mankind in general, I agree with you verbatim et literatem.

E P.

[*Addressed*] James C. Johnston Esqr
<Hayes>
Edenton
Edenton P. Office
No Ca

Henry Clay to Ebenezer Pettigrew UNC

Ashland 1st June 1842.

My Dear Sir

I postponed acknowledging the receipt of your friendly letter of March until my return home, that I might make enquiry as to the State of the fact in respect to two of the mules in the lot which Mr. Weimar delivered to you for me. I have accordingly made enquiry of my Servant who accompanied him, and you are right in your conjecture. The Servant says that two of the mules gave out on the journey from lameness, and not standing the journey well, and Mr. Weimar swaped them for the two which you got. I suspect some fraud in the exchange, but if there were I have not been able to get it out of the Servant, and I have not seen Weimar, of whom, by the by, I know very little He was engaged by my son, in my absence, to take charge of the Mules. I hope the two obtained in the exchange may turn out well, as I feel quite Sure the others will; but I shall regret extremely if you should be disappointed with any of them.

I thank you, my good friend, for your kind wishes for my happiness and prosperity in my retirement.[1] I should have been very happy if it could have been under more auspicious circumstances. But the state of things at Washington, produced by the death of Genl Harrison, and the accession of Mr. Tyler is most deplorable, and such as to leave me no personal regret in / in quitting Washington.

I agree with you in thinking that the moral, political and pecuniary condition of the Country is very discouraging. And what adds to our discouragement is that we cannot distinctly see any termination to the embarrassment which so generally prevails. I thought that North Carolina and Kentucky were probably <su> suffering less than most of the other States, but, on my return home, I find that I was mistaken as to this State. Here, all men in active business, other than Agriculture; all manufacturers of Hemp, all traders to the South, and all who are largely in debt, experience the greatest distress.

It has taken twelve years to bring about this unhappy state of things, by a great maladministration of the General Government.

I hope it will not require as long a term to restore to the Country its lost prosperity; but I am fully persuaded it will be a considerable time before we recover from the errors of our rulers. In the mean time we should not despair. If the good portion of the Community, yielding to Sentiments of despondency, abandon all care of the Government, and of popular elections, the bad will take /undisturbed/ possession and continue to rule. In all situations and conditions in life, there is one line of conduct to which we ought constantly to adhere, and that is, to do our whole duty, honestly and faithfully. Having done that, if things turn out ill, we have nothing to reproach ourselves with. Whereas, if we neglect the / the discharge of our duty, we shall be tortured by the reflection that we might possibly have prevented the evils which have arisen.

I should be very glad to see you under my roof. Do you never think of visiting Kentucky? If instead of going to the North, you would direct your course towards the West, I am persuaded that your health would be benefited, and that you never would have occasion to regret the journey. I hope that we shall meet again; but at all events I request you to believe me, most sincerely and cordially,

Your friend & ob[t] Serv[t]
H. Clay

E. Pettigru Esq.

P.S. I have a lot of Mules about the same size and description as that which I sent you. If any of your neighbours should want such a lot, I should like to supply them.

H. C.

---

[1]Clay resigned from the Senate on March 31, 1842, and began preparing for the Whig party campaign of 1844. Morris, *Encyclopedia of American History*, 186-187.

Mary Blount Pettigrew to James Johnston Pettigrew UNC

[*Washington, D.C.*] June 3[d] 1842

My dear brother,

Only think it is june already and what have I done during this year? It seems as only yesterday since december. I received your very unexpected but truly welcome letter in due time. You asked me about the circus at Plymouth, well, I will give you a description of my journey. When we arrived at that celebrated seaport the worthy inhabitants were all on tip toe in expectation of the show, and the next day mistresses, children and servants quit business and went to see it; what were its merits I do not know as I do not go to such genteel places and withal so suitable to ladies' taste. When we started in the steamboat I was agreably surprised at having the company of Mr and Mrs Singletary and her sister; I found them very pleasant companions. I formed in my mind a match between Mr Aldis and Miss Williams, Mrs S——'s sister; it would be so delightful to have her near home to associate with. she is a plain, amiable girl just such a one as would make a good minister's wife. In the cars there were some southerners whose appearances I like very much. There was a Gen Campbell[1] among them formerly from South Carolina; when Pa went out of the cars he told some other getlemen, that Pa was a very fine old gentleman from N.C. and spoke some more in his praise; you may imagine what a liking I formed for him from that instant; he did not know me. Nothing more of importance happened until we arrived in the mighty Metropolis.

I pass my time very pleasantly. I do'nt find it much trouble to get my lessons and I practice two hours and a half a day and thus doing my duty /as near as I can/ have a good conscience; which you know adds a great deal to ones happiness. I have been to several parties one very delightful one at Mrs Henderson's; you must know what is the cause of all these parties; there is one of the Steam ships here in which there are some handsome midshipmen; the girls are all crasy about them, not <m> I you must understand, althoug/h/ I think them quite ag/r/eable. I expect to go to one more party and then I believe the Capt is going to give a ball on board ship, which I also hope to attend, and then I shall be done.

I suppose you are settled by this time. I hope you are contented, for what happiness can there be without contentment and then I /also/ think it a duty to be so.

Have you heard of the quarrel between Mr [*Henry A.*] Wise and Mr [*Edward*] Stanly? they had like to have fought a duel but have made it up now. I expect they have both lessened themselves in the esteem of their friends.

I have almost read Charles O'Malley[2] since I have been here and am delighted with it. Do'nt you like the blouse that Pa brought to you? I assure you that you are just in the fashio/n./ Does it take at Hillsboro? I must now conclude as my time is limited. I hope you will me directly and a long letter, Remember I have a great deal to do and can not write often, but will do so whenever I can.

Very affectionately your sister
Mary.

[*Addressed*] J. Johnston Pettigrew
Hills-Boro
North Carolina

[1]Mary might refer to Robert Blair Campbell, who had served in Congress as a Whig and was commissioned general of South Carolina troops in 1833. He moved to Lowndes County, Alabama, about 1840. Appointed consul in Cuba in September, 1842, he held various diplomatic posts until 1861 and died in London in 1862. *Biographical Directory of Congress*, 656.

[2]This was probably *Charles O'Malley: The Irish Dragoon*, by Charles Lever. Dated 1841 in the author's first introduction, it is a typical Victorian novel.

Mary Blount Pettigrew to James Johnston Pettigrew UNC

Washington June 23^{d}, 1842

My dear brother,

I received your letter on saturday with two others; which raised my spirits very much, alt/h/ough we had such weather. It rained eight days before these last two, which have been beautiful. I am very sorry to hear you have lost your friend, but hope you will find some one to fill his place. I will do all in my power, to amuse you, with reading my weighty epistles and to employ you in answering them, this vacation.

About the studies in the Navy, I forgot to ask the Col.; but I know that they do not pay attention to the dead languages, but to french and mathematicks. Why do you inquire so particularly? have you any idea of going in to it? if so it is time you should apply, I expect. C. Henderson is at school; <now> not having obtained his warrant yet; the girls would not run away with him until he had on his uniform.

You said you hoped my heart was entire; it most assuredly is; do'nt you go to thinking any thing else. The steam ship has been gone a week, and every thing is back in the regular train.

F[*rancis Theodore*]. Bryan was here a short while since and I spent two days very pleasantly at Mrs Henderson's partly with him; he was quite talkitive much more so than I expected. You recollect some one told /brother C./ it was the contrary with him. He is very much pleased at the idea of going to West-Point. I beged him not to resign his commission in the army when he left the Point.

I am very sorry to hear that you have gone to Dr [*James*] Webb's, and hope you will not be led off by his son; he has a bad character. I hope, my dear brother, you attend to your religious duties; both public and private. I know that boys are exposed to temptation and ridicule, but hope that you are able to withstand them.

I was very glad to have such a long letter from you and hope you will always write such, but I want you to take more pains with your writing. You wrote a very good hand last winter, you must practice and write as good a one now. It would be a very good employment for you, during the holidays to learn on some musical instrument, but I suppose this is impossible; so you will have to sing, as much as you can, and read the remainder of the time. I am very anxious for all my brothers and my sister to cultivate their musical talents; and devote, on an average, three hours a day to /the study of music/ <it> myself.

John Bryan wrote me that Nancy was studying quite /hard/ and taking lessons on the piano. I was delighted to hear it. She is very affectionate and loves me much; she cried a great deal when I left her and not only then, but, at night, some weeks before. How did you get on to Raleigh; did you take good care of her? I beg of you, dear dear brother, not to do any thing to incur Pa's displeasure, recollect how dearly he loves us all, one as much as the others; he would do any thing to benefit us. I know your disposition and that you will do what I ask.

I do'nt envy you your jewish comp[an]ions at all, but it being vacation you can go some where else during the day and leave them. Do do'nt fall dead in love with Miss Mary Webb; she is so beautiful that I think a very great risk to put you in the same precincts. Remember me to Miss Mitchel and Mrs Waters and all inquiring friends. So bon *soir*.

Your truly aff' Sister
Mary

[*Addressed*] J. Johnston Pettigrew
Hillsboro
North Carolina

[The Reverend] Charles Aldis to Ebenezer Pettigrew UNC

Somerset Place, July 6th 1842.

My dear Sir,

In acknowledging the receipt of $100, as your generous contribution towards my Salary, permit me to say that it gratifies me exceedingly to perceive such a strong manifestation of interest on your part towards the Church.

For your unvarying kindness towards myself personally, I desire, also to express my sincere gratitude and my hope that in all our future intercourse, you will never fail to command the best efforts of Dear Sir

Your affectionate Friend & Pastor
Charles Aldis.

E. Pettigrew Esqr

[*Addressed*] The Hon. Ebenezer Pettigrew
Bonarva.

Ebenezer Pettigrew to James Cathcart Johnston UNC

Belgrade July 19, 1842

My dear friend

I wrote you by the last mail but I doubt whether you have received untill this time. in consequence of the mail being stoped by the storm.

I have not been to the Lake since the storm nor have I seen Charles, as we can pass no other way than by water, but I learn today by my Jim that the field is yet under water and that the corn is nearly all dead and dying and there is no hope that I can raise one hundred barrils. I have seen my corn at this place in part and have but a hope of raising three hundred barrils My prospect was fair on the 10th June for 2500 barrils. Seven hundred barrils is the least I can sustain my family with. The Virginia Hodges, left /from New York/ Sunday night before the storm and is on shore <at> at <the South> Chicamacomic banks. This you will say is rather a gloomy prospect and so it is, particularly as it was my last year, and I wanted to say in truth what Genl. Jackson said falsely. I leave my property prosperous & unencumbered, but a wise provedance says no, & I must bow in humble submission, Blessed be the Lord for his mercies.

My wheat sold in New York for $1.30. & I suppose I have about 1000 bushels more for sail.

My health has been a little on the mend for the last week, but I am much plauged now with sore <throt> /throat/.

I think of leaving some time the last of next week perhaps fryday the 29th I cannot get away much sooner in consequence of arrainging matters, and really I dred to leave for my sons, as well as negroes, for depend upon it we have reason to expect a most desperate sickly fall, & I fear a deadly one & God knows who will be able to live. Such a storm & such distruction I never have before seen. Every thing blown to pieces & destroyed:

I understand Charles is well, William has been very puney for the last fortneight or three weeks, but is now much on the mend, He desires me to make his best respects to you and please to accept for yourself the sincere <reg> regard & Esteem of your friend

E Pettigrew

James C. Johnston esqr.

[*Addressed*] James C. Johnston esqr
Hayes
Edenton P. Office

Mary Williams Bryan to Ebenezer Pettigrew A&H

Raleigh July 27th 1842

My dear Brother

I am very sorry to learn from your letter to Mr Bryan rec^{d} some time since that your health continued bad I had thought until that time that it was improving, I fear very much for you should you remain in the low country during the summer & fall, Mr Bryan unites with me in the sincere wish that you would come up and spend it with us—your life is of more value to your children than any thing else, you should therefore use every means of preserving it—I know it is very bad leaving Charles & William, but is it necessary that all should stay & be exposed to the climate? If you *cannot come* let one of them come we shall be most happy to see any or all of you as you can make it convenient—We hear from NewBern that the rains have been excessive & apprehensions are entertained of great mortality in the fall—Mr B left here last friday for NewBern where he is called by the extreme illness of his mother, I have heard since he left that she continues very low, we are very much afraid that she cannot recover—Charles & his family are with Ma' they are all pretty well except Charles who has been quite indisposed for the last week—James is very much engaged in electioneering, we have seen very little of him lately & shall not 'till the election is over—We have good accounts of Richard he has written to Ma' that he expects to be here during this month so we are in daily expectation of him—I am very much afraid Mr Bryan's trip to NewBern will make him sick but he says it is al<l>ways a comfort to him to be in the line of his duty & so it should be to all of us—

I suppose you have heard that Frank is at West Point, he says he has very hard duty to perform now but he seems to be satisfied & I hope he will prove a comfort & honor to us—Our family are well except James whom I kept from school to-day, he has been slightly indisposed for several days, my infant is teething & is not well, Nancy is well now tho' she has been a little sick several times since she came up; she is constantly engaged with her studies & is I think doing well, I am very much pleased with the [*St. Mary's*] school in *every respect* both as a boarding & a day school, I think Nancy has every advantage that she could have if she were a boarder in the school, & certainly some that she could not have except under a parent's roof—I told William therefore that I prefered keeping her with me at any rate until she was older* & after that time (if you wished it) I would have no objection to her boarding in the school—* If she were 14 or 15 I would be willing or in the event of my death or my being unable to attend to attend to her, I think she would be better off there than any where else—There are nearly 20 boarders & upwards of 30 day scholars, there are 6 teachers beside Monsieur Strozzi an Italian who lectures every day in French, this gentleman is very highly recommended & is a candidate for the French Professorship at Chapel Hill which is to become vacant the middle of the session by the resignation of Professor [*John J.*] Roberts who is about to marry & study Divinity—Madame Clement teaches French she gives me a very satisfactory account of Nancy & Betsy, I like all the teachers very much, they all seem devoted to the school; I have been all thro' the building the interior arrangement is admirable, the dormitories are delightful & every thing is conducted with the greatest neatness & regularity—in truth I have heard but one opinion expressed & that is a general approval I have thus endeavoured to give a just account of the school & if it continues as it is which I trust it may it will not be necessary to send our daughters to the North or any where else for their education, but have it upon better terms at home.—Mr & Mrs Lamar of Savannah passed thro' Raleigh last week on their way to Alexandria Mrs Lamar you know is a sister of Mr. Henderson she is the only one of the family I have seen, I was much pleased with her—Be pleased to remember me affectionately to Charles & William and believe me Your very aff. sister

Mary W Bryan

I hope you will visit us this summer give my best love to Mary when you write her—Mamma has lately visited Hillsboro she saw Johnston frequently while there and left him well—Your friend Mr Rayner has taken off Miss Susan[1] they had a very stylish wedding all Mrs Polk's sons were present, they all have all left again Andrew for College, & the others for Tennessee—the old lady's residence looks very lonely again.—

[*Addressed*] Hon. E. Pettigrew
Cool Spring
N. Ca—

---

[1]Kenneth Rayner married Susan Spratt Polk of Raleigh, the daughter of Leonidas and Frances Devereux Polk. Leonidas Polk (1806-1864) was an Episcopal bishop and a lieutenant-general in the Confederate army. Ashe, *Biographical History*, II, 365-366.

Ebenezer Pettigrew to Charles Lockhart and William Shepard Pettigrew UNC

Norfolk Aug 2nd, 1842

My dear Charles,

When I last talked with you respecting geting our corn for the next year it was then my opinion which I believe accorded with yours at the time that it would be best to order from New York three hundred barrils, but I yesterday talked with the Mr Hardys, & they were decidedly of the opinion that it would be a bad opperation altogether. That the corn would come higher than the new corn as there was a promise of very abundant crops so as /to/ bring the price below $2.50; that the corn would not be good having been probably heated & &c. In consequence of this information I thought I would write you today that you might be informed, but you will do as you like on the subject; if you get, it might be well not to get more than would ballast the schooner & /it/ would hardly be worth going /up/ the river <for> with. The corn on the rail road from blackwater is better than I ever saw it & the rain yesterday & the day before which was a full sufficiency for any land will be a great affair for it. I hope it reachd our country. I understand it was very heavy at Halifax. I did /not/ see a single tree or bush justled between B[*lack*].water & Norfolk with the storm. I saw Capt Ballance /at Plymouth/ who took your plank & he says that he was at Alexandria on the day of the storm & that it was as fine a sun shine day as he ever saw, & I also talked with Capt Howil who is concerned with Bryan & Maitland, & he informs me the Virginia H. in going over the bar with the load got a ground & thumped twelve hours and finally had to liter. So that you see we were in great danger of loosing all before the storm. He also told me that he saw the schooner & that she is on the ridge between the sea & sound, & that he expects they will launch her in the sound & that it is his opinion that if the storm had continued an hour longer she would have been driven over into the sound and might had proceeded on her voyage, he also says that if the new sails had been bent they would have been blown away & thereby would have cost more than launching her. I have bought a ream of paper here & taking out two quires from the white half ream, the other half ream is blue & not quite so good, I have requested Mr Hardy to get a box of lemmons & send them /with the paper/ by the first opportunity to Columbia. It might be well for you to direct Mr Dun as soon as they arrive to send word to William that he may get them in as much as lemmons are perishable. I find great difficulty in having a half dozen shirts made. It is not certain yet whether I can have it done here. O this worthless world. I think I shall go to Old Point tomorrow but I am told it is quite cold there now. I hope My dear sons, you guard against these cold changes, depend upon it there lies the danger. I have pretty /well/ got over the fever given me by my ride from B.water

I shall not leave this place untill I get a letter from home which cannot be before Saturday week. I should be glad in that to learn /the particulars/ about the election. I expect nothing but the Legislature will be Locofoco. It is all hopeless. If the strong negroe men should be sick, in ordinary cases where tonics may be wanting the peruvian bark is as good as the Qinine. I mention this /that/ the Qinin may be not used except in cases where needed. It is a matter of argument whether the Bark is not better where the stomach can take it than Qinine.

My health I think improves & strength also I hope my dear sons that you may retain your health which is the prayer of your affectionate father

E Pettigrew

[*Addressed*] Messrs Charles & William Pettigrew
Cool Spring
N. Carolina

Ebenezer Pettigrew to Charles Lockhart and William Shepard Pettigrew UNC

Norfolk Aug 14, 1842

My dear sons

You will probably be surprised to receive a nother letter dated at this place. I have found it agreeable & my health has improved so much that I have not been in haste to get away withall Mr Johnston arrived here on this day week & is disposed to continue longer & how much farther he will go is not yet determined. We were this week in various parts of Princes Ann county (& in the neighborhood of Dr Old (but did not see him) and the prospect of corn was as bad as they can be any where. Hundreds of acres that will produce not a single grain & no storm. Large fields, but wretched farmers, low grounds without ditches.

I fear the latter wheat will go to a bad market, there seems to be a perfect panic on that subject. Mr Johnston had a small cargo here & sold it yesterday for seventy cents & Mr Hardy & himself thought that the account of prices in Petersburg, Richmond & Baltimore & New York would not justify sending to any of those places, to do much better. Since Mr J.s arrival at this place he got letters from Bryan & Maitland N. York giving an account of wheat shipped to that place. The sale was eighty five cents & then to starch maker.

They said it was warm. I learned yesterday from a man who is agent for the underwriters, & came from the banks the day before that the Virginia Hodges was on the way & ready for launching when the last storm came & that she /was/ washed down, but not injured & that she can & will be certainly got off, if the winds will cease so as to give an opportunity to do it.

On my arrival at this place I gave an order to Mesrs Hardy for the Lemmons & they went to the places where the Carolina vessils stoped with direction to be informed, but alas our trade is so down that not one has yet offered. If you see Dr Lewis give my compliments to him & tell him that I received a letter from Dr Coleman dated the 12th saying that the medicines were put up & would be shipped by a vessil shortly to /be/ sent out to Columbia by the Mesrs. Trimble & Wilson.

Since I have been here there has been rain enough & one day last week there fell a great deal so as to stop the stage from Elizabeth to this place carrying away all the Bridges. I fear it has made a bad begining in brick making & interrupted or inconvenienced ditching in the canal, but will contribute to health, which I find by your letter Williams was uninterrupted when you wrote & very glad to learn that yours was restored. I pray God that /with/ both of you it may continue. Give my compliments to M^r & Mrs Davenport & tell Mr D. that I will get him a saddle as requested & that I am exceedingly sorry of Mrs D. having bilious fever, but it is no more than I expected. I hope she is before this restored. I have been twice to Old Point, but W. Shepard was gone before I got there. My health is so improved that were it not for the fear of geting sick again I should return. I eat what I wish with impunity & have fattened very much. In truth I am in as good health as I have been for the last 2 or 3 years.

I suppose you have heard of Ba[r]ny's courting Coffields daughter, by letter in his own hand writing. He has left Edenton, & it was said that he was in Portsmouth the other day. Parson [*Samuel I.*] Johnston has turned him out of the church. He was /a/ vestry man. It is said to be the basest acct of the present day, but if you have not heard of it, it is too long a story for me /to/ commit to paper in a letter. I saw Mr Aldis & Mr Watson on their passing through this place. The former mentioned the subject. When Mr Johnston heard of it he took his bed sick. If that affects him so much I fear if he knew all the acts of his bretheren he would continue in bed his life out, though this act of Barneys exceeds any thing of the kind on record. God help the /would be/ Christians.

Although there is great disaster with crops in some places it /is/ thought that /grain/ will be low. Mr Johnston had a good deal of old corn on hand & he thinks he may raise a half crop on Roanoke, & says he will furnish me with what I may want, therefore I shall look no farther. While on Roanoke since the storm, he sold to a merchant in Halifax corn—at $2.50 a barril, with an injunction that it should be retailed at $3.00 & thereby the price fell from $10.00 to a glut of the article for there was a good deal of old corn on hand. You will direct your next letter to Baltimore, Barnums Hotel.

Mr Johnston is in want of one hundred bushels of wheat for seed and will send his boat with one hundred barrils of corn for the Lake, which you will take up to that place. Mr Johnston wishes Mr Davenport to furnish it /the wheat/ because I have told him that he has none but pure wheat. He expects to send bags for it. Tell Mr Davenport that /the/ price is not an object & if the vessil /(Vir Hodges)/ wants that quantity to fill up he can pay dead freight as it will be allowed. I do not by any means wish Mr Johnston to be disappointed. & that he get the wheat if to be had good let what will happen. His boat will take the corn from Pasquotank, (she is here now) & will be along in a week or ten days. Mr Johnston desires his best Respects to you both & believe me your affectionate father

E Pettigrew

[*Addressed*] Messrs Charles & William Pettigrew
Cool Spring
N. Carolina

Ebenezer Pettigrew to Charles Lockhart and William Shepard Pettigrew UNC

Baltimore Aug 22, 1842

My dear Charles

I received your letter of the 16th at this place yesterday. We (Mr Johnston is with me) left Norfolk on 18th at night and consequently did not get your letter though I waitted untill that time. The cause of which was the steam boat Fox broke her shaft last week & the letters lost a day in going by Elizabeth. From what Mr Thompson told me the boat is by this time repaired.

It was with great sorrow that I learned of your brother Williams continued attacks—I fear he will linger or be feble through the fall, unless he takes a small trip some where. I wish most sincerely that he would go to Old Point & spend a fortnight or three weeks. It would entirely restore him & there would be no dainger in his return at any time of the season. If he /or/ you should go, I should be glad if you or him would call on Mr /& Mrs/ Thompson. They have been very polite to me and expressed a wish that if either of you came that way that <they> /<you>/ would call on them. I am confident you would both be gratified. Also call on the Mesrs Hardy & brothers. They have been very polite & attentive to me.

Before this you will have received my letters of the 14 & 17 & ditto by the Captain of Mr Johnstons boat who will carry you a hundred barrils of corn. I refer you to those letters. In consequence of the disaster to the Fox I expect you did not get mine in time to procure the shingles for Mr Johnstons vessil & if you have not he yet wishes you to procure them & let them remain at Columbia subject to his call. Pray let them be as good two feet as can be had.

It is thought that wheat is at its lowest point for the present, & that there is & has been something like a panick from which there will a measurable recovery, but that both wheat & corn <both> must be ruinously low next year no one I have heard yet speak has the least doubt. Except in one particular section the crops of corn are said to be both north & south unpresedentedly abundant. I find the wheat crop is not so much injured on James river by the freshet & the Eastern shore by rust as was expected. I leave it with you to say where you will ship the next wheat. I think well of Trimble & Wilson. You will be surprised to learn that they got for all that was worth anything of the whea[t] shipped by Capt Myers 82 cents a bushel, when part of it was rotten. I know I made a bad bargain with those persons whose land the canal passes through, but they then hesitated and all I can say is that you will make the best of it.

We found your uncle William at this place & last night Doctor Harrison arrived. The accounts given of their Edenton speculations are perfectly astounding & confirm my opinion in every sense of the word, and are almost incredible to any but one like my self perfectly confirmed in my opinion. It cannot be spread on paper & I will say no more. He whome God intends to destroy he first makes mad. Death & distruction must be close at hand, & there will be none to deliver. I received or found here a long letter from Dr Hardison dated the 9th It is explanatory of things past & in conclusion says he should take it kindly if I would write to him when convenient. I think he now sees clearly that he has made a mistake & would be glad to retrace his steps. While resentfull I thank my God I am not revengefull. The Almighty God says revenge not, vengance is mine. I will repay. I believe it unequivocally.

The distress is & will be excessive in our country & the accounts given of the like in the Cities is equally great. Among the thousands of cases of starvation there is one published like this, A man was seen to steal a pice of meat at the market /in Philadelphia/ & was followed to his house for the purpose of detection, but when they entered they found his starving children *devouring devouring the meat raw*. Dr Harrison who has just passed through Richmond & Peterburg says that the factories there have discharged most of their opperative & that hundreds are starving The like there was never before known. I am told here that numbers went out of this

City in harvest time & worked for their victuals & that hands to work in gardens &c are to be had in any number at twenty five cents a day. It is said here as well as at Norfolk that marketing was never so abundant or so cheap. Mr Johnston & myself took [a] walk through one of the markets saturday evening last & we were perfectly astonished at the piles of every thing to eat, sweet potatoes in great abundance & of good size. Peaches of the finest sort, & any /& every/ thing else in abundance.

My health continues good & I do not know that any disease attends me. I hope my dear Charles you will attend to my former advice as respects your health and that you my dear William <has> before this reaches you have recovered, & that you will if at all lingering take a trip to Old point as expressed in the first of my letter. Make my best respects to Mr & Mrs Davenport, who I shall write /to/ today also Dr Lewis & not to forget my wish expressed to him. Mr Johnston is in fine health & desires me to give to you both his best respect. & believe me my dear sons your affectionate father

E Pettigrew

[*Addressed*] Messrs Charles & William Pettigrew
Cool Spring
N. Carolina

Doctrine Davenport to Ebenezer Pettigrew A&H

Holly Grove August 30 1842

My dear friend

I receved your favour and was very glad to hear from you that your helth was so much improved Mr Johnsons boat has arived and I expect to deliver the hundr'd bushels of wheat to day it keeps very hethy yet and continues to rain it is raining now very hard I saw Mr Charles Pettigrew to day and Mr William they was both very well and all the famly since you left we have had another storm which has runed the foder and the young corne Mr William Pettigrew and my self went to see Mr Wrigs the orther day and spent quite agreeable day their is a little [nuse] stiring in scuppernong Mr Charles Pettigrew told me to day that they told him at the mill that Mr Tully Spriull stold a bag of wheat from the mill Mrs Myrs is dead she was purefactly crazey before her death and Mr Richard Hassel is at the point of death Mrs Myrs has left 2 young babys Mr Charles told me that the last storm did not injer him but / but very little it was worse on Mr Collins than the orther storm as to my part I expect to be broke I sha<n>t raise no corn and wheat is down so low I cant get much for that and what to do I dont no but I must hope for the best <I receved the sadle and bridle and> /I receved the/ bag of coff you sent by Mr Johnsons boat and I am very much oblige to you

Mr Pettigrew dear sir I should like very much to have /some/ of the nice frute in bawltimore for frute have bin very scerce here this sumer the peaches have bin very scerce a bout here and I have not seen a water melon the hole seson I expect their never was such a year a bout here before for we cand get fruit that is fit to /eat/ none as I see a bout here I did not thinke Miss Fanny ever wald leve baltimore she semed to be so wel satisfide at the hotel and had bin there so long Mr Pettigrew I wish you if you please when you return home to bring one dozen spolds of /sowing/ cotton give my recpects Mr Johnson if he is withe you Mary sends her love to you I remain your affectionate friend

Mary sends her <best> respects to Mr Johnson

Doctrine Davenport

[*Addressed*] Mr E Pettigrew
Barnums Hotel
Baltimore
Ma

William Shepard Pettigrew to Ebenezer Pettigrew UNC

Belgrade, Sep. 6, 1842.

Dear Father:

We have recieved several letters from you of late, all of which have arrived in due time. It affords us great pleasure to learn that your health continues to improve, and it is to be hoped, its durability will be commensurate with its improvement.

The day after I wrote my last, we had a storm: Mr Davenport thinks there was the heaviest fall of water he ever knew. I differ from him in this, but it was certainly a great rain, the water in the 15 feet ditch beeing 4 feet deep notwithstanding the tide was low. The Lake was raised but 3 in, occasioned, I presume, by two causes—the rain being lighter there than here, and the wind, in the last of the storm, blowing from South East, and, after the excessive violence had abated, from South, which caused it to run over in quantites to the West so as to injure Mr Collins' shore considerably in places. On Wednesday last there was a heavy rain. The rains interrupt brother Charles in the canal, and have, thus far, prevented me from continuing with the bricks.

Times are hard in Scuppernong, and the prospect is that they will be worse: I cannot think how, many will support themselves

Crilly House, the Pettigrew ancestral home near the village of Aughnacloy in County Tyrone, Northern Ireland. Photograph courtesy of Mrs. John H. Daniels.

This outbuilding at the Pettigrew plantation Belgrade probably dates from 1838. Photograph by Sarah M. Lemmon.

The house at Somerset, built by Josiah Collins III, stands in Washington County on the shores of Lake Phelps. Photograph from the files of the Division of Archives and History.

Hayes, the Chowan County residence of James Cathcart Johnston. Photograph from Frances Benjamin Johnston and Thomas Tileston Waterman, *The Early Architecture of North Carolina* (Chapel Hill: University of North Carolina Press, 1941), 154.

through the year; but the Bible tells us that the Almighty tempers the storm to the shorn lamb. I understand, Capt. Myers will leave next week for the West, to look at the country with the intention of moving should he be pleased. M[rs] Myers died a week or two since. Asa [*illegible*]ly also thinks of moving. I should doubt their being able to sell their land to advantage. Now is the time for those who have money to make their fortunes.

Capt. Rollins will be here next week for the remainder of the wheat. He was not injured by the last storm.

I cannot express, and brother Charles unites with me, my sorrow at the return of sister Nancy's disease. Were I afflicted with a calamity of the sort, I should not consider life worth having. But I sincerely hope she will again be restored:

There is some sickness in Scuppernong, and should it become dry, there will be more. Some predict drought—some a storm, and none, I suppose, know much about it: however, sickness or no sickness I hope it will be dry, that we may execute the work which is before us. The last storm injured the corn at Belgrade by slitting the fodder on the younger corn which had been made between the two storms: immediately after it, I striped what was left, and obtained, together with the old fodder, about ¼ of the quantity saved last year.

On Wednesday & Thursday last brother Charles received from Capt. Wilson, of M[r] Johnston's boat, one hundred bar. of corn (100), and on Thursday M[r] Davenport delivered to the Capt one hundred bush of wheat (100). The articles that were sent were safely delivered; the Lemon Syrup is very good, for which, we are obliged to you. M[r] Collins['s] Castor Oil was sent to him. His family are well.

We are healthy on both places. Brother C— unites with me in love to you & Sister Mary, and best respect to M[r] Johnston.

I am, your affectionate son,
William S. Pettigrew.

E. Pettigrew Esq.

P.S. I am very much obliged to you for your proposal to me to spend a few weeks at Old Point, but must beg leave to decline going as I am now quite restored.

I was sorry to learn, by yours, of Gen. [*Thomas?*] Emory's death.

W. S. P.

[*Addressed*] E. Pettigrew Esq.
Barnum's Hotel
Baltimore
Md.

Ebenezer Pettigrew to Charles Lockhart and William Shepard Pettigrew UNC

Baltimore Sep 12, 1842

My dear son William,

On my return from Washington City la[*s*]t evening I found your letter of the 7th I had gone to Washington on fry day to carry your sister Mary who had been with me some time, it being her vacation. She expects to go to scool the next quarter to a Mrs Wilmer in Alexandria, where you will in future direct your letters. She is well but has a cough that I do not like & it may be necessary to take notice of it. She is a fine girl & I think is gain/ing/ favour with the world, deservedly. She requested me to send her love to her brothers when I wrote. I observe the contents of your letter, your brother Charles' had informed me of the storm. We seem to be domed to distruction in Scuppernong & as for the Lake, I am very willing to have its name changed to Scuppernong. It is certainly no longer Lake Phelps. Grain & Flower are very low here and every where else except with us; I feel much for the poor & what will become of them I cannot think, something must be done or they will starve outright before any thing can be raised from the earth. I am glad to learn that Captain Rollins was not cast away a second time. I fear the wheat will go to a low market let that be where it may.

My dear Son Charles I was not able to go to Alexandria while at Washington and thinking it would serve the interest of Halsey & Pettigrew I gave a draft to Mrs Henderson on Messrs Cassenove & Gardner, for what sum she might want for Marys expenses, which can be paid to you in N. Carolina. It will not exceed I expect two hundred dollars. You have the power to draw on New York for any funds I may have there. I have drawn for but ($200.) two hundred dollars /on N. York,/ & shall not as far as I now know draw for much more. Mr W. W. Lewis is at this place attending the lectures, by his request I had to loan him ($25) twenty five dollars & take an order on his brother the Doctor. I make no comment on all this.

My dear Sons I was taken with my old complaint on wednesday night last & on thursday was confined to the bed untill twelve, but was better in the afternoon so as to ride out with your sister. On fryday was so much better that I went with her to Washington as before remarked; In the afternoon felt badly & in the morning of Saturday very much out of order, but got up to breakfast (though eat nothing) because I had promised to meet Col Henderson at the steam boat at 9 for Alexandria to see Messrs C. G. of what I have written you. But I soon found it was impossible for me to go there & I had to go to bed, & for a few hours I could not be much sicker. For with the diareah I had an excessive sick stomach & vomiting. I had

/not/ done, nor eat anything that I could charge with the cause of my sick/n./ess. I am now better & feel much better today but am fearfull if I had been in our country I should /not/ recover from this attack this fall. I expect to leave for Raliegh by the way of Norfolk tomorrow, where I hope to be by Saturday next, You will therefore direct your letters to that place in future as before advised. When I went to Washington with your sister, Mr Johnston went to Philadelphia to see Joe Blount. I expect him back this evening.

My dear sons I am glad to learn that you are still in health, & that your people are in like manner well; I pray it may continue, but let me suggest to you that there is yet enough of the season left if it turns off dry, (which I think it will) to give a good /deal/ of disease to our country before the 20th of October. If my memory serves me there was little or no sickness in the year 1833 up to the second week of September, you have heard me tell the result after that time. I would therefore advise you to take all the precaution you can possibly.

Make my best respects to Mr & Mrs Davenport who I hope are in health also all enquiring friends

and believe me my dear sons your affect father
E Pettigrew

N.B. I sent a double mould board plough, two saddles & a pair mill stones by the schooner Jerome to Columbia the other day. The mill stones are for Belgrade & the plough is to split the corn ridges before sowing wheat the saddle is for Mr Davenport as marked & the other is for your sister Mary. Tell Mr Davenport that I have engaged for him some seed rye which he wished me to do for him to sow on his Jonny place. It will be sent to Columbia by the first opportunity. E P.

[*Addressed*] Messrs Charles & William Pettigrew
Cool Spring
N. Carolina

Ebenezer Pettigrew to James Cathcart Johnston UNC

Raleigh Sep 24, 1842

Sick, melancholy & miserable. This you will think My dear friend a strange way to begin a letter if you do not make a full allowance for the animal. But you will say from strange animals we must expect strange acts. But to begin. I arrived at Petersburgh in the afternoon of the day I left you & at night took the cars for Raleigh, & did not stop (according to a new arraingment) untill I reached this place which was at 2 oclock in the afternoon of the next day. The trip of 140 miles of R-Road, traviling all night, cold, sick & fatigued almost to death, together with melancholy at leaving my company that I had been enjoying so much, at the same time thinking of the cause of my coming, (my poor little diseased girl,) perfectly unmaned me & I was fit to be nowhere. With the indisposition which is about the same as when I left you, together with the affection of the head which is always attendant on my mental distress renders me very unfit for any thing, but a close room. My dear Nancy is, the Doctor says better than she was and is safe to go about & goes to school & helps herself at the table, but her appearance brought to my mind so vividly all my recollections of my poor James in whom I had taken such excessive interest, that I have no power to resist my feelings. The doctor thinks this disease may be at intervals until Nancy arrives to womanhood. I will say no more on this subject. I shall be out of the way before that time, but I pray God she will have good sense.

William Shepard arrived here yesterday. He says he left Mary well, but seems to know nothing of her cough. That is all in character. He is very cool on the old subject and I think indifferent as to the issue. What a world it is? God has made but a few persons who are fit to stay in it. The others are not at home, & I doubt whether they will ever find any, here or else where.

Mr Stanly is here also. I had an interview with him today. He was very clever, & we talked of Collins & Spruills collision, which he had heard something of. I was as carefull in my relation of the circumstances as a *say all* man could be, but mentioned at one time that Spruill quailed, at which I thaught there was a marked fall of the countenance. I was hurt & embarrassed, for I am alive on that subject & if there was certainly undoubted courage should be almost willing to renew it. The Lord have mercy on a poor old sinner that I am!

I called & gave Mr Iredell the letter yesterday. The family are all well as I was told. I saw them all.

I found no letter here from home & am very anxious to hear. I hope you found all things to your satisfaction, and Miss Helen better please to make my best respects to her & the other Ladies of your family. I forgot entirely to ask you to write to me but hope you would never wait for that request I have been very anxious to know how you are & how you got along.

My arraingement to leave this place is to take the cars on monday the tenth of October & shall get to Sledges near Gaston that night. The next morning leave for Hallifax where I probably shall get to by dinner & shall be glad /to/ meet you if convenient & if not your conveyance at that place. And now my dear friend if anything should occur that would make it desirable that you should not go up at that time pray do inform me & abandon the trip. I have other things to say to you but from the affection of my head can recollect nothing & must conclude by beging you to accept the best wishes of your sincere friend

E Pettigrew

James C. Johnston esqr.

[*Addressed*] James C. Johnston Esqr
Hayes
Edenton Post Office
N. Carolina

William Shepard Pettigrew to Ebenezer Pettigrew UNC

Belgrade, Sep. 27. 1842.

My Dear Father

Your favors from Baltimore & Norfolk were received by last mail: we were very sorry to learn that you had been attacked again with your old disease, but were glad to learn by the same mail that it had left you.

We have been so fortunate, thus far, as to have but little sickness on either Plantation, & I hope, the season is now too far advanced & the weather too cool for us to suffer much from sickness this Fall. The Lake has been more healthy than Belgrade. I have scarcely heard of a case there (I allude to your side) while here there have been four sick. All are well at Mr Davenport/'s/. Mrs D. is doing as well as could be expected. There is no doubt but they have been benefited by the cole-kiln which was burnt there this Fall. He has received his saddle & is pleased with it. It is now quite dry. Mr D. fears, should it continue so, that the old ground will be /too/ solid for the plough to enter, but I think he is mistaken—the ridge is composed of earth thrown up during the last Spring, & the time which has elapsed & the rain which has fallen cannot be sufficient to make it thus hard. Brother Charles is exerting every energy in the canal. With the few that are left, I shall commence gathering corn to-morrow; it is remarkably dry, & is more fit to gather now than when we commenced last year. There is much danger of corn being stolen from the field if one be not vigilant. Mr D. says, Jo. Newberry told him that he ran a man out of Mr Collins' field on Sunday last. Franklin Spruill offers his land for sale a ($12) twelve dollars per acre. Myres is willing to give him ten. Do you not think it is worth purchasing at $12? He estimates 86 acres, but I think there are not more than 75. I understand from Mr Davenport, that

Myres says, if any one will agree to sell him the old ground & as far as a continuation of Mr Clayton's /back/ line, or, as far as a continuation, across Franklin Spruill's land, of the fence on the Eastern side of the Poplar Neck field, that he (Myres) will withdraw from the list of bidders.

It is said that Simmons is hard run.

I was sorry to learn that Mr Johnston was unwell, but hope he has recovered ere this.

Mr Davenport requests me to present to you his & Mrs D's. respects. I hope Sister Nancy is better. Brother Charles unites with me in love to her, yourself & all our relatives in Raleigh.

Please do not neglect to purchase those green goggles of which we were speaking; we should also be glad of a few skains of silk.

I am, your affectionate son,
William S. Pettigrew.

E. Pettigrew Esq.

[*Addressed*] E. Pettigrew Esq.
Raleigh
N. Carolina

William Shepard Pettigrew to
James Johnston Pettigrew UNC

Belgrade, Oct. 4, 1842.

My Dear Brother

Your favor of Aug. 31st was received some time since. It afforded me much pleasure to hear from you, and, particularly, to learn that you were doing well in your studies: I was fearful that you had lost too much time during the past winter to join your class on your return and maintain in it a respectable standing, but I am agreeably disappointed. Then I suppose, four years from this time, we shall have the happiness of greeting another brother as a resident in this section, when that is the case we shall form quite a phalanx of Pettigrews, and should we remain united (which Heaven grant we may) will be in a moral point of view what the Grecian Phalanx was in military affairs.

Brother Charles is using /every/ energy in digging the new canal to the Eastward, which, when completed, will relieve the Lake Plantation & Magnolia from back water; by the end of next Fall it will be completed. Five miles of it will be twenty feet wide and two miles twelve feet wide, the average depth being four feet, the deepest spot, which is opposite Alex Alexander's, is eight feet deep. If we had some of those long, idle fellows who lounge about Hillsboro. it would /be/ of service to them & us, they would be taught a different story from the one they have learnt, they would be instructed in the art of supporting their masters instead of their masters supporting them.

I suppose you have seen or heard from Pa ere this, he last wrote us from Norfolk, at which time, he was on his way to Raleigh; he was complaining then, but the atmosphere of the hills & mountains doubtless soon reinstated him. I am satisfied you will join with me in sorrow at the return of Sister Nancy's disease. Brother Charles would send his love if he knew I were writing you. I shall be glad to hear from you at all times.

I am, your affectionate brother,
William S. Pettigrew.

[*Addressed*] Master J. Johnston Pettigrew
Hillsboro.
N. Carolina.

Ebenezer Pettigrew to Charles Lockhart and William Shepard Pettigrew UNC

Caladonia Mr Johnstons Plantation Octr 15, 1842

My dear Sons

I have at length got as far as this on my way home and hope to be at Plymouth on Fryday night the 21st and should be glad if you will send for me at /that/ place on that day that I may come home on Saturday the 22nd. I should like to <return> have receivd a nother letter from you <at> /after/ that of the 2[7]th before I left Raleigh but I suppose you thaught it would not come in time & did not write. I have had a good deal of anxiety in this latter warm weather for your health, but it has had no unhealthy effect /where I have been/. A great part of the time I was at R. & Hillsboro. I was threatened with chills but they have now left me & I am in good health except a cold & cough which I have had for the last fifteen days. I went to see Johnston the last week I stayed. He <was> is well & exceedingly grown, & seems to be much improved in his mind. Mr Bingham says farthermore that he behaves well & gives him no trouble. He is also, as well as Doctor Webbs /family/ well pleased with each other. In truth the visit to him was highly gratifying. Your poor little sister Nancy is as she has been, with but little change in any way. The Doctor & myself with the corresponding opinion of Dr Potter of Baltimore that she will recover, but her diseased state is truely distressing. Your aunt

Mary says & I am satisfyed by what & all I saw that she is a very good child. I have been around Mr Johnstons fields & there is a great deal of corn in them, withall the field is large indeed. say between fifteen hundred & two thousand acres. It is quite healthy here, but very sickly at Halifax town & else where

I will close my letter my dear sons hoping to see you in a few days. Believe me your affectionate father

E Pettigrew

[*Addressed*] Mrs Charles & William Pettigrew
Cool Spring
N. Carolina

Ebenezer Pettigrew to Charles Lockhart and William Shepard Pettigrew UNC

Rail Road at Black water October the 21, 1842

My dear Sons,

I wrote to you from Mr Johnstons plantation that I should be along tomorrow, but the day before we were to leave to take the boat at Winton Mr Johnston received a letter express that his sister was very ill, & he started post in his own conveyance for home & I took the public conveyance by Hallifax &c &c. On my arrival at this place yesterday I learned that Miss Helen died on Wednesday morning at about the time the express must have arrived at Caledonnia. I was surprised at being informed of the death of Miss Helen by several persons to hear them express a warm sympathy for Mr Johnston. I feel exceedingly for him. It is truly an unfortunate occurrence for us both in as much as I have reason to think that but for my visit to Caledonia he would have been with his sister in the last week of her life. She was the last link between him & the world, and it is uncertain what step he will take next. I had a full intimation of something about to happen to me in which I was innocently to blame in a dream on <Mon> Sunday night at which he laughed hartily.

In consequence of Miss Helens death I shall stop tonight at Mr Johnstons house & send this to you by Jim who will return & you can send him for me again on monday evening next, to stay there /Plymouth/ untill I <return> arrive I have been very anxious to hear from you since the 28th Sep but trust you have been well. My health is good with some threatening of chills without consequences.

God Bless you my dear sons your

affectionate father
E Pettigrew

N.B. I might be well for Jim to leave on monday at such a time as not pass Res[p]asses ferry untill about two hours by [noon?] as I may pass over that way but I do [*not*] much expect it.

[*Addressed*] Messrs Charles & William Pettigrew
Belgrade

Ebenezer Pettigrew to James Cathcart Johnston UNC

Lake Scuppernong Nov. 1, 1842

My dear friend,

I was much gratified on my arrival at Belgrade on tuesday at 3 oclock to find my two sons waiting dinner for me though two hours out of time, which gratification was much hightened by their kind & affectionate reception of me. They were both in fine health & spirits, and I learn from my servant Jim first and after from my son William that Charles who has been all the time engaged in the canal has exercised the most unbounded energy in prosecuting the work and it is Jims opinion that his master Charl'es management in the work has been equal to the labour of six of the best hands in the canal. By great exertions he on friday night compleated it to the end of the Be[*e*]tree canal which was widened to the size of the new one (20 ft) a half mile last spring which makes two and a half miles now finished. It will do some /considerable/ good as it is & the widening the Be[*e*]tree canal to the Lake will be comparatively a light job. In consequence of this all absorbing work & the great importance of making a junction with the creek & the end of the Be[*e*]tree canal we have only begun to sow wheat on saturday last. This defering of the wheat sowing is what I should myself have done & what I have some two or three times done in my opperations in this truely difficult country to overcome. With the amount of teams we have, we can now get get the wheat sown in this month & then we must trust on an all wise providence for the product.

The health of the Lake has been astonishingly great. Scarcely a case of indisposition on my place and but very little at Belgrade / grade. I thank my God for his kind mercies.

I have been astonished at the promptitude with which I have been called on by certain persons without an exception and the kindness of deportment and expressions of gratification at my return as well as restoration to health. You know my sentiments. They have not changed, they cannot be changed & I will say no more on the subject, Than my God, my God what is this world.

My corn is gathered; at Belgrade William got one hundred and sixty <five> barrils and at the Lake Charles actually took from the field but one bushel. Thus you see my prospects on the score of corn are very small, but I have been labouring for the last thirty nine years to meet these times and an indulgent providence has prospered /my/ exertions & I have no right to complain. My sons are of the opinion that we cannot get along with less than five hundred barrils including the hundred received and I should be much obliged by geting a part of that as soon as it can be convenient for you to send it, but pray do not give yourself any inconvenience about it. All the meal eat on both places is ground at the Lake & the fating the Hogs takes what little we have there very fast. Charles requests me to say to you that he has had unavoidable delay in geting such shingles as he wished to get for you, but that when the vessil comes over with the corn, he will have the 25, or 30 thousand, having told Mr Dun his miller that they must be had. On the subject of geting one hundred thousand if you should want them, it might be well for you to see this first parcel before the others are engaged.

I hear very little talk of famine in the neighborhood, for there is a little corn yet with most to take from the fields, also peas & potatoes, & the community are easy untill that is all used up. It is not, nor never can be known how much corn is raised at another place. It is however said by those who say they cannot tell what to think, that it is five hundred barrils. All is darkness & uncertainty. The Lake is within three inches of Lake Phelps high water, but it looks low for Lake Scuppernong. How soon does poor human nature assimilate itself to what is around it—. Since my return I have been along the shore & I do not think in all these high tides for several years & particularly this, that we have lost a cart load of earth off the shore. It shows me without a doubt to *my mind* the correctness of my management of the shore from my first commencement (as soon as I could act) up to this time & on a retrospect of the past and a *knowledge* of the result gives me no little gratification.

Not an hour (except when asleep) has passed away since I parted with you my friend, without my mind turning upon you.

For me to attempt to give you consolation I know would be vain, but I know it is a balm to a wounded heart to believe that ones friends feele all that sympathy & sorrow which human nature can possess. I hope and pray that you will endeavour to remove that weight of grief and permit thereby that power of reason to opperate on your mind of which you possess so much. Your dear sister, that bone of your bone & flesh of your flesh has left you; but where has she gone? To a distant country and you know not into whose hands or protection? No; my dear friend she is gone to her Heavenly father, that blessed God who gave her life in this *world* to fit her for that everlasting Kingdom which he has prepaired from the foundation of the world for those who / who love & serve him, that heavenly world where the tears shall be wiped from every /eye/ and where there is no more sorrow, no more pain, no more death, but where there is joy forever & forever. My dear friend for the last twelve years I have looked on that journey of death as but a travil from my dear children to one I loved more far more. Our dear departed friends cannot come to us, but let us prepare to go to them by /full/filling our duty in that station to which it has pleased God to call us. Let us be resigned to his dispensations & wait with patience for the hour of his coming. I have <have> children who call imperiously on me for my attention & God will desert me when I desert them. My friend a wise God has made you a stewerd over many things let me beseach you to occupy your time in that stewertship that he may say at his coming well done though good and faithfull servant enter thou into the joys of thy Lord.

I hope your health has been as when I left you. Mine has been unimpaired. My sons who are both with me desire me to make their kind regards to you, please to make mine to the Ladies and be assured of the sincere affection & regard of your friend

E Pettigrew

James C. Johnston esqr

[*Addressed*] James C. Johnston Esqr
Hayes
Edenton P. Office

Ebenezer Pettigrew to James Cathcart Johnston UNC

Belgrade Nov. 15, 1842

My dear friend,

Your kind favour of the 4th came to hand by the last mail. It found me I regret to say in rather a feble state. On sunday the 6th I awoke in the morning feeling very badly but could not believe I was sick when before breakfast I was taken with an ague which continued to shake me 2 hours and a half and in all that time I had the /most/ violent bilious vomiting. It was not folowed with much fever & in five days in bed & the use of quinine I have to[t]aly recovered; after I left you I continued to fatten, my appetite being sharp at every meal. You will naturally say that I walked myself into the attack, but I was exceedingly cautious of it & in no instance took a long walk or was at all fatigued in the walks I did take. In my four days sickness I had more calls from A. B. & C. than I had in the whole of the winter of '40-'41 and there has been a request made to me with a request to Charles to use his influence respecting my dear Mary that I was amazed at. 'To change her place of residence from her fathers house'. On that subject I will tell you the rest when I see you. Poor little Nancys health is yet the same if not worse. It is right that Mary should visit her, & taking all things into the account I think it best for the present to take her to Raleigh. So you see my dear friend, plan or move as I will I am headed or put to trouble.

I observe the course with the Revd Mr Johnston. I regret to learn his continued feble state, of health, and more his want of determination, without which a man /is/ constantly under the tyrany of his fellow man, A tyranny which is worse than death. A tyranny without law, and according to the caprice of any upstart.

In this *monstrous* swell that is about to [break], I fear my dear brother will be roaled over & lost, Poor fellow! He is however doing what he ought to do, as he began it. I am not in the least astonished at all the account nor would I be if it was twice as much. You have long known my opinion. It has never changed nor wavered in the least. With so much consummate vanity no good sence can prevail. It will and must have the preponderance yet in some things it will have the entire rule. I thank God that I have got so far through life as this without its geting into my house, and may I have power so long as I do live to drive it out of my sight or to run from it.

As soon as I can get from this trip for my dear Mary I expect to begin to make preparations for commencing on the stuf for my cottage, but it will be a years opperation to get fixed comfortably & I hope you will give me the pleasure of some of your company before that time, if it were but to make suggestions about locality of different houses. Put me to fixing a barn & I think I can get along well, but in a dweling I am wanting.

I know not how to express my gratitude for your kind remarks respecting the corn that /I/ may want during the season and I could not realise my feelings at being told by my sons 'Pa there is not corn enough to last longer than the first day December except what I want to pick the seed corn out of' I should be very much obliged if on the receit of this you would send over the fifty or sixty barrils of corn which you have at your mill, and the other as soon as it comes down the river. And now my dear friend what shall I say about the shingles. I am ashamed to say any thing, but the truth must come. They were expected certainly to be had at the mill for corn long before this, but Charles was down all the latter part of last week and says that enough can be got, but they are not such as he would be willing to send to you, he has now engaged them to be spetially made by a responsable man and they are to be ready certain (which I have no doubt of) in a month, and can certainly be had when the vessil comes with the corn from Plymouth. I regret all this delay & you will reasonably say why was not all this known before? A reasonable question & one I cannot answer & will therefore butt say, why? I have no doubt of them this time & they are on honour to be good.

Mr Davenport is desirous to make a payment on his note with you. I told him that it was not well to plague you with small payments & that I would take it, giving my note to him but I thought from his remarks & looks that he would greatly prefer that the payment should be on his note, & God knows I do not want the money, and will therefore take it to you, and will either call on my way to the north or returning home should you be at home, and should be glad to be informed when you leave home that I might not miss you and thereby loose <the> that pleasure which I should anticipate so anxiously. I will not say when I expect to /be/ along for fear your politeness & good feeling may cause you to interfere with some of your arraingments. I say this knowing that about the close of the year, it is important that ones plans should not be broken in upon.

My dear Friend, It was with great & heart felt gratification that I read your truely Christian remarks on the subject of your late bereavement. With such sentiments you cannot fail to be supported under all & every tryal that poor man is subject to in this world of sorrow. I would to God that I not only could reason in like manner, but /put/ in practice such heavenly sentiments, but this high, excitable temperament of mine, at times, overruns every sentiment of religion, Philosophy, & almost reason & leaves me almost an entire wreck. I feel at times as though I would give the world could I have been more calm & dispationate. The more I look at man the /more/ satisfied I am that he is with a very little improvement or alteration acting under the influence of his nature & hence it is that I estimate different famelies. Nothing can alter /the/ nature of the beast much.

I received a letter dated Octr. 31st from my dear daughter Mary I hope it will not be amiss to extract a part of it. 'I am sincerely sorry for Mr Johnstons bereavement; he must feel dreadfully to think of being alone in the world without one near relative to love & comfort him; but I hope, dear Pa, that he will come to see you often, and we all can make him happier. He was so kind and seemed so good last summer that I really love him, if that be proper and I cannot see any impropriety in it myself.' I will also give you one extract from the Messers Hardy & Brothers dated Oct. 29th

'We hope Sir you are now with Mr Johnston, who is suffering under the afflictive dispensation of divine Providence, in taking from him his amiable Sister, and only *near* relation—' Thus you see my dear friend you are not passing through the world without the good feelings of your fellow man. Yes man, you have all the sympathy & best of feeling from the best, the good, the honorable of mankind, and may God in his infinate mercy give you a long life in this world, and when he /has/ finished your course in this world, may he take you to that heavenly place which /he/ has prepared from the foundation of the world for those who love & serve him, is the prayer of your sincere & affectionate friend

E Pettigrew

James C. Johnston esqr.

N.B. William who is with me, desires me to del[*ive*]r his kind regards to you & that /he/ cannot appretiate too highly that opinion which you were please to express of him, he farther says he is afraid you are mistaken in him & that he would fall short upon scrutiny. I hope you will never be afraid of burdening me with the length of your letters, there can be no burden in a pleasure; at any rate it is a pleasant burden, if such a thing can be. I have been interrupted in writing this letter, but you see I have made out a pretty long one, but be assured I am not writing against length. It is well to be able to talk some which property you have to a sufficient degree, while I overdo the thing entirely & to write well is very desirable; to write at any rate has been to me a sevier business.

The accounts of Virginia Hodges has been settled today and she has cost since she left New York two days before the storm of July including a suit Jack got while at New York at that time $1060—a nice sum to make over the left shoulder. But so let it be. It is bad to get into a bad run of luck.

As ever yours truely
E P.

Pray do not fear taxing me with Postage. I have taken this evening the second ride since I was riding with you and I feel much better by it.

[*Addressed*] James C. Johnston Esqr
Hayes
Edenton Post Office

Mary Blount Pettigrew to William Shepard Pettigrew UNC

Nov 21st [*1842*] Alexandria

My dear brother,

I have commenced two letters to you but none suit me. I am much distressed to learn by Pa's letter that he has had an other attack & is still sick; but I hope ere this he will have recovered. Oh how glad I should be to be there to nurse him; but brother Charles' letter brings the sad intelligence that I am to go to Raleigh instead of home. It has been my delight to think of the time when my school days being finished I should go <th> to live with my dear father and brothers and carry on my studies under their eyes; and to think /in/ how many ways I could add to their happiness. I can but hope that Pa will change his mind before he comes for me. I can not think that I am to be again seperated from him for so long a time. It is far from my thoughts to do any thing in opposition to my dear father's will. You may think by my reluctance to go to Raleigh that my love, for those who have been so kind to me, is lessened, but I assure you it is not so; <but> They have no need of me; I could not reduce Ma's labours;—while at home I think I may be of much use a<n>s you are all alone. It would delight me above all things to have my poor little sister at home with me and would also be a great pleasure to her. I have been wishing for sometime to write to inform Pa when I shall be ready to start; which will be on the twelth of december. Mrs Henderson says she hopes he will remain some days in Washington. We were up there on saturday, when as usual we had a dance. The family are all well and Mrs H—— does not seem to be dreading the winter as much as when we were last there. Mr Gardner looks as well as he has done but they say he has very severe attacks in the night sometimes. The weather has been as cold as we had at any time last winter, but is now much more pleasant. The ladies are beginning to shine forth in all the splendour and colour of winter.

Have you seen Dickens' new work?[1] it is really abominable. Scarcely a thing is said in praise and a great deal in abuse of America. In speaking of the south he is particularly abusive. Although, I think those who made so much noise over him deserve it, yet I can not help feeling incensed at his impudence and ungratefullness. The book arrived in New York on sunday night and <before noon> by monday morning was scatter/ed/ all over the city.

I have been reading the "Southern Matron"[2] and am perfectly delight<ful>ed with it; it is written by a lady of Charleston and is true to <life> /reality/ of a southern life.

Mr Johnston, the Minister of this place, has a bible class here at Mrs Wilmer's, which he makes very interesting. He gives is a lessen in the evidences and some questions, to prove which we find texts of scripture, once a week.

It is approaching nine o'clock and therefore I must close, knowing due allowance will be made for all deficiencies. Give my love to Pa and brother Charles.

Believe me ever, my dear brother, your
affectionate sister
Mary—

[*Addressed*] William S. Pettigrew Esq,
Cool Spring
North-Carolina

---

[1]Charles Dickens visited the United States early in 1842. He published his impressions in *American Notes* late that year. The work was widely criticized and resented by Americans who had lionized the writer on his recent tour. *Encyclopedia Americana* (1977 edition), IX, 76.

[2]Mary refers to Caroline Howard Gilman's *Recollections of a Southern Matron* (1838). Mrs. Gilman, a transplanted northerner, dedicated her writings to the concept that sectional differences disappeared "when seen in a domestic light." Edward T. James (ed.), *Notable American Women, 1607-1950* (Cambridge: Belknap Press of Harvard University Press, 4 volumes, 1971), II, 37-39.

Mary Blount Pettigrew to William Shepard Pettigrew UNC

Raleigh. Dec. 22nd. [*1842*]

My dear brother,

I do not know whether I am your debtor, but you know we must do unto others as /we/ would be done by, Pa left us on monday last; but has not yet, I suppose, reached home. He told me to send my letters via New-Berne; so as to try and find another sure way of communicating between these two almost entirely separated parts of the world. Johnston is here spending his vacation but he says he is very tired of Raleigh and will decamp as soon as possible after Christmas. He says Hillsboro is dull enough but that Raleigh is almost insupportable. He will <stand> spend Christmas as usual with Grandma. I spent the day with her some days ago, and found her in tolerably good health and talking of coming down the country in the spring.

Nancy is almost, if not entirely, well. Ma thinks that all her sickness arose from a tooth which you can now just see. She will commence school again in January; and will endeavour to make up for what she has lost. She has an excellent ear for music and I think will make a good performer. Will you ask Pa if he will not allow her to continue her french. It is useful, you know, and all the other girls study it; so I think it would be better for her to learn it now as she has a good oppotunity.

I commenced this letter to go in the office thursday night, but whilst I was in the midst of it a gentleman came to see us and I was obliged to defer it.

I am very anxious to take music lessons and, if I possibly can will begin in Jan' Mary's piano is a fine instrument. I am taking my vacation now while the boys are here, but as soon as they go, will, or will try, to resume my studies.

John Bryan and myself have been intending to take a great many rides on horseback, but there is always something to prevent and we have not as yet taken a single one.

Ma and father both say that I am old enou/gh/ to go in company, but I have such a dislike to it that I can hardly persuade myself to visit.

Mary and John have gone to dress the church. Mr. Henderson, who I believe was with you at college, came here this morning and made Ma's cedar trees contribute pretty largely for that purpose. He is a devoted beau of Mary's and makes his appearance here once in every twenty four hours.

Mr Hinds [*Hines?*] has a very fine daughter his youngest. She was here this morning and I was much pleased with her for the first visit.

Before you receive this you will have heard that the renowned William H Haywood[1] is the senator of the 'Old North State. I was up at Grand Ma's when she heard /the news./ She was perfectly delighted and said that he was a smart fellow and had out generaled them all. Uncle James, although he voted for [*Romulus M.*] Saunders,—did not seem to mind it much; but Johnston says he was much chagrined and endeavoured to hide it.

Gov. Morehead gave a large party last night but the weather was so bad that it was not well attended.

Uncle James said that Mrs Saunders was very angry because the election turned against her husband; the people say she wrote an angry note to our uncle because he did not vote for him the time before the last; but I believe that is not the case. With my best love to Pa and brother Charles I must conclude this not very well written epistle.

Very affectionately your sister
Mary—

[*Addressed*] William S. Pettigrew Esq.
Cool Spring
North-Carolina

[1]William Henry Haywood, Jr. (1801-1852), a Democrat of Wake County, had been elected to the United States Senate. A lawyer, Haywood previously served in the state legislature. He resigned from the Senate in 1846. *Biographical Directory of Congress*, 1032.

Ebenezer Pettigrew to James Cathcart Johnston UNC

Lake Scuppernong Jan 17, 1843

My dear friend

I have at length arrived at this mortal place for water &c &c &c to which I sumed up courage enough to move for on thursday last having stayed at Belgrade twelve days before I could sum up courage sufficient. The next day I learned that the visitants of the Lake left, so that I did not see them & I have only seen any other of my neighbors at the chapel on sunday last, at which <pla> place I had a short interview.

The affairs of which I am interested are going on well and every exertion is making to prepare for another crop of corn. I observe that though the new canal is not nearer than two & a half miles of the lower edge of the field & four miles of the Lake, yet it has great effect on the field & the old canal so much on /the/ latter that there is little or no water in it when the machienery is not going though it has been so rainey untill just at this time. You are aware that the new twenty feet canal connects with & is up the Bee Tree ten feet canal more than half a mile. Charles is very sanguine on the perfect effect which the new canal when brought up to the Lake will have on all my possessions here. I rejoice to say to you also that his deportment & exibition of kind feelings & *condesention* is all I could ask or would require of any child, & his brother thinks that I am mistaken as to my opinion of the cause of a great deal of his actions & that it arises from an excess of melancholy / melancholy. It was alway a mistery to me how one of my sons could have contempt or bad feeling for me their father. But there is nothing but mistery in the world and very few of those misteries can be solved by human wisdom. If his deportment continues as since I came home I shall have removed from me a weight that was insupportably heavy, though as far as I have been able to observe not as great as almost all the other parents have to bear, for he was certainly economical, industrious, & discreet in all things. I fear you will think that what I have said above will make me relax in my opperation at Magnolia, but not so, the logs are now hauling to the mill & I expect to begin to saw to day, and as the people are literally starving I really <have> can get no work that they may get a mouth full of bread. I think of employing them to clear up the place where my house is to be put. It is an experiment, but the opinion is now that if there was anything offered to the people that they could do to procure bread they would work. You will understand that I am not to be troubled with the work, as I intend to employ one of them to be head of the work, & I am not going an inch farther than I can stop without injury or inconvenience. If all should turn out nothing, it can not be nothing to me as I shall have an approving mind.

My Wheat at Belgrade & particularly at the Lake looks very well, when we consider how cold the first of the season has been. However as the latter has been so mild & the winter is half gone, I flatter my self that we shall not have that excessive cold winter prophesied. As the lower part of my field was sown at the Lake I think with the early rains we had that the wheat would have suffered; as it is it seems not to know that it has rained. So much for the new canal.

Politically, you see that Miss Margrets & my favourite Major Hinton lost his election for Treasurer.[1] After the quarrel or angry debate in the Commons about the time of baloting I had no hope for him. It was enough to rally the party. If I had (in my canvassing) done as some of my whig friends & fools had wished me to do enter in to political discussion with D^r^ [*Thomas H.*] Hall, charging him with voting according to Genl Jacksons will, (just what the people wanted him to do) it would have produced an issue between us in which the talents of no man /in America/ could have sustained me or given me the election, but after I had been elected & removed the delusion from their eyes by sending them information which I did think was the truth, there was no difficulty in electing M^r^ [*Edward*] Stanly against Genl. [*Louis D.*] Wilson & next the same old coon that I contended with. But vanity and selfsufficiency is the curse of the present age & it is as well /to/ let them alone for no good can grow out of any thing that age & experience can say or do. I will drop the subject by saying that Major Hinton was a most estimable man. The state could not get a better for the office which it pleased the Loco focos to dismiss /him from;/ but the Whigs of the last Legislature did no better and may hold their tongues, We the poeple nevertheless have a right to complain.

I observe by a late Inteligencer that Doctor Potter of Baltimore is dead. Poor old man! He died suddenly & I fear went off not in that state of mind best calculated for another world. I cannot know what is after death, but it is an awfull plunge in the dark, and I should greatly prefer to take it with a calm, quiet, & peacefull mind, with a heart of forgiveness to all those who have at any time done me evill by word or deed, & thereby hoping for forgiveness from my mercifull *God* for my *many many* sins, & transgressions. I thank my God I feel at this time at peace in my heart with the world, & all I ask of them is to let me alone and I think I can continue so to my lifes end.

I received a letter dated 29 ult. from my dear little Mary, she says they are all well, & gives some little account of the movements of the place, such as an honourable member of the Senate who has rather more than his share of teeth & who among other uncouth acts, reached over & helped himself out of her plate &c &c.

I have determined that she will come home about the middle of February & her brother Charles has offered his services to bring her home. I think that riding on horse back is indispensable to her health & as I had anticipated she had not been able to ride from the time I left up to that of her writing. I have heard not /a/ word of W. Shepards matrimonial movements. I should not be surprised if he has got clear thirty thousand dollars from his Alabama speculation if he should back out, to the no small gratification of some. I care nothing about it.

I find I have compleated or filled one sheet & must take another to close what little I have to say. I hope you will bear with me & I believe you will, as you have so far born with my almost interminable talking, but I ought to be satisfied with talking & not inflict on you writing also, but I will close as soon as possible this already too long scratch, though I think I have had a thousand things to say to you since we parted, which I hope you /will/ give me an opportunity of saying as many as I can recollect by giving me the pleasure of a visit before the winter is over. It seems to me now like it had been a long time since I saw you, & considering how much I am occupied in my new concern it can be no mistake or vain fancy that I wish to see you, but then my dear friend you are to exercise your own feelings & gratification on that subject. I think from present appearances there will be little if any interruption from another quarter. I think it highly probable that the string is cut. Well, so let it be; I always did dislike being at unprofitable business. I cannot repent for any thing I ever did when I was satisfied that it was for the best.

I am now too old to /be/ runing about after the fashionables, I feel ashamed of it when it is the case. The young people must take care of themselves, & I must be allowed at the age of sixty to do as such myself when it interferes with no one else. In the present case I think I have always been a supernumerary if it could have been known how to get over or round me.

The corn & all the other articles sent by the Queen from Captain Wilson came, safe to hand, & every dispatch was given that could be consistantly. If the Captain had not got on a log between Cross Landing & the mouth of the canal on monday morning, he would have been unloaded early tuesday morning instead of evening, for Charles was down with the flats to where the schooner was coming at sunrise on monday & could have made two loads that day, but she did not arrive untill after ten, & consequently could not make but one or be all night at the second. I hope you found the shingles good. If you should want more I expect they could be had of the same man & I suppose same price.

You wished to know when I was with you how much more corn I should want. From the best calculations I can make, taking all things into the account that is calculating for the old women, & old men & for those who can and will pay and not for the young & worthless part of the population, who I hope will /be/ sustained by the shingle geting establishment I should be glad to get three hundred barrils & should like to have it between the middle of March & /middle of/ April, to suit your convenience. All which corn will amount to the very moderate quantity of seven hundred & twenty seven barrils. Blessed be God for his mercies.

Charles who is with me desires his best respects to you & please to make mine to the Ladies, and now my dear friend please to accept the best wishes for your health & comfort from your sincere friend

E Pettigrew

James C. Johnston esqr

turn over

N.B. I have seen the little doctor since my return. In truth he preached at the Chapel Sunday before last,[2] in consequence of the day being two threatening for the Lake to come out & the minister stayed of course with it. It is the first time I have ever heard him hold forth. Doctrine Davenport was there, & when he heard that the little fellow was to hold forth, he said he would go, he could hear no such D——d little rascal preach the word of God, & when I persuaded him to stay as he had come, he said no, that he had rather go to H——l than hear any such creature preach.

The little creature is the most forlorn looking a groom that I have ever seen. He is unequivocably in a very tight place. Little or no practice No corn, no money, in debt to Mr C.s overseer for F. Fagan $1000. to the same for borrowed money for himself $400 without a dollar to pay it with & the overseer scared to death lest he loose it. What would have become of your $800. if it had been associated with this $1400— Have not Mr C. the Right R. [*Levi S. Ives*] & the little doctor got me out of a *great*, very *great* scrape. Yes they have & no thanks to them.

No one got you out, for you have cut your eyeteeth & they stay cut; as for my part I am always cuting mine for they will not stay cut. Poor creature but I think with assistance I am mending. I think there will be other people in tight places beside the doctor in time.

E P.

P.S. I hope to get a letter by the return mail if not please write me soon.

[*Addressed*] James C. Johnston Esqr
Hayes
Edenton P. Office

[1]Charles L. Hinton of Wake County was state treasurer from 1839 until 1843 and from 1845 until 1851. John Hill Wheeler of Lincoln County held the office in the interim; he was elected on December 22, 1842. Cheney, *North Carolina Government*, 181.

[2]The doctor was probably a lay reader in the Episcopal church.

William A. Dickinson to Ebenezer Pettigrew A&H

Hillabie Talladega C[o] [*Alabama*] 21 January 1843

Dear Sir

Yours dated 15th Nov. 1841 came duly to hand and was happy to learn that you and family were all well, hopeing this will find you all in good health, my family and self are in good health,

I return you my warmest thanks for your very friendly and ready acquiescence in acceeding to my wishes relative to the Land, I gave a Deed for it in the name of John Beasley, as we thought it would answer the purpose better so you can arrange it in the best manner & way you think will answer best, in case of death,

It is now a long time since I had the pleasure of writting you and have now to beg pardon for my long silence rest assured it is not that I have forgotten you for your name is often before us in our North Carolina conversation, it affords me much pleasure to learn that your sons are so acting in their worldly pursuits, as to reflect back that tender feeling into a parents bossom so much happines when he sees his children steering a <staight> straight and honourable course, long may they & you live to be a blissing to each other,

We have sad times in this State, every thing seems turned up side down, money scarce & all kinds of produce low, pork 3 @ 3½¢, corn 37½, cotten 4 @ 5½ to 5⅞ for some prime, people are much in debt & many of them are & has taken the benefit of the general Bankrup Law, I have considerable due me but I see no chance of ever gitting a cent, so here we go, some fast & some slow to destruction,

I am gitting on slow in the Farming business for the want of help it takes hard tuging to settle in /the/ woods, my two sons if they live and are prudent, they will in a few years be a great help, this part of country is setting up fast, the country is very brocken well watered and I believe it is the most healthy part of Alabama, we have three or four Gold Mines in opperation some few making money & others lossing as is usually the case in gold *Digings*, I believe Far[*m*]ing is the safest & most honorable *calling* after all,

We have had a severe winter— forst began in Oct^{r} & has been very cold, but little rain & no snow as yet,

I notice the news you favor me with it would afford me much pleasure to pay you visit once more before we depart from this and for ever,

You surprise me as regards Daniel Woodlys intemperance I am sorry for him I use to drink too much myself at times, he has begun where I leave off—I have not joined the Temprence society, but notwithstading I do not drink any *strong drink*, and has not for some years, the good folks of this region have confered the honor of Justice of the Pease on me, in this State they are elected by Ballot, they are now trying to have me made Post Master, what next I am not able to say, if anything else will duly aprise you of it,

If I have not already offended you by my long silence, you will please write me as soon as you can, your letters always are a source of pleasure

I hear from Hardy H. Phelps occasionally. tell him I wrote him since the death of Allen Bateman & has had no answer, what has become of Charles Wilder, give my respects to your sons, self and family join in wishes for your health & happiness in this & that world to come, and am Dear Sir with the greatest Respect

Your Obd^{t} Sv^{t}
William A. Dickinson

[*Addressed*] Ebenezer Pettigrew Esqr
Coolspring
Washington County
N.C.

Mary Blount Pettigrew to James Johnston Pettigrew UNC

[*Raleigh*] Jany 23^{d} '43

My dear Brother,

I recieved your letter on friday /before/ last and Grandma recieved the one you wrote her some days before. She would not let me see but said she would very willingly let me see it had she not solemnly promised you she would let no one read it; not even uncle James. She is an admirable hand at keeping things secret. As, I <called> came by there this morning from /my/ music lesson, I tried to get in to see Grandma; but after knocking three or four times, came away without succeeding in obtaining admittance. She told me when I wrote to give her love to you and tell you to write to her again soon.

Louis brought me two letters saturday night one from Pa and a long one from brother William; he seemed to be in excellent spirits and spent Christmas with Pa at Mr Johnston's. He seems much delighted with Mr J and says he called him by his first name. Dr Hardison is married and Mr Collins gave him a dinner but it rained so hard they could not attend; was not that unfortunate? however we got our share of the good things for brother C— and W— were both at it and found <them> it pleasant. Pa says that brother Charles has offered to come to Raleigh for me; so I shall go home in Febuary. I suppose I told you while here that I should possibly go home in that month. Pa says he is preparing to live at Magnolia and expects by this time next year to settled there. I am sorry he has determined to live a that place for I fear he will be lonesome. There is one thing that I had forgotten to tell you. brother W.— says that Pa gives you a very high character.

Nancy commenced school to day with great joy. I asked William if J. Iredel was going to Hillsboro, he says that J. Iredel says so, but that he has been saying so for the last three years.

The Legislature is in session yet and will probably adjourn on wednesday. We went the other night and heard an excellent speech from Mr [*Henry Kollock*] Nash, it <is> /was/ the only thing I have heard that was worth hearing. For the last week the ladies have been thronging to the commons but I beleive the Senate is totally deserted. I have not been in the hall since I went with the unfortunate Mr H— and the distinguished Mr J. J. P.

I received a long letter from Eliza the other night but have not answered it yet. A bundle was brought, from C— Hill by Turner and Hughes to day, for W— and what do you think it contained? two collars belonging to said W—who said that John had stolen them.

With love to all inquiring friends I remain

Your affectionate sister
Mary

[*Addressed*] J. Johnston Pettigrew
Hills-boro
N. Carolina

Caroline E. Bateman[1] *to Ebenezer Pettigrew* UNC

Albemarle Jan 25th—[*1843*]

Beloved and respected Sir

Though you may think it bold in me to address you thus and—though you may care nothing about me in any way—Yet believe Sir that you have had my most sincere love and respect.

I have heard of the base falsehood in circulation respecting Mrs Davenport, And am truly sorry that no *Friend* has been Kind enough to let me know it before— Is it necessary Mr Pettigrew for me to assure you that it is false. Do you believe me the despisable wretch that could fabricate so base a thing.

Monday evening is the first time that I have ever heard such a thing spoken of or alluded to—And I would just as soon expected to have heard that Mrs Halsey had sworn that I had commited murder—

I visited both Mrs Halsey and Mrs Davenport yesterday— Mrs Halsey denies *ever* having heard me speak of you or Mrs Davenport except in the most respectful maner— And Mrs Davenport says that she only infered from Mrs Halseys conversation that it was me. I am willing Mr Pettigrew for every one who has *ever* heard me speak of you to tell all they know— *You* then might be convinced that I am not the contemptible being you now think me I have ever wished for your esteem Mr Pettigrew more than any other persons in the wide world— but have ever felt that you disliked me—from your cold and restrained manner—

<A> A word of Kindness from you my dear Sir would be rightly appreciated and never forgotten—

I have been taught to love and respect you Mr Pettigrew from my childhood— I now need no Tutor to make me love my beloved Fathers dearest and best Friend— I know that *you* loved my Father and I well Know that *he* loved and respected you above any one else Is it strange then /that/ I love you—or is it strange that I wish your Esteem. If you believed my Father grateful—think of me the same—for be assured that my Father has left me one treasure—gratitude.

Receive my sincere and grateful acknowledgements for all that is past And believe that a word of advice from you Mr Pettigrew will be most thankfully recieved—

Let me beg of you Mr Pettigrew not to think me guilty of this miserable affair— I am inocent—let who may say to the re[ver]se.

I have always thought that you looked on Mr and Mrs Davenport as children and treated them as such—had I have gone to Baltimore with Mrs Davenport would have expected to have looked on you as she did—as a Father and protector.

I have spoken of Mrs Davenport as an Amiable and inoffensive lady and have had no right to speake otherwise So far as regards her clotheing—I know not how many dresses she has no more than I know how many coats you have And know not whether she got her cloak before or after going to Baltimore I shall be thankful to hear from you. Mr Pettigrew—Will you receive the best wishes and highest respect of—

C. E. Bateman

[*Addressed*] Mr Pettigrew
Present

[1]Caroline E. Bateman has not been further identified.

*Ebenezer Pettigrew to Caroline E. Bateman** UNC

Copy

Lake Scuppernong Jan 26, 1843

My dear Miss Caroline

It is true I have heard of what you refer to in your letter. With respect to the fact from which this whole disturbance derives its source. I have only to say, that it is a matter of the most serious regret, that so kind and so disinterested an act, having only the good of a suffering invalid in view should have been thus distorted. I the more regret that my name has been introduced & used so unwarrantably: I have hoped that as my years increase in number so I would be less and less involved in the petty strife & bickering of which we see so much in the world. And when the glorious sun shall have gone down in gorgeous splender upon my earthly prospects, that I should leave the world with a character untainted by the fowl mouth of slander & uninvolved with its consequences. You must permit me to say that I was astonished at receving your letter; neighborhood talk or slander is an occupation in which I am by no means desirous of being engaged, no notice should be taken of it untill we are directly and individually charged face to face. By engaging in it we but introduce ourselves into a whirlpool which the longer we continue in it involves us the more distructively in its inveloping circles & eventually we are swalowed up with awfull rapidity. Fly from its center; have nothing to say about the slander; is my motto & advice.

My dear Miss Bateman you charge me with having disliked you, this is rather a grave accusation and if you will permit me to say, without sufficent reason. Something more is required to constitute dislike than a retiring manner. In this slanderous and uncharitable world those are friends who do us no harm: for unfortunately some injure us wearing the garb of friendship. I hope therefore that I may have had a more effective friendship than many of whose good feeling you think better than my own. Really there is so little sincerity in the world that I almost consider friendship a negative quality. In this light my dear Madam I hope you will consider me among your friends

E Pettigrew

Ebenezer Pettigrew to William Shepard Pettigrew UNC

Bonarva Feb 3, 1843

My dear William

It is with deep regret I inform you that Edward & Hugh Collins were drownd last evening together with two little negroe boys one of them Harry last son. It would be well if on the receit of this you come in as there will be want of some person to sit up tonight & also a respect which you owe to the family. We are well & send our Love to you Your affect father

E Pettigrew

[*Addressed*] Mr W. S. Pettigrew
Belgrade

*Ebenezer Pettigrew to James Cathcart Johnston** A&H

Lake Scuppernong Feb. 24, 1843

My dear friend

Your favour of the 22nd came to hand by the mail on the next day. To say that on reading it I was mortified would be a light remark, for mortification is my mother & sorrow is my father; but I can truely say that it gave me real *pain* to know that for a single moment instead of the time taken to write a letter, you could have entertained the opinion which it expressed. Why my dear friend so far from your letters, whether long or short, being an infliction, they have always been received & read with the greatest pleasure, and what then? Laid by? By no means, I can say with perfect truth that many of them are read a dozen times, & I rarely travel without /half/ that number in my trunk; Today looking for a letter /in my traveling desk/ from James Pettigrew of Charleston to show to William I counted in the file ten of yours & be assured your last contained too many wholesome truths for it to be either a sweating dose or for me to give it but one reading. Every day proves the correctness of the observances it contains. The people have no reason, & none can be taught <them> but they are starving.

I can but repeat again that knowing the exalted opinion which I have of you in all things, the sincere regard I have for you & at the same time a knowledge of the high esteem you had for me evinced in every way, I did not think it possible I could act in any way so as to seem to neglect you for a moment, for nothing can be farther from my wishes or intention than to injure your feelings in the slightest degree, and I was perfectly thunderstruck at reading the first passage in your letter. I can but say that I am & have been all my life at the rack of immagination to do for the best not only in my business, but to mankind in <all my> every relation<s> of life, but that after all my exertions, my family find falt of me, my neighbours find falt of me; my sons think I might have done differently by them, I have been always finding falt of my self & lastly I am constrained to say, and you too Brutus? Alas! It must be so, and I can /but/ fall decently.—Up to the evening that I wrote you for the last twenty days, I had, had not a moment of time to spare. but before the stars were out of the sky, never taking more than ten minutes to eat & give rally leaving the work (a mile from the house) when it was too dark to distinguish persons twenty steps & the day that /I/ did write to you I left the yard before sunrise, eat my breakfast in the woods & could /not/ return to get my dinner untill half after three, after which I warmed my shivering old limbs, & wrote the confused letter which I presume you have recieved.

In all this hurry & bustle, carrying all before me, for I think my hands never worked better. Stimulated with the thought of preparing a new, for a place to retire too, & shotly to die at & while alive to be retired, there was never a day that my mind did not revolve on you & so far from wishing or in the least thinking to neglect your much esteemed letter; looking with anxiety for an opportunity to answer it, and be assured sooner than giving you cause intentionally to think for a moment that I neglected it I would have droped every thing & complyed with your expectations and my own wish. Hoping you are before this satisfied with my explanation / nation, I will make but one other remark on this painfull subject. I never yet received a letter from you that I did not regret when I got to the end. So far, have they allways been from a sweating dose.—I am much obliged to you for the order on Messrs Bryan & Maitland of Plymouth for the corn. I have no doubt of its being of a good quality & in good order. I received a letter by the last mail from Messrs Hardy & Brothers informing me of a vessil coming to me with two hundred & fifty bus Irish potatoes, & a few other trifles, I think it <very> probable that I shall be able to get him to go for the corn. I shall not let it stay longer at Plymouth than it is possible to get it away. I am very glad to learn that the trunk which Mr Hathaway was puting down when I was at the plantation answers the purpose fully. As respects the money paid for the shingles by Charles Pettigrew It was mine & I shall be glad for it to go /towards/ <the> pay<ment>ing of the corn as you mention. I am very glad they were found good. I can assure you the trouble taken to procure them was a pleasure.

In my letter of the 21st I wrote you something respecting my opperations in timber geting. I have halled up to the mill above three hundred logs, more than two thirds are sawed & in little more than a fortneight I hope to have the others sawed, amounting to more than fifty thousand feet & <more than> sufficient for my dwelling & six out houses, I have sills hewed for all those houses & also for a barn 34 ft. by 144 ft long. All of which, together with the logs for the mill was laid of by my own hand. I have also had forty seven thousand shingles made. In going to the various places when the work was doing, I found it impossible for me to walk all & consequently had ride. My horse being held all day became at length restive & in one case I was thrown from him in the middle of one of the field roads I fell directly on my back, but was not hurt much. But the day in which I received your letter I had a very bad fall, that might have been worse than death. After walking in the plank yard giving some directions, I went into the saw mill & to get a measuring rod I got on a log & in steping down from the log, I steped on the log way from which my foot sliped (the soles of my shoes being frosted) & I fell at my full length across the saw carriage way my thigh across one way & my arm and hand on the other. The injury to my thigh was very sevier & nearly deprived me of walking. It was Gods mercy that both my thigh & arm was not broken, than which I should greatly prefered it had been my neck. Then the agony would have been over.

Untill saturday the weather has been good, except ocasionally very cold, but at this time it is very wet & uncomfortable & it would at this time /be/ exceedingly bad to hall cut logs. Fearing this might be the case I lost not <time> a moment of time & have compleatly compassed my object so far. Up to this time the people who I have employed to clear ground, have behaved well, not one has intruded himself at my house yet. In truth they are distressingly humble, for they have got nothing to eat, no, money & no credit. I learn that a number of those who work at Magnolia have not a mouthfull of meat. In truth those few who have money are like to starve for there is no corn to be bought. Fifty dollars was turned away a few weeks ago from the steam mill, because they had no corn & could get none. Poor women are going from house to house to beg one pint of meal. But let me drop this [picture] & wish that I could die.

My health & vigour was never beter than the last month, but for the last week I have not been so well. I hope you continue to enjoy good health.

My dear Mary who is with me, is in good health She requests me to give her Love to you & to say that she would be very glad <*illegible* see> that you would visit her pa that thereby she might /have the pleasure to/ see you, which would be equally gratifying to my sons who desire their best respects to you and please to assure yourself of the sincere regard & Esteem of your friend

E Pettigrew

[*Addressed*] Copy of a letter
To James C. Johnston esq
Hayes
Edenton P. Offce

Mary Blount Pettigrew to James Johnston Pettigrew UNC

Bonarva March 28th [*18*]'43

My dear brother,

Although I am not in your debt I thought it would be as well to improve the present time and address you a letter, knowing the need of amusement in your delightful city of hills. Pa received your letter last mail. I hope, my dear brother, you will not think hard of me, if as a sister, I give you a little advice. Therefore I will venture to beg that you will take more pains with your letters and write longer ones.

Pa's health is pretty good. He is very much engaged with his preparations for Magnolia, which keeps him in good spirits and makes him much more contented than he otherwise would be. He is having plank sawn for the house, & you know the saw mill is his delight. I wish he could always have some business of importance at it. Our dear father is not near as active as formerly—he has had several falls and yesterday while in the woods came near hurting himself very badly; so much so as in his fall to break his rule, which was in his pocket and has been there for the last forty years.

Brother Charles and I went into Scuppernong last week to see Mrs Lewis and Mrs Halsey—the latter has a piano, and it would be difficult to tell you how much delighted Mr H—— was with it. His daughters were expected home in the spring but have defered their return until after the sickly season. Dr and Mrs Hardison seem to be very well fixed at the cottage. An application has been made to make him postmaster; our former officer thinking the constable's place as more honorable station has resigned.

The season is exceedingly backward so much so that they have not commenced to plant corn yet and the trees look like January. It does seem as if we are to have a dreadful famine; for the wheat promises badly. Pa thinks some enemy is destroying it and I heard Mr Collins says last night he did not expect to raise seed; but it is to be hoped that he has taken too gloomy a view of it. Pa Mr C—— and Mr Davenport are doing all in their power to alleviate the suffering comm/u/nity but there will be great want notwithstanding all efforts. Morals, seem, in these two counties to be in the lowest state of degradation. They are in reality neither savage nor civilised, w/h/iskey is the bane of their existance. Mr and Mrs Daniel

Woodly were at one time both in a fair way to kill themselves shortly but he has joined the temperance society and I do hope will reform but it is a tough job to change bad habits. He is in the other room now; it being the first time he has been here this winter.

Brother William came in this morning. On mondays he holds a levee of Scuppernongers who come for corn. Mr Collins holds one on Wednesdays and we have a good deal of amusement in laughing at their ways. I have taken several rides on horseback with brother C——. I still retain Wild-Cat in my service. He purchased a colt about three years old and I am feeding myself with the hopes of getting possession myself as soon as she is well broken.

My dear Johnston I am more and more delighted with my own dear Lake, it certainly is the most charming spot on the face of the earth, I think I will be perfectly contented to make it my home the rest of my days; only going away during the fall to avoid the musquitoes and to see a little of the world. In all probability. I shall return to school in the spring and improve myself in french and music.

The Bishop will be here on Easter Sunday to remain two or three weeks. His health is better than it was and he thinks he will soon be more sound than before he was sick.

With love from all I remain, your aff' sister

M. B. P.

James J. Pettigrew

[*Addressed*] Johnston Pettigrew
Hillsboro
North-Carolina

John Herritage Bryan to Ebenezer Pettigrew UNC

Raleigh Apl. 1. [*18*]'43

My dear Sir,

I had intended writing you before this but have had nothing worth communicating—I have had so far the worst or poorest circuit that I remember—There is almost literally in some of the Courts no new business—the corps of lawyers is increasing, with the decrease of the means of support. It is greatly to be regretted that labour should be considered unfashionable or at all disparaging particularly in a country professing to be republican.—

I suppose Mary B. informed you in her letter to Mary P. that Frank had attained the topmost round in his class and that too in Mathematics & at West Point.

We have had exhibitions of Animal Magnetism here, I witnessed one, & was much astonished at the experiments—there are certainly many great mysteries in nature yet undiscovered—I understand that the Bishop & Mr Badger would not go to witness any of the experiments.

The differences between Mr Devereux & the Burgwyns[1] were referred to Arbitrators who were Col. Joyner,[2] Gov Morehead & Gov. [*Edward Bishop*] Dudley. I understand they have made their award—I heard Gov. M. say that they had no hesitation in sanctioning Mr Devereux's conduct in regard to the shipments of cotten of which so much complaint was made.—

The breach made by their family quarrel will hardly ever be reconciled I imagine.—

I have reason to believe (between ourselves) that Mr Iredell is very much straitened just now for money—his courts are of very little value to him.—

It is to be hoped that the pressure of the times may produce some good, by compelling people to economize & thus to imitate in some degree their ancestors.—

Tell Mary that her mother & all the children Send their love to her—& also to you & sons—My regards to them & please offer my sincere condolence to Mr Collins.—

very truly
yr friend & relative
Jn H. Bryan

P.S. This Sheet was torn <in two> by mistake.—
Little Charlotte is not well—

[*Addressed*] E. Pettigrew Eqr
Cool Spring
N.C.

---

[1]The suit between the Burgwyns and Thomas Pollock Devereux began in the Superior Court of Jones County. It concerned a dispute over land owned by George Pollock, who died intestate in 1839. Henry King Burgwyn and the other Burgwyns involved were children of John Fanning Burgwyn and Sarah Pierrepoint Hunt Burgwyn, George Pollock's half-sister. Thomas Pollock Devereux's mother, Frances Pollock Devereux, was sister to George Pollock. The court awarded the decision to Devereux. When the Burgwyns appealed to the North Carolina Supreme Court, the lower court's decision was upheld. *Henry K. Burgwyn et al.* v. *Thomas P. Devereux*, 23 N.C. 583-592 (1841); Powell, *DNCB*, I, 278.

[2]Andrew Joyner (1786-1856), lieutenant-colonel of United States Volunteers during the War of 1812, lived in Halifax County. A Whig, he had sat in the state House of Commons and was a state senator at this time. Joyner was a justice of the peace and often acted as an arbitrator in disputes. Ashe, *Biographical History*, III, 236-238.

Joshua Skinner[1] *to Ebenezer Pettigrew* A&H

Athol Apl 24th 1843

Dear Sir

It falls to my lot to inform you of death of Mrs [*Ann Hall*] Blount she died on the 19th Inst about 9 O'clock in the Evening Just two weeks after the death of Mr. [*Clement Hall*] Blount—A few days after you left her she was taken with a violent attack of cholic which produced inflamation in the bowels & violent fever which terminated in death, she suffered great pain for a few days but died easy and composed—Your visit to her was a great comfort & satisfaction to her, she could talk of nothing else, she made a will in a day or two after she was taken sick and after paying her own debts directed the remainder of her property to go towards the discharge of Mr Blounts debts prefering Dr [*James*] Norcom, Whitaker Benbury & Joseph Underhill—a sale of her little effects furniture &c will take place soon after our may court as notice can be given, the crop will be carried on & the hired negroes kept on the farm the remainder of the year—In looking over Mr Blounts papers did /you/ see a note of John D. Collins payable to Mrs. Blount for about $130. I understood Mr B. to say /he/ had such a note some short time before his death—You were saying something to me about the grave yard, will you be so kind as to give me your views how I had best have it done & whether I had better have it enlarged Mr Blount had it laid off & said it was sufficiently large as it enclosed all the family & there would be no other persons to be buried there—please /write/ me when convenient—

With my kindest regards to your sons & family

I am dear sir Very respectfully yours
Joshua Skinner

[*Addressed*] Ebenezer Pettigrew Esq
Lake Pheps
Near Cool Spring
Tyrrell Co

[1]Joshua Skinner has not been identified.

Ebenezer Pettigrew to James Johnston Pettigrew UNC

Lake Scuppernong Ap 30, 1843

My dear Son,

I received a letter mail before last from Mr Bingham dated the 12th Instant, informing me that the day before, you had accidentally sprained your ancle & that he feared it would keep you some days from school I flatter myself however that before this it is pretty well recovered, but I would suggest to you, it is frequently remarked that /a/ sprain is worse than a broken bone & I would then say that you cannot be too carefull untill it gets entirely well & strong how you step, le/a/st another strain of the same ancle might take /you/ off your feet for months.

I was much gratefied also to read in /the first line of/ Mr Binghams letter that you were doing well in your studies & he might say in your deportment. He farther said that he was geting along pretty well in his school, but that he had a few who were infected with laziness & Rowdyism, who he apprehended he would have to dismiss. As for laziness I hope I beleive my dear son I need say to you nothing & farther hope & believe that you are as far from rowdyism, or even countenancing rowdies as you are from any other vice. My reasons for the above opinion I give you more fully in consequence of /the/ present dreadfull insubordination & depravity of youth in the present age Really there appears to be an entire spirit of insubordination / nation pervading all classes of the united states, & the consequences will be (if not soon checked) an entire subvertion of all rule & order. My son the reason I have for hoping & believing that I say of you I will give you in a few words. Your father is /of/ all men one most in favour of law, order & good government & if you please strong government. He will & has allways controaled where it was his province to do so, perfectly regardless of consequences. By this law & order his children that are grown & nearly so, stand before the world as examples for the world; yet without boasting I can say that I am ready to go into the comparison with /any/ person & they may take an equal number from as many families. I know my son that your good sense must see and know what I say to be true, & that you must <[w]ay> /be sensible of/ the lasting benefit of such deportment, & with such before your eyes, cannot, depart from them. But to avoid evil you must shun it, & him that possesses it as you would a biting snake. Go not with him, le/a/st after long assotiation (& /the/ devil enters sooner than one thinks) you become familiar with vice & fall into its embrace. Your uncle Freds remarks when he was driven from West Point I shall never forget. 'The fellow he took the part of & rescued from punishment was a low rowdy & one he had no association with, & rarely spoke to.' <And> If ever I [*saw*] any one who repented his act he did. From having the materials to make one of the finest fellows of the family in my view he has been little else than a scap-goat ever since. Now my son these are remarks made to /you/ as merely precautionary, not for a moment supposing that you take any part with idle fellows & Rowdies. Rely on my word. If you do, you sin against light & knowledge.

A fortnight ago, I was taken with Cholera morbus, & came very near dying, & but for the timely assistance of Doctor Lewis, I think I should. I am now however pretty well recovered. Your brother & sister Mary are also well, & your brother Charles is about to leave with your sister Mary for Washington, City where it is concluded she shall spend another summer. They all send their love to you.

The season has been one of the most backward ever known, but vegetation has at last burst forth, & wheat has much improved, & the young corn seems to puting forth, with considerable force. The country is now in a most wretched state of poverty, & starvation, & if they can possibly get through or keep alive to the coming crop it will be the utmost. The corn I must buy for my self & give to the starving will amount to something like twenty four hundred dollars, & nothing to sell to pay it, but the wheat crop, which looks pretty fair but, under the best circumstances will not be sufficent. You will find by these remarks that money will be a scarce article, & that economy will be possitively requisit is run behind. Having not received a letter from you for some time I should like an answer to this letter. I the mean time I remain your affectionate father

E Pettigrew

Mr J. J. Pettigrew

N.B. Make my best respects to Mr & Mrs Bingham, also Dr Webb & Lady.

[*Addressed*] Mr J. Johnston Pettigrew
Hillsborough
N. Carolina

Hardy and Brothers to Ebenezer Pettigrew A&H

Norfolk, Va 19. May 1843—

E. Pettigrew, Esq— Lake Scuppernong—

Dear Sir,

We wrote you on the 12. inst—with Invo & B/Ldg. corn &c. pr Elvira Jane, and this morning have your favour ofthe 16th At the time we shipped the corn to Little and Great Alligator, it was impossible to obtain any but that we sent—opportunities of shipping to these places seldom offer, and supposing the people were in immediate and great need ofthe corn, we considered it best to send it. It was old, but the quality was very good—heavy white Maryland corn, and but slightly touched with weavel, and very good for bread—They may consider themselves fortunate indeed, ifthey can always get such—We have long thought that nine tenths ofour charities, were improperly bestowed—tending to make those we desire to benefit, more indolent and lazy—they possess very little gratitude—Indeed, some /are/ like Wolves, howling round your enclosure, and will not be satisfied till you have thrown over to them your *last* Sheep. Very few indeed appreciate properly, the favours and charities they recieve—At the time we purchased the last corn for you, we had no expectation that it would further decline soon; for we had to pay 58¢—to execute a part of Mr. Collins' order, bought immediately after yours—Since, however, our reciepts have been very large from the neighbouring rivers, and a cargo of 7000 bushels from New Orleans—and the price has receded to 54 & 55¢—with considerable now afloat, and should not be surprised if should be sold as low as 50¢—before all is disposed of—We hear ofone sale today at /#/ 53¢ Ifyou desire us to send you more, please let us have your order, and it shall be executed on the best terms possible—At present we do not think it can be lower in July.

Very Respectfully Sir, yrfrds & Sts
Hardy & Brothers

#53¢

[*Addressed*] Hon: E. Pettigrew
Cool-Spring
Washington County
No Ca—

William Shepard Pettigrew to Mary Blount Pettigrew UNC

Belgrade, May 20th 1843

My dear Sister

Perhaps you may think me quick on the trigger to renew our correspondence at so early a period after your departure and without allowing you time to write the first letter, which is invariably required among correspondents: with friends & relatives, particularly female relatives, I am not punctilious, but rather cast away forms & ceremonies and allow my association with them to rest upon the feelings of the heart. There is nothing more clearly true than this—for an association between persons of equal ages to be pleasant, they must be free from restraint, not cramped by a fear of transgressing imaginary rules. We were agreeably surprised by Brother Charles' early return. He spred before me a quantity of new clothes; I was renewed if not regenerated.

I was glad to learn that our friends at Washington & Alexandria are well. I shall never think of my visit to the two places in the Winter of —36 & —37 without a glow of pleasure passing my bosom. I never shall forget Gov. [*Joseph*] Kent. Poor old Gov. where is he now—gone—gone—gone, I trust to a better, to a brighter world; but notwithstanding the belief which we entertain that our friends are happier, we wish them back again, we long for them—we sigh; their absence creates an aching void that neither wealth, nor honors, nor new friends can restore—

"The thoughts we hold dearest,
The pledges we gave,
Of love the sincerest,
Must sink in the grave!"

"The ties must be broken,
That friendship has twined,
No vestage or token,
Shall be left behind."

"The brightest, the purest,
Must haste to decay;
All things we love dearest,
Must vanish away"

"Our joys flee from us,
Like phantoms at night;
They smile once upon us,
And then take their flight."

"But as tones of music
Still ring on the ear,
When the loved one that made it,
Is cold on the bier."

"Or as flowers when withered,
Yield sweeter perfume,
Than when they are gathered
In freshness and bloom."

"So surely in Heaven,
Shall memory remain,
And the joys here given,
Shall be felt again."

Nor shall I soon forget the two pleasant days spent at Mr Gardener'^s^, nor that part of one of Scott's novels read by Miss Horner, and, I think, read also by Miss Constance; I was fresh from Scott myself, and had my mind in a good train for appreciating his merits. Miss /C/ is a very agreeable lady. I am much engaged in the corn crop, trusting that a wise Providence will bless my labors with a bountiful harvest. I have not yet complained of the loss last

Summer—nor shall I complain let come what may; I act upon the Christian rule, the Lord giveth & the Lord taketh away. We are only stewards, and if our master, who giveth us all things, sees fit for our misconduct to lessen our wages, let us humbly bow. I thank my Maker, most cordially do I thank him, that he has imbued me with the spirit of resignation. I trust he will give me the power through life to struggle manfully against difficulties; to rise Phenix like from beneath them; although borne down for a while, at length to rise triumphantly; should it ever be my lot to be threatened with poverty, disgrace, or overwhelming sorrow, I trust he will "throw his broad & impenetrable shield around me and bear me aloft."

From my constant occupation in business I have not visited Mr Collins' since you left, nor have I seen one of the grown members of the family. I was at Pa's on the Sunday previous to the last. In the afternoon, as I looked from the window, I saw Mr Collins' three youngest children returning from a walk on the Lakeside, the sweetness of their countenances so forcibly struck me that I rose from my seat immediately, and went out and spoke to them; a sudden impulse of fondness seized me, I thought of their little brothers,[1] the circumstances attending whose death are too deeply impressed upon my mind ever to be eradicated, which circumstances have promoted the friendly feelings that I before entertained for the Parents, Children & Uncle (of course I do not exclude Miss Alethea, whom I esteem very highly). I have seen something of death, and have felt for the bereavement of the survivors & for those who have been snatched from a bright existence: but never, except in the case of a relative, have I felt such poignant sorrow. Death under all circumstances is mournful, & calculated solemnly to impress all whose hearts are not seared. Even the beasts of the field lament over the loss of the companions of their labor, should not man, possessed as he is of some of the attributes of his Maker, feel much more? When the grim monster tears from us friends who have reached the Winter of life, we have less cause for sorrow, for in the ordinary course of nature their days must soon be numbered; but when he cuts down those around whom the roses of life are blossoming, we must repine; when he blights the bud that promises to bloom so beautifully; when he blasts it not in a baren waste but in a genial mead; when he lays the brilliant, the virtuous, the lovely in the tomb, the heart sickens, & human hopes wither. These interesting children, but a short while since, were among us; their cheerful smiles gladdened the hearts of doting parents; their joyous laugh and sprightly step were a source of pleasure to all who knew them; none could be so prejudiced as not to think they were destined to be blessings to their parents & ornaments to their country, that, in after life, they would be bright examples to illustrate the reward of Christian parents who bring up their children in the nurture & admonition of the Lord; to-day they sleep in the silence of the grave, the wind howls over them, the cold rain beats upon the turf beneath which repose their mortal remains, but they hear not the inhospitable blasts of the one nor the chilling drops of the other. Peace, Gentle Spirits!--It is for the living only to grieve.—Philosophy would tell us mourn /only/ for those who are left. But man cannot always be guided by the lessons of philosophy. The morose ascetic may look on with indifference, but he, who is not buried to the world, cannot otherwise than drop a tear. When I stood over their lifeless bodies—when I touched their icy heads, I could but wish for the power of omnipotence to snatch them from the grasp of death. Dear boys, adieu—Those who love you will ever cherish your memories, your forms will be vivid in their minds when years have rolled away; you will be the subjects of their reflections by day, & the companions of their dreams by night; your earthly career is run, but you are only removed from a world of sorrow to one of happiness; could the prayers of friends have detained you your hearts would yet beat animated with the hopes of youth. But the lamentation of friendship can, now, no more reach you than the laugh of indifference. You are the lonely inhabitants of the tomb, there to remain until the ark-angel's trump shall sound to awaken you from your slumbers.

My dear Sister, I should be glad to say much more, but I fear I have already /been/ too prolix, besides, I am trespasing on my own time, having been absent from the business three hours.

Pa & Brother Charles were well when I last saw them.

With very high esteem I am your affectionate brother
Will: S. Pettigrew

Miss Mary B. Pettigrew

P.S. May 21st.—After Brother Charles & I had returned from the chapel this morning, a negro boy brought us three notes from Mr Collins, one for Pa, one for Brother Charles, and one for your humble servant. Mine was couched in the following terms—the others of whose were similar—

The Misses Collins request
the pleasure of Mr Wm Pettigrew's
company, on Thursday evening next,
at eight o'clock—

Edenton.
Saturday, May 20th

You may draw your own inference from this; I presume it is an invitation to Uncle William's wedding, but it is only a presumption, as I have not heard a word relative to it, since you left. I saw Mr & Mrs Collins at the chapel, (Miss Alethea left for Edenton on Wednesday last) and was extremely sorry to see them look so badly. He complains much of his head, which affection, you know, he has, for some time, been suffering from; her eye is not yet well, otherwise, I know of no positive complaint, but she looks wan & care worn. No one knows that I am writing, or they would unite with me in love to you. If my acquaintance with the families at Washington & Alexandria be sufficient, of which you will be the best judge, please present them my kind regards. Farewell—

W. S. P.

[*Addressed*] Miss Mary B. Pettigrew
Care of Gen. Henderson,
Washington City
D.C.

[1]Two of the children, Edward and Hugh, drowned in the Collins canal on February 2, 1843. Powell, *DNCB*, I, 405.

Ebenezer Pettigrew to James Johnston Pettigrew UNC

Lake Scuppernong May 22, 1843

My dear Son

I received in the due course of the mail your letter of May 1st Post marked April 2nd, also your letter dated /May the/ 17th Postmarked May the 11th on the 18th of the same month. There seems to be a strong discrepancy in those dates, but I suppose you are all so busy in Hillsborough, that you have not time to pay much attention to the small matter of dates &c &c in private letters & small correspondence. We poor creatures in the woods may be thankfull if we can get our correspondants to write us in any way or fashion & then thankfull if we have got learning enough to english it.

I was very glad to learn that your foot got well or better so soon, particularly when it seemed to be so bad a sprain, & farther by your last letter that you had taken no part with those rowdies, that Mr Bingham had to drive out from his school. I have no doubt of your being prepared for your examination at Chapel Hill, even if it were in former day. From what I hear generally now talked, I suppose a tolerable intelegent boy might expect to pass who had but turned over the leaves of most of the books.

With respect to your coming home at the vacation. My son, I should be very glad if you could, but I have not the money to spare,

& you will very easily understand how that is, when I inform you that from the total failure of the corn crop last year I not only loose the income from that crop which would have amounted to at least $4000. dollars, but I have to buy corn principly for my self & some for the poor to the amount of about $2400, almost all which I have to ask credit for & rely on the wheat crop to settle. The wheat now looks well but it is uncommonly late, & you know at best a very uncertain crop. I very well recollect the promise I made you to take you to Norfolk to get your cloths, but the expen[*se*] of travil woud amount to the cloths, & you had better get the cloths you may want either /at/ Hilsborough or Raleigh. You had better write me on that subject. I do not wish extravagance, but at the same time I do not wish you by any means to be behind in your dress any but the fools, who I hope you would patern after in no way.

Your sister Mary left for Washington City the first of this month. Your brother Charles who went with her has returned & leaves today for Edenton to witness the nuptial ceremony of your Uncle William Biddle Shepard to Miss Ann D. Collins of that place. Your brothers are both well & would send their love to you if they knew I was writing. I began this letter to write you a fashionable one, but find myself on the third page with my rustic slang. Make my respects to M^{r} & Mrs Bingham also D^{r} & Mrs Webb. & beleive me your affectionate father

E Pettigrew

Mr J. Johnston Pettigrew

N.B. If you should go down to Raleigh to get your cloths it will be necessary that you consult Mr Bryan or you will be cheated most unmercifully. You must get the money before you can get them from any place. We are all starving in this quarter, not a bushel of corn but what we get from another state. The country is entirely used up.

[*Addressed*] Mr J. Johnston Pettigrew
Hillsborough
N. Carolina

Thomas Turner to Ebenezer Pettigrew A&H

Windsor NC June 7 1843

Dear sir

The last mail brought me your kind and acceptable letter of the 29th last month.

I am glad, very glad that I did at last pay you up the money that you so kindly lent me, so long ago, and under circumstances that gave so small promise of repayment. I regret only that I paid you in notes; but the notes are good and I hope they will serve you a good purpose. I am happy however to see that the payment was made at a time when you were wanting it; and I hope the interest made you some amends for the delay of payment. I am heartily thankful to you for that instance of your kindness as well as for your great kindness /in general/ which I have often felt and in a great variety of ways. I wish we lived so nearby together as to enable me to show how much I esteem you, and how happy I should be to render you services and to increase that kind regard which you have ever shown me. But fate has ordered it otherwise, and we must seldom meet again. Yet though we may meet but seldom, I shall frequently call you to mind, and shall thank Heaven for that recollection.

You could not have better entertained me in a letter than you did in the one before me which tells me of your children, their occupation, their whereabouts, and your own affairs. The storms of last year did you great harm. I knew as much before I read it in your letter. Every good hath its evil, and every evil its good. Your abundant crops and great prosperity in a variety of ways subjected you to great damage by those storms. Whereas my great adversity felt them not, except indirectly as they injured my neighbours. I speak of <them> /the storms/ in my common jocose way as /I might of/ persons of great violence, visiting the earth to do what damage they could; but as persons also of great dignity, too great to notice such poor folks as me.—And I relate that they called upon me as they passed, enquired what I had, and finding I had nothing, left me without injury, and passed on to you and Mr Collins, where they delighted to dwell, roll, wallow, revel in the luxuries afforded by plenty.—And then I add how happy is the man of obscurity!! And I thank Heaven! that I had not then either ships to be cast away, or large crops to be ruined! While however I am thus felicitating myself, lo! I feel the rebound of their violence, and find that the injury of my neighbors was an injury to me; and thence I reason myself into the belief that their good is also my good, and that I do but add to my prosperity and happiness whenever I increase or improve their's.— And so good is constantly coming out of what we deem evil, and every thing hath a tongue to persuade us that our true interest lies in a tender concern for the welfare of others, Amen! And stop here, that I may not preach you a sermon, nor seem to be better than I am.

I tell you what my friend, I could wish your children were at home; that your fireside was restored, and that you should once more

"Look for pleasures yet to come
And feel again that home is—home"

I hope you will find a way to realize all that happiness, that cheerful happiness which belongs to so much prosperity, health, children, friends, and virtue. He that cannot be perfectly happy in such circumstances, notwithstanding heavy strokes of misfortune and griefs, events natural in themselves and that sooner or later must have happened,—should suspect something in himself proned to unhappiness and should try to correct it.

As I read over your labors, I cannot persuade myself that you are not a very cheerful, happy, contented man. A mistake was made when labor was imposed on man with intent to curse him; for it is the source of every blessing! But the blow did not miss its full intent. Though it missed to make labor a curse, and made it a blessing, it fell heavily upon our taste for labour, and made us hate it; /and/ therein ever since the curse hath lain.—But when I compare your labors with mine, I am led into another strain of thinking. I have now a use for the addition columns of cents, dollars, eagles. And I find that my labor in the *cent* columns gives almost as much content as yours in the *dollars* and *eagles*. For which I thank Heaven! as it tends to reconcile me to little things, and to naturalize me to my condition and necessities.

I am happy to see that Heaven blesses you with health as well as mental energy to go thro' with your heavy undertakings. As for me, thank Heaven! I had the rheumatics pretty badly last November and was confined the rise of thirty days flat on my back in bed! I hopped about the house some times, but made a bad hand at that!—But I am better of it now, though not entirely well. My brother's health is generally good.—Some times, in the ague and fever season, he takes a chill or two, and /then comes/ a steam engine in his belly.—But Calomel and Quinine soon put the fire out, and he is well again.—He is all the time busy in his profession, and I at almost nothing, but busy for all that.—At the present time we have in the house, and have had for 22 or 23 days a gentleman diseased of dropsy and jaundice, a bad case, has been much worse, and is now almost well. A Doctor's life is a new scene to me.—It is full of pukes, purges, blisters, bleedings, cuppings; feeling the pulse, handling the privts, /and/ bowels; nursings, persuasions, grumblings, aches, cannots, musts, dislikes, pots, vials, lotions, salves, sores, pills, abominable smells, pains of all sort; and sad to tell, it is also full of cries, griefs everlasting lamentations and death!—This is the bad side. The other side is also in extremes.

We love you very much—and when we say that, every thing /else/ follows. Adieu, and Heaven bless you.

Th: Turner.

[*Addressed*] Ebenezer Pettigrew Esq
Cool Spring
Washington County
NC

Henry Alexander to Ebenezer Pettigrew A&H

Philadelpia June 21th 1843

My Dear Sir

I acknowledge that I have neglected you, by not writing sooner, but I had nothing new, I frequntly heard of you, Through Mr [*John Baptist*] Beasley and that you all enjoyed good helth (exsept) you Daughter Nancy, and that she was afflicted with the Desease that your son James was I was truly sorry to here of her misfortin but I am in hopes that you will be abile to have her caured

Mr Beasley informed me that the Storm last year, did more damage than ever had been known in you part of the Country, and that it look more like affamon [*a famine*], than any thing that ever been seen in that parts--and that the poorer clase of people had nothing to buy bread with—But you, and Mr Collins, had bought a large quanty, of Corn & Potatoes. expressly to save them from suffering, (if not from starving) how grate is the reward, to him the feed the hungry & cloth the naked

I am Satified, that affliction of body. mind & disappointment is the lot of the hole human family, and thair is no way to avoid it

I will now give you the cause why I am at this place, last year my son James was attacked with Eplipsy. and in February last it increased to and alaming exstent I then determined as soon is Spring opened to try and see if I could not get him cured, in April, we left home, and went to New Orlens, and thair we took a packit ship, to NewYork, to try what efect a sea voige would have, (but it was of no use to him) we reach this place 27 of May, James has been under the care of Dr. Jackson[1] ever since we have been here, he has had but 3 or 4 Paroxysms, since he has been here, and them very light—I rejois that he is much better and that I look forward with hope and exspation that he will soon be well.

I was taken qute sick on 1st. and was confind for 10 days, but I have got qute well again, except I am weak,

nothing new worth writing, [*President*] John Tyler was here last week, the City Counsel would take no notice of him, This is a Clay City, I thought when I left home that I should visit N. Carolina, and have the pleashr of seeing you all again, but when James is well anuf, to travel we shall go home from here, for the weathe will be too hot to visit

Providence seam to bless our part of the County last year with an abundent Crop, produce of every kind was very low when we left home Cotten 3 to 5 cts. corn 15 cts per Bushel, Bulk pork 2½ to 3 cts. Baken 4 to 5 cts. flower $3.50—and other articles in proportion, thair complant for money for it is very scarce. and all kind of Property is on the decline Please persent my respects to Charles & William and your other children to Mr & Mrs D. Davenport Mr & Mrs Collins, and inquiring friends my son James send his Respects to you all—with much respect I Remain yours

Henry Alexander

E. Pettigrew Esqr.

NB. I should like to here from you I cannot tell when I shall leave here

H. A.

[*Addressed*] Ebenezer Pettigrew Esqr
Cool Spring P.O.
Tyrrell County
N. Carolina

[1]This was probably Dr. Samuel Jackson (1787-1872), a prominent Philadelphia physician. He was on the faculty at the University of Pennsylvania and in 1843 was teaching in the wards of Philadelphia Hospital. *DAB*, IX, 553.

Jesse Alexander[1] *to Ebenezer Pettigrew* A&H

Memphis T. July 10th 1843.

E. Pettigrew Esqr:

Dear sir

Your favor to my father of the 16th of May last, was duly received; previous to its receipt he and my brother [*James*] had left for Philadelphia via New Orleans which place they reached the last of May. I presume ere this you have heard of my brothers bad health, the physicians here recommended him to take a sea voyage, and it was also deemed advisable that he should consult the physicians in Philadelphia—I recd a letter from him a few days since, and am happy to say, that his health was improving, and he entertained great hopes of immediate relief—I have thus briefly alluded to his situation, without particulars, thinking it probable he and father will visit you before they return.

The intelligence of the situation of a portion of your state, had reached us through various channels, as well as in your communication; indeed the present year must be one of extreme distress and without parrallel, much credit is due to to few individuals (from what I have heard) in their liberal and generous course, in such a cricis, in procuring bread for the hungary and saving the penless from stravation.

The extreme pressure that has prevailed for some time, continues here almost without mitigation, and if the reports of the Banks of this state made to the Legislature on the 1st October last, can be relyed on, we have but little prospect of immediate relief. The report showes that the Banks have due them nine and a half millions of dollars with an outstanding circulation of not quite one and a half millions to pay with. Amidst these times the improvements of Memphis continue to progress, and real estate in its immediate vicinity is held at enormus high rates, I suppose in many instances it is in anticipation of the General Goverment establishing here, the Navy Yard and Depot, and probably the Western Armory. That this is one of the most desireable points in the South or West, and it has natural advantages, none, who are acquainted with its location and the country tributary can deny, and that the Goverment in a geographical point of view, and it being at the head of navigation at all seasons, should establish these works here, is equally true, and yet I cannot see how property is to maintain present prices &c.

The crops in this country were very good last year, and provisions of all kinds could be had at low rates, though they have now advanced as is usually the case at this season;—The present crop is not very promising, the drought for the last three weeks has injured corn and cotton materially.

With the exception of the political canvass of this state, which seems to excite attention in every quater, their is no news of importance. Upon this state depends the political complexion of the next U.S. Senate, Tennessee had no senators in Congress at its last session, both parties seem certain of sucess, and from the best information it is believed that the election will be close.

I cannot close this communication without adverting to the situation of my Aunt [*Amelia Spruill*], who deseves my sympathy, and it would afford me pleasure to extend to her any assistance in my power; I have none of this feeling for son [*Anson Spruill*], (although a relation) he is the cause of his mothers distress, and will bring her grey hairs sorrowing to the grave,—it is unnecessary for me to say more on this subject, you know his course and conduct.

The Mississippi river is now falling and the extreme dry and warm weather has produced some sickness, principally diarrhoea, and slight cases of billious fever—

My father and brothers family are in tolerable good health, You will please present my best respects to your sons and accept of my regard and steem—I shall be pleased to hear from you and your sons at all times

Very Respectfully Your friend and obt: Servant
Jesse Alexander

[*Addressed*] E. Pettigrew Esqr.
Cool Spring,
North Carolina,

[1]Jesse Alexander was a son of Henry Alexander.

Ebenezer Pettigrew to Charles Lockhart and William Shepard Pettigrew UNC

Baltimore July 23, 1843

My dear sons

I arrived at this place last night, leaving Norfolk in the morning. While at the latter place I made all the arraingments for articles to be sent, which I hope will be in the first of this week. I also, Charles requested Mr Hardy which he said he would do, to pay your draft on him for $100, if you should draw. I have not been able today to learn any thing of Capt. Rollins, it being sunday, but before I close this letter tomorrow morning will make the enquiry & inform you, though from the course of the winds no hope of him before the middle of the week. In the mean time wheat is falling, & I fear that is not the worst, it is too long in the vessil; half that has arrived here & in shorter passages has been heated & consequently commanded less price. But there is no help for all this, & it is as well to say nothing about it, it will make it no better. My good star is set, I fear to rise no more. William I send now two sets ca[r]t boxes, the tire iron I could not get at Norfolk. I will send it from this place It would be well not to send the boxes & other fellows [*felloes*] before the tire comes, unless it may be wanted by Mr Davenport. I also William send a box of Lemon syrrup say one & a half dozen; a half dozen is for Dr Lewis; 4 bottles for your brother Charls, 4 for you & will you send 4 to Mr Davenport. I have also sent 4 ounces or bottles of Qinine, 3 are for us & one for Mr Davenport if he should want.

Charles there will be a bale of cotton osnaburgs for the negroes shirts, also 200 wt. Collar yarns. you will let Mr Davenport have 50 wt. /of the yarns/ also there will be sent ten barrils of prime pork. one barril is for Mr Davenport, one barril for Calib Phelps, & one barril for Moses Spruill, which three barrils had better go to Belgrade, the seven you know what to do with. The barril of sugar & leather is for you. If Mr Davenport should want a piece of the osnaburgs you can let him have one, I have no recollection of what he said. I have given the Messrs Hardies a memorandum for the [wollen] cloth when it arrives, fifty yards of which is for Mr Davenport. Also for the negroe shoes, both which articles are directed to be sent to you as soon as an opportunity offers after their arrival, which I suppose will be in September. I also ordered one Doz sidlitz powders for you and your brother.

My sons I hope & pay that you will not expose yourselves to sun & fatigue more than you cannot avoid. My health is much as when I left, but rather more of rheumatism. Though in such health as you know; I have suffered far more with fatigue in all the journey than I did in either of the two former falls though so low in health. & I have at no time left home with so much reluctance, & if it would not be disappointing Mr Johnston so much & acting so contrary to any thing like my former life, I would as soon as /the/ wheat is sold return home if I died by it. You /will/ understand that nothing in the world has occured, to cause these remarks, but every thing like the contrary. I can hardly tell why these feelings, but I have not felt any wish to go away this fall. My bowels are in an entire state of quiet since I got here. & very different from when I left.

July 24, 12 oclock M. I have been to Trimble & Wilson's this morning. No Virginia Hodges & the wind a head. They think wheat cannot be above ¢115—& I also called at Mr James Cheston's & son. The former died suddenly about a month a go to the great regret of all. The son told me that wheat was to-day 110 to 112 & heavy, & but little in market also that flower was a shade lower. All tends to give less hope for our wheat, but I will say no more on that subject. William the corn vessil will take a bundle to Mr Davenport containing the curtain stuff &c. also a bundle of shoes for Mr D.

It has been quite seasonable here untill a few days, but is now very dry. I hope & pray that <that> there has been rain with you, though I fear not ne[ar] enough. Mr Johnston is well & sends his respects to you both. Make mine to Mr & Mrs Davenport and believe me your affectionate father

E Pettigrew

N.B. As the mail leaves you the day after this is received you can if any thing should occur add to your letter after it is received.

E P.

Messrs C. L & W. S. Pettigrew

Direct your letters untill farther directed To Barnums Hotel Baltimore.

[*Addressed*] Messrs Charles L. & Wm S. Pettigrew
Cool Spring
North Carolina

James Johnston Pettigrew to Ebenezer Pettigrew UNC

Chapel Hill July 27th 1843.

My dear father,

I went up to Hillsboro' a week before the beginning of the session according to Mr. Bingham's direction, in order to be furnished with some clothes for college. He bought, in addition to what I had already, ½ doz. shirts, 3 pair of drawers, 1 pair of pantaloons, one waistcoat, 4 pair of socks and one dress suit. The amount to pay to the bursar is $31.50 for college charges; board is $10. a month and bed and washing are $10. a session. There several other necessary expenses, for candles, chairs washstand and other furniture; also books. Mr Bingham furnished me with a hundred dollars, although you had not requested him to do it, he said, for which I am very much obliged to him

There is a great deal less depravity and rowdyism here than I expected to find, at least as yet; there is not half the swearing or drinking as at Hillsboro; in fact, I have not seen any brandy or wine since I have been down here. Some of the students had a club the other night for blacking the Freshman class; they blacked John [*Herritage*] Bryan and all the Freshman except myself and one or two others. Col. Jones's son and a young man named Calvert locked me up in their room and I escaped in that manner. There will be more students here this year than last, it is expected, there are about forty in the Freshman class and a great many have joind the other classes. Billy [*William Shepard*] Bryan is considered the smartest boy in his class by far; I cannot say the same of John: he is very much disliked here and that was the reason why they blacked him. Please to give my love to brother Charles and brother William and beleive me

to be your aff. son,
J. Johnston Pettigrew.

[*Addressed*] E. Pettigrew Esq
Cool Spring
North carolina

William Shepard Pettigrew to Ebenezer Pettigrew UNC

Belgrade, Aug. 2, 1843.

My dear Father

We received your favor of the 23d Ult. by last mail and were glad to learn that your health was good. I am a little surprised that you should feel more fatigue this Summer than in the two previous Summers & Falls, but I presume you have arrived at that period of life when it is not intended that a person should perform much service but rather rest from those labors which in youth were a pleasure. I hope the wheat has not been injured by the long voyage, but if it has been, it is as well to bear it patiently, as grief could make no alteration. When the vessel arrives we will dispose of the articles she may bring in the way that you direct. Please accept our thanks for the Lemon Sirup you were so good as to purchase, it will give us many a pleasant draught during the close & sickly weather of Fall.

Since you left, it has been exceedingly dry, until last Tuesday (Aug. 1st) when there was a general and a fine rain. Until which, much of the corn in Scuppernong was in a deplorable state. Mr Davenport sent me word last Saturday that if rain should not come in a week he would be a corn buyer. I do not think his case so deplorable as that, but his crop as well as ours is much injured, not withstanding this rain. We have 30 acres fired half way to the ear; now I take it rain may improve such, but it must be very much injured. Nearly all the field is fired more or less, but none approximates the 30 acres above mentioned. I came from the Lake this morning; it has been more favoured with rain than Belgrade, and may be considered as having a tolerably good crop. I think there is a prospect of showery weather for a short while; if so, it will be worth hundreds of dollars to us; anxious as I am to complete the canal, I am willing to have its progress retarded until the staff of life is provided for. I did not cross the Sound with Mr Riggs, but went as far as James Chesson's and Mr [*Joshua?*] Swift's. The corn in that region looks quite well. Mr Swift has an undertaking before him in which, I fear, he will not succeed, but it is intrinsically a valuable place. If he were a relative of mine I should advise him to push. There is no doubt but his place could be drained if his ditches were larger & deeper. He has a beautiful location for a house. I was much struck with the undulating country about Buncomb Hall.[1] How different must be the state of things at the present time from what they were when the old Col. was in his bloom!

Aug 3d

My dear Father, we were very glad to receive by this afternoon's mail, two letters from you, but regretted greatly the news respecting the wheat. But let us bear these reverses with fortitude, the sun, I hope, will yet shine upon us. I learn from Brother Charles, who is just from Columbia, that the corn vessel has arrived. It is thought that Stanly will get a majority of 300 in Tyrrell. The vote /at Cool Spring,/ at 3 O'clock this afternoon (at which time I left) stood at 119 for Stanly & 6 for Arrington. I fear from what I learn that Stanly will be defeated.[2] We regret to learn that Mr Johnston is unwell, but hope this will find him recovered. Please present him our kind regards, and believe me

most affectionately your son
Will: S. Pettigrew

Brother Charles is well, & requests to be affectionately remembered to you.

P.S. Mr Davenport was here this afternoon, & sends his best respects. He thinks his corn will average 5 barrels per acre. He thinks of writing you by the next mail. I hear nothing from Dr Lewis & the vehicle he wished you to purchas/e/

W. S. P.

[*Addressed*] E. Pettigrew Esq.
Barnum's Hotel
Baltimore
Md

[1]Col. Edward Buncombe (1742-1778) built Buncombe Hall shortly after 1768. No longer standing, it was twelve miles south of Edenton in what was then Tyrrell County. The site is now in northwest Washington County. Haywood, *Builders of the Old North State*, 64-69; Powell, *North Carolina Gazetteer*, 75.

[2]Edward Stanly was defeated by Archibald Hunter Arrington. Arrington (1809-1872) was a Democrat from Nash County. Cheney, *North Carolina Government*, 683; *Biographical Directory of Congress*, 490.

James Alfred Pearce to Ebenezer Pettigrew A&H

Chestertown [*Maryland*] Augt 7th 1843

My Dear Sir

It has been a great while since I saw you or heard from you but I am not one of those with whom to be out of sight is to be out of mind. You have been the subject of many of my quiet thoughts and of frequent conversations with my wife and Judge Chambers.[1] We shall all be glad to see you here again. I am so tied to my home by professional business and the state of my wife's health that I cannot so readily get to see you as you may to visit us. Nevertheless if you will come and spend a week or two with us I will promise to make a trip to N Carolina next year Deo volente

The bushel of wheat which you sent me was sown in ground so heavily limed that it was nearly half destroyed. nevertheless I got 8½ bushels from it—gave some away last fall and raised from 6 seeding last fall The fly injured it very much and it was cut in the midst of the rainy weather. It turned out very well however. The Judge and myself would like to get another parcel from you say 20 bushels. Can you send it to Baltimore Care of Robert D Barry? If you can do so please notify us and say how much I shall remit you for it—The reason why we wish it from you is that after 2 years sowing it becomes assimilated to our climate and loses the property of early maturity which makes it valuable. The judge cut & thrashed his this year before the rains came on It is a small grain & heavy tho it did not weigh as much as my white wheat this year by ¾th.

Mrs Pearce has been very ill this Spring—She has a cough & occasional spitting of blood but her health has been improving from time to time since May—She will be quite well enough to welcome you when you come to see us as I do hope you will.

I believe I sent you a copy of my report on Genl Jacksons fine—If I did not you must tell me that I may do so for I am sure you approve it's doctrines and it is I hope not a reprehensible vanity in me to wish for the approbation of an old and valued friend—

I am looking with interest for the returns from your State. The whigs every where else seem to have resigned themselves to the apathy of despair If *old Rip* should prove to be wide awake we may consider a great political revival is at hand—I much incline to think that after the coming election private personal interests will prove stronger than party divisions and that various factions will spring out of the ambitions of different political favourites. Indeed this will have some effect upon the canvass of 1844. Whatever it is must enure I should think to the benefit of the Whigs who have only one leader & prime favourite now that Black Dan [*Daniel Webster*] has deserted us.

By the by nothing has so much shaken my confidence in the virtue & patriotism of our eminent men as his playing second fiddle to such a scoundrelly ninkompoop as John Tyler. I used to think him the *most honest public man* in the Union He has been seduced not so much by ambition as by hatred He has felt towards Mr Clay as Milton's Satan towards the Sun when he exclaimed after his flight thru chaos "Oh Sun how I do hate thy beams"—

I have done with Congress for some time at least. You would not call to see me there. But you *must* come here

Farewell my dear Sir

Believe me always most truly yrs
J A Pearce

yr wheat 59½ lb to the bushel
Is it not the same with the wheat called in Virga the *May* wheat

[*Addressed*] Hon. E. Pettigrew
Cool Spring
Washington Cy
N Carolina

[1]Ezekiel Forman Chambers (1788-1867), a Whig, served as a United States senator from Maryland, 1826-1834. Afterward he was a district judge and judge of the state court of appeals. *CDAB*, 153.

Mary Blount Pettigrew to James Johnston Pettigrew UNC

Marine Barracks August 10th [*1843*]

My dear Johnston,

Well really you ought to be ashamed to have let your vacation pass and write me only one letter. I suppose you received my last on your arrival at C.H. for I had no idea where a letter would find if I had have had time to write. So, my dear brother, after all you were neglectful not to inform me of your location during the vacation.

Pa left me on monday after spending four days. He did not stay at the hotel but by invitation remained at the Barracks. He did not come on account of his health; that was very good, but is going to Tennesee to look after the lands belonging to our dear mother. Pa said he had not heard from you often; but heard sometimes from Nannie. Will you not, dear J<a>ohnston, write to her? and not once only but persevere until you get her to <aswer> answer promptly. Although her letters as yet may not be interresting to you, when she has practiced and gets older they will become so; I know girls, who have never been obliged to write letters when young, <who> who find it impossible to accomplish that necessary branch decently, when required. I got /a/ letter from her and was much amused to see that it was sent more than a month after it was written. It seemed it was put by to have a postscript added by Ma.

I was glad to observe an improvement in your last letters. You will see by this that I am trying to effect the same in *my* hand writing; but I am afraid I shall be too tired to persevere to the end.

Pa does not expect to commence at Magnolia until the winter, I am sorry for that, for it /was/ a great pleasure to anticipate going into <it next> /the house on my/ return from Washington. I have quantities of plans for furnishing it, not with costly and stilish furnishings, but with plain, such as suits the country, and in place of splendour, to have comforts. When you come down to spend your vacations with us, you will, I think, be charmed with my *judicious* arrangements. Among other things I promise myself a small but beautiful garden, as well as well arranged pantry, with the shelves loaded with good things such as collegiates like.

Mr Johnston did not come to W—— on account of indisposition. He was suffering from "*Tyler's grip*" a <of> disease notice of which you have probably seen in the paper. It is otherwise called Influenza and is pevailing over nearly all the United States, but probably the "Old north—" has been spared this as well as a great many other disagreeabilities. You will certainly think me a little cracked if I digress much more, but let me assure you, not /at/ all so. Mr J— is going to Ohio and will meet Pa somewhere on his return. Mr J— sent me some very valuable books by Pa. I feel much flattered that he should have thought of me.

I have not heard from brother C— in a long time. When brother Wm. wrote last he was in wretched spirits; is it not a dreadful thing?

Your last letter reminds me so much of my Raleigh home, especially in the description of their quarrel for the horses. Oh how natural! In imagination I can see them every one. Did M— ride at all?

Look here, my dear fellow, you seem to be terribly smitten with a certain Smeadesite [*student at St. Mary's School*]. I hope you & John will never duel on that account, especially before she has decided which shall be killed. Do you not know the reason her neck and cheeks where <red> flushed when she rode by Grandma's? Why, my dear soul, it was agitation while passing the place in which *your* eyes, weary with wat/c/hing, were <either> closed or else /in which/ you were looking out for her to pass. You make a mistake as to the shape of her nose, it is turned up a grecian nose is perfectly strait and is considered a great beauty.

So GrandMa and Ma are afraid of their horses? I expect as much but hope they will not carry their fright to such an extent as to be induced to dispose of them. I should like so much to see Ma and all of them. Did you speak to S. Saunders? and did she say any thing about me? Ma writes me that they had all sorts of doings on the fourth of July at Ravenscroft Hall. I suppose they honoured you; if that be not the case, they surely could not have known it was your birthday.

Have you had any warm weather in N.C? If you have any desire for warmer <weat> than you have ever felt come to W—— and spend the last of July and first of August at Browne's I assure you will be gratified to the fullest extent. A gentleman, who could be relied on, told us that the thermometer at the Navy Yard had been at 102. You know I suppose that this city is famous for its dust you will have powers of that when you come on to enjoy the heat. You knew there was a new Secretary of the Navy. I have not heard much about him but hope he will be as efficient as the former [*George Badger*]. Who is your room mate? Write how you like College life. I hope you may find it all you anticipate and also that you will resist its temptations. With this *spicing* of advice let me say Adieu, Votre soeur avec sincerete

M. B. P.

[*Addressed*] Johnston Pettigrew
Chapel Hill
North Carolina

Ebenezer Pettigrew to John Herritage Bryan A&H, BRYAN

Jordan spring near Winchester Aug 15, 1843

My dear Sir,

I have been from day to day ever since I left home siting down to write to you, but puting off from day to day has brought it to the middle of summer. So much for bustle & confusion, the last [note] a situation that I ever wished to be in.

Since I came to Baltimore I enquired of the shoe maker, & he assures me that he put a pair of boots in the box as well as twelve pair of mens & boys shoes, and what could have become of them I cannot conceive. It is a pitty that the conveyance from Baltimore to Raleigh is so confused, for shoes are so easily & cheaply got compaired to Raleigh or any of our little towns. I hope you found the boots at the bottom of the box & that they fited you. I would have had you another pair (summer) made, but as the others were more than six months after engaged before the got in hands, it would have /been/ dead of winter before you could have got them if ever. Say nothing of the cost of the road, in its present fix it is more a curse than an advantage.

I left home for Baltimore to see to a shipment of wheat, which I regret to say arrived to a declining market & from the unusual length of the voyage in not very good order. The first I recollect to have sent to market in the last forty years in which there had to be an abatement / ment in the price for injury by staying too long in the vessil. One week sooner, the time it should have arrived would have made four hundred dollars advantage in the west provinces. Thus you see I have got into run of ill luck. Nearly five thousand bushels of corn to buy from a failure of last years crop, the present a good deal injured by drought my wheat injured by shipping, &c. and the great salvo I have to all this change of times is that it /is/ near the close of all my actions or opperations in this world, for at the end of this year I intend to square up with my sons and take my little interest down the canal where I have made a begining, for a future residence. I wish you to believe that these remarks are not in the spirit of complaining. I have had a great deal of prosperity in the world though checkered with the most heart rending dispensations. But shall we have good from the hand of the Almighty & not evil? and all I can say is amen & amen.

I did not wish to leave home this fall, but my friends & sons advised me to leave under an apprehention that I might get sick, & while I am away I intend to visit my childrens land in Tennessee in truth that is my principle object, & untill it gets cooler I am laging along & at present at this place, where there is at this time a good deal of company, among others chief justice Tanney[1] who looks very little like what he is said to be, also Mr Casinove's family. No one is in my way but I am tired of the bustle, now & for years, I can say with candor & truth, that I look back with longing anxiety to the day of seclusion /& labor/ which I spent on the Lake with my dear ever dear Nancy. *Unknowing & unknown.* I wanted no change, but it was God will & I am bound to submit. I will endeavour to do so without a murmur. But as I draw near to the close of my time I feel more my destitute situation. One year of my former life is worth a whole eternity of this crazy mixture with the world. But I will drop this subject. As my poor wife used to say every one has troubles enough of their own, without burthening them with mine.

If you should have any business in Tennessee, it would give me a great deal of pleasure to attend to it, and you will direct a letter to Dresden Tennessee.

I suppose you will soon begin your fall circuit I hope most sincerly that our low country atmosphere may not disagree with you. I fear a sicklier fall than we have had. Let me suggest to you to be guarded against the first cange of wind to the north, which checks persperation, & causes half our fall attacks.

Please to my kind regards to sister Mary & the children & tell dear little Nancy that I will write to her in a few weeks, & believe me sincerely & truely your

friend & relation
E Pettigrew

[*Addressed*] John H. Bryan esqr
Raleigh
North Carolina

[1]Roger Brooke Taney (1777-1864) was chief justice of the United States Supreme Court after 1836. As United States attorney general and secretary of the treasury, he had supported President Andrew Jackson in the Bank of the United States controversy. *CDAB*, 1042.

Henry Alexander to Ebenezer Pettigrew A&H

Memphis Tenn August 20th 1843.

My dear friend,

your faver May 16th/43 was duly receved, by my son Jesse, while I was abstent at the North and East, on my arivel home, my son said that he had wrote you of my abstence from home—your letter to me is one of Grate Satifaction to me, for it from the hand of soncere and long trid frend, and it contains contains an account of maters and things in Geneal, of that part of the Country & people wheth whom I have been so long aquainted, and in the habit of mixing amoung, in day which are gown by that it; (seames like as if I was coversesing with you) I had heard that the storm las July and August had almost Swep the corn Crop,

you seem to think, (and it was my opinion when I was with /you/) that industry & morrals of the people of Old Tyrrell and Scuppernong are not improving much—pleas say to old Sister Amelia Spruill, if she has not spent all her property, for God Sake to hold on to anuf to feed and Clouth her the ful remaining days which is aloted to her, if I had her out here I would Gladly feed. cloth & take Cere of her—But as for Anson he is not fit to bait a bare trap with for no Drunkard is Good for any thing I was glad to here of the good helth of your famley and hope that it has continud,

I have ackoledg that I did neglect writing of you to long, but I entend hereafter to do better and bee promp to my promus

when in Phildelphia I wrote which I exspect you have Recd Giving you an account for why I was thair, and the helth of my Son James I left Phla on the 9 of July—we had rother and on plesent trip owen to the weather bening hot the Ohio river low, and the Boat much crowded with people—whin I reach home I found Jesse well. James wife & child, the negros had been some sick withe the Influanseea, but have got well,

James helth since he has got home has impruved as fast as could be exspected, the paroxysm are very lite, and much further apart, and seam to be passing of Just as Dr [*Samuel*] Jackson said they would, therefore I have hope and the most flatring exspection that he will soon be well again

The crops are general good in this part of Country, the people are as helthy as are common. at this Season of the year, thair is Grate complant for money, all kind of property, is selling low for cash, (except the rale Estate in Memphis and it naberhood that still continus high) but that will sell much lower than the holders think, when conpll [*compelled*] to be sold (and I think that will not be long past) now for, *Elections* In this state, has Exerted grate intrust as to the majority in the Senate of the unted states, depnded on this state wheather it would be Demeocrat or whig therefore ever thing was dun that could be by both partes

But our whig victory is complete, Gov. James C— Jones (whig) is re-elected over his copetitor Ex-gov James. K. Polk, (dem) by above 4000— votes we have also carried both branches of the Legislator Senate 14 (whigs) 11 (Dem) The house, 40 (whigs) and 35 (dem) which gives us an joint ballet 8— majority, and secures the Election of *Two* whig senaters to the next Congress[1] whigs has Elected 5. and the Democrats 6 members to Congress I am in hopes that you have been abel to Elect Mr Stanly, for from what I learn Mr Arrington is a very poor creatur—

I should been glad to visut you & my frends this summer, but the helth of my son James for bid it, please let me her from as offen convenent I intend to visit you all next year if nothing disipnt [*disappoints*] me my sones send they bet respects to you & sons, Pleas prsent my Respects to Charles & William & your other Children wen you see them and /to/ Mr & Mrs Davenport Mr & Mrs Collins and all inquiring frends and I remain with much respect you frend and abedeand Servent

Henry Alexander

Ebenezer Pettigrew Esqr.

[*Addressed*] E. Pettigrew Esqr
Cool Spring
Tyrrell County
North Carolina

---

[1]Ephraim Hubbard Foster and Spencer Jarnagin, both Whigs, were elected to represent Tennessee in the Senate. *Biographical Directory of Congress*, 907, 1116.

John Herritage Bryan to Ebenezer Pettigrew A&H

Raleigh Aug. 26. [*18*]43

My dear Sir,

We received yours from the vicinity of Winchester & were very glad to hear from you.—I think you have done right to take the journey & hope it will conduce both to your health & your children's interest.—There was no *boots* in the box, it had no doubt been robbed; villainy has free scope in our country—The people are so much engaged in politics, that religion & morals are of minor importance in their eyes.—

I am sorry that you met with delay in the arrival of your wheat, I hope however that you have not got into a current of ill luck as you suppose—Speaking of the Baltimore market reminds me of a matter which I wished to mention to you.—John will graduate next June, and I wish to get him into a good & respectable mercantile house, and I thought it probable that you could select such a one in Baltimore.—

I was at Chapel Hill the other day & was in Johnston's room, he is very well & is doing well in his studies.—

I am much obliged by your offer to attend to our land interest in Tenn.—I have endeavoured to keep the taxes paid & have the Sheriffs recpt. for taxes for this year on 800 acres in Civil Dist. No. 8.—I have another tract besides this & also our interest in Penelopes' share.—Perhaps the tenants pay the taxes on the rest—Mr Gardner can explain it I suppose.—

It would suit us best to sell our interest in these lands as soon as a fair price can be got for them.—I recd a letter dated Apl. 30. '43 from Green Axum proposing to buy one of my tracts, he says he has been living on it for some time & paying *rent*—that he can pay for half of it at $2 per acre /for the upland/ & can secure the balance.—I declined selling at that price; thinking the value would increase &c.—This tract you can easily find & ascertain the value I suppose.--

We are all well—Nancy is doing very well at school now & sends her love to you.—

I returned from Wayne[1] the other day; the village had been nearly drowned, & there was a very bad smell—& we got very little money to console us—the law was never I suppose at so low an ebb as regards the profits &c—

I heard about a fortnight ago that Mr Halsey was at Nag's head in a very low state of health.—

M^rs^ B & the children send their love & best wishes for your health & happiness.—

very truly yr friend & relation
Jn. H. Bryan

[*Addressed*] E Pettigrew Esq
Dresden
Tenn:

[1]Waynesboro, on the Neuse River, was the county seat of Wayne County until 1850. Powell, *North Carolina Gazetteer*, 521-522.

Mary Blount Pettigrew to James Johnston Pettigrew UNC

Marine Barracks Sept. 2nd [*1843*]

My dear Johnston,

See what a *good sister* I am to write to you when you are my debtor! I hope in future you will recollect this instance and follow the good example. Why do you not answer my letter? Are the college duties more than you anticipated? How I envy you your excellent library; I suppose your time is much filled up with reading when not otherwise engaged. Pa came to see me, as I wrote you he intended, and remained four days. I was with him all the time as he staid at Gen. H[*enderson*].'s.

He told me every that was going on. Poor old Miss Hannah Phelps is dead; she died of a lingering illness and during all the time, Mr [*Charles*] Aldis came to see her only once. Pa buried her at Belgrade by her own desire. Although the Ministers were within a mile, at Dr Hardison's, she was buried without the service. It was scandalous. I suppose they thought Pa ought to have sent for them; I do not think so at all, she was a member of the Church and Pa had no more to do with it than any body else. I have received a letter from him since he left; he was at the Shannondale Springs, with Mr Johnston and Mr [*James L.*] Bryan, no relation of our Bryan<'>s and suffering under an attack of the Influenza. I am sorry to say he was in bad spirits.

It is so horribly warm this morning that I can think of nothing but the weather and how to keep cool. So I am afraid my letter will not prove the most interesting ever written.

I fear, dear Johnston, you do not find my correspondence as agreable as formerly, or you would write oftener.

We have delighful fruit here now and a plenty of nice books to read; the best new work I have seen is the Poetry of life, by Mrs Ellis,[1] It is really a sterling work that can be read more than once.

Oh! I forgot to ask you if you heard of Mr Henderson in Raleigh. But I was <was> not there to tell and so I suppose if any thing happened it was kept from the others.

Annie H[*enderson*] has just returned from a jaunt to the springs, she enjoyed herself much and was greatly admired. I go back to school monday week of course with the best intentions.

I am ashamed to send so short a letter and so badly written; <one> but the weather must be my excuse. Do write soon and believe me now as ever your attached sister

Mary Pettigrew

Love to John and William [*Bryan*].

[*Addressed*] Johnston Pettigrew
Chapel Hill
N. Carolina.

[1]This refers to Sarah Stickney Ellis, *Poetry of Life* (New York: J. and H. G. Langley, 1843), a work described by cataloguers as inculcating the domestic virtues.

James Louis Petigru to Ebenezer Pettigrew UNC

Charleston 5 Sept 1843

My dear Cousin,

Since I had the good fortune to make your acquaintance it has been my desire to maintain the intercourse of our families, and have regretted that the opportunities for indulging that feeling have been so rare—My only son is at Princeton College and will graduate at the commencement which takes place on the 27th inst. I have desired him on his way home to pay you a visit.[1] As you live however at a distance from the great thoroughfares by the Portsmouth or Petersburg and Wilmington Roads, he can scarcely do so without the risk of losing his way unless he has some directions for his guide. And it may happen also that you may be from home or not in a situation to receive /from sickness or other cause or accident/ such a visitor if he came without notice. But should it be convenient for you to allow my son an opportunity of seeing his relatives, I would request you to write or cause one of your sons to write to him and give him the proper directions for leaving the Rail Road at the proper point and taking the public conveyance to your house—But in case your neighborhood or the country th/r/ough which he would have to travel is as subject to malaria as our low country it would be by no means /prudent/ for one that has been so long at the North to venture into it as early as the 1st of October—You will take this into consideration too, and if there is danger in the expedition we must depend on some other opportunity for renewing that intercourse which would render our children better acquainted—Perhaps some day you or some of your family may find an inducement to travel to the South, and it would give me no ordinary pleasure to /see/ you or any of them here—

I have had a great deal /of trouble/ since I saw you and am not over with it either, tho I am not distressed and hope if I live 10 years to be able to sit down without the fear of <debt> /a jail/ before me—

Both my daughters are married with consent of friends on all sides, and live near me—Caroline the eldest is Mrs Carson on

Cooper River, where her husband is an opulent planter. Susan the other is Mrs Henry King—Her husband the son of my friend and contemporary at this Bar Mr Mitchell King—Our relative the Sailor has got a step since you saw and is now Commander [*Thomas*] Petigru—He is here at present, but in expectation of orders. My poor wife is a martyr to ill health, and can seldom leave her bed—The grippe has been so prevalent both in town and country that it is like murmur<r>ing against the common lot, to complain of it: but I have had it so very severity as to unfit me for business even after it is gone—So I am going to make a trip to Abbeville to see my sister [*Jane Gibert Petigru North*] there, and try a change of air for a couple of weeks. It will be sometime therefore even if you should write immediately before I could hear from you—but to my son a letter as soon as convenient would would be relieving from uncertainty His address is Daniel Petigru. Nassau Hall Princton. New Jersey—With sentiments of the truest regard I am Dear Ebenezer Your attached relative

J. L Petigru

[*Addressed*] Ebenezer Pettigrew Esqr
Cool Spring
North Carolina

[1]Daniel Petigru did not visit the lake but went to Washington, D.C. See Mary Blount Pettigrew to James Johnston Pettigrew, November 20, 1843, in this volume.

Ebenezer Pettigrew to Charles Lockhart and William Shepard Pettigrew UNC

Nashville Sep 11, 1843

My dear sons,

I arrived at this place on the 8th. from Louisville after a hard ride of about 180 miles /in [4]0 hours/ & /with/ some little fever, which passed off in the course of the night but the water disagrees with me & I am not so well. Spirits would correct it, but I do not wish to take it, having taken but three drinks since I left home. I leave this place this night at 1[2] oclock for Dresden a distance of 130 miles. Since here I have talked with /Mr/ McClimore [*John C. McLemore*] (who was so friendly to me when here before) and he tells me that my agent is a very good man & that I will have no difficulty with him, & that the land which we own is good & rising in estimation fast & <in> that section of the western district he considers higher in estimation than any other in the district but more of that when I have seen it & you.

Mr Johnston was much worried with the journey as well as myself, & I had hoped for his own care & comfort that he would remain here, untill my return, but he insists on going with me to the district. While we are gone <we> Mr [*James L.*] Bryan will go to Florance on business, & meet us on [his] return, when we shall take a line of march back. through Ohio & towards home. I hope to get a letter from you in Dresden, & am very uneasy, least you have it sickly this excessive hot weather, for where I have been it has been insupportable.

I have seen a great deal, and observe more towns declining than advancing. In truth it is universally admited that most of the towns that flourish with the first settlement of the place decline as fast as the population moves farther west, and that they are short lived. This place Nashville is declining, with the rest though much enlarged since I was here (24 years ago). All Kentucky is declining & the crops in general not good, from drought & exhasted land The corn is good in Tennessee, & I heard a gentleman say last night that the expected /the/ price of the neaxt years crop was thirty seven & ½ cents to fifty cents a barril (5 bus) for it. I have seen verry little or none better than ours. We have been called on by the Governor & Judge Catron[1] of the supreme court & wish to call on them, if the weather will allow. It is raining now. Mr Johnston desires his best respects to you both. He is entirely too modest & dificent to get along in this bustle & is very reluctant to call on those Gentlemen. Give my best respect to Mr & Mrs Davenport tell them that I hope most sincerely thay as well as the family have not been sick. I pray God to protect you my dear Sons, your affectionate father.

E Pettigrew

N.B. When you write again direct to Baltimore where I hope to find one or more letters from you.

[*Addressed*] Messrs. Charles & William Pettigrew
Cool Spring
North Carolina

[1]John Catron (1786-1865) of Tennessee was appointed by Andrew Jackson to the United States Supreme Court in 1837. *CDAB*, 151.

Ebenezer Pettigrew to Charles Lockhart and William Shepard Pettigrew UNC

Dresden Tennessee Sep 17, 1843

My dear sons.

After a hard & most miserable ride we arrived at this place on Fryday evening the 15th—On the way from Huntington to Paris, we had an upset, but fortunately no one (4 in number) was much hurt. Mr Johnston sprained his rist, his man Peter hurt his arm, a young gentleman hurt his back & ancle & I sprain'd my little finger, but all our hurts were light. Mr Johnston before was very sick with an affection of the bowels, & I do believe but for the camphor I had with me he would have had colera. The night we upset was one of the darkest & rainy nights I have seen since I left home. No one could see his hand before him, and as the young gentleman said when we left Huntington, we shall meet with disaster & all we can do is to sit quiet & go in for luck. The road is hilly, & full of gulleys, & we had three other hair breadth escapes. We arrived at Paris at 3 at night & the stage continued on, but we determined to go no farther in that way. & let it go. The next day was rainy & Mr J. very bad off. so we laid by, & the following day hired a road waggon & two mules & took char[*illegible*]s, & in that way arrived at Dresden at 3 oclok a distance of 25 miles. Mr Johnston wished to see my land but finding no convenince for both of us to go /to/ it (12 miles) he determined to go a head & left yesterday at 8 oclok for Mills' Point (35 /mils/) & to take a steam boat for Randolph where he has relations. & I expect /to/ leave on Tuesday the 19th for the same place where we shall proceed up the river, winding our way homeward. I have made arrangements to go tomorrow to see our land & should have gone to day, but there is a camp meeting in the neighborhood, & every horse & vehical is /in/ requisition.

Mr Alfred Gardner lives within a mile of this place & I went to /his/ house yesterday, & settled all my accounts with him. I had no trouble, for if I know a perfectly fair, open, plain, straight forward man he is one. He paid me all that is now due me for sale ($245) of Land. & goes with me tomorrow to the land. He gives a high character of our tract; but the other two he thinks worth very little. Of that I shall be a better Judge when I see them. To give you a character of the country would take more power than I have got. It is hilly & washes exceedingly. It is sickly, (though they say not) & the bilious fever is very prevalent, & far more violent, than with us. This town is about half the size of Plymouth & there are to be two persons buryed in it to day. I have not felt at any time in our country more like it than yesterday & today, & am trying to counteract it /by taking/ large doses of Qinine & hope to escape it. This is no place for me to have a bilious fever.

19th I leave in two hours for Mills' Point on the Missisippi. Kept this letter open hoping to get a letter from am exceedingly anxious to hear from you, Feel better than I did when I began this letter. Hope my dear sons that you have retained your health, make my respects to Mr & Mrs Davenport., & God Bless you my dear sons.

your afft. Father
E Pettigrew

[*Addressed*] Messrs Charles & William Pettigrew
Cool Spring
N. Carolina

William Shepard Pettigrew to James Johnston Pettigrew UNC

Belgrade, Sep. 26, 1843.

My dear Brother

It has been so long since a letter has been received of sent that if we ever are to correspond it is high time /for/ a commencement. That friends and relatives, particularly relatives as closely connected as we are, should communicate with one-another, occasionally, when separated, is a fact which all must be sensible of—it will encourage feelings of affection which may otherwise languish, then, it will induce the younger party to listen to the experience of the older and prize his good opinion. However, I trust my brother will never cease to cherish the esteem and harken to the suggestions of those who are his nearest & best friends, those whose happiness is identified with his and whose honour cannot but be so. Wicked young men are every where, there pernicious counsels are always at hand to allure the inexperienced, they will ever scoff at morality, industry, and all other qualifications that are held as praise worthy by the good, but those who wish to attain distinction in any branch of human excellence must despise their temptings. Let one's genius be what it may, it cannot receive its full measure of praise without some degree of morality, nor can genius, itself, reach great eminence except by the aid of close application; no one, ever yet, obtained a thorough knowledge of science by intuition, if that were possible it would give a portion of mankind too great an advantage over their fellows, and produce intolerable vanity in the gifted, which would threaten, if it did not accomplish their ruin, <for> nothing renders persons, blessed with wealth or talents, more odious, than for them to exhibit to others, less fortunate, a consciousness of the fact. It gives me great pleasure to renew my acquaintance with Chapel Hill, even by letter—It stirs a chord of memory,

> "It speaks a tale of other years—
> Of hopes that bloomed to one."

No doubt you are pleased with College life. The morning after I had been admitted I well remember looking out of the window with the lightest heart imaginable, thinking to myself, is it possible I am in College, have I left my master, have I become a gentleman student—no longer to be ordered as William, but to be requested as Mr Pettigrew—then the old Philanthropic, "God bless her," How is she? I love her as though she were /my/ best friend. Wednesday night (the time when we met) was to me the most agreeable portion of the week. Perhaps, however, your numbers are /now/ too great for that patriotic feeling to exist which then animated us. Large bodies will be disorderly; no kindness, no severity can restrain them within those limits, in which all collections of men must be kept to reap the greatest advantage.

Pa, as you are aware, has been from home for some months. We have not heard from him since Aug., it is probable he is now in Tennessee. Mr Collins and family are at the North. Brother Charles and I are alone, but well, not withstanding the sickness which prevails in certain localities, the Lake and Belgrade being blessed with health this season. He requests to be affectionately remembered to you, and together with my self to our cousins. Please let me hear from you soon, and as often as your duties will permit.

Assure yourself, my dear Johnston, of the attachment of your affectionate brother,

Will: S. Pettigrew.

Mr J. Johnston Pettigrew

[*Addressed*] Mr J. Johnston Pettigrew
Student
Chapel Hill
N. Carolina.

William Shepard Pettigrew to Ebenezer Pettigrew UNC

Belgrade, Oct. 3, 1843

My dear Father

We duly received your favor of the 11th ult. It gave us much pleasure to hear from you after so long a silence caused by the distance that has separated us. We are glad yourself and Mr Johnston bore the fatigues of the journey so well, and hope Mr Bryan's health has been improved by the trip; the slight indisposition of which you spoke being nothing more than the most natural of consequences. I feared the lime-stone water would disagree with you. We were glad to learn that our landed interest in Tenn. was thought valuable. Would to Heaven it were doubly so, and could be advantageously disposed of, for land at that distance, say the [least] of it, is a pest. It is cheering to know that our crops are not inferior to those of the West—the land of abundance. I fear some of us are too desponding; fortunes are not realized in a day, nor will the earth invariably yield abundantly; man must labor for his bread, and labor unceasingly if to accumulate wealth is his object: unless he be the child of good fortune, even to retain the comforts, passing over the luxuries of life, he must struggle hard.

In Scuppernong, with some exceptions, it is quite sickly. Dr Lewis thinks more so than in 1833. There is one difference between this year and that—in 1833 it was more general. The Alligators are quite healthy. Some of the boys at the Lake were sufficiently unwell, on sunday last, to require the Dr, but the place nevertheless could not be termed sickly. We are getting on pretty well at Belgrade only one being on the list. Mr Davenport's family have been unhealthy throughout the Fall. He and Mrs D. are, at the present time, confined to their rooms. He has had the "grip" and bilious fever combined. Mr & Mrs D. unite in respects to you. Mr Halsey left, on last Monday week, for the up country; his object is to bring home his children, male & female. He has had a hard time of it this Fall. I have not seen him since with you last Spring, but I learn he looks badly. Mr [*John Baptist*] Beasley has lost his son Ebenezer, and has also been quite sick himself. His son John has returned to N.C., where he thinks of remaining.

Will you be so good as to purchase for me a pair of boots or shoes, either will answer, and a pair of suspenders, as both those articles /which I have/ are becoming old and broken; I could do without them some time yet, but this is the most favorable opportunity I shall have.

I dislike to trouble you again with my ring-worm, but I am so much annoyed with it that I hope you will pardon me. The Land's Sarsaparilla you were so good as to send was of much service, and I cherish the hope that six bottles more together with Land's Remedy for Salt Rheum, which he states has been successful in 14,000 cases without having failed in one, will relieve me of a scourge which has followed /me/ so long. [L]and's Remedy for Salt Rheum is an external application.

Dr Lewis & brother request me to make you their best respects.

I hope this may find yourself & friends well, and pleased with your long trip. Brother Charles & myself are well, and unite in kind regards to Mr Joh[nsto]n and best respects to Mr Bryan. Please assure yourself of our warmest attachment.

I remain your affectionate son,
Will: S. Pettigrew

[*Addressed*] E. Pettigrew Esq.
Barnum's Hotel
Baltimore
Md

Ann Blount Shepard Pettigrew to
[William Shepard Pettigrew] UNC

Raleigh Sunday. Oct th29. 1843

Dear Brother

I received your letter and was very glad. I am very sorry to inform you of the death of Uncle Charles Shepard he died last thursday night at nine O Clock the very night on which Cousin Alexander [*Blount*] was married he was taken sick Monday and he was sick a little more than a week. Grand Ma is quite sick today.

I have not heard from Pa since he left the Lake but I hope that I will hear from him soon. I want to see you very much I hope that you will make a visit to Raleigh this winter I think you would like it very much though there is not many interesting things. Our vacation will commence next wednesday and we will have a month. I study music and French I like them both very much. Mr Smedes is going to New York this vacation. I suppose that you are very expert in playing on the Violin. Mr Smedes has a great many scholars. Mr Smedes and Madam seem to be the greates governor's of the school for the girl's are very much afraid of them. You must excuse my bad writing for I had a bad pen. All the Children are very well except George and the babe they both have very sore eye's. We have had the Tyler Gripp, it is very bad for I have had it. We all send our love to you and Brother Charles

Your affectionate Sister N[*ancy*].
A. B. S. Pettigrew.

William A. Dickinson to Ebenezer Pettigrew A&H

Hillabie [*Alabama*] 31st October 1843

E. Pettigrew Esqr

Dear Sir

It is now a long time since I had this pleasure, my last was dated 21 Jany 1843 since when I have not heard from you, I am somewhat fearfull you are not in agood humor with me If I have <in> in way given offence I sincerely beg your pardon, but I am not concious of it, trusting this will find you and your family all well, I had a letter from Hardy H. Phelps a few months ago and was glad to learn that you were then all well, since my arrival here I have been very busy in clearng and preparing ground for the plough, but up to this time it appears I have made but little progress as it takes both time and hard work to tame wild ground to get it in a fitting state to make a return, the land here is generally poor and of very uneven quality being all mostly upland. I am rather affraid it will hardly pay for the clearing times are exceedingly dull, and the people generally are a curious mixture of half savage, & half civilised noways suiting neither my ways nor my of thinking, anything like the society I have been long accustomed, it seems thy have no idea of such a thing as sociability in their composition, every thing is much in the same way with me as when I last wrote you I find it will be a considerable time before I can be able to make a surplus from farming to go to market, our State Alabama is much like all other South & Western States terribly crippled by Bank speculation and rascallity, your old N. Carolina seems to be as well off as ever and I belive as good a State to live and make a living as any, you have better Land particularily the lower part of it, than any I have ever seen and all those that can stay ought to stay and behoove themselves, I have nothing particular to inform you of from this wild region, Hardy Phelps gave me some particulars regarding Charles Bateman & others I am sorry for the misfortunes of mankind ingeneral, but barefaced and oppen rascallity ought to be whipped and punished according to its deserts. I should like to know the whole particulars either through you or my old corresponded the Ex. Post Master [*Hardy H. Phelps*], I shall as I have been for a considerable time in trouble conserning your silence untill I have again the pleasure of your letters My Family and self are in good health, only I suffer from lameness in my Ancles, I wonder what has become of my old crony Chas Weldn & Wife, by your giving me the news of the place as you did in former times will be gladly receivd, please write soon. wishing you and your family good health here and happiness in the wold to come. Believe me Dear Sir

Your most Obd^t Sv^t
William A. Dickinson.

P.S. my fingers are quite stiff to what they use to be

[*Addressed*] Ebenezar Pettigrew Esqr
Lake Phelps
Coolspring P.O.
Washington C^o
N.C.

Ebenezer Pettigrew to James Johnston Pettigrew UNC

Lake Scuppernong Nov. 1, 1843

My dear Son,

I returned home on the 22nd Ult. & found your two letters of the 27th July & 26th Sep. I am glad to find that you are fairly located, & hope you will take the benefit of your situation. You can get the cloak you mention in your last letter, & any thing else that you may stand in need of also get your cloths at Hillsboro as you have requested. It is my particular wish that /you/ shall want for nothing that will make you comfortable, & appear as well and as genteel as any rational, & moderate boy at the Hill. All I ask of you my dear Johnston is, to be prudent, & economical in the use of money, for one hundred & fifty reasons but one is sufficient, which I will give you which is this. My pecuniary funds are at this time in a very moderate state, from the disasters of the seasons, but at the same time I am not in distress, & do not wish you to undergo any degradation or mortification, for want of money & therefore I want you at all times to let me know how you stand, & call on me for such sums as you may want. I suppose the vacation will take place about the end of this month; if you wish to go down to Raleigh to see your Grand-Ma or your sister you can do so, at the same time taking care to get back in time to begin the session. I repeat again do not want for warm cloths & good strong shoes, nor any thing that you think you aught to have. On the reciet of this write to me, how you stand in your money matters, & how much you will want for the next session & whether you will /go/ down to Raleigh, that I may know where to write you.

My health has been generally good, & I thank my God that I found your brothers Charles & William well, and that with a little indisposition of your brother William they had been both well, also no serious sickness with the negroes since the fall, though it has been one of the most sickly ever known in this country. M^r^ & Mrs Davenport have been at the point of death, & were not out of bed this week, & the children have been sick over & over again & are yet sick, but they are all on the mend.

On my canal Danl Woodley lost his third daughter, Hardy Woodley lost his wife, George Davenport lost one of his oldest sons, & Charles Phelps at the mouth of Mr Collins canal lost a child. Almost every one has been sick, but blessed be God all are now on the recovery & I hope no more will get sick, as the season is far advanced.

It was too dry for the corn in July, & it gathers very little more than a half crop, & it is expected to be very low in truth there is no demand any where for it at this time.

Your brother Charles finished the canal on the 10th Oct^r^ & it is a great work, & of great advantage to all our interests. Since that he has sown the wheat; & also your brother William expects to finish this week. Your brother Charles sends his love to you and assure yourself of the sincere affection & love of your father

E. Pettigrew

Mr James Johnston Pettigrew

[*Addressed*] J. Johnston Pettigrew
Chapel Hill
North Carolina

Ebenezer Pettigrew to John Herritage Bryan A&H, BRYAN

Lake Scuppernong Nov. 6, 1843

My dear Sir,

I received with the deepest sorrow the information in your letter from Newbern of the death of our brother Charles, & while I sorrow for my own bereavement I grieve *more* much *more* for /the/ suffering & sorrow of his nearer relatives & more particularly of our poor old Mother. I can but say under such, we have lived too long. Pray make my affectionate regards to her & tell her that my sorrow for her bereavement is more than I have words to express & that she has to look to that blessed book, which tells us not to sorrow as one without hope, but to look to him who is our only hope in time of need.

I regreted very much to learn from Frederick Shepard, (who I traviled with from Portsmouth to Elizabeth City on my way home) that you had two attacks of bilious fever this fall, & that you looked badly. I hope most sincerely that you have before this entirely recovered & that sister Mary & the children have had their health this fall. We have had in this section of the country a most wretched sickly season, some say surpassing any before known, but though with all this floating disease both my dear Sons have been well except some little complaining of William, also very little sickness of my people. Blessed be God for his mercies, & I know not words to express my humble thankfulness for them. My own health while gone was in general good, & without any bilious affection, untill since my return which was the 22nd last month. I have been threatend with the prevailing disease, but with care & the use of Qinine have kept it off & in the last few days feell pretty well.

While last in Baltimore (the 20th Oct.) I made the necessary enquiry respecting the geting a young man into a counting house. The first, was of the Cashier of the Planters & Farmers Bank, a gentleman with whom I have had several /years/ acquaintance. He told me that he had, had a son, who /he/ wished to get into an establisment of that kind, and after keeping him waiting six months, he succeeded on the following terms. Viz, He must board & cloth the son (he 16 years old) the first year, & receive for his services $50—<the first year.> The second year, board & cloth his son & receive for his services $100—and after that if he was appoved of he would be no cost to him. But thinking it would be well to make farther enquiry I consulted a Mr Cheston who is a floure merchant & miller a man of great worth & he told me that it was a very difficult matter to get a young man in a good establishment, & mentioned the terms above. I therefore have no doubt of their correctness.

While at Dresden Tenn. I received your two letters to me at that place & made all the necessary inquiry respecting your remaining land, & was on part of that belonging to my children a few (say 2) hours. It was amasingly hot and as much as a mans life was worth to be going about in those stagnant rivers, & lagoons at that season of the year & I had to apply for all the necessary information respecting yours, mine, & all the rest to our agent Mr Gardner, & who I am bound to say, from the respect paid to him in his agencies f[rom] all manner of persons his candor in settling with me, his general manner & appearance, is a perfectly honest man, if there is any to be found. Mr Gardner went with me to look at the land, consequently had a days conversation with him. I passed through the land sold by William Shepard to Mr Etheridge from Currituck, dined at his house. He is geting in a very comfortable situation also was in sight of Clemens' on the land you sold to him. Passed from thence through the lands of our poor brother Charles, saw where some one had been pillaging it, & learned it was

Clemens, at which Mr Gardner determined to sue him, but low & behold he had no power to sustain a suit for he did not know where or whether the division of the land was recorded, & wished me to make the necessary enquiry & inform him. When I saw Frederick the other day & asked him, he made very light of it & said the gave a coppy of it /to/ William, & that he had sold his, intimating thereby that he had no interest in it. I then at Elizabeth ask William & /he/ said he supposed the dividers would return it to court & there the thing rests, in a perfect fog. The high lands in that section of the state are settling up fast, & their crop for exportation is tobacco, and it requires timber for Hogsheads and more particularly for flat boats to carry it down the river Obion which is in progress of improvement, & now navigated. The low grounds of that river will be valuable alone for its timber of which there is a great abundance of /the/ finest I ever saw & without the power to stop pillage it must in time be all taken away & thereby render the land entirely valueless. I should be glad if you can find this necessary paper or where it has been put. If it can be hunted up I will write Mr Gardner concerning it. He was so confident when I left that he could get the paper necessary, and without which he could not sustain a suit, that the last words he said to me was that /he/ would have a writ on Clemens at the next court for his trespas on brother Charles land. If you have ever had a /plot of the/ devision of the land you can find who were the deviders of the land with Frederick Shepard & we might probably learn from some of them what was done with the paper. And in looking over the sttlement of William Shepard, with the heirs of his fathers estate you could perhaps find if there was a charge for registration, you know for myself I have never had nor seen any of the accounts & can know nothing about the estate. Mr Gardner told me that Penelope's land could be sold for a tolerable price if the purchasers could get a /good/ title. Whether such a thing can be done with so many grown & minor heirs I do not know.

And now my dear Sir Please to make my kind regards to sister Mary & the children & tell dear little Nancy that I will write to her by the next mail and assure yourself of the sincere Esteem and regard of your friend & relation

E Pettigrew

John H. Bryan esqr

[*Addressed*] John H. Bryan Esqr
Raleigh
North Carolina

Ebenezer Pettigrew to James Louis Petigru[1]* UNC

[*November, 1843*]

My dear cousin

Your kind and very gratifying letter awaited my arrival at home some time after its reception. However my eldest son, Charles, informed me that without delay, he had written to his cousin and had given him the requiste information for performing the journey to my residence.

He has not received an answer, but hopes the letter was received in due time, and my sons and my self wish that no long time will intervene before this promise of a visit will be redeemed. I can assure you that you can not have a more sensible appreciation of the pleasure and advantage resulting from the intercourse of our families than myself: Nor a greater regret /that/ the opportunities for indulging it so rarely occur.

If we would seriouly think of it, <ath> although many miles divide us, yet time, which is the great consideration, does not place us far asunder: At most we are only a few days apart, the improvements <have> of modern times almost annihilate distance For the last three years my hea[l]th has been in an enfeebled state and I have found it necessary to seek a more invigorating climate. I have done so and have invariably returned home much restored. This fall I left North Carolina in July and did not return home untill the 22^{d} October. My inclination and some little business induced me to go westward, /to visit/ western Pennsylvania, Ohio, Kentucky and Tennessee. Ours is certainly a great and growing country; "Onward" is truly with them the watch word.

I regret exceedingly that you should have become involved, and hope that you are not as seriouly so as you apprehend. A year or two of the active energy, you usually display, m/a/y perhaps enable you to arrange all you difficulties. But all is not evil with us, you have reason to be happy that a portion of your family are settled in life.

Your daughters are happily married and that of course must relieve you of some thoughts that at times trouble the mind of a parent in reflecting upon the destiny of that tenderest portion of his family.

Sincerely do I regret the protracted and now almost hopeless illness of your suffering wife. Could there be hope, I would most ardently wish her better.

My two older sons are living at my two respective plantations, /(and it is scarcely saying too much),/ they are prudent and industrious. At the end of the year I contemplate resigning to them the weight of business of those plantations, and shall myself retire to a place situated between the two.

My eldest daughter, Mary, will quit school in a few weeks; my youngest Ann, who is about thirteen, is pursuing her education at the female school in Raleigh. My younger son Johnston has just entered the University of North Carolina. Thus you observe that in a few years my family will be grown and begin all of them to supply the place and be exchanged for their parents. How many scenes have passed before us since we occupied the places of our children!

Let me assure you my good cousin James, that it would give me *no ordinary* pleasure to welcome you or any of your family to my house in North Carolina. Remember myself and my sons affectionately to the members of your family and with the truest regard I remain

[1]This copy is not in Ebenezer Pettigrew's handwriting.

William Shepard Pettigrew to Mary Blount Pettigrew UNC

Belgrade, Nov. 11, 1843

My dear Sister

Uncle William, Pa & Brother Charles have just left for the Lake, and I am alone, exposed to those feelings which solitude after one has been in society is so well calculated to produce. Company operates on me differently—sometimes it makes me happy, sometimes miserable: if I am talkative the former, if silent the latter. I am now in the latter state. I fear I am calculated only for solitude. I fear this gloomy, retiring nature, occasioned more by my silince in company than any other cause, which causes me to shun my fellow man, will wean every one from me whose friendship I esteem, and leave me a recluse. Solitude is to be my lot; may God give me strength to bear, and even love it! Then, come sorrow, here is your home! Perhaps it may be better it should be so, in order to wean me from a world which is too enticing: perhaps when pleasure has closed its door my thoughts may dwell more on that home to which we are all traveling; were I prepared for that abode, oh! how happy should I be to enter it, there to rest my weary, thrice weary spirit; my wind-sheet would be the most acceptable apparel for this dyeing body.

Religion is truly the greatest blessing given to man: wander where he may, to the icy regions of the North or sunny plains of the South, among the forests of the West or the smiling fields of the East, if he have the benign spirit it will accompany him; in solitude or in society, in the grave or on earth its consolations are always present.

We regretted very much to learn of Uncle Charles' death: he was a great loss to his family, and the State of which he was an ornament. I trust he was prepared for the change. Poor Grand Ma how heavy this affliction must be upon her.

On Thursday last I had the pleasure of dining at Mr Collins' in company with our Uncle & Aunt, Miss Mullen[s] & others. It was one of the most pleasant evenings I have spent in many a day. I had the good fortune to sit by Miss Alethea at the table, and after dinner was accidentally again seated near her; we had a good deal of conversation which made the evening pass delightfully on my part. She is very agreeable. She says she has not received a letter from you although she has written you; but pardons you on the ground of your school duties. She was disappointed at Pa's returning without you, and appears to prize you highly. She also told /me/ our Aunt wished you in company with herself to visit them at Elizabeth. Aunt Shepard is cheerful. Mrs [*Louisa McKinley Collins*] Harrison was also of the dinner party.

My spirits are reviving: I feel like a different being from the one that commenced this letter; but the hour is late and I must take leave of you. With this, I imagine, closes my part of our correspondence until you leave school. I lose you as a correspondent with sorrow. If your time will permit, it will give me pleasure to hear from again before the 1st Dec.

Good night, my dear Sister, and cherish as much as you are able the affection of your brother

Will: S. Pettigrew.

Miss Mary B. Pettigrew

[*Addressed*] Miss Mary B. Pettigrew
Care of Gen. A. Henderson
Washington City
D.C.

James L. Bryan to Ebenezer Pettigrew A&H

Windsor 13 Novem 1843.

My Dear sir

I thank you for your very friendly letter of the 2d inst which was handed to me by Mr Hurlbut. just as Mr Johnston and myself were <were> leaving Barnum Hotel for the Steam Boat Georgia on our return home—I was much gratified to learn that our journey was attended with such good feelings towards each other, and I must express to you that I have never spent a more pleasant and agreeable time than I did while in your company, and I shall always remember the many acts of your kindness and friendship extended to me during our sojourn to gether, and the interest you felt and the attention paid to me, particularly while we were at Harrisburg as well as every where else,—and I feel rejoiced that we have reached our respective homes without meeting with any accident, <and>—

I was much pleased to hear that both of your sons remained well this fall and that your negroes had escaped with so little sickness; Also to hear that Mr Davenport and his family were still alive and that you entertained hopes of their recovery, I have never had the pleasure of a personal acquaintance with Mr Davenport, but the high terms you always spoke of him, the community in which he resides would have sustained a serious loss by his death, and I hope and trust that he and his family will speedily recover—

I reached home last thursday after having parted with Mr Johnston at Edenton the night previous, On my arrival here I found my sister and other relatives in as good health as I had any right to expect considering there has been so much sickness in every part of the county this fall, not a single individual on my Lot escaped, but none had been seriously sick, And I feel thankful to the Giver of all good that they escaped so well; I understand that the County was never more sickly and it is supposed that at least three fourths of the whole population of the County have been sick this summer & fall, it is now our Court week and I am certain that I have not seen a dozen persons who have escaped, the weather is now very cold which I hope will be the means of restoring health— The crops are said to be very abundant, but the farmers here complain of low prices, and no money—last year they complained of nothing to eat, so we cannot be satisfied with our situation—

The day after you left us at Balto Mr Johnston & myself left for New York, before we got to Phila Mr Johnston did not feel very well & we remained there two days & then proceeded on our journey—I found my brother and his family very well and regreted that you could not accompany us they would have been very much pleased to have seen you, Mrs Bryan desired me to present her regards to you & say that she will with pleasure attend to the purchase of a Piano Forte whenever you may order one—

While in New York I went to almost every carriage Repository in the City but could not find any thing in the way of a carriage that answered exactly your description, I however found a Phaton that I thought might answer, it has a drawer seat which can be made by pushing it back from the Spatter board to answer for 4 persons, it is one of the most convenient things of the kind that I ever saw; it was made for John L. Stephens (the traveller) & by his directions and used by him only a month, and is in every respect as good as new—the cost of which including Pole, shafts, Boxing & insurance $163.62/100;—/which is $75 cheaper than a new one./[1] I have shipped it to Bryan & Maitland Plymo with diretions to advise you on its arrival—Now my dear sir, if on examination of this Phaton it should not answer you both as to quality and price, I *do not wish you to take it because I purchased it*, as I can dispose of it without any loss or trouble to me at the cost or even an advance—Should it answer, you can remit the amt to Bryan & Maitland New York—With my kind regards to your sons.—

I remain truly yr fd
Jas. L Bryan

[*Addressed*] Ebenezer Pettigrew Esq
Cool Spring
North Carolina

[1] Ebenezer Pettigrew appears to have purchased the phaeton for Dr. Lewis for $163.62, receiving the money from the latter in three installments during 1844, judging from notations on the back of this letter.

John Lloyd Stephens, a noted American traveler, explorer, and author, was best known for his discoveries, with Frederic Catherwood, of Mayan ruins in Central America and Yucatan. From 1839 to 1842 he conducted two Mayan expeditions, with a brief interlude in New York City in the fall of 1841. Victor Wolfgang von Hagen, *Maya Explorer* (Norman: University of Oklahoma Press, 1948), 301.

Ebenezer Pettigrew to James Alfred Pearce A&H

Lake Scuppernong Nov. 20, 1843

My dear sir,

Your favour of the 7 Aug. was received in my absence. I left home in the middle of July & did not return untill the 22nd October, & though intending /to answer your letter/ from mail to mail (we have but one a week) I have not found time untill now. I thank you for your kind invitation to visit you this fall. I know nothing that could have given me pleasure than to have spent some days with you & Mrs [*Martha Laird*] Pearce, as well as my friend Judge C[*h*]ambers, & I could easily have had the time, for I stayed at Baltemore two weeks in the last of July & first of August preparetory to leaving for the west, but my friends with whom I was about to travil would not have listened to my leaving /for/ any where else. I mention my traviling to the west. I know you do not expect me to write any thing of what I saw or heard, and it was a great deal in a journey of three thousand miles from Baltemore by land & by water, in the states of Virginia Kentucky, Tennessee, Ohio & Pensylvania & on the rivers in view of the states of

Arkansas, Missouri, Illinois & Indiana. You know I am a bungler at giving my ideas on paper & it is labour, that I dislike to undertake, but whether bunglingly or not, it is no labour /for me/ to talk, & if I had an opportunity it would give me a great pleasure to pour into you as far as you would listen, what I saw, & what my conclusions are on all that vast country & people. In a word, I will compare them to the River (the great Mississippi) which they navigate. If it fills on the one side it never fails to open its way on the other, for its waters will go ahead, and with great respect, I will add; a great many of them are as uncertain as the channel of that great river, which the Pilots say who navigate it is always changing, & never continues in one place.

I traviled through the country with great good feeling for the people & some of their locations & if I had /not/ lived so long & done so much in the swamps of North Carolina, I think it likely I should move, but my plantations are like sickly children. The more we nurse them the more strongly we become attached to them & strange as it may seem, if it should please God to relieve us from our anxious charge, by taking our dear little invalid unto himself we grieve more for it than one much more promising for this wicked worlds troubles. So it is & so it ought to be, if it was not right, the Almighty & mercifull God would have had it otherwise. I began to write you a letter but find I am begining a sermon, & will turn the subject, for I have seen too much of preaches of /the/ present day to think of commencing the business. It is very gratifying to believe that my friends have not forgoten me, & that you make me a subject of conversation with Mrs Pearce & Judge Chambers, because I flatter my self it is saying something favourable, & if not it is of my excentricities, of which I fear I have & must have a goodly number.

I enquired in Baltemore of the health of yourself & Mrs P. and was much gratified to learn that Mrs P. health was much improved, which your letter in part confirms. I hope most sincerely that it may continue.

I observe your remarks respecting wheat, I shipped mine this year to Baltemore, but it was not good. A great deal of the wheat from Scuppernong is shipped to Baltemore, & mostly consigned to Trimble & Wilson. & you could at all times during the season get it by geting your friend to apply to those gentlemen. All raised in this section almost without an exception is of my kind of wheat. & generally good. Of that however those gentlemen would be judges.

We were visited last year by storms & sweept from the face of the earth. This year we had it too dry at hilling time of our corn & it is much shortend, perhaps two thirds of a crop, & no price for that. So that farming is a [*torn*] business, but I know no better & can do nothing else.

I observe your remark that you are done with politicks at least for a time. I was much gratified to hear from several sourses at Baltemore that they intended to send you to the Senate from Maryland. I receved /& read/ with great /pleasure/ your report on Genl Jacksons claim, & have heard it spoken of in in the most flatering manner by good Judges. I had intended writing acknowledging its receit & thanking for it for it was passed on. It has been in this country very sickly, few falls as much so. But my two sons who remaind the whole fall had with little exception good health. Mine is pretty well restored & I expect this winter to begin a new place for my future residence [*Magnolia*], being about to give up my other two to my sons. But of that more hereafter. I shall always and at any time be glad to see you. And now my friend excuse this miserable & unpremedetated scrawl, & Please to make my kind regards to Mrs Pearce, my respects to Judge Chambers and assure yourself of the sincere Esteem & regard of your friend

E Pettigrew

Hon. J. A. Pearce

N.B. I have had a good deal of anxeiety to know something about the mud machine of which I send to you & Judge Chambers a modle when you write me again, which I hope will not be long first, please to say something, about I should also like to know how the Judge <aprove> aproves of his reaping machine.

E P

[*Addressed*] Hon James A Pearce
Chestertown
Maryland

Mary Blount Pettigrew to James Johnston Pettigrew UNC

Breschard Academy Nov 20th [*1843*]

I hope, my dear Johnston, you have not given me up as one of the "lost sheep of the house of P——. I admit I ought to have written to you before, but—My excuse although a true one will not do to be written on paper as it is the excuse of all lazy people. Mind that is not saying that I am of that denomination.

I have just recieved a letter from brother C——. All well. He is coming for me next week, instead of Pa. Uncle W. B. Shepard and lady were at the lake he with Pa and brother W—— dined with them. Dr and Mrs Hardison were there and so the room was full. Mr Collins has as many in family as usual. I should like to know if he has the same as last year and what sort of geniuses he has been able to collect this time. You know I suppose that Mr. Aldis was married and of course he will not return; and they do not, generally, keep a teacher more than one winter.

Pa is going to send north to get me a piano. Is it not good in him? He was in Baltimore, not long since, on his way home from the West; but did not come here, as he recieved a letter saying Mr and Mrs Davenport were very ill and Mr D——, very much frightened I expect, was continually calling out for him. He hurried home and found them convalescing.

Our cousin Dan [*Daniel Petigru*], brother C—— says, did not go to the Lake, notwithstanding a very pressing letter he wrote him. That does not raise him much in my estimation, and besides he was in Washington sometime ago and did [*not?*] call on *me*. I was really <ver> glad of it, as my ease, in company, is not quite sufficient yet to make me desire it. I wish with all me heart it was; but I tremble and suffer when I am about to enter the room as if it was my last effort.

Give my love to Father [*John Herritage Bryan*] and thanks for the pamphlet. He should have answered my letter before this but, if he has [*not*] yet done it, I would advise him to wait until he has express orders from myself in person. I suppose you will have vacation by the end of this month and will go to Raleigh; therefore I will direct to the care of Father.

I was greatly pleased, my dear brother, with what you wrote me relative to the boys.

Our poor Uncle Charles' death is a great blow to Grandma and his poor wife. He died the very night and about the same time that Alex. Blount was married. I was glad to learn that father was with him at the time.

Bettie and Nannie have their vacation now; it is a pity for It would be much more pleasant for them when we all are there.

Charley Henderson is just William's age but looks like a grown person. He has gone back to College at Princeton which he says is decidedly the best in the Union. He<s> says also that a great many boys go there from C.H. of course I did my best for the latter and I really do not beleive Princeton better. *You know my facility for judges is very great.* Charley is in the Junior class and the youngest <boy> man in college. If I were to call him a boy I am doubtful whether he would forgive me or not as his ideas of dignity are wonderfully extensive.

The weather is delightful and the members coming one by one. I saw three consequential looking being on the avenue and had a mind to stare at them. You can tell one the instant you see him. I don't know why it is, unless because they are from home and think themselves rather larger than other people think them. A Mr Barringer[1] is a member of Congress now. I saw him in the

Legislature last winter. You never write on this side of your letters and I do not know whether you like it or not. Any how I must stop and bid you farewell until I meet you in Raleigh.

Au revoir Your affectionate sister M.

[*Addressed*] Johnston Pettigrew
Care of J. H. Bryan Esq.
Raleigh
N C.

---

[1]Daniel Moreau Barringer (1806-1873) of Cabarrus County was elected to Congress as a Whig in 1843. He served three terms and was then appointed minister to Spain, serving 1849-1853. Powell, *DNCB*, I, 99-100.

John Herritage Bryan to Ebenezer Pettigrew A&H

Raleigh Nov. 26. 1843

My dear Sir,

I received your Kind letter of the 6th inst. postmarked the 10th, just before I left for Wayne County Court, and as you stated that you should write by next mail to Nancy, I concluded to defer writing until we heard from you again.—

I was taken sick with the old fashioned "burning ague" directly after my return from Wayne & Johnston Augt. Courts, and was confined to my room & the house about 9 or 10 days—I am now as well as usual.

Nancy received your letter on the 24th; we are sorry to learn that Mary does not return this way as well all wish to see her.—I am much obliged by your inquiries & the information relative to our Western lands & a suitable place for John in Baltimore.—I have a copy of the division of the land, which I expect was made from a copy of the original, the division appears to have been made in May 1826 & is signed by W. B. G. Killingsworth, M Woodfin & Elisha Harbour; it ought to have been recorded in both the counties of Weakly & Obion [*Tennessee*]; & it probably was.—

Nancy was taken with the grippe early in Octo. for about a week, after she got over it, she had fever for two or three days; we had Dr Beckwith[1] to see her while she had fever, and after three or four days her fever left her—she took oil & quinine—she now has sore eyes but they are now nearly well.—Last tuesday (21st) Mrs B. thought that she discovered that she was slightly nervous & thinks she is still so; but that it has not increased—she grows very fast. Her nervousness is not perceptible to a casual observer, Mrs B. thinks it affects her speech a little, by making her talk thick—she hopes when her health is fully restored, (and she is now improving daily) that it will disappear.—She has not been confined to her bed at any period of her sickness & says she feels very well—Mrs B. thought however, you had better know *all* about her.—

Mrs Shepard & Mrs B. are in great affliction as you have supposed—poor Charles (I expect) died very unexpectedly to himself, he left no will.—

I have had a wretched circuit—sickness & death has prevented business from being done—we have not done upon the whole circuit as much as has sometimes been done at one court—

Johnston is here & is looking very well, I learn that he got the first honor in his class—as Wm Bryan did in his.—

Nancy will write in a few days.—My kind regards to Charles & W^{m}.—Their Aunts love to them & yourself.—

Very truly Yr friend & relation
Jn. H. Bryan

P.S. Our neighbour Mrs Polk is very low—her disease I expect is consumption.—
Our little George has been & is now quite sick—

[*Addressed*] E Pettigrew Esqr
Cool Spring
N.C

[1]John Beckwith (1785-1870) was a physician and surgeon noted for his successful eye operations. He lived in Raleigh from 1823 until 1845. Powell, *DNCB*, I, 126.

*Ebenezer Pettigrew to Alfred Gardner** A&H

Lake Scuppernong Cool Spring P. Offce Dec 7, 1843

My dear Sir,

I arrived at this place on the 22nd October, The day previous, I met in the stage with Frederick Shepard (who now lives in Mobile), and mentioned to him the division of his fathers lands in your district. He seemed to be very indifferent in his remarks, saying that he had taken the earliest opportunity to get clear of his, but did say as respects the division, that he had given to William Shepard who was one of the executors of his fathers estate a copy of the division & there his information stoped. I have since seen William Shepard & he seems to know very little about the division papers. But farther said the deeds for the lands, to his father &c. he had registered in Parris [*Tennessee*] & that /the/ commissioners who were appointed to divide the land he supposed returned /<a plot> a

plot of the/ division & survey to the court, and that it was registered, but of that he knew not. But if all the necessary steps had not been taken, it was not too late, in as much as all the proceedings had been sanctioned, by the parters either setling their lands or appointing agents on them. /N. 2/ On the recet of this will you be so good as to employ a lawyer, (your brother John) and proceed to get the thing straight, by first examining the offices to see what is done. /N. 1/ Since my return I have been examining a copy of the division given me by Fred. Shepard, and find in the Plot of the survey the following. 'The above map contains a true representation of a division of the 24 tracts of land belonging to the heirs of William Sheapard: Moses Woodfin
Elisha Harbour Commissioners
Wm B. G. Killingsworth

Now I presume the origional of this paper is some where, as also some of the parters whose names are attached to it are yet to be be found, and you will please get it put straight. I expect it is vain to say that I /with/ others will <not> pay my part of the cost. <If others> What others do not pay of their quota, I will, as well as my own, and therefore do not delay. <in>

I was about to write on the above subject, & the trespass in his land, to Charles Shepard, when I received the news of his death. He died the 26th October with bilious fever. leaving a wife & two or three children.—Since my return I learn that this country had never been more sickly, attended with a considerable number of deaths. But Blessed be to my kind father in Heaven, My two sons, who attended to my business, during the whole fall together with my negroes had little or no sickness, and I found all things had gone on well. From the allmost entire loss of the corn crop of 1842, & but ⅔ of one this year in consequence of the drought, Our country is in a very embarrassed pecuniary state, & it is my opinion will not recover from it in less than ten years.

My dear sir, I left Dresden [*Tennessee*] with regret /from the kindness which I meet with from those I became acquainted with/ <for> I should have been glad to remained there some weeks, & even longer. Please to remember to all my acquaintence, particularly to your brothers Jeptha & John, also Mr Hall & make my kind regards your companion Mrs G. & children, hoping that you are all in good health, & that Mrs Gardner did not get sick at the camp meeting which she was at when I was there. And now please to accept for yourself my thank for your kindness to me. and assure yourself of the sincere Esteem of your fd & sert

E Pettigrew

NB I shall be glad to hear from you as soon as convenent. I expect there were letters came for me after I left Dresden if so & they are not sent to the general P.O. will you take them out, carge my account with the postage & then open them & read them. They are from my sons, /Bless God/ we have no secrets /to keep/ & by those letters you will see what my sons are. You can <keep them or> then destroy them. or retain them. E P.

[*Addressed*] Copy to
Alfred Gardner esqr
Dresden Tennessee

Ebenezer Pettigrew to James Johnston Pettigrew UNC

[*December 15, 1843*]

My dear Johnston

I received your letter of the 30th Nov. in due course and was glad to find that you had come down to Raleigh to visit your poor Old Grandma, who in her late misfortune needs all the sympathy of her relations & friends.

You had stated in your former letter what Cloths you had got, all of which is right & meets with my entire approbation. You must be comfortable & appear respectably clad, & it is my wish & desire that you should. In a letter from Mr Bingham at the time of yours, he informed me that you had got necessary articles, & that you were very prudent in choice, which gratified me very much. I hope you will continue to be so, & you will have no reasonable want that I shall not wish to satisfy.

I regret exceedingly to learn from your letter and one also from Mr Bryan that your poor little sister Nancy has symptoms of her old disease. Tell your aunt Mary that I will write her in a week /or two/ and ask her in the mean time not to seem to act towards Nancy as to let her know that any thing was the matter with her, & not to let the doctors dose her, but to give about a grain of Qinine three times a day. The Qinine will strengthen her, for I apprehend it has come on her by weekness, from fast growing, & the indisposition which she has had. And it is not well to talk of that disease to the person who has it, in as much as it is produced sometimes by sympathy.

You will observe at the head of this letter a check on the Bank of Baltimore for a hundred dollar, which is to commenc the next year with. You will get your Uncle Bryan to assist you in negotiating it with the Bank at Raleigh, & you had better take notices, how it is done that you may know in future. You will write me directly on your receit of the check that I may be satisfied of its not miscarrying.

Your brother Charles left on the 27 Nov. for New York & returning to bring home your sister Mary & I expect them on Saturday, that is tomorrow.

You will be surprised to see from whence I date this letter, I have commencd in earnest to make a place here & have moved for my first house the shanty that I built for the canal, in which I am writing this letter, at the same time I have six carts hauling earth from the bank of the canal to the place where my house is to be put as well as a number of other hands cuting stumps and clearing the way for other houses.

And now my dear son I hope you will in /all/ things act worthy, of your father & particularly of your dear ever dear mother. Make my kindest regards to your Grandma, aunt & uncle Bryan, sister Nancy, & all your little cousins, & believe me to be your affectionat father

E. Pettigrew

J. Johnston Pettigrew

N.B. Your brother William sends his Love to you & all the family.

Magnolia December 15, 1843

N.B. It is highly probable I shall see you before you get this letter therefore do not negotiate the draft untill you are about to leave for Colledge.

E. P.

[*Addressed*] Mr J. Johnston Pettigrew
Care of John H. Bryan esq
Raleigh
North Carolina

Josiah Collins to William Shepard Pettigrew UNC

Somerset Place 23rd Decr 1843

My dear Sir

If you are not otherwise more pleasantly engaged will you do me the pleasure of joining our circle on Monday to partake of our Christmas dinner? I shall expect your brother to make one of our number on that day with Mr Riggs so that we may expect a grave party from so many *old* men

Very truly yours
Josiah Collins

Wm S. Pettigrew Esqr

We dine at ½ past 3 p.m.

[*Addressed*] Wm S. Pettigrew *Esqr*
Belgrade

*William Shepard Pettigrew to Josiah Collins** UNC

Copy

Belgrade, Dec. 23d, 1843

My dear Sir

I am very much obliged to you for your polite invitation to me to join your party at Christmas, and it will give me great pleasure to accept it; I assure /you/ I could not spend my time more agreeably. I think we old gentlemen will by the grayness of our heads & the gravity of our manners keep in check the effervescence of the youthful. Please present my regards to the ladies, and believe me

very sincerely yours
Will: S. Pettigrew

[*Addressed*] Josiah Collins Esq.
Somerset Place

Receipt for Pianoforte UNC

[*December 27, 1843*]

Received Norfolk Va. 27. Decr. 1843, in good order & well conditioned, from Hardy & Brothers, on board Schr Columbia, myself master, one box containing a Piano Forte and one box containing a Stool for same, for E. Pettigrew, Esq. which I promise to deliver in like good order & condition, unto Mr. William Dunn or to his assigns, at Columbia, N.C. He or they paying freight for same as customary

M Bowers

Norfolk 27. Decr. 1843—

Dear Sir,

Above we hand you Capt. Bower's Rect for a Piano & Stool, Shipped for your account, pr Sch. Columbia, & consigned to Mr. Wm. Dunn, Columbia, N.C. as directed by your Son, Mr. Charles L. Pettigrew, who came down with the Piano (we think) in the Steam Boat from Washington City—For freight to the Steamer, & expenses here, we debit your a/ct with five dollars.

Our receipts of Corn have been very large recently, and Northern Vessels being very scarse, the price receded to 35¢—& some sales at 33¢—But the Stock has passed off, and today the demand is active at 38¢—with indications of a further improvement. soon.

Very Respy Sir,
Yr frds & Sts
Hardy & Brothers

Hon: E. Pettigrew.

[*Addressed*] Hon: E. Pettigrew
Cool-Spring
Washington County
N° Ca—

INDEX

F

G

H

Q

R

S

T

U

V

W